Lieber Herr Geus!

AF698554

Mit den besten Grüßen

&

Wünschen

Ihr

Hatem Elliesie

Bibliografische Information der Deutschen Nationalbibliothek
Die Deutsche Nationalbibliothek verzeichnet diese Publikation in der Deutschen Nationalbibliografie; detaillierte bibliografische Daten sind im Internet über http://dnb.d-nb.de abrufbar.

Gedruckt mit Unterstützung der Gesellschaft
für Arabisches und Islamisches Recht (GAIR e.V.).

Gedruckt auf alterungsbeständigem,
säurefreiem Papier.

ISSN 0942-2323
ISBN 978-3-631-57848-3

www.peterlang.de

Beiträge zum Islamischen Recht VII

Leipziger Beiträge zur Orientforschung

Herausgegeben von Hans-Georg Ebert
Begründet von Günter Barthel

Band 26

PETER LANG
Frankfurt am Main · Berlin · Bern · Bruxelles · New York · Oxford · Wien

Hatem Elliesie (Hrsg./ed.)

Beiträge zum Islamischen Recht VII

Islam und Menschenrechte / Islam and Human Rights / الإسلام وحقوق الإنسان

PETER LANG
Internationaler Verlag der Wissenschaften

INHALTSVERZEICHNIS
TABLE OF CONTENTS

ABKÜRZUNGSVERZEICHNIS / LIST OF ABBREVIATIONS 9

EINFÜHRUNG / INTRODUCTION 21

- **Vorwort des Herausgebers** 23
  Hatem Elliesie, Berlin
- **Editor's Foreword** 27
  Hatem Elliesie, Berlin
- **Die Gesellschaft für Arabisches und Islamisches Recht: 10 Jahre in der Retrospektive** 31
  Mathias Rohe, Erlangen
- **The *Gesellschaft für Arabisches und Islamisches Recht:* 10 Years in the Retrospective** 35
  Mathias Rohe, Erlangen

BEITRÄGE ZUR ISLAMRECHTLICHEN METHODIK SOWIE ZUR RECHTSPHILOSOPHIE / CONTRIBUTIONS TO ISLAMIC LEGAL AND THEOLOGICAL APPROACHES AND PHILOSOPHY OF LAWS 39

- **Islam and Human Rights: Introductory Remarks and Reflections** 41
  Abdullahi Ahmed An-Na'im, Atlanta
- **Islam und Menschenrechte: Betrachtungen zum Verhältnis von Religion und Recht** 49
  Muhammad Kalisch, Münster
- **Hermeneutik, Koraninterpretation und Menschenrechte** 73
  Assem Hefny, Kairo / Leipzig / Marburg
- **„Westliche" *versus* „islamische" Menschenrechtskonzeptionen?** 99
  Heiner Bielefeldt, Berlin

MENSCHENRECHTSSITUATIONEN IN AUSGEWÄHLTEN ISLAMISCH GEPRÄGTEN REGIONEN UND LÄNDERN / HUMAN RIGHTS SITUATIONS IN SELECTED PREDOMINANTELY ISLAMIC REGIONS AND COUNTRIES 121

- **Islam and Human Rights in the Constitutions of African States: Agenda for Good Governance** 123
  Mashood Baderin, London
  - **Islam, Islamic Law and Human Rights in the Nigerian Context** 155
    Isa Hayatu Chiroma / Hatem Elliesie, Maiduguri / Berlin
  - **Mufti Act of Zanzibar and the Fundamental Rights and Freedoms of Moslems on the Isles** 173
    Chris Maina Peter, Dar es Salaam
  - **Sudan under the Constraints of (International) Human Rights Law and Humanitarian Law: The Case of Darfur** 193
    Hatem Elliesie, Berlin
- **Remarks on Human Rights and Islam in the Middle East** 219
  Ann Elizabeth Mayer, Philadelphia
  - **Governmental Human Rights Structures and National Human Rights Institutions in the Middle East** 239
    Anna Würth / Claudia Engelmann, Berlin
  - **Zwischen Einschränkung und neuen Entwicklungen: Das Grundrecht auf heterosexuelle Selbstbestimmung in den Verfassungssystemen arabischer Staaten** 257
    Naseef Naeem, Berlin / Göttingen
  - **The Human Rights Dilemma in Egypt: Political Will or Islam?** 281
    Bahey eldin Hassan, Kairo
- **Human Rights and Islam in South East Asia: The Case of Indonesia** 299
  Tim Lindsey, Melbourne
  - **Human Rights Standards in Afghan Courtrooms: The Theory and Reality of the Right to a Fair Trial** 329
    Tilmann Röder, Heidelberg / Kabul
  - **Sharia and Implementation of Human Rights norms of Equality and Non Discrimination in the Family: A Case Study of Family Law in Pakistan** 361
    Ayesha Shahid / Javaid Rehman, Hull / London
  - **Civil Society and Legislation: Developments of the Human Rights Situation in Iran in 2008** 387
    Irene Schneider, Göttingen

INTERAKTION ISLAMISCH GEPRÄGTER LÄNDER UND ORGANISATIONEN MIT INTERNATIONALEN MENSCHENRECHTSINSTITUTIONEN / INTERACTIONS OF PREDOMINANTLY ISLAMIC COUNTRIES AND ORGANISATIONS WITH INTERNATIONAL HUMAN RIGHTS INSTITUTIONS 415

- **Der Frauenrechtsausschuss der Vereinten Nationen in der Interaktion mit islamisch geprägten Staaten** 417
  Hanna Beate Schöpp-Schilling, Wohltorf / New York
- **Die Organisation Islamischer Konferenz im UN-Menschenrechtsrat: Menschenrechte als Instrument staatlicher Politik** 457
  Theodor Rathgeber, Kassel

MENSCHENRECHTE UND ISLAMISCHES RECHT UNTER DEM BLICKWINKEL DES (INTERNATIONALEN) PRIVATRECHTS / HUMAN RIGHTS AND ISLAMIC LAW IN LIGHT OF THE (INTERNATIONAL) PRIVATE LAW 475

- **Ordre Public, Menschenrechte und Scharia** 477
  Peter Scholz, Berlin
- **Religionsfreiheit und islamisch geprägtes Erbrecht: gesetzliche Regelungen und Rechtsprechungsauslegung im heutigen Ägypten und Tunesien** 499
  Imen Gallala, Hamburg

BEITRAGENDE AUTORINNEN UND AUTOREN 523

ZUSAMMENFASSUNGEN 529

CONTRIBUTING AUTHORS 539

SUMMARIES 545

559 **المؤلفون المشاركون** ٢١

568 **خلاصة الموضوعات** ١٢

573 **الإسلام وحقوق الإنسان: تأملات وملاحظات تمهيدية** ٧
عبد الله أحمد النعيم (أتلانتا)

576 **جمعية دراسات الشريعة الإسلامية وقوانين البلاد العربية في العشر سنين الماضية** ٤
ماتياس روهي (أرلانجن)

579 **كلمة مسؤول التحرير** ١
حاتم الليثي (برلين)

ABKÜRZUNGSVERZEICHNIS / LIST OF ABBREVIATIONS

Aufgrund der weltweiten und interdisziplinären Bandbreite an mitwirkenden Autor(inn)en in dieser Publikation bot es sich an, nachstehendes Abkürzungsverzeichnis aufzunehmen.

The worldwide and interdisciplinary scope of contributors found in this volume has necessitated the list of abbreviations found below to facilitate better understanding.

A

A.A. / a.A.	andere Auffassung
a.a.O.	am angegebenen Ort
Abs.	Absatz
AC	Constitution of the Islamic Republic of Afghanistan
ACHPR	African Charter on Human and Peoples' Rights
AD / A.D.	Anno Domini
ÄEG	Ägyptische Gesetz Nr. 77 von 1943 über die Erbschaft
AEMR	Allgemeine Erklärung der Menschenrechte
AFP	Agence France Press
AG	Amtsgericht
ägypt.KassGH	ägyptischer Kassationsgerichtshof
ägypt.OVerfG	ägyptischer Oberster Verfassungsgerichtshof
ägypt.ZGB	ägyptisches Zivilgesetzbuch
AH	Anno Hegirae
AHDR	(World Bank's) Arab Human Development Reports
AI	Amnesty International
AIBA	Afghan Independent Bar Association
AIHRC	Afghanistan's Independent Human Rights Commission
AJIL	American Journal of International Law
akad.	akademisch
AL	Arab League / Arabische Liga
a.M.	am Main
APuZ	Aus Politik und Zeitgeschichte
arab.	arabisch / Arabic
Art.	Artikel / Article
AU	African Union / Afrikanische Union

Islam und Menschenrechte (Islam and Human Rights / الإسلام وحقوق الإنسان)
Hatem Elliesie (Hrsg./Editor), © Peter Lang Verlag: Frankfurt a.M. 2010, S. 9-19

Aufl.	Auflage(n)
AYIHL	African Yearbook on International Humanitarian Law
AYLH	Association of Young Legal Historians
Az.	Aktenzeichen

B

BAKWATA	Baraza Kuu la Waislam wa Tanzania
Bearb.	Bearbeiter(in)
Bd.	Band / Bände
BGB	Bürgerliches Gesetzbuch
BGBl.	Bundesgesetzblatt
BGH	Bundesgerichtshof
BGHZ	Entscheidungen des Bundesgerichtshofs in Zivilsachen
B.I.I.C.L.	British Institute of International and Comparative Law
BRD	Bundesrepublik Deutschland
bspw.	beispielsweise
Bull. Civ.	Bulletin des arrêts des Chambres civiles de la Cour de Cassation
BVferG	Bundesverfassungsgericht
BVerfGE	Entscheidungen des Bundesverfassungsgerichts
bzgl.	bezüglich

C

ca.	circa
CAT	Convention against Torture and Other Cruel, Inhuman or Degrading Treatment or Punishment
CC	Cour de Cassation / (Iranian) Civil Code
CCM	Chama Cha Mapinduzi
CE	Common Era / Christian Era
CEDAW	Committee / Convention on the Elimination of Discrimination against Women
CERD	Committee on the Elimination of Racial Discrimination
CIA	Central Intelligence Agency
CIBEDO	Christlich-Islamische Begegnungs- und Dokumentationsstelle
CIHRS	Cairo Institute for Human Rights Studies
CIRI	Cingranelli-Richards Human Rights Index

CMRA	Child Marriage Restraint Act of 1929
CNMS	Centrum für Nah- und Mittelost-Studien
CNN	Cable News Network
COC	tunesisches Gesetzbuch für Obligations- und Vertragsrecht
Cp. / cp.	compare
CPA	Comprehensive Peace Agreement
CRC	Convention on the Rights of the Child
CRIDHO	Cellule de recherche interdisciplinaire en droits de l'homme
CSO	civil society organisation

D

d.	died
D.C.	District of Columbia
DEDAW	Declaration on the Elimination of Discrimination against Women
ders.	derselbe
d.i.	das ist
Dir.	Direktor
d.h.	dass heisst
DMMA	Dissolution of Muslim Marriages Act of 1939
Doc.	Document
Dok.	Dokument
Dr.	Doktor / doctor
Draft Bill	lāyeḥeh-ye ḥemāyat az ḫānevādeh

E

EAMWS	East African Muslims Welfare Society
ECOSOC	(UN) Economic and Social Council
Ed. / ed.	Editor
Eds. / eds.	Editors
e.g.	exempli gratia
EGBGB	Einführungsgesetz zum Bürgerlichen Gesetzbuch
em.	emeritiert; emeritus
EMHRF	Euro-Mediterranean Foundation of Support to Human Rights Defenders
EMPINX	Empowerment Rights Index
Entsch.	Entscheidung(en)

EOHR	Egyptian Organization for Human Rights
EPLF	Eritrean People's Liberation Front
et al.	et alii
etc.	et cetera
et seq.	et sequens
et seqq.	et sequentes
e.V.	eingetragener Verein
evtl.	eventuell
EU	European Union / Europäische Union
EUGRZ	Europäische Grundrechte-Zeitschrift
EUMC	European Monitoring Centre on Racism and Xenophobia

F

f.	folgend(e)
FamRZ	Zeitschrift für das gesamte Familienrecht
FAZ	Frankfurter Allgemeine Zeitung
FCO	Family Courts Ordinance of 2002
FES	Friedrich Ebert Stiftung
ff.	folgende
FGG	Gesetz über die Angelegenheiten der freiwilligen Gerichtsbarkeit
Fn. / fn.	Fußnote / footnote
FPA	Family Protection Act of 1975
FROLINAT	Front de Libération Nationale du Tchad
FS	Festschrift

G

GA	Georgia [State]
GAIR	Gesellschaft für Arabisches und Islamisches Recht
GDP	Gross Domestic Product
gest.	gestorben
GG	Grundgesetz
ggf.	gegebenenfalls
GoS	Government of Sudan
GURLAC	Group of Latin America and Caribbean Countries
GWA	Guardian and Wards Act of 1890

H

h.	hiğrī (qamarī)
HE	Her Excellency / His Excellency
h.M.	herrschende Meinung
hon./h.c.	honoris causa
HRQ	Human Rights Quarterly
Hrsg.	Herausgeber
HRW	Human Rights Watch
http	hypertext transfer protocol
https	hypertext transfer protocol secure

I

i.a.	inter alia
ICC	International Coordination Committee / International Criminal Court
ICCC	Interim Criminal Code for Courts
ICCPR	International Covenant for Civil and Political Rights
ICESCR	International Covenant for Economic, Social and Cultural Rights
ICHRP	International Council on Human Rights Policy
ICJ	International Court of Justice
ICLQ	The International and Comparative Law Quarterly
ICRC	International Committee of the Red Cross
ICTR	International Criminal Tribunal for Rwanda
ICTY	International Criminal Tribunal for the former Yugoslavia
ICYFDC	Islamic Conference Youth Forum for Dialogue and Cooperation
IDP	Internally Displaced People
i.e.	id est
ILM	International Law Materials
ILO	International Labour Organization
IMF	International Monetary Fund / international military forces
INC	Interim National Constitution of the Republic of Sudan
insb.	insbesondere
IPR	Internationales Privatrecht
IPrax	Praxis des Internationalen Privat- und Verfahrensrechts
i.R.	im Ruhestand

irak.	irakisch
IRNA	Iran's official news agency
ISAF	International Security Assistance Force
ISESCO	Islamic Educational, Scientific and Cultural Organization
	J
JEM	(Sudan) Justice and Equality Movement
JICJ	Journal of International Criminal Justice
JORT	Journal Officiel de la République Tunisienne
JSSP	Justice Sector Support Program
JURA	Juristische Ausbildung
JZ	Juristen Zeitung
	K
KAAD	Katholischer Akademischer Ausländer-Dienst
KAS-AI	Konrad Adenauer Stiftung - Auslandsinformationen
KCA	Kadhi's Court Act
kg	Kilogramm / kilogramme
	L
LE	livre égyptienne
Lfg.	Lieferung
LL.M.	Legum Magister; Master of Laws
LOJC	Law on the Organization and Jurisdiction of Courts
	M
M.A.	Magister Artium; Master of Arts
MAoZ	Mufti Act of Zanzibar of 2001
m.E.	meines Erachtens
MENA	Middle East and North Africa
MERIP	Middle East Research and Information Project
MFLC	Marriage and Family Law Commission of 1955
MFLO	The Muslim Family Laws Ordinance of 1961
Mich. JIL	Michigan Journal of International Law
MNLF	Moro National Liberation Front
MP	Member of Parliament

MPIL	Max-Planck-Institut für ausländisches öffentliches Recht und Völkerrecht
MPR	Majelis Permusyawaratan Rakyat
MPU	Majelis Permusyawaratan Ulama
MRR	VN-Menschenrechtsrat / UN Human Rights Council
MSA	Haager Abkommen über die Zuständigkeit der Behörden und das anzuwendende Recht auf dem Gebiet des Schutzes der Minderjährigen vom 5.10.1961 (Minderjährigenschutzabkommen)
m.w.N.	mit weiteren Nachweisen

N

N.B.	Nota bene
NC	Constitution of the Federal Republic of Nigeria
NCW	National Council for Women
NDS	National Directorate of Security
NGO	Non-governmental Organisation
NHRI	National Human Rights Institution
NHRIs	National Human Rights Institutions
NJW	Neue Juristische Wochenschrift
NNPC	Northern Nigeria Penal Code of 1960
No. / no.	Number / number
n.p.	unpaginated
NPA	National Plan Of Action
Nr.	Nummer
NZZ	Neue Zürcher Zeitung

O

OAU	Organisation of African Unity
OIC	Organization of the Islamic Conference
o.g.	oben genannt(e/n)
o.J.	ohne Jahresangabe(n)
OP	Optional Protocol
OP-CRC-AC	Optional Protocol to the Convention on the Rights of the Child on the Involvement of Children in Armed Conflict
OUA	Organisation de l'Unité Africaine

P

p.	page
PAN	Partai Amanat Nasional
para.	paragraph
PAS	Partai Islam Se-Malaysia
PCr.L.J	Pakistan Criminal Law Journal
PDF	Popular Defence Force
PerDa	Peraturan Daerah
pers.	persisch / Persian
PhD	philosophiae doctor
PHYSINT	Physical Integrity Rights Index
PKB	Partai Kebangkitan Bangs
Pl.	Plural
PLD	Pakistan Legal Decisions
PNCSW	Pakistan National Commission on the Status of Women
pp.	pages
PPP	Partai Persatuan Pembangunan
Prof.	Professor
PRT	Provincial Reconstruction Team
PUOICM	Parliamentary Union of the OIC member states

R

RANHAM	National Action Plan for Indonesian Human Rights
rer. pol.	rerum politicarum
Res.	Resolution
RevICJ	Review of the International Commission of Jurists
Rez.	Rezension
RG	Reichsgericht / Reichsgesetz
RGZ	Revolutionary Government of Zanzibar
RiA	Recht in Afrika
Rn.	Randnote
Rp	Rupiah
RSF	Reporters Sans Frontieres
Rz.	Randziffer

S

S.	Seite(n)
S. / s.	siehe / see
SAA	Shariʿat Application Act of 1937
SFDA	Sudan Federalist Democratic Alliance
SJEM	Sudan Justice and Equality Movement
SLM	Sudan Liberation Movement
S.M.Z.	Serikali ya Mapinduzi ya Zanzibar
s.o.	siehe oben
sog.	sogenannt(e/n)
SPLA	Sudan People's Liberation Army
SPLM	Sudan People's Liberation Movement
SSP	Justice Sector Support Program
SSPC	Sokoto Shariʿa Penal Code
St.	Sankt / Saint
StAZ	Zeitschrift für Standesamtswesen, Familienrecht, Staatsangehörigkeitsrecht, Personenstandsrecht, internationales Privatrecht des In- und Auslands
s.u.	siehe unten

T

T.	tome
TOP	Tagesordnungspunkt
TPI	Tribunal de Première Instance
TPersG	tunesisches Gesetzbuches zum Personalstatut
TPLF	Tigray People's Liberation Front

U

u.	und
u.a.	unter anderem
UDHR	Universal Declaration of Human Rights
u.g.	unten genannt(en)
UK	United Kingdom
UN	United Nations
UNAMA	United Nations Assistance Mission in Afghanistan

UNAMA LSOP	United Nations Assistance Mission in Afghanistan, Legal System Observation Program
UNESCO	United Nations Educational, Scientific and Cultural Organization
UNHCHR	United Nations High Commissioner for Human Rights
UNHRC	United Nations Human Rights Council
UNICEF	United Nations Children's Fund
U.N.T.S.	United Nations Treaty Series
UNYB	Max Planck Yearbook of United Nations Law
u.ö.	und öfters
UPR	Universal Periodic Review
ursp.	ursprünglich
US	United States of America
USA	United States of America
USD	United States Dollar
usw.	und so weiter

V

v.	verse(s) / versus
VASA	Vereinigung Arabischer Studenten und Wissenschaftler
VCLT	Vienna Convention on the Law of Treaties
vgl.	vergleiche
Virg. JIL	Virgina Journal of International Law
VN	Vereinte Nationen
vol.	volume
VRÜ	Verfassung und Recht in Übersee

W

WEOG	Western European and Others Group
WLUML	Women Living Under Muslim Laws
WOCMES	World Congress of Middle Eastern Studies
WPFCA	West Pakistan Family Courts Act of 1964
www.	World Wide Web

Z

ZaöRV	Zeitschrift für ausländisches öffentliches Recht und Völkerrecht
Z.B. / z.B.	zum Beispiel

Ziff.	Ziffer(n)
ZGB	Zivilgesetzbuch
ZPO	Zivilprozessordnung
z.T.	zum Teil
ZVglRWiss.	Zeitschrift für Vergleichende Rechtswissenschaft
z.Z.	zur Zeit

Einführung

Introduction

مقدمة

Islam und Menschenrechte (Islam and Human Rights / الإسلام وحقوق الإنسان)
Hatem Elliesie (Hrsg./Editor), © Peter Lang Verlag: Frankfurt a.M. 2010, S. 21-37

Vorwort des Herausgebers

Menschenrechte stellen sowohl in ihrem materiellen Gehalt als auch in ihrer formell-rechtlichen Ausprägung einen gängigen Untersuchungsgegenstand wissenschaftlicher Studien dar. Diese liegen in den unterschiedlichsten Akzentuierungen vor. Naturrechtliche und philosophische Begründungsmuster, der Universalitätsanspruch, die Bedeutung von Menschenrechten in Form von nationalen, meist verfassungsrechtlich gewährleisteten Bürgerrechten, aber auch die Systematisierung von Menschenrechten im Rahmen des jeweiligen Staatsorganisationsrechts können thematischer Schwerpunkt oder methodischer Rekurs akademischer Arbeiten sein, um nur einige Aspekte zu nennen.

Die Einbeziehung des Islam in diesen Kontext macht das komplexe Themenspektrum nicht einfacher, zumal der »Islam« nicht als einheitlicher Block, einem monolithischen Gebilde gleich, existiert. Zu unterschiedlich ist das, was man an einem bestimmten Ort und einer bestimmten Zeit für sich als „islamisch“ begreift. Folglich wäre es auch verfehlt, wenn man den Diskurs „Islam und Menschenrechte“ pauschal und undifferenziert auf die vermeintlich antagonistischen Begriffspaare »islamische Menschenrechte« und »westliche Menschenrechte« reduziert. Menschenrechtsvorstellungen spiegeln grundsätzlich kulturelle Wertvorstellungen wider, die Ähnlichkeiten wie auch Unterschiede aufweisen. Trotz der dramatisch erscheinenden religiösen Dimension hängen Menschenrechtsverletzungen in der islamischen Welt aber nicht *per se* mit ihren soziokulturellen oder gar soziorelígiösen Traditionen zusammen. Das Verständnis dessen, was man in islamisch geprägten Regionen der Welt als »Menschenrecht(e)« versteht, zu verstehen hat oder möglicherweise verstehen will, unterliegt verschiedenartigen Prozessen. Je nach Kontext können kulturprägende Faktoren, theologische Dogmatik aber auch ideologische Programmatik richtungsweisend sein. Diese gilt es stets in kritische Überlegungen einzubeziehen. Durch die Konfrontation mit anderen Sichtweisen kann man die jeweiligen Verständnishorizonte besser erfassen. Punktuelle Selbstreflexion kann dabei das eigene Verständnis verändern. Es sollte aber nicht zwangsläufig darum gehen, einen umfassenden Relativismus zu erwirken. Es gilt vielmehr anzuerkennen, dass heutige Rechtssätze vor dem Hintergrund verschiedener Kulturen und religiöser Ausprägungen unterschiedlich interpretiert werden können. Die Frage nach dem Verhältnis von „Islam und Menschenrechten“ sollte daher auch stets im Diskurs mit islamische Wissenschaftler und nicht nur über deren Ansichten hinweg gestellt und herausgearbeitet werden.

Islam und Menschenrechte (Islam and Human Rights / الإسلام وحقوق الإنسان)
Hatem Elliesie (Hrsg./Editor), © Peter Lang Verlag: Frankfurt a.M. 2010, S. 23-26

Unter dieser Prämisse steht auch die konzeptionelle Gestaltung des vorliegenden Bandes: Die einzelnen Artikel sollen in ihrer Aussagekraft wirken, kontrastieren, durch andersartige methodische Ansätze neue Perspektiven eröffnen und über den eigenen wissenschaftlichen Zirkel hinaus den Diskurs nach Möglichkeit bereichern. Ein notwendigerweise begrenzter Band kann dabei sicherlich nur einen Ausschnitt des Spektrums liefern. Das Bestreben lag indes darin, ein internationales Forum zu bieten, um unterschiedlichste Facetten der Thematik vorzustellen und zu diskutieren.

Dass das seit vielen Jahren behandelte Thema „Menschenrechte und Islam" nichts an seinem Reiz verloren hat, lässt sich an der 10. Jahrestagung der Gesellschaft für Arabisches und Islamisches Recht e.V. veranschaulichen: Zehn Jahre nach der ersten Tagung der Gesellschaft in Bonn entschied man sich, das Thema wieder aufzugreifen und zum alleinigen Gegenstand der gemeinsam mit dem Deutschen Institut für Menschenrechte organisierten *Jubiläums*tagung am 19. und 20. Oktober 2007 in Berlin zu machen. Ein Teil der Beiträge des vorliegenden Bandes basieren auf dieser Tagung und wurde durch weitere interessante Abhandlungen ergänzt. Man kann also nicht – wie bisher üblich – von einem reinen Konferenzband, sondern viel eher von einem Jubiläumsband sprechen. Das besondere Ereignis aufgreifend, freue ich mich auf den nachfolgenden einleitenden Beitrag „Die Gesellschaft für Arabisches und Islamisches Recht: 10 Jahre in der Retrospektive" verweisen zu können, in dem Mathias Rohe als Gründungsmitglied und Erste Vorsitzender der Gesellschaft einen Rück-, Ein- und Ausblick der Aktivitäten der Gesellschaft bietet.

In den ersten die islamrechtlich-theologischen Methodik und Rechtsphilosophie betreffenden thematischen Block führt Abdullahi Ahmed An-Na'im mit seinem Artikel „Islam and Human Rights: Introductory Remarks and Reflections" ein. Daran schließen sich Beiträge von Muhammad Kalisch („Islam und Menschenrechte: Betrachtungen zum Verhältnis von Religion und Recht"), von Assem Hefny („Hermeneutik, Koraninterpretation und Menschenrechte") und von Heiner Bielefeldt („‚Westliche' versus ‚islamische' Menschenrechtskonzeptionen?") an.

Um Sinn, Funktion und Relevanz der »Menschenrechte« in der sich annähernden Welt und Gesellschaft der Gegenwart sowie ihren dogmatischen wie praktischen Stand in ihrem jeweiligen Kontext besser begreifen zu können, ist es unerlässlich, auch den *status quo* in einigen ausgewählten islamisch geprägten Staaten und Regionen nachzuzeichnen. Eine Konzentration auf die sog. arabischen Kernländer würde allerdings nur eine verengte Sichtweise aufzeigen. Ich habe daher bei der Gliederung des zweiten Abschnittes dieser Publikation drei regionale Schwerpunkte gesetzt, der seinerseits jeweils aus einem Überblicksartikel zu Afrika (Mashood Baderin), dem Nahen Osten/Nordafrika (Ann Elizabeth Mayer) und Asien (Tim Lindsey) besteht. Diese Artikel werden dann jeweils durch ausgewählte länderspezifische Studien, zu Nigeria (Isa Hayatu Chiroma / Hatem Elliesie), Sansibar (Chris Maina Peter), dem Sudan (Hatem Elliesie); Ägypten (Bahey eldin Hassan), zu staatlichen Menschenrechtsstrukturen und nationalen Menschenrechtsinstitutionen in der MENA-Region (Anna Würth / Claudia Engelmann), zum Grundrecht auf heterosexuelle Selbstbestimmung in den Verfassungssystemen arabischer Staaten (Naseef Naeem) sowie Afghanistan (Tilmann Röder), Pakistan (Ayesha Shahid / Javaid Rehman) und Iran (Irene Schneider), ergänzt.

Inhaltlich anknüpfend an die Beiträge von Javaid Rehman / Ayesha Shahid und Irene Schneider zu frauenrechtlichen Aspekten beleuchtet Hanna Beate Schöpp-Schilling die Thematik auf einer institutionell übergeordneten Ebene, nämlich dem „Frauenrechtsausschuss der Vereinten Nationen in der Interaktion mit islamisch geprägten Staaten“. Gemeinsam mit dem Beitrag von Theodor Rathgeber zur „Organisation der Islamischen Konferenz im Menschenrechtsrat der Vereinten Nationen: Menschenrechte als Instrument staatlicher Politik” wurde an dieser Stelle der dritte Themenkomplex aus einer über- und zwischenstaatlichen, institutionellen Betrachtungsweise beleuchtet.

Abgerundet wird der vorliegenden Band mit Beiträgen von Peter Scholz („Ordre Public, Menschenrechte und Scharia“) und Imen Gallala („Religionsfreiheit und islamisch geprägtes Erbrecht: gesetzliche Regelungen und Rechtsprechungsauslegung im heutigen Ägypten und Tunesien“) in dem hierfür vorgesehenen, abschließenden Themenkomplex: Menschenrechte und Islamisches Recht unter dem Blickwinkel des (Internationalen) Privatrechts.

In diesem Zusammenhang sei noch angemerkt, dass die Verfasser der jeweiligen Aufsätze allein die Verantwortung für die von ihnen vorgebrachten Auffassungen und den jeweiligen Inhalt tragen, welche nicht unbedingt der Meinung des Herausgebers oder gar der Gesellschaft für Arabisches und Islamisches Recht entsprechen. Die Transliteration orientiert sich, soweit es sich um relevante *termini technici* oder Zitierung von Autoren und u.a. arabischsprachigen Werken handelt, an der Norm der Deutschen Morgenländischen Gesellschaft. Bei der Darstellung von Eigennamen wurde entweder den Vorgaben der Beitragenden entsprochen oder darauf geachtet, dass die Namen in der Form dargestellt werden, wie sie sich seither etabliert haben. Ähnlich wurde auch mit der Wiedergabe deutscher sowie englischer Namen und Ortsbezeichnungen ins Arabische verfahren, wobei sich die Orthographie weitgehend an der ägyptisch-arabischen Lautung orientiert. Soweit sich darüber hinaus in der deutsch- oder englischsprachigen Literatur bestimmte Schreibweisen arabischer Bezeichnungen oder Begriffe eingebürgert haben, wurden diese übernommen.

Schließlich ist es dem Herausgeber ein Bedürfnis, sich bei allen zu bedanken, die einen Anteil am Zustandekommen dieses Bandes gehabt haben. Ein besonders tief empfundener Dank gilt dem Reihenherausgeber der *Leipziger Beiträge zur Orientforschung,* Prof. Dr. Hans-Georg Ebert, für die Anregung, die Herausgeberschaft dieses speziellen VII. Bandes in der Unterreihe *Beiträge zum Islamischen Recht* zu übernehmen. Auch ohne den dankenswerten Beistand zahlreicher Kollegen hätte der vorliegende Band in dieser Form nicht zeitnah umgesetzt werden können. Die technischen Ratschläge, das kritische Korrekturlesen und die konstruktiven Hinweise insb. von Sina Nikolajew, Joy Gebhardt, Bawar Bammarny und Zeus Wellnhofer weiß ich sehr schätzen. Herrn Benjamin Kloss vom Peter Lang Verlag bin ich für seine Bemühungen und das Verständnis in gleicher Weise verbunden.

Ein ganz besonderer, herzlicher Dank richtet sich selbstverständlich an die Autorinnen und Autoren. Ihnen sei an dieser Stelle nochmals für die Bereitschaft sich am Diskurs innerhalb dieses Bandes zu beteiligen, die ihnen abgeforderte Zeit und Arbeitskraft ausdrücklich gedankt. Ihren interessanten Beiträgen und der gute Zusammenarbeit ist das erfolgreiche Zustandekommen dieser Publikation maßgeblich zuzuschreiben.

Vielen Dank! Many thanks! شكرا جزيلا!

Berlin, im Sommer 2009 *Hatem Elliesie*

Editor's Foreword

The concept of Human Rights remains a prevalent subject of research in various academic studies in and of itself: rationale based on Natural Rights and philosophical patterns, the claim of the universality of Human Rights, Human Rights' significance in terms of national inalienable rights, and also their systematization within the scope of the respective *Staatsorganisationsrechts,* to name a few. Islam, as it relates to these concepts, compound the complexity of the intricate spectrum of themes, since the idea of »Islam« itself does not consist of a singular, compact definition. One's understanding of »Islam« is both multifarious and fluid in time and place, to say the least.

Hence, it would be inappropriate to reduce the discourse of "Islam and Human Rights", categorically and undifferentiated, to the seemingly stark and oversimplified juxtaposition between »Islamic Human Rights« und »Western Human Rights«. Even though the term »Human Rights« portends an alleged, accepted clear definition, upon closer examination this is not the case. Human Rights perceptions reflect, fundamentally, cultural ideas and moral concepts which feature similarities as well as differences. Despite the dramatic religious dimension, the notion of Human Rights abuses in the 'Islamic World' is neither *per se* related to its socio-cultural nor even to its socio-religious traditions. The understanding of what one comprehends, is obliged to conceive, or possibly means to avow one's self to, as »Human Right(s)« in Islamic or predominantly Islamic regions of the world, is subject to diverse processes and influences. Determining processes in this context may derive not only from factors devised by cultural patterns and/or dogmatic aspects of theology, but also ideological pragmatics. It is imperative to include those facets into one's critical considerations. By dint of the confrontation with other views, one is each time able to further refine one's definition; of Human Rights, of Islam, and of Human Rights in an Islamic setting. In doing so, more acute self-reflection might change one's own understanding. This should not, however, necessarily lead to a broadstroke generalization or a relativism, so to speak, of distinct ideas. Rather, it is necessary to establish that contemporary legal norms can be interpreted differently against the background of diverse cultures and religious characteristics. Therefore, the matter of the relationship of "Islam and Human Rights" ought to be questioned, explored and worked out between scholars of 'Western' training and those of predominantly Islamic countries, and not simply presumed that the 'Western' thinking is imposed on scholars of predominantly Islamic countries.

Islam und Menschenrechte (Islam and Human Rights / الإسلام وحقوق الإنسان)
Hatem Elliesie (Hrsg./Editor), © Peter Lang Verlag: Frankfurt a.M. 2010, S. 27-30

The composition of the collection is based upon this premise. Each article provides its own statement; at times contrasting and/or providing new perspectives through varying methodological approaches. The volume can by no means – and neither does it attempt to – impart a conclusive view of such a broad, and oftentimes controversial, subject matter. The purpose, rather, lies in facilitating the formation of an international forum aiming to discuss the various facets of Islam, Human Rights and the practice of Human Rights in the 'Islamic World'. The ideal result would be to enrich the discourse even further, and broaden it beyond one's own academic circle.

That the interest (and controversy) in "Human Rights and Islam" remains in the forefront is exemplified by the 10th Annual Conference of the *Gesellschaft für Arabisches und Islamisches Recht* (German Association of Arabic and Islamic Law) again choosing it as its primary concern; just as it had ten years ago, at its initial conference in Bonn, Germany.

Some of the volume's contributions are based on the aforementioned conference, which was organized in collaboration with the German Institute for Human Rights, and took place in Berlin, on 19 and 20 October 2007. The supplementations of these contributions by further enlightening discourse warrants its designation as a 'Jubilee Edition', and not merely a 'Conference Edition', as is the custom. That said, I am pleased to give special mention to the contribution "The *Gesellschaft für Arabisches und Islamisches Recht:* 10 Years in the Retrospective" in which Mathias Rohe presents, as founding member and Chairman of the Association, a comprehensive look at the association: looking back at its beginnings, providing an insight of its aims and accomplishments, and looking forward to the association's prospects ahead.

Abdullahi Ahmed An-Na'im provides a prelude to the key issue "Islam and Human Rights" with his article "Islam and Human Rights: Introductory Remarks and Reflections". The first section includes contributions dealing with Islamic legal and theological Approaches and Philosophy of Laws, namely those of Muhammad Kalisch ("Islam and Human Rights: Considerations on the Relationship of Religion and Law"), Assem Hefny ("Hermeneutics, Quran Interpretation and Human Rights") and Heiner Bielefeldt ("'Western' versus 'Islamic' Human Rights Conceptions?").

In order to better understand the sense, function and relevance of Human Rights in theory as well as in practice, and keeping in mind a constantly 'shrinking' globalized world, it is absolutely necessary to take into account the current state of affairs in a number of predominantly Islamic states and regions. A concentration on the so-called 'core Arabic countries' would only demonstrate a narrowed point of view. To counter this, I have therefore established three regional emphases, each with their own introductory article, namely on Africa (Mashood Baderin), the Middle East (Ann Elizabeth Mayer) and South East Asia (Tim Lindsey).

Each emphasized region is complemented by three essays dealing with the MENA's governmental Human Right's structures and institutions (Anna Würth / Claudia Engelmann), the Basic Right of heterosexual Self-Determination in the constitutional Systems of Arabic States (Naseef Naeem), Egypt (Bahey eldin Hassan); and Nigeria (Isa Hayatu Chiroma / Hatem Elliesie), Sansibar (Chris Maina Peter), the Sudan (Hatem Elliesie); as well as Afghanistan (Tilmann Röder), Pakistan (Javaid Rehman / Ayesha Shahid) and Iran (Irene Schneider).

Rehman / Shahid and Schneider's contributions focus on women's rights in Pakistan as well as in Iran. Hanna Beate Schöpp-Schilling's contribution, which follows, jumps off of this topic, but from another perspective: that of an organization's, "The UN Committee on the Elimination of Discrimination and its Interaction with Muslim States". After this, comes Theodor Rathgeber's paper, "The Organisation of Islamic Conference in the Context of the Human Rights Council: Human Rights as Instruments of Government Politics", completing the third section and highlighting the topic from an institutional point of view.

The closing chapter, "Human Rights and Islamic Law in light of the (International) Private Law", with contributions by Peter Scholz ("Ordre Public, Human Rights and Sharia") and by Imen Gallala ("Freedom of Religion and Islamic Law-based Succession Law: Statutes and Judicial Interpretations in Contemporary Egypt and Tunisia") completes the collection.

It must be noted that the authors are solely responsible for the views expressed in their respective pieces and specific content, and that these do not necessarily correspond with the opinions and notions either of the editor or that of the *Gesellschaft für Arabisches und Islamisches Recht.*

The transcription used throughout the book follows the standard of the *Deutsche Morgenländische Gesellschaft* as far as it is a matter of relevant *termini technici* or citations of authors and Arabic works, among others. Names have been either displayed in the way prescribed by the contributors, or in consideration of how names have been commonly written in the Latin script. Accordingly, the manner of presentation of German or English names and places into the Arabic characters has been handled in the same fashion; whereas, the orthography is based on Egyptian Arabic Phonology, for the most part. Moreover, common spellings of Arabic descriptions and terms into the German or English literature have been assumed in the way they are generally used.

In closing, I would like to thank all who have helped bring this volume to completion. Profound gratitude is reserved for the editor of the series *Leipziger Beiträge zur Orientforschung*, Prof. Dr. Hans-Georg Ebert, for initiating the energy and enthusiasm which brought about my conceptual and editorial undertaking and eventual publishing of this book in the sub-series *Beiträge zum Islamischen Recht*, as its seventh volume. It is also necessary to mention here that without the assistance of numerous colleagues, the culmination of the project would not have been possible. The technical suggestions and constructive guidance from Sina Nikolajew, Joy Gebhardt, Bawar Bammarny and Zeus Wellnhofer are very much appreciated. I am also extremely grateful to Benjamin Kloss of Peter Lang Publishing for his support and understanding.

Very many special and warm thanks, of course, to the authors, whose time, attention and collaboration are essentially what brought this discourse to its successful fruition.

To each and every one of you,

Many thanks! Vielen Dank! شكرا جزيلا!

Berlin, Summer 2009 *Hatem Elliesie*

Die Gesellschaft für Arabisches und Islamisches Recht: 10 Jahre in der Retrospektive

Mathias Rohe, Erlangen

Wird man die sieben Personen zusammenbringen, die zur Gründung eines Vereins nötig sind? Nur sehr kurz stellte sich diese Frage im Jahre 1997, als einschlägig interessierte und versierte Wissenschaftler und Praktiker (oft in Personalunion) die Gründung der Gesellschaft für Arabisches und Islamisches Recht (GAIR) ins Auge fassten. 28 Gründungsmitglieder zeigten am 24. Oktober des Jahres, dass die Zeit für die Einrichtung einer solchen wissenschaftlichen Gesellschaft im deutschsprachigen Raum reif war. Mittlerweile ist die Mitgliederzahl auf über 170 angewachsen – der Bedarf scheint nicht geringer geworden zu sein.

In vielen Bereichen des arabischen und islamischen Rechts ist noch Grundlagenarbeit zu leisten. Die Bündelung der Kräfte in einer wissenschaftlichen Gesellschaft erleichtert dies erheblich. Umso höher ist die Arbeit der Pioniere einzuschätzen, welche häufig unter schwierigen Arbeitsbedingungen grundlegende Werke fortdauernder Validität erarbeitet haben. Hier ist nicht zuletzt unser im Jahre 2006 verstorbener Gründungsvorsitzender Prof. Dr. Ernst Klingmüller zu nennen, der juristische und islamwissenschaftliche Interessen in Studium und wissenschaftlichem Werk trefflich verbunden hat. Als er im Jahre 2001 aus Altersgründen den Vorsitz unserer Gesellschaft aufgab, durfte ich seine Nachfolge übernehmen, er selbst blieb der Gesellschaft über den Vorsitz unseres Kuratoriums verbunden. Diese Nachfolge hat mittlerweile unser hochverdientes, im Jahre 2008 mit einem Symposium zu ehrendes Mitglied Prof. hon. Dr. Hilmar Krüger angetreten. Über seinen Tod hinaus hat Prof. Dr. Ernst Klingmüller in seiner bekannten großzügigen Weise weitere Forschungsarbeiten durch die Einrichtung der Klingmüller-Stiftung ermöglicht (näheres auf der GAIR-Homepage unter: http://www.gair.uni-erlangen.de/Klingmueller-Stiftung.html).

Die GAIR lebt. Sie lebt vom ehrenamtlichen Engagement der Mitglieder, des Vorstandes und des Kuratoriums. Keine großen Geldbeträge sind zu verwalten – wissenschaftliche Gesellschaften in Deutschland stützen sich in aller Regel auf Expertise und Einsatzbereitschaft ihrer Mitglieder, nicht auf finanzielle Pfründen. Immerhin gelingt es uns, mit Hilfe der Mitgliedsbeiträge jährlich eine meist zweitägig angelegte Tagung an wechselnden Standorten abzuhalten, auf der typischerweise ein bestimmter Themenbereich und eine bestimmte Rechtsordnung im Mittelpunkt stehen. In den vergangenen Jahren wurden so die Rechtsordnungen von Afghanistan, Ägypten, Irak, Iran, Libanon, Nigeria,

Islam und Menschenrechte (Islam and Human Rights / الإسلام وحقوق الإنسان)
Hatem Elliesie (Hrsg./Editor), © Peter Lang Verlag: Frankfurt a.M. 2010, S. 31-33

Pakistan, Sudan, Syrien, der Türkei, den Vereinigten Arabischen Emiraten sowie unter anderem die Themenbereiche Klassisches Islamisches Recht / Islamische Rechtsgeschichte; Einflüsse des Islam auf das moderne Rechtsleben (insbesondere in *Arabischen Staaten*); Gutachtenwesen (*iftā*ʾ) in Vergangenheit und Gegenwart; Strafrecht im Islam; Menschenrechte und Islam; (Internationales) Privatrecht in sowie zu islamisch geprägten Ländern; *Islamic Banking* und *Islamic Finance;* Schiedsgerichtsbarkeit; Schutz des geistigen Eigentums, Urheberrecht, Handels- und Wirtschaftsrechts in und zu islamisch geprägten Staaten im Nahen- und Mittleren Osten; sowie Islamisches Recht in Deutschland und Europa aus wissenschaftlicher und rechtspraktischer Sicht beleuchtet. Im letzten Jahr konnten wir die sehr erfolgreiche 10. Jahrestagung gemeinsam mit dem Deutschen Institut für Menschenrechte in Berlin ausrichten. Das Symposium zu Ehren von Hilmar Krüger anlässlich seines 70. Geburtstags im Jahre 2008 hat die Deutsch-Türkische und die Deutsch-Iranische Juristenvereinigung mit der GAIR zusammengeführt. Tagungsbände, zum erheblichen Teil unter der Ägide unseres Vorstandsmitglieds Prof. Dr. Hans-Georg Ebert herausgegeben, bringen die gewonnenen Erkenntnisse einem breiteren Publikum nahe. Ich selbst habe sie erfreut in Bibliotheken zwischen Boston, London und Tokio vorfinden können. Zudem ist eine stattliche Zahl von weiteren Informationsseminaren und Symposien zu nennen: Zu Ehren unseres stellvertretenden Vorsitzenden Prof. em. Dr. Omaia Elwan, akad. Dir. i.R. fand 1999 ein hochkarätig besetzte einschlägiges Symposion an der Universität Heidelberg statt; 2-tägige Informationsseminare zum arabisch-islamischen Recht (2002) und iranisch-islamischen Recht (2005) wurden, insbesondere durch Hatem Elliesie konzipiert, initiiert, und mit weiteren höchst engagierten Nachwuchsmitglieder an der Universität Mannheim in Zusammenarbeit mit der *European Law Students' Association* organisiert und durchgeführt. Nicht zuletzt ist das Panel „Islamic Law in a Comparative Perspective“ auf dem *First World Congress for Middle Eastern Studies* im Jahre 2002 in Mainz zu nennen.

All dies mag auch aufzeigen, was wir nicht sind: Wir sind kein Interessenverband, keine „Lobby“, die sich in tagesaktuelle Mediendebatten einschalten wollte, sondern eine Vereinigung, die sich zum Ziel gesetzt hat, einen wichtigen Bereich des Rechts *sine ira et studio* mit wissenschaftlicher Gründlichkeit und Blick auf praktische Realitäten zu erforschen und bekannt zu machen. Der Satzungszweck benennt das Anliegen, zum gegenseitigen Verständnis der Rechtssysteme und der Rechtspraxis des europäischen und des islamischen, insbesondere des arabischen Raumes beizutragen. Mit der gebotenen Nüchternheit werden hierbei auch offensichtlich bestehende Missverständnisse ebenso wie tatsächlich bestehende Probleme aufgearbeitet. Weder kann es unser Anliegen sein, bestehende Konfliktlagen blauäugig zu ignorieren, noch wäre es angebracht, in einen verbreiteten faktenresistenten Alarmismus einzustimmen. Information und auf solide Arbeiten gegründete Einschätzungen der Lage(n) ist das, was wir zu bieten haben.

Drei Besonderheiten zeichnen die GAIR aus: Erstens hat sie seit ihrer Gründung und bis heute erfolgreich die Interessen von Praktikern und Wissenschaftlern einen und eine enge Zusammenarbeit fördern können. Zum zweiten baut sie Brücken zwischen Vertreterinnen und Vertretern von Rechts- und Islamwissenschaften. *Last, but not the least:* Wir sind eine erfreulich jung gebliebene Gesellschaft mit großer Resonanz unter Studierenden und jungen Nachwuchswissenschaftlern.

Diese Zeilen sind in Graz entstanden, wohin der Verfasser an der dortigen Leopold-Franzens-Universität zu einem einschlägigen Vortrag eingeladen war. Dies richtet zugleich den Blick auf einige Zukunftswünsche: Es wäre zu begrüßen, wenn es uns gelänge, uns noch stärker in Nachbarländern und international mit Interessierten zu vernetzen. Damit könnten wir weiterhin und vermehrt einen Beitrag zur Erhaltung einer großen auf den Islam und die *Arabische Welt* gerichteten Wissenschaftstradition leisten.

The *Gesellschaft für Arabisches und Islamisches Recht*: 10 Years in the Retrospective

Mathias Rohe, Erlangen

The question of forming the aforementioned association came up, but for a moment, as respective interested and versed academics and legal practitioners envisioned the founding of the "Association for Arabic and Islamic Law (*Gesellschaft für Arabisches und Islamisches Recht* – GAIR)" in 1997. Twenty eight (28) founding members agreed on the 24 October of the same year that the time has come for such an academic association in Germany. Meanwhile, membership has increased to over one hundred and seventy (170) and it appears that the demand is flourishing.

In numerous areas of Arabic and Islamic Law, much of the groundwork still needs to be done. A concerted effort in an academic association alleviates this load considerably. The preliminary work of the pioneers must be all the more appreciated, as this was often done under difficult working conditions, while continually striving to maintain its validity. It is, especially in this context, worth noting that our founding Chairman Prof. Dr. Ernst Klingmüller, who passed away in the year 2006, exemplified this manner. He faithfully combined scientific, legal, as well as Islamic interests in his studies and in his academic work. I have had the honour and privilege of taking on his position as Chairman, which he relinquished due to old age. He remained affiliated with the association as Chairman of our Board of Trustees until his death. This function has now been taken over by our well-deserved, Prof. hon. Dr. Hilmar Krüger, who is to be honoured in a symposium in 2008. It should also be mentioned that in light of his absence, Prof. Dr. Ernst Klingmüller's well-known generosity made further research possible by the establishment of the *Klingmüller-Stiftung* (details on the GAIR-Homepage under: http://www.gair.uni-erlangen.de/Klingmueller-Stiftung .html).

The GAIR lives on through the voluntary engagement of its members, the Executive Committee and the Board of Trustees. No large sums of money need to be administered. Academic associations in Germany normally rely on the expertise and eager participation of its members, not on (financial) endowment. The membership fee allows for a yearly two-day Conference, held in alternating venues, wherein a particular subject matter and a certain legal system is made the focal point of examination. In this manner, a vast range of topics have been presented and examined; including, but not limited to, the following: legal orders of Afghanistan, Egypt, Iraq, Iran, Lebanon, Nigeria, Pakistan, Sudan, Syria, Turkey, the United Arab Emirates; the themes of Classical Islamic Law/history

Islam und Menschenrechte (Islam and Human Rights / الإسلام وحقوق الإنسان)
Hatem Elliesie (Hrsg./Editor), © Peter Lang Verlag: Frankfurt a.M. 2010, S. 35-37

of Islamic Law; the impact of Islam on contemporary legal practice (particularly within *Arabic States*); the Method of giving Legal Interpretation (*iftāʾ*) in the past and present; Criminal Law in Islam; Islam and Human Rights; International Private Law in, and in light of, predominately Islamic countries; Islamic Banking and Islamic Finance; Arbitration; Protection of Intellectual Property Rights and Commercial Law in, and in view of, predominately Islamic states in the Middle East; as well as Islamic Law in Germany and Europe from a Scientific and Legal Practice point of view. In 2007, we were able to arrange our very successful 10th annual conference in collaboration with the German Institute for Human Rights in Berlin, Germany. The symposium, in honour of Hilmar Krüger, on the occasion of his 70th birthday in 2008, brought the GAIR together with the *Deutsch-Türkische Juristenvereinigung* (Association of German-Turkish Jurists) and the *Deutsch-Iranische Juristenvereinigung* (Association of German-Iranian Jurist). Proceedings, in considerable parts, issued under the aegis of our executive committee member, Prof. Dr. Hans-Georg Ebert, made the insight more accessible to the general public. I, myself, was pleased to be able to find them in libraries in Boston, London and Tokyo. Moreover, a sizeable number of additional seminars and symposia need to be mentioned; most especially, the renowned symposium in honour of our Deputy Chairman, Prof. em. Dr. Omaia Elwan, akad. Dir. i.R., which took place at the University of Heidelberg in 1999 as well as two (2) two-day seminars at the University of Mannheim conceptualized, initiated and organised by Hatem Elliesie and by highly committed young members' in collaboration with the European Law Students' Association on Arabic-Islamic Law in 2002 and Iranian-Islamic Law in 2005. Lastly, a panel discussion entitled "Islamic Law in a Comparative Perspective" on the occasion of the First World Congress for Middle Eastern Studies in 2002 in Mainz, Germany.

All this demonstrates what we are not: We are neither a pressure group, nor a lobby, which aims to join the daily media dispute; but, rather, an association which has as its aim to research exhaustively and realistically an important field of law *sine ira et studio* and make it known to the public. The purpose of the GAIR-statute is that one contributes to the mutual understanding of the legal systems and the legal practices of the European and Islamic – especially the *Arabic* – areas. With reason, obviously existing misunderstandings are reappraised as much as factual existing problems. It can neither be our concern to naively ignore existing conflicts, nor would it be appropriate for us to join into an alarmism which disregards the facts. What we have to offer is information and an evaluation of the situation(s) based on solid, well thought out analysis.

The GAIR is characterized by three distinctions: firstly, it has been able to promote a close cooperation of interests of both those of practitioners and those of academics ever since its foundation. Secondly, it forges links between representatives of jurisprudence and Islamic sciences. And – last, but not the least – we are, pleasantly, a dynamic association with a sizeable following of students and ambitious young scholars.

All this arose in Graz (Austria) where the author was invited to a pertinent lecture at the local *Leopold-Franzens-Universität.* This brings up the point: It would be welcomed if an even broader network of the neighbouring countries and of interested international entities and individuals could be established. By doing so, a contribution to the maintenance of a large scientific tradition focusing on Islam and the *Arabic World* could further enhanced.

Islam und Menschenrechte (Islam and Human Rights / الإسلام وحقوق الإنسان)
Hatem Elliesie (Hrsg./Editor), © Peter Lang Verlag: Frankfurt a.M. 2010

BEITRÄGE ZUR ISLAMRECHTLICHEN METHODIK SOWIE ZUR RECHTSPHILOSOPHIE

CONTRIBUTIONS TO ISLAMIC LEGAL AND THEOLOGICAL APPROACHES AND PHILOSOPHY OF LAWS

مساهمات في منهج البحث القانون الإسلامي وفلسفة القانون

Islam und Menschenrechte (Islam and Human Rights / الإسلام وحقوق الإنسان)
Hatem Elliesie (Hrsg./Editor), © Peter Lang Verlag: Frankfurt a.M. 2010, S. 39-119

Islam and Human Rights: Introductory Remarks and Reflections*

Abdullahi Ahmed An-Na'im, Atlanta

The implementation of International Human Rights norms in any society requires thoughtful and well-informed engagement of religion (broadly defined) because of its strong influence on human belief systems and behaviour, regardless of the formal characterization of the relationship between religion and the state society. While it is true that the behaviour of believers is not always motivated by total fidelity to their faith, religious considerations are too important for the majority of people for Human Rights scholars and advocates to continue to dismiss them simply as irrelevant, insignificant, or problematic.

In emphasizing the need for advocates of Human Rights to seriously engage religion, I do not assume that there is either immediate compatibility or permanent contradiction between Human Rights and any religion. On the contrary, my suggestion is premised on the paradox of the reality of tension between the two, on one hand, and the importance of reconciliation on the other. This paradox is often depicted in terms of the polar extremes posed by the universality of Human Rights and the relativity of religion. In my view, to posit such a dichotomy is misleading, because of the interdependence between the two. While the universality of Human Rights cannot be realized among believers unless they accept it as consistent with their religious beliefs, the integrity of religious faith and its relevance to the lives of its adherents is dependent on the effective protection of Human Rights. Accordingly, it is more useful to see this relationship in terms of synergy and mutual influence, than to envision its as one of the permanent antagonism.

My argument is that the terms of this debate should be expanded, to include the role of local and global social, economic and political factors, instead of focused purely theological analyses of the relationship between religion and Human Rights. In my view, this approach is more conducive to mediating between the polar extremes of universality and relativity by emphasizing of common features of human experiences over differences in abstract theological terms. This mediation is more likely to be effective when the focus is on actual perception and practice of Muslims and other believers in their specific context. In other words, I am advocating that religious factors be understood in their proper perspective

* This article is – for the purpose of this volume – revised and modified version of a paper presented on the 94th annual meeting of the American Society of International Law held in Washington D.C. on 5-8 April 2000.

Islam und Menschenrechte (Islam and Human Rights / الإسلام وحقوق الإنسان)
Hatem Elliesie (Hrsg./Editor), © Peter Lang Verlag: Frankfurt a.M. 2010, S. 41-47

or context, instead of disregarded altogether or granted exaggerated impact as theological ideals.

For the purpose of this introductory remark to the Jubilee-Edition of the *Gesellschaft für Arabisches und Islamisches Recht* (German Association of Arabic and Islamic Law) in celebration of its 10th anniversary, its necessary to distinguish between the two senses in which the term *Human Rights* is often used. In one sense, the term *Human Rights* refers to historical struggles for freedom and social justice in general. While prevalent in popular discourse, this general sense of the term is not useful for an analysis of the compatibility of Human Rights with any specific religious, political or ideological tradition, as each of these paradigms would claim its own understanding of Human Rights. As used here, the term *Human Rights* refers to the particular conception of freedom and social justice that was articulated in the Universal Declaration of Human Rights (UDHR) of 1948, and more specifically defined in subsequent treaties and effectuated through a variety of implementation mechanisms.

The key feature of Human Rights as defined in the UDHR is that these rights are *due to all human beings by virtue of their humanity, without distinction on such grounds as race, sex (gender), religion, language or national origin.* There is no doubt that the most immediate antecedents and articulation of this concept of Human Rights have emerged from Western (European and American) experiences since the late 18th century. As commonly acknowledged, however, those experiences were premised on the Enlightenment, rather than Christian or Jewish theologies, though the latter have tended to reconcile themselves with the former over time. In particular, the concept of Human Rights as defined in the UDHR is essentially a "universalization" of the idea of fundamental constitutional rights as developed by *Western* countries, although the actual set of rights provided for the Declaration surpasses what can be found under constitutional system of any country, *Western* or *non-Western*.

It is important to note here that while it is not binding as such under International Law, the UDHR is clearly the enabling document for efforts to define Human Rights and devise mechanisms and strategies for their implementation. Given the realities of national sovereignty and international relations, it was imperative to strike a balance between the need for international supervision and respect for the domestic jurisdiction. Thus, in universalizing certain notions of Fundamental Rights, International Human Rights systems seek to make these rights binding under International Law, while leaving application on the ground to the agency of the nation-state. The mitigation of this paradox of self-regulation by states of their own Human Rights performances requires a clear understanding of domestic and international factors and processes, including religion and the role of religious institutions, which influence the actual conduct of states in this regard.

Since there is no reliable international mechanism for "enforcing" Human Rights standards against the will of national governments,[1] the crucial question is how to encourage governments to ratify Human Rights treaties, and motivate them to comply with the obligation to protect these rights within their respective territories. An effective and sustainable way of doing this is to generate a local constituency to advocate for the ratification and implementation of Human Rights within the national context. Even if the elite in control of government want to respect some Human Rights, it is unlikely to do so against the wishes of its own population. For such a local constituency to emerge and be effective in its advocacy of Human Rights, these rights must be seen by the general public as consistent with its own religious beliefs. In other words, International Human Rights norms are unlikely to be accepted by governments as legally binding, and respected in practice, without strong legitimation within national politics. Popular perceptions of Human Rights as consistent with the religious beliefs of the population are essential for the legitimization of these rights in each country. Even in so-called secular states, such as the United States and France a clear understanding and appreciation of the political and sociological importance of religion is essential to efforts to influence the Human Rights policies and practices of the state.

As noted earlier, I am not suggesting that consistency between religion and Human Rights can be assumed, or taken for granted, in any part of the world. On the contrary, one can easily identify some fundamental tensions, if not open conflict, between religious precepts and Human Rights norms. Therefore, a key question in the universality debate is whether the secular Western origins of Human Rights, as defined by the UDHR, necessarily mean that these rights are not (or cannot be) truly universal.

The response I am proposing to this question is based on the following interrelated propositions:

1. The moral or philosophical foundation and political justification of the conception of Human Rights as defined by the UDHR *can be* found in different religious and cultural traditions. However, since the traditional

1 Some scholars may argue that "humanitarian interventions" and actions by the UN Security Council are examples of coercive measures for the protection of Human Rights against the will of national governments. In my view, however, these mechanisms apply only in extreme cases and are to depend on the political calculations of the major countries to qualify as part of a reliable system for the regular international enforcement of human rights norms.

theology of the major religions of the world, including Christianity, is not readily consistent with this specific conception of Human Rights, reconciliation will require a reinterpretation of some of the precepts of those religions.

2. Reconciliation is necessary because of the fundamental value of international protection of Human Rights in checking the abuse of the powers of the state. Since the European model of the nation-state has been universalized through colonialism, there is need for effective protection against excessive or abusive state power. The corresponding universalization of fundamental constitutional rights through the UDHR is the best available means of providing that protection.
3. While there will necessarily be a theological dimension to the reinterpretation of religious precepts, the process itself must be understood in the specific political, social and economic context of the community of believers. The concrete historical context in which believers live is integral to all human understandings of religion, explained below in terms of an anthropological approach to religion. This context is also the framework within which the reinterpretation of religious precepts can emerge and be accepted in practice.

Like other believers, Muslims have always sought to experience their faith in terms of individual and collective conformity with its normative system, commonly known as *šarīʿa,* which is supposed to regulate their daily live as Muslims: While Muslims tend to ascribe divine authority to historical formulations of *šarīʿa* by jurists of the eighth and ninth centuries, it is clear that the precise content of that normative system has always been, and will continue to be, the product of human understanding in specific historical context.[2] As *Bernard Weiss* explained in the same year the *Gesellschaft für Arabisches und Islamisches Recht* hold its first annual conference also dealing in parts with the subject matter of this Jubilee Edition,[3] "[a]lthough the law (*šarīʿa*) is of divine provenance, the actual construction of the law is human activity, and its results represent the law of God *as humanly understood.* Since the law does not de-

---

2 On the origins and development of that historical understanding of *šarīʿa* see *Abdullahi Ahmed An-Na'im,* Toward an Islamic Reformation: Civil Liberties, Human Rights and International Law, Syracuse 1990, Chapter 2.

3 See *Hatem Elliesie,* "Editor's Foreword", in: *Hatem Elliesie* (Hrsg./Editor), Beiträge zum Islamischen Recht VII, Islam und Menschenrechte (Islam and Human Rights / الإسلام وحقوق الإنسان), Frankfurt a.M. 2010, p. 27.

scend from heaven ready-made, it is the human understanding of the law – the human *fiqh* – that must be normative for society".[4]

While readily understandable, the common confusion between *šarīʿa* as divinely ordained, on the one hand, and human efforts to discover what it means, on the other, needs to be clarified if Islam itself is to play a positive role in the lives of Muslims today. Given drastic changes in the social, economic, and political circumstances of Islamic societies throughout the world, an understanding of *šarīʿa* that was developed more than a thousand years ago is bound to face some practical difficulties today. Yet, significant reform of any problematic aspect of *šarīʿa* cannot occur as long as pre-existing human formulations of it are taken to be divine. As a result of this "man-made" deadlock, Muslims everywhere continue to subscribe to a concept of *šarīʿa* that none of them are willing or are able to live by. For example, religious condemnation of *ribā* is understood to mean that the payment of any interest on loans is totally prohibited. Similarly, religious objections to *ġarar* is taken to invalidate contracts of insurance where the obligations of the parties are contingent on whether or not something happens in the future. In practice, however, Muslim individuals and their governments routinely charge and pay interest on loans, and conclude and enforce contracts of insurance because it is impossible to have viable economic systems today without these practices. This discrepancy between theory and practice can be bridged through an appreciation of the fact that all specific definitions of concepts such as *ribā* and *ġarar* are necessarily the product of human understanding in specific historical context, not divine decree.

Failing to distinguish between the two meanings of Human Rights noted earlier, some Muslims claim that historical formulations of *šarīʿa* have always secured Human Rights in theory, though such a situation may not have materialized in practice. While relatively true in a limited sense, this claim is seriously misleading. It is true that by securing a relatively advanced degree of protection for the rights of women and non-Muslims, historical formulations of *šarīʿa* did provide for better protection of Human Rights than other normative systems in the past. For example, from the very beginning, *šarīʿa* was understood to require an independent legal personality for women, and the protection of certain minimum rights for them in inheritance and family relations, beyond what was possible under other major normative systems until the nineteenth century. Similarly, *šarīʿa* guarantees specific rights for the so-called People of the Book (*'ahl al-kitāb*) more than what had been provided for under other majority normative systems in the past. But since the rights of women and non-Muslims under

4 *Bernard Weiss,* The Spirit of Islamic Law, Athens, GA, USA: University of Georgia Press, 1998, p. 116.

šarīʿa are not equal to those of men and Muslims, respectively, the level of protection of rights under *šarīʿa* is not sufficient when judged by the standards set by the UDHR, which require equal rights for all human beings, without distinction on such ground as sex, religion, or belief.[5]

A possible response to this criticism of *šarīʿa* is the argument that Muslims (and other believers) should strive to live by the dictates of their religion, not according to some fallible, humanly devised set of Human Rights norms. However, since divine commands are always understood and applied by human beings, the contrast between orthodox perceptions of "the dictates of religion" and new or unorthodox views on the matter is really between two *human understandings* of what the religion requires of its adherents. Accordingly, a reinterpretation of Islamic sources that demonstrates agreement with Human Rights norms should be considered on its own terms, rather than dismissed as un-Islamic because it is inconsistent with previously established human understandings of *šarīʿa*. What I wish to emphasize here is the possibility of establishing the religious legitimacy of such an interpretation through what might be called an anthropological approach to Islam.

As I have explained elsewhere,[6] this approach is premised on an organic and dynamic relationship between the sacred texts of a religion, the *Qurʾān* and *sunna* in the case of Islam, on the one hand, and the comprehension, imagination, judgement, behaviour, and practical experience of human beings, on the other. Such an approach is not only justified, but in fact required by the terms of the *Qurʾān* which in numerous verses invites individuals, or the community, to reflect and reason independently. Indeed, 2 : يوسف and 3 : الزخرف by saying

"إِنَّا أَنْزَلْنَاهُ قُرْآنًا عَرَبِيًّا لَعَلَّكُمْ تَعْقِلُونَ"
(يوسف : 2)

"إِنَّا جَعَلْنَاهُ قُرْآنًا عَرَبِيًّا لَعَلَّكُمْ تَعْقِلُونَ"
(الزخرف : 3)

are proclaiming that human reflection and understanding is the whole purpose of revealing the *Qurʾān*.

---

5 For a detailed discussion of discrepancies between historical formulation of *šarīʿa* and modern international standards, see *Abdullahi Ahmed An-Naʿim,* Toward an Islamic Reformation: Civil Liberties, Human Rights and International Law, Syracuse 1990, pp. 4-7.

6 *Abdullahi Ahmed An-Naʿim,* "Towards an Islamic Hermeneutics for Human Rights", in *Abdullahi Ahmed An-Naʿim* (Editor), Human Rights and Religious and Religious Values: An Uneasy Relationship, Amsterdam / et al. 1995, chapter 16.

The rich diversity of opinion among Muslim jurists over almost every significant legal principle or issue of public policy clearly indicates a dynamic relationship between *Qur'ān* and *sunna* on one hand, and human comprehension, imagination and experience, on the other.

Since the historical context of the community and the personal experiences of individual believers substantially influence human perception and behaviour, drastic changes in the conditions of individual and communal life should lead to reconsideration of the meaning and implications of the divine message. By the same token, one must appreciate the differential impact of these factors on the perception and orientation of each community of Muslims today. To emphasize the importance of the specific historical context within which Islamic principles are understood and practiced is to call for clear understanding of the nature of these factors and care consideration of their consequences for each society. In other words, one should address the issue for each Islamic society in its own context, instead of treating all such societies in the same way.

This contextualization is particularly important because of the role of the state as the framework for the articulation and implementation of public policy for Islamic societies today. Whatever role *šarīʿa* may play in the lives of contemporary Muslims, that role will necessarily be mediated through the agency of their respective national states, rather than by the autonomous action of the global Muslim community as such. As an essential political institution, any state has to balance a variety of competing claims and interests. It is true that some of those claims and interests will probably reflect the religious sentiments of the population. But in view of the religious and political diversity of the population of Islamic countries today, and the complexity of their regional and global economic and security concerns, it is totally unrealistic to expect any state to be solely motivated by the religious sentiments of even the vast majority of its population.

I am therefore calling for an engagement of religious discourse to enhance the legitimacy and practical efficacy of Human Rights in all societies, each in relation to its own religion. I have presented here a possible approach to this engagement in relation to Islam because I am a Muslim advocate of Human Rights in the hope of persuading others to engage in a similar process in relation to their own religious traditions, whatever that may be. The need and possibility of this engagement is not peculiar to Islam, and the response must therefore apply to other religious traditions as well.

Islam und Menschenrechte: Betrachtungen zum Verhältnis von Religion und Recht

Muhammad Kalisch, Münster

A. Was ist eigentlich „der Islam"?

Von „dem Islam" zu reden ist genauso sinnvoll oder unsinnig wie von „dem Christentum" oder „dem Judentum" zu sprechen. Der Islam hat wie alle Religionen vielfältige Ausprägungen erfahren und dieser Prozess ist in allen Religionen nicht abgeschlossen. Ständig entstehen neue Varianten und Strömungen innerhalb der verschiedenen Religionen.[1]

Man kann sich mit dem Islam als einem historisch gewachsenen Phänomen auseinandersetzen. Da gibt es bestimmte theologische und juristische Denkrichtungen, die man analysieren und hinsichtlich bestimmter Fragestellungen dann bewerten kann. Die Frage etwa, ob die ḥanafitische Rechtsschule in der Form, wie sie von klassischen ḥanafitischen Autoren verstanden worden ist, mit den Menschenrechten übereinstimmt, lässt sich klar analysieren. Von diesen Autoren gibt es Schriften, die man hinsichtlich dieser Fragestellung auswerten kann.

Muslime haben sich untereinander oft das Recht auf das „Muslim sein" abgesprochen. Das gilt nicht nur für den Fall der islamischen Philosophen, deren Ablehnung als Muslime durch den aš'aritischen Theologen al-Ġazālī in seiner Schrift *Tahāfut al-Falāsifa*[2] große Bekanntheit erfahren hat, sondern es gilt ebenso für das Verhältnis von Sunniten und Schiiten, Aš'ariten und Mu'taziliten usw.

Kennzeichnend für die meisten Strömungen des Islam ist ein Verständnis dieser Religion, in dem das Recht eine große Rolle spielt. Welche Rolle das allerdings genau ist und vor allen Dingen, welche Normen dieses Recht im Einzelnen ausmachen, ist hoch umstritten.

---

[1] Ann Elizabeth Mayer verwendet daher im Diskurs dieser Buchpublikation, wenngleich in einem eher politischen Kontext aus einem anderen methodischen Fokus, den Begriff *"Islams"*; siehe *Ann Elizabeth Mayer,* "General Remarks on Human Rights and Islam in the Middle East", in: *Hatem Elliesie* (Hrsg./Editor), Beiträge zum Islamischen Recht VII, Islam und Menschenrechte (Islam and Human Rights / الإسلام وحقوق الإنسان), Frankfurt a.M. 2010, S. 217. So auch *Tim Lindsey,* "Human Rights and Islam in South East Asia: The Case of Indonesia", in: *Hatem Elliesie* (Hrsg./Editor), Beiträge zum Islamischen Recht VII, Islam und Menschenrechte (Islam and Human Rights / الإسلام وحقوق الإنسان), Frankfurt a.M. 2010, S. 299 ff. (vgl. Seite 320).

[2] *Abū Ḥāmid Muḥammad al-Ġazālī,* tahāfut al-falāsifa, 4. Aufl., Bairūt 1990, S. 254.

B. Islamisches Recht

Der Islam ist eine Gesetzesreligion in der das Heil, das Bestehen vor Gott, stark von der Beachtung des religiösen Gesetzes abhängig ist. Die aus dem Christentum wohlbekannte Frage, was Vorrang hat, Glaube oder Werke, ist auch eine zentrale Frage der islamischen Theologie. Die größten theologischen Strömungen des Islam, die sunnitische Theologie wie die *I͟tnā ʿAšarīya* (12er Šīʿa), haben sich letztlich für den Vorrang des Glaubens eingesetzt und lehnen eine ewige Verdammnis für den reuelos sterbenden Sünder ab, sofern dieser den rechten Glauben besitzt,[3] aber auch in diesen Theologien wird die Wichtigkeit der Einhaltung des Gesetzes betont und bei Nichteinhaltung eine zeitlich begrenzte Höllenstrafe im Jenseits angedroht. Gesetz ist dabei im Islam nicht nur ein religiöses Gesetz, das bestimmte Riten und grundsätzliche ethische Verhaltensnormen regelt. Das religiöse Gesetz des Islam ist umfassend und regelt sämtliche Bereiche des Lebens, vom Ritus bis zur Frage der Leitung des Staates.

Auch wenn in der islamischen Mystik der „*Ṣūfī*" dem „*Kūfī*"[4] gegenübergestellt und oft eine gewisse Distanz gegenüber der Rechtsgelehrsamkeit ausgedrückt wurde, echte *bī-šarʿ Ṣūfī*s, d.h. Mystiker, die das religiöse Gesetz abgelehnt haben, waren immer eine Minderheit. Dem religiösen Gesetz ablehnend gegenüber standen offensichtlich auch viele Anhänger der *Ġulāt*, der frühislamischen Gnosis.[5] Diese frühislamische Gnosis ist jedoch von allen anderen Gruppierungen heftig bekämpft worden und obwohl sie selbst in der *Šīʿa* ihren Ursprung hat[6] ist sie von der späteren *Šīʿa* als Irrlehre verworfen worden.[7] Gesetzesfeindlichkeit war im Islam immer eine Mindermeinung. Erst in der Neuzeit ist eine Diskussion entstanden, innerhalb der Muslime dann auch säkularistische Positionen vertreten haben.[8] Ein überzeugter Muslim wie Ismail

---

3 *Saʿd ad-dīn Masʿūd b. ʿUmar at-Taftāzānī*, šarḥ al-ʿaqā'id, Istanbul [ohne Jahresangaben], S. 150. *Muḥammad b. Muḥammad b. an-Nuʿmān al-Mufīd*, awā'il al-maqālāt, 2. Aufl., Bairūt 1993, S. 47.

4 Annemarie Schimmel, Mystische Dimensionen des Islam, Frankfurt a.M. 1995, S. 36. *Kūfī* bedeutet „aus Kūfa stammend" oder „zu Kūfa gehörig" und ist eine Anspielung darauf, dass Kūfa als bedeutendes Zentrum des islamischen Rechts galt und insbesondere der große Rechtsgelehrte Abū Ḥanīfa aus Kūfa stammte.

5 Siehe zu den Ġulāt: *Heinz Halm*, Die islamische Gnosis – Die extreme Schia und die ʿAlawiten, Zürich / München 1982.

6 So die gängige Meinung. Zu fragen wäre allerdings, ob nicht vielleicht umgekehrt die Šīʿa oder der Islam überhaupt ihren Ursprung in dieser Gnosis haben.

7 Siehe z.B. *Muḥammad b. Muḥammad b. an-Nuʿmān al-Mufīd*, taṣḥīḥ iʿtiqādāt al-Imāmīya, 2. Aufl., Bairūt 1993, S. 131.

8 Wobei eine solche Position nicht unbedingt die Ablehnung des Gesetzes bezüglich des Ritus (*ʿibādāt*) impliziert.

Fenni Ertuğrul (1855-1946) etwa konnte zu Beginn der türkischen Republik in einer Schrift zur Verteidigung des Islam anmerken, dass nunmehr auch in Bezug auf das Recht europäische Autoren keinen Anlass zur Kritik mehr haben könnten, da die türkische Nationalversammlung jetzt auf der Grundlage des Schweizer Gesetzes, welches das Vollkommenste aller Zivilgesetze (*medeni kanunların en mükemmeli*) sei, ein Zivilgesetzbuch erstellt habe.[9]

Eine andere Frage ist, wie ernst die Muslime im Laufe ihrer Geschichte eigentlich wirklich ihre Gesetzestradition genommen haben. Ohne Zweifel finden sich in den Werken des *fiqh* über die Jahrhunderte hinweg bestimmte Ansichten und die heutigen islamistischen Bewegungen fordern, zumindest teilweise, eben dieses *fiqh* wieder so anzuwenden, wie es in diesen Büchern steht. Hat man dies in der Vergangenheit wirklich so getan? Ein sehr gutes Beispiel, das Zweifel an der Vorstellung einer stets gesetzestreuen Haltung in der Praxis auch unter Frommen aufwirft, ist etwa die Frage der Frauenbeschneidung.[10]

In den *al-Fatāwā l-Hindīya*, einem ḥanafitischen Rechtswerk aus dem Indien des 17. Jahrhunderts, das bis in die Gegenwart in ḥanafitischen Ländern hohe Autorität besitzt, finden wir die Aussage, dass Beschneidung für Frauen eine *sunna* sei, zumindest aber eine edle Tat.[11] Frauenbeschneidung wird in den traditionellen Rechtswerken generell als *sunna* oder sogar Pflicht betrachtet.[12]

Frauenbeschneidung hat sich aber in der islamischen Welt nur dort durchgesetzt, wo sie auch in vorislamischer Zeit schon fest verwurzelt war. In den meisten Gegenden der islamischen Welt ist sie unbekannt. Man hat dort die in den Rechtswerken aufgeführte Meinung einfach ignoriert und auch einige der Gelehrten haben sich offensichtlich nicht für deren Anwendung eingesetzt. Einerseits hat man eine Rechtsmeinung über Jahrhunderte tradiert, andererseits hat man sie offensichtlich selbst auf der Ebene der Gelehrten praktisch missachtet. Es wäre interessant, einmal genauer zu erforschen, ob solch eine Haltung nicht auch in Bezug auf andere Vorschriften eingenommen wurde und ob sich

---

9 *İsmail Fenni Ertuğrul*, "Dini hükümlerin zamana göre değişmesi", in: İsmail Kara, Türkiye'de İslamcılık Düşüncesi II, İstanbul 1987, S. 181.

10 Vgl. hierzu *Dörthe Engels*, Die islamrechtliche Beurteilung der Mädchenbeschneidung: Eine kritische Analyse des Beschlusstextes der Gelehrtenkonferenz „Verbot des Missbrauchs des weiblichen Körpers" vom 22. bis 23. November 2006 an der Azhar-Universität in Kairo im Kontext moderner Entwicklungen in der islamischen Rechtsfindungspraxis [Magisterarbeit am Institut für Islamwissenschaft an der Freien Universität Berlin], Berlin 2008.

11 *Niẓām ad-dīn al-Burhānpūrī*, al-fatāwā l-hindīya, Bd. 5, 4. Aufl., Bairūt [ohne Jahresangaben], S. 357.

12 Vgl. *Muḥammad b. ʿAlī aš-Šaukānī*, nail al-auṭār, Bd. 1, Miṣr 1938, S. 112. S. auch *Taqī d-dīn Aḥmad ibn Taimīya*, al-fatāwā l-kubrā, Bd. 1, Bairūt 1965, S. 51.

Hinweise auf eine Begründung durch Gelehrte für eine solche Haltung finden. Dass Muslime in der Praxis das islamische Recht mit unterschiedlichen Begründungen nicht eingehalten haben, wird schon bei al-Ġazālī erwähnt.[13]

Die Frage, was eigentlich islamisches Recht ist, ist nicht leicht zu beantworten. Im Prinzip gibt es drei methodische Ansätze, sich mit dem islamischen Recht auseinanderzusetzen:

1. Die engste und unflexibelste Strömung trachtet danach, die Texte des *Qur'ān* und der Ḥadīṯwerke möglichst wörtlich zu verstehen und auf weitere Rechtsquellen weitgehend zu verzichten. *Iǧtihād*[14] nach dem Verständnis dieser Strömung besteht hauptsächlich darin, Rechtsmeinungen, die von den Ḥadīṯüberlieferungen abweichen, durch ein möglichst wörtliches Verständnis dieser *aḥādīṯ* zu ersetzen. Der Ḥadīṯüberlieferung und der formalen, ganz überwiegend an der Überlieferungskette orientierten Ḥadīṯkritik wird großes Vertrauen entgegengebracht. Das flexible Element dieser Strömung besteht in dem stetigen neuen Bezug auf die Quellen, das unflexible Element in dem Umgang mit den Quellen, der sich am äußeren Wortlaut des Textes orientiert und bezüglich der Ḥadīṯüberlieferung kaum eine inhaltliche Kritik übt. Diese Strömung ist im Sunnitentum eng mit der Methodik der *Ẓāhirīya*[15] verbunden. In der *Šī'a* wird dieses Denken von der *Aḫbārīya*[16] repräsentiert.
2. Die zweite Strömung orientiert sich an den traditionellen Methodiklehren wie sie von den verschiedenen Rechtsschulen hervorgebracht wurden. *Qur'ān* und Ḥadīṯüberlieferung werden wie Gesetzestexte behandelt. Diese müssen auf der sprachlichen Ebene ausgelegt und zueinander in Beziehung gesetzt werden (z.B. *lex generalis* zu *lex specialis*) und außerdem kann es Rechtslücken geben, die im Wege der Analogie (*qiyās*) oder weiterer Rechtsquellen ausgefüllt werden müssen. Diese Strömung kennt eine gewisse Flexibilität, betont jedoch, dass der Wortlaut der

---

13 Vgl. die Ausführungen von al-Ġazālī in *Abū Ḥāmid Muḥammad al-Ġazālī*, al-munqiḏ min aḍ-ḍalāl, Bairūt 2004, S. 81 ff.

14 *Iǧtihād* bedeutet selbständige Rechtsfindung. Höchste Form des *iǧtihād* ist *al-iǧtihād al-muṭlaq* (absoluter *iǧtihād*), bei welcher der *muǧtahid* völlig frei ist und mit einer eigenen Rechtsmethodik eigene Rechtsnormen ableitet.

15 Eine heute faktisch ausgestorbene Rechtsschule, die auf Dāwūd al-Iṣfahānī (gest. 270 / 883) zurückgeführt wird. Sie lehnt alle Rechtsquellen außer *qur'ān, sunna* und dem Konsens der Prophetengefährten ab.

16 Als *Aḫbārīya* wird eine im 11./17. Jahrhundert entstandene Strömung der Iṯnā 'Ašarīya bezeichnet, die sehr formalistisch denkt und sich gegen die Vernunft als Rechtsquelle ausspricht.

nuṣūṣ[17] die Grenze der Auslegung darstellt. So wird beispielsweise eine Änderung der Erbrechtsregel, dass die Frau nur die Hälfte des Anteils des Mannes erbt, mit eben dieser Begründung der Festschreibung durch einen naṣṣ abgelehnt.[18]

3. Die flexibelste Strömung schließlich geht davon aus, dass zumindest allen Regelungen in *Qur'ān* und *sunna,* die nicht die *ʿibādāt*[19] betreffen, eine *ratio legis* zugrunde liegt, die durch die Vernunft erkannt werden kann und die die Grundlage der Auslegung bildet. Entscheidend ist es, den Sinn der Norm zu verstehen und eine Regelung zu finden, die dem Sinn entspricht, selbst wenn sie unter Umständen dem äußeren Wortlaut des *Qur'ān* widerspricht.[20] Weiterhin wird die Überlieferung der Worte und Taten des Propheten sehr kritisch betrachtet und vieles in der Überlieferung eher als spätere Rückprojektion theologischer und juristischer Ansichten auf den Propheten gewertet. Die Anhänger dieser Strömung können durch ihre Methodik ohne Probleme eine Übereinstimmung von islamischem Recht und moderner Menschenrechtsvorstellung herbeiführen, da dieser ja selbst eine Auslegung möglich ist, die den Wortlaut der *nuṣūṣ* missachtet.

Vom Ergebnis her ist diese dritte Strömung in der Lage eine Harmonisierung von islamischem Recht und moderner Menschenrechtskonzeption herbeizuführen. Dieser letzte Ansatz erlaubt eine enorme Freiheit. Was die *ratio legis* (*ḥikma tašrīʿīya*) einer Norm ist und welche Folgerungen daraus zu ziehen sind, ist eine sehr subjektive Angelegenheit. Wenn man davon ausgeht, die Normen in *Qur'ān* und *sunna* seien das Verständnis von Gerechtigkeit aus der Entstehungszeit dieser Normen, dann kann man sie jederzeit durch ein moderneres Verständnis des Gerechtigkeitsbegriffes ersetzen. Da trotzdem vieles unterschiedlich betrachtet wird, braucht man ein Legislativorgan und dann ist man eigentlich schon fast bei säkularer Demokratie angelangt.[21]

Rechtsphilosophische Grundlage einer flexiblen Auslegung des islamischen Rechts ist die theologische Diskussion über die Erkenntnisfähigkeit der Ver-

---

17 Pl. von *naṣṣ,* darunter sind die Texte von *Qur'ān* und *sunna* zu verstehen.

18 Eine umfangreiche Kritik an modernem *iǧtihād* gegen den Wortlaut des *naṣṣ* (einschließlich des genannten Beispiels aus dem Erbrecht) findet sich bei al-Qaraḍāwī, vgl. *Yūsuf al-Qaraḍāwī*, al-iǧtihād fī š-šarīʿa al-islāmīya, al-Kuwait 1985, S. 139 ff.

19 Die Fragen des Ritus.

20 Die Vertreter dieser Richtung knüpfen im Sunnitentum an die Methodik der *ahl ar-ra'y* an und in der *Šīʿa* an der in den šīʿitischen Schulen anerkannten Rechtsquelle *ʿaql* (Vernunft).

21 Zu den rechtsphilosophischen Folgerungen hieraus siehe Gliederungspunkt „D. Menschenrechte und Religion" auf Seite 65 ff.

nunft im Bereich von „gut“ und „böse“ (*al-ḥusn wa-l-qubḥ*). Hierzu werden traditionell drei Positionen vertreten,:

1. Die Ašʿariten sind der Auffassung, das „gut“ und „böse“ durch die Vernunft nicht erkannt werden können und auch den Handlungen nicht wesensmäßig zu Eigen sind.[22] Eine Handlung ist allein deshalb „gut“, weil Gott sie geboten hat und allein deshalb „böse“, weil Gott sie verboten hat. Einen unschuldigen Menschen zu töten, ist nur deswegen „böse“, weil Gott dies verboten hat. Hätte er es befohlen, wäre es „gut“. Die menschliche Vernunft kann zwar erkennen, ob eine Handlung vollkommen oder mangelhaft ist und ebenso, ob sie von der menschlichen Natur als angenehm oder unangenehm empfunden wird. Diese Erkenntnis ist jedoch nicht als Erkenntnis der moralischen oder juristischen Qualität der Handlung zu werten. Einzig und allein das Urteil Gottes entscheidet über die Qualifizierung einer Handlung als „gut“ und „böse“. Ungerechtigkeit wird von al-Ġazālī lediglich definiert als die Verfügung über fremdes Eigentum ohne Erlaubnis. Da Gott aber Schöpfer aller Dinge und somit auch deren Eigentümer ist, kann er aus diesem Grunde niemals ungerecht sein.[23] Die Begriffe Ungerechtigkeit bzw. Gerechtigkeit werden hier also lediglich als bloße Worthülsen verstanden, die völlig willkürlich durch Gott mit Inhalt gefüllt werden können.
2. Die *Māturīdīya*[24] und die *Salafīya*[25] sind hingegen der Ansicht, dass „gut“ und „böse“ den Handlungen wesensmäßig zu Eigen sind und von der Vernunft erkannt werden können. Nach dieser Ansicht verbietet Gott eine Handlung, weil sie „böse“ ist und gebietet eine Handlung, weil sie „gut“ ist. Nicht das Urteil Gottes bestimmt die Qualität einer Handlung, sondern Gottes Urteil richtet sich nach der Qualität der Handlung. Allerdings wird in diesen Schulen betont, dass Gott anders handeln könnte, wenn er wollte.

---

[22] Vgl. zur ašʿaritischen Ansicht *Abū Isḥāq aš-Šāṭibī*, al-muwāfaqāt fī uṣūl aš-šarīʿa, Bd.1, Bairūt 2001, S. 66 und ausführlicher *Abū Ḥāmid Muḥammad al-Ġazālī*, al-mustaṣfā min ʿilm al-uṣūl, Bd.1, Bairūt [ohne Jahresangaben], S. 55 ff.

[23] *Abū Ḥāmid Muḥammad al-Ġazālī*, iḥyāʾ ʿulūm ad-dīn, Bd.1, Istanbul 1985, S. 117.

[24] Vgl. zur Position der Māturīdīya *ʿAbd al-ʿAlī al-Anṣārī*, fawātiḥ ar-raḥamūt bi-šarḥ musallam aṯ-ṯubūt, Bd.1, Bairūt [ohne Jahresangaben], S. 25 ff. und *ʿAbd al-Wahhāb Ḫallāf*, ʿilm uṣūl al-fiqh, 17. Aufl., al-Kuwait 1987, S. 99.

[25] Vgl. zur Position der Salafīya *Muḥammad b. ʿAlī aš-Šaukānī*, iršād al-fuḥūl, Bairūt [ohne Jahresangaben], S. 7 ff.

3. Die *Muʿtazila*[26] und die *Šīʿa*[27] schließlich teilen die Ansicht der *Māturīdīya* und der *Salafīya*, gehen allerdings noch einen Schritt weiter und vertreten die Ansicht, dass Gott gar nicht anders handeln kann. Gott ist gerecht und kann niemals ungerecht sein. Daher kann er nur „das Böse" verbieten und „das Gute" gebieten.

Die Theorie der *Māturīdīya, Salafīya, Muʿtazila* und *Šīʿa* bietet einen innerislamischen geistesgeschichtlichen Ansatz für ein auf die Vernunft gestütztes Recht. In der Vergangenheit waren die Frage nach der Erkenntnisfähigkeit der Vernunft bezüglich „gut" und „böse" und die Frage, ob „gut" und „böse" den Handlungen wesensmäßig zu Eigen seien oder nicht rechtsphilosophische Vorfragen, die zwar in keinem größeren Werk über *ʿilm al-kalām* oder *uṣūl al-fiqh* fehlen durften, aber erkennbar keine praktische Relevanz hatten. Auch in der Rechtsableitung spielte diese rechtsphilosophische Fragestellung praktisch keine Rolle. Die traditionelle Literatur zu diesem Thema bezieht bezüglich der Frage, wie weit nun tatsächlich die Erkenntnisfähigkeit der Vernunft reicht ebenfalls keine klare Stellung. Kann sie nur die Qualität genereller Fragen erkennen (z.B. Ungerechtigkeit oder Lügen ist „böse") oder kann sie auch bei einzelnen konkreten Handlungen deren Qualität erkennen. Dies liegt meines Erachtens darin begründet, dass diese Fragen ursprünglich nicht in einem juristischen, sondern in einem theologischen Kontext diskutiert wurden. Sie waren keine Diskussionsgegenstände in Bezug auf praktische Rechtserkenntnis, sondern sie waren wichtige Prämissen in der äußerst umstrittenen Problematik der Prädestination, Willensfreiheit, Theodizee und göttlichen Gerechtigkeit.[28] Erst als im 19. Jahrhundert unter muslimischen Intellektuellen die Frage nach einer Reform des islamischen Rechts immer heftiger diskutiert wurde, wurde diese Frage als eine Frage juristischer Praxis und Rechtsableitung entdeckt, wobei man dann von einer weiten Erkenntnisfähigkeit der Vernunft bezüglich „gut" und „böse" ausging. Der spätosmanische Gelehrte Seyyid Bey (1873-1924) etwa entwickelte unter Berufung auf die māturīditisch-muʿtazilitische Lehre ein

---

26 Vgl. zur Position der Muʿtazila *Abū l-Ḥusain al-Baṣrī*, al-muʿtamad fī uṣūl al-fiqh, Bd. 2, Bairūt 1983, S. 322 ff. und *ʿAbd al-ǧabbār b. Aḥmad*, al-muġnī fī abwāb at-tauḥīd wa-l-ʿadl, Bd. 6/1, al-Qāhira 1962.

27 Vgl. zur Position der Iṯnā ʿAšarīya (12er Šīʿa) z.B. *al-ʿAllāma al-Ḥillī*, kašf al-murād fī šarḥ taǧrīd al-iʿtiqād, Qum 1422 *h.*, S. 417 ff.; *Muḥammad Riḍā al-Muẓaffar*, uṣūl al-fiqh, Qum [ohne Jahresangaben], S. 164 ff.; *Muḥammad Baqir aṣ-Ṣadr*, durūs fī ʿilm al-uṣūl, Bd. 2, 6. Aufl., Qum 1421 *h.*, S. 288 ff. Vgl. zur Position der Zaidīya z.B. *Ṣārim ad-Dīn Ibrāhīm b. Muḥammad al-Wazīr*, al-fuṣūl al-luʾluʾīya fī uṣūl fiqh al-ʿitra az-zakīya wa-aʿlām al-umma al-muḥammadīya, Bairūt 2001, S. 398 f.; *al-Ḥusain b. Badr ad-Dīn*, yanābīʿ an-naṣīḥa, Ṣanʿāʾ 1998, S. 138 ff.

28 Vgl. hierzu *Aḥmad b. Muḥammad b. Ṣalāḥ aš-Šarafī*, šifāʾ ṣudūr an-nās bi-šarḥ al-asās – šarḥ al-asās al-kabīr, Bd.1, Ṣanʿāʾ 1991, S. 152.

dynamisches Konzept des *fiqh,* das letztlich zu einer parlamentarischen Demokratie führt.[29] Er war für kurze Zeit Justizminister unter İsmet İnönü.

An dieser Stelle noch eine kurze Bemerkung zur islamischen Philosophie und deren Verhältnis zum islamischen Recht: Der Philosoph Ibn Rušd (520-595/1126-1198) war mālikitischer Rechtsgelehrter und *Qāḍī* von Córdoba und Sevilla. Sein Werk *Bidāyat al-Muǧtahid wa-Nihāyat al-Muqtaṣid* zählt bis heute zu den Standardwerken der sunnitischen Rechtstradition. Er hat deutlich zum Ausdruck gebracht, dass es für ihn ein Verständnis der Wahrheit durch die Philosophen gibt, welches einer kleinen Elite vorbehalten ist, während die Massen die religiösen Texte so hinnehmen sollten, wie diese wörtlich zu verstehen seien. Für Ibn Rušd war Religion eine in allegorische Darstellung verpackte massenkompatible Darstellung der Wahrheit. Dabei geht es ihm in seiner Argumentation in *Faṣl al-Maqāl* um die Frage der Deutungshoheit im Bereich der Metaphysik. Das islamische Recht ist für ihn eine gegebene Größe, deren Gültigkeit für ihn feststeht.[30] Ihm geht es darum, nachzuweisen, dass die Religion *(aš-šarʿ)* die philosophische Erkenntnis der Wahrheit zulässt, ja ausdrücklich dazu auffordert. Dabei fordert er von den einfachen Menschen, diese sollten einfach nur glauben, was in *Qurʾān* und *sunna* vorgegeben ist. Er fordert sogar die Regierenden auf, die Bücher des Abū Ḥāmid (d.h. al-Ġazālīs) denen zu verbieten, die dafür nicht geeignet seien wie auch die Bücher der Philosophie (*kutub al-burhān*) ungeeigneten Personen nicht zugänglich gemacht werden dürfen und er bekräftigt, dass er selbst es nicht als erlaubt betrachtet hätte, auch nur einen Buchstaben darüber zu schreiben, wären diese Probleme nicht schon so allgemein bekannt[31]. Ibn Rušd plädiert für die Freiheit des Philosophen, den *Qurʾān* allegorisch zu deuten und ein philosophisches Verständnis der Wahrheit zu erlangen, während er gleichzeitig für das Volk die Beschränkung auf den Wortlaut des *Qurʾān* fordert. So schreibt er:

---

29 Siehe hierzu *Seyyid Bey*, "Hilafetin şerî mahiyeti", in: İsmail Kara: Türkiye'de İslamcılık Düşüncesi I, 2. Aufl., İstanbul 1987.

30 Siehe seine Ausführungen in *Ibn Rušd*, faṣl al-maqāl wa-taqrīr mā baina š-šarīʿa wa-l-ḥikma min al-ittiṣāl, 8. Aufl., Bairūt 2000, S. 30, S. 35 und S. 50, wo *fiqh* kurz als Wissenschaft angesprochen und nicht in Frage gestellt wird. Vgl. auch *Ibn Rušd*, al-kašf ʿan manāhiǧ al-adilla fī ʿaqāʾid al-milla, Bairūt 2002, S. 95 ff. über die Propheten.

31 *Ibn Rušd*, faṣl al-maqāl wa-taqrīr mā baina š-šarīʿa wa-l-ḥikma min al-ittiṣāl, 8. Aufl., Bairūt 2000, S. 49.

واذا تقرر[و] هذا، فقد ظهر لك من قولنا ان ههنا ظاهرًا من الشرع لا يجوز تأويله. فان كان تأويله في المبادئ فهو كفر، وان كان فيما بعد المبادئ فهو بدعة. وههنا ايضاً ظاهر يجب على اهل البرهان تأويله، وحملهم ايَّاه على ظاهره كفر. وتأويل غير اهل البرهان له واخراجه عن ظاهره كفر في حقّهم او بدعة.

Wenn dies nun feststeht, so wird dir aus unserem Wort deutlich, dass es in der Religion (šarʿ[32]) äußere Wahrheit (ẓāhir) gibt, die nicht allegorisch verstanden werden darf. Bezieht sich dessen allegorische Auslegung (taʾwīl) auf die Grundprinzipien, so ist dies Unglaube (kufr) und bezieht es sich auf das, was jenseits der Grundprinzipien liegt, so ist es unerlaubte Neuerung (bidʿa). Es gibt aber auch äußere Wahrheit, die allegorisch zu interpretieren für die Philosophen (ahl al-burhān) Pflicht ist und es ist Unglaube (kufr), dass sie dies gemäß dem äußeren Wortlaut verstehen. Ebenso ist dessen allegorische Deutung und das Herausnehmen aus dem äußeren Wortlaut durch Nichtphilosophen für diese Unglaube oder unerlaubte Neuerung.[33]

Unglaube ist also nicht gleich Unglaube, sondern richtet sich nach der Verständnisfähigkeit der Menschen, wobei Ibn Rušd offensichtlich doch recht elitär denkt und nicht davon ausgeht, dass es Sinn macht, zu versuchen, möglichst vielen Menschen die Philosophie nahe zu bringen. Ibn Rušd verhält sich wie ein Priester der Mysterienreligionen der Antike, der versucht, den eigentlichen Gehalt der Religion von allen Menschen abzuschirmen, die er für die Erkenntnis dieser Wahrheiten noch nicht reif genug hält und die deswegen einen Mythos präsentiert bekommen. Er ist auch im Hinblick auf sein elitäres, undemokratisches Menschenbild auf einer Linie mit seinem großen Vorbild Aristoteles, für den es ja auch Sklaven „von Natur aus" gab und der Ungleichheiten wie er sie in seiner Gesellschaft vorfand akzeptierte.[34] Ibn Rušd scheint diese Theorie einer strikten Trennung zwischen philosophischer Elite und unverständiger Masse wirklich geglaubt zu haben, wenngleich dem Betrachter natürlich nicht verborgen bleibt, dass seine Betonung von Rechtgläubigkeit und Autorität von Offenbarung und Propheten ganz im Stile von Fiqh-, Qurʾān- und Ḥadīṯ-gelehrten, sowie die geforderte Selbstisolierung der Philosophen, deren Bücher nicht den Massen zugänglich gemacht werden dürfen, wie ein Angebot an die traditionelle Gelehrsamkeit gewertet werden könnte, den kleinen Kreis der Philosophen in Ruhe zu lassen, der im Gegenzug dafür die Autorität der Religionsgelehrten nicht in Frage stellt.

Ibn Sīnā (370-428/980-1037) war im ḥanafitischen Recht ausgebildet.[35] Auch für ihn gab es die Unterscheidung zwischen den Philosophen und der Masse.

---

32 Šarʿ ist hier mit Religion zu übersetzen, weil Ibn Rušd die Aussagen zur Glaubenslehre meint, welche in *Qurʾān* und *sunna* vorhanden sind.

33 *Ibn Rušd*, faṣl al-maqāl wa-taqrīr mā baina š-šarīʿa wa-l-ḥikma min al-ittiṣāl, 8. Aufl., Bairūt 2000, S. 46.

34 Siehe hierzu *Otfried Höffe*, Aristoteles, 2. Aufl., München 1999, S. 262 ff.

35 *Gotthard Strohmaier*, Avicenna, München 1999, S. 21.

Prophetentum und islamisches Recht werden von ihm ebenfalls nicht in Frage gestellt und im *Kitāb aš-Šifā'* erläutert er Sinn und Notwendigkeit der Sendung von Propheten.[36] Er verteidigt die Religion, erscheint dabei aber distanzierter als Ibn Rušd, der sich in *Faṣl al-Maqāl* als Verteidiger der Rechtgläubigkeit im Tonfall eines Rechtsgelehrten äußert. Ibn Sīnā geht es nur darum, in einem relativ emotionslosen Stil die Berechtigung und den Sinn von Religion und Prophetie neben der Philosophie darzustellen. Noch distanzierter ist al-Fārābī (257-337/870-950), der ebenfalls das Prophetentum als Realität anerkennt. In seiner Schrift *Iḥṣā' al-ʿUlūm* äußert er sich kurz zu *fiqh* und *kalām*, die er nicht als spezielle islamische Phänomene anspricht. Er spricht dabei von *wāḍiʿ aš-šarīʿa* (der Recht Setzende) und *wāḍiʿ al-milla* (Gründer der Glaubensgemeinschaft).[37] Wie auch in *Ārā' Ahl al-Madīna al-Fāḍila* geht er nicht spezifisch auf den Islam ein, der für ihn keine Sonderstellung einzunehmen scheint. Šihāb ad-Dīn Yaḥyā as-Suhrawardī (549-587/1154-1191) spricht zwar vom „Herrn dieser *šarīʿa*" (*ṣāḥib hāḏihī š-šarīʿa*),[38] anerkennt Prophetentum und Offenbarung, doch seine Beziehung zur Religion lässt sich am besten so beschreiben, wie einer der gründlichsten Kenner Suhrawardīs dies tut:

> *A less tangible, but quite real, connection is Suhrawardī's curious aloofness from Islam. It is true that the sources portray him as a man zealous in his piety. He could debate the fuqahā', seems to have been accepted as a religious scholar, was certainly a Sufi – yet in his philosophical and mystical writings Islam seems to play no real part. When he mentions Muḥammad, it is with great respect, but he does not often do so. The heroes of Islam, apart from some Sufis, have no place in his pantheon.*[39]

Die islamische Philosophie ist eine Fortsetzung der Antike. Islamische Philosophen anerkennen Prophetentum und Offenbarung als einen allegorischen Zugang zur metaphysischen Wahrheit für die Massen. Das islamische Recht wird dabei als das allgemein akzeptierte Rechtssystem betrachtet, durch das die Ordnung aufrechterhalten wird und spirituelle Praktiken für die Läuterung der Seele und deren Aufstieg bereitgestellt werden. Ein wirkliches Verständnis der Wahrheit aber bietet nur die Philosophie und es ist gut vorstellbar, dass manche islamischen Philosophen aus Furcht vor den religiösen Eiferern nicht alles aufgeschrieben oder ausformuliert haben, was sie wirklich dachten. Was das islamische Recht betrifft, so scheinen sie es aber wirklich für ein gutes Instrument zur Ordnung des Gemeinwesens gehalten zu haben. Aus der Sicht

---

36 *Ibn Sīnā*, al-ilāhīyāt min kitāb aš-šifā', 2. Aufl., Qum 1428 *h.*, S. 487 ff.

37 *Abū Naṣr al-Fārābī*, iḥṣā' al-ʿulūm, Paris 2005, S. 107f.

38 *Šihāb ad-Dīn Yaḥyā as-Suhrawardī*, ḥikmat al-išrāq, Provo 1999, S. 161.

39 *John Walbridge*, The Wisdom of the Mystic East – Suhrawardī and Platonic Orientalism, Albany 2001, S. 41.

der Antike und des Mittelalters ist das auch verständlich. Viele Fragen, die uns heute bezüglich des islamischen Rechts beschäftigen, etwa die mindere Rechtsstellung der Frau, Körperstrafen oder Sklaverei waren für Antike und Mittelalter nicht ungewöhnlich und die Regelungen des islamischen Rechts waren für ihre Zeit durchaus fortschrittlich. Den islamischen Philosophen ging es um Metaphysik und Erkenntnis, nicht um Sozialreform. Ihre politische Philosophie hielt sich im Rahmen des damaligen Weltbilds.

C. Die Menschenrechte und das islamische Recht

Der Begriff der „Menschenrechte" existiert nicht in der islamischen Rechtstradition. Allein die Tatsache, dass der Begriff nicht existiert, sagt aber noch nichts darüber aus, ob nicht dessen Inhalt oder Teile von dessen Inhalt nicht doch in der islamischen Tradition vorgefunden werden können.

Die islamische Rechtstradition kennt die Vorstellung, dass das Individuum Träger von Rechten ist und dass diese Rechte nur im Rahmen der islamischen Rechtsvorschriften angetastet werden dürfen. Der Mensch ist Rechtssubjekt mit einklagbaren Rechten. Manche dieser Rechte waren für die Zeit der Entstehung dieses Rechtssystems durchaus fortschrittlich.

Dennoch ist, was das klassische islamische Recht der verschiedenen Rechtsschulen angeht, die Frage nach dem Verhältnis von Islam und Menschenrechten schnell beantwortet. Identifiziert man die von diesen Rechtsgelehrten erarbeiteten Normen mit dem islamischen Recht, so stößt man neben vielen fortschrittlichen Ansätzen auf eine Reihe von Punkten, in denen diese Normen mit dem modernen Menschenrechtsbegriff nicht übereinstimmen. Hierzu zählen insbesondere:

- Entwürdigende und quälende Strafen[40]
- Ungleichbehandlung von Mann und Frau[41]
- Einschränkung der Religionsfreiheit[42]
- Einschränkung der Meinungsfreiheit[43]
- Sklaverei

Traditionelle islamische Juristen verteidigen in der Regel bis heute diese Abweichungen von den Menschenrechten mit Ausnahme der Sklaverei. Hier hat

---

[40] Prügelstrafen, Abtrennung von Gliedmaßen.

[41] Kein gleicher Erbteil, keine dem Mann gleichwertige Zeugenaussage, kein eigenständiges Recht auf Ehescheidung, Aufenthaltsbestimmungsrecht des Mannes, Züchtigungsrecht des Mannes bei Verfehlung in der Ehe.

[42] Todesstrafe für Apostasie vom Islam, Einschränkung der freien Religionsausübung für nichtmuslimische Minderheiten auf islamischem Territorium.

[43] Staat hat die Pflicht, „falsche Auffassungen" zu unterbinden.

sich weitgehend die Ansicht durchgesetzt, dass der Islam eigentlich eine Abschaffung der Sklaverei intendiere. Ein zeitgenössischer traditioneller islamischer Jurist wie Hayreddin Karaman meint, dass das islamische Recht hier irregegangen sei (*sapmıştır*) und ist offenkundig abgestoßen davon, dass viele traditionelle Bücher der islamischen Rechtswissenschaft das Kaufrecht sehr häufig am Beispiel des Sklavenkaufs erörtern.[44] In der Frage der Sklaverei wird allgemein argumentiert, dass der Islam hier eine vorislamische Institution lediglich übernommen und reformiert habe, ohne die Institution als solche zu loben oder als positiv darzustellen. Vielmehr stellten die Regelungen aus *Qur'ān* und *sunna* zur Sklaverei darauf ab, Sklaverei zu minimieren. Aus all diesen Punkten sei zu folgern, dass der Islam eigentlich als Endziel die endgültige Abschaffung der Sklaverei wolle. Mit ähnlichen Argumenten könnte man z.B. auch begründen, dass der Islam eigentlich die volle Gleichberechtigung der Frau wolle, was aber in traditionellen Kreisen generell abgelehnt wird.

Es gibt in der Gegenwart den Versuch, eine islamische Menschenrechtslehre zu entwickeln, wie etwa die Islamische Deklaration der Menschenrechte durch das *Islamic Council*. Solche Versuche sind interessant unter dem Aspekt, dass sie überhaupt eine Auseinandersetzung mit dem Menschenrechtsgedanken im traditionellen Islam anregen, machen aber gleichzeitig deutlich, dass diese islamischen Menschenrechtsbegriffe etwas anderes sind als der Menschenrechtsbegriff der Allgemeinen Erklärung der Menschenrechte. Das ist ohnehin logisch, denn universelle Menschenrechte können sich ja schlecht nach Religion oder Kulturkreisen unterscheiden. Der Versuch einer islamischen Menschenrechtslehre – nicht zu verwechseln mit dem Versuch, die universellen Menschenrechte aus dem Islam abzuleiten - ist daher nichts anderes als ein Versuch, die universellen Menschenrechte einschränken zu wollen. In der Islamischen Erklärung der Menschenrechte des *Islamic Council* heißt es gleich zu Beginn unter I a):

> *Das menschliche Leben ist heilig und unverletzlich, und jede Anstrengung soll zu seinem Schutz unternommen werden. Insbesondere soll niemand Verletzungen oder dem Tod ausgesetzt werden, es sei denn, das islamische Gesetz erachtet derartige Maßnahmen für den Schutz und die Sicherheit der Gesellschaft als unumgänglich.*

Hier wird ein grundsätzliches Menschenrecht auf Leben und Unverletzlichkeit postuliert, jedoch im Rahmen der Vorschriften des islamischen Rechts. Dieses kennt sowohl die Todesstrafe (unter anderem auch für die Apostasie des Muslims) wie auch Strafen, die die körperliche Integrität verletzen. Wir haben

---

[44] Siehe *Hayreddin Karaman*, İslam'da İnsan Hakları – Din, Vicdan ve Düşünce Hürriyeti, 2. Aufl., Istanbul 2004, S. 138.

es hier eben nicht mit einem allgemeinen grundsätzlich gültigen Menschenrecht zu tun, das über jeglichem Gesetz steht und nicht eingeschränkt werden darf, sondern mit einem Recht, das seine konkrete inhaltliche Ausformung erst durch zahlreiche Einzelgesetze erfährt. Der Gedanke der Menschenrechte wie er in der allgemeinen Erklärung der Menschenrechte beschrieben wird, besteht aber eben darin, dass die Menschenrechte ein Maßstab sind, an dem staatliche Gesetze und Hoheitsakte zu messen sind. Sie sind gedacht als unantastbare Rechte, die eben nicht zur Disposition eines Gesetzgebers stehen. Die Menschenrechte islamischer Menschenrechtslehren dagegen sind keine höherrangigen Rechte. Sie sind keine subjektiven Rechte, denen gegenüber jedes anders lautende Gesetz oder jeder anders lautende Hoheitsakt eines Staates zurückweichen müsste, sondern deskriptive Wiedergabe dessen, was dem Einzelnen faktisch an Recht neben verschiedenen einschränkenden Regelungen noch verbleibt.

Nun ist eine Einschränkung der Grundfreiheiten auch gemäß der Allgemeinen Erklärung der Menschenrechte zulässig. Dort heißt es in Art. 29 Ziffer 2:

> *Jeder Mensch ist in Ausübung seiner Rechte und Freiheiten nur den Beschränkungen unterworfen, die das Gesetz ausschließlich zu dem Zwecke vorsieht, um die Anerkennung und Achtung der Rechte und Freiheiten der anderen zu gewährleisten und den gerechten Anforderungen der Moral, der öffentlichen Ordnung und der allgemeinen Wohlfahrt in einer demokratischen Gesellschaft zu genügen.*

Dass insbesondere Freiheitsrechte niemals schrankenlos gültig sein können, ergibt sich aus der Natur der Sache. Ausübung eigener Freiheiten berührt leicht die Freiheit anderer. In vielen Fällen sind daher Gesetze notwendig, die die Freiheiten des Einzelnen einschränken, um optimale Freiheit für alle zu gewährleisten. Hier ist wichtig zu beachten, dass die allgemeine Erklärung der Menschenrechte die Notwendigkeit solcher Einschränkungen zu dem Zweck sieht, die Anerkennung der Rechte und Freiheiten anderer zu wahren. Weiterhin wird auf gerechte Anforderungen der Moral, der öffentlichen Ordnung und der allgemeinen Wohlfahrt in einer demokratischen Gesellschaft verwiesen. Es geht also um optimale Menschenrechtsverwirklichung für alle Menschen. Das traditionelle islamische Recht hingegen nimmt vielfach Einschränkungen von Menschenrechten vor, die gerade nicht eine optimale Verwirklichung dieser Rechte für alle Menschen bezwecken, sondern einfach die Menschenrechte generell oder für einzelne Gruppen einschränken. So gibt es eben auch unterschiedliche Regeln für Freie und Sklaven, Männer und Frauen, Muslime und Nichtmuslime. Das traditionelle islamische Recht kennt auch keine demokratische Gesellschaft.

Das Verständnis von Menschenrechten oder Grundrechten bei traditionellen islamischen Juristen entspricht einem undemokratischen Verständnis, das selbstverständlich von der Überlegenheit der islamischen Religion ausgeht. So schreibt zum Beispiel der zeitgenössische zaiditische Gelehrte ʿAlī b. ʿAbd al-Karīm al-Faḍīl Šaraf ad-Dīn zur Glaubensfreiheit des Menschen und zum Straftatbestand der Apostasie (*irtidād*):

وهو حر في عقيدته لقوله تعالى (فمن شاء فليؤمن ومن شاء فليكفر، لا إكراه في الدين) ٢٥٦ / البقرة.

Er ist frei in seinem Glauben, wegen Gottes Wort: (Wer nun will, der soll glauben, und wer will, der soll ungläubig sein; Es gibt keinen Zwang im Glauben[45]) [vgl.] 256 : (*al-Baqara*) البقرة

وهو حر في الدفاع عنها ولذلك وجب الجهاد، وإذا عجز عن الدفاع وجب عليه الهجرة بدينه إلى الأرض التي يأمن فيها على دينه لقوله تعالى: (إن الذين توفاهم الملائكة ظالمي أنفسهم قالوا فيم كنتم قالوا: كنا مستضعفين في الأرض قالوا ألم تكن أرض الله واسعة فتهاجروا فيها فأولئك مأواهم جهنم وساءت مصيرا إلا المستضعفين من الرجال والنساء والولدان لا يستطيعون حيلة ولا يهتدون سبيلا فأولئك عسى الله أن يعفو عنهم وكان الله عفوا غفورا) ٩٧، ٩٨، ٩٩ / النساء.

Er ist frei darin, diesen zu verteidigen. Deswegen ist der ǧihād verbindlich. Ist ihm die Verteidigung nicht möglich, so muss er mit seiner Religion auswandern zu dem Ort, wo er in seiner Religion sicher ist, wegen Gottes Wort:(Diejenigen, die die Engel abberufen, während die sich selbst Unrecht tun, (zu jenen) sagen sie: „Worin habt ihr euch befunden?“ Sie sagen: „Wir waren Unterdrückte im Lande.“ Sie (die Engel) sagen: „War Allahs Erde nicht weit, so dass ihr darauf hättet auswandern können?“ Jene aber, - Ihr Zufluchtsort wird die Hölle sein, und (wie) böse ist der Ausgang! Ausgenommen die Unterdrückten unter den Männern, Frauen und Kindern, die keine Möglichkeit haben auszuwandern und auf dem Weg nicht rechtgeleitet sind. Jenen wird Allah vielleicht verzeihen. Allah ist Allverzeihend und Allvergebend.) [vgl.] 97, 98, 99 : (*an-Nisāʾ*) النساء .

أما اذا دخل في الإسلام بحريته واختياره، أو كان فيه مسلما، فهو ملزوم بقوانينه وأحكامه التي منها عقوبة القتل للمرتد صيانة للحرية في الدين من التلاعب والاستهتار، ولأن الدين الإسلامي هو الدين الحق الخاتم لكل الديانات. ولكنه لا يقتل إلا بعد استتابته ومحاولة استصلاحه، فإن لم يتب نفذ فيه حكم المرتد وقتل حداً شرعيا وجزاء وفاقا.

Tritt er aber durch seine Freiheit und seine freie Entscheidung in den Islam ein oder war er bereits darin ein Muslim, so ist er gebunden an dessen Gesetze und Normen, zu denen die Todesstrafe für den Apostaten gehört, zur Bewahrung der Freiheit in der Religion vor Veralberung und Geringschätzung und weil die islamische Religion die wahre Religion ist, welche alle anderen Religionen abschließt. Jedoch wird er nur nach Aufforderung zur Reue und dem Versuch seiner Besserung getötet. Bereut er nicht, so wird die Norm für den Apostaten vollstreckt als festgelegte Strafe der šarīʿa (ḥadd šarʿī) und als angemessene Vergeltung.

أما حكم الذين لا يؤمنون بدين الاسلام فإن كانوا من أهل الكتاب، فقد ضمن لهم الإسلام حريتهم في الدين، ما لم يحاربوا، فإذا حاربوا خيروا بين ثلاثة خيارات: الإسلام - ولهم ما للمسلمين وعليهم ما على المسلمين- أو الجزية - ولهم حريتهم في دينهم وممتلكاتهم أو الحرب - وهو ما اختاروه لأنفسهم.

---

45 Für die Übersetzung von Versen aus dem Qurʾān wird die Übersetzung des Zentralrats der Muslime in Deutschland verwendet.

Was nun die Norm für diejenigen betrifft, die nicht an die Religion des Islam glauben, so garantiert ihnen der Islam ihre Glaubensfreiheit, wenn sie zu den Schriftbesitzern (ahl al-kitāb) gehören, solange sie nicht bekämpfen. Wenn sie bekämpfen, so haben sie die Wahl zwischen drei Möglichkeiten: der Islam – und ihnen steht zu, was den Muslimen zusteht und ihnen obliegt, was den Muslimen obliegt – oder die ǧizya – und ihnen steht ihre Glaubensfreiheit und ihr Eigentum zu – oder der Krieg – und dies ist, was sie für sich selbst wählen.

وأما حكم من لا دين له من السماء، أو الذين لا يؤمنون بأي دين من الأديان فقد أمر الله بدعائهم إلى الإسلام بالحكمة والموعظة الحسنة، فإن حاربوا بعد ذلك حوربوا لقوله تعالى: (وقاتلوا في سبيل الله الذين يقاتلونكم ولا تعتدوا إن الله لا يحب المعتدين) ١٩٠ / البقرة.

Was nun diejenigen betrifft, die keine himmlische Religion oder gar keine Religion haben, so befiehlt Gott, sie zum Islam mit Weisheit und schöner Ermahnung aufzurufen. Wenn sie danach bekämpfen, so werden sie bekämpft, wegen Gottes Wort: (Und kämpft auf Allahs Weg gegen diejenigen, die gegen euch kämpfen, doch übertretet nicht! Allah liebt nicht die Übertreter.) [vgl.] 190 : (*al-Baqara*) البقرة

أمّا من كان في شبه الجزيرة العربية بلا دين سماوي، أو بلا دين مطلقاً، فلن يقبل منه إلا الإسلام لكونه آخر الديانات السماوية الحافلة بكل المصالح للعباد- أو السيف لقوله تعالى: (وقاتلوهم حتى لا تكون فتنة ويكون الدين لله) ١٩٣ / البقرة، وكل ذلك حفاظاً على أمن الدعوة الإسلامية وعلى سلامتها في عقر دارها وأرضها.

Wer sich auf der arabischen Halbinsel ohne himmlische Religion oder irgendeine Religion befindet, von dem wird nur der Islam akzeptiert – weil dieser die letzte der himmlischen Religionen ist und alle menschlichen Interessen beachtet – oder das Schwert, wegen Gottes Wort: (Und kämpft gegen sie, bis es keine Verfolgung mehr gibt und die Religion (allein) Allahs ist) [vgl.] 193 : (*al-Baqara*) البقرة. *All dies zur Wahrung der Sicherheit des islamischen Anspruchs und seines Wohlergehens im eigenen Gebiet.*[46]

Diese Ansicht eines traditionellen zaiditischen Rechtsgelehrten findet sich so oder in ähnlicher Form auch bei den traditionellen Gelehrten anderer Schulen. Es geht nicht um universelle Menschenrechte, sondern um ein Rechtsdenken, in dem zwar allen Menschen gewisse Rechte eingeräumt werden, nur eben nicht gleiche und unantastbare Rechte, wobei der Wahrheitsanspruch des Islam völlig unreflektiert als Grundlage rechtlicher Überlegungen akzeptiert wird. Das Menschenbild der allgemeinen Erklärung der Menschenrechte kennt Rechte, die jedem Menschen unveräußerlich zukommen, weil er Mensch ist. *ʿAlī b. ʿAbd al-Karīm al-Faḍīl Šaraf ad-Dīn* spricht hier hingegen von Rechten, die vom islamischen Recht dem Einzelnen eingeräumt werden. Diese haben nichts damit zu tun, dass jemand ein Mensch ist, sondern einzig mit der Frage, welches Verhältnis der Mensch zum Islam hat. Im Falle von Nichtmuslimen, die nicht zu den Schriftbesitzern gehören, scheint *ʿAlī b. ʿAbd al-Karīm al-Faḍīl Šaraf ad-*

46 *ʿAlī b. ʿAbd al-Karīm al-Faḍīl Šaraf ad-Dīn*, az-Zaidīya – naẓarīya wa-taṭbīq, ʿAmmān 1985, S. 100 f.

Dīn sogar den Standpunkt zu vertreten, diese hätten nur die Wahl zwischen Annahme des Islam und dem Tod.

Traditionelles islamisches Recht, wie es sich in den Rechtsschulen herausgebildet hat, ist ohne Zweifel mit dem modernen Menschenrechtsgedanken unvereinbar. Identifiziert man aber das islamische Recht nicht mit den traditionellen Rechtsauslegungen und folgt man einer flexiblen Auffassung in der Rechtsmethodik, dann kann man alle traditionellen Auffassungen, die den Menschenrechten widersprechen, durch menschenrechtskonforme Normen ersetzen. Man kann auch ganz einfach so argumentieren, dass der *Qur'ān* Gerechtigkeit und Vernunft fordert und da die Menschenrechte das moderne Verständnis von Gerechtigkeit repräsentieren, seien diese nun zeitgenössisches islamisches Recht.

Damit gelangt man zu einem der weiteren Kernprobleme des islamischen Rechts überhaupt. Das islamische Recht ist kein festgelegtes Rechtssystem. Im Zivilrecht haben die Fiqh- und Fatwāwerke in späterer Zeit praktisch den Rang von Gesetzen eingenommen.[47] Die Rechtsschulen haben in der islamischen Rechtsgeschichte einen erheblichen Beitrag zur Rechtssicherheit geleistet und umgekehrt hat sicherlich die Zunahme der Rechtssicherheit zum Erfolg der Rechtsschulen beigetragen. Mit dem Sieg der Rechtsschulen nahm die Rechtssicherheit zu und die Flexibilität und Dynamik des Rechts ab. Identifiziert man das islamische Recht mit den Rechtsschulen, dann findet man in diesen Rechtsschulen ausdifferenzierte Normen, die eine relativ große Rechtssicherheit gewähren. Die Rechtsschulen sind aber immer angegriffen worden, weil sie das Ergebnis einer historischen Entwicklung waren und durch sie der Rückgriff auf die eigentlichen Quellen unmöglich wurde. Dafür aber gebe es gar keine Legitimation.[48] Die Freigabe des *iğtihād* jedoch ist untrennbar verbunden mit einer großen Zunahme der Vielfalt der Rechtsmeinungen, selbst dann, wenn man einer relativ konservativen Rechtsmethodik folgt, die sich noch eng an den *naṣṣ* anlehnt. Akzeptiert man hingegen modernistische Methodiklehren, die auch Rechtsableitung entgegen dem wörtlichen Verständnis des *naṣṣ* zulassen, so kann letztlich alles islamisches Recht genannt werden. Hinsichtlich der Methodiklehren ist dabei noch zu erwähnen, dass diese selbst auch wieder das Produkt historischer Entwicklung sind. Mit anderen Worten: Islamisches Recht kann alles Mögliche bedeuten, da die Freiheit des *iğtihād* sich in unterschiedlichsten Ansichten manifestiert.

---

47 *Hayreddin Karaman*, Anahatlarıyla İslam Hukuku, Bd.1, Istanbul 1987, S. 88.

48 Siehe hierzu etwa die Schrift von *Muḥammad b. ʿAlī aš-Šaukānī*, al-qaul al-mufīd fī adillat al-iğtiād wa-t-taqlīd, 3. Aufl., al-Kuwait 1983.

Die traditionelle Position der islamischen Gelehrten ist, dass es sich beim islamischen Recht um ein von Gott gesetztes Recht handelt und daher sei es menschlichem Recht überlegen und dürfe nicht durch menschliches Recht ersetzt werden.[49] Diese Position ist selbst wenn man die zugrunde liegenden theologischen Prämissen akzeptiert (*Qur'ān* = Wort Gottes, *Muḥammad* = unfehlbarer Gesandter Gottes) schon bezüglich traditioneller Methodiklehren so nicht haltbar, da die konkrete Norm immer erst durch einen Reflexionsvorgang des *muǧtahid* erlangt wird. Anders ausgedrückt: Tatsächlich verbindliche Norm ist das, was der *muǧtahid* aufgrund seiner Auslegung für den Willen Gottes hält. Ob dies tatsächlich der Wille Gottes ist, ist eine andere Frage. Bezüglich dieses Problems sind in der Methodenlehre zwei Schulen entstanden. Die *Muṣawwiba* lehrt, dass jeder *muǧtahid* Recht habe, Gott also verschiedene Lösungen zulasse, während die *Muḫaṭṭi'a* lehrt, es gebe nur eine richtige Lösung und ein diese verfehlender *muǧtahid* irre und sei höchstens entschuldigt, wenn er seinen *iǧtihād* mit entsprechender Sorgfalt betrieben habe.[50] Man war sich also einig, dass die konkrete Norm nicht von Gott stammt, sondern vom *muǧtahid.* Trotzdem wird bis heute die Auffassung vertreten, islamisches Recht zeichne sich dadurch aus, dass es von Gott gesetztes Recht sei. Dies ist dadurch zu erklären, dass trotz aller Vielfalt in der Rechtsauslegung in der Vergangenheit bestimmte Normen niemals angetastet wurden und Traditionalisten hinterfragen diese Normen bis heute nicht. Für sie endet die Freiheit des *iǧtihād* bei bestimmten traditionellen Auffassungen, die sie nicht zu hinterfragen wagen. Modernisten hingegen haben eine weitere Auffassung vom *iǧtihād* und dementsprechend werden nun auch Normen hinterfragt, über die in der Vergangenheit nie gestritten wurde. Dadurch aber stellt sich in der Tat die Frage, ob es dann überhaupt noch Sinn macht, von islamischem Recht zu sprechen.

D. Menschenrechte und Religion

Das islamische Recht kann man mit den Menschenrechten versöhnen, wenn man gemäß dem zuvor beschriebenen flexiblen Ansatz in der Rechtsmethodik vorgeht.[51] An dieser Stelle aber stellen sich nun einige weitere Fragen.

I. Zur Vereinbarkeit mit der historisch-kritischen Forschung

Die erste Frage lautet:

49 Siehe z.B. *ʿAbdalkarīm Zaidān*, al-madḫal li-dirāsat aš-šarīʿa al-islāmīya, 6. Aufl., Bairūt 1982, S. 39 ff.

50 Zu den Lehren der *Muṣawwiba* und *Muḫaṭṭi'a* siehe *Aḥmad b. Yaḥyā ibn al-Murtaḍā*, minhāǧ al-wuṣūl ilā miʿyār al-ʿuqūl fī ʿilm al-uṣul, Ṣanʿā' 1992, S. 766 ff.

51 Siehe innerhalb dieses Beitrages Seite 53.

Lässt sich der flexible Ansatz in der islamischen Rechtsmethodik mit der historisch-kritischen Forschung vereinbaren?

Der flexible Ansatz des islamischen Rechts geht davon aus, dass die Vernunft die *ratio legis* einzelner Normen des *Qur'ān* und der *sunna* erkennen und dementsprechend das Recht anpassen und weiterentwickeln kann. Insbesondere bezüglich der *sunna* tendiert modernistisches islamisches Denken dazu, das als nicht authentisch abzulehnen, was nicht mit dem *Qur'ān* und der Vernunft übereinstimmt.

Ein solches Rechtsdenken geht also eigentlich von einer Rechtserkenntnis durch Vernunft aus, die man nur in den religiösen Texten wieder finden möchte. Die Interpretation des *Qur'ān* ist am bereits bekannten Ergebnis orientiert und die Authentizität der Überlieferung vom Propheten wird gemessen an einem Maßstab, der bereits vorgibt, wie der Prophet gewesen sein muss. So sympathisch die Ergebnisse einer solchen Vorgehensweise aus rechtsphilosophischer Sicht auch sein mögen, die Vorgehensweise selbst ist wissenschaftlich nicht haltbar. Historisch-kritische Forschung muss ergebnisoffen sein und kann daher nicht von einem als gegeben vorausgesetzten Prophetenbild ausgehen. Sie muss vielmehr erst versuchen, aus den bekannten Fakten einen historischen Muḥammad zu rekonstruieren. Ein solcher Versuch aber führt zu Ergebnissen, die auch für den flexiblen Ansatz in der islamischen Rechtsmethodik untauglich sind. Hält man mit einem konservativen Ansatz die islamische Geschichtsschreibung für im Kern zutreffend, dann gelangt man zu Ergebnissen wie etwa Tilman Nagel in seiner Muḥammad-Biographie.[52] Die dunklen und negativen Seiten, die dem Propheten durch die islamische Überlieferung zugeschrieben werden, stellen dann ein schweres Problem dar, weil die Vermutung dahin geht, dass gerade negative Berichte, die von den eigenen Parteigängern berichtet werden, mit hoher Wahrscheinlichkeit authentisch sind. Es lässt sich nicht vermeiden, dass dann ein Bild von Muḥammad entsteht, das einen brutalen Machtmenschen zeichnet. Der Muḥammad der islamischen Überlieferung kann nicht das Vorbild für eine moderne Ethik oder ein modernes Recht sein.

Folgt man dem Ansatz der „Revisionisten", die die islamische Geschichtsschreibung weitgehend oder vollständig für Fiktion halten, bis hin zur Leugnung der Geschichtlichkeit Muḥammads, dann bricht jeglicher historischer Hintergrund zusammen. Es ist unklar, ob Muḥammad überhaupt existiert hat und wenn er existiert hat, dann ist der historische Muḥammad eine unbekannte Persönlichkeit, die nicht mehr zu rekonstruieren ist. Ebenso unklar ist auch die Entstehungsgeschichte des *Qur'ān*. Für den Ansatz der Revisionisten ist die Weltreligion Islam, wie Judentum und Christentum auch, das Ergebnis eines langen

---

52 *Tilmann Nagel*, Mohammed – Leben und Legende, München 2008.

historischen Prozesses. Theologisch könnte man dies so neu deuten, dass sich in diesem Prozess ein Wirken des *Logos* oder kosmischen Muḥammad (*al-ḥaqīqa al-muḥammadīya*) manifestiert. Allerdings wird man dann konsequenterweise nicht begründen können, warum dieses Wirken der *Weltseele* in irgendeiner Weise besser sein sollte als deren Wirken zu irgendeiner anderen Zeit an irgendeinem anderen Ort. Der Islam würde dadurch zu einer religiösen Tradition wie alle anderen auch.

Historisch-kritische Forschung kann nicht mit dem Offenbarungsbegriff der traditionellen islamischen Theologie arbeiten. Ihre Grundannahme besteht darin, geschichtliche Prozesse ohne übernatürliche Eingriffe zu erklären. Anders könnte Geschichtswissenschaft auch gar nicht betrieben werden, denn nur, wenn man davon ausgeht, dass alle historischen Prozesse sich im Rahmen der allgemein bekannten Gesetzmäßigkeiten der Natur bewegen, lassen sich Quellen beurteilen und Schlussfolgerungen ziehen. Unterstellt man die Möglichkeit eines übernatürlichen Geschehens, dann entfiele jeglicher Maßstab. Offenbarung kann im Rahmen historisch-kritischer Arbeit lediglich als subjektive spirituelle Erfahrung verstanden werden. Dementsprechend ist der *Qur'ān,* selbst wenn er tatsächlich nur die spirituelle Erfahrung Muḥammads enthält und nicht das Ergebnis eines viel längeren Prozesses darstellt, nicht das Wort Gottes.

In jedem Falle entzieht die historisch-kritische Forschung durch ihre erkenntnistheoretischen Voraussetzungen wie auch durch ihre Ergebnisse nicht nur dem islamischen Recht – darüber hinaus jedem religiösen Recht – die Grundlage, sofern es sich nicht auch durch die Vernunft begründen lässt.

II. Zur Ableitung des modernen Menschrechtsgedankens aus heiligen Schriften

Die zweite Frage lautet:

Macht eine Ableitung des modernen Menschenrechtsgedankens aus heiligen Schriften überhaupt Sinn?

Abgesehen von den Problemen, welche von der historisch-kritischen Methode aufgeworfen werden, existiert grundsätzlich das Problem, ob eine Ableitung moderner Rechtsvorstellungen aus heiligen Texten Sinn macht. Wenn man durch die Vernunft zu der Überzeugung gelangt ist, dass die Menschenrechte gut und richtig sind, dann ist es gleichgültig, ob man sie in einer religiösen Tradition finden oder aus einer religiösen Tradition ableiten kann oder nicht. Wenn das Urteil der Vernunft bestand hat, dann ist das Urteil der religiösen Tradition bedeutungslos. Die Vernunft ist der entscheidende Faktor. Dies muss man sich vor Augen führen, wenn religiös-apologetische Argumentation die Ableitung der Menschenrechte aus der eigenen Tradition behauptet. Wenn man die Menschenrechte will, weil die Vernunft diese fordert, dann hängt ihr Bestand nicht davon ab, ob man sie nun aus religiöser Tradition begründen kann oder nicht. So gesehen ist es also völlig irrelevant, ob man die Menschenrechte aus einer religiösen Tradition ableiten kann und eigentlich nur Zeitverschwendung, dies zu versuchen. Im Übrigen ist das Unterfangen einer Ableitung der Menschenrechte aus religiösen Texten methodisch fragwürdig. Wir können nicht wissen, was Muḥammad, falls er denn gelebt haben sollte, wirklich gedacht hat. Den modernen Menschenrechtsgedanken können weder er oder wer auch immer sonst für die Entstehung der heiligen Texte des Islam verantwortlich ist, gehabt haben, denn er findet sich darin bekanntlich nicht. Wie diese Menschen heute denken würden, ist eine hypothetische Fragestellung, auf die es keine sichere Antwort geben kann. Dass die Autoren der Schriften die dort aufgeführten Rechtsregeln als Gerechtigkeit verstanden haben, ergibt sich aus diesen Texten. Insofern kann man immer argumentieren, in ihrem Sinne zu handeln, wenn man auf eine Weiterentwicklung des Gerechtigkeitsgedankens verweist und diese Regeln gemäß heutigem Gerechtigkeitsverständnis modifiziert. So kann man sogar argumentieren, wenn man ganz traditionell islamisch Gott als Autor des *Qur'ān* betrachtet und davon ausgeht, dass Gott hier eine Offenbarung auf dem Verständnisniveau von Menschen des 6./7. Jahrhunderts gesandt hat, die durch menschlichen *iǧtihād* stets aktualisiert werden muss, was durch die zahlreichen Verweise des *Qur'ān* auf Vernunft und Gerechtigkeit begründet werden kann. Eine solche Theologie bezüglich der Offenbarung ist aber schwerlich haltbar.

Der Menschenrechtsgedanke liefert nur noch weitere philosophische Argumente gegen ein Offenbarungsverständnis, das in Offenbarung ein direktes Wort Gottes sieht. Warum hat Gott den Menschenrechtsgedanken nicht direkt offenbart, so dass kein Zweifel daran bestehen kann, dass er für Gleichberechtigung von Mann und Frau, für Meinungsfreiheit und gegen Sklaverei ist? Warum hat Gott dies nicht von Anfang an klar verkündet? Stattdessen setzen sich Bibel und *Qur'ān* mit dem ethischen Standard ihrer Zeit auseinander.

Ob dabei Bibel und *Qur'ān* immer den höchsten Standard in der Diskussion ihrer Zeit vertreten, ist eine andere Frage: Origenes[53] etwa meinte, dass ein Christ, der das Alte Testament wörtlich verstehe, erröten müsse, angesichts der so viel feiner und vernünftiger wirkenden Menschengesetze etwa der Römer oder Athener.[54] Warum hört Offenbarung zu einem Zeitpunkt auf, wo noch so viel zu verbessern gewesen wäre? Was nützt eine direkte Offenbarung Gottes, wenn sie ohnehin nur das verkündet, was zu gewissen Zeiten ethischer Standard

---

53 Origenes (ca. 185-254): altkirchlicher Theologe mit großer Nähe zur Gnosis und zum Neuplatonismus. Sein Hauptinteresse galt dem allegorischen Sinn der Schrift.

54 *Karlheinz Deschner*, Kriminalgeschichte des Christentums, Bd.1, Hamburg 1989, S. 249.

war? Sie bringt keine neue Erkenntnis und fördert dann doch lediglich das Missverständnis der Fundamentalisten, diesen Standard der Vergangenheit für alle Zeiten festschreiben und geistigen Fortschritt verhindern zu wollen.

Die drei monotheistischen Religionen Judentum, Christentum und Islam in ihrer klassischen Form leiden unter zwei gravierenden Fehlern:

- Die Vorstellung einer Auserwähltheit und Überlegenheit,

sowie

- die Vorstellung, dass es Texte gibt, die direkt von Gott stammen, die „Wort Gottes“ sind.

Die Vorstellung der Auserwähltheit und Überlegenheit führt in ihrer schlimmsten Form zu Gewalt gegen und Unterdrückung von Andersgläubigen. In ihrer mildesten Form führt sie mindestens zu Abgrenzung, zu einem Denken in der Form „wir“ und „die anderen“, das stark zu einer Herabsetzung neigt. Wenn man selbst zur auserwählten und überlegenen Gruppe gehört, dann haftet „den anderen“ eben mindestens der Makel an, eben nicht zu dieser Gruppe zu gehören, da hilft auch alle Beteuerung der grundsätzlichen Gleichheit aller Menschen nichts.

Die Vorstellung vom „Wort Gottes“ hat im schlimmsten Falle zur Herausbildung von Dogmen und zur Verfolgung von Ketzern und Andersgläubigen geführt. Im mildesten Fall hat sie viele intelligente Menschen davon abgehalten, einfach ihrer Vernunft zu folgen und dazu gebracht, ihre Zeit damit zu verschwenden, ihre Vernunfterkenntnisse oder eigene spirituelle Erfahrungen unbedingt mit dem „Wort Gottes“ harmonisieren zu wollen. Diese Vorstellung hat selbst bei rationalistischen Theologen immer als Zensurschere im Kopf gewirkt, die völlige geistige Freiheit verhindert hat. Die Illusion von der einen absoluten Wahrheit vertreten von einer Religion ist eine furchtbare Wahnvorstellung der drei monotheistischen Religionen, die in dieser Beziehung gegenüber der Antike und älteren Religionen einen Rückschritt darstellen. Ein echter Meister unter Schamanen etwa würde niemals die Gültigkeit der Erfahrung eines anderen Menschen bestreiten oder Dogmen zulassen.[55]

Der Begriff der Offenbarung ist nur noch haltbar, wenn man darunter subjektive spirituelle Erfahrung versteht. Religiöse Texte und Traditionen sind das Ergebnis subjektiver menschlicher spiritueller Erfahrung und können deswegen auch keinen Anspruch auf Absolutheit erheben. Auch aus diesem Grunde ist es unsinnig, unbedingt aus einem bestimmten Text den modernen Menschenrechtsgedanken herausarbeiten zu wollen. Sinnvoll ist einzig eine rechtshistorische Ana-

---

[55] *Michael Harner*, The Way of the Shaman, 3. Aufl., New York 1990, S. 45.

lyse, was die Quellen aussagen und wie sich z.B. das islamische Recht im Laufe der Zeit entwickelt hat. Es ist sinnvoll und hilfreich, zu versuchen, die Vergangenheit zu verstehen. Was wir als Menschen heute wollen hingegen, ist einzig eine Frage unserer Vernunft.

III. Zur Bedeutsamkeit für die Religion(en)

Die dritte Frage lautet:

Was bedeutet all dies für die Religionen?

Wenn man die Menschenrechte anerkennt, kommt man nicht darum herum, ebenfalls anzuerkennen, dass diese nicht aus den Religionen stammen. Die heiligen Schriften der Religionen kennen die Menschenrechte nicht. Das bedeutet nicht, dass sie diese vollständig negieren, nur enthalten sie eben nicht die moderne Menschenrechtsvorstellung und widersprechen ihr teilweise. Der moderne Menschenrechtsgedanke ist ein Ergebnis der Aufklärung. Entscheidende Schritte zu seiner Entwicklung waren die *Virginia Bill of Rights* aus der Gründerzeit der USA und die *déclaration des droits de l'homme et du citoyen* der französischen Revolution. In den Religionen sind sicher wichtige philosophische und juristische Beiträge zum Rechtsdenken geleistet worden und es mag auch Fortschritt gebracht worden sein, doch Tatsache bleibt, dass der moderne Menschenrechtsgedanke nicht von den Vertretern der Religionen entwickelt worden ist. Vielmehr sind nach der Entwicklung des Menschenrechtsgedankens manche Vertreter der Religionen auf den nunmehr fahrenden Zug aufgesprungen. Im Allgemeinen aber ist der moderne Menschenrechtsgedanke von den Vertretern der Religionen eher blockiert worden.[56] Was den Islam angeht, so ist es evident, dass die Verfechter eines vollständig oder weitgehend traditionellen islamischen Rechts Gegner des modernen Menschenrechtsgedankens sind.

Die Idee des Menschenrechtsschutzes war zunächst mit einem innerstaatlichen Menschenrechtsschutz verknüpft. Der Gedanke eines internationalen Menschenrechtsschutzes schließlich ist gerade einmal wenige Jahrzehnte alt, wie folgendes Zitat von Bruno Simma in seiner Einleitung zu den Beck-Texten Menschenrechte von 1985 deutlich macht:

---

[56] Für die Entwicklung im Christentum siehe *Otfried Höffe*, Vernunft und Recht – Bausteine zu einem interkulturellen Rechtsdiskurs, 2. Aufl., Frankfurt a.M. 1998, S. 83 ff. Siehe ebenfalls *Karlheinz Deschner*, Abermahls krähte der Hahn, 4. Buch, III. Teil, 3. Aufl., Rastatt 1988, S. 485 ff.

> *Noch vor wenigen Jahrzehnten hätte man in den Registern der völkerrechtlichen Lehr- und Handbücher vergeblich nach dem Stichwort „Menschenrechte" gesucht.*[57]

Dass es um die praktische Durchsetzung dieses internationalen Menschenrechtsschutzes bis heute eher schlecht bestellt ist, exemplifizieren die nachfolgenden Studien ab Seite 121. Es bedarf daher an dieser Stelle keiner weiteren Erläuterung. So sehr man auch in religiösen Traditionen Ansätze eines modernen Menschenrechtsgedankens suchen und vielleicht auch teilweise finden mag, es bleibt die Tatsache, dass es weder jüdische, noch christliche noch islamische Gelehrte waren, die den modernen Menschenrechtsgedanken entwickelten. Durch die Aufklärung und den Menschenrechtsgedanken ist in der Menschheitsgeschichte ein eigenständiger Entwicklungsschritt vollzogen worden, der unabhängig von einer bestimmten Religion stattgefunden hat. Dieser Schritt hat die Vertreter der Religionen in zwei Lager gespalten: in die Befürworter dieses Prozesses der Aufklärung, die diese durch moderne Interpretation mit der Aufklärung versöhnen wollen und die Gegner der Aufklärung, die sich auch gegen den modernen Menschenrechtsgedanken stellen. Die Religionen mögen sich mit dem Menschenrechtsgedanken versöhnen lassen, sie sind aber nicht dessen Urheber.

Akzeptiert man die Aufklärung und insbesondere den Menschenrechtsgedanken als das, was sie tatsächlich sind, nämlich ein eigenständiger geistiger Entwicklungsschritt in der Menschheitsgeschichte,[58] dann stellt dies für alle Religionen eine Relativierung dar, weil damit unweigerlich die Erkenntnis verbunden ist, dass dieser wichtige Schritt in der Menschheitsgeschichte, ohne die Religionen gemacht wurde. Der Menschenrechtsgedanke ist ein Ergebnis der Vernunft und bedurfte der Religionen nicht, um zu entstehen. Bereits aus dieser Tatsache heraus ist jede Vorstellung absurd, eine bestimmte Religion sei allen anderen überlegen, repräsentiere gar die absolute Wahrheit oder stelle den Entwicklungshöhepunkt der Menschheit dar. Der Menschenrechtsgedanke wie auch die historisch-kritische Methode machen deutlich, dass es sich bei Religionen um spirituelle Traditionen handelt. Jedes Individuum muss für sich selbst entscheiden, ob es etwas aus diesen Traditionen übernehmen möchte oder nicht und wenn ja, was es übernehmen möchte. Das ist ein Menschenrecht. Die Erkenntnis aber, dass Religionen historisch gewachsene spirituelle Traditionen sind und

57 *Bruno Simma / Ulrich Fastenrath* (Hrsg.), Menschenrechte – Ihr internationaler Schutz, 2. Aufl., München 1985, S. XXIII.

58 Vgl. hierzu *Abdullahi Ahmed An-Na'im,* "Islam and Human Rights: Introductory Remarks and Reflections", in: *Hatem Elliesie* (Hrsg./Editor), Beiträge zum Islamischen Recht VII, Islam und Menschenrechte (Islam and Human Rights / الإسلام وحقوق الإنسان), Frankfurt a.M. 2010, S. 41 (42).

letztlich nie aufgehört haben, sich zu verändern und neue Unterformen zu entwickeln, wie auch die Erkenntnis, dass menschliche Entwicklung auch nach der Entstehung der großen Religionen und ohne deren Beitrag weitere Fortschritte macht, bedeuten letztendlich, dass Religion in ihrer traditionellen Form vor unserer modernen Erkenntnis keinen Bestand haben kann.

Islam und Menschenrechte (Islam and Human Rights / الإسلام وحقوق الإنسان)
Hatem Elliesie (Hrsg./Editor), © Peter Lang Verlag: Frankfurt a.M. 2010

Hermeneutik, Koraninterpretation und Menschenrechte*

Assem Hefny, Kairo / Leipzig / Marburg

A. Einleitung

Der vorliegende Aufsatz soll sich mit den Themenbereichen Hermeneutik und Koran, Problemen der Koraninterpretation sowie Menschenrechten und Islam beschäftigen. Dabei wird der Versuch unternommen, hermeneutische Prinzipien als eine Auslegungskunst bei der Interpretation koranischer Verse zu berücksichtigen. Daran anschließend sollen wichtige Fragestellungen in Bezug auf die Koraninterpretation in historischer und aktueller Sicht aufgegriffen werden. Es folgt eine Auseinandersetzung zur Möglichkeit einer Vereinbarung von Menschenrechten und Islam aufgrund einer hermeneutischen Interpretation des Korans, dargestellt am Beispiel der Apostasie.

B. Hermeneutik und Koran

Die Hermeneutik als die Kunst oder Lehre des Verstehens bzw. der Auslegung und Interpretation[2] ist für das Verstehen des Korans von großer Relevanz. Das Verfahren des „hermeneutischen Zirkels", wonach „das Ganze aus dem Einzelnen und das Einzelne aus dem Ganzen"[3] zu verstehen ist, lässt sich beim Interpretieren des koranischen Textes sinnvoll zur Anwendung bringen. Der „hermeneutische Zirkel" kann auf den Koran folgendermaßen angewandt werden: Das einzelne koranische Wort gehört in den Zusammenhang des Satzes, der wiederum in den Zusammenhang des Textes gestellt werden soll. Der koranische Text seinerseits gehört in den Zusammenhang des gesamten Korantextes, der im Zusammenhang aller heiligen, von Gott offenbarten Schriften steht. Darauf bauend lässt sich ein Verstehen des Korans nur dadurch vollenden, wenn zunächst das *Gott-Mensch-Verhältnis* sowie die Sprache und die Historizität der Offenbarung erfasst werden. Dieser Weg des Verstehens geht wiederum kreisförmig vom Ende bis zum Anfang zurück. Was das *Gott-Mensch-Verhältnis* anbelangt, stellen sich u.a. folgende Fragen:

---

* Bei dieser Veröffentlichung handelt es sich um meinen überarbeiteten und erweiterten Beitrag, der am 20.Oktober 2007 in Berlin auf der 10. Jahrestagung der Gesellschaft für Arabisches und Islamisches Recht (GAIR) gehalten wurde. Für die Durchsicht des Manuskripts und die kritischen Hinweise bin ich Herrn Prof. Dr. Hans-Georg Ebert dankbar.

2 Vgl. *Hans-Georg Gadamer*, Wahrheit und Methode: Grundzüge einer philosophischen Hermeneutik, Tübingen 1999, besonders S. 296 ff.

3 Ibidem, S. 270 ff. und 296.

Islam und Menschenrechte (Islam and Human Rights / الإسلام وحقوق الإنسان)
Hatem Elliesie (Hrsg./Editor), © Peter Lang Verlag: Frankfurt a.M. 2010, S. 73-97

- Warum sendet Gott dem Menschen eine Botschaft herab?
- Zielt Gott auf die Qual oder die Freude des Menschen ab?

Bezüglich der Sprache und Historizität der Offenbarung sind u.a. folgende Fragen entscheidend:

- Inwieweit kann der Mensch die Sprache des heiligen Textes verstehen?
- Ist die Herabsendung koranischer Botschaften vom historischen Kontext abhängig?

Diese Fragen stehen meines Erachtens im Mittelpunkt einer hermeneutischen Koraninterpretation, deren Inhalt und Methoden von der Antwort darauf bestimmt werden. Aus diesen Gründen unternimmt die vorliegende Studie den Versuch, eine Antwort auf die oben gestellten Fragen zu geben.

I. Hermeneutik und ta'wīl

Im Laufe der Untersuchung wird der Begriff Hermeneutik durch einen islamischen, vom Ziel und Verfahren her ähnlichen ersetzt, und zwar den Begriff *ta'wīl*. Die *ta'wīl*-Methode ist von frühislamischen Koraninterpreten erarbeitet, jedoch aus verschiedenen Gründen nicht weiterentwickelt worden. Neben *ta'wīl* fand und findet weiterhin eine andere, weniger bedeutende Interpretationsmethode des Korans, der sog. *tafsīr*, Beachtung. Unter *tafsīr* ist die Suche nach der direkten Bedeutung des Wortes bzw. des Textes auf der sprachlichen Ebene zu verstehen, während *ta'wīl* weit über diese Stufe hinausgeht. *Ta'wīl* beschäftigt sich sowohl mit der sprachlichen Dimension des koranischen Textes, indem die direkten und indirekten sprachlichen und metaphorischen Beziehungen der Texteinheiten zueinander unter die Lupe genommen werden, als auch damit, was im Text hinsichtlich von Entstehungszusammenhängen bzw. historischem Kontext verborgen ist.[4] Damit erscheint *tafsīr* als Vorstufe von *ta'wīl*, um zum verborgenen Sinn gelangen zu können. Die große Bedeutung von *ta'wīl* lässt sich auch durch seine Häufigkeit im Koran belegen, denn der Begriff taucht in 17 Versen auf, während *tafsīr* lediglich ein einziges Mal erwähnt wird.

Die *ta'wīl*-Methode beim Interpretieren heiliger Texte wurde jedoch aus verschiedenen Gründen zu Gunsten von *tafsīr* in den Hintergrund gedrängt, sodass sich die Spuren über die Jahrhunderte verwischt haben. Auf die Gründe dieser Entwicklung wird im Folgenden eingegangen.

1. Ta'wīl und Verfälschung

Im Laufe der islamischen Geschichte erfuhr der Begriff *ta'wīl* eine negative Konnotation, da er als Verfälschung oder Entstellung des Textes verstanden wurde. Diese Tatsache ist sowohl auf politische als auch auf interpretatorische

---

4 Vgl. *Ǧalāl ad-Dīn as-Sīūṭī*, al-itqān fi ʿulūm al-qurān [Die Genauigkeit in den Koranwissenschaften], 3. Aufl., Maktabat Muṣṭafā al-Babī al-Ḥalabī: Kairo 1951, S. 77. Stichwort: *tafsīr* und *ta'wīl*.

Ursachen zurückzuführen. Der Fachausdruck *ta'wīl* hatte am Anfang eine neutrale Bedeutung und fand in mehreren Zusammenhängen Anwendung. Als die Umayyaden in ihrem Krieg (Schlacht von Ṣiffīn[5]) gegen den vierten Kalifen ʿAlī b. Abī Ṭālib (gest. 661) Blätter aus dem Koran an die Spitzen ihrer Speere steckten, womit sie ihren Willen, das Buch Gottes als Schiedsrichter[6] zu nehmen, andeuteten, soll ʿAlī b. Abī Ṭālib folgenden berühmten Satz ausgesprochen haben:

"بالأمس حاربناهم على تنزيله واليوم نحاربهم على تأويله"[7]

„Früher haben wir gegen sie wegen seiner Herabsendung gekämpft
und heute wegen seiner Deutung"[8]

Ta'wīl bedeutet hier nichts weiter als das mögliche unterschiedliche Verständnis des Korans.[9] Die neutrale Bedeutung des Begriffs *ta'wīl* lässt sich durch den bekannten Koraninterpreten Muḥammad b. Ǧarīr aṭ-Ṭabarī (gest. 923) bestätigen. Er benutzt diesen Begriff sowohl im Titel seines exegetischen Werkes als auch im Text, wenn er mit der Interpretation eines Koranverses beginnt[10]. Allerdings ist *ta'wīl* beim späteren Koraninterpreten Abū ʿAbdullāh al-Qurṭubī (gest. 1272) nicht zu finden,[11] was sich vermutlich auf die Bedeutungsverschlechterung des Begriffs zurückführen lässt.

---

5 Mehr zu dieser Schlacht siehe *Gudrun Krämer*, Geschichte des Islam. München 2005, S. 39-41.

6 Diese Geschichte steht bis heute im Mittelpunkt des Diskurses über die Fragestellung: Wer regiert? Gott oder Mensch?

7 Vgl. *Muḥammad b. Ǧarīr aṭ-Ṭabarī*, tārīḫ al-rusul wal-mulūk [„Geschichte der Gesandten und Könige"]. Bearb. von *Muḥammad Abū al-Faḍl Ibrāhīm*. 5. Bd., 4. Aufl., Dār al-Maʿārif: Kairo 1979, S. 48.

8 ʿAlī b. Abī Ṭālib gilt als der erste Minderjährige, der den Islam angenommen hat. Als Anhänger und Cousin des Propheten verteidigte er die neue Religion nach besten Kräften. Damals gehörten Muʿāwiya b. Abī Sufyān (gest. 680) und seine Familie *banū 'umaiya* [= die Umayyaden] noch zu den Gegnern des Islam. Auf diese alte Feindschaft deutet ʿAlī b. Abī Ṭālib mit seinem o.g. Spruch hin.

9 Vgl. *Naṣr Ḥāmid Abū Zaīd*, naqd al-ḫiṭāb ad-dīnī [„Kritik des religiösen Diskurses"], Neue Ausgabe mit einem dokumentierten Kommentar, Maktabat Madbūlī: Kairo 2003, S. 119 ff.

10 Vgl. *Muḥammad b. Ǧarīr aṭ-Ṭabarī*, ǧāmiʿ al-bayān ʿan ta'wīl āyi al-Qur'ān [„Die umfassende Darstellung zur Deutung der Koranverse"]. Bearb. von *Maḥmūd Muḥammad Šākir*, 6. Bd., Dār al-Maʿārif: Kairo 1971.

11 Vgl. *Abū ʿAbdullāh Muḥammad b. Aḥmad al-Qurṭubī*, al-ǧamiʿ li 'aḥkām al-Qur'ān [„Das Umfassende der Koranvorschriften"]. Bearb. von *Hišām Samīr al-Buḫārī*, Dār Aʿlām al-Kutub: Riad 2003.

Abū Zaīd meint, der Bedeutungswandel von *ta'wīl* kam zuerst zustande, als Muḥammad b. Ǧarīr aṭ-Ṭabarī beim Interpretieren des 7. Verses der 3. Sure[12] erwähnte, dass mit denjenigen, in deren Herzen es Neigung zur Abkehr gibt und die beim *ta'wīl* jenen koranischen Versen folgen, die unterschiedlich zu deuten sind, die Kharijiten (*al-Ḫawāriǧ*)[13] gemeint sind.[14] Danach wurden dem Begriff *ta'wīl* politische Schattierungen zuerkannt.

2. Ta'wīl und Politik

Die verfeindeten Gegner am Ende der Kalifatszeit des dritten Kalifs ʿUṯmān b. ʿAffān (gest. 656) sowie zurzeit von ʿAlī b. Abī Ṭālib deuteten den Koran mittels *ta'wīl*-Verfahren gemäß den jeweiligen Interessen. ʿAbdullāh Šiḥāta meint dazu, dass die politischen Konflikte unter den Muslimen im ersten Jahrhundert des umayyadischen Kalifats (660-750) zur Entstehung mehrerer gegnerischer Gruppierungen geführt hätten. Diese Gruppierungen versuchten ihre Standpunkte religiös durch eine entsprechende Koraninterpretation zu bestätigen, was logischerweise extreme Meinungsverschiedenheiten zur Folge hatte. Dadurch entstanden zwei Hauptrichtungen: Die eine bevorzugte die wortwörtliche Deutung des heiligen Textes, während die andere der Vernunft den höchsten Stellenwert beimaß und demgemäß die *ta'wīl*-Methode auferlegte. Die erste Richtung wird mit den Salafīten, die zweite mit den Muʿtazilīten in Verbindung gebracht. In diesem Sinne haben sich Interpretationen in Polemik verwandelt. Nicht den Text an sich zu verstehen, sondern die eigene Richtung zu verteidigen, wurde das Ziel.[15]

---

12 Auf diesen Vers wird nachfolgend auf Seite 78 f. ausführlicher eingegangen.

13 Die Kharijiten sind eine islamische Gruppe, die das Handeln als eine unverzichtbare Voraussetzung des Glaubens betrachtet. Ein die religiösen Pflichten nicht praktizierender Muslim gilt für sie als ungläubig. Die Kharijiten lehnten die Aufforderung der Umayyaden, den Koran als Schiedsrichter in ihrem Krieg (Schlacht von Ṣiffīn im Jahre 657) gegen den vierten Kalifen ʿAlī b. Abī Ṭālib zu nehmen, ab. Weil ʿAlī dieser Aufforderung nachgekommen ist und die von Gott vorgeschriebene Vergeltung für die Tötung des dritten Kalifs ʿUṯmān b. ʿAffān n (gest. 656) nicht geübt hatte, haben sie ihn für ungläubig erklärt. Sie gelten deshalb als Gegenpol zu den Schiiten. Mehr dazu; siehe: The Encyclopaedia of Islam, Web CD Edition, Brill Academic Publishers 2003 (Stichwort: K͟hāridjites – G. Levi Della Vida, IV:1074b).

14 Vgl. *Naṣr Ḥāmid Abū Zaīd*, naqd al-ḫiṭāb ad-dīnī, a.a.O. (Fn. 9), S. 219 f. sowie *Muḥammad b. Ǧarīr aṭ-Ṭabarī*, ǧāmiʿ al-bayān… a.a.O. (Fn. 10), S. 198.

15 Vgl. *ʿAbdullāh Šiḥāta*, manhaǧ al-'imām Muḥammad ʿAbdu fī tafsīr al-Qur'ān al-Karīm [„Die Methode des Imams Muḥammad ʿAbdu bei der Koraninterpretation des adligen Korans"], al-maǧlis al-aʿlā li riʿāyat al-funūn wal 'adāb wal ʿulūm al-iǧtimāʿīya [„Der höchste Rat zur Förderung von Künsten, Philosophien und sozialen Wissenschaften"], Kairo 1984, S. 52 u. 153.

Islam und Menschenrechte (Islam and Human Rights / الإسلام وحقوق الإنسان)
Hatem Elliesie (Hrsg./Editor), © Peter Lang Verlag: Frankfurt a.M. 2010

Die politischen Konflikte zwischen den gegnerischen islamischen Richtungen sowie deren Verteidigung durch den heiligen Text setzten sich fort. Das 9. Jahrhundert erlebte eine uneingeschränkte Unterstützung der rationalen Richtung der Muʿtazilīten, hauptsächlich durch den 7. abbasidischen Kalifen ʿAbdullāh al-Ma'mūn (gest. 833). Im 10. Jahrhundert standen Abū al-Faḍl Ǧaʿfar al-Mutawakkil (gest. 861) und seine Nachfolger dagegen in Wort und Tat hinter der streng konservativen salafītischen Interpretation. In diesem Klima fiel es sowohl den Laien als auch den meisten Gelehrten schwer, zwischen Politischem und Religiösem zu unterscheiden. Dies führte dazu, dass *ta'wīl* mit negativen Konnotationen wie beispielsweise der Verfälschung in Verbindung gebracht wurde. Hinzu kommt, dass die Schiiten einige Koranverse mittels *ta'wīl*-Methode auf eine Art und Weise interpretiert hatten, die die Sunniten vollkommen ablehnten. Aus diesen Gründen trat *tafsīr* in den Vordergrund als Beweis für eine „unvoreingenommene Sachlichkeit".[16]

C. Probleme der Koraninterpretation

I. Die Verstehbarkeit des Korans

Die Frage, ob und inwieweit die menschliche Vernunft den Koran verstehen kann, bedarf einer Erörterung und Antwort. Denn erst unter der Prämisse einer grundsätzlichen Verstehbarkeit ist der Mensch zu einer uneingeschränkten Auseinandersetzung mit dem Koran fähig. Allerdings steht diese schwierige Frage mit einer anderen, noch „heikleren" in engem Zusammenhang, und zwar mit der Frage der Heiligkeit des koranischen Textes. Diese Frage ist zunächst in den Mittelpunkt zu stellen.

1. Inwiefern ist der Koran heilig?

Die Heiligkeit des Korans bedarf einer Begriffsbestimmung. Viele strenge Islamgelehrte sind der Meinung, der koranische Text sei so heilig, dass man ihn wortwörtlich annehmen müsse. Diese theologische Ausrichtung glaubt „blind" an die überlieferte Tradition (*an-naql*), obwohl gerade diejenigen Gelehrten, auf die sehr oft Bezug genommen wird, sich mit dem Text durchaus „vernünftig" und auch kritisch auseinandergesetzt haben und auseinandersetzen. Der koranische Text ist meines Erachtens als Gottes Wort zwar heilig, aber nur in dem Sinne, dass er geachtet, respektiert und hoch geschätzt werden soll. Letztendlich handelt es sich jedoch um eine sprachliche Botschaft an den Menschen. Diese Botschaft beinhaltet Anweisungen bzw. Vorschriften, die der Mensch zu respektieren hat, was notwendigerweise die menschliche Fähigkeit

---

16 Vgl. *Naṣr Ḥāmid Abū Zaīd*, iškāliyyat ta'wīl al-qur'ān qadīman wa ḥadīṯan (Problematik der Koraninterpretation, früher und heute), http://maaber.50megs.com/issue_july05/spot lights1.htm (zuletzt aufgerufen am 25. März 2008).

zum Verstehen dieser Botschaft voraussetzt. Da der Mensch mit Gott nicht reden kann, um zu erfahren, was Gott genau mit diesem oder jenem Vers meint, bleibt ihm nur die Option übrig, sich mit dem koranischen Text zu beschäftigen. Der Koran ist letzten Endes in einer menschlichen Sprache, deren Regeln der Mensch aufgestellt hat, herabgesandt worden. In diesem Sinne gehört der koranische Text also dem Menschen und unterliegt deshalb jeder Art der Untersuchung. Dadurch verliert er nicht an Heiligkeit im oben erwähnten Sinne.

Naṣr Ḥāmid Abū Zaīd meint dazu, dass der Koran ein heiliger Text bezüglich seines Wortlautes sei. In Bezug auf sein Verstehen ist er hingegen relativ und veränderlich. In diesem Sinne „vermenschlicht" sich der koranische Text,[17] nicht weil er von Menschen verfasst ist, wie viele übereilt verstanden haben oder verstehen wollten, sondern weil er von Menschen und durch menschliche Mechanismen verstanden und interpretiert wird.

2. Die Fähigkeit des Menschen zum Verstehen des Korans

Der Koran schreibt dem Verstand bzw. dem Nachdenken[18] in mehreren Versen eine bedeutungsvolle Rolle zu und lässt den Verständigen[19] ein besonderes Lob zuteil werden. Ganz zu schweigen davon, dass das erste geoffenbarte Wort ein Befehl zum Lesen[20] ist. Darin ist erkennbar, dass den koranischen Vorschriften nicht wortwörtlich nachzugehen ist. In diesem Zusammenhang sei ein sehr interessanter Spruch vom vierten Kalif ʿAlī b. Abī Ṭālib erwähnt. Als Reaktion auf den Wunsch seiner Gegner, den Koran als Schiedsrichter zu nehmen, soll er gesagt haben:

"القرآن بين دفتي المصحف لا ينطق وإنما يتكلم به الرجال".[21]

„Der koranische Text schweigt. Von den Menschen wird er zum Sprechen gebracht".

ʿAlī b. Abī Ṭālib meinte damit, dass der koranische Text nur durch uns Menschen zu verstehen ist, d.h. der Koran sagt, was ihn der Mensch sagen lässt. Dennoch wird auch weiterhin die Meinung vertreten, dass der Mensch nur zum Verstehen der „klaren" Verse fähig ist. Diese eingeschränkte menschliche Fähigkeit zum Verstehen des Korans geht zum größten Teil auf die Interpretation des 7. Verses der 3. Sure (آل عمران) zurück, wonach

---

17 Vgl. *Naṣr Ḥāmid Abū Zaīd*, naqd al-ḫiṭāb ad-dīnī, a.a.O. (Fn. 9), S. 119 u. 126.

18 Im Koran ist die Aufforderung zum Nachdenken zehnmal erwähnt. Vgl. z.B. Sure 7 (الأعراف), Vers 176; Sure 10 (يونس), Vers 24 und Sure 16 (النحل), Vers 44.

19 Die Bezeichnung *die Verständigen (ulū al-albāb)* taucht im Koran sechzehnmal auf. Vgl. z.B. Sure 2 (البقرة), Verse 179, 197 und Sure 3 (آل عمران), Verse 7, 190.

20 Vgl. Sure 96 (العلق), Vers 1.

21 Vgl. *Muḥammad b. Ǧarīr aṭ-Ṭabarī,* ǧāmiʿ al-bayān..., a.a.O. (Fn. 10), S. 48 f. u. 66.

"هُوَ الَّذِي أَنْزَلَ عَلَيْكَ الْكِتَابَ مِنْهُ آيَاتٌ مُحْكَمَاتٌ هُنَّ أُمُّ الْكِتَابِ وَأُخَرُ مُتَشَابِهَاتٌ فَأَمَّا الَّذِينَ فِي قُلُوبِهِمْ زَيْغٌ فَيَتَّبِعُونَ مَا تَشَابَهَ مِنْهُ ابْتِغَاءَ الْفِتْنَةِ وَابْتِغَاءَ تَأْوِيلِهِ **وَمَا يَعْلَمُ تَأْوِيلَهُ إِلا اللَّهُ وَالرَّاسِخُونَ فِي الْعِلْمِ يَقُولُونَ** آمَنَّا بِهِ كُلٌّ مِنْ عِنْدِ رَبِّنَا وَمَا يَذَّكَّرُ إِلا أُولُو الأَلْبَابِ"

„Er ist es, Der auf dich das Buch herabsandte. In ihm sind eindeutig klare Verse - sie sind die Mutter des Buchs - und andere, mehrdeutige. Diejenigen nun, deren Herzen zum Abweichen neigen, suchen vor allem das Mehrdeutige darin, um Uneinigkeit zu verursachen und es (nach eigenem Gutdünken)[22] auszulegen. ***Seine Deutung kennt jedoch niemand außer Allah. Und die mit fundiertem Wissen sprechen:*** 'Wir glauben daran. Das eine wie das andere ist von unserem Herrn'. Aber nur die Verständigen beherzigen es“[23].

(Sure 3 [آل عمران], Vers 7)

Es ist erkennbar, dass in den hervorgehobenen arabischen Stelle die Gliedsätze:

“الرَّاسِخُونَ فِي الْعِلْم„ und “وَمَا يَعْلَمُ تَأْوِيلَهُ إِلا اللَّهُ„

mit einer Konjunktion, und zwar „و“ [= und] verbunden sind. Über die Lesart dieser Stelle sind sich die Koraninterpreten jedoch bis zur heutigen Zeit uneinig. Manche schreiben eine Pause nach dem ersten Gliedsatz vor, damit die Bedeutung so sein soll, dass nur Gott die Korandeutung kennt, während die tiefgründig Wissenden nur die nachstehende Aussage aussprechen. Laut dieser Interpretation ist der Mensch nur zur Deutung einiger Koranverse fähig, was suggeriert, dass dies eine göttliche Vorherbestimmung sei. Demnach brauche sich der Mensch keine Mühe zu geben, die mehrdeutigen Verse zu deuten, denn sein Versuch wäre bereits im Vorfeld zum Scheitern verurteilt.

Andererseits betrachten einige Interpreten das „و“ [= und] als eine echte Konjunktion. Ausgehend davon teilen diejenigen mit tiefgründigem Wissen mit Gott die Fähigkeit, den Koran zu deuten. Die entsprechende Übersetzung wäre:

„Seine Deutung kennt jedoch niemand außer Allah und die mit fundiertem Wissen. Diese sprechen [...]“

Die zweite Interpretationsvariante, die leider immer noch wenige Befürworter hat,[24] scheint durchaus plausibel zu sein. Es würde der Gerechtigkeit Gottes

22 Im Original geht es hier um den umstrittenen Begriff *ta'wīl*.

23 Für den Koran in Deutsch wird *Max Henning*, Der Koran, Arabisch-Deutsch, aus dem Arabischen (Überarbeitung und Einleitung von *Murad Wilfried Hofmann*), 3. Aufl., Istanbul 2002 berücksichtigt.

24 Mehr zur Interpretation dieses äußerst umstrittenen Verses siehe alle berühmten Koraninterpretation, insbesondere *Ismāʿīl b. Kaṯīr*, http://quran.al-islam.com/Tafseer/DispTafsser.asp?nType=1&bm=&nSeg=0&l=arb&nSora=3&nAya=7&taf=KATHEER&tashkeel=1 sowie *Muḥammad b. Ǧarīr aṭ-Ṭabarī*, http://quran.al-islam.com/Tafseer/DispTafsser.asp?l=arb&taf=TABARY&nType=1&nSora=3&nAya=7 (beide zuletzt aufgerufen am 12. April 2008).

widersprechen, dass Gott dem Menschen eine undeutbare und unverständliche Botschaft herabgesandt hätte. In diesem Falle wäre die Frage nach dem Offenbarungsgrund legitim. Eine Anerkennung der Fähigkeit von Gelehrten mit tiefgründigem Wissen zur uneingeschränkten Korandeutung würde den Weg für die Entwicklung des Islamischen Rechtes ebnen. Möglich wäre auch ein neuer Umgang mit islamwissenschaftlichen Forschungsvorhaben. In einem solchen Klima könnte das *ta'wīl*-Verfahren seine verlorene Bedeutung zurückerlangen.

In diesem Zusammenhang ist die Wiederbelebung des historischen Aspektes als eines der Hauptprinzipien des *ta'wīl*-Verfahrens eine unabdingbare Notwendigkeit.

II. Hintergründe der Herabsendung (*asbāb an-nuzūl*)[25]

Der Koran wurde Stück für Stück, d.h. „in Raten", herabgesandt; und dabei wurde auf die Bedürfnisse und Forderungen der Menschen reagiert. Abū Zaīd formuliert:

> „Da er Antworten auf die Fragen der Gemeinde gab, entwickelte sich der gesetzliche Charakter des Korans langsam und spiegelte auf diese Weise das dialektische Verhältnis vom Gottes Wort und den menschlichen Interessen wider".[26]

Diese Tatsache setzt eine Lektüre unter historischem Aspekt voraus. Einen Text unter historischem Aspekt zu lesen, bedeutet nach Wilhelm Egger, nach „der Verankerung der Textaussagen in der Historie"[27] zu fragen. Es handelt sich hierbei um die zu erklärende Beziehung zwischen Text und Ereignis, d.h. um die Hintergründe der Herabsendung. Diese Beziehung ist für eine hermeneutische Interpretation des Korans von zentraler Bedeutung. Ein Interpret muss den Versuch unternehmen, die Lebensumstände der Koranoffenbarung nachzuerleben und auszulegen.

1. Abrogation (*an-nasḫ*)

Beim Interpretieren des Korans ist dieses Prinzip sehr problematisch, da keine einheitliche Meinung über die chronologische Reihenfolge der Koranverse herrscht. Folglich besteht nicht die Möglichkeit zu einer endgültigen Entscheidung, welcher Vers welchen abrogiert hat. Beispielsweise gibt es im Koran etwa 100 Verse, die zum Frieden, zu einem guten Umgang mit den Nicht-Muslimen, zur Beschränkung des Krieges auf die Verteidigung usw. aufrufen.

---

25 Es wird hier um die Hintergründe der Herabsendung fast nur aus theoretischer Sicht gehen. Eine praktische Behandlung folgt unten am Beispiel der Apostasie.

26 *Naṣr Ḥāmid Abū Zaīd*, naqd al-ḫiṭāb ad-dīnī, a.a.O. (Fn. 9), S. 124.

27 *Wilhelm Egger*, Methodenlehre zum Neuen Testament: Einführung in linguistische und historisch-kritische Methoden, Freiburg im Breisgau / et al. 1987, S. 195.

Die Fanatiker und Extremisten sind der Auffassung, dass alle diese Verse durch den sog. Schwert-Vers abrogiert seien, obwohl sie sich nicht darüber einig sind, um welchen Vers es sich genau handelt. Allerdings existiert eine einheitliche Meinung, dass der betreffende Vers in der Sure 9 (التوبة) enthalten ist.[28] Darüber hinaus vertreten viel islamische Gelehrte die Ansicht, dass es im Koran überhaupt keine Abrogation gibt.[29]

2. *Asbāb an-nuzūl* statt Abrogation

Asbāb an-nuzūl gilt als ein deutlicher Beweis für die Orts- und Zeitbezogenheit des koranischen Diskurses. Diese diskursbezogene Natur des Korans im Gegensatz zum textbezogenen Charakter, der die Abrogation zum Gegenstand hat, bestätigt die Wichtigkeit und Notwendigkeit von *asbāb an-nuzūl* als Mittel zur Einsicht in die Bedeutung koranischer Textstellen. Die diskursive Methode berücksichtigt die Historizität der Verhältnisse und der Rezipienten, während die zweite Methode sich vor allem mit dem Text befasst. *Asbāb an-nuzūl* schafft einen dynamischen Deutungsprozess, während die Abrogation keinen freien Raum für eine Entwicklung des Rechtssystems lässt. In diesem Sinne kann eine auf *asbāb an-nuzūl* basierende Untersuchung der Verse des *ǧihād* bzw. des Kampfes gegen die Nichtmuslime eine endgültige Lösung für die Problematik des friedlichen Zusammenlebens zwischen Muslimen und Nichtmuslimen bringen. Diese Verse bedürfen einer hermeneutischen, *ta'wīl*-bezogenen Untersuchung mit besonderer Berücksichtigung ihrer Historizität, um zu einem zeitgerechten Urteil zu gelangen. Hierbei kann die Geschichte der Sklavereiabschaffung als vorbildhaftes Beispiel genommen werden. Der Koran enthält mehrere Vorschriften bezüglich der Sklaven, obwohl diese nicht mehr existieren, da er die Bedingungen eines allmählichen und indirekten Sklavereiverbots geschaffen hat. Dies macht deutlich, dass es im Koran zahlreiche Vorschriften gibt, die nur eine historische Bedeutung und keinen Anspruch auf gegenwärtige Wirkung haben. Die daraus zu ziehende logische Schlussfolgerung ist:

Die islamischen Vorschriften in Bezug auf die weltlichen Angelegenheiten sind zeitlich und örtlich veränderbar.

---

[28] Der Schwert-Vers soll einer der Verse 5 (المائدة), 29, 36 oder Vers 41 der 9. Sure (التوبة) sein. Mehr dazu s. *Yūsuf al-Qaraḍāwī*, al-ǧadal ḥawla āyat as-sayf [„die Polemik um den Schwert-Vers"], http://www.islamonline.net/Arabic/contemporary/2003/07/article04c.shtml (zuletzt aufgerufen am 14. April 2008).

[29] Vgl. als Beispiel *Ṭāhā Ǧābir al-ʿAlwānī*, maqāṣid aš-šarīʿa [„Grundziele der Scharia"], in: *ʿAbd al-Ǧabbār ar-Rifāʿī* (Hrsg.), silsilat afāq at-taǧdīd [„Serie der Erneuerungshorizonte"], Dār al-Fikr: Damaskus 2002, S.109.

Hier gilt die islam-rechtliche *Grund-und-Folge-Regel* (*al-ʿilla wa-l-maʿlūl*). Die Gründe unterscheiden sich nach Ort und Zeit, daher müssen sich auch die Folgen unterscheiden. Dadurch ist eine zeitgerechte Koraninterpretation erreichbar. Aus den genannten Gründen ist zu schlussfolgern, dass der Abrogation als Mittel zur Deutung des Korans kein großer Wert beigemessen werden sollte.[30]

Die Wiederbelebung der Theorie der *asbāb an-nuzūl* als eine Grundlage einer Koraninterpretation würde die Bedingungen zur Akzeptanz der historisch-kritischen Methode unter den muslimischen Gelehrten schaffen, denn beide Verfahren – das westliche wie auch das islamische – verfolgen im Wesentlichen das gleiche Ziel.

III. Inwieweit ist die historisch-kritische Methode für eine zeitgemäße Koranexegese wichtig?

Die historisch-kritische Methode dient als Bezeichnung für einen Methodenapparat zur Untersuchung von Texten. Bekannt ist sie vor allem als eine Methode der biblischen Exegese. Tatsächlich wird die historisch-kritische Methode überall dort angewandt, wo schriftlich überlieferte Traditionen in mehreren, voneinander abweichenden Varianten vorliegen. Bezogen auf die Exegese der Bibel wird von den folgenden Methodenschritten Gebrauch gemacht: „Textkritik, Literaturkritik, Form- und Traditionsgeschichte/-kritik, Redaktionsgeschichte/-kritik".[31]

Offensichtlich können nicht alle Aspekte der historisch-kritischen Methode auf den Koran angewendet werden. Allerdings wären der Aspekt der Textkritik im Sinne einer kritischen Betrachtung vorhandener Interpretationen und der Aspekt der Traditionsgeschichtskritik für die Untersuchung des koranischen Textes von großem Nutzen. Denn diese beiden Aspekte sind Gegenstand des zuvor erläuterten *asbāb an-nuzūl*-Verfahrens.

Vielversprechend ließe sich meines Erachtens das Prinzip der Traditions-Geschichtskritik auf die Untersuchung des Verhältnisses zwischen Kultur und Interpretation anwenden.

1. Kultur und Interpretation

Die Interpretation ist eine menschliche Tätigkeit. Nur im Rahmen seiner Bildung, Kompetenz, Intelligenz und seines Wissens kann der Interpret einen Text auslegen. Alle diese Aspekte sind mit der Kultur bzw. den vorhandenen Wissensquellen des Interpreten eng verknüpft. Deshalb liegt jedem Verständnis schon immer ein Vorverständnis in Form von gewissen Vorurteilen zugrunde.

[30] Aus dem oft angeführten Beispiel des Weinverbots als ein Beleg für die Abrogation ist meines Erachtens eher die Schlussfolgerung eines prozesshaften Vorgangs zu ziehen.

[31] *Wilhelm Egger*, Methodenlehre zum Neuen Testament..., a.a.O. (Fn. 27), S. 160.

Denn die Interpreten sind immer in einen bestimmten Zusammenhang, der von Sprache, Situation und Tradition beeinflusst wird, eingebunden.

Ein anschauliches Beispiel dafür findet sich u.a. in der Interpretation des 5. Verses der 4. Sure (النساء). Beeinflusst von der vorislamischen Haltung der Gesellschaft gegenüber der Frau als Eigentum des Mannes, sei es der Vater, Bruder oder Ehemann, haben viele berühmte Koraninterpreten unter dem koranischen Wort *sufahā'* *(Schwachsinnige* bzw. *Urteilsunfähige)*[32] in diesem Vers Frauen und Kinder verstanden:

"وَلا تُؤْتُوا السُّفَهَاءَ أَمْوَالَكُمُ الَّتِي جَعَلَ اللَّهُ لَكُمْ قِيَامًا وَارْزُقُوهُمْ فِيهَا وَاكْسُوهُمْ
وَقُولُوا لَهُمْ قَوْلا مَعْرُوفًا"

„Und gebt nicht ***den geistig Behinderten*** *das Vermögen, das Allah euch für ihren Unterhalt gegeben hat. Versorgt sie damit, kleidet sie, und sprecht freundlich mit ihnen".*

(Sure 4 , [النساء] Vers 5)

Muḥammad b. Ǧarīr aṭ-Ṭabarī (gest. 923), Abū ʿAbdullāh Muḥammad b. Aḥmad al-Qurṭubī, (gest. 1272) und auch Ismāʿīl b. Kaṯīr (gest. um 1373) erwähnen,[33] dass mit den *sufahā'* nach Ansicht einiger Gelehrter (so Muǧāhid b. Ǧabr al-Makkī – gest. 722/723) die Kinder und die Frauen gemeint seien. Obwohl diese Ansicht nicht von vielen Interpreten vertreten wird, spiegelt sie dennoch eine bestimmte damalige Sichtweise des Mannes in Bezug auf die Frau wider, zumal die Interpretationen selbstverständlich eine Männerdomäne waren. Solche extreme Meinungen haben Spuren bei einigen gegenwärtigen muslimischen Gelehrten hinterlassen, die nach wie vor gegen eine Gleichberechtigung der Geschlechter polemisieren. Nach Immanuel Kant (gest. 1804) haben die Dinge an sich eine eigene Bedeutung. Sie können für uns jedoch eine andere Bedeutung annehmen, denn ihre Bedeutung zeigt sich in unserer Wahrnehmung und Bewertung. Kant schreibt:

> „Es sind uns Dinge als außer uns befindliche Gegenstände unserer Sinne gegeben; allein von dem, was sie an sich selbst sein mögen, wissen wir nichts, sondern kennen nur ihre Erscheinungen, d.i. die Vorstellungen, die sie in uns wirken, indem sie unsere Sinne affizieren."[34]

---

32 Das Wort *sufahā'* wurde in der zitierten Übersetzung mit „geistig Behinderte" wiedergegeben. Hier hat sich der Übersetzer m.E. für eine plausible Interpretation entschieden.

33 Vgl. die Interpretation dieses Verses bei *Muḥammad b. Ǧarīr aṭ-Ṭabarī,* ǧāmiʿ al-bayān..., a.a.O. (Fn. 10); sowie *Abū ʿAbdullāh Muḥammad b. Aḥmad al-Qurṭubī,* al-ǧamiʿ li 'aḥkām al-Qur'ān, a.a.O. (Fn. 11).

34 *Immanuel Kant:* Werke in zwölf Bänden. *Wilhelm Weischedel* (Hrsg.) Bd. 5, Frankfurt a.M. 1977, S. 152.

Das bezieht sich auch auf den Koran[35] und die *šarīʿa*. Beide „schweigen". Sie sprechen nur, wenn der Mensch ihnen Fragen stellt. Er kann jedoch nur solche Fragen stellen, die seinem Wissensstand entsprechen. Genauso kann er die erhaltenen Antworten nur gemäß seiner Kenntnisse bzw. Bildung verstehen.

2. Macht und Interpretation

Neben der Kultur spielt auch die Macht eine beeinflussende Rolle bei der Interpretation. Denn der politische Aspekt gilt als ein wichtiger Faktor bei der Steuerung der Interpretation. Dies verdeutlicht sich bei der Interpretation von Versen in Bezug auf die gegenseitige Beratung (*aš-šūrā*) und Gottes Herrschaft (*al-ḥākimiyya*). Ṭāhā Ǧābir al-ʿAlwānī bestätigt diese Tatsache, indem er sagt:

"لقد حاول العلماء في تاريخنا أن يجعلوا من أنفسهم قوة مشاركة لرجال السلطة، ورديفا لهم،
ففسروا 'أولي الأمر' بالعلماء والأمراء."

"In unserer Geschichte hatten die Gelehrten versucht, die Macht mit deren Inhabern zu teilen und sich mit ihnen gleichzusetzen. Demnach hatten sie *ulū al-ʾamr*[36] als Gelehrte und Herrscher interpretiert."[37]

Diese Interpretationsrichtungen bergen die Gefahr einer Vermischung zwischen Politischem und Religiösem in sich und führen zu Unklarheiten bei der Rolle von Politikern und Religionsgelehrten. Ein solches Umfeld entzieht dem Säkularismus den Boden, während der Aufruf zur Gründung eines „Religionsstaates" entstehen kann. Eine hermeneutische Lesart des Korans ist daher für die Bestimmung des Politischen und des Religiösen von großem Nutzen. Sie basiert auf der Unterscheidung zwischen zwei Arten von Koranversen.

3. Arten der Verse

Um eine zeitgerechte, Hermeneutik-orientierte Koraninterpretation, die der menschlichen Vernunft eine Rolle bei der Weltverwaltung zuschreibt, zu erreichen, ist zwischen **zwei Arten von Versen** zu unterscheiden:

-**Verse,** die sich mit den rituellen Verpflichtungen (*ʿibādāt*) befassen,

und

-**Verse,** die sich mit den zwischenmenschlichen Beziehungen (*muʿāmalāt*) beschäftigen.

Die Verse über die rituellen Handlungen lassen sich nicht hinterfragen, da man den Grund bzw. das Ziel der Art und Weise einer rituellen Handlung nicht erkennen kann. Man glaubt daran (oder nicht). Im Gegensatz dazu regeln die

---

[35] Vgl. den auf Seite 78 zitierten Spruch des vierten Kalifs: „Der koranische Text schweigt. Von den Menschen wird er zum Sprechen gebracht".

[36] "*Ulū al-ʾamr* " bedeutet die Befehlshaber oder diejenigen, die das Sagen haben.

[37] *Ṭāhā Ǧābir al-ʿAlwānī*, lā ikrāha fī ad-dīn [„Kein Zwang in der Religion], iškālīyat ar-ridda wa-l-murtaddīn min ṣadr al-islām ilā al-yaum [„Die Problematik der Apostasie und Apostaten vom Frühislam bis zur Gegenwart"], 2. Aufl., Maktabat aš-Šurūq ad-Dawlīya: Kairo 2006, S. 165.

muʿāmalāt konkrete Lebensverhältnisse. Dabei muss der Grund bzw. das Ziel der Gesetzgebung gesucht und nicht nur die Textoberfläche betrachtet werden. Beim Interpretieren solcher Verse sind auch das Wohl und das Interesse des Menschen im Auge zu behalten.

D. Menschenrechte und Islam

I. *Gott-Mensch-Beziehung* und Hintergrund der Menschenrechte

Einige westliche Denker halten eine Vereinbarung von Islam und Menschenrechten deswegen für ausgeschlossen, weil die meisten Muslime bei der Konzipierung von Menschenrechten nur auf Gott Bezug nehmen würden. Die muslimischen Gelehrten seien der Auffassung, der Mensch erhalte seine Rechte von Gott. Ferner gingen die meisten von ihnen davon aus, die Menschenrechtsidee habe einen islamischen Hintergrund.[38] In der Präambel der Menschenrechtserklärung des Islamrats für Europa wird erwähnt, dass der Islam dem Menschen die Würde und damit auch die Menschenrechte gegeben habe. Mit ihm seien die Menschenrechte 'bereits vor 14 Jahrhunderten erklärt' worden.[39] Im Gegensatz dazu geht die Menschenrechtsvorstellung im *Westen* von der absoluten Unantastbarkeit des Individuums aus, auch gegenüber Gott selbst,[40] da der Mensch immer im Mittelpunkt stehe. Eine hermeneutische Interpretation einiger Koranverse könnte diese Problematik lösen. Im Koran heißt es nämlich

" إِنَّا عَرَضْنَا الأَمَانَةَ عَلَى السَّمَاوَاتِ وَالأَرْضِ وَالْجِبَالِ فَأَبَيْنَ أَنْ يَحْمِلْنَهَا وَأَشْفَقْنَ مِنْهَا وَحَمَلَهَا الإِنْسَانُ"

„Sehe, Wir boten die Verantwortung[41] den Himmeln und der Erde und den Bergen an;
doch weigerten sie sich, sie zu tragen, und schreckten davor zurück.
Der Mensch lud sie sich jedoch auf.“
(Sure 33 [الأحزاب], Vers 72)

---

[38] In diesem Zusammenhang meint Hans-Georg Ebert zu Recht, dass „ein unterschiedlicher Ausgangspunkt in der Menschen- und Grundrechtsdiskussion“ nicht zwangsläufig unterschiedliche Standpunkte zur Folge hat. Vgl. *Hans-Georg Ebert*, Das Personalstatut arabischer Länder, Problemfelder, Methoden, in: *Hans-Georg Ebert* (Hrsg.), Perspektiven. Leipziger Beiträge zur Orientforschung, Bd. 7, Frankfurt a.M. 1996, S. 42.

[39] Vgl. *Lorenz Müller,* Islam und Menschenrechte, Sunnitische Muslime zwischen Islamismus, Säkularismus und Modernismus, Hamburg 1996, S. 125; und die Präambel der Menschenrechtserklärung des Islamrats für Europa in der Übersetzung von *Martin Forstner*, Islam und Menschenrechte, CIBEDO-Texte, Nr. 15/16, Frankfurt a.M. 1982, S. 20.

[40] Vgl. *Bassam Tibi [Bassām Ṭībī],* Im Schatten Allahs. Der Islam und die Menschenrechte. Erweiterte Taschenbuchausgabe, 2. Aufl. München 1999, S. 89.

[41] In den meisten Koranübersetzungen wird *amāna* mit *Treuhänderamt* übersetzt. In der Übersetzung von *Max Henning*, a.a.O. (Fn. 23) ist jedoch ein genaueres Verständnis dieses Begriffs erkennbar.

Eine hermeneutische Betrachtungsweise dieses Verses im Lichte zusammenhängender Verse könnte genau bestimmen, inwieweit der Mensch die weltliche Macht innehaben kann. Die zentrale Rolle des Menschen ist aus diesem Vers[42] ableitbar. Es sollte eine an den „Zielen der *šarīʿa*" orientierte Deutung des Begriffs *amāna* zugrunde gelegt werden. *Amāna* im Sinne von *anvertrautem Gut* würde so die „Verantwortung" für die Verwaltung der Welt bedeuten. Die Übernahme dieser schwierigen Verantwortung haben – wie der Vers lautet – Himmel, Erde und Berge trotz ihrer äußerst großen Stärke zurückgewiesen. Im Gegensatz dazu habe sie der Mensch auf sich genommen, weil er sie mittels des ihm von Gott verliehenen Verstandes erfüllen kann. Das lässt sich dadurch beweisen, dass Gott dem Menschen alles in der Welt dienstbar gemacht hat.[43] Aus diesem Versverständnis zeigt sich, dass der Mensch im Mittelpunkt der Welt steht und alle Offenbarungen auf sein Wohl und Interesse abzielen. Dies dient weiter als Beweis dafür, dass der Islam die Stellung und Würde des Menschen auf die höchste Stufe erhöht, was sich logischerweise auch auf die Stellung der Welt bezieht, wo der Mensch lebt. Das führt uns zum Ergebnis, dass die westliche Würdigung des Menschen und dessen Rechte mit dem Islam auf keinen Fall im Widerspruch stehen. Gott sagt:

"وَلَقَدْ كَرَّمْنَا بَنِي آدَمَ وَحَمَلْنَاهُمْ فِي الْبَرِّ وَالْبَحْرِ وَرَزَقْنَاهُمْ مِنَ الطَّيِّبَاتِ
وَفَضَّلْنَاهُمْ عَلَى كَثِيرٍ مِمَّنْ خَلَقْنَا تَفْضِيلا"

„Und wahrlich, Wir zeichneten[44] die Kinder Adams aus und trugen sie über Land und See und versorgten sie mit guten Dingen und bevorteilten sie gegenüber den meisten Unserer Geschöpfe".

(Sure 17 [الإسراء], Vers 70)

Es lässt sich folgende Hypothese aufstellen: Wäre das Prinzip einer zentralen Rolle des Menschen der Ausgangspunkt der Methodik des Islamischen Rechts gewesen, hätte die *šarīʿa* eine andere Entwicklung genommen. Denn in diesem Falle wäre der Mensch und nicht die religiösen Ge- und Verbote der Mittelpunkt ihrer Auseinandersetzung gewesen. Die intensive Beschäftigung mit den religiösen Vorschriften hat aus dem Menschen einen „Untertan" und keinen Herrscher gemacht, was in der herkömmlichen Interpretation der Gottesherr-

42 Neben diesem Vers sind die Verse 30 der 2. Sure (البقرة) und 26 der 38. Sure (ص) über die menschliche Nachfolgerschaft Gottes in der Welt zur Bestätigung der zentristischen Rolle des Menschen im irdischen Leben zu berücksichtigen.

43 Vgl. Sure 22 (الحج), Vers 65.

44 Im arabischen Original wird das Verb *karrama* im Sinne von *würdigen* bzw. *ehren* benutzt.

schaft[45] zum Ausdruck kommt. Völlig geändert hätte sich auch die Ansicht der Theologen unter anderem zu den Fragen der menschlichen Willensfreiheit und der Vorherbestimmung, deren vage Auffassung die Lethargie sowie die Bereitschaft zur Unterwerfung zur Folge hatte.

II. Die Beziehung zwischen Koraninterpretation und Menschenrechten

Es ist nicht zu leugnen, dass Koran und Sunna in ihrem herkömmlichen Verständnis Aussagen enthalten, die gemäß ihrem Wortsinn als menschenrechtswidrig bezeichnet werden können[46]. Die *šarīʿa* und die Islamische Jurisprudenz (*fiqh*) basieren auf dem Verständnis und der Deutung von Koran und Sunna. Diese Quellen bilden den geistigen Hintergrund der formulierten Menschenrechtserklärungen unterschiedlicher islamischer Organisationen in den vergangenen Jahrzehnten. Menschenrechte in islamischen Ländern können – dieser Theorie folgend – nur im Rahmen der im Koran und im islamischen Gesetz festgelegten Gebote gewährt und eingefordert werden. Diese Auffassung zeigt sich auch im Art. 24 der „Kairoer Erklärung der Menschenrechte" von 1990, wonach „alle Rechte und Freiheiten, die in dieser Erklärung genannt werden, der islamischen *šarīʿa*" unterstehen; sowie im Art. 25, der statuiert: „Die islamische *šarīʿa* ist die einzige zuständige Quelle für die Auslegung oder Erklärung jedes einzelnen Artikels dieser Erklärung".[47] In diesem Zusammenhang meint Bassam Tibi [Bassām Ṭībī] zu Recht, „Islamisches Recht ist interpretativ, d.h. es basiert auf der Deutung des Korans und der Sunna [...]. Formalisiertes Recht gibt es im Islam nicht. Es gibt aber Rechtsschulen, die den Status von Konfessionen haben".[48] Aus diesen Gründen wird eine neue Interpretation des Korans aus hermeneutischer Sicht unabdingbar, wobei das Wohl des Menschen im Mittelpunkt stehen sollte.

III. Šarīʿa und Wohl des Menschen

Die islamischen Gelehrten sind sich einig, dass der göttliche Wille nur das Wohl des Menschen zum Ziel habe, dass die *šarīʿa* aber zugleich als ewig, als für jeden Ort und jede Zeit passend, zu gelten habe. Ausgehend von dieser Überzeugung erarbeiteten die *fiqh*-Gelehrten die hauptsächlichen Werte und daraus abgeleitete Bestimmungen. Die zu bewahrenden Werte der *šarīʿa* sind Religion,

---

45 Mehr zur „Gottesherrschaft" siehe *Abu Zaid* [Abū Zaīd], Islam und Politik. Kritik des religiösen Diskurses [Aus dem Arabischen von *Chérifa Magdi*], Frankfurt a.M. 1996, S. 63-81.

46 Vgl. *Lorenz Müller*, Islam und Menschenrechte..., a.a.O. (Fn. 39), S. 190.

47 Die deutsche Übersetzung der zwei Artikel stammt aus der Zeitschrift *Gewissen und Freiheit*, 19. Jahrgang, Nr. 36, Bern 1991, S. 90 ff.

48 *Bassam Tibi*, Im Schatten Allahs..., a.a.O. (Fn. 40), S. 188.

Leben, Verstand, Ehre und Vermögen.[49] Ferner besteht Konsens unter den *fiqh*-Gelehrten über einige allgemeine Regeln: „Die Not kennt kein Gebot“; die Bestimmungen ändern sich nach Ort und Zeit; die Gewohnheit dient der Gesetzgebung als Quelle genauso wie der Text.[50] Hier ist u.a. folgender Koranvers zu erwähnen:

"يُرِيدُ اللَّهُ أَنْ يُخَفِّفَ عَنْكُمْ وَخُلِقَ الإِنْسَانُ ضَعِيفاً"

„Allah will es euch leicht machen;
denn der Mensch wurde schwach erschaffen.“
(Sure 4 [النساء], Vers 28)

Das „menschliche Interesse“ (المصلحة) gilt als Bestandteil der *šarīʿa* und wurde unter den Gelehrten in unterschiedlicher Weise erfasst und z.T. mit dem Analogieschluss (*qiyās*) als Rechtsquelle in Verbindung gebracht.[51]

Selbst Ibn al-Qaiym al-Ǧawziya (gest. 1350), der mit seinem Lehrer Aḥmad b. Taimiya (gest. 1328) als Autorität für die salafītische traditionelle Richtung gilt, unterstreicht die Grundziele (Intentionen) der islamischen *šarīʿa* bzw. deren Aufgabe, die Interessen der Menschen im Dies- und Jenseits zu erfüllen. Für ihn ist die *šarīʿa* angefüllt mit Barmherzigkeit, Gerechtigkeit und Nützlichkeit. Wenn sich eine Angelegenheit von Gerechtigkeit in Unrecht, vom Allgemeinwohl in Übel wandelt, gehört sie nicht mehr zur *šarīʿa.*[52] Aḥmad ar-Raisūnī vertritt diese Ansicht und betont, dass die *šarīʿa* ihre Grundlagen in der Logik, in den Zielen, Interessen und Weisheiten haben müsse. Jedes *šarīʿa*-Urteil ist demgemäß begründbar.[53] Muḥammad Abdu (gest. 1905) betrachtet das „allgemeine Interesse“ (المصلحة) als ein Prinzip für die politischen und zivilen Bestimmungen. Er verlangte von den Richtern, die Urteile den weltlichen Interessen und dem allgemeinen Nutzen anzupassen.[54]

---

49 Vgl. *Muḥammad Abū Ḥāmid al-Ġasālī*, al-mustaṣfā fī ʿilm al-ʾuṣūl [„Das Raffinierte in der islam-rechtlichen Methodiklehre“], S. 174; eine digitalisierte Version ist nachlesbar unter www.al-mostafa.com (zuletzt aufgerufen am 29. April 2008).

50 Mehr dazu *Muḥammad Rašīd Riḍa*, tārīḫ al-ʾustāḏ al-ʾimām Muḥammad ʿAbdu [„Geschichte des Imams Muḥammad ʿAbdu“], al-Manār: Kairo 1931.

51 Mehr dazu *Abū Isḥāq aš-Šāṭibī*, al-muwāfaqāt fī ʾuṣūl aš-šarīʿa [„Die Gemeinsamkeiten in den Prinzipien der Scharia“], S. 148 ff. Eine digitalisierte Version [ohne Jahresangabe] ist ebenfalls nachzulesen unter www.al-mostafa.com (zuletzt aufgerufen am 29. April 2008); siehe auch *Lorenz Müller*, Islam und Menschenrechte…, a.a.O. (Fn. 39), S. 99 f.

52 Vgl. *Ibn al-Qaīyim al-Ǧawzīya,* iʿlām al-muwaqqiʿīn ʿan rabb al-ʿālamīn [„In-Kenntnisssetzung derjenigen, die über den Herrn aller Welten Zeugnis ablegen“], 3. Aufl., Dār al-Ǧīl: Kairo [ohne Jahresangabe], S. 3.

53 Vgl. *Aḥmad ar-Raisūnī*, maqāṣid aš-šarīʿa [„Intentionen der Scharia“]; in: *ʿAbd al-Ǧabbār ar-Rifāʿī* (Hrsg.), silsilat afāq at-taǧdīd, a.a.O. (Fn. 29), S. 175 und 212.

54 Vgl. *ʿAbdullāh Šiḥāta*, manhaǧ al-ʾimām..., a.a.O. (Fn. 15), S. 60.

Naǧm ad-Dīn aṭ-Ṭūfī widerspricht der These, dass die *šarīʿa* die Interessen bzw. das Wohl des Menschen besser kennen würde als der Mensch selbst. Nur der Sinn der rituellen Handlungen bleibt der Vernunft verborgen. Die weltlichen Interessen hingegen kann der Mensch dank seiner Vernunft durch die Erfahrung feststellen. Er vertritt die Ansicht, dass im Falle eines Widerspruchs zwischen einem eindeutigen, „stark" überlieferten Text und dem Wohl des Menschen Letzteres in den Vordergrund zu stellen, der Text auszusetzen bzw. einzufrieren ist, denn die *šarīʿa* sei im Prinzip zur Realisierung der Menscheninteressen herabgesandt worden.[55] Darüber hinaus könne der Wille Gottes nie der Logik und der Weisheit widersprechen.

Ṭāhā Ǧābir al-ʿAlwānī betont drei hehre Grundziele der *šarīʿa*, nämlich die Einheit Gottes (*al-waḥdāniyya*), die Würdigung (*at-tazkiya*) des Menschen und die Entwicklung der Erde (*al-ʿumrān*). Diese drei Grundziele gelten für ihn als Verfassungsprinzipien, von denen die Verfassungsartikel und die rechtlichen Regeln abzuleiten seien.[56]

Wären diese drei hohen Grundziele (*maqāṣid*) berücksichtigt worden, hätte sich das Islamische Recht unmittelbar durch *iǧtihād* (Rechtsfortbildung)[57] erneuern und der Zeit anpassen können. Die Anwendung der *maqāṣid*-Theorie würde auch die Ansicht über die kultischen Pflichten ändern. Anstatt diese zu erfüllen, um von der Verantwortung befreit zu werden, würden ihre spirituellen Werte, ihre Ziele und ihre Wirkung im Mittelpunkt stehen. Demnach könnte der bewaffnete *ǧihād* beispielsweise als ein Mittel angesehen werden, um Frieden und Freiheit für das Praktizieren religiöser Pflichten zu schaffen. Dies bedeutet zugleich, der bewaffnete *ǧihād* sei nicht nötig, solange dessen Ziel friedlich erreicht werden könne, was z.Z. in nicht-islamischen Ländern zum größten Teil gegeben sei. Diese Sichtweise bedarf allerdings einer geeigneten Atmosphäre.

Die erwünschte kritische, von der *maqāṣid*-Theorie im Umgang mit der Welt begründbare Mentalität erfordert entsprechende Bedingungen und ein Umfeld, welches zunächst geschaffen werden müsste. Es ist kaum denkbar, dass in der

---

55 Vgl. *Naǧm ad-Dīn aṭ-Ṭūfī*, at-taʿyīn fī šarḥ al-ʾarbaʿīn [„Die Festlegung in der Erklärung der 40 Ḥadīṯe), Muʾassasat ar-Raīyān: Beirut [ohne Jahresangabe], S. 246, 279 sowie 280.

56 Vgl. *Ṭāhā Ǧābir al-ʿAlwānī*, maqāṣiḍ aš-šarīʿa, a.a.O. (Fn. 29), S. 97, 100 und 103.

57 Der Begriff *iǧtihād* ist vom arabischen Substantiv *ǧuhd* [„Mühe"] abgeleitet und bedeutet, dass sich die Rechtsgelehrten bemühen bzw. anstrengen, ein zeitgerechtes Rechtsurteil über neue Fragen zu finden. Mehr zum Begriff *iǧtihād* und dessen Verfahren siehe *Birgit Krawietz*, Der Prophet Muḥammad als Muftī und Muǧtahid, in: *Hans-Georg Ebert/Thoralf Hanstein* (Hrsg.), Leipziger Beiträge zur Orientforschung; Beiträge zum Islamischen Recht III, Bd. 13, Frankfurt a.M. 2003, S. 55-71, besonders S. 64 ff.; sowie *Lorenz Müller*, Islam und Menschenrechte…, a.a.O. (Fn. 39), S. 93 ff. Siehe auch unter Gliederungsabschnitt D., Kapitel IV. (Vereinbarung des Islam mit den Menschenrechten).

gegenwärtigen, diktatorisch regierten arabisch-islamischen Welt eine kritische und kreative Mentalität entstehen kann. Es fehlen Meinungsfreiheit und eine offene Diskussion, angefangen in der Familie mit den Eltern über die Schule mit den LehrerInnen bis hin zum Staat mit seinen politisch Herrschenden. Kurz gesagt: Die Rückständigkeit ist nicht von der kulturellen, sozialen und politischen Umwelt, auf die sich die entsprechende Vernunft gründet, zu trennen.

IV. Vereinbarung des Islam mit den Menschenrechten

Das Verhältnis des Islam zu den Menschenrechten muss im Lichte der Intentionen der *šarīʿa* (*maqāṣid šarīʿa*; s.o.) diskutiert werden. Als eine hauptsächliche Intention der islamischen Religion kann das Allgemeinwohl des Menschen gelten. Gott übermittelt seinem Propheten Muḥammad:

"وَمَا أَرْسَلْنَاكَ إِلا رَحْمَةً لِلْعَالَمِينَ"

„Und Wir entsandten dich fürwahr als eine Barmherzigkeit für alle Welt."

(Sure 21 [الأنبياء], Vers 107)

Ferner muss davon ausgegangen werden, dass die religiöse Pflichtenlehre des Islam, welche die muslimischen Rechtsgelehrten vor Jahrhunderten entwickelt haben, *in ihrer Gesamtheit* für die Muslime des 21. Jahrhunderts nicht notwendig verbindlich sein kann, denn diese Lehre beruht darauf, wie die *fiqh*-Gelehrten den Koran und die Sunna gemäß der damaligen Situation und den damals herrschenden Traditionen verstanden haben. Da die gegenwärtigen Religionsgelehrten wie deren Vorgänger über menschliche Vernunft verfügen, sich jedoch in anderen Lebensverhältnissen befinden, haben sie logischerweise den gleichen Anspruch, Koran und Sunna zu verstehen und zeitgemäß zu interpretieren. Dabei kommt dem *iǧtihād* (Rechtsfortbildung) ein zentraler Stellenwert zu, denn der *iǧtihād* spielte eine wichtige Rolle bei der Entwicklung der islamischen Jurisprudenz. Viele muslimische Juristen im 9. und 10. Jahrhundert waren der Ansicht, dass alle grundsätzlichen Rechtsfragen so weit beantwortet worden seien, dass *iǧtihād* nicht mehr nützlich sei. Für die zukünftig möglichen Fragen reiche die Nachahmung (*taqlīd*) aus. Lorenz Müller meint zu Recht, dass die sog. „Schließung des Tores des *iǧtihād*" der Grund dafür war, dass man aufhörte zu versuchen, den Koran zeitgemäß zu interpretieren.[58] Dies bewirkte eine Lähmung verstandesmäßiger Aktivitäten, sodass eine Entwicklung eines allgemeinen Menschenrechtskonzepts blockiert wurde.

---

58 Vgl. *Lorenz Müller*, Islam und Menschenrechte…, a.a.O. (Fn. 39), S. 93 ff., so auch im Vortrag von Lorenz Müller auf der 1. Jahrestagung der GAIR in Bonn am 6. Juli 1998 zum Thema „Die Menschenrechte im Islam".

1. Religionsfreiheit und Todesurteil

Vorab wird an dieser Stelle deutlichst darauf hingewiesen, dass mit der hier zu zeigenden Glaubensfreiheit kein Aufruf zum Glaubenswechsel beziehungsweise zur Apostasie intendiert ist und auch nicht intendiert werden soll, was von einigen Demagogen hineininterpretiert werden könnte. Ziel ist lediglich, eine koranische Tatsache (gerade im und auch für den akademischen Diskurs) ans Licht zu bringen und den Gedankenaustausch weiter zu befruchten!

Viele muslimische Gelehrte sind von der Religionsfreiheit fest überzeugt. Sie äußern sich allerdings dazu nicht offen aus Angst, dass Muslime dies als Ermunterung zum Religionswechsel verstehen würden. Diesem Argument ist folgendes zu entgegnen: Muslime, die ihre Religion verlassen wollen, sollen es tun, denn weder Gott noch der Mensch legen nach islamischer Vorstellung Wert auf diejenigen, die nicht aus innerer Überzeugung an ihre Religion glauben.

In diesem Zusammenhang ist zu empfehlen, die mutmaßliche Strafe der Apostasie aus einem anderen Blickwinkel heraus zu betrachten: Nicht ausgehend von der Angst, dass Muslime Nichtmuslime werden könnten, sondern ausgehend von der Möglichkeit, dass Nichtmuslime den islamischen Glauben annehmen werden. Nichtmuslime werden nicht selten von der Vorstellung abgeschreckt, dass die Annahme des Islam keinen Weg zurück – aus welchen Gründen auch immer – eröffnen würde, sondern das Todesurteil als Drohung steht. Das Tor jeder Religion muss in zweifacher Richtung offen bleiben. Es ist dann die freie Entscheidung des eigenverantwortlichen Menschen, für welche Richtung er sich bewusst entscheidet.

2. Religionsfreiheit in Koran und Sunna

Die Frage der Religionsfreiheit im Islam muss anhand aller koranischen Verse, die von der Freiheit des Denkens und von der Verantwortung des Menschen handeln, betrachtet werden. Dass der Mensch für seine Taten verantwortlich ist, setzt seine Freiheit voraus, ansonsten wäre Gott ungerecht, indem er den unfreien Menschen für seine Taten verantwortlich macht.

Viele der zitierten Koranverse, die sich um die Glaubensfreiheit drehen, deuten darauf hin, dass diese Freiheit im Islam nicht eingeschränkt ist. Oft wird der Vers „Kein Zwang im Glauben" (Sure 2 [البقرة], Vers 256) genannt. Auch der Vers „Und sprich: 'Die Wahrheit ist von eurem Herrn. Wer nun will, der glaube, und wer will, der glaube nicht'" (Sure 18 [الكهف], Vers 29). Weiter sagt Gott: „Sprich: 'O ihr Ungläubigen! Ich verehre nicht, was ihr verehrt, Und ihr verehrt nicht, was ich verehre. Und ich werde kein Verehrer dessen sein, was ihr verehrt, und ihr werdet kein Verehrer dessen sein, was ich verehre. Euch euer Glaube und mir mein Glaube!'" (Sure 109 [الكافرون], Verse 1-6).

Der Koran erwähnt die Apostasie an mehreren Stellen und sieht dafür eine Strafe nur im Jenseits vor, ohne auf irgendwelche Maßnahmen im Diesseits hinzuweisen. Als Beispiele dafür sind folgende Verse zu nennen:

- „Wer sich aber von euch von seinem Glauben abtrünnig machen lässt und als Ungläubiger stirbt, **deren Werke sind vergeblich im Diesseits und im Jenseits, und sind sie Bewohner des Feuers und verweilen ewig darin.**“ (Sure 2 [البقرة], Vers 217)
- „An einem Tag, da manche Gesichter weiß und manche Gesichter schwarz sein werden. Und was jene anlangt, deren Gesichter schwarz wurden: 'Wurdet ihr ungläubig, nachdem ihr geglaubt hattet? **So kostet die Strafe, weil ihr ungläubig wurdet'.**“ (Sure 3 [آل عمران], Vers 106)
- „Siehe, diejenigen, welche glauben und danach ungläubig werden, dann wieder glauben und dann an Unglauben noch zunehmen, **denen verzeiht Allah nicht, und er leitet sie nicht des Weges.**“ (Sure 4 [النساء], Vers 137)

Aus dem Dargelegten zeigt sich, dass die Todesstrafe für die Apostasie keine koranische Grundlage hat.[59] Alle Koranverse in Bezug auf Apostasie nennen weder explizit noch implizit eine weltliche Strafe dafür. Frank Griffel betont diese Tatsache ausdrücklich, indem er sagt: „Der Koran fordert niemanden auf, einen Apostaten zu bestrafen oder gar zu töten“.[60]

Die Todesstrafe beruht allerdings auf zwei *ḥadīṯen* (Prophetenüberlieferungen). Der Prophet soll gesagt haben: „Das Blut eines Muslims, der bezeugt, dass es keinen Gott außer Allah gibt, und dass ich Sein Gesandter bin, ist unantastbar außer in drei Fällen: Wenn ein Verheirateter Unzucht begeht; im Falle einer unberechtigten Tötung; und **wenn ein Muslim seine Religion verlässt und sich gegen die Gemeinde wendet**“.[61] D.h. eine Bedingung dabei ist, dass der Apostat die Sicherheit und die Stabilität der Gesellschaft gefährdet. Die *fiqh*-Gelehrten sahen und sehen z.T. bis heute darin Staats- oder Hochverrat, was in vielen Ländern mit dem Todesurteil bestraft wurde und immer noch wird. Den Gelehrten ging es dabei nicht primär um die Glaubensfreiheit, sondern um die politischen Folgen der Apostasie. Diese und nicht der Abfall vom Glauben

---

[59] Mehr zu den Versen über die Apostasie und deren jenseitige Strafe siehe *Ṭāhā Ǧābir al-ʿAlwānī,* lā ikrāha fī ad-dīn, a.a.O. (Fn. 37), S. 85-95.

[60] *Frank Griffel*, Apostasie und Toleranz im Islam, die Entwicklung zu al-Ġazālīs Urteil gegen die Philosophie und die Reaktion der Philosophen, Leiden / Boston / Köln 2000, S. 28.

[61] Ḥadīṯ Nr. 1322 bei *Abū ʿĪsā at-Tirmiḏī,* http://hadith.al-islam.com/Display/Display.asp?hnum=1322&doc=2&IMAGE=%DA%D1%D6+%C7%E1%CD%CF%ED%CB (zuletzt aufgerufen am 27. August 2008).

werden somit bestraft.[62] In diesem Zusammenhang sollen die sog. Apostasiekriege, die der erste Kalif Abū Bakr (gest. 634) gegen die Apostaten geführt hat, verstanden werden.[63] Ṭāhā Ǧābir al-ʿAlwānī hat alle Personen, die vom Propheten wegen der Apostasie zum Tod verurteilt worden waren, erwähnt und festgestellt, dass sie alle neben dem Religionswechsel ein mit der Todesstrafe zu belegendes Verbrechen begangen hatten, d.h., sie wurden nicht nur wegen Apostasie getötet.[64]

Es ist an dieser Stelle zu betonen, dass das Plädoyer für die Menschenrechte vor allem in Bezug auf die Glaubensfreiheit weder die Freiheit des Verrates noch die der Spionage meint, was Muslime des Öfteren damit verbinden.

Im erwähnten Sinne hat die gemäß dem Islam strafbare Apostasie mit der Freiheit nichts zu tun, denn der Angriff auf den Staat und nicht der Glaubenswechsel wird bestraft. Daraus ist der Schluss zu ziehen, dass eine nicht mit politischen Folgen verbundene Apostasie nicht von den Menschen im Diesseits zu bestrafen ist. Ferner ist eine als Angriff auf die islamische Ordnung und ihre wichtigsten Grundlagen (Hochverrat) angesehene Apostasie nicht notwendigerweise mit der Todesstrafe zu belegen. Es handelt sich vielmehr um eine politische, möglicherweise gesetzeswidrige Angelegenheit, deren Strafe im Ermessen des Gesetzgebers – also orts- und zeitabhängig – liegt.

Der zweite *ḥadīṯ* besagt: „Wenn jemand seine Religion fallen lässt, so tötet ihn".[65] Ṭāhā Ǧābir al-ʿAlwānī hat sich mit diesem *ḥadīṯ* ausführlich auseinandergesetzt und demonstriert, dass er schwach überliefert ist. Für ihn gilt dieser *ḥadīṯ* als *āḥād*[66] (ohne verlässliche Überliefererkette).[67] Außerdem sollte diese Überlieferung im Lichte der o.g. Prophetenüberlieferung verstanden werden, die den Angriff gegen die Gemeinde als Bedingung für die Bestrafung des Apostaten vorsieht.[68]

---

62 Vgl. *Baber Johansen*, Zwischen Verfassung, Kodifizierung und Šarīʿa: Die Apostasie in Gesetzgebung und Rechtsprechung einiger arabischen Staaten, in: *Hans-Georg Ebert/ Thoralf Hanstein* (Hrsg.), Leipziger Beiträge zur Orientforschung, Bd. 15; Beiträge zum Islamischen Recht IV, Frankfurt a.M. 2004, S. 23 ff (27 f.)

63 Vgl. *Ṭāhā Ǧābir al-ʿAlwānī*, lā ikrāha fī ad-dīn, a.a.O. (Fn. 37), S. 149.

64 Ibidem, S. 106 f.

65 Ḥadīṯ Nr. 3993 bei *Abū ʿAbd ar-Raḥmān an-Nisāʾī*, http://hadith.al-islam.com/Display/Display.asp?hnum=3993&doc=3&IMAGE=%DA%D1%D6+%C7%E1%CD%CF%ED%CB (zuletzt aufgerufen am 27. August 2008).

66 Hans-Georg Ebert übersetzt *āḥād* mit „Einzelüberlieferungen, Traditionen ohne verlässliche Überliefererkette". Vgl. *Hans-Georg Ebert*, Das Personalstatut arabischer Länder, Problemfelder, Methoden, a.a.O. (Fn. 38), S. 163.

67 Vgl. *Ṭāhā Ǧābir al-ʿAlwānī*, lā ikrāha fī ad-dīn, a.a.O. (Fn. 37), S. 123-144.

68 Ibidem, S. 155.

Hierbei läuft man Gefahr, die Sunna des Propheten dem Koran gleichzustellen. Ohne Zweifel gilt die Sunna als die zweite Rechtsquelle im Islam. Allerdings genießt sie im Allgemeinen nicht die Authentizität und Verbindlichkeit des Korans.[69] Darüber hinaus obliegen die authentischen, stark überlieferten *aḥadīṯ* (Pl. von *ḥadīṯ*) des Propheten den Prinzipien und Methoden der Interpretation, insbesondere dem geschichtlichen Kontext. Das Erkennen des Grundes einer Prophetenüberlieferung ist dafür von großem Nutzen, um über die Vorläufigkeit bzw. die Ewigkeit des daraus erschlossenen Urteils entscheiden zu können.

Muḥammad ʿĀbid al-Ǧabrī stellt die Glaubwürdigkeit der erwähnten Tradition in Frage, weil dessen Authentizität durch den Koran nicht bestätigt wird. Er weist darauf hin, dass die mekkanischen Suren des Korans, zu einer Zeit, da die islamische Religion und die islamische *umma* noch schwach waren, einige Handlungen wie Diebstahl und außerehelichen Geschlechtsverkehr verurteilen,[70] aber ohne dafür eine weltliche Strafe zu bestimmen. Die medinensischen Suren hingegen erklären solche Taten als Delikte mit einer festgelegten Strafe.[71] Diese Entwicklung von der Verurteilung zur Bestrafung ist in Bezug auf die Apostasie nicht nachweisbar, denn die mekkanischen Verse verurteilen den Apostaten und bedrohen ihn mit schweren Strafen im Jenseits,[72] während die medinensischen Verse nur diese Verurteilung bzw. die spätere Strafe Gottes am Jüngsten Tag bestätigen, ohne eine einzige weltliche Strafe zu nennen.[73] Dies gibt zu erkennen, dass Gott die Apostasie im Diesseits nicht bestrafen will. Zudem sei in diesem Zusammenhang auf die Verse zur Glaubensfreiheit verwiesen.

In der Auseinandersetzung mit dieser Tradition im Besonderen und mit den Prophetenüberlieferungen im Allgemeinen kann die Methodik der Hintergründe der Herabsendung (*asbāb an-nuzūl*) Beachtung finden. Es muss auch hier nach dem Kontext der Überlieferung gefragt werden. Dies hat der zweite Kalif ʿUmar b. al-Ḫaṭṭāb (gest. 644) getan, indem er die Todesstrafe für Apostasie aussetzte und den Apostaten stattdessen mit einer lebenslangen Haftstrafe „als Denkzeit" belegte.[74] Die Aussetzung der *ḥadd*-Strafe für Diebstahl im Kriegsfalle wurde so von ʿUmar b. al-Ḫaṭṭāb auf die Apostasie ausgedehnt. Der Kalif verstand diesen

---

69 Ṭāhā Ǧābir al-ʿAlwānī bezeichnet es als Seuche, dass der *ḥadīṯ* gegenüber dem Koran in den Vordergrund gestellt wird; ibidem, S. 125.

70 Vgl. Sure 17 (الإسراء), Vers 32.

71 Vgl. Sure 24 (النور), Vers 2 und Sure 5 (المائدة), Vers 38.

72 Vgl. Sure 16 (النحل), Vers 106.

73 Vgl. *Muḥammad ʿAbid al-Ǧabrī*, ḥadīṯ al-murtad yaftaqid al-miṣdaqīya [„Dem Apostat-*ḥadīṯ* fehlt die Glaubwürdigkeit"], http://www.aljabriabed.net/mortadd3.htm (zuletzt aufgerufen am 17. September 2007.)

74 Ausführlich zur ʿUmar b. al-Ḫaṭṭābs Einstellung zur Apostasie siehe *Ṭāhā Ǧābir al-ʿAlwānī*, lā ikrāha fī ad-dīn, a.a.O. (Fn. 37), S. 122 f.

ḥadīṯ als eine politische Anweisung von einem Imām bzw. einem Staatsoberhaupt, nicht jedoch als einen ewig gültigen göttlichen Befehl. Die kritische Betrachtung des Korans und der Sunna im historischen Kontext führten ʿUmar b. al-Ḫaṭṭāb zu dieser Einsicht. Die Methode bedarf heutzutage der Wiederbelebung.

In diesem Zusammenhang vertritt Yūsuf al-Qaraḍāwī die Ansicht, dass der heilige Text, sei er Koran oder Prophetenüberlieferung, immer Gegenstand der Untersuchung sein kann. Dabei ist zwischen den endgültigen und den vorläufigen Vorschriften, zwischen dem, was der Prophet als politischer Führer gesagt und getan hat, und dem, was als religiöse Vorschrift gilt, zu unterscheiden.[75]

Es existiert unter muslimischen Gelehrten die Meinung, dass der Unglaube und die Apostasie die abscheulichste Sünde sei, die Gott nicht vergibt. Im Koran heißt es: „Siehe, Allah vergibt es nicht, dass Ihm Götter zur Seite gesetzt werden: Doch im Übrigen vergibt Er alles, wem Er will. Wer Allah Götter an die Seite setzt, der ist weit abgeirrt“ (Sure 4 [النساء], Vers 116). Trotzdem werden im Koran ausdrücklich bestimmte Strafen für weniger „abscheuliche Sünden“ wie Diebstahl und Unzucht festgeschrieben.[76] Insofern ist erkennbar: Wäre die Apostasie vom Menschen zu bestrafen, hätte Gott dies im Koran erwähnt. Es widerspricht dem Gerechtigkeitsprinzip Gottes, hätte er diese Sünde nicht als „weltliche“ Straftat erklärt, wenn sie denn eine wäre. Aber im Koran steht klar und deutlich, dass die Bestrafung der Apostasie nur Gott im Jenseits zustehe.

Es bleibt allerdings die Aufgabe der *fiqh*-Gelehrten und der Gesetzgeber, zwischen demjenigen, der seine Religion aus innerer Überzeugung ohne politische Ziele wechselt, und demjenigen, der die Apostasie mit dem Kampf gegen die „islamische“ Gesellschaft verbindet, zu unterscheiden.

V. Ablehnungsgründe der Universalität der Menschenrechte

Lorenz Müller meint zu Recht, dass viele Länder der Auffassung sind, die in der Allgemeinen Menschenrechtserklärung von 1948 enthaltenen Grundsätze spiegeln nicht die Werte ihrer Kultur wider, sondern vielmehr die des *Westens*. In der Anlegung eines *westlichen Maßstabes* sieht die *arabisch-islamische Welt* eine Einmischung in ihre inneren Angelegenheiten. Dies mag ein Grund sein, warum Muslime gegen die Übernahme *westlicher Menschenrechtskonzeptionen* eintreten. Hinzu kommt der historische Faktor. Denn das Verhältnis zwischen

[75] Vgl. *Yūsuf al-Qaraḍāwī,* as-sīyāsa aš-šarʿīya fī ḍauʾ nuṣūṣ aš-šarīʿa wa-maqāṣidihā [„Die islam-rechtliche Politik im Lichte der Texte der *šarīʿa* und deren Grundziele“], 2. Aufl., Maktabat Wahba: Kairo, 2005, S. 26.

[76] Vgl. Sure 24 (النور), Vers 2 und Sure 5 (المائدة), Vers 38.

Orient und Okzident ist in vielfacher Weise belastet. Darüber hinaus werden die Menschenrechte nach westlichem Muster nicht selten mit Säkularismus in Verbindung gebracht.[77] Säkularismus wird im Orient aus verschiedenen Gründen mit Ketzerei gleichgesetzt und ist daher bereits als Begriff problematisch. Mithin werden die Menschenrechte als Deckmantel für kulturelle Kolonialisierung und Missionierung betrachtet.[78]

Eine Universalität der Menschenrechte kann dem folgenden *ḥadīṯ* entnommen werden: „Der Prophet sagt: ‚Die Weisheit ist jedem Gläubigen wie ein verlorener Sohn. Er sollte ihn annehmen, egal wo er ihn findet'".[79] Dies könnte auch als Aufforderung verstanden werden, Demokratie und Menschenrechte[80] nach *westlichem Konzept* als eigenen Wert oder – um in der Sprache der Tradition zu bleiben – als anwendbare Weisheit zu begreifen.

Allerdings bestehen Hindernisse bei der Realisierung der Menschenrechte in der *arabisch-islamischen Welt* nicht nur in religiösen Vorbehalten. Die autoritären Herrschaftssysteme in Verbindung mit patriarchalischen Gesellschaftsidealen erschweren oder verhindern die Verankerung und Durchsetzung der Menschenrechte. Michael Thumann bringt dies zum Ausdruck, wenn er schreibt: „Dabei sind die gemäßigten Islamisten wahrscheinlich ein geringeres Hindernis für die Demokratisierung als die dickfelligen Oberhäupter der mächtigen Familien".[81]

VI. Postulate

➊ Muslime können und dürfen die Auseinandersetzung mit Fragen der Menschenrechte nicht deshalb vernachlässigen, weil deren Wurzeln bei „den anderen" zu suchen sind. Mit der Verteidigung einer eigenen Identität hat dies nichts zu tun, sondern würde eher Rückständigkeit und Widerstand gegen eine Entwicklung bedeuten. Es wäre töricht, sich den Verfechtern der Stagnation bzw. der Erstarrung im Namen der Religions- und Identitätsverteidigung anzuschließen.[82]

---

77 Mehr dazu siehe *Lorenz Müller*, Islam und Menschenrechte…, a.a.O. (Fn. 39), S. 15, 16 und 18.

78 Vgl. zu den Auswirkungen der historischen Gegnerschaft von Islam und Christentum *Hartmut Bobzin*, „Heiliger Krieg. Zum Verhältnis von Islam und Christentum", in: *Peter Billing / Gert Krell* (Hrsg.), Krieg und Frieden am Golf, Frankfurt a. M. 1991, S. 11-19.

79 Ḥadīṯ Nr. 2611 bei *at-Tirmiḏī*: http://hadith.al-islam.com/Display/Display.asp?hnum=2611&doc=2&IMAGE=%DA%D1%D6+%C7%E1%CD%CF%ED%CB (zuletzt aufgerufen am 30. April 2008).

80 Es geht hier um die Menschenrechte im Allgemeinen, nicht um einzelne inhaltliche und kulturelle Vorbehalte.

81 *Michael Thumann*, Erst das Recht macht die Demokratie, in: *Michael Thumann* (Hrsg.), Der Islam und der Westen, Berlin 2003, S. 127 ff. (S. 134).

82 Vgl. *Naṣr Ḥāmid Abū Zaīd*, Problematik der Koraninterpretation…, a.a.O. (Fn. 16).

❷ Das Problem des Verständnisses einer Gottes- und/oder „Textherrschaft" (*al-ḥākimiyya*) bedarf einer umfassenden Lösung. Die Herrschaft des heiligen Textes sollte mit einer entsprechenden Lesart und einer Rationalität verbunden sein, die dem Menschen den ihm gebührenden Interpretationsrahmen lässt.

❸ Die Sunna erfordert eine umfassende Analyse. Sie benötigt eine eigene Interpretationswissenschaft analog zur Beschäftigung mit dem Koran. Alle Prophetenüberlieferungen müssen im Lichte ihrer Historizität, d.h. unter Berücksichtigung ihrer zeitlichen und örtlichen Hintergründe behandelt werden. Ferner sind die medinensischen Überlieferungen von den mekkanischen in Bezug auf ihre Wirkung und ihre Grundlage zu unterscheiden.

❹ Die Menschenrechte in ihrer gegenwärtigen Form sind Resultat eines langen Prozesses. Viele Beispiele zeigen dies; so ist die Rassentrennung in öffentlichen Parks, Bädern und in den Schulen in den USA, dem Protagonisten der Universalität von Demokratie und Menschenrechten, erst in der zweiten Hälfte des 20. Jahrhunderts aufgehoben worden. Das Wahlrecht wurde den Frauen in Deutschland 1919, in Frankreich 1940 und in der Schweiz erst 1971 zugestanden. Hinzu kommt, dass die Konkretisierung des Inhalts der Menschenrechte nicht nur als ein Problem des Orients wahrgenommen werden sollte. Unterschiedliche Ansichten über den Inhalt der Menschenrechte werden auch in anderen Regionen vertreten. Das Spektrum ist dabei breit: Es reicht vom Umgang mit gleichgeschlechtlichen Partnerschaften über die Anhäufung von personenbezogenen Daten bis zur Folter „für einen höheren Zweck". Die Universalität der Menschenrechte, aber auch deren Inhalt und deren Verwirklichung bleiben Gegenstand der Diskussion.[83]

[83] Vgl. *Hans Hattenhauer*, Europäische Rechtsgeschichte, Heidelberg 1992, S. 632.

„Westliche“ versus „islamische“ Menschenrechtskonzeptionen?

Heiner Bielefeldt, Berlin

A. Einführung

Die nach dem „Wendejahr“ 1989 aufgekeimte Hoffnung, dass die internationale Menschenrechtspolitik sich fortan auf einen globalen Konsens würde stützen können, ist längst zerstoben. An die Stelle der alten Konfrontation zwischen Ost und West, die die Entwicklung des Menschenrechtsschutzes in den Vereinten Nationen über Jahrzehnte blockiert oder zumindest enorm verlangsamt hatte, sind neue, regionale Gruppierungen getreten, die vielfach gegensätzliche Interessen in der Menschenrechtspolitik durchsetzen wollen und sich dabei von unterschiedlichen Menschenrechtskonzeptionen leiten lassen. Die Ersetzung der Menschenrechtskommission der Vereinten Nationen durch den Menschenrechtsrat im Jahre 2006 hat daran nichts geändert.[1]

Die Interessenslagen sind komplex und die Lagerbildungen nicht immer übersichtlich.[2] Auch innerhalb der westlichen Gruppe streitet man nach wie vor über das Verhältnis der bürgerlichen und politischen zu den wirtschaftlichen, sozialen und kulturellen Menschenrechten. Das sozialdemokratisch geprägte Schweden steht dabei – für manche überraschend – oft an der Seite der USA, Großbritanniens und anderer wirtschaftsliberaler Gegner einer stärkeren justiziellen Durchsetzung sozialer Menschenrechte. In Fragen der Terrorismusbekämpfung ist nach dem 11. September 2001 eine Entfremdung zwischen den USA und der (intern wiederum keineswegs immer einigen) Europäischen Union unübersehbar geworden. Der „Westen“ tritt also durchaus nicht immer einheitlich auf. Ähnliches gilt für die so genannte Dritte Welt. Wenn es beispielsweise um die Rechte sexueller Minderheiten gibt, befinden sich Brasilien und Südafrika, die in Fragen sozialer Menschenrechte miteinander kooperieren, in völlig unterschiedlichen Lagern. Einen in sich geschlossenen „Süden“ gibt es offenbar genauso wenig wie einen stets einheitlich auftretenden „Westen“. Auch die Organisation der Islamischen Konferenz (OIC), in der so unterschiedliche Staaten wie die Türkei, Saudi-Arabien und Malaysia zusammen arbeiten, bildet

---

1 Vgl. *Andreas Zumach*, „Von der Menschenrechtskommission zum Menschenrechtsrat“, in: *Heiner Bielefeldt / Franz-Josef Hutter / Sabine Kurtenbach / Carsten Tessmer* (Hrsg.), MenschenrechtsFragen. Zum 65. Geburtstag von Volkmar Deile, Karlsruhe 2008, S. 14-24.

2 Vgl. die Berichte von *Theodor Rathgeber* zu den Sitzungen der früheren UN-Menschenrechtskommission bzw. des seit 2006 bestehenden UN-Menschenrechtsrats, die in den Ausgaben der Jahrbuchs Menschenrechte (hrsg. vom Deutschen Institut für Menschenrechte u.a. Frankfurt a.M.) der letzten Jahre regelmäßig erschienen sind.

Islam und Menschenrechte (Islam and Human Rights / الإسلام وحقوق الإنسان)
Hatem Elliesie (Hrsg./Editor), © Peter Lang Verlag: Frankfurt a.M. 2010, S. 99-119

keine uniforme politische Größe in der Menschenrechtspolitik.[86] Die im Rahmen der OIC in Kairo 1990 veröffentlichte „Erklärung der Menschenrechte im Islam“ ist aufgrund ihrer durchgängigen Orientierung an der *šarīᶜa* mit den Verfassungsordnungen einiger der OIC-Mitgliedstaaten wie etwa der Türkei oder Tunesiens eigentlich überhaupt nicht kompatibel.

Bei aller Komplexität der Debattenlagen ist der Eindruck, dass in vielen Fragen vor allem die westliche Gruppe und die Organisation der Islamischen Konferenz gegeneinander stehen, gleichwohl nicht falsch. Abgesehen von konkreten Interessensgegensätzen sind auch die konzeptionellen Unterschiede in der Menschenrechtspolitik hier oft besonders ausgeprägt. An hochsymbolischen Konflikten wie dem Streit um die Muḥammad-Karikaturen treten sie offen zu tage. Hartnäckige Anhänger der sowohl im Ganzen als auch im Detail längst widerlegten Huntington-These eines globalen Kulturkampfs sehen sich dadurch immer wieder bestätigt.

Es wäre freilich politisch fatal, die Chancen menschenrechtlicher Konsensbildung durch ein kulturalistisch-ideologisches Lagerdenken von vornherein preiszugeben, das sich leicht zu einer *self-fulfilling prophecy* entwickeln kann. Um nicht einer Lagermentalität zu verfallen, gilt es zunächst, die bestehenden Konfliktlinien genauer zu beschreiben. Dabei wird deutlich, dass – wie soeben kurz skizziert – auch innerhalb der jeweiligen „Blöcke“ ernst zu nehmende politische Differenzen in Menschenrechtsfragen bestehen.

Zu berücksichtigen ist darüber hinaus vor allem, dass die vielfach autoritären Regierungen keineswegs vorbehaltlos mit den Gesellschaften gleichgesetzt werden dürfen, die zu repräsentieren sie beanspruchen. Die iranische Friedensnobelpreisträgerin Shirin Ebadi (Šīrīn ᶜEbādī), die gelegentlich bei „side events“ anlässlich der Sitzungen des Menschenrechtsrats in Genf auftritt, steht mit ihren emanzipatorischen Ansichten großen Teilen der iranischen Gesellschaft weitaus näher als die Regierung der Islamischen Republik Iran. Die Stellungnahmen der pakistanischen Rechtsanwältin Asma Jahangir (ᶜAṣma Ǧahāngīr), UN-Sonderberichterstatterin für Religionsfreiheit, dürften vielen Pakistanis ungleich sympathischer sein als die reaktionären Positionierungen, die die pakistanische Regierung im Menschenrechtsrat vorträgt.

Außerdem gilt es, die Idee der Menschenrechte gegenüber die ideologische Okkupation durch die jeweiligen „Lager“ in ihrer Eigenständigkeit zur Geltung zu bringen. Zu konzeptioneller Klarheit im Umgang mit dem Anspruch der

86 Vgl., hierzu weiterführend: *Theodor Rathgeber*, „Die Organisation Islamischer Konferenz im UN-Menschenrechtsrat: Menschenrechte als Instrument staatlicher Politik“, in: *Hatem Elliesie* (Hrsg.Editor), Islam und Menschenrechte (Islam and Human Rights / وحقوق الإنسان الإسلام), Frankfurt a.M. 2010, S. 457-473.

Menschenrechte, die dafür unerlässlich ist, will der vorliegende Aufsatz einen Beitrag leisten. Dabei konzentriere ich mich auf einen einzigen Punkt, nämlich die Dekonstruktion kulturalistischer Vereinnahmungen der Menschenrechte. Andere für das interkulturelle Verständnis der Menschenrechte wichtige Streitfragen – etwa zum Verhältnis zwischen Individuum und Gemeinschaft, zur Relation zwischen Rechten und Pflichten oder zum Verhältnis von säkularen Menschenrechtsnormen und religiös-rechtlichen Vorgaben (z.B. der *šarīʿa*) können im engen Rahmen des vorliegenden Textes nicht behandelt werden. Ich habe mich andernorts dazu ausführlich geäußert.[4]

Zunächst soll die Menschenrechtsidee in ihrem normativen Profil kurz erläutert werden (Kapitel **B.**). Anschließend geht es mir um eine Dekonstruktion sowohl westlicher (Kapitel **C.**) als auch islamischer (Kapitel **D.**) Vereinnahmungen der Menschenrechte. Der Aufsatz endet mit einigen Überlegungen, die vom Rawlsschen Konzept des „overlapping consensus" inspiriert sind (Kapitel **E.**).

B. Zur normativen Bestimmung der Menschenrechte

Zur Klärung des Menschenrechtsbegriffs möchte ich drei Aspekte hervorheben, die *in ihrer Verbindung* das normative Profil der Menschenrechte ausmachen. Es sind dies: (I) der universale Geltungsanspruch der Menschenrechte, (II) ihre inhaltliche Zielrichtung auf eine an der Würde des Menschen orientierte Ordnung gleicher Freiheit und gleichberechtigter Partizipation sowie schließlich (III) ihre politisch-rechtliche Durchsetzungsintention.

I. Der universale Geltungsanspruch der Menschenrechte

Bei den Menschenrechten handelt es sich, wie schon der allgemeine Sprachgebrauch zeigt, um grundlegende Rechte, die jedem Menschen zukommen. Im Unterschied zu solchen Rechtskategorien, die an bestimmte Rollen oder Funktionen in der Gesellschaft anknüpfen – etwa an die Rolle von Mietern oder Vermietern, an die Mitgliedschaft in bestimmten Verbänden und Berufsgruppen oder an den Besitz einer bestimmten Staatsangehörigkeit – sind die Menschenrechte schon *mit dem Menschsein* des Menschen gegeben. In einer aus dem 18. Jahrhundert überkommenen Metapher spricht man noch heute gelegentlich davon, dass die Menschenrechte dem Menschen „angeboren" seien. So beginnt Artikel 1 der Allgemeinen Erklärung der Menschenrechte der Vereinten Nationen von 1948 mit dem Satz:

---

4 Vgl. *Heiner Bielefeldt,* Philosophie der Menschenrechte. Grundlagen eines weltweiten Freiheitsethos, Darmstadt 1998; *Heiner Bielefeldt,* Muslime im säkularen Rechtsstaat. Integrationschancen durch Religionsfreiheit, Bielefeld 2003.

„Alle Menschen sind frei und an Würde und Rechten gleich geboren."[5]

Die Geburtsmetapher verweist auf das *Faktum des Menschenseins* als den Anknüpfungspunkt für die Anerkennung grundlegender Rechte. Auch wenn diese Metapher angesichts der mittlerweile bestehenden Eingriffsmöglichkeiten in vorgeburtliches Leben vielleicht naiv anmutet, behält sie ihren Sinn, indem sie deutlich macht, dass die Menschenrechte nicht das Ergebnis von Leistung oder Verdienst sind, sondern jedem Menschen zustehen, und zwar allein schon deshalb, weil er ein Mensch ist.

Der Blick auf die Geschichte zeigt, dass Bekenntnisse zur Universalität der Menschenrechte offensichtlich nicht immer ganz ernst gemeint waren. Unter den Verfassern der ersten Menschenrechtsdokumente des späten 18. Jahrhunderts finden sich sogar Sklavenbesitzer. Der Universalismus der Menschenrechte stellt indessen ein kritisches Prinzip dar, das sich immer auch gegen Inkonsequenzen und Halbherzigkeiten in der Formulierung bzw. Positivierung von Menschenrechtsnormen richtet und oft genug eine Wirkung entfaltet hat, die über die Absichten ihrer Autoren weit hinausgeht. Zur Geschichte der Menschenrechte gehört daher auch die Kritik an den jeweils herrschenden Menschenrechtsnormen, wie sie von verschiedenen Befreiungsbewegungen – z.B. der Frauenbewegung, der Anti-Sklaverei-Bewegung, den Gewerkschaften oder den Selbstorganisationen von Behinderten – vorgetragen wurde und wird.

So wurde die androzentrische Verkürzung der *déclaration des droits de l'homme et du citoyen* von 1789 bereits von der jungen feministischen Bewegung der Revolutionszeit als Unrecht entlarvt und im Jahre 1791 mit einer von Olympe de Gouges verfassten *déclaration des droits de la femme et de la citoyenne* beantwortet, in der die Autorin gleiche Rechte für Frauen **und** Männer verlangt und so mit dem menschenrechtlichen Universalismus sehr viele entschiedener ernst macht.[6]

II. Inhaltliche Zielrichtung der Menschenrechte

Menschenrechte, auch dies ist bereits im Begriff impliziert, gelten für jeden Menschen gleichermaßen, sind also Gleichheitsrechte. Sie erlauben keine Diskriminierung nach Stand, Geschlecht, Religionszugehörigkeit, ethnischer Her-

[5] Zitiert nach *Christian Tomuschat* (Hrsg.), Menschenrechte. Eine Sammlung internationaler Dokumente zum Menschenrechtsschutz, 2. erweiterte Auflage Bonn 2002, S. 39. Alle weiteren Zitate aus UN-Menschenrechtsdokumenten sind, sofern nicht anders vermerkt, der von Tomuschat herausgegebenen Sammlung entnommen.

[6] Abgedruckt ist die Erklärung der *Olympe de Gouges* – in Gegenüberstellung zur offiziellen Menschenrechtserklärung von 1789 – im Anhang der Studie von *Ute Gerhard,* Gleichheit ohne Angleichung. Frauen im Recht, München 1990, S. 263 ff. Vgl. auch den Kommentar, ibidem, S. 49 ff.

kunft usw. Als fundamentale Rechte des Menschen schlechthin sind sie das genaue Gegenteil von Privilegien, nämlich Gleichheitsrechte. Während der Begriff des Privilegs im Kontext der traditionellen europäischen Ständegesellschaft einen *Rechts*begriff darstellt, hat er für unser heutiges, menschenrechtlich geprägtes Empfinden bezeichnenderweise *Unrechts*charakter. Die menschenrechtliche Gleichheit meint nicht etwa Gleichförmigkeit oder Uniformität, sondern *gleiche Freiheit*, und zwar nicht nur die gleiche Freiheit persönlicher Lebensführung, sondern auch die *gleichberechtigte Partizipation* an den Belangen der Gemeinschaft, insbesondere auch in der Politik. Inhaltlich sind Menschenrechte demnach durch ihre emanzipatorische Stoßrichtung gekennzeichnet, die man im Anschluss an die berühmte Trias der Französischen Revolution mit „Freiheit, Gleichheit, Brüderlichkeit" umreißen kann (wobei es angemessen wäre, den Begriff der „Brüderlichkeit" heute durch „Solidarität" zu ersetzen).[7]

Das politisch-rechtliche Prinzip gleicher Freiheit und Partizipation verweist auf die Würde des Menschen, die in Menschenrechten zur Geltung gebracht werden soll. Menschenrechte bringen die wesentliche Gleichheit der Menschen als sittlicher Subjekte dadurch zur Geltung, dass sie einem jeden gleiche Freiheit und gleichberechtigte Partizipation ermöglichen. Diese komplexe normative Konstellation – die innere Verbindung von Würde und Recht sowie die Strukturierung des Menschenrechtsdenkens nach den Prinzipien von Freiheit, Gleichheit und Brüderlichkeit (bzw. Solidarität) – kommt in Artikel 1 der Allgemeinen Menschenrechtserklärung zum Ausdruck, der feststellt:

> „Alle Menschen sind frei und an Würde und Rechten gleich geboren. Sie sind mit Vernunft und Gewissen begabt und sollen einander im Geist der Brüderlichkeit begegnen."

III. Politisch-rechtliche Durchsetzungsintention der Menschenrechte

Menschenrechte stellen eine *politisch-rechtliche Kategorie* dar. Ihr Geltungsanspruch beschränkt sich nicht auf einen humanitären Appell, sondern findet Gestalt in politisch-rechtlichen Institutionen und Verfahren, die sich auf nationaler, regional-völkerrechtlicher und internationaler Ebene herausgebildet haben bzw. derzeit noch entwickelt werden. Im modernen Verfassungsstaat sind Menschenrechte teils als einklagbare Grundrechte verankert, die, wie es in Artikel 1 Absatz 3 des Grundgesetzes der Bundesrepublik Deutschland heißt, „Gesetzgebung, vollziehende Gewalt und Rechtsprechung als unmittelbar geltendes Recht" binden. Als bisher erfolgreichstes Beispiel einer regional-völkerrechtlichen Normierung von Menschenrechten gilt die Europäische

---

7 Zur Trias von Freiheit, Gleichheit und Solidarität (bzw. Partizipation) vgl. *Wolfgang Huber / Ernst Eduard Tödt*, Menschenrechte. Perspektiven einer menschlichen Welt, Stuttgart 1977, S. 80 ff.

Menschenrechtskonvention, die im Rahmen des Europarates 1950 entstanden und seit dem Jahre 1953 in Kraft ist. Nach dem Ende des Ost-West-Konflikts sind ihr mittlerweile auch fast alle osteuropäischen Staaten beigetreten. Die Europäische Menschenrechtskonvention eröffnet den im Bereich der Mitgliedsstaaten lebenden Menschen die Möglichkeit, ihre Rechte ggf. vor dem Europäischen Gerichtshof für Menschenrechte in Straßburg einzuklagen. Vergleichbare (wenn auch bislang weniger effiziente) regional-völkerrechtliche Menschenrechtskonventionen bestehen auch im interamerikanischen Raum, in Afrika sowie innerhalb der Arabischen Liga.

Den Auftakt für die Etablierung von Menschenrechtsstandards im Rahmen der Vereinten Nationen bildet die bereits erwähnte Allgemeine Menschenrechtserklärung vom 10. Dezember 1948. Aus ihr sind in der Folgezeit mehrere internationale Menschenrechtskonventionen hervorgegangen, die für die Vertragsstaaten auch völkerrechtlich verbindlich sind, darunter der Internationale Pakt über bürgerliche und politische Rechte sowie der Internationale Pakt über wirtschaftliche, soziale und kulturelle Rechte (beide von 1966, in Kraft getreten 1976). Da es einen internationalen Gerichtshof für Menschenrechte bislang nicht gibt, obliegt die Überwachung dieser (und zahlreicher anderer) Konventionen eigens eingesetzten unabhängigen Prüfungsausschüssen, deren Durchsetzungsmöglichkeiten derzeit allerdings noch viel zu wünschen übrig lassen.

Aus dem spezifisch politisch-rechtlichen Charakter von Menschenrechten ergeben sich zugleich auch immanente *Grenzen* ihres normativen Anspruchs. Auf diese *Grenzen* hinzuweisen ist gerade im Blick auf interreligiöse oder interkulturelle Debatten wichtig, werden doch nach wie vor Bedenken laut, Menschenrechte seien eine moderne globale „Humanitätsreligion", die die Vielfalt der Religionen bzw. Kulturen überwölben oder gar überwinden solle. Manche Befürworter der Menschenrechte geben solchen Befürchtungen Nahrung, indem sie den Anspruch der Menschenrechte überziehen und etwa mit Bassam Tibi die Idee der Menschenrechte als „religion civile"[8] bezeichnen. Will man sich gegen den Vorwurf wehren, menschenrechtliches Engagement sei eine moderne Fortsetzung religiöser Kreuzzüge oder eine Variante eurozentrischer Zivilisationsmission, so gilt es, den Geltungsanspruch der Menschenrechte klar zu limitieren und auf die politisch-rechtliche Ebene zu konzentrieren (vgl. dazu auch nachfolgend, Kapitel E., Abschnitt 2).

Geht von man der *Verbindung* der drei genannten Aspekte – des universalen Geltungsanspruchs, der emanzipatorischen Stoßrichtung („Freiheit, Gleichheit, Solidarität") und der politisch-rechtlichen Durchsetzungsintention – aus, so er-

[8] *Bassam Tibi,* Im Schatten Allahs. Der Islam und die Menschenrechte, München / Zürich 1994, S. 280.

weisen sich Menschenrechte als eine spezifisch *moderne* Idee.[9] Ein entscheidender Durchbruch fand in den großen demokratischen Revolutionen des späten 18. Jahrhunderts statt, in denen die ersten politisch wirksamen Menschenrechtsdokumente entstanden, darunter die *Virginia Bill of Rights* von 1776 und die *déclaration des droits de l'homme et du citoyen* von 1789. In das internationale Recht fanden Menschenrechte weitaus später Eingang, nämlich erst mit Gründung der Vereinten Nationen.

Menschenrechte gehören somit der Moderne an. Es wäre aber ein Missverständnis, wollte man die Modernität der Menschenrechte im Sinne einer einlinigen Fortschrittsgeschichte konzipieren und pauschal gegen vormoderne Traditionen von Ethik und Recht stellen. Denn Menschenrechte bieten eine Antwort gerade auch auf massive *Unrechtserfahrungen* der Moderne. Dies kommt ebenfalls in der Allgemeinen Menschenrechtserklärung von 1948 zu Wort, wenn die Präambel von „Akten der Barbarei" spricht, „die das Gewissen der Menschheit tief verletzt haben", und damit insbesondere an die Gräueltaten des Nationalsozialismus erinnert. Von Anfang an stellen Menschenrechte einen Protest gegen konkret erfahrenes Unrecht dar, und zwar nicht zuletzt gegen solche strukturellen Unrechtserfahrungen, die sich aus dem Umbruch der Gesellschaft zur Moderne und den damit einhergehenden Krisen und Erschütterungen ergeben haben. Mit den Worten des Politikwissenschaftlers Reza Afshari: "Although [Human Rights] originated in the West, their particular substantive foundation belongs to a moral vision that was the result of accumulated experiences in dealing with the abuses of the modern state and market economies."[10]

C. Okzidentalistische Vereinnahmung der Menschenrechte

Aus der kaum bestreitbaren Tatsache, dass Menschenrechte historisch zunächst in Europa und Nordamerika zum Durchbruch gelangt sind,[11] wird oft der Schluss gezogen, sie seien an die kulturellen, philosophischen und meta-

9 Die normativen Komponenten, aus denen das moderne Menschenrechtsdenken entstanden sind, lassen sich historisch natürlich viel weiter zurückverfolgen. Weder die biblische Idee der Gottesebenbildlichkeit jedes Menschen noch auch die Magna Charta von 1215 können jedoch im engeren Sinne als Menschenrechte verstanden werden: Im ersten Fall fehlt die unmittelbare politisch-rechtliche Durchsetzungsintention, im zweiten Fall fehlt der universale Geltungsanspruch.

10 Vgl. *Reza Afshari*, „An Essay on Islamic Cultural Relativism in the Discourse of Human Rights", in: Human Rights Quarterly, 16, Baltimore 1994, S. 235 ff. (248).

11 So auch *Abdullahi Ahmed An-Na'im*, „Islam and Human Rights: Introductory Remarks and Reflections", in: *Hatem Elliesie* (Hrsg./Editor), Beiträge zum Islamischen Recht VII, Islam und Menschenrechte (Islam and Human Rights / الإسلام وحقوق الإنسان), Frankfurt a.M. 2010, Seite 41 f. (42); *Muhammad Kalisch*, „Islam und Menschenrechte: Betrachtungen zum Verhältnis von Religion und Recht", in: Ibidem, Seite 49 ff. (71).

physischen Voraussetzungen des „westlichen" Denkens notwendig gebunden. Diese These findet sich in vielen Varianten. Verbreitet ist z.B. die Überzeugung, Menschenrechte entstammten letztlich der christlichen Tradition und könnten nur in ihrem Horizont angemessen verstanden werden. In diesem Sinne schreibt der katholische Moralphilosoph Jozef Punt: „In der Scholastik vorbereitet, im Humanismus übersteigert und in der Aufklärung säkularisiert, ist die Einsicht in die Würde und Freiheit des natürlichen Menschen letztlich eine religiös-philosophische Kategorie, die zwar auf das Christentum und die Stoa zurückgeht, die aber im christlichen Abendland doch vor allem durch die biblische Lehre der Schöpfungsordnung und der Gottesebenbildlichkeit lebendig geblieben und durch die Jahrhunderte hindurch weitergetragen wurde."[12] Georg Picht verweist in einer ideengeschichtlichen Studie auf die Rolle der stoischen Philosophie, deren metaphysischer Rahmen nicht nur für die Erklärung der Genese, sondern auch für das aktuelle Verständnis der Menschenrechtsidee unverzichtbar sei: „Stellt man die Grundlehren der europäischen Metaphysik in Frage, so erschüttert man zugleich die Menschenrechtsdoktrin."[13]

Die historische Herleitung der Menschenrechte aus der Reformation wird etwa von Wolfgang Fikentscher vertreten, der den Ursprung menschenrechtlicher Forderungen in den Befreiungskampf der niederländischen Protestanten gegen die katholischen Spanier datiert.[14] Auch er sieht die christliche Herkunft und Deutung als „für Grund- und Menschenrechte konstitutiv" an.[15] Ludger Kühnhardt schließlich verortet den Ursprung der Menschenrechte in der neuzeitlichen Wendung des abendländischen Naturrechtsdenken. Er schreibt: „Der geschichtlich entscheidende geistige Durchbruch zur Idee unveräußerlicher Menschenrechte wurde durch das Werk John Lockes (1632-1704) geleistet."[16]

Problematisch an diesen und ähnlichen Herleitungen der Menschenrechte ist, dass sie implizit oder explizit zu einer Vereinnahmung der Menschenrechtsidee in den geistig-kulturellen Horizont der christlich-abendländischen Tradition führen. Für Menschen anderer kultureller Herkunft oder Orientierung hat dies

---

12 *Jozef Punt*, Die Idee der Menschenrechte. Ihre geschichtliche Entwicklung und ihre Rezeption durch die moderne katholische Sozialverkündigung, Paderborn 1987, S. 87.

13 *Georg Picht*, „Zum geistesgeschichtlichen Hintergrund der Lehre von den Menschenrechten", in: *Georg Picht*, Hier und Jetzt. Philosophieren nach Auschwitz und Hiroshima, Stuttgart 1980, S. 116 ff. (131).

14 Vgl. *Wolfgang Fikentscher*, „Die heutige Bedeutung des nicht-säkularen Ursprungs der Grundrechte", in: *Ernst-Wolfgang Böckenförde / Robert Spaemann* (Hrsg.), Menschenrechte und Menschenwürde. Historische Voraussetzungen – säkulare Gestalt – christliches Verständnis, Stuttgart 1987, S. 43-73.

15 *Wolfgang Fikentscher*, Die heutige Bedeutung..., a.a.O., (Fn. 14), S. 60.

16 *Ludger Kühnhardt*, Die Universalität der Menschenrechte. Studie zur ideengeschichtlichen Bestimmung eines politischen Schlüsselbegriffs, München 1987, S. 81.

zur Folge, dass sie, wenn überhaupt, dann nur als Trittbrettfahrer „westlicher Wertvorstellungen“ an Menschenrechten teilhaben können. Die Universalität der Menschenrechte erweist sich dann aber entweder als von vornherein illusionär, oder sie wird mit dem globalen Durchsetzungsanspruch einer bestimmten Religion oder Kultur vermischt und gerät damit zu einer Kategorie imperialistischer Zivilisationsmission. Die erstere Konsequenz zieht Picht, für den „die Utopie einer globalen Menschenrechtsordnung nur als leerer Wahn betrachtet werden“ kann.[17] Die zweite Möglichkeit klingt bei Fikentscher an, wenn er mit spitzer Ironie vermerkt, dass „die meist säkular gesonnenen 'westlichen' Reformer“ in den Ländern der Dritten Welt *nolens volens* christliche Werte propagieren: „Unwissend betreiben sie mit ihren politischen Bestrebungen christliche Mission.“[18]

Gewiss sind Menschenrechte nicht in einem kulturellen, philosophischen und religiösen Vakuum entstanden, sondern mit geistig-kulturellen Strömungen in Christentum, hellenistischer Philosophie, Renaissance und Aufklärung vielfältig verwoben. Der Aufweis solcher historischer und ideengeschichtlicher Bezüge darf allerdings nicht zu dem Kurzschluss führen, die Idee der Menschenrechte sei gleichsam im kulturgenetischen Potential der abendländischen Tradition von Anfang an grundgelegt und deshalb substantiell und exklusiv an den Horizont westlicher Kultur gebunden. Gegen eine solche „kulturessentialistische“ Sicht sollte man sich klarmachen, dass das Aufspüren ideengeschichtlicher Motive, die in der einen oder anderen Weise in die Formulierung von Menschenrechten eingegangen sind, stets *von heute aus,* d.h. *im Rückblick* geschieht. Im Blick zurück in die Geschichte aber werden wir allzu leicht zu „Hegelianern“, die allenthalben Kontinuitäten und Linien zur Moderne hin entdecken und den Fahrplan der Geschichte bis in die Urquellen zurück verfolgen. So entsteht dann der Eindruck, die moderne Demokratie habe in der Athener Volksversammlung genauso ihren Vorläufer wie die modernen Grundrechtsgarantien in der englischen *Magna Charta* von 1215.

Gegen eine derart „hegelianisierende“ Geschichtsbetrachtung gilt es, immer wieder an die Kontingenz der Geschichte zu erinnern, die sich nicht gleichsam naturwüchsig als Entfaltungsprozess kultureller Potentiale vollzieht, sondern auch ganz anders hätte verlaufen können. Diese Kontingenz zu vergegenwärtigen, wäre zugleich ein erster Schritt zur Überwindung kulturessentialistischer Vereinnahmungen der Menschenrechte bzw. positiv ausgedrückt: zur Offenheit für mögliche alternative Wege zur Anerkennung der Menschenrechte.

---

17 *Georg Picht,* Zum geistesgeschichtlichen Hintergrund…, a.a.O., (Fn. 13), S. 127.

18 *Wolfgang Fikentscher,* Die heutige Bedeutung…, a.a.O., (Fn. 14), S. 64.

Außerdem dürfen neben den Elementen historischer Kontinuität die Aspekte von Diskontinuität nicht aus dem Blick geraten. Auch im Westen mussten (und müssen!) Menschenrechte *erkämpft* werden; sie sind den westlichen Gesellschaften nicht wie eine reife Frucht in den Schoß gefallen, sondern wurden gegen erbitterte Widerstände durchgesetzt.[19] Bemerkenswert ist, dass zu den Gegnern menschenrechtlicher Freiheiten lange Zeit auch die christlichen Kirchen zählten, die sich – abgesehen von einigen Freikirchen – erst spät zu einer Anerkennung der Menschenrechte durchgerungen haben. Nachdem die römischen Päpste die Menschenrechte im allgemeinen und die Religionsfreiheit im besonderen im 19. Jahrhundert wiederholt kompromisslos abgelehnt hatten, zeichnete sich erst im 20. Jahrhundert in der katholischen Kirche ein allmählicher Wandel ab, der schließlich zur offiziellen Anerkennung von Menschenrechten und Religionsfreiheit auf dem Zweiten Vatikanischen Konzil führte.[20] Die Tatsache, dass mit den Kirchen gerade die berufenen Vertreter der abendländisch-christlichen Kultur sich lange Zeit der Anerkennung der Menschenrechte verweigerten, ist ein Indiz dafür, dass Menschenrechte auch im Westen nicht von vornherein als jene „self-evident truths" gegolten haben, als die sie in der Amerikanischen Unabhängigkeitserklärung behauptet werden.

Für die praktische Durchsetzung der Menschenrechte ist gewiss von Vorteil, wenn die christlichen Kirchen inzwischen im Ethos der Menschenrechte heute ein eigenes ethisches Anliegen in neuer Gestalt wiederentdecken und ihr Engagement für die Wahrung von Würde und Recht des Menschen aus ihrem christlichen Auftrag her begreifen und begründen.[21] Eine solche „Aneignung" der Menschenrechtsidee darf aber nicht zu deren einseitiger Vereinnahmung zu exklusiv „christlichen Werten" führen, wie dies etwa in den zitierten Aussagen von Picht und Fikentscher anklingt. Im Bemühen, eine Brücke zwischen Tradition und Moderne zu schlagen, darf das Bewusstsein dafür nicht verloren gehen, dass Menschenrechte nicht nur von Christen, sondern oft auch von erklärten Nicht-Christen erkämpft worden sind, und zwar nicht nur mit Billigung, sondern vielfach gerade auch gegen die ausdrückliche Missbilligung der Kirchen.

---

19 Vgl. *Dieter Senghaas*, Wohin driftet die Welt? Über die Zukunft friedlicher Koexistenz, Frankfurt a.M. 1994, S. 112: „Die Rechtsstaatlichkeit oder die von einzelnen einklagbaren Menschenrechte sind westliche Errungenschaften, die in langwierigen politischen Konflikten während des Modernisierungsprozesses in Europa erkämpft wurden. Sie sind also keineswegs das eherne Erbe einer ursprünglichen kulturgenetischen Ausstattung Europas."

20 Näheres bei *Konrad Hilpert*, Die Menschenrechte. Geschichte – Theologie – Aktualität, Düsseldorf 1991, S. 137 ff.

21 Ibidem, S. 161.

Erst die Vergegenwärtigung nicht nur der Kontinuitäten, sondern auch der geschichtlichen Brüche und Umbrüche schafft die Voraussetzung dafür, dass die Aneignung der Menschenrechte durch die christlichen Kirchen als das Ergebnis einer komplizierten „Lerngeschichte" begreifbar wird.[22] Und erst in der selbstkritischen Offenlegung dieser Lerngeschichte entsteht zugleich die Offenheit für mögliche neue Lernerfahrungen. Diese prinzipielle Offenheit aber ist die Voraussetzung für ein ernsthaftes Menschenrechtsgespräch mit Angehörigen anderer religiöser oder weltanschaulicher Überzeugung, die ihre eigenen – vielleicht ähnlichen, vielleicht aber auch anderen – Lernerfahrungen im Umgang mit Menschenrechten einbringen können.

Gegen eine vorschnell-harmonisierende Integration der Menschenrechtsidee in das Gesamt der westlichen Kultur und Geschichte spricht schließlich auch die Tatsache, dass Menschenrechte erst in der *Moderne* zum Durchbruch gelangt sind. Und zwar geschah dies zu einem Zeitpunkt, als die religiös-kulturelle Zentrierung der europäischen Gesellschaften in eine Krise geraten war. In der Krise der traditionellen normativen Ordnungen und den daraus resultierenden Bedrohungen der Humanität bestand zugleich die Chance, dass die sittliche Verantwortung des Menschen als innerer Grund aller ethischen und rechtlichen Normen in neuer Weise zu Bewusstsein kam. Man kann diesen Prozess der Innewerdung menschlicher Mündigkeit als „Aufklärung" bezeichnen. Ohne eine so verstandene Aufklärung sind universale Menschenrechte als politisch-rechtlicher Freiheitsanspruch eines jeden Menschen undenkbar.

Es wäre indessen verfehlt, den Begriff der Aufklärung auf eine bestimmte Epoche der europäischen Geschichte – auf das „siècle des lumières" – zu verkürzen, generell mit der westlich-modernen Zivilisation gleichzusetzen oder gar mit bestimmten westlichen Philosophien abschließend zu identifizieren. Die Vereinnahmung der Menschenrechte in eine auf diese Weise verdinglichte Vorstellung westlich-moderner „Aufklärung" wäre für den menschenrechtlichen Universalismus um nichts weniger problematisch als ihre Reduzierung auf einen partikularen Kanon „abendländischer Werte". Außerdem geraten die Begriffe von „europäischer Aufklärung" und „westlicher Moderne" in solch verdinglichter Gestalt entweder zum Programm einer imperialistischen Zivilisationsmission oder zu Ausgrenzungskategorien, unter Berufung auf die Menschen nicht-westlicher Herkunft – insbesondere Muslime – pauschal als „unaufgeklärt" diskreditiert und von der Mitgestaltung der modernen multikulturellen Gesellschaft ausgeschlossen werden könnten.[23] In aggressiver Form zeigt sich eine

22 Ibidem, S. 161 f.

23 Vgl. *Heiner Bielefeldt,* Das Islambild in Deutschland. Zum öffentlichen Umgang mit der Angst vor dem Islam, Berlin 2007.

solche Ausgrenzung bei Hans Ebeling, wenn er alle „religiös grundierten ‚Kulturen‘“ summarisch als „prämodern“ bezeichnet[24] und gegen den nach seiner Meinung insbesondere von Seiten des Islams drohenden Fundamentalismus eine westliche „Aufklärung“ mobilisiert, die nicht nur von vornherein eurozentrisch definiert, sondern zugleich auch mit militärischen Konnotationen aufgeladen wird. Ebelings Polemik gegen den Multikulturalismus kulminiert in der Forderung, „dass heute die Aufklärung eine Funktion übernehmen muss, die spätestens seit Karl Martell und der Schlacht zwischen Tours und Poitiers (732) auf der Länge eines nicht unbedeutenden Jahrtausends gerade das Christentum wahrgenommen hatte“.[25]

Eine solche Verdinglichung des Aufklärungsbegriffs zu einer quasi-kulturalistischen Kategorie wäre indessen letztlich das Ende von Aufklärung, sofern man darunter den Anspruch rückhaltloser und beständiger Selbstkritik, verbunden mit der Bereitschaft zu kommunikativer Auseinandersetzung versteht. Menschenrechte stellen demgegenüber den Versuch dar, den religiösen, weltanschaulichen und kulturellen Pluralismus der modernen Gesellschaft dadurch „aufklärerisch“ zu bewältigen, dass sie ihn um der mündigen Verantwortung und Würde des Menschen willen politisch-rechtlich anerkennen und schützen. In dieser Weise innerlich auf den Pluralismus als Ausdruck menschlicher Würde und Freiheit bezogen, sind Menschenrechte selbst mit einer Vielzahl philosophischer und weltanschaulicher Letztdeutungen vereinbar, einschließlich solcher Deutungen, die sich aus religiösen Traditionen speisen. In dieser Perspektive aber besteht keine Rechtfertigung dafür, die legitimen Interpretationen von Menschenrechte von vornherein auf die Religionen und Philosophien europäischen Ursprungs zu beschränken, weil nur sie angeblich zur Aufklärung fähig seien. Im Gegenteil: Die Möglichkeit, in Menschenrechten humane Anliegen der eigenen Tradition in moderner Gestalt wiederzuerkennen und zur „Aufklärung“ der Tradition fruchtbar zu machen, kann – auch um der Universalität der Menschenrechte willen – kein Privileg des *Westens* sein.

D. Islamistische Vereinnahmungen der Menschenrechte

Gegen die „westlich“ verstandenen Menschenrechte werden seit einigen Jahrzehnten alternative Menschenrechtskonzeptionen zur Geltung gebracht, die sich auf „nicht-westliche“ kulturelle oder religiöse Quellen berufen. Paradigmatisch dafür stehen einige „islamische Menschenrechtserklärungen“ muslimischer Autoren oder islamischer Institutionen. Da auch sie in der Regel einen uni-

24 *Hans Ebeling*, Der multikulturelle Traum. Von der Subversion des Rechts und der Moral, Hamburg 1994, S. 68.

25 Ibidem, S. 75.

versalen Geltungsanspruch erheben, spiegeln sie die kulturimperialistischen Tendenzen, wie sie sich aus einer Okzidentalisierung der Menschenrechtsbegriffe ergeben können, unter anderen Vorzeichen – und oft auch verschärft – wider. So betont Abūl l-Aʿlā al-Maudūdī, ein Vierteljahrhundert nach seinem Tode längst zum Klassiker des Islamismus avanciert, in seinem Buch *Human Rights in Islam*: "The people in the West have the habit of attributing every good thing to themselves and try to prove that it is because of them that the world got this blessing [...]".[26] Gegen die, wie er meint, primär europäisch geprägten internationalen Menschenrechtsnormen setzt Abūl l-Aʿlā al-Maudūdī eine exklusiv „islamische" Menschenrechtskonzeption, die im Ergebnis allerdings gewiss nicht weniger essentialistisch gehalten ist als die von ihm kritisierten Ideologen des Westens. Abūl l-Aʿlā al-Maudūdī sieht die Menschenrechte sowohl als Konzept als auch in ihren einzelnen Verbürgungen unmittelbar in den Quellen des Islams – also in Koran und Sunna – begründet. Aus dem göttlichen Ursprung der Menschenrechte schließt Abūl l-Aʿlā al-Maudūdī auf deren zeitlose Gültigkeit und Unveränderlichkeit: „The rights which have been sanctioned by God are permanent, perpetual and eternal. They are not subject to any alterations or modifications, and there is no scope for any change or abrogation."[27]

Abūl l-Aʿlā al-Maudūdī führt eine Reihe einzelner Rechte auf – die Rechte auf Leben, Sicherheit, individuelle Freiheit, Gerechtigkeit, die Gleichheit der Menschen usw. –, die er jeweils mit Belegstellen aus dem Koran theologisch untermauert. Mit der koranischen Begründung der Menschenrechte verbindet er den Anspruch, dass der Islam auch in historischer Perspektive die Errungenschaft der Menschenrechte für sich reklamieren kann. Während der Westen Menschenrechte nicht vor dem 17. Jahrhundert gekannt habe,[28] seien sie im Islam von Anfang an grundgelegt und praktiziert worden.

Die Behauptung, die Menschenrechte seien erstmals im Islam formuliert worden, hat auch Eingang in einige halb-offizielle Menschenrechtsdokumente islamischer Konferenzen und Organisationen gefunden. So heißt es in den Abschlussthesen eines im Dezember 1980 in Kuwait durchgeführten Seminars über Menschenrechte im Islam:

> "Islam was the first to recognise basic human rights and almost 14 centuries ago it set up guarantees and safeguards that have only recently been incorporated in universal declarations of human rights."[29]

---

26 *Abul Aʿla al-Maududi* [Abūl l-Aʿlā al-Maudūdī], Human Rights in Islam, Leicester 1976, S. 13.

27 Ibidem, S. 15.

28 Ibidem, S. 13.

29 Human Rights in Islam. Report of a Seminar held in Kuwait, December 1980, veröffentlicht von der Internationalen Juristenkommission 1982, S. 9.

Markanter noch beginnt die im Jahre 1981 vom Islamrat für Europa – einer nicht-staatlichen islamischen Organisation – vorgelegte *Allgemeine Islamische Menschenrechtserklärung* mit den Worten:

> „Vor vierzehn Jahrhunderten legte der Islam die ‚Menschenrecht' umfassend und tiefgründend als Gesetz fest."[30]

Wie die Vereinnahmung der Menschenrechte in einen Kanon „westlicher Werte" im Ergebnis auf die Relativierung des menschenrechtlichen Universalismus oder seine Verkehrung in imperialistische europäische Zivilisationsmission hinausläuft, so nimmt analog auch der islamistisch vereinnahmte Menschenrechtsbegriff entweder partikularistische oder imperialistische Züge an. Dies zeigt sich in der Verquickung menschenrechtlicher und islamrechtlicher Begriffe, wie sie für die Menschenrechtserklärung des Islamrats von 1981 charakteristisch ist.[31] Indem sich die Erklärung – jedenfalls in ihrer arabischen Fassung – wiederholt auf die *šarīʿa*, die islamische *umma* und die islamische Armensteuer (*zakāt*) bezieht, werden die Menschenrechte einseitig „islamisiert". Von der menschenrechtlichen Universalität kann folglich allenfalls insofern noch die Rede sein, als auch die göttliche Botschaft des Islams an die gesamte Menschheit gerichtet ist.

Deutlicher noch als in der Erklärung des Islamrats von 1981 kommt die Islamisierung menschenrechtlicher Begriffe im Entwurf einer *Erklärung der Menschenrechte im Islam* zum Ausdruck, der von den Außenministern der OIC im August 1990 in Kairo angenommen wurde.[32] Sowohl die Erklärung im Ganzen als auch die einzelnen Rechte stehen unter dem Vorbehalt, dass sie mit der *šarīʿa* übereinstimmen müssen. Artikel 24 bestimmt in diesem Sinne: „Alle Rechte und Freiheiten, die in dieser Erklärung genannt werden, unterstehen der islamischen *šarīʿa*." Und der abschließende Artikel 25 bekräftigt noch einmal:

> „Die islamische *šarīʿa* ist die einzige zuständige Quelle für die Auslegung oder Erklärung jedes einzelnen Artikels dieser Erklärung."

Angesichts des nachdrücklich behaupteten Vorrangs der *šarīʿa* können Menschenrechte in ihrer Eigenstruktur – geschweige denn in ihrem kritischen

---

30 Zitiert nach der Übersetzung von *Martin Forstner*, in: CIBEDO-Dokumentation Nr. 15/16 (Juni/September 1982), S. 20.

31 Zur Kritik an der Erklärung des Islamrats vgl. *Martin Forstner*, „Inhalt und Begründung der Allgemeinen Islamischen Menschenrechtserklärung", in: *Johannes Hoffmann* (Hrsg.), Begründung von Menschenrechten aus der Sicht unterschiedlicher Kulturen, Frankfurt a.M. 1991, S. 249-273. Vgl. Auch die Studie von *Ann Elizabeth Mayer*, Islam and Human Rights. Tradition and Politics, Boulder 1991.

32 In deutscher Übersetzung vorliegend in: Gewissen und Freiheit (Halbjahreszeitschrift der Internationalen Vereinigung zur Verteidigung und Förderung der Religionsfreiheit), Bd. 36 (1. Halbjahresband 1991), S. 93-98.

Anspruch – von vornherein nicht zur Geltung kommen. Im Gegenteil besteht eher der Eindruck, dass die islamische Menschenrechtserklärung von Kairo zur Rechtfertigung autoritärer Freiheitsbeschränkungen herhalten kann, wenn beispielsweise die Rechte auf Leben und auf körperliche Unversehrtheit (Artikel 2) oder auf Meinungsfreiheit (Artikel 22) Vorbehaltsklauseln zugunsten der *šarīʿa* enthalten.

Während Abūl l-Aʿlā al-Maudūdī in seinem Kapitel über die Gleichheit der Menschen bezeichnenderweise lediglich vier Diskriminierungsverbote auflistet – nämlich Hautfarbe, Rasse, Sprache und Nationalität, nicht aber Religionszugehörigkeit und Geschlecht![33] –, proklamiert die Kairoer Erklärung in Artikel 1 die gleiche Würde aller Menschen „ohne Ansehen von Rasse, Hautfarbe, Sprache, Geschlecht, politischer Einstellung, sozialem Status oder anderen Gründen". Auf diese weitreichende Gleichheitsvorstellung folgt jedoch der Hinweis: „Der wahrhafte Glaube ist die Garantie für das Erlangen solcher Würde auf dem Pfad zur menschlichen Vollkommenheit." Selbst wenn man – in wohlwollender Interpretation – davon ausgeht, dass die Gleichheit der Würde uneingeschränkt gelten soll, bleibt indes unklar, ob aus der gleichen Würde auch *gleiche Rechte* folgen. In Bezug auf das Geschlechterverhältnis wird jedenfalls die ungleiche Rollenverteilung und Rechtsstellung festgeschrieben, wenn es in Artikel 6 heißt:

> „a) Die Frau ist dem Mann an Würde gleich, sie hat Rechte und auch Pflichten; sie ist rechtsfähig und finanziell unabhängig, und sie hat das Recht, ihren Namen und ihre Abstammung beizubehalten.
>
> b) Der Ehemann ist für den Unterhalt und das Wohl der Familie verantwortlich."

Prägnant zeigt sich der Widerspruch zu den Menschenrechtsstandards der Vereinten Nationen bei Artikel 10, der anstelle eines allgemeinen Rechts auf Religionsfreiheit den Vorrang des Islams behauptet. Dort heißt es:

> „Der Islam ist die Religion der reinen Wesensart. Es ist verboten, irgendeine Art von Druck auf einen Menschen auszuüben oder seine Armut oder Unwissenheit auszunutzen, um ihn zu einer anderen Religion oder zum Atheismus zu bekehren."

Auch wenn in dieser Formulierung kein unmittelbares Verbot der Konversion vom Islam zu einer anderen Religion ausgesprochen ist, läuft der Artikel doch zumindest auf eine Ächtung jeder Missionstätigkeit unter Muslimen und damit auf eine Beschränkung der Religionsfreiheit hinaus. Die Kairoer Erklärung erweist sich damit als ein politisches Dokument, das die inhaltliche Kontinuität

---

33 Vgl. *Abūl l-Aʿlā al-Maudūdī*, Human Rights in Islam, a.a.O. (Fn. 26), S. 23.

mit den universalen Menschenrechtsstandards der Vereinten Nationen bewusst preisgibt.

Aus der Kairoer Erklärung von 1990, die als bloße Deklaration zunächst nicht auf völkerrechtliche Verbindlichkeit hin angelegt war, ist im Jahre 2005 – als erste menschenrechtliche Spezialkonvention der OIC – eine spezifisch Islamische Kinderrechtskonvention entstanden, die aufgrund ihrer autoritäre Interpretation des Kindeswohls mit der Kinderrechtskonvention der Vereinten Nationen völlig unvereinbar ist.

Der Anspruch auf eigenständige „islamische“ Menschenrechte klingt auch im europäischen islamischen Schrifttum immer wieder an. So bekennt sich etwa Murad Hofmann zu islamisch konzipierten Menschenrechten, von denen er zugleich betont, dass sie bei aller inhaltlichen Nähe mit den international anerkannten Menschenrechte doch „nicht voll mit den Menschenrechtspakten der Vereinten Nationen übereinstimmen“.[34] Worin die Differenzen konkret bestehen, wird nicht näher ausgeführt. Auch die *Islamische Charta*, die der Zentralrat der Muslime in Deutschland, einer der islamischen Spitzenvereinigungen, im Februar 2002 vorgelegt hat,[35] verbindet die Anerkennung der Menschenrechte in Artikel 13[36] mit einem doppelten – materialen und formalen – Vorbehalt. Zum einen bleibt es beschränkt auf einen nicht näher definierten „Kernbestand“ der Menschenrechte. Zum anderen wird die Menschenrechtserklärung mit dem Adjektiv „westlich“ versehen. Sofern dabei (wie man vermuten darf) die Allgemeine Menschenrechtserklärung der Vereinten Nationen von 1948 gemeint ist, legt deren Qualifikation als „westliches“ Dokument den Eindruck nahe, dass ihr Geltungsanspruch als für Muslime nicht unmittelbar verbindlich angesehen wird.

Auf der anderen Seite finden sich auch unter Muslimen sehr entschiedene Verteidiger des menschenrechtlichen Universalismus, die kurzschlüssige Verschmelzung der Menschenrechtsidee mit den religionsrechtlichen Quellen des Islams einer systematischen Kritik unterziehen.[37] Es wäre deshalb verfehlt, die hier genannten Dokumente als repräsentativ für den „islamischen Menschen-

---

34 *Murad Wilfried Hofmann,* Der Islam im 3. Jahrtausend. Eine Religion im Aufbruch, Kreuzlingen 2000, S. 104.

35 Zu beziehen ist die Islamische Charta beim Zentralrat der Muslime in Deutschland (ZMD, Postfach 12 24, D-52232 Eschweiler); sie ist auch im Internet verfügbar.

36 „Zwischen den im Koran verankerten, von Gott gewährten Individualrechten und dem Kernbestand der westlichen Menschenrechtserklärung besteht kein Widerspruch.“

37 Vgl. z.B. die Beiträge der muslimischen Diskussionspartner – insbesondere *Mohamed Talbi, Mohamed Charfi* und *Ali Merad* – in dem Band von *Johannes Schwartländer* (Hrsg.), Freiheit der Religion. Christentum und Islam unter dem Anspruch der Menschenrechte, Mainz 1993.

rechtsansatz“ zu betrachten, den es in solch monolithischer Gestalt – Gott sei Dank – genauso wenig gibt wie ein einheitlich „westliches“ Menschenrechtsverständnis.[38]

E. Menschenrechte als Kern eines interkulturellen „overlapping consensus“

Kulturalistische Deutungen stellen die derzeit am stärksten verbreitete Variante des Relativierung der Menschenrechte dar. Zum Teil laufen sie auf eine direkte Preisgabe des menschenrechtlichen Universalismus hinaus, zum Teil verknüpfen sie die Menschenrechte derart mit einem kulturellen oder religiösen Erbanspruch, dass die universale Geltung der Menschenrechte unter der Hand zur Zumutung einer kulturellen oder religiösen Konversion (z.B. zu „westlichen Werten“ oder zu islamischen Normen) gerät. Die Alternative zur kulturalistischen Vereinnahmung besteht darin, die politisch-rechtliche Eigenstruktur der Menschenrechte ernst zu nehmen. Damit ist die Möglichkeit keineswegs ausgeschlossen, zwischen Menschenrechten einerseits und spezifischen religiös-weltanschaulichen bzw. kulturellen Perspektiven andererseits zu vermitteln.

Zur Beschreibung dieser Vermittlung bietet sich der Begriff des „overlapping consensus“ an, den John Rawls geprägt hat.[39] Rawls hat diesen Begriff freilich für eine etwas anders gelagerte Debatte eingeführt, nämlich um die Rolle der leitenden politischen Gerechtigkeitsvorstellung in einer modernen liberalen Gesellschaft zu klären, in der unterschiedliche Weltanschauungen nebeneinander oder auch gegeneinander stehen. Die Rawlsschen Überlegungen zur politischen Gerechtigkeit als Zentrum eines *overlapping consensus* in der pluralistischen Gesellschaft lassen sich indessen auch für das interkulturelle Verständnis universaler Menschenrechte fruchtbar machen. Drei Aspekte möchte ich in freiem Anschluß an Rawls herausheben: (I) den eigenständigen kritischen Anspruch der Menschenrechte, (II) ihre begrenzte normative Reichweite als politisch-rechtliches Konzept und (III) die Möglichkeit, sie über die politisch-rechtliche Ebene hinaus umfassender auszudeuten.

I. Der eigenständigen kritischen Anspruch der Menschenrechte

Rawls betont, dass die von ihm rekonstruierte politische Gerechtigkeitsvorstellung mehr als ein bloßer Kompromiss zwischen sämtlichen in der Gesellschaft vorhandenen Wertorientierungen sein soll. Die liberalen Prinzipien politischer Gerechtigkeit bringen nämlich einen *eigenständigen normativen An-*

---

38 Zur Vielfalt islamischer Begründungsansätze für Menschenrechte und Demokratie vgl. grundsätzlich: *Gudrun Krämer*, Gottesstaat als Republik. Reflexionen zeitgenössischer Muslime zu Islam, Menschenrechten und Demokratie, Baden-Baden 1999.

39 Vgl. *John Rawls*, Political Liberalism, New York 1993, S. 133 ff.

spruch zum Ausdruck, der mit autoritären Ideologien oder konservativen Wertorientierungen in der Gesellschaft durchaus konflikthaft zusammenstoßen kann und in diesem Fall *Vorrang* beansprucht. Der Begriff des „overlapping consensus" ist daher nicht ein deskriptiver, sondern ein normativer Begriff. Er bezeichnet nicht einen faktischen Konsens, sondern die normative Zielvorstellung eines Konsenses, der zwar eine Vielfalt weltanschaulicher Überzeugungen freisetzt, gleichzeitig aber auch Grenzen der Toleranz markiert.[40]

Analog gilt auch für die Menschenrechte, dass sie als universale Freiheitsrechte zu manchen autoritären Bestandteilen religiöser, weltanschaulicher und kultureller Traditionen in Widerspruch stehen. Menschenrechte enthalten mithin eine „kulturkritische" Komponente, durch die sie zum Ferment gesellschaftlichen und kulturellen Wandels werden können. Um es mit Walter Kälin zu sagen: „Menschenrechte sind auf Emanzipation angelegt, sie sind immer auch Stachel im Fleisch einer Kultur, welcher die eigenen Traditionen und Gewohnheiten angenehm geworden sind."[41]

Die Anerkennung der Menschenrechte durch die katholische Kirche ging dementsprechend einher mit einer durchgreifenden Revision traditioneller kirchlicher Positionen zu Fragen der Religionsfreiheit und des Verhältnisses von Staat und Kirche. Auch im islamischen Denken können Menschenrechte ohne Bereitschaft zu Selbstkritik und politisch-rechtlichen Reformen etwa im Familienrecht auf längere Sicht keine Heimat finden. Der in der Idee des menschenrechtlichen Universalismus intendierte Konsens meint deshalb nicht lediglich die Schnittmenge der weltweit faktisch vorhandenen kulturellen Wertorientierungen,[42] sondern beinhaltet die *normative Zumutung* der wechselseitigen Anerkennung von Menschen unterschiedlicher Orientierung und Lebensweise auf der Grundlage gleicher Freiheit und gleichberechtigter Partizipation. Der menschenrechtliche *overlapping consensus* ist folglich kein interkultureller Minimalkonsens, sondern impliziert umgekehrt einen kritischen Maßstab moderner Interkulturalität.[43]

Die von Menschenrechten freigesetzte Interkulturalität ist kein vorbehaltloser Multikulturalismus, der gegebene Lebensformen oder Wertorientierungen allein

---

40 Ausgeschlossen aus dem Rawlsschen "overlapping consensus" sind in seiner Terminologie "unreasonable doctrines". Vgl. ibidem, S. 58 ff.

41 *Walter Kälin,* „Menschenrechte in der kulturellen Vielfalt", in: *Stefan Batzli u.a.* (Hrsg.), Menschenbilder, Menschenrechte. Islam und Okzident: Kulturen im Konflikt, Zürich 1994, S. 17 ff. (20).

42 So aber der Ansatz von *Alison Dundes Renteln,* International Human Rights. Universalism Versus Relativism, Newbury Park u.a. 1990.

43 Vgl. *Heiner Bielefeldt,* Menschenrechte in der Einwanderungsgesellschaft. Plädoyer für einen aufgeklärten Multikulturalismus, Bielefeld 2007.

schon deshalb anerkennt, weil sie als Bestandteile kultureller Tradition firmieren. Normative Prämisse des Menschenrechtsdenkens ist vielmehr die Einsicht, dass *unter den Bedingungen der Moderne* die Pluralität kultureller Lebensformen und religiöser und weltanschaulicher Orientierungen nur dann produktiv gestaltet werden kann, wenn Menschen einander – auch in ihrer Differenz – dadurch anerkennen, dass sie einander gleiche Freiheit und gleichberechtigte Mitwirkung zuerkennen. Dieser spezifisch moderne politisch-rechtliche Achtungsanspruch wiederum kann nur zum Tragen kommen, wenn er zugleich kritisch auf vorgegebene Traditionen zurückwirkt, die sich den Ideen mündiger Selbst- und Mitverantwortung auf Dauer nicht verweigern können.

II. Begrenzte normative Reichweite als politisch-rechtliches Konzept der Menschenrechte

Der „kulturkritische" Anspruch der Menschenrechte ist freilich in seiner Reichweite begrenzt, weil Menschenrechte keine umfassende Weltanschauung bilden. Auch dies ist ein Aspekt, der sich von der Rawlsschen Idee des *overlapping consensus* übernehmen lässt. Rawls betont nämlich, daß sich die von ihm rekonstruierte liberale Gerechtigkeitsvorstellung auf die „basic structure of society" konzentriert[44] und keineswegs eine umfassende gleichsam weltanschauliche Orientierung bieten will. In ihrer Differenz zu den miteinander konkurrierenden „comprehensive doctrines" der weltanschaulich pluralistischen Gesellschaft soll die politische Gerechtigkeit selbst gerade nicht als umfassende Doktrin, sondern als verbindliche Rahmenordnung fungieren.[45]

Entsprechendes gilt für Menschenrechte, die – wie bereits zuvor dargestellt wurde – als politisch-rechtliches Konzept in ihrer normativen Reichweite von vornherein begrenzt sind. Menschenrechte geben keine Antwort auf die Frage nach dem Sinn menschlichen Lebens, Leidens und Sterbens. Sie enthalten keine umfassenden Weisungen für die rechte Lebensführung als Individuum und in der Gemeinschaft. Sie bieten keine Riten und Symbole, durch die Menschen über die politisch-rechtliche Gleichberechtigung hinaus einander Achtung bezeugen und Verbundenheit oder auch Differenz zum Ausdruck bringen können. Menschenrechte stehen deshalb nicht unmittelbar in Konkurrenz zu umfassenden religiösen bzw. weltanschaulichen Überzeugungen oder kulturellen Lebensformen, auch wenn sie mit ihrem emanzipatorischen Anspruch durchaus kritisch auf diese zurückwirken können.

Das Menschenrechtsdenken konzentriert sich zunächst auf politisch-rechtliche Standards einschließlich des darin sich ausdrückenden modernen politischen

---

44 Vgl. *John Rawls,* Political Liberalism, a.a.O. (Fn. 39), S. 11 u.ö.
45 Ibidem, S. 154 ff.

Freiheitsethos. In dieser normativen Begrenzung geben Menschenrechte einer Vielfalt religiöser und weltanschaulicher Überzeugungen bzw. kultureller Lebensformen Raum. Menschenrechte wollen weder ein umfassendes Ethos[46] oder eine globale Einheitskultur durchsetzen noch gar eine für die gesamte Menschheit verbindliche Weltanschauung oder „Zivilreligion" zustandebringen. Wer Menschenrechte zu einer Art moderner Humanitätsreligion stilisiert, unterminiert durch solche Überziehung ihren spezifisch politisch-rechtlichen Geltungsanspruch und verbaut zugleich die Chancen ihrer faktischen Akzeptanz. Der in den Menschenrechten intendierte *overlapping consensus* verlangt auch keine umfassende Ökumene der Religionen, Weltanschauungen und Kulturen. Vielmehr steht es den Menschen frei, ihre individuelle und gemeinschaftliche Identität auch *gegeneinander* zu bestimmen und Grenzen wechselseitigen Verstehens zuzugestehen, solange die politisch-rechtliche Gleichberechtigung gewahrt bleibt.

III. Möglichkeit die Menschenrechte über die politisch-rechtliche Ebene hinaus umfassender auszudeuten

Auch wenn das Menschenrechtsdenken sich auf politisch-rechtliche Standards konzentriert, ist es freilich offen für weitergehende Ausdeutungen. Wie die von Rawls eruierten Gerechtigkeitsprinzipien über ihre politisch-rechtliche Orientierungsfunktion hinaus im Rahmen unterschiedlicher „comprehensive doctrines" interpretiert werden können (ohne selbst eine „comprehensive doctrine" darzustellen), so besteht auch hinsichtlich der Menschenrechte die Möglichkeit, sie von verschiedenen religiösen, philosophischen oder kulturellen Perspektiven aus zu verstehen und zu vertiefen.

Eine solche Vertiefung ist nicht nur möglich, sondern sinnvoll, sofern sie dazu verhilft, über die unerlässliche Ebene politischer Pragmatik und positiv-rechtlicher Regelung hinaus als humanes Sinnangebot umfassend zu explizieren und damit die Attraktivität des Menschenrechtskonzepts zu erhöhen. Vor allem die den Menschenrechten normativ zugrundeliegende Idee der unantastbaren Menschenwürde bietet Anknüpfungsmöglichkeiten für eine Beheimatung der Menschenrechte in unterschiedlichen religiösen, weltanschaulichen und kulturellen Traditionen.[47]

---

[46] In dieser Hinsicht bleiben Menschenrechte hinter dem von Hans Küng unternommenen Versuch zur Formulierung eines interreligiös und interkulturell konsensfähigen Weltethos zurück. Vgl. *Hans Küng,* Projekt Weltethos, 3. Auflage, München / Zürich 1991. Menschenrechte gehen andererseits aber über die Erklärung ethischer Prinzipien hinaus, insofern sie auf die Etablierung politisch-rechtlicher Durchsetzungsinstrumente zielen.

[47] Vgl. eine im Rahmen der UNESCO erstellte Textsammlung, die Affinitäten zwischen Menschenrechten und unterschiedlichen Traditionen belegen will: *UNESCO,* Le droit

Um der Universalität der Menschenrechte willen darf ihre umfassende Ausdeutung allerdings nicht in Vereinnahmung umschlagen. Es kann deshalb nicht darum gehen, die Struktur moderner Menschenrechte unmittelbar in der Bibel, im Koran, in den heiligen Schriften der Hindus, in den Lehren des Konfuzius oder in den Erzählungen afrikanischer Völker aufzuspüren und somit Menschenrechten ein je eigenes religiöses bzw. kulturelles Fundament zu verschaffen. Sonst droht die Idee der Menschenrechte in eine Vielzahl religiös, weltanschaulich oder kulturell begründeter Konzepte auseinander zu brechen, die außer dem gemeinsamen Namen nichts mehr verbindet. Deshalb gilt, was oben über die Möglichkeiten der Inkulturation von Menschenrechten in die „westliche Tradition" gesagt wurde, analog auch für andere Traditionen – einschließlich eines islamischen Zugangs zu den Menschenrechten: Ein Brückenschlag zur Tradition kann nur geschehen als *rückblickende kritische Vermittlung vom hermeneutischen Ort der Moderne aus.*[48] Auf diese Weise lassen sich in unterschiedlichen Traditionen humanitäre Haftpunkte für menschenrechtliches Denken finden, die aber gerade nicht kurzschlüssig zu exklusiven „Wurzeln" oder Quellen der Menschenrechte stilisiert werden können.

d'étre un homme. Recueil de textes preparé sous la direction de Jeanne Hersch, Paris: 1968.

48 Vgl. hierzu bspw. *Assem Hefny*, „Hermeneutik, Koraninterpretation und Menschenrechte", in: *Hatem Elliesie* (Hrsg./Editor), Beiträge zum Islamischen Recht VII, Islam und Menschenrechte (Islam and Human Rights / الإسلام وحقوق الإنسان), Frankfurt a.M. 2010, Seiten 73-97.

MENSCHENRECHTSSITUATIONEN IN AUSGEWÄHLTEN ISLAMISCH GEPRÄGTEN REGIONEN UND LÄNDERN

HUMAN RIGHTS SITUATIONS IN SELECTED PREDOMINANTELY ISLAMIC REGIONS AND COUNTRIES

اوضاع حقوق الإنسان
في عدد من الدول والمناطق ذات الطابع الإسلامي

Islam und Menschenrechte (Islam and Human Rights / الإسلام وحقوق الإنسان)
Hatem Elliesie (Hrsg./Editor), © Peter Lang Verlag: Frankfurt a.M. 2010, S. 121-414

Islam and Human Rights in the Constitutions of African States: Agenda for Good Governance*

Mashood Baderin, London

A. Introduction

As the principles of constitutionalism and rule of law are being promoted globally, both have, consequently, become well recognised fundamental elements of democratic governance in many African countries today.[1] Conventionally, constitutionalism and rule of law are related doctrines that are generally perceived as modern secular principles for the promotion of good governance, supremacy of law, guarantee of human rights, equality and non-discrimination in governance. Apart from different international cooperative efforts in that regard, national constitutions have become important domestic instruments for providing for human rights guarantees and principles of good governance within the domestic law of modern nation states. Thus, in the last two decades or more, "Africa has witnessed an upsurge in the demand for constitution-based governance that broadly reflects, in terms of process and outcome, the will of the people"[2] and manifests, in terms of aspiration, the peoples' desire for good governance in Africa. Laudably, in line with modern global constitutional practices, the constitutions of many African states today accommodate principles of rule of law and constitutional rights provisions similar to the substantive rights guaranteed under the Universal Declaration of Human Rights of 1948,[3] all with the ultimate objective of fostering good governance in the respective states and in Africa generally.

---

* I thank Taymour Harding for providing me with research assistance on this chapter. Responsibility for all views expressed in the chapter are, however, wholly mine.

1 See e.g. *Abdullahi Ahmed An-Na'im* (Ed.), Human Rights under African Constitutions: Realizing the Promise for Ourselves, Philadelphia 2003; *Hassen. Ebrahim / Kayode Fayemi / Stephanie Loomis,* Promoting Constitutionalism and Democracy in Commonwealth Africa [A Background Paper accompanying Commonwealth Human Rights Initiative's Recommendation to the Commonwealth Head of Governments Meeting 1999], http://www.humanrightsinitiative.org/publications/const/constitutionalism_boolet_1999.pdf (accessed on 6 November 2009); *John Hatchard / Muna Ndulo / Peter Slinn,* Comparative Constitutionalism and Good Governance in the Commonwealth: An Eastern and Southern African Perspective, Cambridge 2004.

2 *Hassen Ebrahim / Kayode Fayemi / Stephanie Loomis,* Promoting Constitutionalism..., supra, footnote 1, on p. 8.

3 Adopted by the UN General Assembly on 10 December 1948, G.A. Res. 217A (III), U.N. Doc A/810 on 71.

Islam und Menschenrechte (Islam and Human Rights / الإسلام وحقوق الإنسان)
Hatem Elliesie (Hrsg./Editor), © Peter Lang Verlag: Frankfurt a.M. 2010, S. 123-153

Within the ongoing constitutional development and aspiration for good governance in Africa, many African states also provide a role for Islam and/or Islamic Law and institutions, in one form or another, in their modern constitutions. Currently, there are more than 10 African states in this category as indicated below in the table provided in the second part of this chapter. In many cases, such provisions have apparently been incorporated into the constitutions of the relevant African states through legitimate constitutional processes in the respective states. This is not unique to African states, but reflects the constitutional dispensation of other Muslim states in other parts of the world, especially the Middle East. This practice of providing a role for Islam and/or Islamic Law and institutions in the modern constitutions of different Muslim states, has been described as "Islamic theocratic constitutionalism"[4] or "constitutional Islamization",[5] and considered by some commentators as a challenge to the perceived secular characteristics of conventional global constitutionalism.[6]

This raises the question of how the doctrines of modern constitutionalism and rule of law (which are often perceived as strictly secular doctrines) can practically accommodate a constitutional role for Islamic principles (which are essentially religious in nature) as is currently reflected in some African states as well as in other parts of the Muslim world. It generates a complex discourse regarding what Abdullahi Ahmed An-Na'im has described as "the relationship between Islam, as an ancient and extremely diverse religious tradition, on the one hand, and constitutionalism as a modern secular doctrine of governance and rights, on the other."[7]

- How can this relationship be perceived?
- Does a constitutional role for Islam and/or Islamic Law and institutions inherently create an obstruction to the concepts of modern constitutionalism and rule of law in modern nation states or can such constitutional roles for Islamic principles serve as a possible means for promoting good governance, rule of law and the guarantee of human rights within the constitutional dispensation of modern nation states, particularly Muslim states in Africa?

---

4 *Larry Catá Backer*, "Theocratic Constitutionalism: An Introduction to a New Global Legal Ordering", in: Indiana Journal of Global Legal Studies, volume 16, no.1, pp. 85-172.

5 *Clark B. Lombardi / Nathan J. Brown*, "Do Constitutions requiring Adherence to Shari'a threaten Human Rights?: How Egypt's Constitutional Court reconciles Islamic Law with the liberal Rule of Law", in: American University International Law Review, volume 21, issue 3, pp. 379 et seqq. (on p. 381).

6 See e.g. *Larry Catá Backer*, Theocratic Constitutionalism..., supra, footnote 4.

7 *Abdullahi Ahmed An-Na'im*, African Constitutionalism and the Role of Islam, Philadelphia 2006, p. 8.

There are different points of view on these questions, as is usually the case with most complex discourses. For example, in their analysis of the constitutional provision on Islamic Law under the Egyptian constitution, Clark B. Lombardi and Nathan J. Brown identified two clearly opposing views in that regard. They observed notably that, on the one hand, there are those who "fear that constitutional Islamization clauses will hinder a country's ability to develop democratic governance structures, to conform to human rights norms, or to engage fully in global economy," while, on the other hand, there are also those who disagree with that view and argue to the contrary that "the trend towards constitutional Islamization is not, in itself, harmful."[8] As a matter of course, there are a variety of other grey views floating between these two opposing positions.

Within the context of the Egyptian Constitutional Court's interpretation of Article 2 of the Egyptian Constitution, which provides a major role for Islamic Law,[9] in relation to ensuring the human rights guarantees under the same constitution, Clark B. Lombardi and Nathan J. Brown have expressed the view that:

> "If a court has sufficient prestige and independence, it will have considerable flexibility to interpret and apply Islamic Law in a way that is consistent with its overarching constitutional philosophy. A progressive court can thus Islamize state law in a way that is consistent with democracy, international human rights and economic liberalism."[10]

This chapter concurs with that view and proposes further that apart from the positive role that the courts in relevant Muslim states can play in harmonising the relationship between Islam and modern constitutional objectives of human rights and good governance through progressive judicial interpretations, the constitutional role accorded Islam can also serve as a possible means for promoting good governance, rule of law and the guarantee of human rights within the overall constitutional dispensation of the relevant states. It is submitted that such provisions can be perceived as placing both a moral and legal responsibility on the political leadership to ensure good governance as required by Islamic Law and at the same time empowering the Muslim populace of the relevant states to constitutionally demand for good governance, rule of law and respect for human rights from the political leadership. Such prospects are achievable through what

---

8 *Clark B. Lombardi /Nathan J. Brown,* Do Constitutions requiring Adherence to Shari'a..., supra, footnote 5, pp. 379 et seqq. (on pp. 382-383).

9 Article 2 of the Egyptian Constitution provides that:
الإسلام دين الدولة، واللغة العربية لغتها الرسمية، ومبادئ الشريعة الإسلامية المصدر الرئيسى للتشريع.
("Islam is the religion of the state and Arabic its official language.
Principles of Islamic Law (*šarīʿa*) are the principal source of legislation.")

10 *Clark B. Lombardi /Nathan J. Brown,* Do Constitutions requiring Adherence to Shari'a..., supra, footnote 5, pp. 379 et seqq. (on p. 386).

I call the evolutional interpretations of Islamic Law and political theory as analysed later below. Thus, rather than construing it as an aberration or impediment to modern constitutionalism, this chapter asserts that the constitutional role of Islam can be utilised positively in conjunction with the human rights provisions in the constitutions of relevant African states to promote an agenda for good governance and rule of aw in Africa.

B. African Constitutions with combined Provisions on Islam and Human Rights

For a conceptual appreciation of the relevant constitutional provisions, I provide a list of African constitutions with combined provisions on Islam and Human Rights with summarised contents of the relevant sections in the table below, before proceeding to examine the questions of Islam and constitutionalism, historical and evolutional interpretations of Islamic Law, and Islam and good governance, respectively.

ALGERIA (1976 Constitution [as amended])	
Constitutional Provisions on Islam, Islamic Law and/or Islamic Institutions	**Constitutional Human Rights Provisions**
Preamble ("its identity is Islam", "being a land of Islam");	**Preamble** ("social justice, equity and freedom for all", "fundamental law which guarantees the individual and collective rights and liberties");
Section 2 ("Islam is the Religion of the State"); **Section 9** (Prohibits "practices contrary to Islamic ethics"); **Section 73** (The President shall "be Muslim"); **Section 76** (Presidential oath to "respect and glorify the Islamic religion"); **Section 171** (Creation of a "High Islamic Council"); **Section 178** ("Any Constitutional revision cannot infringe on Islam as the Religion of the State").	**Section 20** ("Right to a prior, fair and just compensation" in case of expropriation); **Section 22** (Prohibits "Abuse of Power"); **Section 27** ("Right of Self Determination" and prohibition of "any racial discrimination"); **Section 29-69** (Constitutional Bill of Rights); **Section 76** (President oath to "Protect the fundamental Human and Citizen's Rights and Liberties"); **Section 122** (Parliament to legislate on "fundamental Human Rights and Duties of the Individuals"); **Section 139** (Judiciary to protect Liberties and safeguard Fundamental Rights); **Section 151** ("Right for Defence recognized and guaranteed in penal Matters"); **Section 178** ("any Constitutional revision cannot infringe on Fundamental Liberties, and Citizen's Rights").

EGYPT (1971 Constitution [as amended])	
Constitutional Provisions on Islam, Islamic Law and/or Islamic Institutions	**Constitutional Human Rights Provisions**
Preamble ("in the name of Allāh and with His assistance", "acknowledgment of Allāh's right and His Heavenly Messages"); **Section 2** ("Islam is the Religion of the State and Arabic its official language. Principles of Islamic Law [*šarīʿa*] are the principal source of legislation"); **Section 11** ("without violation of the rules of Islamic Jurisprudence").	**Preamble** (recognises "Human Dignity", "Rule of Law", "Political and Social Freedom"); **Section 4** (Right to "Social Justice, "property and the preservation of labourers' rights"); **Section 13** (Right and Duty to Work); **Section 14** (Right to Public Office); **Section 17** (Right to "social and health insurance services"); **Section 18** (Right to Education); **Section 34** (Right to Private Ownership and Inheritance); **Section 40-72** (Constitutional Bill of Rights); **Section 156** (Cabinet shall "protect the rights of the citizens and the interests of the State"); **Section 194** (The *Šūrā*-Council shall promote the "public rights, freedoms and duties"); **Section 208**; ("Freedom of the Press"); **Section 210** (Journalists have the right to obtain news and information")

KENYA (1963 Constitution [as amended])	
Constitutional Provisions on Islam, Islamic Law and/or Islamic Institutions	**Constitutional Human Rights Provisions**
Section 66 (1)[11] (Establishment of Kadhi's courts); **Section** 66 (5) ("The jurisdiction of a Kadhi's court shall extend to the determination of questions of Muslim law relating to personal status, marriage, divorce or inheritance in proceedings in which all the parties profess the Muslim religion.").	**Section 70-82** ("Protection of Fundamental Rights and Freedom of Individuals")

11 N.B.: Section 209 of the new Draft Harmonised Constitution of Kenya (2009) is currently under debate.

<table>
<tr><th colspan="2">LIBYA
1969 Constitution (superseded, in principle, by the Declaration on the Establishment of the Authority of the People [DEAP] 1977)</th></tr>
<tr><th>Constitutional Provisions on Islam, Islamic Law and/or Islamic Institutions</th><th>Constitutional Human Rights Provisions</th></tr>
<tr><td>1969 CONSTITUTION:
Section 2 ("Islam is the Religion of the State"); Section 6 ("Its inspiration is its Arabic and Islamic Heritage"); Section 8 ("Inheritance is a Right which will be governed by the Islamic Šarīʿa").
1977 DEAP:
Preamble ("with the help of Allāh and adherence to His Holy Book as the everlasting source for guidance and as the ordinance of society"); Section 2 ("The Holy Qurʾān is the Constitution".</td><td>Section 4 (Right and Duty to Work); Section 5 ("All citizens are equal before the law"); Section 8 (Right to Private Ownership); Section 11 (Right to political Asylum); Section 12 (Right to Inviolability of the Home); Section 13 (Freedom of Opinion); Section 14 (Right to Education); Section 15 (Right to Health Care); Section 27 (Judiciary shall protect "the rights, dignity and freedom of individuals"); Section 28 (Freedom of the Judiciary).</td></tr>
</table>

<table>
<tr><th colspan="2">MAURITANIA
(1991 Constitution [as amended])</th></tr>
<tr><th>Constitutional Provisions on Islam, Islamic Law and/or Islamic Institutions</th><th>Constitutional Human Rights Provisions</th></tr>
<tr><td>Preamble ("solemnly proclaims its attachment to Islam");</td><td>Preamble (solemnly proclaims its attachment to principles of democracy as defined by the Universal Declaration of Human Rights and by the African Charter of Human and Peoples Rights as well as other international conventions with Mauritania has signed");</td></tr>
<tr><td>Section 1 ("Social Islamic Republic"); Section 5 ("Islam shall be the Religion of the People of the State"); Section 23 (The President "shall be a Muslim"); Section 94 Creation of "High Islamic Council").</td><td>Section 1 ("Equality before the Law"); Section 2 ("The People shall be the Source of Power"); Section 3 (suffrage rights and the Right to Vote); Section 4 (Rule of Law); Section 10 (Public and Individual Freedoms): Section 11 (political rights); Section 12 (Right to Public Office); Section 13 (Right to "presumption of innocence, personal liberty, privacy and non-violence"); Section 14 ("Right to Strike"); Section 15 ("Right to Property and Inheritance"); Section 16 (Right to Protection of Family); Section 21 (Right to Protection for Foreigners); Section 57 (the law shall protect fundamental rights and duties); Section 89 (Independence of the Judiciary); Section 91 (Right to Personal Liberty).</td></tr>
</table>

MOROCCO (1996 Constitution)	
Constitutional Provisions on Islam, Islamic Law and/or Islamic Institutions	**Constitutional Human Rights Provisions**
Preamble ("Islamic sovereign state");	**Preamble** ("reaffirms its determination to abide by the universally recognised human rights");
Section 6 ("Islam is the Religion of the State"); **Section 19** (The King is "Commander of the Faithful" and defender of the Islamic faith); **Section 106** "no prescriptions related to the religion of Islam may be subject to a constitutional revision.).	**Section 3** (Right to Political Organization); **Section 5** (Right to Equality before the Law); **Section 6** (Freedom of Worship); **Section 8** (Right to Civil and Political Rights); **Section 9** (Right to Freedom of Movement, Opinion, Expression and Association); **Section 10** (Right to Personal Liberty and Inviolability of the Home); **Section 11** (Right to Privacy of Personal Correspondence): **Section 12** (Right to Public Office); **Section 13** (Right to Education and Employment); **Section 14** (Right to Strike); **Section 15** (Right to Private Property and Free Enterprise); **Section 46** (Parliament shall protect Individual and Collective Rights.

SUDAN (2005 National Interim Constitution)	
Constitutional Provisions on Islam, Islamic Law and/or Islamic Institutions	**Constitutional Human Rights Provisions**
	Preamble (Committed to "uphold values of justice, equality, human dignity and equal rights and duties of men and women");
Section 5 (1) Islamic šarīʿa as source of legislation; **Section 20 (2)** ("Zakāt is a duty on Muslims"); **Section 156 (d)** ("the judicial discretion of courts to impose penalties on non-Muslims shall observe the long-established šarīʿa principle that non-Muslims are not subject to prescribed penalties"); **Section 157** (Non-Muslims not to be "adversely affected by the application of the šarīʿa law in the National Capital"); **Section 201 (2)** (establishment of Islamic banking system); **Section 202 (1)** (use of "Islamic financing instruments to implement the national monetary policy in Northern Sudan").	**Section 1 (2)** (committed to the respect and promotion of human dignity; and is founded on justice, equality and the advancement of Human Rights and Fundamental Freedoms"); **Section 6** (Religious Rights); **Section 7** (Right to Nationality and Citizenship); **Section 11(1)** (Right to Clean and Diverse Environment); **Section 12** (Right to Social Justice and Employment); **Section 13** (Right to Education); **Section 15** (Family Rights); **Section 25** (respect for role of the State in the promotion of the welfare of the people and protection of their Human Rights and Fundamental Freedoms"); **Section 27 to 48** (Constitutional Bill of Rights).

TUNISIA (1959 Constitution [as amended])	
Constitutional Provisions on Islam, Islamic Law and/or Islamic Institutions	**Constitutional Human Rights Provisions**
Preamble ("In the name of God, the Compassionate and Merciful"; "to remain faithful to the teachings of Islam");	**Preamble** ("guarantee for the respect of rights and duties of all citizens");
Section 1 ("its religion is Islam"); **Section 38 and 40** (The religion of the President is Islam).	**Section 5** ("inviolability of the human person and freedom of conscience, and protects the free exercise of beliefs"); **Section 6** (Right to Equality before the Law); **Section 7** (Right to exercise guaranteed rights"); **Section 8** (Right to Freedom of Opinion, Expression Assembly, Association and Union); **Section 9** (Right to Inviolability of the Home and Privacy of Correspondence); **Section 10** (Freedom of Movement and Domicile); **Section 11** (Freedom from Expatriation); **Section 12** (Right to Presumption of Innocence); **Section 14** (Right to Property); **Section 17** (Right to Political Asylum).

COMOROS (2001 Constitution)	
Constitutional Provisions on Islam, Islamic Law and/or Islamic Institutions	**Constitutional Human Rights Provisions**
Preamble ("To draw on Islam for continuous inspiration for the principles and rules governing the Union")	**Preamble** ("attachment to the principles and fundamental rights [...] notably those relating to the rights of children and women"); **Section 4** (Right to Suffrage); **Section 5** (Right to Nationality); **Section 6** (Right to Political Organisation); **Section 7** (Freedom of Movement and Settlement); **Section 31** (Constitutional court to guarantee basic rights of individuals and public freedoms).

SOMALIA (2001 Constitution)	
Constitutional Provisions on Islam, Islamic Law and/or Islamic Institutions	**Constitutional Human Rights Provisions**
Preamble (based on the Islamic šarīʿa);	**Preamble** (based on "sanctity of human life through the entrenchment of fundamental rights and individual freedoms");
Section 5 (Islam is the Religion of State); **Section 10 (6)** (The Republic has place in Islamic world); **Section 12 (7)** (Payment of Zakāt is a cornerstone of Islam); **Section 15 (3)** ("learning of and training in the Islamic religion compulsory"); **Section 16 (3)** (encourage observance of Islamic behaviour), **Section 33** (no renunciation of Islam by Muslims); **Section 41 (1)** (A Member of legislative house must be Muslim); **Section 82 (2)** (The President must be Muslim); **Section 127 (1)** (no amendment contradicting Islamic šarīʿa); **Section 128 (1)** (Constitution must be based on Islamic principles); **Section 129** (Presidential oath "to be true to the Islamic religion"); **Section 130 (5)** (current law not conflict with the Islamic šarīʿa).	**Section 8** (equal rights and obligations); **Section 10 (2)** ("Shall respect the Universal Declaration of Human Rights"); **Section 20** (Right and Duty to Work); Art. **21-36** (Constitutional Bill of Rights and Duties); **Section 127 (d)** (no amendment contradicting fundamental rights and individual freedoms); **Section 130 (5)** (current law no conflict with fundamental rights and individual freedoms).

GAMBIA (1997 Constitution [as amended])	
Constitutional Provisions on Islam, Islamic Law and/or Islamic Institutions	**Constitutional Human Rights Provisions**
	Preamble ("will ensure for all time respect for and observance of human rights and fundamental freedoms for all");
Section 7 (f) ("The šarīʿa as regards matters of marriage, divorce and inheritance among members of the communities to which it applies."); **Section 137 (1)** ("A Cadi Court shall be established in such places in The Gambia as the Chief Justice shall determine."); **Section 137 (A)** ("There shall be a Cadi Appeals Panel.").	**Section 17-38** ("Protection of Fundamental Rights and Freedoms"); **Section 39** ("Right to Vote"; **Section 132(1)(b)** (High court to "to interpret and enforce the fundamental rights and freedoms".).

NIGERIA (1999 Constitution)	
Constitutional Provisions on Islam, Islamic Law and/or Islamic Institutions	**Constitutional Human Rights Provisions**
	Preamble (recognises "principles of freedom, equality and justice");
Section 237 (2b) (Judges of the Court of Appeal to include "not less than three" judges "learned in Islamic personal law"); **Section 260** ("There shall be a Sharia Court of Appeal of the Federal Capital Territory, Abuja"); **Section 262** (The Sharia Court of Appeal of the Federal Capital Territory has jurisdiction to determine questions of Islamic personal law); **Section 275** ("There shall be for any State that requires it a Sharia Court of Appeal for that State."); **Section 277** (The Shari Court of Appeal of a State has jurisdiction to determine questions of Islamic personal law); **Third Schedule:** **Part I, Section 20 (g)** (One Grand Kadi to be appointed to the National Judicial Council); **Part II, Section 5 (c),** (Grand Kadi of a State to be on the State Judicial Service Commission.).	**Section 17** ("The State social order is founded on ideals of Freedom, Equality and Justice"); **Section 33 to 46** ("Fundamental Rights" provisions.).

C. Islam and Constitutionalism: Friends or Foes?

Two main questions need be addressed in relation to Islam and constitutionalism within the context of this chapter. The first is whether Islamic principles should actually have a role within the constitutions of modern nation states, while the second is whether or not Islam itself is amenable to the concept and principles of constitutionalism at all. We will address each of these questions in turn.

I. Should Islamic Principles have a Role in the Constitutions of Modern States? – Three theoretical perspectives

The question of whether Islamic principles should have a role in modern constitutionalism may be addressed from three theoretical perspectives, namely, the separationist, accomodationist and double-edged theoretical perspectives, respectively.[12]

[12] See *Mashood A. Baderin*, "Religion and International Law: Friends or Foes", in: European Human Rights Law Review, volume 5, London 2009, pp. 637-658 for an analysis of

1. The Separationist theoretical perspective

The argument from a strict separationist theoretical perspective would be that, generally religion should have no role in modern constitutionalism at all, and thus, Islam and/or Islamic Law and institutions should have no role in the constitutions of modern nation states. The separationist theory promotes a strictly secular approach to law and constitutionalism, consequently religion is expected to be completely restricted to the private sphere of individuals and not allowed into the public sphere of governance and constitutional provisions, with the aim of ensuring neutrality in the political order. This theoretical perspective draws largely from the Western, particularly American, liberal concept of separation between church and state. The theory is hinged mainly on the need to ensure neutrality in the public sphere of governance and constitutionalism. It has been argued, therefore, that "including in a constitution a proclamation that the country is a "Christian" or "Islamic" state is unhelpful" for assuaging the fears and apprehensions of other religious and non-religious minority groups within the state and involving them meaningfully in the political system and nation building.[13]

Thus, the pragmatic separationist challenge against a religious role in modern constitutionalism is that a constitutional order that recognises and gives a particular dominant religion a role in the constitutional order, would have innately created room for discrimination against other religions and beliefs within the system. Consequently, the separationist theoretical perspective is that only a strictly secular constitutional order that is free from any religions leanings or influence can ensure a neutral politico-legal system that would facilitate good governance within the principles of modern constitutionalism. While the neutrality argument of the separationist theory has been generally challenged as being inherently subjective,[14] it would, on balance, still be reasonable to argue that the onus does rest on advocates and implementers of any relevant religion to demonstrate, both theoretically and practically, that any constitutional role for such a religion can be discharged in a manner that is consistent with modern constitutional objectives of ensuring respect for fundamental human rights, rule of law,

---

these three theoretical perspectives respectively in the context of the relationship between religion and international law generally.

13 *John Hatchard / Muna Ndulo / Peter Slinn,* Comparative Constitutionalism..., supra, footnote 1, on p. 25 (footnote 47).

14 See e.g. the observation of Richard Falk in the text to the following footnote 15. See also, *Mashood A. Baderin,* Religion and International Law..., supra, footnote 12, pp. 637 et seqq. (on pp. 645-646), for other critiques of the neutrality argument of the separationist theory.

equality, non-discrimination and promotion of good governance generally. This brings us to the accomodationist theoretical perspective on the question.

2. The Accomodationist theoretical perspective

Contrary to the separationist theory, the argument from the accomodationist theoretical perspective would be that, because religion is an important aspect of human existence that cannot be easily excluded from the public sphere, particularly in predominantly Muslim societies, Islamic principles should have a role and be conveniently accommodated in the modern constitutions of Muslim states as is the case currently in some African countries. The accomodationist theory is based on the view that religion generally plays a positive and important ethical/normative role in human society in a way that can benefit the general political dispensation and should therefore be accommodated in modern constitutionalism. Proponents of this view assert that religious considerations are so important for the majority of the world's population that they cannot be considered irrelevant to the public sphere of governance and constitutionalism. This theory is reflected in a notable observation by Richard Falk that:

> "Historically, the exclusion of religion from political life was seen as a vital step in the struggle to establish humane governance. However, the best secular thinking has fallen short of providing either a plausible path to such governance or a sufficiently inspiring vision that would mobilize a popular grassroots movement for global reform. This failure is partially due to the exclusion of religious and spiritual dimensions of human experience from the shaping of the vision and practices associated with the quest for global humane governance. The challenge is to infuse the struggles of the peoples of the world for democracy, equity, and sustainability with a vision of human existence that is human-centered yet recognizes the relevance of the spiritual sensibilities in the major world religions, moving us beyond a society based on reason and machines."[15]

It is important to emphasise that the strength of the accomodationist theory lies mainly in the proposition that religion is relevant and can indeed contribute positively to the realisation of modern constitutional objectives of ensuring respect for fundamental human rights and promotion of good governance generally. Richard Falk had noted in his observation above that "the best secular thinking has fallen short of providing either a plausible path to [humane or good] governance or a sufficiently inspiring vision that would mobilize a popular grassroots movement for global reform", and argued that "[t]his failure is partially due to

---

15 *Richard Falk*, "Religion and Global Governance: Harmony or Clash", in: International Journal on World Peace, volume 19, St. Paul (Minnesota, USA) 2002. See excerpt at: http://www.quetia.com/googleScholar.qst;jsessionid=LxjQ9jFnx1LvfbSTpCJ7Q5lMjSV4pyHgW2pRTncQSLpKTMMQwc22!202834244?docId=5000662721 (accessed on 6 November 2009).

the exclusion of religious and spiritual dimensions of human experience from the shaping of the vision and practices associated with the quest for global humane [or good] governance". While this can be seen as an indictment against a strict separationist theory in modern constitutionalism, yet, it is equally a potent challenge to advocates of the accomodationist theory in modern constitutionalism to demonstrate practically that, where accommodated, religion can indeed contribute positively to the realisation of humane and good governance in the modern world. In the context of the question under consideration, current empirical evidence in respect of most African and other Muslim states that provide a role for Islam and/or Islamic Law and institutions in their constitutions indicates apparently that this onus has not yet been fully discharged by the relevant states through the positive utilization of the constitutional role of Islam to ensure respect for fundamental human rights, rule or law, equality, non-discrimination and promotion of good governance generally within their respective constitutional orders. This brings us to the third theoretical perspective, i.e., the double-edged theoretical perspective.

3. The Double-edged theoretical perspective

The double-edged theory is both a pragmatic and relative theoretical perspective that lies between the separationist and accomodationist theories. Pragmatically, it proposes that religion is generally like a double-edged sword that could either be utilised positively or negatively when given a role in law generally and in modern constitutionalism specifically. Thus, in relation to the question of whether Islam should have any role in the constitutions of modern nation states, the double-edged theoretical response would be both "Yes" and "No" depending largely on the utilitarian consideration of how such a constitutional role could be potentially utilised by both the political leadership and the populace within the constitutional order. Where there is potential to utilize such a constitutional role to ensure good governance within the political order, then, "Yes", it should be accommodated, but where it is evident that such constitutional role would be utilized to restrain good governance within the political order, then, "No", it should not be accommodated. It is in this double-edged sense that the role of Islam in the constitution of Muslim states generally may be seen as being contingent.[16] Thus, in the context of the question at hand, the double-edged perspective would also require, at least, a demonstrable expectation that Islam can indeed play a positive role in ensuring good governance to justify its role in the constitutional order of respective modern states.

---

16 See e.g. *Abdullahi Ahmed An-Na'im*, African Constitutionalism..., supra, footnote 7, p. 99 et seqq.

Relatively however, the double-edged theoretical perspective to the question would equally demand that the concept of constitutionalism be contextualised in relation to the normative and legitimacy role that Islam actually plays in predominantly Muslim societies including the relevant African countries in whose constitution it is given a role. In that regard, it has been argued that rather than promoting an abstract transplantation of the concept, "constitutionalism needs to come to terms with the indigenous values and institutions of those societies" in which it is expected to operate.[17] It is in that contextualised sense that commentators on constitutionalism in Africa talk sometimes of "African constitutionalism", and argue that constitutions "must be locally-focused and take into account the specificities of the society to be governed by the rules".[18] Such contextualisation is what actually differentiates between a constitution, as a mere transplanted set of rules or legal document, and constitutionalism, as a process towards realising a constitutional order that reflects the aspirations of the populace and expresses the general will of the people. Today, many of the countries that provide a role for Islam in their constitutions have majority Muslim populations. Thus, where the constitutional role for Islam in the constitutions of those states has been achieved through legitimate constitutional processes, it is arguable that such provision would be a reflection of the general will of the majority populace and must thus be accommodated on grounds of legitimacy.

Nonetheless, one cannot but agree with the assertion that while it is necessary for a constitution to reflect the aspiration of the majority for legitimacy, "in doing so, it also has to take into account the fears and concerns of the minorities"[19] and the general modern constitutional objective of respect for human rights and good governance generally. Thus, even in the context of African constitutionalism, it has been observed that while African constitutions must reflect cultural legitimacy (which may include a role for Islam in the constitutions of African Muslim states), this must be within modern constitutional principles of inclusivity, transparency, accessibility and accountability,[20] among others, for the promotion of good governance generally in the respective states. Thus, while Islam

---

[17] Ibidem, p. 99.

[18] *John Mukum Mbaku*, "Constitutionalism and Governance in Africa", in: West Africa Review, issue 6 (2004), http://www.westafricareview.com/issue6/mbaku.html (accessed on 6 November 2009). See also *Francis Mading Deng*, Identity, Diversity, and Constitutionalism in Africa, Washington D.C. 2008; *Joseph Oloka-Onyango*, Constitutionalism in Africa: Creating Opportunities, Facing Challenges, Kampala 2001.

[19] *Hassen Ebrahim / Kayode Fayemi / Stephanie Loomis*, Promoting Constitutionalism…, supra, footnote 1, on p. 7.

[20] Ibidem, pp. 11-16, where the principles of Inclusivity, Transparency, Accessibility, Accountability and others have been discussed as important elements of constitutionalism in Commonwealth countries.

may be recognised as playing a legitimacy role in the relative sense of the double-edged theory, that role must be facilitative to realising the principal objective of good governance in the constitutional order, which still places the onus of a positive demonstration on the relevant states that Islam can indeed play a contributing role in ensuring good governance to justify its role in the constitutional order of respective modern states. This brings us to the second question of whether Islam is itself amenable to the concept of constitutionalism in that regard.

II. Does Islam recognise the concept of Constitutionalism?

It is often presumed that the concepts of constitutionalism and rule of law are completely modern "Western" secular concepts and thus unknown to Islam or to Islamic Law at all. That presumption is however easily refutable by reference to a historical document, that has come to be known as the "Constitution of Medina", which was formulated by the Prophet Muḥammad around 622 CE when he migrated from Mecca to Medina and was appointed as the leader of the Medinan community. Muhammad Hamidullah has described that document as the first written constitution in the world.[21] Many Muslim and non-Muslim commentators consider the document as the earliest rudimentary demonstration of constitutionalism in governance.[22] The Muslim community *(umma)* was first recognised as a polity when the Prophet Muhammad and the early Muslims migrated from Mecca to Medina (then called Yaṯrib) after the 13th year of his mission. The city of Medina was then inhabited by a mixture of Jewish and Christian tribes, local Muslim converts and local pagan tribesmen between whom tribal wars were very rampant.[23] After his arrival in Medina, Prophet Muḥammad was recognised as the administrative leader of the city and he, consequently, enacted "the Constitution of Medina" as the binding instrument for governing the city.

This established an era of peaceful co-existence between the Muslims, Jews, Christians, and the local tribesmen in Medina, and a common reference point for communal rights and duties for all the inhabitants of the city.[24] The constitutional order thus created was a radical departure from the chauvinistic and war-

21 *Muhammad Hamidullah,* The First Written Constitution in the World , Lahore 1981.

22 See e.g. *Mohamed Berween,* "Al-Wathiqah: The First Islamic Constitution", in: Journal of Muslim Minority Affairs, volume 23, number 1, London 2003, pp. 103-120. *William Montgomery Watt,* Islamic Political Thought, Edinburgh 1980, pp. 130-134; *Ali Bulaç,* "The Medina Document", in: *Charles Kurzuman,* (Ed.) Liberal Islam, A Sourcebook, Oxford 1998, pp. 169-178; *Marshall G. S. Hodgson,* The Venture of Islam, Chicago 1974, Volume 1, pp. 193 et seqq.

23 Cp. *William Montgomery Watt*, Muhammad at Medina, Karachi 1981, pp. 155-158.

24 Ibidem, pp. 221-228.

mongering attitude of the traditional Arab society, which obtained among the different groups in Medina before the Prophet's arrival. Although the term community *(umma)* was used in the "Constitution of Medina" to describe the new polity that had emerged, it will be correct to refer to that polity as a "state" in the context of modern international law. All the elements of statehood were present. There was a population consisting of Muslims and non-Muslims, whom the document referred to as one (political) *umma*[25], there was a defined territory,[26] there was a government[27] and there was capacity to enter into relations with other states as depicted by the provisions of the document and demonstrated in subsequent treaty relations with other political powers in existence then. Commenting on this early Medinan state, Marshall G. S. Hodgson, rightly identified that "the political structure which Muhammad was building was by now clearly a state, like the states in the nations round about Arabia, with an increasingly authoritative government, which could no longer be ignored with impunity".[28] Formal recognition of the Medinan state and the political leadership of Prophet Muḥammad were demonstrated later by the political authorities of Mecca and the other political powers around the Arabian Peninsula through different bilateral peace treaties and treaties of cooperation.[29]

That enactment of the "Constitution of Medina" by the Prophet during the very foundation of the nascent state in Medina can be seen not only as an important reference point for the recognition of the concept of constitutionalism in Islam, but a positive step towards recognition and promotion of peaceful co-existence, Human Rights and basic principles of good governance in Islamic political theory and practice. The document clearly defined certain basic rights and duties of the individuals and groups within the community as well as some fundamental

---

25 The opening parts of the document provided that:

"(1) This is a document by Muhammad the Prophet, between the believers and Muslims of Qurayš and Yaṯrib, and those who followed them and joined them and struggled with them.

(2) They are one community *(umma)* to the exclusion of all men.

[...]

(25) The Jews [...] are one community *(umm)* with the believers. (The Jews have their religion *(dīn)* and the Muslims have theirs [...])".

26 It is reported that the Prophet actually ordered a companion named Kaʿab b. Mālik to plant some indicators to define the territorial boundaries of Medina. Cp. *Muhammad Hamidullah,* Le Prophet de l'Islam, Paris 1959 cited in: *Mohammad Talaat al-Ghunaimi,* The Muslim Conception of International Law and the Western Approach, The Hague 1968, p. 54. See also *Ali Bulaç,* The Medina Document, supra, footnote 22, on p. 170.

27 The document addressed, *inter alia,* issues on defence, legislation and administration of justice.

28 *Marshall G. S. Hodgson,* The Venture of Islam, supra, footnote 22, p. 193.

29 See *Mohammad Talaat al-Ghunaimi,* supra, footnote 26, pp. 54-70

rule of law that could be easily referred to by every member of the community. For example, Mohammad Talaat al-Ghunaimi [Muḥmmad Ṭalaʿat al-Ġunaimī] has pointed out the importance of the "Constitution of Medina" in ensuring respect for individual rights within the community then, by referring to the statement of one of the Muslim leaders, Abū Bakr, (the succeeding Caliph after the Prophet) to a man called Pinḥas (Hebrew: פנחס / Arabic بنحاس), a Jewish Arab of the Banū Qainuqāṯ, during a quarrel between the two. Abū Bakr was reported to have said to Pinḥas in anger, during the quarrel, that: "if it were not for the charter (i.e. the Constitution of Medina) between us and you, I would have cut off your head." It was also on the basis of the violation of provisions of the "Constitution" that some of the Jewish tribes were reported to have been expelled from Medina on grounds of actions that were comparable to the crime of treason in modern times.[30]

From the above historical analysis, it is clear that the concept of constitutionalism is, at least, not completely alien to Islam. But can this be interpreted conclusively as Islam being fully amenable to modern constitutionalism? In that regard, Abdullahi Ahmed An-Na'im has observed notably and rightly that "some [traditional] interpretations of Islam are seriously problematic from a [modern] constitutional point of view, while others are at least consistent with the principle, if not positively supportive of it",[31] which leads us to our next analysis on the need to distinguish between historical and evolutional interpretations of Islamic Law and political theory. Such distinction is of utmost importance if Islam is to contribute positively to the realisation of good governance in Africa through the constitutional role accorded to it in relevant African constitutions.

D. Historical and evolutional interpretations of Islamic Law and political theory

Essentially, constitutionalism and good governance are associated with legal/political theory and practice. Thus, it would be necessary to focus more specifically on Islamic Law and political theory rather than on Islam generally in the context of the interpretation of Islamic norms in relation to constitutionalism and good governance. One of the major misunderstandings about Islam is the erroneous view that its laws, norms, and practices are all completely divine, immutable, monolithic and inflexible, which often leads to an adumbration of the evolutional nature of Islamic Law and political theory in relation to modern constitutionalism. Generally, all Islamic norms, including Islamic Law and po-

30 Ibidem, pp. 56-61; cp. also *William Montgomery Watt*, Muhammad at Medina, supra, footnote 23, pp. 208-220.

31 *Abdullahi Ahmed An-Na'im*, African Constitutionalism…, supra, footnote 7, p. 9.

litical theory are derived from two main sources, namely the Qur'ān and the authentic Traditions (*sunna*) of the Prophet Muḥammad, jointly referred to as the *šarīʿa,* and both of which Muslims consider to be divine and immutable sources. Specifically, Islamic Law and political theory are derived from the divine *šarīʿa* based on human jurisprudence called *"fiqh"* (literally understanding), reached through the process of *iǧtihād* (juristic reasoning). That is, human juristic understanding of the divine sources using different well defined classical and post-classical jurisprudential methods and principles formulated by Muslim jurists over time. Based on their human understandings of the provisions of the divine *šarīʿa* through careful and dedicated study, the classical Islamic jurists compiled books of *fiqh* (jurisprudence) containing their interpretations and views on different issues as evidenced by the different schools of Islamic jurisprudence (*maḏāhib*) that were consequently established around the 10th century, namely the Ḥanafī, Mālikī, Šāfiʿī and Ḥanbalī Sunnī schools, as well as the different Šīʿa schools. These jurisprudential rulings and views by the classical Islamic jurists, unlike the *šarīʿa* itself, are neither divine nor immutable, but have become accepted by Muslims as established legal treatises in different parts of the Muslim world today, including relevant African states.

In that regard, Islamic Law as derived rulings from the *šarīʿa* can be perceived either in a historical or evolutional sense. Perceived in a strict historical sense, Islamic Law is often restricted to the traditional rulings of the classical Islamic jurists, while Islamic political theory is often based on the practices of early Muslim leaders as if those rulings and practices were immutable, like the divine *šarīʿa* itself. This creates a reductionist perception of Islamic Law that is hinged on the disputed theory of the closing of the gate of juristic reasoning (*iǧtihād*) advocated around the 13th Century.[32] This theory is to the effect that Islamic Law and practice must be restricted to the legal rulings of the classical jurists as recorded in the legal treatises of the established schools of Islamic jurisprudence dating back to the 10th Century, which, in essence, represents Islamic legal theory and practice as systems stuck in the past without possibility of change.

Conversely, the evolutional perception of Islamic Law is the opposite of the historical perception, and it is to the effect that while the rulings and practices of the classical jurists and leaders provide a rich source of jurisprudence and precedent they do not estop the continual development of Islamic Law and practice based on relevant contemporary jurisprudence (*fiqh*) through the continuing

[32] See e.g. *Wael Hallaq,* "Was the Gate of Ijtihad Closed?", in: International Journal of Middle East Studies, volume 16, number 1, Cambridge / et al. 1984, pp. 3-41; *Shaista P. Ali-Karamali / Fiona Dunne,* "The Ijtihad Controversy", in: Arab Law Quarterly, volume 9, number 3, London / et al. 1994, pp. 238-257.

process of legal reasoning (*iğtihād*). In essence, the evolutional perception represents Islamic Law and practice as systems that evolve in necessary response to the dynamic nature of human life and experiences.

While there are commentators who advance a strict historical perception of Islamic Law and practice, there is abundant theoretical and practical evidence to establish that the system has not actually been inherently static or immutable, but has responded and adjusted to the factors of time and circumstances since its inception. This is particularly in respect of temporal matters pertaining to inter-human relations (*muʿāmalāt*) which are more affected by the dynamic nature of human life, in contrast to matters of strict religious observances and acts of worship (*ʿibādāt*) which are more relatively stable. It is in the different aspects of human relations (*muʿāmalāt*) that the evolutional nature of Islamic Law has been well manifested in theory and practice over the years, since its emergence in the 7th century. There are many relevant established jurisprudential principles and maxims of Islamic Law depicting this evolutional and flexible nature of Islamic Law both in theory and practice. A relevant Islamic legal maxim in that regard is that Islamic legal rulings may change with relevant changes in time and place within the context of the *šarīʿa*.[33] Obviously, constitutionalism and good governance falls within the realm of inter-human relations in Islamic Law and political theory and should thus be amenable to evolutional interpretations of the *šarīʿa* that are consistent with modern constitutional objectives of ensuring respect for fundamental Human Rights, rule or law, equality, non-discrimination and promotion of good governance generally, rather than to static historical interpretations that are inimical to it.

Adopting an evolutional perception does not necessarily mean that all the classical interpretations of Islamic Law and practice would be totally discarded. Rather, particular traditional interpretations of Islamic Law and practice that conflict with modern constitutional objectives of good governance would need to be re-considered contextually and the relevant sources re-interpreted in an evolutional manner to meet with modern constitutional objectives of ensuring respect for fundamental human rights, rule or law, equality, non-discrimination and promotion of good governance in modern nation states. Said Ramadan [Saʿīd Ramaḍān] has observed in that regard that while all historical jurisprudential works of the classical Islamic jurists of the past "are very rich and indispen-

[33] Cp. also *Hatem Elliesie*, "Editor's Foreword", in: *Hatem Elliesie* (Hrsg./Editor), Beiträge zum Islamischen Recht VII, Islam und Menschenrechte / Islam and Human Rights / الإسلام وحقوق الإنسان, Frankfurt am Main 2010, p. 27; *Abdullahi Ahmed An-Na'im*, "Islam and Human Rights: Introductory Remarks and Reflections", in: *Hatem Elliesie* (Hrsg./ Editor), ibidem, pp. 35 (on p. 44); and, particularly *en détail*, *Assem Hefny*, "Hermeneutik, Koraninterpretation und Menschenrechte, ibidem, pp. 73-97.

sable, they must always be [...] open to reconsideration"[34] in response to contemporary questions and experiences. Thus, the evolutional perception looks both backwards, to benefit from the richness of the historical jurisprudential works of classical Islamic jurists, and forwards to meet the needs of contemporary times.

Such evolutional interpretations of Islamic Law and practice are currently reflected in the legislative and judicial practices of some Muslim states as well as in the juristic views of many contemporary Islamic jurists and scholars in different parts of the Muslim world. Mohammad Hashim Kamali illustrates this in his observation in that regard as follows:

> "In modern times legal interpretation or reasoning [in Islamic Law] has occurred in the following three ways: statutory legislation, judicial decision and learned opinion (fatwa) [*fatwā*], and scholarly writings. Instances of legislative interpretation, which Noel Coulson referred to as "neo-ijtihad [*iǧtihād*]," can be found in the modern reforms of family law in many Muslim countries, particularly with reference to polygyny and divorce, both of which have been made contingent upon a court order, and therefore are no longer the unilateral privilege of the husband. Current reformist legislation on these subjects derives some support from the jurists' doctrines of the Maliki and Hanafi schools, but these reforms are essentially based on novel interpretation of the Quran's relevant portions. Numerous instances of independent reasoning are also found in the views of the ulama [*ʿulamāʾ*; religious scholars], such as the collections of published opinions of Muhammad Rashid Rida in the 1920s and those of the late shaykh of Azhar, Mahmud Shaltut, in the 1950s. In the 1967 case of Khursid Bibi vs. Muhammad Amin, the supreme court of Pakistan's decision to validate a form of divorce, known as khula [*ḫulʿ*], that can take place at the wife's initiative, even without the consent of the husband, can be cited as an example of judicial ijtihad [*iǧtihād*]. Another example of ongoing reinterpretation is the scholarly contribution of the Egyptian scholar Yusuf al-Qaradawi, who validated air travel by women unaccompanied by male relatives. According to the rules of fiqh that were formulated in premodern times, women were not permitted to travel alone. Al-Qaradawi based his conclusion on the analysis that the initial ruling was intended to ensure women's physical and moral safety, and that modern air travel fulfills this requirement. He further supported this view with an analysis of the relevant hadiths [*ḥadīṯ*] on the subject and arrived at a ruling better suited to contemporary conditions."[35]

---

34 *Said Ramadan,* Islamic Law: Its Scope and Equity, London 1970, p. 36.

35 *Mohammad Hashim Kamali,* "Law and Society: The Interplay of Revelation and Reason in the Shariah", in: *John Louis Esposito* (Ed.), The Oxford History of Islam, Oxford 1999, pp. 107 et seqq (on p. 118).

Such evolutional interpretations of Islamic Law and practice are well justified within the context of the overall objectives of the *šarīʿa* or the higher intents of Islamic Law (*maqāṣid aš-šarīʿa*) which is understood by both the classical and contemporary Islamic jurists to be the promotion of human welfare/benefit (*maṣlaḥa*) and prevention of harm (*mafsada*).[36] Ibn al-Qayyim al-Ğawziyya, the renowned 13th/14th Century Islamic jurist of the Ḥanbalī School of jurisprudence stated in that regard that:

> "Islamic Law is structured and founded upon wise purposes and the best interests of God's servants both in this world and the next. The Law is pure justice, pure mercy, pure benefit, pure wisdom. Hence, anything which embodies injustice rather than justice, cruelty rather than mercy, harm rather than benefit, or folly rather than wisdom does not originate from the Law, even if it happens to have been interpolated therein by means of interpretation."[37]

Although some Muslim states and commentators continue to advance a strict historical perception of Islamic Law and political theory in different parts of the Muslim world, which may be practically problematic in relation to modern constitutional objectives of respect for fundamental human rights and good governance, there is currently a strong wave of scholarship advocating the evolutional interpretation of Islamic Law in ways that would facilitate the realization of the humane objectives of the *šarīʿa* in the modern world in a way that is consistent with modern constitutional objectives of promoting human rights and good governance.

From the evolutional perception of Islamic Law, I have argued elsewhere that:

> "Islam can, and should, serve as a positive factor for the promotion of human rights and development in Muslim States. The *Qur'an* and the *Sunnah* (i.e. the *Shari'ah*), which constitute the main sources of Islamic religious, moral and legal norms contain relevant provisions that support the guarantee of human rights and promotion of development in Muslim States. Also, the methods and relevant principles of Islamic Law can be positively employed to ensure the practical realisation of that objective."[38]

---

36 For some contemporary writings on *maqāṣid aš-šarīʿa,* see e.g. *Jasser Auda,* Maqasid al-Shariah as Philosophy of Islamic Law: A Systems Approach, London 2008; *Gamal Eldin Attia,* Towards Realization of the Higher Intents of Islamic Law: Maqāṣid al-Shari'ah: A Functional Approach, London 2007.

37 *Ibn al-Qayyim al-Ğawziyyah,* 'iʿlām al-muwaqqiʿīn ʿan rabb al-ʿālamīn, volume 3, Maktabat al-Kulliyyāt al-Azhariyya: Cairo 1968, p. 3, Translation cited in *Gamal Eldin Attia,* Towards Realization…, supra, footnote 35, p. 7.

38 *Mashood A. Baderin,* "The Role of Islam in Human Rights and Development in Muslim States", in: *Javaid Rehman / Susan C. Breau* (Eds.), Religion, Human Rights and International Law, Leiden / et al. 2007, pp. 321 et seqq. (on p. 324).

It is in a similar vein that I strongly submit in this chapter that African states that have provided a constitutional role for Islam should adopt the evolutional interpretation of Islamic Law and legal theory towards the realization of good governance in the respective states. There are many relevant provisions in the Qur'ān and the *sunna* as well as relevant practices from early Islamic history to support this as analysed below. [39]

E. Advancing Islam as Agent for Good Governance in Africa

While human rights provisions in a country's constitution apparently signifies good governance ideals, constitutional provisions on Islam is not seen apparently as such, but needs to be substantiated. Thus, this section advocates that Islam can indeed be utilised as an agent for good governance in those states that provide a constitutional role for it in Africa, if there is positive will on the part of both the leadership and the populace in that regard.

Under Islamic political thought, governance is characterised in two inter-related ways. Firstly, governance is representative in nature, (*niyābī*) in the sense that it is perceived as consisting of a binary Trust (*amāna*) primarily from God and subsequently from the populace to those in authority. The Qur'ān confirms in many verses that God is the sovereign of the whole universe[40] but has created human beings as vicegerents on earth and thereby entrusted them generally with governance on earth.[41] This is expressed, for example, in the narrative of the creation of Adam whereby he is referred to as vicegerent of God on earth.[42] As descendants of Adam (Banū 'Ādam), all human beings are entitled to participate in governance on earth, which thus creates a subsequent Trust from the populace to whomever they appoint as their leaders. This subsequent Trust from the popu-

---

39 See also *Muhammad S. El-Awa*, On the Political System of the Islamic State, Indianapolis, 1980.

40 *Sura 5* (المائدة): *Verse 18*:

وَقَالَتِ الْيَهُودُ وَالنَّصَارَى نَحْنُ أَبْنَاء اللّهِ وَأَحِبَّاؤُهُ قُلْ فَلِمَ يُعَذِّبُكُم بِذُنُوبِكُم بَلْ أَنتُم بَشَرٌ مِّمَّنْ خَلَقَ يَغْفِرُ لِمَن يَشَاء وَيُعَذِّبُ مَن يَشَاء
وَلِلّهِ مُلْكُ السَّمَاوَاتِ وَالأَرْضِ وَمَا بَيْنَهُمَا وَإِلَيْهِ الْمَصِ.

Sura 3 (آل عمران): *Verse 26:*

قُلِ اللَّهُمَّ مَالِكَ الْمُلْكِ تُؤْتِي الْمُلْكَ مَن تَشَاء وَتَنزِعُ الْمُلْكَ مِمَّن تَشَاء وَتُعِزُّ مَن تَشَاء
وَتُذِلُّ مَن تَشَاء بِيَدِكَ الْخَيْرُ **إِنَّكَ عَلَىَ كُلِّ شَيْءٍ قَدِيرٌ.**

41 Cp. *Sura 6* (الأنعام): *Verse 165*:

وَهُوَ الَّذِي جَعَلَكُمْ خَلاَئِفَ الأَرْضِ وَرَفَعَ بَعْضَكُمْ فَوْقَ بَعْضٍ دَرَجَاتٍ لِّيَبْلُوَكُمْ فِي
مَا آتَاكُمْ إِنَّ رَبَّكَ سَرِيعُ الْعِقَابِ وَإِنَّهُ لَغَفُورٌ رَّحِيمٌ.

42 *Sura 2* (البقرة): *Verse 30:*

وَإِذْ قَالَ رَبُّكَ لِلْمَلاَئِكَةِ **إِنِّي جَاعِلٌ فِي الأَرْضِ خَلِيفَةً** قَالُواْ أَتَجْعَلُ فِيهَا مَن يُفْسِدُ فِيهَا
وَيَسْفِكُ الدِّمَاء وَنَحْنُ نُسَبِّحُ بِحَمْدِكَ وَنُقَدِّسُ لَكَ قَالَ إِنِّي أَعْلَمُ مَا لاَ تَعْلَمُونَ.

lace to the leadership is signified in practice by the oath of allegiance (*mubayaʿa*) undertaken by the populace to the elected leader, which is a form of "social contract" between the leadership and the populace.[43] Thus, while the political leadership would be accountable to God in the hereafter for the primary Trust, they are also accountable to the human populace here now in this world for the subsequent Trust reposed in them. The Qur'ān provides in that regard:

> "God commands you to render the Trusts back to those whom they are due; and when you judge between people, you should judge with justice; Verily, how excellent is the teaching which God gives you, for God hears and sees all things".[44]

In his book on Islamic political theory, *al-siyāsa aš-šarʿiyya*, Ibn Taymiyya al-Ḥarrānī, the 13th/14th Century Islamic jurist, observed that this Qur'ānic verse relates to those in authority and that it obliges them to make over the Trust to those entitled to it (i.e. the populace who elected them to power) and that they have a duty to administer justice and rule fairly in that regard.[45] The Prophet Muḥammad made this obligation of the political leadership clearer in a statement where he is reported to have said:

> "Each of you is [like] a shepherd and each of you is accountable regarding his flock. The leader of a people is [like] a shepherd and is accountable regarding his subjects [...]"[46]

To effectively discharge the obligation, this Trust of leadership must be rendered back to the populace in form of good governance by the political leadership.

Secondly, governance, from an Islamic perspective, is temporal in nature (*muʿāmala*) but underpinned by God-consciousness. It is not strictly sacrosanct and can thus be questioned by the governed. Therefore the populace should not just sit down and watch the political leadership mismanage resources without asking questions. Being temporal but underpinned by God-consciousness, governance in Islam can best be described as "anthropo-theocentric" (human and God centred), having horizontal and vertical dimensions for serving God through humanity. To demonstrate the anthropo-theocentric nature of governance in Islamic political thought, the concept of *as-siyāsa aš-šarʿiyya* was developed by Islamic jurists in the 11th Century as a means of responding to the dynamic nature of governance. The principles of governance are therefore not

---

43 See e.g. *Qamaruddin Khan*, The Political Thought of Ibn Taymiya, Delhi, 1992, p. 162.

44 *Sura 4* (النساء): *Verse 58:*

إِنَّ اللَّهَ يَأْمُرُكُمْ أَن تُؤَدُّواْ الأَمَانَاتِ إِلَى أَهْلِهَا وَإِذَا حَكَمْتُم بَيْنَ النَّاسِ
أَن تَحْكُمُواْ بِالْعَدْلِ إِنَّ اللَّهَ نِعِمَّا يَعِظُكُم بِهِ إِنَّ اللَّهَ كَانَ سَمِيعًا بَصِيرًا.

45 *Ibn Taymiyya al-Ḥarrānī,* al-siyāsa aš-šarʿiyya, Cairo, 1951, p. 3.

46 Reported by *al-Buḫārī and Muslim.*

static under Islamic Law, but must respond to the needs of time within the relevant provisions of the *šarīʿa* and Islamic jurisprudence.[47]

As Islam emphasizes the need for God-consciousness or piety (*taqwā*) in every human endeavour,[48] including governance, the political leadership, particularly, is expected to be God-conscious, but so also is the populace generally. Although piety (*taqwā*) alone cannot guarantee good governance, it is believed in Islam that genuine God-consciousness can prevent abuse of authority by the leadership and also promote allegiance on the part of the populace, both of which are essential for effective good governance.

It is historically established that in its golden ages, based on its relevant principles and teachings, Islam demonstrated good governance both in theory and practice. While the Qurʾān does not specify a particular form of government, it does provide relevant social and political norms that can be used positively to promote effective good governance in modern times. Reference to such relevant Islamic ideals and teachings can make significant impacts on the attitudes of both the political leadership and the populace for the promotion of good governance in predominantly Muslim states, particularly in those states that provide a constitutional role for Islam. An example in that regard is the introduction of the concept of *"Islam Hadhari"* ("Civilizational Islam") as state policy towards realising good governance in Malaysia. In a paper delivered by the country's former Prime Minister, Abdullah bin Haji Ahmad Badawi, at the Victoria University in Wellingon, New Zealand in March 2005, he observed as follows:

> "We view Islam Hadhari [*Ḥaḏārī*] as the way to good governance, that is to say the way in which the government hopes to administer to the wellbeing of the country and the welfare of its multi-religious and multi-racial population. The teachings of Islam are undoubtedly the foundation and inspiration for our actions but the benefits are intended for equitable sharing by all Malaysians, Muslims as well as non-Muslims alike".[49]

---

47 Cp. in this context also *Assem Hefny,* "Hermeneutik, Koraninterpretation und Menschenrechte", in: *Hatem Elliesie* (Hrsg./Editor), Beiträge zum Islamischen Recht VII, Islam und Menschenrechte / Islam and Human Rights / الإسلام وحقوق الإنسان, Frankfurt a.M. 2010, pp. 73-97.

48 See e.g *Sura 49* (الحجرات): *Verse 13:*

يَا أَيُّهَا النَّاسُ إِنَّا خَلَقْنَاكُم مِّن ذَكَرٍ وَأُنثَى وَجَعَلْنَاكُمْ شُعُوبًا

وَقَبَائِلَ لِتَعَارَفُوا إِنَّ أَكْرَمَكُمْ عِندَ اللَّهِ أَتْقَاكُمْ إِنَّ اللَّهَ عَلِيمٌ خَبِيرٌ.

49 Speech by Malaysian Prime Minister, *Abdullah bin Haji Ahmad Badawi,* at Victoria University of Wellington, New Zealand on 31 March 2005, para. 6; http://www.pmo.gov.my/WebNotesApp/PMMain.nsf/0/d33361f0890dd06548256fe700190019?OpenDocumen t (accessed on 6 November 2009). See also generally, *Mohammad Hashim Kamali,* IAIS

There is no doubt that the main challenge confronting most African countries today is averting "bad governance" and realising "good governance". According to the United Nations Development Programme (UNDP) the greatest "challenge for all societies is to create a system of governance that promotes, supports and sustains human development – especially for the poorest and most marginal."[50] Thus, the promotion of "good governance" is currently a big international agenda. The practical difference between "good governance" and "bad governance" is illustrated by Robert I. Rotberg as follows:

> "Good governance is essential if citizens of nation-states [...] are to maximise their inalienable rights as subjects, taxpayers or mere residents of the polities to which they owe, or are compelled to pay, allegiance. From their greatest need, freedom from attack (security), to mundane but real needs, such as well-maintained roads and availability of potable water, citizens look to [...] their modern nation-states [...] for high quality performance. Where that high-quality performance – good governance – is delivered, citizens can go about their personal business and pursuits with enhanced expectations of success, opportunity and satisfaction. Where bad governance prevails, however, citizens suffer increasingly severe consequences – death, injury, intensified morbidity, diminished personal accomplishments, lowered expectations of achievement, hunger, and sometimes starvation"[...] "good governance does not occur by chance. It must be nourished explicitly and consciously. The intervention of human agency is therefore critical."[51]

In essence, good governance must ensure the fulfilment of two fundamental and inherent freedoms for the populace, at all costs. These are Freedom from Fear (Security) and Freedom from Want (Sustenance). This can only be achieved through the concerted efforts of both the political leadership and the populace. As noted by Robert I. Rotberg above, "The intervention of human agency is therefore critical." From an Islamic perspective, this is very much confirmed by the Qur'ānic provisions that: "Verily, God will never change the condition of a people until they change it by themselves"[52] and "[...] that Man can have nothing but what he strives for",[53] respectively.

Malaysia: Exploring the Intellectual Horizons of Civilisational Islam, Selangor (Arah Publications) 2008.

50 S. *UNDP*, Good Governance – and sustainable Human Development", http://mirror.undp.org/magnet/policy/chapter1.htm (accessed on 6 November 2009).

51 *Robert. I. Rotberg*, On Improving Nation-State Governance, in: Daedalus, volume 136, number 1, Cambridge (Winter) 2007, pp. 152 et seqq. (on p. 152 and on p. 153).

52 *Sura 13* (الرعد): *Verse 11:*

لَهُ مُعَقِّبَاتٌ مِّن بَيْنِ يَدَيْهِ وَمِنْ خَلْفِهِ يَحْفَظُونَهُ مِنْ أَمْرِ اللَّهِ إِنَّ اللَّهَ لاَ يُغَيِّرُ مَا بِقَوْمٍ حَتَّى يُغَيِّرُواْ مَا بِأَنْفُسِهِمْ

وَإِذَا أَرَادَ اللَّهُ بِقَوْمٍ سُوءًا فَلاَ مَرَدَّ لَهُ وَمَا لَهُم مِّن دُونِهِ مِن وَالٍ.

53 *Sura 53* (النجم): *Verse 39:* وَأَن لَّيْسَ لِلْإِنسَانِ إِلَّا مَا سَعَى.

In relation to good governance in Africa, these two Qur'ānic verses reflect the need for positive change on the part of both the political leadership and populace to enable a real move towards effective good governance. If the political leaders would not change, the populace should change their attitude of suffering in silence by asking questions and by demanding that the Trust that they imposed in the political leadership should be discharged efficiently. It is evident that bad governance puts a strain on the populace generally, but it particularly hits the weak and the vulnerable in society much harder. Therefore, Islam does not condone bad governance as is reflected in the Qur'ān [Sura 4 (النساء): Verse 75] as follows:

وَمَا لَكُمْ لاَ تُقَاتِلُونَ فِي سَبِيلِ اللّهِ وَالْمُسْتَضْعَفِينَ مِنَ الرِّجَالِ وَالنِّسَاء وَالْوِلْدَانِ الَّذِينَ يَقُولُونَ رَبَّنَا أَخْرِجْنَا
مِنْ هَذِهِ الْقَرْيَةِ الظَّالِمِ أَهْلُهَا وَاجْعَل لَّنَا مِن لَّدُنكَ وَلِيًّا وَاجْعَل لَّنَا مِن لَّدُنكَ نَصِيرًا.

> "And why would you not fight in the cause of God and of those who being weak, are ill-treated (and oppressed), Men, Women, and Children, whose cry is 'Our Lord! Save us from this town, whose people (leaders) are oppressors; and raise for us from You, a Saviour and raise for us from You a Helper."

Islam therefore supports the concept of a "Welfare State", where everyone is assured of at least the minimum basic necessities of life that ensures human dignity. Where people can sleep peacefully at night, have food on their table, and be able to earn sustenance through legitimate work without difficulty. Under the Islamic political concept of *as-siyāsa aš-šarʿiyya,* the classical Islamic jurists emphasised that the primary objective of governance was to promote human welfare (*maṣlaḥa*) and they identified many necessary factors for realising that objective based on relevant Islamic injunctions, some of which are as follows.

I. Elimination of Corruption

One important factor of good governance is the need to eliminate corruption, which is actually the opposite of human welfare. The prohibition of corruption is reiterated in many parts of the Qur'ān.[54] There is no doubt that corruption is the main cause of bad governance in most parts of the world today, particularly in Africa. It is a big challenge that must be confronted if bad governance is to be averted. There is deep-rooted corruption from top to bottom, and everyone, particularly the weak and vulnerable, suffers the consequences in one form or the

---

54 *Sura 7* (الأعراف): *Verse 85:*

وَإِلَى مَدْيَنَ أَخَاهُمْ شُعَيْبًا قَالَ يَا قَوْمِ اعْبُدُواْ اللّهَ مَا لَكُم مِّنْ إِلَهٍ غَيْرُهُ قَدْ جَاءتْكُم بَيِّنَةٌ مِّن رَّبِّكُمْ فَأَوْفُواْ الْكَيْلَ
وَالْمِيزَانَ وَلاَ تَبْخَسُواْ النَّاسَ أَشْيَاءهُمْ وَلاَ تُفْسِدُواْ فِي الأَرْضِ بَعْدَ إِصْلاَحِهَا ذَلِكُمْ خَيْرٌ لَّكُمْ إِن كُنتُم مُّؤْمِنِينَ.

Sura 2 (البقرة): *Verse188:*

وَلاَ تَأْكُلُواْ أَمْوَالَكُم بَيْنَكُم بِالْبَاطِلِ وَتُدْلُواْ بِهَا إِلَى الْحُكَّامِ لِتَأْكُلُواْ فَرِيقًا مِّنْ أَمْوَالِ النَّاسِ بِالإِثْمِ وَأَنتُمْ تَعْلَمُونَ.

other every day. Sincere God-consciousness in line with Islamic injunctions can help stem the evil of corruption as Islam strongly admonishes that:

وَمَا كَانَ لِنَبِيٍّ أَن يَغُلَّ وَمَن يَغْلُلْ يَأْتِ بِمَا غَلَّ يَوْمَ الْقِيَامَةِ ثُمَّ تُوَفَّى كُلُّ نَفْسٍ مَّا كَسَبَتْ وَهُمْ لاَ يُظْلَمُونَ.

[Sura 3 (آل عمران): Verse 161]

> "Anyone who misappropriates his Trust shall bring forth what he misappropriated on the Day of Judgement, and every soul shall be paid (by God) for whatever it earned and no one shall be dealt with unjustly."

II. Maintenance of Justice and the Rule of Law

The maintenance of justice and rule of law is an absolute value of Islam, which must be maintained under any circumstance without any discrimination whatsoever. This is also evidenced in many verses of the Qur'ān, for example:

إِنَّ اللّهَ يَأْمُرُ بِالْعَدْلِ وَالإِحْسَانِ وَإِيتَاء ذِي الْقُرْبَى وَيَنْهَى عَنِ الْفَحْشَاء وَالْمُنكَرِ وَالْبَغْيِ يَعِظُكُمْ لَعَلَّكُمْ تَذَكَّرُونَ.

[Sura 16 (النحل): Verse 90]

> " God commands justice, the doing of good and liberality to kith and kin, and He forbids all shameful deeds and injustice and rebellion. He instructs you, that you may receive admonition."

يَا أَيُّهَا الَّذِينَ آمَنُواْ كُونُواْ قَوَّامِينَ بِالْقِسْطِ شُهَدَاء لِلّهِ وَلَوْ عَلَى أَنفُسِكُمْ أَوِ الْوَالِدَيْنِ وَالأَقْرَبِينَ إِن يَكُنْ غَنِيًّا
أَوْ فَقَيرًا فَاللّهُ أَوْلَى بِهِمَا فَلاَ تَتَّبِعُواْ الْهَوَى أَن تَعْدِلُواْ وَإِن تَلْوُواْ أَوْ تُعْرِضُواْ فَإِنَّ اللّهَ كَانَ بِمَا تَعْمَلُونَ خَبِيرًا.

[Sura 4 (النساء): Verse 135]

> " O Believers! Be maintainers of justice, bearers of witness for God's sake, even though it be against your own selves, your parents, or your near relatives, and whether it be against (the) rich or (the) poor; for God can best protect both. Follow not the lusts (of your hearts) lest you swerve; and if you distort justice, verily God is well-acquainted with all that you do."

يَا أَيُّهَا الَّذِينَ آمَنُواْ كُونُواْ قَوَّامِينَ لِلّهِ شُهَدَاء بِالْقِسْطِ وَلاَ يَجْرِمَنَّكُمْ شَنَآنُ قَوْمٍ
عَلَى أَلاَّ تَعْدِلُواْ اعْدِلُواْ هُوَ أَقْرَبُ لِلتَّقْوَى وَاتَّقُواْ اللّهَ إِنَّ اللّهَ خَبِيرٌ بِمَا تَعْمَلُونَ.

[Sura 5 (المائدة): Verse 8]

> " O Believers! stand out firmly for God as witnesses to fair dealing (equity); and let not the hatred of a people to you make you swerve to depart from justice: Be just; that is closer to piety; and fear God for God is well acquainted with all that you do."

III. Consultation and Participation

The Qur'ān states clearly in Sura 42 (الشورى): Verse 38 that the Muslims conduct their affairs by "mutual consultation" and the Prophet Muhammad was specifically directed to consult the Muslim populace in their affairs in Sura 3

(آل عمران): Verse 159.[55] This emphasises the need for consultation (*šūrā*) in governance and the two verses are often referred to by different institutions, organisations and scholars as the Islamic basis for promoting democratic governance and public participation in many Muslim countries today.

The concept of consultation (*šūrā*) under Islamic political thought means that the leadership should carry the populace along, and not take them by surprise on any issue. The populace must be kept informed and the leadership must call for and welcome their counsel regularly. This was demonstrated by Caliph Abū Bakir in his acceptance speech on his appointment as the first Caliph after the death of the Prophet. He addressed the populace as follows:

> "I have been chosen as your chief although I am better than none of you. Thus, if I do good work it is incumbent on you to extend your help and support to me; if I go wrong it is your duty to put me on the right path. Truth and righteousness are a trust and untruth is a breach of trust. The weak among you are strong to me unless I give them full justice, and the strong among you are weak to me unless I receive what is due from them."[56]

By inviting the populace to support him when he did well and to correct him when he did wrong, Caliph Abū Bakir above recognized consultation and participation as important element of good governance in Islam.

IV. Accountability

I have addressed the issue of accountability to God in the hereafter and to the populace here now when addressing the nature of governance as a Trust under Islamic political thought earlier above by reference to the Qur'ānic provision which says:

> "God commands you to render the Trusts back to those whom they are due; and when you judge between people, you should judge with justice; Verily how excellent is the teaching which Allah gives you, for Allah hears and sees all things."[57]

---

55 *Sura 42* (الشورى): *Verse 38:*
وَالَّذِينَ اسْتَجَابُوا لِرَبِّهِمْ وَأَقَامُوا الصَّلَاةَ وَأَمْرُهُمْ شُورَى بَيْنَهُمْ وَمِمَّا رَزَقْنَاهُمْ يُنفِقُونَ.
Sura 3 (آل عمران): *Verse 159:*
فَبِمَا رَحْمَةٍ مِّنَ اللَّهِ لِنتَ لَهُمْ وَلَوْ كُنتَ فَظًّا غَلِيظَ الْقَلْبِ لَانفَضُّواْ مِنْ حَوْلِكَ فَاعْفُ عَنْهُمْ
وَاسْتَغْفِرْ لَهُمْ وَشَاوِرْهُمْ فِي الأَمْرِ فَإِذَا عَزَمْتَ فَتَوَكَّلْ عَلَى اللَّهِ إِنَّ اللَّهَ يُحِبُّ الْمُتَوَكِّلِينَ.

56 *Akbar Shah Najeebabadi*, The History of Islam, volume 1, Riyadh 2000, p. 276.

57 *Sura 4* (النساء): *Verse 58:*
إِنَّ اللَّهَ يَأْمُرُكُمْ أَن تُؤدُّواْ الأَمَانَاتِ إِلَى أَهْلِهَا وَإِذَا حَكَمْتُم بَيْنَ النَّاسِ
أَن تَحْكُمُواْ بِالْعَدْلِ إِنَّ اللَّهَ نِعِمَّا يَعِظُكُم بِهِ إِنَّ اللَّهَ كَانَ سَمِيعًا بَصِيرًا.

This covers both political and judicial accountability. The acceptance speech of Caliph Abū Bakir cited earlier above also demonstrates a sense of accountability. The second Caliph ʿUmar was also reported to have declared similarly one of his speeches after his appointment.

> "Oh People, it is your duty, if I show evil qualities, to reprove me for them. You must see that I do not exact from you any tax or anything of what God has given you, except that which He allows. You must see that when I have control of the money nothing should be spent improperly".[58]

A classical practice in Islam was to give leadership advice to persons appointed to public offices before they step into office and also from time to time thereafter. This was the practice of the Prophet Muḥammad during his lifetime and which was followed by the Caliphs after him. An example of such leadership advice is the one given by the fourth Caliph ʿAlī b. Abī Ṭālib to Mālik b. Aštar when he appointed the latter as Governor of Egypt. Excerpts of the advice, which is considered as a summary of the Islamic principles of good governance as dictated by Islam, is as follows:

> "Malik […] You must always appreciate and adopt a policy which is neither too severe nor too lenient, a policy which is based on equity and justice and which will be largely appreciated and liked. Remember that the disapproval of common men, have-nots and depressed persons overbalances the approval of a few important persons, and the displeasure of a few big people will be excused by Allah if the masses are happy with you. Do not give cause to the people to envy each other, man versus man, tribe versus tribe or one section of the society versus the other".
>
> "[…] Gather honest, truthful and pious people around you as your advisers and friends. Train them not to flatter you and not to seek your favour by false praises. Try to realise that a ruler can create goodwill in the minds of his subjects. He can make them faithful and sincere only when he is kind and considerate, when he reduces their troubles and difficulties, and when he does not oppress or tyrannise them, and when he never asks for things beyond their capacities. Be afraid of bloodshed. […] Do not strengthen your position by shedding the blood of others unnecessarily and illegally, for it weakens the State. Do the right thing at the right time and in the right way. If people are unanimous about a thing, do not force your opinion upon them. Follow carefully the advice contained in these orders. Through them I have done my duty so that you may not go astray".[59]

---

58 See e.g. *Muḥammad Ḥusayn Haykal*, ʿUmar al-Fārūq, Cairo 1945.

59 See e.g. *Imam Ali,* Nahjul Balagah: The Peak of Eloquence, Letter 53, http://peakofel quence.tripod.com (accessed on 6 November 2009).

It is instructive to note that the UNDP has also identified nine indices for good governance, namely Participation, Rule of Law, Transparency, Responsiveness, Consensus, Equity, Effectiveness and Efficiency, Accountability, and Strategic Vision,[60] which can be broadly compacted into the identified four factors of good governance under Islamic political thought analysed above.

F. Conclusion

This chapter has endeavoured to demonstrate with relevant evidences and arguments that it is very possible for the constitutional role accorded to Islam and/or Islamic Law and institutions in relevant African states to be exploited in conjunction with the human rights provisions in those constitutions to promote good governance in the relevant states. Based on the arguments herein, it is submitted that no government in any of the relevant African states can justifiably claim that Islam, Islamic Law or Islamic institutional provisions in its constitution creates an impediment for the pursuance of human rights and good governance.

What is needed is positive political will on the part of the leadership and collective positive affirmation on the part of the populace in promoting an agenda for good governance by reference to the Islam and human rights provisions in the constitutions of the relevant states. Practically, one can make reference to Morocco as one African country that has demonstrated some good leadership example in that regard by reference to the Moroccan Family Code adopted in 2004. The preamble of the Code states that the King of Morocco provided the Commission that drafted the Code

> "with his constant enlightened guidance and advice [...] and insisted upon their fidelity to the provisions of Sharia (religious law) and Islamic principles of tolerance, and encouraged the use of ijtihad (juridical reasoning) to deduce laws and precepts, while taking into consideration the spirit of our modern era and the imperatives of development, in accordance with the Kingdom's commitment to internationally recognized human rights"[61]

The preamble further states that the Code was:

> "drafted in a modern legal jurisprudential style in conformity with Islam's tolerant rules and exemplary purposes while providing balanced, fair and pragmatic solutions resulting from enlightened open *ijtihad* (juridical reasoning). This code stipulates that human and citizenship rights are accorded to all Moroccans, women and men equally, in respect of the holy divine religious references."[62]

---

60 See *UNDP*, Good Governance…, supra, footnote 50.

61 Moroccan Family Code / مدونة الاسرة المغربية الجديدة (2004), Preamble, par. 4. Cp. English translation, available at: www.globalrights.org/site/DocServer/Moudawana-English_Translation.pdf (accessed on 6 November 2009).

62 Ibidem, Preamble, par. 5.

This approach is commendable and very much in consonance with the evolutional perception of Islamic law and political theory discussed earlier above. That approach must certainly be encouraged in all other relevant African Muslim states to utilize the provisions on Islam and human rights in their constitutions as an agenda for good governance in the respective states.

Islam und Menschenrechte (Islam and Human Rights / الإسلام وحقوق الإنسان)
Hatem Elliesie (Hrsg./Editor), © Peter Lang Verlag: Frankfurt a.M. 2010

Islam, Islamic Law and Human Rights in the Nigerian Context

Isa Hayatu Chiroma / Hatem Elliesie, Maiduguri / Berlin

A. Introduction

With the swearing in of elected executives of Nigeria's Republic in May 1999, the political system witnessed a paradigm shift. After the election victory of President Olusegun Obasanjo, Nigeria returned to democracy after years of military dictatorship.[1] Barely five months after the new civilian government was inaugurated, the governor of the northern Nigerian state Zamfara proclaimed *šarīʿa* (legal system) as the controlling legal system for the state, implementing the provisions of *šarīʿa* / Islamic Law[2] in the penal code. The implementation had a domino-effect on other states with a predominantly Muslim population in northern Nigeria.[3]

The application of the Islamic Criminal Law in Nigeria's northern states is not new since it has legal and historical antecedents. *Šarīʿa* has always been an essential element of the legal system of Northern Nigeria.[4] Although the 1979 Nigerian Constitution limited the application of the Islamic criminal justice system, Islamic Personal Law, i.e. civil matter such as marriage and succession was still applicable. With the reintroduction and expansion of state-run *šarīʿa* penal laws after May 1999, the imposition of sentences developed threefold: (1) sentences more severe than are provided for under the Penal Code, (2) sentences not provided for at all and (3) sentences that are not found in any penal law in Nigeria.[5]

---

1 *Lennart Lehmann,* "'Shariacracy' in Nigeria: Difficult Balance between Sharia and Human Rights", in: Qantara, Bonn 2005, http://www.qantara.de/webcom/show_article.php/_c-476/_nr-341/i.html (accessed on 15 June 2009); see also *Kaniye S.A. Ebeku,* "Making a Democratic and Legitimate Constitution in Nigeria: Lessons from Uganda", in: Recht in Afrika (Law in Afrika · Droit en Afrique), Cologne 2005, pp. 23-61.

2 The term "Islamic Law" and "*šarīʿa* (law)" are used interchangeably within this article as understood in the Nigerian context.

3 Cp. *Vincent O. Nmehielle,* "Sharia Law in the Northern States of Nigeria: To Implement or not to Implement, the Constitutionality is the Question", in: Human Rights Quarterly, volume 26, London 2004, p. 730 et seq.; *Sanusi Lamido Sanusi,* Shariacracy in Nigeria: The intellectual Roots of Islamist Discourses, http://www.nigerdeltacongress.com/ sarticles/shariacracy_in_nigeria.htm (accessed on 15 June 2009).

4 *Ruud Peter,* Islamic Criminal Law in Nigeria, Ibidan / et al. 2003, p. 5; Cp. *G. Ezejiofer,* "The Federation of Nigeria", in: *Antony Niclas Allott* (Ed.), Judicial and Legal Systems in Africa, London 1970, pp. 40 et seqq. (pp. 65-70).

5 *Vincent O. Nmehielle,* Sharia Law…, supra, footnote 3, on p. 732.

Islam und Menschenrechte (Islam and Human Rights / الإسلام وحقوق الإنسان)
Hatem Elliesie (Hrsg./Editor), © Peter Lang Verlag: Frankfurt a.M. 2010, S. 155-171

Seeing that Section 38 of the 1999 Constitution of the Federal Republic of Nigeria (NC) guarantees every citizen the right to freedom of religion, including the freedom to manifest one's belief in worship, practice and in the observance of the tenets of one's religion of choice, some Muslims considered the return of democratic rule in Nigeria as an opportunity to implement full Islamic Law as stipulated by the Holy *Qur'ān* and the *sunna*. On the other hand, when some Northern states reintroduced Islamic Law, this process did not enjoy popularity with some other parts of the Nigerian society. The non-Muslim citizens were especially apprehensive that Islamic Law would not guarantee fundamental human rights and freedoms. Several people raised concerns as to the conformity of some provisions of the various state penal laws with subordinate law and the 1999 NC.[6] Furthermore, the society has been, and still is, engaged in debates about the function, interpretation and status of Islamic Criminal Law regulations in multicultural, multireligious Nigeria.[7]

B. Genesis of Islamic Criminal Law in Nigeria

I. Pre-colonial developments

Šarīʿa has been applied in the northern part of the country before, during and since the colonial period.[8] It dates back to the 11th century.[9] The administration machinery of this *šarīʿa* legal system was first established in the Borno caliphate and subsequently in Kano and Katsina.

Akintunde Olusegun Obilade asserts that long before the 19th century, the principal law administered by the courts in most parts of the territory, now constituting the northern part of Nigeria, was Islamic Law based on the Mālikī *madhab* (school of thought).[10] In this context, one has to note, that, contrary to the general belief, *šarīʿa* was never applied beyond the northern parts of the country.

6 *Mashood A. Baderin,* International Human Rights and Islamic Law, Oxford / New York 2003, p. 31.

7 See, for example, *Abdulmumini A. Oba,* "Religious Rights and the Corporate World in Nigeria – Products and Personal Perspectives, in: Recht in Afrika (Law in Afrika · Droit en Afrique), Cologne 2004, pp. 195 et seqq.

8 Cp. *Human Rights Watch,* 'Political Shari'a'? Human Rights and Islamic Law in Northern Nigeria, http://www.hrw.org/reports/2004/nigeria0904/ (accessed on 15 June 2009).

9 See *Joseph Schacht,* An Introduction to Islamic Law, Oxford / New York 1982, p. 86.

10 *Akintunde Olusegun Obilade,* The Nigerian Legal system, London 1979, p. 17. See also *Emmanuel H. Ofori-Amankwah,* Criminal law in the Northern States of Nigeria, Zaria 1986, pp. 52-59; *Kharisu Sufiyan Chukkol,* "The Penal Code, Origin and Application", in: *Mahmood Yakubu / et al.* (Eds.), Understanding Shari'ah in Nigeria, Ibadan 2001, p. 163; *Abdulmalik Bappa Mahmud,* A Brief History of Shari'ah in the Defunct Northern Nigeria, Jos 1988, p. 1; *Bashir Yusuf Ibrahim,* "Application of the Shari'a Penal Law and Justice in

II. Developments during the colonial period

When northern and southern Nigeria was formally unified in 1914, Lord Lugard came upon a system of Islamic Law fully operational in the north,[11] with a native court system that satisfactorily handled most of the litigations in the north parts of Nigeria. Colonial laws continued to recognize *šarīʿa*, but certain aspects of it were modified or restricted. *Šarīʿa* courts – then known as area courts – had jurisdiction only over matters of personal status law, such as divorce, inheritance, and domestic disputes. Criminal matters were dealt with under the Penal Code for Northern Nigeria; although strongly influenced by the British legal system, the penal code included many components of *šarīʿa*.[12] Even after the introduction of English Law by the British, Islamic Law continued to be subject to the *repugnancy test* of 'natural justice, equity and good conscience'.[13]

The British left the local emirs in power. They exerted power through the existing administrative and judicial structures. The Native Courts' Proclamation of 1900 was based on this principle. The Native Court Proclamation was changed several times before it was replaced by the Native Courts Ordinance of 1933. These changes introduced a hierarchy of courts and systems of appeal within the native court system;[14] caning and capital punishment were not allowed, and Islamic Law was enforced within those limits in Nigeria up to 1956 under the umbrella of 'native law and custom'.

In 1956, the Muslim Court of Appeal was established to hear and determine appeals of regional matters involving questions of Islamic personal (status) law from any native court in the region. The court's jurisdiction substantially covered Islamic marriage and its dissolution, family relations, guardianship of infants, Islamic trust, gifts, succession, maintenance, etc. The Northern Nigeria Penal Code of 1960 (NNPC) recognized some Islamic offences such as adultery and being found drunk in public places. In 1960, the Sharia Court of Appeal was established to repeal and replace the Muslim Court of Appeal of 1956 with jurisdiction to hear and determine appeals with respect to regional matters in cases

---

Northern Nigeria: Constitutional Issues and Implications", in: *Joy Ezeilo / et al.* (Eds.), Shari'a Implementation in Nigeria Issues & Challenges on Women's Rights and Access to Justice, Enugu / Lagos 2003, p. 130.

11 *Elliot A. Keay / Sam S. Richardson*, The Native Courts and Customary Courts of Nigeria, London 1966, p. 27 and p. 231.

12 *Human Rights Watch*, 'Political Shari'a'..., supra, footnote 8.

13 See generally on the "Repugnancy Test" *Andrew Edward Wilson Park*, The Sources of Nigerian Law, Lagos 1963; *Elliot A. Keay / Sam S. Richardson*, The Native Courts..., supra, footnote 11, on p. 2.

14 *Ruud Peters*, Islamic Criminal Law in Nigeria, Ibadan 2003, pp. 6-7.

involving questions regarding Islamic personal (status) law from decision of the Native Courts and Provisional Courts of the then Northern Region of Nigeria.

III. Post-independence developments

The *šarīʿa* application in Nigeria changed in 1959 when Nigeria's independence from the United Kingdom was underway. The then legislature of Northern Nigeria promulgated the criminal law code to conform to the constitution. The constitution provided that "no person should be convicted of any offence unless such offence was defined and the punishment for it provided in a written law". In other words, statutory criminal law had to replace native law as well as *šarīʿa* criminal law. The northern Nigeria legislature, in the face of this dilemma, enacted the Northern Nigerian Penal Code of 1960 (NNPC), a body of laws based on the Sudanese and Indian corpus of criminal legislation.[15] In civil matters, the native courts retained their jurisdiction and continued to apply *šarīʿa* related cases.

Nowadays, Nigeria features a federal system of government with a vertical separation of power. Accordingly, the regular court system is composed of federal and state trial courts, state appeals courts, the Federal Court of Appeal, and the Federal Supreme Court. There are *šarīʿa* and customary (traditional) courts of appeal in states that use *šarīʿa* for civil or criminal matters. Courts of first instance include magistrate or district courts, customary or traditional courts, *šarīʿa* courts, and for some specified cases, the state high courts. The NC also provides that the government establish a Federal Sharia Court of Appeal and Final Court of Appeal, but these courts have not been established, so far.[16]

As already indicated on page 155, twelve northern states[17] reintroduced *šarīʿa* penal codes between 2000 and 2002, amending the existing NNPC with provisions for *šarīʿa* criminal law. These penal codes added new Qur'ānic-based *ḥudūd* offences.[18] The reintroduction of *šarīʿa* penal law codes by various states

---

15 Cp. *Suleiman Kumo,* "The Status of Islamic Law in Nigeria", in: The Islamic Quarterly, volume 24, issue 1 & 2, London 1980, pp. 6-7. See also, re the interplay of politics and religion in Nigerian constitutional history, *Andrew Ubaka Iwobi,* "Tiptoeing Through A Constitutional Minefield: The Great Shari'ah Controversy in Nigeria", in: Journal of African Law, volume 48, issue 2, London, pp. 112-115.

16 *Andrew Ubaka Iwobi,* Tiptoeing..., supra, footnote 15, on p. 5. Cp. also *United States, Department of State, Bureau of Democracy, Human Rights, and Labor,* 2008 Human Rights Report: Nigeria, 25 February 2009 (retrieved on 20 March 2009), http://www.state.gov/g/drl/rls/hrrpt/2008/af/119018.htm (accessed on 15 June 2009).

17 These states are: Borno, Bauchi, Gombe, Jigawa, Kaduna, Kano, Katsina, Kebbi, Niger, Sokoto, Zamfara and Yobe.

18 These offences comprise e.g. *zinā* (s. pp. 162-165), *sariqa* (s. pp. 165-166), *ḥirāba / muḥāraba / qaṭʿ aṭ-ṭarīq* (s. pp. 166-167) and *qaḏf* (s. on p. 163).

in Nigeria generates debates from the religious, political, legal and intellectual circles.[19] Both within Nigeria and in the international community, the Zamfara proclamation as well as similar proclamations of the other northern states generated "sharp outcry" of dissent.[20] These debates dealt predominantly with the questionable legal status as well as the relevance of *šarīʿa* penal law codes in present day Nigeria. Arguments have been advanced for and against the introduction of *šarīʿ*a penal law codes, such as:

- Whether or not the *šarīʿa* penal law codes are in conflict with existing constitutional provisions.[21]
- Whether or not the *šarīʿa* penal law codes are in violation of certain fundamental rights as enshrined in the 1999 Constitution of the Federal Republic of Nigeria.[22]
- Whether the issue of the death penalty, as contained in the *šarīʿa* penal law codes, is in accordance with the democratic principles of the national state.

Proponents of *šarīʿa* argued for the introduction of the *šarīʿa* penal law codes based on the provisions of Section 4 para. 7, Section 6 para. 5, Section 10, Section 38 and Section 277 NC. However, there is neither a consensus nor an answer to its constitutionality. The courts in Nigeria have not, until now, made any statement as to the validity of *šarīʿa* penal law codes.

C. Nature and Scope of Islamic Criminal Law

Due to the focus of this article as a case study, and in addition to the book's chapter *"Beiträge zur islamrechtlichen Methodik sowie zur Rechtsphilosophie"* ("Contributions to Islamic Legal and theological Approaches and Philosophy of Laws") on pages 39-119, it is appropriate to consider, albeit briefly, the nature and scope of Islamic (Criminal) Law applied in the aforementioned northern states of Nigeria.[23]

---

19 *Allan Christelow,* "Islamic Law and Judicial Practice in Nigeria: An Historical Perspective", in: Journal of Muslims Minority Affairs, volume 22, issue 1, London 2002, pp. 197-198. See also *John N. Paden,* Muslim Civic Cultures and the Conflict Resolution, the Challenge of Democratic Federalism in Nigeria, Washington D.C. 2005, pp. 157-159.

20 *Vincent O. Nmehielle,* "Sharia Law..., supra, footnote 3, on p. 733. Cp. also *Danny Mc Cain,* "Which Road Leads beyond the Shariʿah Controversy? A Christian Perspective on Shariʿah in Nigeria", in: *Philip Ostein / Jamila M. Nasir / Franz Kogelmann* (Eds.), Comparative Perspectives on Shariʿah in Nigeria, Ibadan / et al. 2005, pp. 7-26.

21 E.g. Sections 1, 10, 36, 38, of the 1999 Constitution of the Federal Republic of Nigeria.

22 E.g. equality before the law (s. on p. 169) torture or cruel, degrading or inhumane punishment (s. on p. 169), etc.

23 Cp. footnote 17.

I. Nature of Islamic Law

Islamic Law can simply be defined as a "divine law" or "sacred law". It is an all-embracing body of religious duties, the totality of Allāh's commands that regulate the life of every Muslim in every aspect; it comprises an equal footing of the ordinances regarding worship and ritual, as well as political and – in the narrow sense – legal rules.[24]

1. Primary Sources: *Qur'ān* and *Sunna*

The primary sources, accepted universally by all Muslims, are the *Qur'ān* and *sunna*. The *Qur'ān* is the holy scripture of Islam, believed by Muslims to be the direct and unaltered word of Allāh. The *sunna* consists of the religious actions and quotations of the Prophet Muḥammad; narrated through his companions and Šīʿa-Imams.

2. Further Source(s) / analogical reasoning

As Islamic regulations stated in the primary sources do not explicitly deal with every conceivable eventuality, jurisprudence must refer to resources and authentic documents to find the correct course of action. According to Sunni schools of law (*maḏāhib*), the secondary source of Islamic Law is consensus (*iǧmāʿ*) of the scholars, representing a common denominator of doctrine achieved in each generation, expressing the synchronous aspect of the living tradition of each school.[25]

What one understands under the "umbrella term *qiyās*" is not only a source in Sunni Islam but also that of analogical reasoning. Generally speaking, *qiyās* is the process of legal deduction according to which the jurist, confronted with an unprecedented case, bases his or her argument on the logic used in the *Qur'ān* and *sunna*. *Qiyās* must not be based on arbitrary judgment, but rather be firmly rooted in the primary sources. It covers, according to the prevailing view, the *argumenta a minore ad maius, a maiore ad minus,* the *a fortiori*-argument as well as the *reductio ad absurdum (qiyās al-ʿaks)* and the *qiyās aš-šabah* where the cause (*ʿilla*) is missing.[26]

---

24 *Joseph Schacht,* An Introduction to Islamic Law, supra, footnote 9, p. 1. Likewise *Muhammad Kalisch,* "Islam und Menschenrechte: Betrachtungen zum Verhältnis von Religion und Recht", in: *Hatem Elliesie* (Hrsg./Editor), Beiträge zum Islamischen Recht VII, Islam und Menschenrechte (Islam and Human Rights / الإسلام وحقوق الإنسان), Frankfurt a.M. 2010, pp. 49 et seqq. (on p. 50 / "B. Islamisches Recht").

25 *Joseph Schacht,* An Introduction to Islamic Law, supra, footnote 9, p. 30.

26 *Wael B. Hallaq,* "Non-Analogical Arguments in Sunni Juridical Qiyas", in: Arabica, volume 36, Leiden 1989, pp. 286 et seqq. (on p. 289); *Birgit Krawietz,* Hierachie der Rechtsquellen im tradierten sunnitischen Islam, Berlin 1999, p. 205 et seq.; *Mathias Rohe,* Das islamische Recht: Geschichte und Gegenwart, München 2009, p. 62.

II. Scope of Islamic Criminal Law

Whenever there is a need to arrange matters of personal status in predominantly Islamic countries, one may take recourse to the classical doctrine of Islamic Law. This differs, of course, from each of the respective legal systems,[27] most notably in criminal matters. The importance placed on the substance of Islamic Law must not overshadow the significance of the status given to *šarīʿa* law by the state. Indeed, its status constitutes a determinant factor that measures the true extent of the role accorded to the religion within the legal 'cogs' of the state's internal system. The challenge posed to Human Rights in various Muslim states is not derived directly from Islamic doctrine; but, rather, from the integration of its provisions into the substantive law.[28] Thus, some classical doctrines of Islamic legal issues will be exemplified and juxtaposed with corresponding relevant matters of particular Nigerian contemporary interest in the course of the following sub-chapters.

1. General Classification of Islamic Criminal Law

Crimes in Islam are classified[29] into three categories: The first and most serious crimes (*ḥadd* or *ḥudūd* crimes), crimes demanding retaliation (*qiṣāṣ* crimes) least serious crimes (*taʿzīr* crimes).[30] The focus, however, will be on the former, the so called *ḥudūd* crimes.

2. Most serious crimes (*ḥadd* or *ḥudūd* crimes)

Ḥadd or *ḥudūd* crimes are crimes which are specifically mentioned in the *Qur'ān* and the *aḥadīṯ* transgressing the limits which God Himself has placed on people's behaviour. Punishment for those offences are prescribed in the respective source of Islamic Law. They are thus considered to be crimes directly disobeying the law; and offenders of *ḥadd* or *ḥudūd* crimes are punished with the most severe punishments. Some legal scholars are including murder and apostasy (*ridda*) among the categories of *ḥudūd* crimes.[31] Following acts, however, are, indisputably, subsumed under the *ḥadd* category:[32]

---

[27] Likewise *Hatem Elliesie*, "Editor's Foreword", in: *Hatem Elliesie* (Hrsg./Editor), Beiträge zum Islamischen Recht VII, Islam und Menschenrechte (Islam and Human Rights / الإسلام وحقوق الإنسان), Frankfurt a.M. 2010, on p. 27.

[28] *Nisrine Abiad*, Sharia, Muslim States and International Human Rights Treaty Obligations: A comparative Study, London 2008, p. 32.

[29] See *Safia M. Safwat*, "Offence and Penalties in Islamic Law", in: The Islamic Quarterly, volume 26, issue 3, London 1982, pp. 153-154; *Jamila Hussain*, Islamic Law and Society, Sydney 1999, p. 134; *Mathias Rohe*, Das islamische Recht..., supra, footnote 26, pp. 122-140.

[30] See *Yahaya Yunusa Bambale*, Crimes and Punishments under Islamic Law, Zaria 2003, p. 26.

[31] *Mathias Rohe*, Das islamische Recht..., supra, footnote 26, p. 122.

[32] Cp. Ibidem; *Jamila Hussain*, Islamic Law..., supra, footnote 29, p. 134 et seq.

a. *Zinā* (rape, adultery and fornication)

Zinā includes adultery, rape and fornication between unmarried persons,[33] although the Mālikī legal scholar ad-Dasūqī classified rape under the heading of *ḥirāba*[34]. If the offender is not married, he is punished, under Classical Islamic Law, with 100 lashings.[35] If he is married, the punishment is stoning to death; since, in contrast to the *Qur'ān,* on the authority of *ḥadīṯ,* the proper punishment by the majority of Islamic legal scholars is stoning to the death.[36] A verdict for adultery or fornication requires the confirmation of the crime by four male witnesses or the confession of the offender(s).

Both the Kano Penal Code[37] and the Niger Penal Code[38] lay down that *zinā* can only be proven by confession or four witnesses.[39] If proven, the following punishments are stipulated:[40]

- *Unlawful sexual intercourse* is to be punished in some Nigerian states according to the aforementioned doctrine. Men are, in addition, punished by imprisonment for one year.[41]
- *Rape* is regarded as a special case of *zinā* and is made punishable by the same punishments, except that the Kano Penal Code, following the Northern Nigeria Penal Code of 1960 (NNPC), extends the imprison-

33 Cp. in this context also *Naseef Naeem,* "Zwischen Einschränkung und neuen Entwicklungen: Das Grundrecht auf heterosexuelle Selbstbestimmung in den Verfassungssystemen arabischer Staaten" ("Between Limitation and new Developments: The Basic Right of heterosexual Self-Determination in the constitutional Systems of Arabic States"), in: *Hatem Elliesie* (Hrsg./Editor), Beiträge zum Islamischen Recht VII, Islam und Menschenrechte (Islam and Human Rights / الإسلام وحقوق الإنسان), Frankfurt a.M. 2010, on pp. 257-280.

34 As to *ḥirāba* cp. p. 166 et seq.

35 Sura 24 (النور), Verse 2 states:

الزَّانِي لا يَنكِحُ إلا زَانِيَةً أَوْ مُشْرِكَةً وَالزَّانِيَةُ لا يَنكِحُهَا إِلا زَانٍ أَوْ مُشْرِكٌ وَحُرِّمَ ذَلِكَ عَلَى الْمُؤْمِنِينَ

> " As for the fornicatress and the fornicator, flog each of them, [giving] a hundred stripes, and let not pity for them detain you in the matter of obedience of Allāh, if you believe in Allāh and the last day, and let a party of believers witness their chastisement."

36 *Jamila Hussain,* Islamic Law…, supra, footnote 29, p. 136.

37 Cp. Section 127 (Explanation) Kano Penal Code; Section 396 Code of Criminal Procedure.

38 Cp. Section 68 (A) (3) (b) Niger Penal Code.

39 The Zamfara Penal Code is silent in this respect.

40 As to the following s. *Ruud Peters,* Islamic Criminal…, supra, footnote 14, pp. 19 et seqq.

41 Section 125 Kano Penal Code. Section 127 Zamfara Penal Code does not stipulate that the imprisonment is only for men; Section 68 (A) (2) (c) Niger Penal Code does not mention imprisonment at all.

ment of the rapist for life.[42] The Kano and Zamfara Penal Codes also oblige the perpetrator to pay compensation up to the amount of the proper bride price.

The fact that rape is assimilated to *zinā* puts women at a great disadvantage because, in principle, both parties to *zinā* are liable for punishment. Furthermore, if a woman reports to the police that she is a victim of rape, this can easily be construed as a confession to unlawful intercourse which makes her liable to the *ḥadd* punishment, unless she can prove that intercourse took place without her consent. The burden of proof lies with her.[43]

aa) *Zinā* case tried in Zamfara state

According to classical Mālikī doctrine, the pregnancy of an unmarried woman is proof of *zinā*. Although the *šarīʿa* penal law codes have been silent on this point, this rule was applied in a case tried in a Zamfara court. A teenage single mother, Bariya Ibrahim Magazu, claimed at trial that she was raped by three men. In September 2000, she was found guilty, because she could not prove that her father pressured her to engage in sexual activity with the men. She was found guilty of two offences: having pre-marital sex, and bringing false charges against the men that she claimed were responsible. She was sentenced to 180 lashes,[44] to be administered on 27 January 2001.

On 13 January 2001 the execution of Bariya Ibrahim Magazu's sentence was postponed and reduced to 100 lashes as she was no longer found guilty of defamation (*qaḏf*), after apparently having withdrawn her claims against the three men for lack of evidence. The sentence was carried out in public on 22 January 2001.

bb) *Zinā* case tried in Sokoto state

On 9 October 2001 Safiya Hussaini of the village Tungkar Tudu was sentenced to death by stoning by a Sharia-Court in Gwadabawa in the northern state of Sokoto for allegedly having a child with a married neighbour. She had the child after her divorce. Both the presumed father Yakubu Abubakar and Safiya Hussaini were charged by the offence of *zinā*, illegal sexual intercourse, which Section 128 and Section 129 of the Sokoto Shariʿa Penal Code (SSPC) makes

---

42 Section 126 et seq. Kano Penal Code; Section 128 et seq. Zamfara Penal Code.

43 *Ruud Peters*, Islamic Criminal…, supra, footnote 14, p. 19.

44 The number of lashes is composed of one hundred (100) for *zinā* and eighty (80) for defamation.

punishable with caning of 100 lashes or stoning to death.[45] While the court acquitted Yakubu Abubakar, the court convicted Safiya Hussaini,[46] but she appealed this sentence. She won the appeal, now withdrew her confession made during the trial and asserted that the father of her child was her former husband and not Yakubu Abubakar as well as, among other reasons, alleging that she had sex out of wedlock before Islamic Law took effect using the *nulla poena sine lege* principle.[47]

cc) *Zinā* case tried in Katsina state

In March 2002, a *šarīʿa* court in Funtua in the northern state of Katsina sentenced Amina Lawal (Kurami) to death by stoning for adultery and for conceiving a child out of wedlock. The father of the child was not prosecuted due to lack of evidence. Amina Lawal's defenders put forward a similar argument as pleaded in the case of Safiya Hussaini during her trial, but it was rejected. Her conviction was overturned and she has since remarried. BAOBAB for Women's Human Rights, an NGO based in Nigeria,[48] took up her case which

---

45 *Section 128 SSPC:*

Whoever, being a man or a woman fully responsible, has sexual intercourse through the genital of a person over whom he has no sexual rights and in circumstances in which no doubt exits as to the illegality of the act, is guilty of the offence of zina.

Section 129 SSPC:

Whoever commits the offence of zina shall be punished

(a) with canning of one hundred lashes if unmarried and shall be liable to imprisonment for a term of one year; or

(b) if married, with stoning to death.

46 The charges against Safiya Hussaini were based on the preliminary police investigation, during which she acknowledged that she had intercourse with Yakubu Abubakar on four occasions, and as a result, had become pregnant and given birth. During the police investigation, however, Yakubu Abubakar denied having sexual relations with her. Subsequently, four prosecution witnesses testified to the truthfulness of Safiya Hussaini's acknowledgement and Yakubu Abubakar's denial. Thereupon Yakubu Abubakar was given the opportunity to challenge all the testimonies, whereas Safiya Hussaini was allowed to do so only with regard to two witnesses, both of them police officers. In response to the charges brought against her during the trial, she stuck to her previous statement. In more detail see *Rudolph Peters,* "The Re-Islamization of Criminal Law in northern Nigeria and the Judiciary: the Safiya Hussaini Case", in: *Muhammad Khalid Masud / Rudolph Peters / David S. Powers* (Eds.), Dispensing Justice in Islam: Qadis and their Judgements, Leiden / Boston 2006, pp. 219 et seqq. (on p. 226 et seq.).

47 Ibidem, pp. 227 et seqq.; *Ruud Peters,* Islamic Criminal..., supra, footnote 14, p. 20.

48 BAOBAB operates from a national office in Lagos and with outreach teams in 14 states across Nigeria. These are: Adamawa, Borno, Edo, Kaduna, Kano, Katsina, Kogi, Kwara, Lagos, Osun, Oyo, Plateau, Taraba and Zamfara. The organization works with women, legal and paralegal professionals, human rights NGOs and members of the general public, see http://www.baobabwomen.org (accessed on 15 June 2009).

was argued by Nigerian lawyers trained in both secular and (classical) Islamic Law. Amina Lawal's lawyers included Hauwa Ibrahim, a prominent human rights lawyer known for her *pro bono* work for people condemned under Islamic Law. In their successful defense of Amina Lawal, lawyers used the notion of 'extended pregnancy', arguing that under *šarīʿa*, a five year interval is possible between human conception and birth.[49] On 25 September 2003 Amina Lawal had her sentence overturned by the Sharia Court of Appeal, and is now free. The five-judge panel stated that she was not given "ample opportunity to defend herself" in the previous proceedings.

b. Theft (*sariqa*)

According to Sura 5 (المائدة) Verse 38, the punishment for theft (*sariqa*) is the cutting off of the hand:

وَالسَّارِقُ وَالسَّارِقَةُ فَاقْطَعُواْ أَيْدِيَهُمَا جَزَاء بِمَا كَسَبَا نَكَالاً مِّنَ اللّهِ وَاللّهُ عَزِيزٌ حَكِيمٌ.

While the consequence of theft is expressed comparatively clear, what *sariqa* constitutes in detail remains open. Contours of the offence were established in the literature until the end of the 2nd/8th century and, on this basis, further developed a comprehensive casuistry until the 4th/12th century.[50]

aa) *Sariqa* regulations in Kano and Zamfara state

The provisions in the *šarīʿa* penal law codes regarding theft, for which the *hadd* punishment of amputation[51] of the right hand from the wrist[52] is incurred, are also very similar to classical Mālikī doctrine. The Kano and Zamfara Penal Codes[53] define it as

> "Covertly, dishonestly and without consent taking any lawful and movable property belonging to another, out of its place of custody [*ḥirz*] and valued not less than the minimum stipulated value [*niṣāb*] without any justification."

The *niṣāb* is defined as

> "minimum amount of property [...] which, if stolen, shall attract *hadd* punishment".[54]

---

49 Five years prior to the date of her daughter's birth, she was still married to her husband.

50 See *Mathias Rohe,* Das islamische Recht..., supra, footnote 26, pp. 127-134; *Joseph Schacht,* An Introduction to Islamic Law, supra, footnote 9, pp. 179-180.

51 Section 135 of the Kano Penal Code and Section 147 of the Zamfara Penal Code (but not the Niger amendment) also list eight defence pleas that under classical Mālikī law preclude the application of the penalty of amputation. If such pleas are accepted, the offender will be punished by imprisonment not exceeding one year and by fifty lashes.

52 Section 134 of the Kano Penal Code and Section 145 of the Zamfara Penal Code stipulate in the event subsequent recidivism the left foot, the left hand and the right foot will be amputated. With regard to the classical Islamic doctrine (in general) cp. *Joseph Schacht,* An Introduction to Islamic Law, supra, footnote 9, p. 179 et seq.

53 Section 133 of the Kano Penal Code and Section 144 of the Zamfara Penal Code.

54 Section 46 of the Kano Penal Code and Section 46 of the Zamfara Penal Code.

This is a circular definition which is not of great help for a legal practitioner. In classical Mālikī law the amount was precisely defined in terms of gold and silver. If the *niṣāb* is not assigned a monetary value, this may result in legal uncertainty, especially since so much depends on its definition.[55]

bb) *Sariqa* judgement in Sokoto state

In a judgement pronounced on July 2001, a Sokoto Sharia-Court presided by judge Bawa Sahabi Tambuwal fixed the *niṣāb* on 869 Naira (ca. 4 €uro), which seems to be rather low. Comparably, the Section 68 A (2) (a) of the Niger Penal Code does not adopt the *šarīʿa* definition, but refers to the Sections 287-290 of the NNPC, stipulates that the stolen goods must have a minimum value of 20,000 Naira (about 90 €uro) and that it must have been stolen from proper custody.[56]

c. Violent street robbery (*ḥirāba / muḥāraba / qaṭʿ aṭ-ṭarīq*)

The synonymously used terms *ḥirāba, muḥāraba* and *qaṭʿ aṭ-ṭarīq* are stipulated in Sura 5 (المائدة) Vers 33 et seqq. subsumed with differing exactitude.[57] This crime is, by classical doctrine, regarded as related to theft on one side and homicide on the other, but is not subsumed under these, except in the case of active repentance before arrest; the penalties inflicted differ according to various facts of the case:

- If only plunder has happened, and the value of the loot, when divided by the number of culprits, at least equals the minimum amount required for the *ḥadd* for theft (*sariqa*) to be applicable, the right hand and the left foot are to be cut off.
- If only homicide has happened, execution with the sword takes place, not as retaliation but as *ḥadd.*
- If both plunder and homicide have happened, execution by crucifixion alive is prescribed.[58]

In nowadays Nigeria, *ḥirāba* is, according to Section 139 Kano Penal Code and Section 152 Zamfara Penal Code, defined as follows:[59]

> Whoever acting alone or in conjunction with others in order to seize property or to commit an offence or for any other reason voluntarily causes or attempts to cause to any person death or hurt or wrongful restraint or fear of instant death or of instant hurt or of instant wrongful restraint in circumstances that renders such person helpless or incapable of defending himself commit the offence of *ḥirāba.*[60]

---

55 *Ruud Peters,* Islamic Criminal…, supra, footnote 14, p. 21.

56 Ibidem.

57 *Mathias Rohe,* Das islamische Recht…, supra, footnote 26, pp. 124; *Jamila Hussain,* Islamic Law…, supra, footnote 29, p. 135.

58 *Joseph Schacht,* An Introduction to Islamic Law, supra, footnote 9, p. 180 et seq.

59 *Ruud Peters,* Islamic Criminal…, supra, footnote 14, p. 23.

60 The wording derives not from Section 296 of the NNPC.

As in the classical doctrine, the penalties are imprisonment for life (the modern understanding of banishment) if neither property nor life was taken, amputation of the right hand and left foot if property was taken, and death if a life was taken.[61]

The Niger Penal Code also imposes alternate amputation in cases in which grievous hurt was inflicted during the attack. The Zamfara Penal Code makes a distinction between the case in which only a life has been taken and the case which both a life and property have been taken. In conformity with the classical doctrine, the penalty in the latter case is crucifixion. Nowhere, however, does the Zamfara Penal Code define this punishment, which is a serious omission since the matter is controversial in classical Mālikī doctrine. Some Mālikī authorities held that crucifixion means that the convict's body is exposed on a cross after his having been put to death, whereas others claimed that the convict must first be crucified and then put to death. Section 256 (d) of the Bauchi Penal Code speaks of "death by impalement (crucifixion)", but does not further define the nature of this punishment.[62]

D. Application of Islamic Law in a Constitutional Democracy: Issues and Challenges

The question of whether or not the reintroduction of Islamic Law in the northern states (with a Muslim majority) is constitutional is hotly debated and highly politicized. Since the reintroduction of the criminal component of Islamic Law in Nigeria, fundamental questions have been raised, such as:

- Whether or not the implementation of criminal aspect of Islamic Law is in conformity with the 1999 Constitution of the Federal Republic of Nigeria.
- Whether or not Islamic Law guarantees Human Rights and freedom within the sphere of its operation in a constitutional democracy.

If there are conflicts between the *šarīʿa* penal law codes of the northern states mentioned in footnote 17, there are two ways to resolve them: litigation or negotiation. Neither the courts of law nor the federal government of Nigeria did anything to answer these fundamental questions. However, many scholars[63] argued

[61] Section 140 Kano Penal Code, Section 153 Zamfara Penal Code, Section 68 A (2) (b) Niger State Penal Code.

[62] As to this chapter see *Ruud Peters,* Islamic Criminal..., supra, footnote 14, p. 24.

[63] See *Joy Ngozi Ezeilo*, Human Rights Protection in Administration of Sharia Justice System, Enugu 2005, pp. 2-229, *Andrew Ubaka Iwobi,* Tiptoeing..., supra, footnote 15, on pp. 112-164; *Ruud Peters,* Islamic Criminal..., supra, footnote 14, pp. 1-71; *Joy Ezeilo / et al.*, Shariʿa..., supra, footnote 10, pp. 2-273; *Philip Ostien / et al.*, Comparative Perspec-

extensively in favour or against the constitutionality of the reintroduction of Islamic Criminal Law in Nigerian constitutional democracy. The main contending issues were:

- Can the introduction of Islamic Criminal Law be regarded as part of the realization of Right to Freedom of Religion as enshrined in the 1999 Constitution of the Federal Republic of Nigeria under a constitutional democracy?
- Can a State House of Assembly enlarge the jurisdiction of a Sharia Court of Appeal amend or enact a new Evidence Act which is contained in the exclusive legislative list?

The incompatibility of provisions of *šarīʿa* penal law with respect to *nulle proseque* and the *prerogative of mercy*, as contained in the 1999 Constitution of the Federal Republic of Nigeria, is a further area of concern. Despite opposing views as to the constitutionality of Islamic Criminal Law, the courts had little or no opportunity[64] to clearly subject the reintroduction as well as enactments of Islamic penal laws in Nigeria to a constitutional validity test.

Article 10 of the 1999 Constitution of the Federal Republic of Nigeria reads:

> "The Government of the Federation or of a State shall **not adopt any religion as state religion**."

The issue, however, is not as clear as it *prima facie* would seem to be, since *šarīʿa* has for a long time – as already mentioned in the Introduction of this article on page 155 – been accepted as a part of the legal systems of the northern states in the domain of family, private and commercial law. There is, on the other hand, no doubt about the unconstitutionality of the implicit introduction of the Mālikīt Law of Evidence: The 1999 Constitution of the Federal Republic of Nigeria stipulates that legislation on evidence is a prerogative of the federal legislature. Some of the *šarīʿa* penal law codes of the northern states are diametrical opposed to Human Rights guaranteed in the 1999 Constitution of the Federal Republic of Nigeria.[65]

---

tives on Shari'ah..., supra, footnote 20, pp. 1-381; *Muhamed Tawfiq Ladan*, A Handbook on Sharia Implementation in Northern Nigeria: Women and Children's Rights Focus, Kaduna 2005, pp 1-191; *John N. Paden,* Muslim Civic Cultures and the Conflict Resolution, the Challenge of Democratic Federalism in Nigeria, Washington D.C. 2005, pp.157-182.

64 Except in the aforementioned cases of Safiya Hussaini and Amina Lawal, where, on appeal, the court reversed the judgement in cases of *zinā* on ground of error of law.

65 Cp. *Human Rights Watch,* 'Political Shari'a'..., supra, footnote 8; *Ruud Peters,* Islamic Criminal..., supra, footnote 14, p. 31 et seq.

I. Equality before the Law

One of the prominent principles in human rights discourse is that all persons are equal before the law and entitled to the same legal protection. This principle is embodied in Section 42 NC.[66] The same principle is expressed in international human rights instruments such as Art. 14 and Art. 16 of the International Convention for Civil and Political Rights (ICCPR).[67]

Section 68 (A) (3) (b) of the Niger Penal Code, for example, stipulates that in the requirement for proving the offence of *zinā,* in the case of unlawful sexual intercourse, the testimony of men is of greater value than that of women. On the other hand, men are placed in a disadvantageous position in Section 125 of the Kano Penal Code, where the punishment for *zinā* committed by unmarried men is caning as well as imprisonment for one year, whereas unmarried women are "only" to be punished by caning. According to Ruud Peters, on the whole, there is little gender bias in the texts of the new *šarīʿa* penal law codes. However, where the codes are silent, the courts apply classical Mālikīte doctrine, which in certain points is discriminatory. The most prominent form of gender discrimination is the application by lower *šarīʿa* courts, unwarranted by the new *šarīʿa* penal law codes, of classical Mālikīte doctrine that – as seen in the aforementioned Bariya Ibrahim Magazu case in the Zamfara state on page 163 – extramarital pregnancy denotes proof of unlawful intercourse.[68] However, now that two Sharia Courts of Appeal have reserved trial court sentences of stoning based on extramarital pregnancy, it seems that this is no longer admitted as proof.[69]

II. Torture or cruel, degrading or inhuman Punishment

Torture or cruel, degrading or inhuman punishment is outlawed by both Section 34 (1) NC and the CAT[70] ratified by Nigeria on 28 June 2001. They lay down that no person shall be subject to torture or to inhuman or degrading punishment and that states shall take measures to prevent public servants from committing acts of torture or administering such punishment.[71]

---

66 *Human Rights Watch,* 'Political Shariʿa'..., supra, footnote 8.

67 *Article 14 ICCPR:*

"All persons shall be equal before the courts and tribunals. [...]."

Article 16 ICCPR:

"Everyone shall have the right to recognition everywhere as a person before the law."

68 *Ruud Peters,* "The Reintroduction of Sharia Criminal Law in Nigeria: New Challenges for the Muslims of the North", in: *Silvia Tellenbach / Thoralf Hanstein* (Eds.), Beiträge zum Islamischen Recht IV, Frankfurt a.M. 2004, pp. 9 et seqq. (on p. 16).

69 Ibidem; *Rudolph Peters,* The Re-Islamization..., supra, footnote 46, pp. 219 et seqq.

70 As to the official text of the CAT, the United Nations Convention against Torture and other Cruel, Degrading Inhuman Punishment or Treatment, see http://www2.ohchr.org /english/law/pdf/cat.pdf (accessed on 15 June 2009).

71 Section 34 of the 1999 Nigerian Constitution; Article 1 (1) and Article 16 (1) of the CAT.

Here, we have one of the most conspicuous examples of conflict between the new *šarīʿa* penal law codes and human rights principles. The *sariqa* punishment of amputation or death by stoning and crucifixion in cases of *ḥirāba, muḥāraba* or *qaṭʿ aṭ-ṭarīq* have to be considered as torture.[72]

F. Problems of Islamic Law Implementation in Nigeria

As seen, the introduction of *šarīʿa* penal law codes conflict in some areas with the 1999 Constitution of the Federal Republic of Nigeria and international human rights instruments ratified by Nigeria. Thus, one has to notice that the implementation of Islamic Criminal Law since the year 2000 was confronted with numerous problems as well as challenges.

The first *šarīʿa* penal law code enacted in Zamfara shows every sign of hasty drafting: incorrect cross-references, incorrect and defective wording, omissions and contradictions. In spite of these defects, five other states have adopted the Zamfara code verbatim or with minor changes.[73]

The *šarīʿa* penal law codes were introduced with little to no preparation. The judiciary was not trained to work with these codes, and are sufficiently equipped to enforce these laws. Consequently, most of the judgements passed by judges were done without recourse to provisions of *šarīʿa*; and where recourse was made to *šarīʿa* laws, they were either procedural error, lack of due process or wrong application of provisions of law. It is striking that in both the Safiya Hussaini case in Sokoto state and the Amina Lawa case in Katsina state the sentence of the trial court were quashed mainly on technical and procedural grounds.

G. Conclusion

The *šarīʿa* penal law codes violate basic human rights on several points and infringe on federal legislative prerogatives, e.g. in the field of evidence, as well as contradict the principle that offences and their punishments must be founded in written law.[74] It is obvious in the *šarīʿa* penal law codes' question of constitutionality that there is a difference between lower courts and the courts of appeal with regard to the enforcement of *ḥadd* or *ḥudūd* crimes. The lower *šarīʿa* courts seemed to be quite willing to pronounce a sentence of death by stoning on the basis of what, even according to classical Islamic standards, are rather thin grounds, by superficially referring to some texts from Mālikī compendia. The Sharia Courts of Appeal seemed to adopt the opposite attitude, trying to prevent

72 *Ruud Peters*, The Reintroduction…, supra, footnote 68, p. 13 et seq.

73 *Idem*, Islamic Criminal…, supra, footnote 14, p. 45.

74 Most of the *šarīʿa* penal law codes contain provisions that acts and omissions, that are punishable under Islamic Law, may be punished by the *šarīʿa* courts, even if the penal code does not mention them; *Ruud Peters*, Islamic Criminal…, supra, footnote 14, p. 44.

the application of the *ḥadd* or *ḥudūd* punishments for *zinā* (unlawful intercourse) as much as possible. The courts used all possible arguments and stretched the classical doctrine to the utmost in order to quash the trial court judgment. One of the reasons may have been affected by political motives. If they upheld the trial court judgements, then the cases would be submitted to the Supreme Federal Court, which might test the constitutionality of the *šarīʿa* penal law codes. This would therefore provide an opportunity for the Federal Supreme Court to find that *šarīʿa* penal law codes are null and void. In order to prevent this scenario, it is likely that the Sharia Courts of Appeal set aside the decisions of the lower courts.[75]

Since, except in the state of Zamfara and Niger, the *šarīʿa* penal law codes were enacted against the wish of the authorities under strong popular pressure, its abolition would mean political suicide. Hence, it is important to realize that *šarīʿa* application in the northern parts of Nigeria is inevitable, especially where Muslims constitute a sizeable number.

One of the major problems of implementation of the *šarīʿa* penal law codes in Nigeria is the failure of these states to address the issues of economic and social justice. Furthermore, it is important to note that the lax attitude of the police combined with the religious fervour of the population in many northern states have led to the emergence of Islamic vigilante groups known as *Hisba.* In many instances these groups have begun to take the law into their own hands, which has often resulted in violence and disorder.

---

[75] Cp. *Rudolph Peters*, The Re-Islamization…, supra, footnote 46, on p. 240 et seq.

Mufti Act of Zanzibar
and
the Fundamental Rights and Freedoms of Muslims on the Isles

Chris Maina Peter, Dar es Salaam

> *"On the face of it [,] Zanzibar appears to be an idyllic island in the sun. One observer wrote that Zanzibar had tremendous potential as a political entity. Tribalism is not a problem; the people are united by the common language of KiSwahili; and over 95% of them are Muslim, which should make for a more harmonious society. And yet, its history over the past four decades has been anything but harmonious."*
>
> Abdul Sheriff
> 1 June 2000[1]

A. Introduction

The enactment of the Mufti Act in Zanzibar in 2001 (MAoZ)[2] was received with mixed feelings. This is because of two main reasons. Firstly, for the first time, a purely religious office, the Mufti, being the religious leader of all Muslims in the Isles, was being legislated under the secular law. Secondly, it was the fate of the newly emerged splitter religious groups which were in effect challenging the legitimacy of the Office of the Mufti.[3] These two reasons led to the speculations on the mischief to be cured by this cause of action by the Revolutionary Government of Zanzibar (RGZ), the *Serikali ya Mapinduzi ya Zanzibar* (S.M.Z.)

This article attempts to examine the aforementioned Act. It will speculate on the reasons behind it, its contents and effects on the majority of Zanzibaris who happen to be Muslims.[4] Moreover, it will evaluate its efficacy, and, in particular, whether it has managed to smoothly regulating the relations between Muslims in

---

1 *Abdul Sheriff*, "Preface" in: *Mohamed Ali Bakari*, The Democratisation Process in Zanzibar: A Retarded Transition, Hamburg 2001, n.p.

2 Cp. the Establishment of the Office of Mufti Act, 2001 / Act No. 9 of 2001.

3 *Nota bene:* The emergence of new radical Muslim groups was not happening in Zanzibar only, but almost all over the Muslim world. Cp. *Sallie Simba Kayunga*, "New Islamic Movements and Political Activism in Africa", in: *Lawford Imunde* (Ed.), Die Rolle der Zivilgesellschaft un der Religion bei der Demokratisierung Afrikas (Loccumer Protokolle 55/00), Loccum, 2000, on p. 333; *John A. Rowe*, "Islam Under Idi Amin: a Case of deja vu?", in: *Holger Bernt Hansen / Michael Twaddle* (Eds.), Uganda Now: Between Decay & Development, London / et al. 1988, pp. 267 et seqq.

4 The overwhelming majority of Muslims in Zanzibar are *Ahl as-Sunna* or *al-Ibāḍiya*. The number of *Šīʿa* followers is negligible although there have been frequent visits to Zanzibar by *Šīʿa* scholars mainly from Iran who have been offering generous scholarships to Iran for young Islamic students. See, inter alia, *Human Rights Documentation Center*, Racial Discrimination: The Record of Tanzania, St. Louis 2001, on p. 33.

Islam und Menschenrechte (Islam and Human Rights / الإسلام وحقوق الإنسان)
Hatem Elliesie (Hrsg./Editor), © Peter Lang Verlag: Frankfurt a.M. 2010, S. 173-192

their daily life in the Isles and what role the government assumes under the MAoZ. The underlying theme is the centrality and importance of the Right of Freedom of Religion and Belief of the citizen.[5] However, this contribution will commence with a brief political and constitutional background on Zanzibar within the United Republic of Tanzania.

B. Brief Historical Background to Zanzibar

The history of Zanzibar goes far beyond its December 1963's independence, the January 1964 revolution and the Union in April 1964. The earliest written record about Zanzibar was the Periplus of the Erythraean Sea, which was written around A.D. 60. Ancient peoples such as the Sumerians, Assyrians, Hindus, Egyptians, and Southern Arabians are known to have visited the East African Coast.[6] They met the indigenous tribes of Zanzibar such as Wahadimu and Watumbatu.[7] People from the Persian Gulf brought Islam to "زنگبار" (pers.) and Zanzibaris adopted the new religion from the beginning of the 10th century.[8]

Vasco da Gama was the first European to visit East Africa in 1498 after circumnavigating the Cape of Good Hope. In the early 16th century, the Portuguese overthrew the Zenj Empire and made themselves the masters of the East African coast, including Zanzibar in 1503. In the 17th century there was an insurrection in the coastal states, including Pemba, and the Arabs attacked Zanzibar in 1652, capturing Mombassa, Pemba and Kilwa in 1698 and 1699. All of the islands became subject to the Imām of Muscat (Masqaṭ).[9]

Sayyid Saʿīd b. Sulṭān, the founder of modern Zanzibar was elected to the Imamate in 1804 and transferred the capital of the Sultanate ʿUmān from Masqaṭ to Zanzibar in 1832.[10] It was during his reign that Zanzibar became, both politically and commercially, the principal town in East Africa.[11]

---

5 The freedom of religion or belief is a right which is protected in all universal and regional legal instruments on civil and political rights as well as it is recognised in the majority of national constitutions of the countries of the world. It is therefore important to ensure that the respective state or its government(s) do not veil this freedom. Cp. Borislav Petranov, "Freedom of Religion or Belief," in: Interrights Bulletin, volume 11, no. 3, London 1997, pp. 1 et seqq.

6 Cp. *Thomas Arnold*, Spread of Islam in the World: A History of Peaceful Preaching, New Delhi 2001, p. 342.

7 See *Godfrey Dale*, The Peoples of Zanzibar, New York 1969.

8 *A Guide to Zanzibar*, 1933 (Available at Zanzibar Archives).

9 *Abdul Sheriff*, Slaves, Spices & Ivory in Zanzibar: Integration of an East African Commercial Empire into the World Economy, 1770-1873, Dar es Salaam / et al. 1987, p. 137; *Esmond Bradley Martin*, Zanzibar: Tradition and Revolution, London 1978, pp. 24-54.

10 See *Haroub Othman*, Zanzibar's Political History: The Past Haunting the Present? Dar es Salaam 1992, p. 2; *Mohamed Ali Bakari*, The Democratisation Process in Zanzibar…, su-

In 1861, by an award of Lord Canning, who was then the Governor-General of India, the territories held by the Sultanate ʿUmān in Africa became independent of Masqaṭ. Moreover, the opening of Suez Canal in 1869 plus the inauguration of monthly steam services between Aden (ʿAdan) and Zanzibar in 1872, brought Zanzibar closer to Europe.[12]

In 1890, by what was called *Vertrag zwischen Deutschland und England über die Kolonien und Helgoland* (Heligoland Treaty), the Imperial German Government obtained a cession of the Sulṭān's territory on the East Coast between the Rivers Umba and Ruvuma, for the sum of four million Marks. In the same year, Zanzibar and Pemba were proclaimed British Protectorates and thus the administration effectively fell out of the Sulṭān's control. In 1891, a regular form of government was set up and Sir Lloyd Mathews becoming the First Minister and Treasurer.[13]

C. Muslims and Islam in Zanzibar

As a result of the aforementioned historical background, Zanzibar is 98% Muslim.[14] Therefore, for Zanzibaris, like other Muslims throughout the world,[15] Islam is not only a religion but a way of life. This is evident in everyday life on the isles; right from the dressing code (which is not written anywhere) to the number of mosques built. The dominance of the Islamic faith is clearly indicated

pra, footnote 1, on p. 47. See also: *Emily Ruete,* Memoirs of an Arabian Princes from Zanzibar: An Autobiography of Salme, Princes of Oman and Zanzibar, Zanzibar 1998.

11 *A. J. Shaaban,* The Political History of Zanzibar [Paper presented on a seminar held at Bwawani Hotel, Zanzibar, November 2001], Zanzibar 2001; *Donald Barton,* An Affair With Africa: Tanganyika Remembered, Hertford, 2004, pp. 248-255; *Abdul Sheriff,* Historical Zanzibar: Romance of the Ages, London 1995, p. 10.

12 *A Guide to Zanzibar,* supra, footnote 8.

13 On the history of Zanzibar, its laws and politics from this specific time until independence on 10 December 1963 cp., among others, *Amir A. Mohammed,* A Guide to a History of Zanzibar, Zanzibar 1997; *Daudi Mukangara,* "Race, Ethnicity, Religion and Politics in Zanzibar", in: *T. L. Maliyamkono* (Ed.), The Political Plight of Zanzibar, Dar es Salaam 2000, on pp. 35 et seqq.; *Suleiman Said Shabal,* Zanzibar: The Rise and Fall of an Independent State 1895-1964, Dubai 2002; *Ibrahim F. Shao,* The Political Economy of Land Reforms in Zanzibar: Before and After the Revolution, Dar es Salaam 1992; *John Middleton / Jane Campbell,* Zanzibar: Its Society and Its Politics, London / et al. 1965; *H.E. Kingdon,* The Conflict of Laws in Zanzibar, Zanzibar 1940; *J. H. Vaughan,* The Dual Jurisdiction in Zanzibar, Zanzibar 1935; *Michael F. Lofchie,* "Party Conflict in Zanzibar", in: Journal of Modern African Studies, volume 1, issue 2, London 1963, pp. 185 et seqq.

14 Cp. footnote 4.

15 Cp. *Mamadou S.C. Janneh,* "Islam and Human Rights?", in: Africa Legal Aid Quarterly, Maastricht, January-March 1998, on pp. 39 et seqq.; *M.H. Al-Khayat,* Health as a Human Right in Islam, Geneva 2004.

during the Holy Month of Ramaḍān when almost all hotels and food and beverages providing outlets are virtually closed.

With Islam being a way of life, it is quite understandable that matters of personal status are subject to Islamic Law.[16] Special courts – Kadhi's Courts – were established,[17] as part of the Judiciary of Zanzibar, to deal with Islamic related matters of personal status[18] such as marriage, divorce, inheritance and other Muslim related issues.

I. Islamic Jurisdiction: The Kadhi's Courts

Kahdi's Court is the oldest judicial institution in Zanzibar.[19] The courts have become very important, if not indispensable, judicial organs in Zanzibar's legal system.[20] Their role, however, is changing. Before 1963 they used to enjoy, under the disguise of Sultan Courts, very wide powers. The current Khadi's Courts were re-established under the *Kadhi's Courts Act of 1985*.[21] Unlike its predecessor, which could hear and determine any civil suit applying *šarīa* as far as both of the parties

---

16 Just as *Isa Hayatu Chiroma / Hatem Elliesie,* "Islam, Islamic Law and Human Rights in the Nigerian Context", in: *Hatem Elliesie* (Hrsg./Editor), Beiträge zum Islamischen Recht VII, Islam und Menschenrechte (Islam and Human Rights / الإسلام وحقوق الإنسان), Frankfurt a.M. 2010, p. 155 (footnote 2), the term "Islamic Law" and "*šarīʿa* (law)" will be used interchangeable within this article. Throught the paper, local legal terms, such as *Kadhi* and *Ulamaa* , etc. will be written in Kiswahili orthography.

17 The Kadhi's Courts were established for the first time in Zanzibar in 1897. They were known then as "Sulṭān's Courts" and were to be re-established later towards independence through the Courts Decree of 1963. The current Kadhi's Courts in Zanzibar and Pemba are governed by the Kadhi's Court Act No. 3 of 1985.

18 In more detail cp. *Imen Gallala,* "Religionsfreiheit und islamisch geprägtes Erbrecht: gesetzliche Regelungen und Rechtsprechungsauslegung im heutigen Ägypten und Tunesien", in: *Hatem Elliesie* (Hrsg./Editor), Beiträge zum Islamischen Recht VII, Islam und Menschenrechte (Islam and Human Rights / الإسلام وحقوق الإنسان), Frankfurt a.M. 2010, pp. 499 et seqq. See also *Erin Stiles,* Broken Edda and Maritial Mistakes: "Two Recent Disputes from an Islamic Court in Zanzibar", in: *Muhammad Khalid Masud / Rudolph Peters / David S. Powers* (Eds.), Dispensing Justice in Islam: Qadis and their Judgements, Leiden / Boston 2006, pp. 95 et seqq.

19 See *Masoud Othman Othman*, "The Zanzibar Judicial System", in: *Chris Maina Peter / Immi Sikand* (Eds.), The Judiciary in Zanzibar, Zanzibar 2006, pp. 15 et seqq.

20 Cp. *Augustiono Ramadhani,* "Judicial System in Tanzania: Zanzibar", in: Eastern Africa Law Review, 1978-81, volumes 11-14, Dar es Salaam, 1978-81, pp. 225 et seqq. (on p. 231); *Anne Lutun / Ismail Kaaya,* Study on Kadhi's Court and Its Implications to Human Rights in Tanzania, Dar es Salaam 2007, pp. 20-21; *Asina Abdillah Omari,* Culture, Religion and Human Rights: The Situation of Muslim Women in Relation to Marriage and Divorce in the Coast Region of Tanzania (LL.M. thesis, University of Dar es Salaam), Dar es Salaam 2005.

21 Act No. 3 of 1985.

are Muslims, the existing Khadi's Courts have very limited jurisdiction. They form another subordinate court limb to the High Court. There is the established Chief Kadhis' Court which is an appellate institution. Any appellate Kadhi or the Chief Kadhi can sit, hear and determine appeals from a District Kadhi's Court. Appeal from the Chief Kadhis' Court lies with the High Court. Such appeals are heard by a judge of the High Court sitting with four Sheikhs (*šaiḫs*) who are well informed and trained in Islamic Law and decisions are made on a majority basis.

The decision of the High Court on cases originating from Kadhis' Court is final and cannot be taken to the Tanzania Court of Appeal.[22] This position is expressed by Article 99 (2)(b) of the 1984 Zanzibar Constitution. This position was recognised by the Court of Appeal itself but given a wider interpretation in the case of *Mohamed Rafik Ishaq & Another v. Anwar Hussein Jaffer & 2 Others* where this Court, referred to the aforementioned Article 99 (2) (b) as well as to Section 10 of the 1985 Kadhi's Court Act (KCA), quoting that

> " [i]t is clear that this Court has no jurisdiction to hear appeals emanating from the Kadhi's Courts 'on matters of Islamic Law' or just 'Islamic matters' as the Constitution of Zanzibar puts it."[23]

In the end, however, the Court of Appeal went on to hear and determined that appeal as the question of property possession does not fall within the ambits of Section 6 (1) KCA, which reads:

> " A Kadhi's Court shall have and exercise jurisdiction in the determination of a question of Muslim law relating to personal status, marriage, divorce or inheritance in proceedings in which all the parties profess the Muslim religion."

This is perhaps a genuine case calling for interference of the Court of Appeal. However, it may seem an exception to the general rule. It is not often that the highest judicial organ interferes, especially in normative matters of faith. Otherwise, the Kadhi's Courts enjoy a lot of respect and acceptability in Zanzibar notwithstanding the emerging cosmopolitan way of life developing in Zanzibar under the guise of globalisation.[24]

---

22 The Court of Appeal of Tanzania established under Article 117 of the 1977 Constitution of the United Republic of Tanzania. Its functions are governed by Appellate Jurisdiction Act No. 15 of 1979 as *Union Matter* and thus covers both parts of the Union. On the Zanzibar side, there are certain restrictions to this Court. The Court of Appeal does not have jurisdiction on conciliation of any dispute between the Government of the United Republic and the RGZ under Article 126 of the Constitution; on interpretation of the Constitution of Zanzibar; and over Islamic matters from Kadhis' Courts of Zanzibar.

23 This case is reproduced in: *Salum Toufiq*, "The Zanzibar Court System", in: *Chris Maina Peter / Immi Sikand* (Eds.), The Judiciary…, supra, footnote 19, pp. 31 et seqq. (on p. 42).

24 On the position of the Kadhi's Court in the Zanzibar judicial system cp., *inter alia*, *Masoud Othman*, "The Zanzibar Judicial System", supra, footnote 19; *Salum Toufiq*, The

II. Quest to Join the Organisation of Islamic Conference (OIC)

It is the Islamic nature of Zanzibar which led the RGZ to join the OIC (Organisation of Islamic Conference),[25] a decision which led to both constitutional and political controversy in Tanzania. In 1993, the RGZ, applied – on its own initiative – and had been admitted into the OIC.[26] This was not taken lightly by the Union government and by the higher echelons of the ruling party,[27] the *Chama Cha Mapinduzi* (CCM). This decision was not only taken as a violation of the Constitution on the aspects of the Union, but also as considered to be conflicting with the secular nature of the Tanzanian State. A Parliamentary Committee was appointed to investigate this issue[28] and a private citizen attempted to impeach the Union President for allowing Zanzibar to violate the Constitution.[29] Notwithstanding the legal and constitutional angle taken by those involved in its interrogation, it had serious religious ramifications.[30]

Zanzibar Court System, supra, footnote 23; *James S. Read*, "Justice on Appeal: A Century Plus of Appeal Courts and Judges in Tanzania" in: *Chris Maina Peter / Helen Kijo-Bisimba* (Eds.), Law & Justice in Tanzania: Quarter of a Century of the Court of Appeal, Dar es Salaam 2007, pp. 55 et seqq.

25 Cp. *Theodor Rathgeber*, "Die Organisation Islamischer Konferenz im UN-Menschenrechtsrat: Menschenrechte als Instrument staatlicher Politik", in: *Hatem Elliesie* (Hrsg./Editor), Beiträge zum Islamischen Recht VII, Islam und Menschenrechte (Islam and Human Rights / الإسلام وحقوق الإنسان), Frankfurt a.M. 2010, pp. 457-473; *Lawrence E.Y. Mbogoni*, The Cross Versus the Crescent: Religion and Politics in Tanzania from 1880s to the 1990s, Dar es Salaam 2004, pp. 144-150.

26 See *Joseph Oloka-Onyango / Maria Nassali*, Constitutionalism and Political Stability in Zanzibar: Search for a New Vision, Kampala 2003, p. 14; *Hamza Mustafa Njozi*, Muslims and the State in Tanzania, Dar es Salaam 2003, pp. 52-57.

27 Former President of the United Republic of Tanzania and Chairman of Chama Cha Mapinduzi the late Mwalimu Julius K. Nyerere made spirited efforts to ensure that Zanzibar withdrew from the OIC as he believed it was unconstitutional. Cp. *Mwalimu Julius K. Nyerere*, Our Leadership and the Destiny of Tanzania, Harare 1995; see also *Evarist Kagaruki*, "Tanzania Should Join Organisation of Islamic Conference" in: Sunday Citizen (Tanzania), 13 July 2008, on p. 8.

28 On this Committee headed by Philip Marmo see *Issa G. Shivij*, Pan Africanism or Pragmatism? Lessons of Tanganyika – Zanzibar Union, Addis Ababa / et al. 2008, p. 232.

29 See *Mwalimu Paul Mhozya v. The Attorney General*, High Court of Tanzania at Dar es Salaam (Civil Case No. 206 of 1993). This case is discussed at length in *Robert V. Makaramba*, "Religion, Rule of Law and Justice in Tanzania," in: *Rwekaza Mukandala et al* (Eds.), Justice, Rights and Worship: Religion and Politics in Tanzania, Dar es Salaam 2006, pp. 360 et seqq. (on p. 367).

30 See *Issa G. Shivji*, Let the People Speak Let the People Speak: Tanzania Down the Road to Neo-Liberalism, Dakar 2006, p. 218.

III. (Official) Islamic Leadership in Zanzibar Tanzania

While all other major religious organisations have global leadership,[31] that is not the case with *Islam*[32].[33] This problem is more evident at a national level. In Tanzania, for example, there are two Islamic centres of power: The Mufti of Zanzibar Sheikh Harith b. Kheref and the Mufti of Tanzania Mainland Sheikh Issa Shaaban b. Simba.[34] Due to this fact, one is able to witness that manipulative ruling parties and/or governments have taken advantage of this vacuum to take over and control Muslim organisations, of which the Tanzania Muslim Council (*Baraza Kuu la Waislam wa Tanzania* – BAKWATA) has been a good example, indicated to have been established by the State through marginalization of the East African Muslims Welfare Society (EAMWS).[35]

IV. (Non-Mainstream) Splitter Muslim Groups in Zanzibar

It is this state of affairs which has given rise to a number of Muslim splitter organisations. In Tanzania, these organisations manifest themselves during common Muslim festivities. For example, the beginning and the end of the Holy Month of *Ramaḍān* and the celebration of the *ʿīd al-fiṭr* has been controversial in both on the Tanzania Mainland and Zanzibar. Splitter groups do not follow in the sighting of the moon (*ru'yat al-hilāl*) as dictated upon by the local organisation but insist in pursuing what one's understand in Wahhābī in Saudi Arabia.

---

31 For instance, the Catholic Church has the Pope as its global leader whose guidance is respected by all Catholics. On this, see *Carl Bernstein / Marco Politi,* His Holiness: John Paul II and the Hidden History of Our Time, London / New York 1996; *David Yallop,* In God's Name: An Investigation into the Murder of Popoe John Paul I, London 2007.

32 The exception may be a branch of the Ismailis (*al-ismāʿīliyun*), the *nizārīs*, a *šīʿa* denomination considered as a sect of Muslims who regard the Agha Khan (Āġā Ḫān) as its global spiritual leader. See *Werner Schmucker,* "Sekten und Sondergruppen", in: *Werner Ende / Udo Steinbach* (Eds.), Der Islam in der Gegenwart, 5th edition, Munich 2005, pp. 716 et seqq.

33 The term "*Islam*" will be used to refer to the religion in general, see *Ann Elizabeth Mayer,* "General Remarks on Human Rights and Islam in the Middle East", in: *Hatem Elliesie* (Hrsg./Editor), Islam und Menschenrechte (Islam and Human Rights / الإسلام وحقوق الإنسان), Frankfurt a.M. 2010, on p. 219; *Muhammad Kalisch,* "Islam und Menschenrechte: Betrachtungen zum Verhältnis von Religion und Recht", in: Ibidem, on p. 49.

34 See *Anne Robi,* "Mufti Asks for Time to Probe Bakwata Conflict", in: Daily News (Tanzania), 14 June 2008, on p. 2; *idem,* "Mufti Shakes Up Bakwata Leadership", in: Sunday News (Tanzania), 14 June 2008, on p. 1.

35 Cp. *Athuman J. Liviga,* "Religion and Governance in Tanzania: The Pre-Liberalisation Period", in: *Rwekaza Mukandala / et al* (Eds.), *Justice…*, supra, footnote 29, pp. 320 et seqq. (on p. 330). See also *Mohamed Said,* The Life and Times of Abdulwahid Sykes (1924-1968): The Untold Story of the Muslim Struggle Against British Colonialism in Tanganyika, London 1998, pp. 282-315.

As both governments support the 'official' Muslim leadership, they have tended to unleash the police force to harass these "opposing" groups, beating and at times imprisoning their followers. However, it is important to note that the rise of the splitter Muslim groups in Zanzibar led to the enactment of Act No. 9 of 2001, officially establishing the Office of the Mufti, the spiritual leader of all Muslims on the Isles. The aim being to control what was viewed as a resurgence of Islamic radicalism.[36]

D. The 2001 Mufti Act of Zanzibar

Previously, in the light of history, the functions of the Mufti were placed under the *Commission for Wakf and Trust Property*. The Chief Kadhi had a mandate to deal with issues, which are now the concern of the Office of Mufti. The remnants of this history are reflected in the *Commission for Wakf and Trust Property Act of 1980*, which states that the Chief Kadhi will be the Chairman of the Commission. It was envisaged that with the enactment of the *Kadhi's Courts Act* in 1985, the *Wakf and Trust Property Act* in 1980 and the MAoZ in 2001, there would be a clear separation of functions between judicial and religious matters, but this does not seem to be the case: The Chief Kadhi is the Head of the Kadhi's Courts, the Chairman of the Commission for Wakf and Trust Property and is a member of the Ulamaa.[37]

I. The Mufti and the Functions of his Office

The Mufti Act 2001 (MAoZ) is a brief legislative provision with a total of 16 Sections. It creates the Office of the Mufti of Zanzibar and other officers related to his office, his powers and the functions of his office and the financing of his office. Thus, the Mufti, who is essentially spiritual, is turned into a statutory organ under RGZ.[38] The Mufti is a Presidential appointee and is the Head of the Office of Mufti.[39] The qualification for appointment is to be Zanzibari, who in the opinion of the President of Zanzibar, "is qualified and has adequate knowl-

36 Cp. *Bjorn Moller*, Religion and Conflict in Africa: With Special Focus on East Africa, Copenhagen, p. 86.

37 Under Section 2 of the Establishment of the Office of Mufti Act, 2001 (Act No. 9 of 2001) "Ulamaa", in this particular context, means religious scholars who had adequate knowledge of various Islamic religious matters.

38 The status of the office of the Mufti of Zanzibar was the centre of discussion in the meeting between civil society organisations on the Isles and the visiting President of the Federal Republic of Germany, the late Dr. Johannes Rau. See the paper titled "Relationships Between Religious Groups in Zanzibar Society" presented by the CSOs at that meeting held at Zanzibar Serena Hotel on 22 March 2004.

39 Section 4 (1) MAoZ.

edge in Islamic 'Shariah' and other religious matters" and, furthermore, has the "command of respect among Islamic scholars."[40] The Mufti is assisted in his daily work by a Deputy Mufti, who is also appointed by the President and his station of duty is Pemba.[41] According to the Act, the Deputy Mufti has to have the equal qualifications as the Mufti. The functions and powers of the Mufti are clearly stipulated in the MAoZ.[42] These are to:

(a) give "fatwa" on any issue raised to him relating to any Islamic question, which needs to be decided;
(b) keep record of all "fatwa" issued by his office;
(c) settle any religious dispute arising among Muslims and any religious dispute arising between Muslims and other religions in consultation with other leaders of that other religions;
(d) organize Islamic research and prepare curriculum of education for Ulamaa in Zanzibar;
(e) approve lecturers of Islamic religion from outside Zanzibar;
(f) coordinate and supervise the preparation of lectures, workshop, seminar and other Islamic activities;
(g) control and approve the importation, supply and translations of all Islamic books;
(h) coordinate the activities of various Islamic groups within Zanzibar;
(i) coordinate and announce the sighting of a new moon;
(j) coordinate and supervise the activities of all mosques of Zanzibar and to keep records of all mosques and Ulamaa of Zanzibar; and
(k) approve the registration of Islamic Societies in accordance with the Societies Act of 1995.

It is clear from the above provision that the Mufti has a coordinating as well as a decision-making role. The Mufti is statutorily mandated to work "hand in hand" with the Office of Chief Kadhi, who administers Islamic Law in cases concerning Islamic personalstatus matters, involving Muslim parties, and the Executive Secretary of the *Wakf and Trust Commission*, who "administers wakf and trust property".[43] The Mufti serves on the *Wakf and Trust Property Commission* in the capacity of a Chairman.[44] The Office of Mufti also conducts reconciliation among parties for matters which fall under its jurisdiction as stipulated in the founding legislation.

II. Secretary to the Mufti

Administrative matters for the Office of Mufti are handled by Secretary who is an appointee of the Minister responsible for matters relating to the management

---

40 Section 4 (2) MAoZ.
41 Section 5 (1) MAoZ.
42 Section 9 (1) MAoZ.
43 Section 9 (3) MAoZ.
44 Ibidem.

of the Office of Mufti.[45] The Minister appoints the Executive Secretary in consultation with the Mufti. In order to qualify for appointment as a Secretary, a person must hold "sufficient knowledge in Islamic Shariah and public administration".[46] The Secretary handles the day-to-day administration of the Office of Mufti and also serves as principal assistant to the Mufti.[47] The Office of Mufti currently has a work force of 23 both for the Unguja and Pemba offices. The Office of Mufti has four units, namely: Administration; Fatwa; International Relations; and Research. The heads of these units shall be appointed by the Mufti.[48]

III. Regulations Made under the Mufti's Act

Three Government Notices have been issued by the Minister responsible for the Office of the Mufti to facilitate the functions of the Office of the Mufti. These are (1) Regulations of the Ulamaa Council[49]; (2) Regulations on Confirmation of Islamic Organisations before Registration[50] and (3) Regulations on Allowing and Coordinating Public Lectures[51].[52]

1. The "Ulamaa" Council

The Ulamaa Council is established as an advisory body to the Mufti.[53] It is composed of experts in Islamic matters.[54] In reality and for practical reasons, there are actually two Ulamaa Councils in Zanzibar. One for Unguja Island and the other for Pemba Island.[55] While both Councils are chaired by the Mufti, their memberships differ to some extent.[56]

---

45 Section 7 (1) MAoZ.

46 Section 7 (2) MAoZ.

47 Section 7 (3) MAoZ. The Secretary will be assisted by an Assistant Secretary who will be based in Pemba as per Section 7 (4) MAoZ.

48 Section 8 MAoZ.

49 Government Notice No. 98 of 2002 made under Section 15 (1) MAoZ.

50 Government Notice No. 99 of 2002 made under Section 15 (1) MAoZ.

51 Government Notice No. 100 of 2002 made under Section 15 (1) MAoZ.

52 I am grateful to Mr. Mahadhi Juma Maalim, the Permanent Secretary, Ministry of State (President's Office) Constitutional Affair and Good Governance in the Revolutionary Government of Zanzibar for providing me with Volume CXI No. 5977, Official Gazette of the Revolutionary Government of Zanzibar of 13 December 2002 which contains all the three Government Notices relating to the Office of the Mufti.

53 Regulation 3 of the Ulamaa Council.

54 According to Section 2 of the Act Establishing the Office of the Mufti of 2001 an "Ulamaa" means "a religious scholar who had adequate knowledge of various Islamic religious matters".

55 Regulations 4 (1) and (2) of the Ulamaa Council.

56 The Unguja Ulamaa Council consits of: The Mufti as Chair; the Mufti's Secretary as Secretary; the Chief Kadhi; the Executive Secretary of the Wakf and Trust Commission; the Principal of the Islamic College of Zanzibar; and one Sheikh from each of Districts of Unguja appointed by the Minister in consultation with the Mufti. The Pemba Ulamaa

The main function of the Ulamaa Councils is to advise the Mufti on various Islamic issues submitted to him for purposes of issuance of "Fatwa"[57] and may do any other work as directed by the Mufti.[58]

2. Regulation of Registration of Islamic Organisations

In Zanzibar, the way people organise, associate and exercise their right to organise is dependent upon their beliefs. The rules do not apply equally to all Zanzibaris. They are constructed in such a way that that of the Muslims' is constrained a great deal. Some stringent rules have been put in place solely to govern Muslims. The law provides that ten or more Muslims may organise themselves into an Islamic organisation and submit their application for registration to that effect.[59] Any Islamic organisation seeking registration in Zanzibar has to be confirmed to a *bona fide* organisation before be registered.[60] The Mufti has a duty to provide his views on registration of any Islamic organisation within two weeks[61] and, where he rejects to confirm a particular organisation, he has a duty to provide his reasons in writing.[62] Appeals from the decision of the Mufti go to the Minister responsible for the Office of the Mufti[63] and might end up in the High Court of Zanzibar.[64] The Mufti is the Custodian of the Role of all registered Islamic organisations in Zanzibar.[65] In a way, the Mufti becomes the agent of the RGZ and reports to the Police organisations which are not properly registered and their activities.

Council has the Mufti as Chair; Mufti's Secretary as Secretary; Chief Kadhi; the Executive Secretary of the Wakf and Trust Commission; the Deputy Mufti; and one Sheikh from each District of Pemba in Consultation and agreement with the Mufti. See Regulations 4 (1) and (2). In addition, the Mufti and the members of the Ulamaa Councils may invite any person a sitting of the Council to assist in deliberations relating to a specific issue although that invitee shall have no voting rights. See Regulation 4 (3) of the Ulamaa Council.

57 According to Regulation 2 a of the Ulamaa Council, Fatwa is the final decision on any Islamic issue submitted to the Mufti for a decision. According to Regulation 8 of the Ulamaa Council any Fatwa issued by the Mufti on any issue is final and has to be respected.

58 Regulation 7 of the Ulamaa Council.

59 Regulation 4 of Government Notice No. 99 of 2002. This application must be accompanied by the Constitution of that organization which shall explain clearly the main aims and objectives of the organisation seeking registration, see Regulation 8 (1) of Government Notice No. 99 of 2002.

60 Regulation 5 (1) of Government Notice No. 99 of 2002.

61 Regulation 5 (2) of Government Notice No. 99 of 2002.

62 Regulation 5 (3) of Government Notice No. 99 of 2002.

63 Regulation 6 of Government Notice No. 99 of 2002.

64 Regulation 7 of Government Notice No. 99 of 2002.

65 Regulation 9 of Government Notice No. 99 of 2002.

3. Allowing and Coordinating Public Lectures

Any Muslim or Islamic organisation planning to hold any public lecture is supposed to notify the Mufti in a special form prescribed by the law.[66] If the lecturer is from outside Zanzibar, that notice should be given to the Mufti no less than 24 hours before the delivery of such lecture, for the Mufti to be able to confirm, the lecturer's qualifications in due time.[67]

It is prohibited for any person or Islamic organisation to hold a lecture without the permission of the Mufti of Zanzibar.[68] The Mufti is empowered to stop any lecture which, in his view, is aimed at opposing or contradicting Islamic Law or laws of the country.[69] When the Mufti allows an Islamic lecture to be held, he will inform the Police to this effect.[70] It is the duty of the Police to ensure that the allowed lecture follows the agreed procedure.[71] Any person or group or organisation whose application to hold a lecture has been rejected by the Mufti may appeal to the Minister responsible for Office of the Mufti and the Minister's decision on this issue shall be final.[72] The ouster clause notwithstanding, in practice a person, a group or organisation whose application has been rejected by both the Mufti and the Minister may still proceed and challenge the same in the courts of law.

4. Offences under the Act

The Act provides two types of offences:

- Firstly, it is an offence to fail to comply with the summons of the Mufti issued under the law and upon conviction one is liable to a fine of not less than one hundred thousand shillings, or to imprisonment for a term of three months, or both.[73]
- Secondly, whoever fails to comply with the order, directive or prohibition or conditions given by the Mufti commits an offence and shall be liable to a fine of not less than two hundred thousand shillings, or to imprisonment for a term of six months, or both.[74]

---

66 Regulation 4 of Government Notice No. 100 of 2002.

67 Regulation 5 of Government Notice No. 100 of 2002. Under Regulation 6 (3) the Mufti may actually refuse a lecture from outside Zanzibar, who in his opinion, does not have educational credentials in Islam and has no sufficient knowledge in religious matters.

68 Regulation 6 (1) of Government Notice No. 100 of 2002.

69 Regulation 6 (2) of Government Notice No. 100 of 2002.

70 Regulation 8 (1) of Government Notice No. 100 of 2002.

71 Regulation 8 (2) of Government Notice No. 100 of 2002.

72 Regulation 10 of Government Notice No. 100 of 2002.

73 Section 14 (1) MAoZ.

74 Section 14 (2) MAoZ.

Saying this, it should be pointed out that issues of belief which are voluntary in nature are shifted into the criminal jurisdiction of the government and people are heavily penalised. This takes religious and related issues of belief into new uncommon heights as it might be a limitation of religious freedom.

E. Implications of the 2001 Mufti Act of Zanzibar

I. Is Zanzibar Secular?

The main implication of the MAoZ is to put into question the genuineness of the secular nature of the Zanzibar. Section 3 (1) MAoZ establishes the Office of the Mufti of Zanzibar which "shall be a department of the Government". That means that the office of the Mufti – the spiritual leader of all Muslims in Zanzibar – will be funded by the taxpayer; making the Mufti and all employees of his Office civil servants. Over and above that, the Office of the Mufti will be provided with an office and other facilities as a department of the Government.

Like any other department of the government, the Office of the Mufti, prepares its own budget and submits it to the Minister responsible for religious matters for his approval.[75] The Minister is also empowered by the founding legislation to make regulations for the effective execution of the Act establishing the Office of the Mufti.[76] The Minister of State appoints the Secretary to the Mufti, a religious (and civil) post.[77] The enormous powers given to the RGZ and its functionaries by the MAoZ undermines any legitimacy left in the spiritual hat of the Mufti of Zanzibar, to a large extent.

Two crucial issues to be questioned arise out of this arrangement, namely:

- Why should one religion be funded from the taxpayer's money and not those of other religions and what is the justification of this kind of discrimination?
- And even more important, with the Mufti and his whole workforce being paid by the Government in Zanzibar and the funds for running the Office of Mufti coming directly from the Government through the annual budget estimates approved by the Zanzibar House of Representatives, is it possible to talk of secularism in Zanzibar? Is there any demarcation between the Government and Islam in Zanzibar? Is it idle imagination to characterise Islam as a Government religion in Zanzibar and Zanzibar an Islamic country?

---

75 Section 12 (1) MAoZ.
76 Section 15 (1) MAoZ.
77 Section 7 (1) MAoZ.

Incidentally, when the Office of the Mufti – the leader of Muslims in Zanzibar – was established in 2001, it was placed under the Ministry of Justice and Constitutional Affairs that happened to be headed, at the time, by a Christian cabinet Minister. Some Zanzibaris felt offended; notably the Imāms. This led some Muslim leaders in Zanzibar to call upon the RGZ to amend the Constitution and turn Zanzibar into an Islamic state. This type of reaction is quite understandable because under the MAoZ, and at this particular time, the possibility that the Muslims be led by a non-Muslim was quite plausible.

II. Challenges: The Government Appointment of Zanzibar's Mufti

The enactment of the Office of the Mufti of Zanzibar has had serious implications to the everyday life of Muslims on the Isles. Its very legitimacy is questionable. However, there are other equally serious implications of the coming into being of this law. Section 4 MAoZ provides:

> (1) There shall be a Mufti of Zanzibar who shall be appointed by the President and who shall be the head of the office of Mufti.
> (2) The Mufti shall be appointed from amongst Zanzibari who in the opinion of the President is qualified and has adequate knowledge in Islamic "shariah" and other religious matters and that he commands respect among Islamic scholars and Muslim community in general.
> (3) The President shall adopt means of obtaining public opinion on a person qualified for the post of Mufti.

This provision has two basic problems. Firstly, it obviously mixes public administration/governance and religion. It instructs a secular administrator/leader to appoint a leader for Muslims. Here lies a presumption that the President of Zanzibar shall always be a Muslim and there is no chance of a person of another faith to rule Zanzibar. If a non-Muslim is elected to the Presidency of Zanzibar, then, accordingly, it would follow that the Muslims in Zanzibar will have their spiritual leaders appointed by a non Muslim – an infidel.

In addition, even if the President is Muslim, this in itself does not give a temporal leader the right or legitimacy to appoint a spiritual leader for a religious group. Therefore, in whatever fashion this law is read, it is fundamentally faulty and cannot stand the test of legitimacy.

III. Restrictions to Zanzibari Muslim's Freedom to assemble peacefully

The powers of the Mufti have also come under scrutiny, particularly in relation to freedom of Muslims to assemble and organise. According to Section 10 of the new law any public gathering of Muslims in Zanzibar has to be specifically sanctioned by the Office of the Mufti. The law states:

(1) Mufti shall have the following powers:
   (a) [...]
   (b) [...].
   (c) to approve any Islamic activities, (including Ijitimai and lectures) or any Islamic gathering in Zanzibar [...]

The earliest victims of this provision were a group of Muslims who wanted to exercise their right to celebrate the end of the Holy Month of *Ramaḍān* earlier than other Muslims. This group, calling itself *Answer Sunnah,* did not seek the permission of the Mufti. Hence, the police set on them with tear gas, buttons and rubber bullets; injuring a considerable number of them. This tendency of attacking believers, ostensibly on the orders of the Office of the Mufti, has triggered the increased attendance of Muslims at prayers as a show of resilience against perceived religious persecution. And this is just the beginning of the problems related to the application of the MAoZ 2001.

This provision has two basic problems.

- It conflicts with both the Constitution of the United Republic of Tanzania of 1977 and Constitution of Zanzibar of 1984. Both Constitutions are providing in their respective Article 20 for the freedoms of peaceful assembly, association and cooperation. Included here is the right of every person to freely express his/her views publicly, to form or join legal associations and organizations for purposes of preserving their interests. It is therefore illegal and unconstitutional to subject these freedoms to the whims of one person.
- The limitation of these freedoms targets the majority section of the population, the Muslims. Thus, one consequence is that non-Muslim Zanzibaris are able continue enjoying their religious freedoms of expression, participating in religious motivated gatherings. This is discriminatory and a discrimination of this nature is prohibited by Article 13 of the 1977 Constitution of the United Republic of Tanzania as well as Article 12 of the 1984 Constitution of Zanzibar.[78] Therefore, the promise by the Chief Justice of Zanzibar that "the Government of Zanzibar shall ensure that every citizen shall have equality of rights, obligations and opportunities before the law",[79] remains a dream having been shattered by the MAoZ 2001.

---

[78] On the freedom of religion in Zanzibar see *Ali Ali Hassan,* "The State and Accession of Individual to Fundamental Rights and Freedoms in Zanzibar", in: *Haroub Othman / Chris Maina Peter* (Eds.), Perspectives on Legal Aid and Access to Justice in Zanzibar, Zanzibar 2003, pp.62 et seqq. (on p. 70).

[79] See *Mahmoud Hamid Hamid,* "Access to Justice: A Legal Right," in: Ibidem, pp. 80 et seqq. (on p. 84).

There are many other areas in this law which experts in matters of religion will have noted. There is, in the very least, a conflict between the provisions of the Constitution(s) and that of the MAoZ which desperately need to be qualified. We have people wishing to enjoy their fundamental rights under the Constitution and, in particular, the freedoms of assembly and association on one hand, and, on the other, we are facing the fact that – despite the mentioned legitimacy problem of the MAoZ – the Police Forces attacking them to enforce the MAoZ. This is a situation requiring its addressing urgently; bearing in mind that the Constitution(s) are the supreme law which cannot be subjected to any other inferior law.

F. The Government *versus* the Mufti under the Law

There is no doubt that the stature of the Mufti as the supreme spiritual leader of Muslims in Zanzibar is highly influenced by the control which the RGZ and its various subordinate institutions and functionaries, such as the President of Zanzibar who is also the Chairman of the Revolutionary Council to the Minister responsible for the Mufti's Office and the Zanzibar House of Representatives which determines the funding of the Mufti's Office.

I. The Powers of the President

The President of Zanzibar has enormous powers over the Office of the Mufti. Apart from designating it as part of the civil service of Zanzibar,[80] it is the President who appoints the Mufti.[81] Though the MAoZ provides that a Mufti shall be appointed among persons who are qualified and with adequate knowledge in "Islamic Shariah" and other religious matters,[82] the appointment is discretionary.[83] It depends on the whim of the person holding the office of the President of Zanzibar. The Mufti, once appointed does not enjoy any tenure. He can be removed from office by the President at any point[84].[85]

II. The Minister and the Office of the Mufti

The Minister responsible for the Office of the Mufti is equally given wide powers over this office. It is the Minister who appoints the Secretary to Mufti, albeit

80 Under Section 3 (1) MAoZ the Office of the Mufti is established as a Department of the Government.

81 Section 4 (1) MAoZ

82 Section 4 (2) MAoZ

83 Section 4 (3) MAoZ

84 Under Section 6 MAoZ the Mufti can be terminated by the President and no reasons thereof need to be given.

85 What has been said for the Mufti applies equally to Deputy Mufti who is based on Pemba Island, cp. Section 5 and Sections 6 MAoZ.

in consultation with the Mufti.[86] The Minister also appoints the Assistant Secretary to the Mufti who is based on Pemba Island.[87] According to the MAoZ, the Mufti is merely left with the power to appoint the heads of various sections within his office.[88] Other officers in his office are appointed in accordance with the civil service recruitment rules.[89]

When the Mufti is of the opinion that Zanzibar should join any zonal or international Islamic organisations which deal with various Islamic developments, he has to seek the approval of the Minister.[90] At the same time, the funds of his office have to be submitted to the Minister for approval[91] and it is the Minister who shall ensure that the Office of the Mufti is properly audited in accordance with government regulations.[92] Also, the Minister – as the oversight authority – has to ensure that every year the Office of the Mufti prepares the following documents for the Zanzibar House of Representatives: Annual Report of Revenue and Expenditure, Annual Report of Properties and Liabilities and Report of Audited Accounts.[93]

According to the Regulations made under Act 9 of 2001 the Minister responsible for Office of the Mufti is given more and a wider range of powers over the Office of Mufti. This includes the powers to appoint some of the Members of the Ulamaa Councils, institutions which advises the Mufti. In general, one can say with sincerity that the Mufti of Zanzibar has no breathing space as he is suffocated from all directions by the government, its institutions and personnel.

G. Conclusion

For all intents and purposes, the MAoZ is a poorly conceived and highly questionable legislation.

Firstly, by providing the Office of Mufti with accommodation, furniture, salaries etc.; all from taxpayers' money, this legislation does not auger well with the concept of good governance. Since the law provides that only one religion (Islām) access to public coffers to which everybody contributes.

86 Section 7 (1) MAoZ.
87 Section 7 (4) MAoZ.
88 Section 8 (1) MAoZ.
89 Section 8 (2) MAoZ.
90 Section 10 (1) (e) MAoZ.
91 Section 12 (1) MAoZ.
92 Section 13 (2) MAoZ.
93 Section 13 (3) MAoZ.

Secondly, it violates both the 1977 Constitution of the United Republic of Tanzania and the 1984 Constitution of Zanzibar. It removes Zanzibari Muslims their Right to Freedom of Assembly and Association, a right guaranteed by the two constitutions and which is enjoyed by non-Muslim Zanzibaris. In this context, it is noteworthy, to emphasise that legislation of this nature in the East African region are currently highly criticised for being unconstitutional. For instance, recently the Constitutional Court of Uganda in the case of *Muwanga Kivumbi v. Attorney General* declared Section 32 of Uganda's Police Act unconstitutional. Underlining the importance of the Right to Freedom of Assembly and Association, Hon. Mr. Justice Byamugisha stated that

> " [t]he justification for freedom of assembly in countries which are considered free and democratically governed [...] is to enable citizens to gather and express their views without government restrictions. The government has a duty of maintaining proper channels and structures to ensure that legitimate protest, whether political or otherwise, can find a voice. Maintaining the freedom to assemble and express dissent remains a powerful indicator of the democratic and political health of a country."[94]

As Mashood A. Baderin pointed out:

> " The concept of Human Rights has, today, become an important form of social ordering which no State can ignore. This status of Human Rights as a form of social ordering is boosted by the fact that there is a strong link between respect for Human Rights and development within a States."[95]

Hence, one has to admit that the RGZ cannot and definitely should not afford to ignore this crucial point(s). In a secular state, there must be a clear separation between public administration and the Basic Right's of religious freedom, e.g. dealing with issues of worship. Questions of personal beliefs and worship should be – within the constitutional framework –regarded as private matters of each citizen. Therefore, the citizen has a clear duty and right to separate allegiance to the temporal leadership and to God. In the Holy Bible, for example, this separation is captured very well:

> " And Jesus answered and said to them, *'Render to Caesar the things that are Caesar's, and to God the things that are God's.'* And they marvelled at Him."[96]

---

[94] This judgement is partly reproduced in *Sunday Monitor* (Uganda), 1 June 2008. I would like to thank Alhaj Salum Toufiq Ali of Zantel, Zanzibar, for providing me with this important decision of the Uganda Constitutional Court.

[95] *Mashood A. Baderin,* "The Role of Islam in Human Rights and Development in Muslim States", in: *Javaid Rehman / Susan C. Breau* (Eds.), Religion, Human Rights and International Law, Leiden / et al. 2007, on p. 321.

[96] See The Gospel According to Mark, Chapter 12 Verse 17, *C.I. Scofield*, The Holy Bible (King James Version), Michigan 1996, p. 1062.

Accordingly, one should *give to Caesar what is Caesar's* and *God what is God's*.[97] Failure to maintain a balance between God and the government of the day or to allow freedom of belief and worship without due regard to the rights of others can be quite disastrous and lead to undesirable consequences.[98] In case of Zanzibar, the separation between *Caesar* and *God* is compromised by the MAoZ which almost means that everything goes to *Caesar* and nothing goes to *God* as the way to *God* is through *Caesar*. This arrangement does not augur well with the dictates of a secular State and has to be seriously addressed. It is just logical that Muslims in Zanzibar should seek a more legitimate way of electing their spiritual leader other than having one imposed on them by the law of the land. Not even the Constitution – source and supreme law of a country – should be allowed to do that.

Thirdly, it undermines the *secular nature* of the Zanzibari society. It does not make sense for a law to provide that the president of the government to be given

97 Issues of belief are, of course, sensitive and personal and it is not always easy to maintain a clear balance between the two, *God* and *Caesar*. Cp. *Robert F. Drinan*, Can God & Caesar Coexist? Balancing Religious Freedom & International Law, New Haven / et al. 2004. See also *Bahiyyih G. Tahzib*, Freedom of Religion or Belief: Ensuring Effective International Legal Protection, The Hague / et al. 1995; *Edward G. Hoseah*, "The Freedom of Conscience and Religion: Some Reflections", in: The Tanzania Lawyer, June-October 2002, on p. 15 et seqq.; *Nabil Hilmy*, "Historical Development of Human Rights and its Influence on Some Aspects of Islamic Law", in: Africa Legal Aid Quarterly, October-December 2000, pp. 14 et seqq.; *Makau Mutua*, "Limitations on Religious Rights: Problematising Religious Freedom in the African Context", in: *Johan van der Vyer / John Witte* (Eds.), Religious Human Rights in Global Perspective: Legal Perspective, The Hague / et al. 1996, pp. 417 et seqq.; *Jochen A. Frowein*, "Religion and Religious Symbols in European and International Law," in: *Winfried Brugger / Michael Karayanni* (Eds.), Religion in the Public Sphere: A Comparative Analysis of German, Israel, American and International Law, Berlin / Heidelberg 2007, pp. 243 et seqq.; *Martin Riesebrodt*, "Religion in Global Perspective", in: *Mark Juergensmeyer* (Ed.), The Oxford Handbook of Global Religions, Oxford 2006, pp. 597 et seqq.; *Cornelus de Jong*, The Freedom of Thought, Conscience and Religion or Belief in the United Nations (1946-1992), Antwerpen / et al. 2000; *Natan Lerner*, Religion, Secular Beliefs and Human Rights: 25 Years After the 1981 Declaration, Leiden / Boston 2006; *Carrie Gustafson / Peter Juviler* (Eds.), Religion and Human Rights: Competing Claims?, New York / London 1999.

98 For instance, where a Muslim preacher on Tanzania Mainland declared that Jcsus was not Son of God in an open sermon, the matter went up to the highest court of the land. See *Court of Appeal of Tanzania at Dar es Salaam*, Criminal Appeal No. 53 of 2001 (*Dibagula v. Republic*). This case has been digested in *Gamaliel Mgongo Fimbo*, The Mind of a Legal Luminary: Digest of Selected Decisions of Hon. Justice Barnabas Albert Samatta, Dar es Salaam 2007; *Hamza Mustafa Njozi*, Muslims..., supra, footnote 26, on p. 200; *Robert V. Makaramba*, "Religion, Rule of Law and Justice in Tanzania", in: *Rwekaza Mukandala / et al* (Eds.), Justice, Rights and Worship: Religion and Politics in Tanzania, supra, footnote 29, on p. 360 and on p. 380.

the responsibility of choosing a leader for a specific religion. This is exactly what the MAoZ does. The Mufti – the spiritual leader of all Muslims in Zanzibar – is appointed by the President of Zanzibar. In fact, as explained earlier, the significance limits the possibility of a non-Muslim ever becoming the President of Zanzibar. If, somehow, a non-Muslim ascends into power, which is feasible under the Constitution, it means that the Muslims in Zanzibar will have their leader chosen by a non-Muslim. This can not be considered a well thought out legislation – discrepancies and tension are preassigned.

Sudan under the Constraints of (International) Human Rights Law and Humanitarian Law: The Case of Darfur*

Hatem Elliesie, Berlin

A. Introduction: (International) Human Rights and Humanitarian Law

The term 'Human Rights' may be used in either an abstract and philosophical sense – as already addressed in previous contributions within this volume – as denoting a 'special kind of moral claim'[1] that humans may invoke; or, more pragmatically, as the manifestation of these claims in positive law; for example, as constitutional guarantees that serve as the basis to hold governments accountable under national legal process.

I. Human Rights and (International) Human Rights Law

To avoid confusion, the first understanding of the term will be referred to as 'Human Rights', and the second as 'Human Rights Law'.[2] The latter is closely linked to the emergence of the nation state. The implication of this state-centeredness is that states are the primary duty-bearers with respect to these rights. Thus, 'Human Rights Law' represents the state's obligations at a given time, while 'Human Rights' serve as a moral measure against which the nature and the extent of these obligations may be assessed, an ideal towards which to strive, and an inspiration to improve the current state of affairs.[3] "*International*

---

* This article is a revised version of the paper "Anmerkungen zum Menschenrechtsschutz im westlichen Sudan" presented by the author on the occasion of the 10th annual conference of the *Gesellschaft für Arabisches und Islamisches Recht e.V.* (German Association of Arabic and Islamic Law) organised in collaboration with the German Institute for Human Rights on 19 and 20 October 2007 in Berlin.

1 *Başak Çali / Saladin Meckled-García,*, "Lost in Translation: the Human Rights Ideal and International Human Rights Law", in: *Saladin Meckled-García / Başak Çali* (Eds.), The Legalization of Human Rights: Multidisciplinary Perspectives on Human Rights and Human Rights Law, London 2006, p. 11. See, in this context, also *Romuald R. Haule,* "Some Reflections on the Foundation of Human Rights: Are Human Rights an alternative to moral Values?", in: Max Planck UNYB, vol. 10, Leiden / Boston 2006, pp. 367-394.

2 See explicitly *Frans Viljoen,* International Human Rights Law in Africa, Oxford / New York 2007, p. 4.

3 *Christof Heyns,* "A 'Struggle Approach' to Human Rights", in: *Christof Heyns / et al.* (Eds.), Human Rights, Peace and Justice in Africa: A Reader, Pretoria 2006, pp. 15 et seqq.; *Malcolm N. Shaw,* International Law, 5th edition, Cambridge / et al. 2003, p. 250; *Raúl Emilio Vinuea,* "Interface, Correspondence and Convergence of Human Rights and International Humanitarian Law", in: Yearbook of International Humanitarian Law, volume 1, The Hague / Cambridge 1998, pp. 69 et seqq. (on p. 71).

Islam und Menschenrechte (Islam and Human Rights / الإسلام وحقوق الإنسان)
Hatem Elliesie (Hrsg./Editor), © Peter Lang Verlag: Frankfurt a.M. 2010, S. 193-217

Human Rights Law", however, differs from *national* "Human Rights Law" as to its source, in that its concretized content is found mainly in provisions of international human rights treaties.[4]

II. (International) Human Rights Law and Humanitarian Law

Although International Human Rights Law and Humanitarian Law have much in common, they also differ in significant aspects: 'International Human Rights Law' and 'Humanitarian Law' are, traditionally, two distinct bodies of law. The traditional distinction between both is, generally speaking, that the former applies in peacetime, and the latter in time of war. The law of armed conflict primarily confers rights on states that are designed to further military efficiency,[5] originated in notions of honourable and civilized behaviour that should be expected in armed conflicts. From a purist's human rights point of view, based on respect for human life and well-being, the use of force is, in and of itself a violation of Human Rights. By way of contrast, Human Rights Law has less clearly defined origins and has had to develop within the constraints of sovereignty. Their focus has been on conferring rights on individuals to protect them from arbitrary actions by the state.[6] While this is broadly correct, such a statement does not allow for the frequent difficulty of distinguishing between peace and war, and the increasing application of 'Human Rights' in armed conflicts of non-international nature. In such situations, 'Humanitarian Law' operates through the 1977 Geneva Protocol II, and Common Article 3 of the 1949 Geneva Conventions. Thus, one is able to ascertain that the Common Article 3 has brought 'Humanitarian Law' closer to 'Human Rights Law', because it is concerned with the treatment of a state's own nationals; a sphere of alleged interference into the *domaine réservé* of a state,[7] as mirrored in Art. 2 (7) UN-Charter.[8]

---

4 Cp. *Manfred Nowak,* Introduction to the International Human Rights Regime, Leiden / Boston 2003, p. 36; *Frans Viljoen,* International Human Rights..., supra, footnote 2, p. 5 et seq.; *Thomas Buergenthal,* International Human Rights in a Nutshell, 2nd edition, St. Paul 1995, pp. 21 et seqq.

5 See *Chris af Jochnik / Roger Normand,* "The Legitimiation of Violence: A critical History of the Laws of War", in: Harvard International Law Journal, volume 35, Cambridge 1994, pp. 49 et seqq. (on p. 58).

6 See *International Criminal Tribunal for Rwanda, Chamber I,* Case ICTR-96-4 (The Prosecutor vs. Jean Paul Akayesu), Judgement, Arusha, 2 September 1998, para. 630; cp. also *Louise Doswald Beck / Sylvian Vite,* "International Humanitarian Law and Human Rights Law", in: International Review of the Red Cross, volume 293, Cambridge 1993, pp. 95 et seqq. (on p. 101); *Anthony Cullen,* "The Definition of Non-International Armed Conflict in the Rome Statute of the International Criminal Court: An Analysis of the Threshold of Application Contained in Article 8(2) (f)", in: Journal of Conflict & Security Law, volume 12, number 3, Oxford 2007, pp. 419 et seqq. (on p. 445).

7 *Cordula Droege,* "The Interplay between International Humanitarian Law and International Human Rights Law in Situations of Armed Conflict", in: Israel Law Review,

III. General Application of Human Rights Law and Humanitarian Law

The 'state sovereignty-objection' against the application of both regimes by derogating 'Human Rights' in times of 'public emergency', which include situations of armed conflict, is, however, a common misconception. Derogations are only permissible as long as the requisite situation calls for it. However, the case in its entirety must remain consistent with the states' other obligations under International (Human Rights) Law and do not involve discrimination solely on the ground of race, colour, sex, language, religion, or social origin.[9] While this view may comply with the overall state practice, some states do not reveal the existence of conflicts in their territory, 'state sovereignty' in the African context is no longer sacrosanct. It is now understood that the source of sovereignty is not 'the sovereign', but the 'people'.[10] In other words, it is the people's sovereignty rather than the sovereign's sovereignty.[11] Evidence of this people-centered understanding of sovereignty, as opposed to the usually raised *domaine réservé* objection, can also be found in the Interim National Constitution of the Republic of Sudan (INC),[12] in numerous other African constitutions[13] and in the African

---

volume 40, number 2, Jerusalem 2007, p. 310 et seq.; *Malcolm N. Shaw,* International Law, supra, footnote 3, p. 254; *Michael Reisman,* "Sovereignty and Human Rights in Contemporary International Law", in: American Journal of International Law, volume 84, issue 4, Washington D.C. 1990, pp. 866 et seqq. (on p. 869); *Frans Viljoen,* International Human Rights..., supra, footnote 2, p. 31; *Manfred Nowak,* Introduction..., supra, footnote 4, p. 33.

8 *Article 2 UN-Charter:*

(7) Nothing contained in the present Charter shall authorize the United Nations to intervene in matters which are essentially within the domestic jurisdiction of any state [...].

9 Cp. Art. 4 of the International Covenant on Civil and Political Rights (ICCPR); Art. 15 of the European Convention for the Protection of Human Rights and Fundamental Freedoms; Art. 27 of the American Convention on Human Rights. Art. 2, 60 of the African [Banjul] Charter on Human and Peoples' Rights.

10 *Frans Viljoen,* International Human Rights..., supra, footnote 2, p. 464.

11 See also *Michael Reisman,* Sovereignty and Human Rights..., supra, footnote 7, on p. 869; *Andreas von Arnauld,* "Souveränität und responsibility to protect", in: Die Friedens-Warte (Journal of International Peace and Organization), volume 84, issue 1, Berlin 2009, pp. 11 et seqq. (on p. 13 et seq.).

12 In the Sudan, member state of the African Union, sovereignty is, *expressis verbis,* "vested [also] in the *people* and shall be exercised by the State in accordance with the provisions of the Constitution and the law [...]"; see Art. 2 INC in conjunction with Art. 27 (1) INC.

13 In particular constitutions of 'Francophone' countries, which, following the French constitutional tradition, declare that "sovereignty belongs to the people", and is exercised on their behalf by elected representatives; see Art. 3 of the 1996 Chad Constitution; Art. 4 of the 2001 Congo Constitution; Art. 7 of the 2004 Burundi Constitution.

Union Constitutive Act,[14] which accepts the right of the Union to use military force in member states in order to restore grave Human Rights violations. In other words, African Union states, in general, and Sudan, in specific, have accepted the principle that individual rights may have to be protected against the abuse of state sovereignty.[15]

This raises the question as to the relationship between (International) Human Rights Law and Humanitarian Law norms. Three possible situations may occur:

- Some rights may exclusively be matters of Humanitarian Law;
- others may exclusively be matters of Human Rights Law;
- yet others may be matters of both these branches.

The International Court of Justice (ICJ) recognized a parallel application of both branches, namely Human Rights Law and, as *lex specialis,* Humanitarian Law,[16] breaking the aforementioned traditional *quasi* 'strict' classification. Hence, the ongoing conflict in the Sudan is put under both of these constraints.[17] In strict adherence to legal methodology, the specific regulations of the Humanitarian Law obligations are going to be set (C.I.) before focusing on binding norms of Human Rights Law (C.II), after illustrating the conflict (B.).

B. The Conflict in the Western most parts of Sudan (Darfur)

Post-colonial Sudan, currently Africa's largest country covering about two and a half million square kilometres, is not only vast in size, but is also blessed with a great diversity of natural resources, and of cultures and social structures. This diversity involves a wide-ranging mixture of population groups[18] exercising dif-

---

14 See Art. 4 (h) AU Constitutive Act.

15 Cp. *Frans Viljoen,* International Human Rights..., supra, footnote 2, p. 464.

16 *International Court of Justice,* Legality of the Threat or Use of Nuclear Weapons, Advisory Opinion of 8 July 1996, para. 24 et seqq., in: International Legal Materials (ILM), volume 35, issue 4, Washington D.C. 1996, pp. 809 et seqq. (on p. 820); *idem,* Legal Consequences to the Construction of a Wall in the Occupied Palestine Territory, Advisory Opinion of 9 July 2004, para. 105 et seq., in: ILM, volume 43, issue 5, Washington D.C., 2004, pp. 1009 et seqq. (on p. 1038 et seq.); *Eve La Haye,* War Crimes in Internal Armed Conflicts, Cambridge 2008, p. 74.

17 Cp. in this context also *Mohamed Abdelsalam Babiker,* Application of International Humanitarian and Human Rights Law to the Armed Conflicts of the Sudan, Antwerp / Oxford 2007, p. 74; *Michael Bothe,* "International Legal Aspects of the Darfur Conflict", in: *August Reinisch / Ursula Kriebaum* (Eds.), The Law of International Relations – Liber Amicorum Hanspeter Neuhold, Utrecht 2007, pp. 1 et seqq. (on p. 4).

18 When the CERD Committee examined the last Sudanese state report (combining its 9th to 11th reports) in 2001, it expressed general concern about the lack of information concern-

ferent languages, customs and lifestyles.[19] However, aside from the 11-years' timeframe, post-colonial Sudan has been continuously involved in one of the longest lasting, internal armed conflicts on the African Continent, mainly carried out between different Islamic-oriented regimes in the North on one hand, and of people of predominantly Christian faith and so-called animists, on the other.[20] This mostly religiously-inspired and race-based conflict gained international attention due to the ghastliness of the atrocities carried out and has thus made Sudan a pariah state in the eyes of many countries.[21] Finally, in 2005, the North-South civil war has been repacified through the so-called Comprehensive Peace Agreement (CPA).[22] Yet, this had led to an even stronger desire for autonomy in

ing the demographic composition of the population. The primary focus of its concluding observations was on the Nuer and Dinka ethnic groups in the Upper Nile Region, omitting any reference to the western region of Darfur; UN-Doc. CERD/C/304/Add.116, para. 8 et seq. Unsurprisingly, no reports were submitted at the height of the Darfur crisis. As to the demographic composition in Darfur, see *Sanā' Ḥamad al-ʿAwaḍ,* "al-ḫarīṭa ad-dīmūğrāfīya li-ʾiqlīm ad-Dārfūr", in: as-Siyāsa ad-Dawliya, 43/167, Cairo (January) 2007, pp. 202-207.

19 *Hatem Elliesie,* "Quo Vadis bilād as-Sūdān? The Contemporary Framework for a National Interim Constitution", in: Recht in Afrika (Law in Africa · Droit en Afrique), volume 8, issue 1, Cologne 2005, p. 63.

20 See *Hanspeter Mattes*, "Sudan", in: *Udo Steinbach* (Ed.), Politisches Lexikon – Nahost / Nordafrika, 3rd edition, Munich 1994, pp. 242-244; *idem,* "Sudan Sommer 2004: Frieden im Süden, Krieg im Westen, Konflikt mit der Opposition", in: Nord-Süd aktuell, volume 18, issue 2, Hamburg 2004, pp. 276 et seqq. (pp. 277-280). He cites in this particular context three major factors: „[1] The Arabic-Islamic identity, primarily of the northern Sudanese; [2] the aftermath of colonial times; [and 3] the characteristically nature of southern Sudan, i.e. its certain religious-, ethnic- and economic conditions". Additionally: *Rainer Tetzlaff,* "Bürgerkrieg und Staatsbildung im Sudan: Ein Land auf der Suche nach seiner kulturellen Identität", in: *Markus Wauschkuhn / Karl Wohlmuth* (Eds.), Die Sudanforschung in der Bundesrepublik Deutschland, Munich / Hamburg 1995, pp. 383 et seqq. (on p. 389).

21 *Jok Madut Jok,* Sudan, Race, Religion and Violence, Oxford 2007, p. 15.

22 Cp. *Hatem Elliesie,* "Friedensprozess und Verfassungsentwicklung im Sudan", in: Verfassung und Recht in Übersee (VRÜ), volume 38, issue 3, Baden-Baden / Hamburg 2005, pp. 276-307; *idem,* Quo Vadis bilād as-Sūdān?..., supra, footnote 19, pp. 63 et seqq.; *Sarah M. H. Nouwen,* "Sudan's divided (and divisive?) Peace Agreements", in: Hague Yearbook of International Law (Annuaire de La Haye de Droit International), volume 19, The Hague 2006, pp. 111 et seqq.; *Philipp Dann / Zaid Al-Ali,* "The Internationalized Pouvoir Constituant – Constitution-Making Under External Influence in Iraq, Sudan and East Timor", in: Max Planck UNYB, volume 10, Leiden / Boston 2006, pp. 423 et seqq. (on p. 443); *Fred L. Morrison,* "The World's most complex Constitution: The Interim Constitutional Framework of the Sudan", in: *August Reinisch / Ursula Kriebaum* (Eds.), The Law of International Relations – Liber Amicorum Hanspeter Neuhold, Utrecht 2007, p. 229 et seq.

the peripheral regions. Simultaneously, we have been made witness to a deepening chasm of conflict among the groups based on tribal, ethnical, geographic, and religious lines ever since.

This contribution draws the attention to the Western most parts of the Sudan where – unlike the southern parts of the country – the *lingua franca* is Arabic, and the peoples[23] are almost entirely Muslim.[24] This said, one could understandably assume that these facts would serve as an unobstructed basis of peaceful coexistence. Yet, the incidents are much more complex.

I. Origins of the Conflict in Darfur

What one is able to witness is a devastating humanitarian situation in this particular region. The interest of international politics and that of indigenous groups' claiming political influence and ownership of resources result in gruesome violence. The mechanisms with which acts of force are carried out, the resulting social and economic dynamics, and the manner in which it is locally embodied, have garnered local and international human rights concern because of obvious racism exhibited by combatants in the region.[25]

1. Context: The Libyan (and Chadian) impact

As historical analysis makes apparent, the mass human rights abuses that are occurring today in the region of Darfur can be traced back to the Chadian-Libyan boundary dispute of the Aouzou Strip.[26] Libyan troops and armed groups of Chadian civil war parties, such as the *Front de Libération Nationale du Tchad* (FROLINAT), used Darfur as a retreat, springboard and combat zone for their own national ambitions. Libya, on the other hand, used the northwestern corner of Darfur as a backdoor to attack Chad. Libya's leader, Muʿammar al-Qaḏḏāfī,

---

23 See *Sanāʾ Ḥamad al-ʿAwaḍ,* al-ḫarīṭa ad-dīmūġrāfīya…, supra, footnote 18, pp. 202-207; *ʿAbdullāh al-ʾAšʿal,* ʾazmat Dārfūr bayna muḥāwalāt at-tadwīl wa-ǧuhūd at-taswīya, Dār Naṣr: Cairo 2007, p. 9.

24 *Helen Fatima Idris,* "The Status and Use of African Languages versus Arabic in Sudan: A sociolinguistic Survey in Nyala, Darfur", in: *Akinbiyi Akinlabi / Oluseye Adesola* (Eds.), Proceedings of the 4th World Conference of African Linguistics, New Brunswick 2003, Cologne 2004, p. 497. See also *Andrew S. Natsios,* "Moving Beyond the Sense of Alarm", in: *Samuel Totten / Eric Markusen* (Eds.), Genocide in Darfur, Oxon / New York, pp. 25 et seqq. (on p. 29); *ʿAbdullāh al-ʾAšʿal,* ʾazmat Dārfūr bayna muḥāwalāt at-tadwīl wa-ǧuhūd at-taswīya, Dār Naṣr: Cairo 2007, p. 11.

25 *Jok Madut Jok,* Sudan, Race, Religion and Violence, supra, footnote 21, p. 17.

26 See in more detail: *Bernard Lanne,* Tchad-Libye: La querelle des frontières, Paris 1986, pp. 228 et seqq.; *John Wright,* Libya, Chad and the Central Sahara, Totowa 1989, pp. 126-133; *M. W. Daly,* Darfur's Sorrow: A History of Destruction and Genocide, Cambridge / et al. 2007, p. 206-207. Furthermore, *Christine Gray,* International Law and the Use of Force, 3rd edition, Oxford / New York 2008, pp. 96-98.

had equipped and sent out the so-called *al-faylaqa al-ʾislāmīya* (Islamic Legion) first to Chad, and then to Sudan's northwestern region. In his mind, the *al-faylaqa al-ʾislāmīya* was to be a tool for the revolutionary unification and arabization of the region. Thus, Libya was not orchestrating a simple border raid on a poor country; it was pursuing a new strategy of pan-Arabism couched in an emotionally charged ideology. For that reason, Colonel Muʿammar al-Qaḏḏāfī supported the creation of the *at-taǧammuʿ al-ʿarabī* (Arab Union), a militantly racist and Pan-Arabist organization, which stressed the "ʿArab" character of the province.[27]

The United States and its ally, the then-president of Sudan Ǧaʿfar Muḥammad an-Numairī, bolstered Hissène Habré's government in Chad against Libya's expansionist policies. While US-military assistance flowed into southern Chad through Darfur, the Libyan leader Muʿammar al-Qaḏḏāfī formed the aforementioned Islamic Legion first to take control of northern Chad, and then to push southward. The recruits to this Islamic Legion came from many Arabic-speaking groups of the Sahel and the Sudan, including pastoralists who straddled the Chad-Darfur border. The ideology they were inculcated with was not just pan-Islamic, but pan-Arabic, stemming from al-Qaḏḏāfī's political vision of creating an 'Arab belt' across the Sahel. With the dismantling of the Islamic Legion following Libya's defeat in 1988, many former members – armed trained, and imbued with a new ideology – crossed into Darfur.[28] This racial salience led to a realignment of the non-*ʿArab* defined groups in Darfur (the Zaġāwa and Fūr[29] in particular).[30]

The extent to which Libya's Islamic Legion and missionary *daʿwa* were inspired by a racist ideology is less important than the effect of that ideology, which rationalized the Sahelian chaos of the 1970's and 1980's by reducing it to "Arabs" versus "Africans". The sharp distinction between "Arabs" and "Africans" in the ethnically mixed Darfur region had not been incorporated into a broader discourse until Libya produced an ideology of pan-Arabism.[31] This led to animosi-

27 Cp. *Gérard Prunier,* Darfur – The Ambiguous Genocide, Revised and Updated Edition, London 2007, p. 45; *Touko Piiparinen,* "Reconsidering the Silence over the ultimate Crime: A functional Shift Crisis Management from the Rwandan Genocide to Darfur", in: Journal of Genocide Research, volume 9, issue 1, London / et al. 2007, p. 71.

28 *Douglas H. Johnson,* "Darfur: Peace, Genocide & Crimes Against Humanity in Sudan", in: *Preben Kaarsholm* (Ed.): Violence, Political Culture & Development in Africa, Oxford / et al. 2006; pp. 92 et seqq. (on p. 94).

29 Cp. *Sanāʾ Ḥamad al-ʿAwaḍ,* al-ḫarīṭa ad-dīmūǧrāfīya..., supra, footnote 18, p. 205.

30 *Douglas H. Johnson,* The Root Cause of Sudan's Civil Wars, Oxford / et al. 2003, p. 140.

31 Cp. *Andrew S. Natsios,* Moving Beyond..., supra, footnote 24, on p. 30; *M. W. Daly,* Darfur's..., supra, footnote 26, p. 265; *Heather J. Sharkey,* "Arab Identity and Ideology in

ties based on racial and ideological polemics, including the idea of *taʿrīb* (Arabization), which were comparable to the Hutu power ideology in Rwanda.[32] Combined with the social tensions resulting from a failed land reform in the same decade,[33] the spiral of violence spun increasingly faster. Given the deficiency of effective governance in the region, the possession of firearms soared[34] and local conflicts increased. Tribes that defined themselves primarily by their local context were now increasingly involved in a militant ethno-political conflict of an even more complex structure between Tripoli, N'Djamena and Khartoum.[35]

2. Context: Ecological disequilibrium

This increase in violence coincided with a sharp decline in rainfall throughout the 1970s, affecting northern Darfur at first, but moving progressively south-

Sudan: The Politics of Language, Ethnicity, and Race", in: African Affairs 107/426, London 2007, pp. 21 et seqq. (on p. 27).

32 *Hatem Elliesie / Urs Behrendt / Niway Zergie Aynalem,* "Different Approaches to Genocide Trials under National Jurisdiction on the African Continent – The Rwandan, Ethiopian and Sudanese Cases", in: Recht in Afrika (Law in Afrika · Droit en Afrique), Cologne 2009, p. 21 et seqq. (on p. 46).

33 The *qānūn al-ʾarāḍī ġayr al-musaǧǧala* (Unregistered Land Act of 1970) declared that all waste, forest and unregistered land belongs to the state. Before the act's passage, the central government avoided interfering with customary rights to unregistered land, and in the late 1980s again adhered to this policy; *Jon D. Unruh,* "Postwar Resource Tenure Issues in the Settlement of Sudan's Dislocated Population", in: North East African Studies, volume 9, no. 1, East Lansing 2002, pp. 1 et seqq. (on p. 5).

34 *Muḥammad ʿAbdullāh ad-Dawma,* "ḥimāyāt al-muwāṭinīn fī Dārfūr: waǧib man? an-niẓām as-sūdānī wa-l-quwwāt ad-dawlīya", in: *Muḥsin ʿAwaḍ / ʿAlāʾ Šalabī* (Eds.), min ʾaǧl salām Dārfūr (buḥūṯ wa-munāqašāt nadwa ḥawla mawāqif ʾakṯar fāʿilīya li-munaẓẓamāt ḥuqūq al-ʾinsān fī Dārfūr – al-Qāhira, 11-12 May 2007), Al-Munaẓẓama al-ʿArabīya li-Ḥuqūq al-ʾInsān: Cairo 2008, pp. 42 et seqq. (on p. 44); *Khalid Y. Khalafalla,* "Der Konflikt in Darfur", in: APuZ, issue 4, Bonn 2005, pp. 40 et seqq.; *Douglas H. Johnson,* The Root Causes…, supra, footnote 30, p. 139 et seq.

35 *Günter Lerch,* "Begehrte Randprovinz: Die Katastrophe in Darfur ist auch das Ergebnis von vielerlei Einmischungen", in: FAZ, no. 157, Frankfurt a.M., 10 July 2007, on p. 8; *Hatem Elliesie,* "Die Darfur-Krise im Sudan und das Völkerrecht: Eine Herausforderung für die Vereinten Nationen (UN) und den Internationalen Strafgerichtshof (ICC)", in: VRÜ, volume 40, issue 2, Baden-Baden / Hamburg 2007, pp. 199 et seqq. (on pp. 201-202); *Gérard Prunier,* Darfur…, supra, footnote 27, pp. 54 et seqq.; *Ayesha Kajee,* "The Regional and International Dimension of the Crisis in Darfur", in: Brian *Raftopoulos / Karin Alexander* (Eds.), Peace in the Balance: The Crisis in Sudan, Cape Town 2006, pp. 71 et seqq. (p. 78 et seq.); *Alex de Waal,* "Briefing Darfur, Sudan: Prospects for Peace", in: African Affairs 104/414, Oxford (January) 2005, p. 127 et seq.; *Marina Peter,* Studien zur länderbezogenen Konfliktanalyse – Sudan, Bonn 2004, p. 16. See also *International Crisis Group,* Dafur's Fragile Peace Agreement, Africa Briefing N° 39, Nairobi / Brussels, 20 June 2006, p. 13 et seq.

wards. The deterioration of resources caused by droughts precipitated a movement of people out of the north and into the southern farming belt.[36] In the west, refugee movements from Chad further complicated the situation, as many armed nomadic peoples resettled in Darfur during the Chadian Civil War.[37] The abolition of tribal administration structures, whose authorities had routinely negotiated, mediated and regulated intra- and inter-tribal conflicts, such as those of sedentary agriculturalists groups (of which the Fūr[38] are the most prominent), like the Baqqāra and other semi-nomadic pastoralists,[39] led to a situation that destabilized the once-effective conflict resolution processes.

3. Context: Abolishment of customary rights

In addition, the 1970 *qānūn al-ʾarāḍī ġayr al-musağğala*[40] abolished customary rights of land use and access to land, and set the foundation for the central state leasing of land for large-scale farming schemes[41]. Furthermore, the *qānūn at-taʿaddī al-ğināʾī* (Law of Criminal Trespass of 1974) strengthened the rights of leaseholders to their lands, further restricting the right of access by nomads and smallholding farmers. After the abolition of the native administration in the 1970s, replaced, mainly by province councils with strong connections to the central Nile region, very weak governmental structures were set up in the 1980s lacking full administrative or economic autonomy and relying on grants from the central government.[42] It became obvious that the overriding power disrupted the traditional conflict resolution mechanisms.[43] Independent of the Khartoum political class, the local tribal leaders initiated traditional negotiations for peacemaking in late May 1989 by launching the conference of reconciliation

36 *Ulrich Braukämper,* "Wanderungen und Transhumanzzyklen von Rindernomaden in Darfur (Sudan)", in: Paideuma, volume 35, Stuttgart 1989, pp. 17 et seqq. (on p. 36).

37 *Andrea Behrends,* "The Darfur Conflict and the Chad/Sudan Border – Regional Context and Local Re-configurations", in: Sociologus (Journal of Empirical Social Anthropology), volume 57, issue 1, Berlin 2007, pp. 99 et seqq. (on p. 113); *Sharif Harir,* "'Arab Belt' versus 'African Belt'. Ethno-Political Conflict in Dar Fur and the Regional Cultural Factors", in: *Sharif Harir / Terje Tvedt* (Eds.), Short-Cut to Decay, The Case of the Sudan, Uppsala 1994, pp. 144 et seqq. (on p. 164).

38 Cp. *Sanāʾ Ḥamad al-ʿAwaḍ,* al-ḫarīṭa ad-dīmūğrāfīya..., supra, footnote 18, p. 205.

39 *Ulrich Braukämper,* Wanderungen und Transhumanzzyklen von Rindernomaden in Darfur..., supra, footnote 36, on p. 19.

40 Unregistered Land Act of 1970, cp. footnote 33.

41 See *ʿAbdullāh al-ʾAšʿal,* ʾazmat Dārfūr bayna muḥāwalāt at-tadwīl wa-ğuhūd at-taswīya, Dār Naṣr: Cairo 2007, p. 10.

42 *Douglas H. Johnson,* The Root Cause..., supra, footnote 30, p. 130.

43 Ibidem, on p. 94; *Julie Flint / Alex de Waal,* Darfur: A Short History of a Long War, Cape Town / et al. 2005, p. 58; *Olaf Köndgen,* Tragödie in Darfur, in: KAS-AI, issue 4, Bonn 2004, p. 4 et seq.

"*muʾtamar at-taṣāluḥ*",[44] which did not live up to their expectations. Instead, the ruling class amended the *al-qānūn al-madanī al-muʿāmalāt* (Civil Transactions Act) in 1990 to prohibit the recognition of customary land rights in courts throughout the country. The cumulative effect of these legal and administrative reforms was that, not only did political power continue to be concentrated in the central government, but control of the very land on which people lived and depended was transferred to those with access to that governmental power.[45]

4. Context: Repercussion of the war's intensity

The whole state of affairs was exacerbated by the downfall of the *Därg*-regime in Ethiopia brought about by the **ህዝባዊ ወያነ ሓርነት ትግራይ**, *həzbawi wäyyanä ḥarənnät Təgray* (Tigray People's Liberation Front – TPLF), and the **ህዝባዊ ግንባር ሓርነት ኤርትራ**, *həzbawi gənbar ḥarənnät Ertəra*[46] (Eritrean People's Liberation Front – EPLF) in 1991. By virtue of the downfall of Mängəśtu Ḫāylä-Maryam's Regime, Dr. John Garang de Mabior, the former leader of the *Sudan People's Liberation Army/Movement* (SPLA/M),[47] lost his major backing in his power struggle against neo-secessional trends within his own ranks as well as with his confrontation with the central Government of Sudan (GoS).[48] Even before the military *coup d'état* in Sudan in 1989, former Prime Minister Ṣādiq al-Mahdī's regime backed the first militia conducting operations in the region Baḥr al-Ġazāl against the ethnic group of Dinkas, which dominated the SPLA. Most members of that militia were recruited out of the Arabic speaking ethnic group of the Baqqāra, based in Darfur and southern Kurdufān.[49] This specific group,

---

44 Cp. *Gérard Prunier,* Darfur…, supra, footnote 27, p. 68.

45 *Douglas H. Johnson,* The Root Cause…, supra, footnote 30, p. 130.

46 Təgrəñña. In Arabic entitled as *"al-ǧabha aš-šaʿbīya li-taḥrīr Irītrīyā"*.

47 John Garang de Mabior Grang died on 30 July 2005 in a helicopter crash returning from a meeting in Rwakitura with long-time ally President Yoweri Kaguta Museveni of Uganda. The accident with the Ugandan Presidential helicopter resulted in massive rioting in cities on both northern and southern Sudan. His position as Sudanese First Vice President and the Leader of the SPLM/A were transferred to Salva Kiir Mayardit, his second in command.

48 *Hatem Elliesie,* Die Darfur-Krise im Sudan und das Völkerrecht…, supra, footnote 35, on p. 202; *Yehudit Ronen,* "Ethiopia's Involvement in the Sudanese Civil War", in: North East African Studies, volume 9, no. 1, East Lansing 2002, pp. 103 et seqq. (on p. 114). See also: *Asgede Hagos,* "Arabism: Ethiopia's Wartime Bogeyman in Eritrea", in: Eritrean Studies Review, volume 1, no. 1, Asmara / et al., pp. 119 et seqq. (on p. 133); *Thomas Zittelmann,* Des Teufels Lustgarten: Themen und Tabus der politischen Anthropologie Nordostafrikas (unpublished postdoctoral thesis [Habilitationsschrift]), Freie Universität Berlin, Fachbereich Politik- und Sozialwissenschaften, Berlin 1999, p. 363.

49 Cp. *ʿAbd an-Naʿīm Ḍayfī,* Dārfūr – at-taʾrīḫ wa-ṣ-ṣirāʿ wa-l-mustaqbal (qiṣṣat ʾiqlīm Dārfūr wa-ṣ-ṣirāʿ), Dār ar-Rašād: Cairo 2008, p. 40; *M. W. Daly,* Darfur's…, supra,

also known as *murāḥilīn,* were militia horsemen who, to this day, have not been disarmed in spite of the escalating virulence. On the contrary, the tribal group of Baqqāra, based in southern Darfur and known as the Rizayqāt,[50] were victorious in their armed struggle for scarce resources in northern Darfur.[51] They formed a structurally non-coherent alliance with like-minded tribes – the so-called *Ǧannǧawīd.*

II. Outcome of the devastating parameters

These tribes were originally referred to as *fursān* or *muǧāhidīn,* and characterized themselves as Arabic descendants. Contrary to what has often been written, these militia groups are no more a "popular" and "organic" expression of all the tribes in Darfur characterized as ʿArab(ic) of descent; than the dreaded Rwandese Hutu paramilitary *Interahamwe*[52]. Both paramilitary groups are organized, politicized and militarized; which, though recruited among people of a (pretended) certain "ethnic origin", do not "naturally" represent them.[53] The formation of the *Ǧannǧawīd* in its current form consists of three main categories[54]:

- The first category includes militias that are only loosely affiliated with the government which received weapons and other supplies from the

footnote 26, p. 264. See also *John Harker,* Human Security in Sudan: The Report of a Canadian Assessment Mission, Ottawa 2000, p. 3; *Fouad Ibrahim,* "Introduction to the Conflict in Darfur/West Sudan", in: *Agnes van Ardenne-van der Hoeven / Mohamed Salih / Nick Grono / Juan Méndez,* Explaining Darfur, Amsterdam 2006, pp. 9 et seqq (on p. 13); *Mohamed Salih,* "Africa's Governance Deficit, Genocide, and Ethnocide", in: Ibidem, pp. 27 et seqq. (on p. 33).

50 For both the Baqqāra and the Rizayqāt, see: *Sanāʾ Ḥamad al-ʿAwaḍ,* al-ḫarīṭa ad-dīmūǧrāfīya..., supra, footnote 18, p. 206; *Ulrich Braukämper,* Wanderungen und Transhumanzzyklen von Rindernomaden in Darfur..., supra, footnote 36, on p. 18 & 21.

51 *Hatem Elliesie,* Die Darfur-Krise im Sudan und das Völkerrecht..., supra, footnote 35, on p. 202; *Farah Arbab,* "Darfur: The Fight for Peace", in: Strategic Studies, volume 24, issue 4, Islamabad 2004, p. 144 et seqq. (on p. 149); *Ulrich Braukämper,* Wanderungen und Transhumanzzyklen von Rindernomaden in Darfur..., supra, footnote 36, on p. 22. Cp. also *ʿAṭā al-Baṭaḥānī,* "naḥw muḫaṭṭaṭ li-taḥdīd ʾanwāʿ wa-marāḥil an-nizāʿāt fī Dārfūr", in: *ʿAbd al-Ġaffār Muḥammad ʾAḥmad / Leif Manger* (Eds.), Dārfūr – ʾiqlīm al-ʿaḏāb: ʾiškālīyat al-mawqiʿ wa-ṣirāʿ al-hawīyāt, Manšūrāt Ruwwāq: Cairo 2006, pp. 75 et seqq. (on p. 92).

52 Kinyarwanda, meaning "those who stand together" or "those who work together" or "those who fight together".

53 *Hatem Elliesie / et al.,* Different Approaches to Genocide..., supra, footnote 32, p. 48 (footnote 181); *Hatem Elliesie,* Die Darfur-Krise im Sudan und das Völkerrecht..., supra, footnote 35, on p. 203; *Gérard Prunier,* Darfur..., supra, footnote 27, p. 97; *Mohamed Salih,* Africa's Governance Deficit..., supra, footnote 49, on p. 33.

54 Cp. also *ʿAbd an-Naʿīm Ḍayfī,* Dārfūr – at-taʾrīḫ ..., supra, footnote 49, pp. 39-41.

state and at the request of state authorities. These militias are thought to operate primarily under a tribal management structure, but also acted on their own initiative to undertake small-scale actions to loot property for personal gain.[55]

- A second category includes militias that are organized in paramilitary structures and act in conjunction with regular forces. Officers in the regular army may head some of these militias, even while they are also controlled by senior tribal leaders. Although militias in this category are thought to operate within a defined command structure, they do not act on legal grounds.[56]
- Finally, the third category of militia includes members of the border intelligence and the *quwwāt aš-šaʿb al-musallaḥa* (Popular Defence Force – PDF).[57] The existence of the PDF is granted by Sudanese Law.[58]

There also appear to be links existing between all three categories.[59]

II. Responses to the Root Causes of the Conflict

Even before 2003, the social, economic and political marginalization of the western most provinces led to the formation of groups opposing the regime in Khartoum to various degrees.

1. Ḥarakat Taḥrīr as-Sūdān

After the deterioration of the situation in Darfur, an armed group referred to as *Darfur Liberation Movement* was formed on 26 February 2003 aiming to overthrow the GoS and to end underdevelopment as well as negligence of the region.

---

55 *International Commission of Inquiry on Darfur,* "Report of the International Commission of Inquiry on Darfur to the United Nations Secretary-General", Geneva 2005, p. 33, para. 106. Cp. also *Thomas Schmidinger,* "Sudan – Der Staat als Warlord", in: Blätter für deutsche und internationale Politik, Bonn 2005, issue 2, pp. 194 et seqq. (on p. 197).

56 *International Commission of Inquiry on Darfur,* Report…, supra, footnote 55, para. 107.

57 President ʿUmar Ḥasan Aḥmad al-Bašīr confirmed that in order to rein the *Ǧannǧawīd,* they were incorporated in "other areas", such as the armed forces and the police; CNN-Interview on 31 August 2004, transcript at http://edition.cnn.com/2004/WORLD/africa/08/31/amanpour.bashir/index.html, accessed on 15 August 2008.

58 Article 6 of the 1989 Popular Defences Forces Act (*qānūn ad-difāʿ aš-šaʿbī)* and Article 122 of the 1998 Sudanese Constitution.

59 *International Commission of Inquiry on Darfur,* Report…, supra, footnote 55, para. 109 et seq.; *Hatem Elliesie,* Die Darfur-Krise im Sudan und das Völkerrecht…, supra, footnote 35, on p. 205. See also *Manjoj Kumar Sinha,* "Crisis in Darfur: International Response", in: Indian Journal of International Law, volume 45, issue 3, New Dehli 2005, p. 389 et seq. (esp. on p. 390); *Kurt Beck,* "Die Massaker in Darfur", in: Zeitschrift für Genozidforschung, volume 5, issue 2, Paderborn 2004, p. 52 et seqq. (on p. 54).

On the occasion of the adoption of its political charter on 14 March 2003, the movement renamed itself as *ḥarakat taḥrīr as-Sūdān* (Sudan Liberation Movement – SLM)[60] due to its overall Sudanese objective.[61] Its current manifesto states that it does not aim to form an independent state; but, rather, calls for a federal system, equal distribution of wealth and power, and the restoration of democracy predicated on full acknowledgement of Sudan's ethnic, cultural, social and political diversity. Viable unity, therefore, must ultimately be based on the right to self-determination.[62] Its manisfesto bears striking resemblance to the SPLM's original vision of a united 'New Sudan'.[63]

2. At-Taḥāluf al-Fīdirālī as-Sūdānī ad-Dīmūqrāṭī

Aside from the military wing of the SLM, the Sudanese Liberation Army (SLA), other guerrilla movements arose, such as the *at-taḥāluf al-fīdirālī as-sūdānī ad-dīmūqrāṭī* (Sudan Federalist Democratic Alliance – SFDA). These groups were mainly composed of people belonging to the Fūr-tribe fighting for the rights of the Fūr and the development of Darfur.

3. Ḥarakat al-ʿAdl wa-l-Musāwāt as-Sūdānīya

Following the same concept of a 'New Sudan', people affiliated with the Zaġāwa tribe established the *ḥarakat al-ʿadl wa-l-musāwāt as-sūdānīya* (Sudan Justice and Equality Movement – SJEM or JEM). In comparison to the other two movements, which were perhaps more militant,[64] the *ḥarakat al-ʿadl wa-l-musāwāt as-sūdānīya* considered themselves a 'pathfinder' of a political party. JEM situates the struggle within a wider context: the marginalized majority against the hegemony of the three ethnic groups – Šāyqīya, Ǧaʿlīn, and Danāqla – and the neglect of development of the regions as demanded by the *al-kutub as-sawdāʾ* (Black Books), published in 2000 and 2003.[65]

---

60 *Hanspeter Mattes*, "Sudan Sommer 2004: Frieden im Süden, Krieg im Westen, Konflikt mit der Opposition", in: Nord-Süd aktuell, Hamburg 2004, issue 2, pp. 276 et seqq. (on p. 289).

61 *ʿAṭā al-Baṭaḥānī*, naḥw muḫaṭṭaṭ li-taḥdīd ʾanwāʿ wa-marāḥil an-nizāʿāt fī Dārfūr, supra, footnote 51, on p. 89.

62 *Robert O. Collins*, "Disaster in Darfur: Historical Overview", in: *Samuel Totten / Eric Markusen* (Eds.), Genocide in Darfur, Oxon / New York, pp. 3 et seqq. (on p. 10); *Mohamed Abdelsalam Babiker*, Application of International Humanitarian and Human Rights Law to the Armed Conflicts of the Sudan, Antwerp / Oxford 2007, p. 22.

63 *Julie Flint / Alex de Waal*, Darfur..., supra, footnote 43, p. 58; *M. W. Daly*, Darfur's..., supra, footnote 26, p. 280.

64 *ʿAṭā al-Baṭaḥānī*, naḥw muḫaṭṭaṭ li-taḥdīd ʾanwāʿ wa-marāḥil an-nizāʿāt fī Dārfūr, supra, footnote 51, on p. 89.

65 S.www.sudanjem.com/sudan-alt/arabic/books/black_book/black_book_first/kitab.htm (for the first part, *al-kitāb al-ʾaswad ǧuzʾ al-ʾawwal*) and <www.sudanjem.com/sudan-alt/ara

III. The Humanitarian Disaster and its Aftermath

While foreign governments, conflict-resolution experts, and international media focused on southern Sudan and the ongoing peace progress, as well as on the Middle East, Darfur received scant attention.[66] Sporadic foreign media attention in Sudan concentrated on the north-south peace negotiations in Naivasha, Kenya.[67] Although it was clear that violence and displacement were increasing across Darfur, the precise nature and extent of the events remained unknown. Sudanese authorities denied reports as rumours.[68] Over time, international reaction to the burgeoning crisis in Darfur was negligible, even with 300,000 people dead (if not much more), 2,500,000 internally displaced people (IDP), and more than 300,000 people who fled to neighbouring Chad.[69] The industrial democracies officially maintained ignorance of anything that might stand in the way of the peace settlement between the GoS and SPLM, and the flow of oil from Sudan (which by late 2003 already amounted to some 300,000 barrels per day).[70] When the world commemorated the 10th anniversary of the 1994 Rwandan genocide in April 2004, the international media could no longer avoid comparing the human rights disasters in Rwanda and in western Sudan.[71] Given their interest in Chad, the French media were among the first to give a separate picture of the Darfur situation. UN Undersecretary-General for Humanitarian Af-

---

bic/books/ black_book/black_book_second/kitab aswad2.htm> (for the second part, al-kit āb al-ʾaswad ǧuzʾ aṯ-ṯānī), accessed on 10 March 2008.

66 *M. W. Daly,* Darfur's…, supra, footnote 26, p. 273.

67 Cp. *Hatem Elliesie,* Friedensprozess und Verfassungsentwicklung im Sudan…, supra, footnote 22, pp. 283-294; *idem,* Quo Vadis bilād as-Sūdān?..., supra, footnote 19, on p. 68.

68 *Gérard Prunier,* Darfur…, supra, footnote 27, p. 125; *Jonathan P. Howard,* "Survey Methodology and the Darfur Genocide", in: *Samuel Totten / Eric Markusen* (Eds.), Genocide in Darfur, Oxon / New York, pp. 59 et seqq. (on p. 60).

69 Cp. *Muḥammad ʿAbdullāh ad-Dawma,* ḥimāyāt al-muwāṭinīn fī Dārfūr…, supra, footnote 34, on p. 45; *Constantin Schreiber,* "Ein Leben auf der Flucht", in: Das Parlament, no. 39, Berlin, 22 September 2008, on p. 3; *Annette Weber,* "Verschärfte Situation – entspannte Reaktion. Darfur ist kein Land in Afrika", in: *Deutsches Institut für Menschenrechte / Volkmar Deile / et al.,* Jahrbuch Menschenrechte 2008, Frankfurt a.M. 2007, pp. 145 et seqq. (on p. 147); *M. Rafiqul Islam,* "The Sudanese Darfur Crisis and Internally Displaced Persons in International Law: The least Protection for the most Vulnerable", in: International Journal of Refugee Law, volume 18, no. 2, Oxford 2006, pp. 354 et seqq.; *Toby N. Jack,* "Sudan's Genocide: Punishment before Prevention", in: Penn State International Law Review, volume 24, issue 3, Carlisle 2006, on p. 707; *International Crisis Group,* A New Sudan Action Plan, Africa Report N° 24, Nairobi / Brussels, April 2005, p. 2; *Andrew S. Natsios,* Moving Beyond…, supra, footnote 24, on p. 30.

70 *M. W. Daly,* Darfur's…, supra, footnote 26, p. 287.

71 *Hatem Elliesie / et al.,* Different Approaches to Genocide…supra, footnote 32, on p. 51; *Robert O. Collins,* Disaster in Darfur…, supra, footnote 62, p. 14.

fairs and Emergency Relief Coordinator, Jan Egeland, warned the Security Council that the situation amounted to "ethnic cleansing"[72] – a term with uncertain legal meaning, if any.[73] Widespread crimes committed by Sudanese government forces and the *Ǧannǧawīd* included targeted killings, summary execution, rape of thousands of civilians, destruction of hundreds of villages, theft of millions of livestock and the forced displacement of the aforementioned estimated number of people.[74] Victims of attacks by the *Ǧannǧawīd* described regularly that GoS military assisted the *Ǧannǧawīd* by bombing villages and attacking civilians by helicopters.[75] The rebel movements, on the other hand, were responsible for attacks on civilians and humanitarian aid workers, as well as summary executions of captured combatants, which may amount to war crimes.[76]

C. Sudan's Benchmark Obligations and Legal Constraints

In view of the disastrous situation in Darfur in specific, and the decades long civil war in general, it is noteworthy to allude to Sudan's obligation under international law: The state of Sudan is bound e.g. to the International Covenant on Civil and Political Rights (ICCPR[77]), the International Convention on the Elimination of All Forms of Racial Discrimination (CERD[78]), as well as to the Convention on the Rights of the Child (CRC[79]), the Optional Protocol to the Convention on the Rights of the Child on the Involvement of Children in Armed Conflict (OP-CRC-AC[80]), the Convention on the Prevention and Punishment of

---

72 Jan *Egeland*, "Sudan: Envoy warns of ethnic cleansing as Security Council calls for ceasefire", available at http://www.un.org/apps/news/storyAr.asp?NewsID=10307&Cr=sudan &Crl=, accessed on 15 August 2008.

73 *Stehpen A. Kostas*, "Making Determination of Genocide in Darfur", in: *Samuel Totten / Eric Markusen* (Eds.), Genocide in Darfur, Oxon / New York, pp. 111 et seqq. (on p. 112).

74 Cp. *Hatem Elliesie / et al.*, Different Approaches to Genocide…, supra, footnote 32, on p. 51 (footnote 202).

75 *Andrew S. Natsios*, Moving Beyond…, supra, footnote 24, p. 33. In this context, see also *ʿAṭā al-Baṭaḥānī*, naḥw muḫaṭṭaṭ li-taḥdīd ʾanwāʿ wa-marāḥil an-nizāʿāt fī Dārfūr, supra, footnote 51, on p. 92; *Kurt Pelda*, "Ein weiteres Massensterben in Darfur?", in: Neue Zürcher Zeitung (NZZ), no. 221, Zurich, 23 September 2006, on p. 6.

76 *United Nations Security Council Panel of Experts on the Sudan*, Letter dated 30 January 2006 from the Chairman of the Security Council Committee established pursuant to Resolution 1591 (2005) concerning the Sudan addressed to the President of the Security Council, UN-Doc. S/2006/65, Annex, Report, 30 January 2006, http://daccessdds.un.org /doc/UNDOC/GEN/N05/632/74/PDF/N0563274.pdf?OpenElement (accessed on 15 August 2008), p. 59.

77 Consent by accession on 18 March 1986.

78 Consent by accession on 21 March 1977.

79 Consent b ratification on 3 August 1990.

80 Consent by ratification on 26 July 2005.

the Crime of Genocide[81] and, moreover, to the Geneva Conventions[82] that set the standards in international law for humanitarian treatment of the victims of war.

For all intents and purposes, adherence to those treaties should be implicit. One of the oldest principles of International Law, the axiom *pacta sunt servanda* is also, *expressiv verbis,* enshrined in Article 26 of the Vienna Convention on the Law of Treaties[83], to which the Sudan is a party. This basic principle, based on good faith, underlies every international agreement. It entitles states to require that obligations be adhered to and to rely upon the obligations being respected. This good faith basis of treaties implies that a party to the treaty cannot invoke provisions of its municipal (domestic) law as justification for a failure to perform.[84] Likewise, the Common Article 1 of the Geneva Convention stresses the underlying obligation by stating that "[t]he High Contracting Parties undertake to respect and to ensure respect for the present Convention in *all circumstances*".[85] Accordingly, and particularly in the "case of armed conflict not of an international character", the Common Article 3 of the Geneva Conventions constitutes an integral part of Humanitarian Law:[86] This norm is not only peremptory in the normative field of public international law's Law of Treaties but also

---

[81] Consent by accession on 13 October 2003. *Nota bene:* This paper will not address the question of genocide (intent); in this regard, see *Hatem Elliesie / et al.,* Different Approaches to Genocide..., supra, footnote 32, pp. 21-67; *Claus Kress,* "The Darfur Report and Genocidal Intent", in: JICJ, volume 3, no. 3, Oxford 2005, pp. 562-578.

[82] The whole set referred to as the "Geneva Conventions" consists of the 'First Geneva Convention' for the Amelioration of the Condition of the Wounded in Armies in the Field; the 'Second Geneva Convention' for the Amelioration of the Condition of Wounded, Sick and Shipwrecked Members of Armed Forces at Sea; the 'Third Geneva Convention' relative to the Treatment of Prisoners of War; and the 'Fourth Geneva Convention' relative to the Protection of Civilian Persons in Time of War.

[83] *Article 26 Vienna Convention on the Law of Treaties:*

> Every treaty in force is binding upon the parties to it and must be performed by them in good faith.

[84] *Article 27 Vienna Convention on the Law of Treaties:*

> A party may not invoke the provisions of its internal law as justification for its failure to perform a treaty. [...]

[85] *Manfred Mohr,* "Durchsetzungsmechanismen des humanitären Völkerrechts – eine aktuelle Bestandsaufnahme", in: *Jana Hasse / Erwin Müller / Patricia Schneider* (Eds.), Humanitäres Völkerrecht. Politische, rechtliche und strafgerichtliche Dimension, Baden-Baden 2001, pp. 158 et seqq. (on p. 163 et seq.).

[86] *Lutz Lehmler,* Die Strafbarkeit von Vertreibungen aus ethnischen Gründen im bewaffneten nicht-internationalen Konflikt: Zugleich ein Beitrag zur neueren Entwicklung des Völkerstrafrechts, Baden-Baden 1999, p. 266; *Christopher Greenwood,* "Anwendungsbereich des humanitären Völkerrechts", in: *Dieter Fleck* (Ed.), Handbuch des humanitären Völkerrechts in bewaffneten Konflikten, München 1994, p. 34 (41/211).

jus cogens-rooted in Customary International Law,[87] consequently binding all states[88] as confirmed by the International Criminal Tribunal for the former Yugoslavia (ICTY) in its 2 October 1995 *Tadić-Decision,* referring to the 27 June 1986 ICJ's finding *La República de Nicaragua vs. United States of America.*[89]

I. Humanitarian Law

Under Humanitarian Law, specifically, there are, as a further matter of principle, two bodies of norms having a different scope of application: namely, rules for international and for non-international armed conflicts. Thus, the existence of armed conflict is fundamental to determining the applicability of Humanitarian Law.[90] This is still true, despite the fact that in recent times there has been a remarkable approximation between both bodies.

1. Classifying the Conflict / Scope of Application

Two thresholds which determine the applicable legal regime have to be ascertained:

- The threshold between an armed conflict and a situation of violence which does not reach the level of an armed conflict (low level violence).
- The threshold between international and non-international armed conflict.[91]

In essence, the Darfur conflict is above the threshold of low-level-violence and has to be considered an 'armed' one. Despite the massive transboundary tide of

---

87 Cp. *Theodor Meron,* "War Crimes in Yugoslavia and the Development of International Law", in: American Journal of International Law (AJIL), volume 88, issue 1, Washington D.C. 1994, p. 78 et seqq. (on p. 80 et seq.); *Christopher Greenwood,* "Customary Law Status of the 1977 Geneva Protocol", in: *Astrid J.M. Delissen / Gerald J. Tanja* (Eds.), Humanitarian Law of Armed Conflict, Challenges Ahead, Essays in Honour of Fits Kalshoven, Dodrecht / Boston / London 1991, pp. 93 et seqq. (on p. 98).

88 See *Lutz Lehmler,* Die Strafbarkeit..., supra, footnote 86, p. 266; *Hans-Peter Gasser,* "Armed Conflict within the Territory of a State", in: *Walter Haller / Alfred Kölz / Georg Müller / Daniel Thürer* (Eds.), Im Dienst an der Gemeinschaft (Festschrift für Dietrich Schindler zum 65. Geburtstag), Basel / Frankfurt a.M. 1989, p. 225 et seqq. (on p. 227).

89 Cp. *International Court of Justice,* ICJ Reports 1986, p. 114.

90 *Anthony Cullen,* The Definition..., supra, footnote 6, on p. 419.

91 As to the term "non-international conflict" (in the sense of the Common Article 3 of the Geneva Conventions) see particularly *Commission of Experts,* Preliminary Report of the Independent Commission established in accordance with Security Council Resolution 935 (1994), UN-Doc. S/1994/1125 Annex, New York 4 October 1994, p. 20, para. 91; *idem,* Final Report of the Commission of Experts established pursuant to Security Council Resolution 935 (1994), UN-Doc. S/1994/1405 Annex, New York 9 December 1994, p. 22, para. 108 et seq.

refugees which affects the social, economic and internal stability of some bordering states respectively, the question whether it is still a non-international one depends on the scope of involvement, significantly that of neighbouring Chad.[92]

Foreign intervention on behalf of armed opposition groups would push the conflict beyond the internal threshold and into the sphere of an international conflict, at least between the forces of the legal government and those of the intervening state.[93] Under the Common Article 2 of the Geneva Conventions, an international armed conflict, by definition, must involve a declared war, or, in its absence, any other armed conflict between two or more states. So far, no state providing assistance to the Sudanese opposition groups has officially declared war against Sudan as a result of its support for armed groups.

However, one has to consider that the ICTY has recently expanded the aforementioned definition in the *Tadić-Case* by setting out a third situation of armed conflict taking place *on the territory of one state* and *between its nationals*. Such a conflict may be *internationalized* if "some of the participants in the internal armed conflict act on behalf of that other State".[94] Thus, in the absence of a declaration of war or direct military confrontations between the Sudan and its neighbours, the pertinent question is, what objective tests can be applied in order to determine the nature of external involvement of states in controlling the Sudanese armed groups to the extent that they can be regarded as acting on their behalf?[95]

In the *Tadić-Case* the Trial Chamber used a strict test of '*effective control*'[96] in order to determine what level of control on the insurgents was exerted by other states. This test, however, was turned on appeal. Instead, the Appeal Chamber applied the test of '*overall control*'[97] to render an international armed conflict, which is *prima facie* internal.[98] In analyzing the *exact* measure of control re-

[92] Cp. *Simon Massey / Roy May*, "The Crisis in Chad", in: African Affairs, 105/420, London 2006, pp. 443-449; *International Crisis Group*, Dafur's Fragile Peace Agreement, supra, footnote 35, p. 13.

[93] Cp. *ICTY, Appeals Chamber*, Judgement, Case IT-94-1-A (Prosecutor v. Tadic), The Hague, 15 July 1999, p. 34 (para. 84).

[94] Ibidem.

[95] *Mohamed Abdelsalam Babiker*, Application of International Humanitarian and Human Rights Law to the Armed Conflict of the Sudan, Antwerp / Oxford 2007, p. 57.

[96] See *Daryl A. Mundis*, "Crimes of the Commander: Superior Responsibility under Article 7 (3) of the ICTY Statute", in: *Gideon Boas / William A. Schabas* (Eds.), International Criminal Law Developments in the Case Law of the ICTY, Leiden 2003, pp. 239 (on pp. 250 et seqq.).

[97] *ICTY, Appeals Chamber*, Judgement, Case IT-94-1-A..., supra, footnote 93, para 146 et seqq.

[98] Ibidem, pp. 35 et seqq. (para. 88-97).

quired for military groups, it stated that "it is not sufficient for the group to be financially or even militarily assisted by a state".[99] It must be proved that the state wields overall control over the group, not only equipping and financing the group, but also by coordinating or helping in the general planning of its military activity.[100]

Following the *Tadić-Test,* it is pertinent to argue that the Sudan's neighbours do not wield an '*overall control*'. Thus, at the time of the writing of this article, the armed conflict had to be considered, *de jure*, as one of a non-international nature.[101]

2. Applicable norms to non-international armed conflicts

The treaty norms, also considered to constitute international customary law, applicable to a non-international armed conflict are Common Article 3 of the Geneva Conventions and Protocol II additional hereto,[102] prohibiting e.g.

> "(a) violence to life and person, in particular murder of all kinds, mutilation, cruel treatment and torture;
> (b) taking of hostages;
> (c) outrages upon personal dignity, in particular humiliating and degrading treatment;

[against p]ersons taking no active part in the hostilities, including members of armed forces who have laid down their arms and those placed '*hors de combat*' by sickness, wounds, detention, or any other cause. [They] shall in all circum-

---

99 Ibidem, p. 55 (para. 130).

100 Ibidem, pp. 56 et seqq. (para. 131 and para. 137).

101 Likewise *Mohamed Abdelsalam Babiker,* Application of International Humanitarian and Human Rights Law to the Armed Conflict of the Sudan, Antwerp / Oxford 2007, p. 57 et seq., *Michael Bothe,* International Legal Aspects..., supra, footnote 17, on p. 4; *Hatem Elliesie,* Die Darfur-Krise im Sudan und das Völkerrecht..., supra, footnote 35, on p. 209; *Anthony Cullen,* The Definition..., supra, footnote 6, on p. 419. See also *Yolanda Gamarra / Alejandra Vicente,* "Securing Protection to Civilian Population: The Doubtful United Nations Response in Sudan", in: The Global Community Yearbook of International Law & Jurisprudence, Dobbs Ferry 2004, pp. 195 et seqq. (on p. 200); *Hennie Strydom,* „The Lesson of Darfur", in: African Yearbook on International Humanitarian Law, Western Cape / Johannesburg 2006, pp. 148 et seqq. (on p. 149); *Christopher Greenwood,* Anwendungsbereich des humanitären Völkerrecht, supra, footnote 86, 41/210 et seq.

102 Cp. *Michael Cowling,* "International Lawmaking in Action – The 2005 Customary International Humanitarian Law Study and Non-International Armed Conflicts", in: African Yearbook on International Humanitarian Law, Western Cape / Johannesburg 2006, pp. 65 et seqq. (on p. 75); *David Weissbrodt / Connie de la Vega,* International Human Rights Law, Philadelphia 2007, p. 213.

stances be treated humanely, without any adverse distinction founded on race, colour, religion or faith, sex, birth or wealth, or any other similar criteria."[103]

It is noteworthy to point out that, unlike human rights treaties, those humanitarian law treaties are clearly binding for both parties of the conflict; for government (affiliated) forces and for non-state actors. Such reciprocity in rights and obligations enhances the prospects of compliance to the rules by either side,[104] in particular, in favour of the suffering civilians, which appear to be the principal objects of the attacks in such internal armed conflicts. This seems to be the rule much more than the exception. The protection of civilian populations from attacks and the effects of hostilities is *jus cogens* in Humanitarian Law,[105] to which even individuals are bound in their combat operations in international armed conflicts. In the course of an *argumentum a maiore ad minus,* the same applies for conflicts of a non-international nature.[106] Consequently, neither the civilian population nor individual civilians may be made the object of attack. The starvation of civilians as a method of combat is, in this context, also forbidden. It is equally forbidden to attack, destroy, remove or render unusable objects indispensable to civilian survival, such as food-stuffs, agricultural areas, drinking water installations, irrigation works and the like, nor may a threat to do anything that would have this effect be used as a measure of pressure against the civilian population which supports the rebels.[107]

---

103 Common Article 3 of the Geneva Conventions.

104 *Hans-Peter Gasser,* "International Humanitarian Law and Human Rights Law in Non-international Armed Conflicts: Joint Venture or Mutual Exclusion?", in: German Yearbook of International Law, Berlin 2002, pp. 149 et seqq. (on p. 158).

105 Cp. in this context also *Art. 13 Protocol II:*

(1) The civilian population and individual civilians shall enjoy general protection against the dangers arising from military operations. To give effect to this protection, the following rules shall be observed in all circumstances.

(2) The civilian population as such, as well as individual civilians, shall not be the object of attack. Acts or threats of violence the primary purpose of which is to spread terror among the civilian population are prohibited.

(3) Civilians shall enjoy the protection afforded by this part, unless and for such time as they take a direct part in hostilities.

106 Cp. *Dietrich Schindler,* "Different Types of Armed Conflicts according to the Geneva Conventions and Protocols", in: *Haagse Academie voor Internationaal Recht / UN* (Eds.), Recueil des cours / Académie de Droit International de La Haye 1979 II, The Hague / et al. 1980, pp. 121 et seqq. (on p. 151 et seq.); *Lutz Lehmler,* Die Strafbarkeit..., supra, footnote 86, p. 37.

107 *Eve La Haye,* War Crimes in Internal Armed Conflicts, Cambridge 2008, p. 66; *Leslie C. Green,* The Contemporary Law of Armed Conflict, 3rd edition, Manchester 2008, p. 353 et seq.

As already indicated on page 207, there are consistent accounts of a recurrent pattern of attacks on villages and settlements, sometimes involving aerial attacks by helicopter gunships or fixed-wing aircraft, including bombing and strafing with automatic weapons. A majority of the attacks reported are ground assaults by the GoS military, the *Ǧannǧawīd* or a combination of the two. Hundreds of incidents have been reported involving the killing of civilians, massacres, summary execution, rape and other forms of sexual violence, torture, abduction, looting of property and livestock, as well as deliberate destruction of torching of villages.[108] It is important to note in this context, clarifying a mis-conception, that certain individuals within the civilian population, who do not come within the definition of civilians, do not deprive the population of its civilian character.[109] Moreover, military engagement between the GoS and rebel forces have resulted in severe violations of the rights of civilian populations, demonstrating a complete disregard by the warring parties of their obligations regarding the security of civilians.[110] Rebel forces have also been engaged in indiscriminate attacks resulting in civilian injuries, deaths and destruction of private property.[111]

Ultimately, there is no doubt that the parties of the conflict the government (affiliated) forces and non-state actors, have acted *contra legem*. Intentional, deliberate and willful killing and targeting of civilians is a war crime, and a crime against humanity when – as is the case in Darfur – committed as part of a widespread or systematic attack directed against a civilian population. The Statute of the International Criminal Court (ICC) lists as war crimes in internal conflicts several serious violations of Common Article 3 of the Geneva Convention, including violence to life and person such as murder, outrage upon personal dignity, and summary execution. Although the signature has not yet been followed

[108] *International Commission of Inquiry on Darfur,* Report…, supra, footnote 55, para. 186.

[109] *UN, International Criminal Tribunal for Rwanda* (ICTR), *Trial Chamber,* Judgement, The Prosecutor v. Jean-Paul Akayesu (Case No. ICTR-96-4-T), Arusha, 2 September 1998, para. 582. See also *ICTR,* Judgement, The Prosecutor v. Georges Anderson Nderubumwe Rutaganda (Case No. ICTR-96-3), Arusha, 6 December 1999, para. 72; *ICTR,* Judgement, The Prosecutor v. Alfred Musema (Case No. ICTR-96-13-A), Arusha 27 January 2000, para. 207 and *ICTR*, Judgement, The Prosecutor v. Clément Kayishema and Obed Ruzindana, (Case No. ICTR-95-1-T), Arusha, 21 May 1999, para. 128: "The targeted population must be predominantly civilian in nature but the presence of certain non-civilians in their midst does not change the character of that population." See also *ICTR*, Judgement, The Prosecutor v. Laurent Semanza (Case No. ICTR-97-20-T), Arusha, 15 May 2003, para. 330.

[110] *International Commission of Inquiry on Darfur,* Report…, supra, footnote 55, para. 189.

[111] Ibidem, para. 190.

ratification of the ICC's Statute, the Sudan is obliged not to do anything which would defeat its object and purpose pending a decision on ratification.[112]

II. Human Rights Law

Having examined the Humanitarian Law to the internal armed conflict, this subchapter addresses, with respect to methodological considerations in a second tier,[113] Human Rights Law. There is, however, a convergence between the provision of Humanitarian Law and the content of human rights conventions. In Practice, Human Rights Law has a significant role to play in internal armed conflicts, in particular when the government refuses to recognise the applicability of Common Article 3,[114] as the continued unwillingness of senior Sudanese officials reflected in obfuscating, denying and evading responsibility for the atrocities. Moreover, not only does the Preamble of Protocol II recognize the application of Human Rights Law in armed conflicts, but also, for the first time, an International Humanitarian Law Convention refers specifically to international instruments relating to human rights and expressly calls for their application in armed conflicts.[115]

1. Classifying the Conflict /Scope of Application

Human Rights Law does not require any threshold for its application as is the case with Humanitarian Law; it applies irrespective of the classification of the armed conflict, and indeed applies whether or not an armed conflict exists.

2. Applicable norms to non-international armed conflicts

Also indicated before on pages 194 et seqq., by the same token of their Humanitarian Law obligation, states are responsible under International Human Rights Law to guarantee the protection and preservation of fundamental freedoms at all times, in war and peace alike. UN General Assembly Resolution 2444 (XXIII) of 19 December 1968 recognized, on respect for Human Rights Law in armed conflict, the principle of civilian immunity and affirmed that "it is prohibited to launch attacks against civilian populations as such". The obligation of the state

---

[112] See also *Markus Böckenförde / Simone Malz / Verena Wiesner* (Eds.), Max-Planck Compilation of International Human Rights Treaties – Sudan, 2nd edition, Heidelberg 2008, p. 9; *Hatem Elliesie,* Die Darfur-Krise im Sudan und das Völkerrecht..., supra, footnote 35, on p. 209; *Yolanda Gamarra / Alejandra Vicente,* Securing Protection to Civilian Population..., supra, footnote 101, on p. 200.

[113] Cp. page 196.

[114] Cp. *D. O'Donell,* "Trends in the application of international humanitarian law by UN human rights mechanisms", in: International Review of the Red Cross, Geneva 1998, pp. 481 et seqq.

[115] Mohamed Abdelsalam Babiker, Application of International Humanitarian and Human Rights Law to the Armed Conflict of the Sudan, Antwerp / Oxford 2007, p. 74.

to refrain from any conduct that violates Human Rights Law, as well as the duty to protect those living within its jurisdiction, is inherent in this principle.[116] There is little doubt that the amount of state practice and the *opino juris* fulfils the criteria of an extensive and virtually uniform practice coupled with the belief that this principle is legally obligatory.[117] This was reached by the ICTY Appeals Chamber in its seminal *Tadić-Decision* and has been constantly reaffirmed by Trial Chambers ever since.

Furthermore, based upon Chapter II (Power Sharing Agreement) para. 1.6.1. CPA,[118] Article 27 (3) INC stipulates that

> " [a]ll rights and freedoms enshrined in international human rights treaties, covenants and instruments ratified by the Republic of the Sudan shall be an integral part of this Bill."

Thus, Article 27 (3) INC expands national Human Rights Law contained in the Bill of Rights and, at the same time, elevates certain international norms to constitutional status, directly applicable in Sudan.[119] Hence, the Sudan, as a party to some human rights treaties, is obliged to respect Human Rights Law and fundamental freedoms of all persons within its jurisdiction, as set out, *inter alia*, in the ICCPR, CERD, CRC, the African Charter on Human and Peoples' Rights (ACHPR):

As described earlier, the attacks by the GoS troop's affiliated *Ǧannǧawīd* units have to be considered in most cases as ***discriminatory acts*** pursuant to Article 5 CERD in that they are based on racial motivations. Discriminatory practices by the GoS of moving the resident population out by force and resettling the area with so-called *ʿArab* people would make displacement permanent and violate Article 2 CERD. The ***indiscriminate and arbitrary attacks*** on civilians in Darfur are in violation of the non-derogable right articulated in Article 6 (1) ICCPR, Article 4 ACHPR and Article 38 (4) CRC. Those attacks against civilians, including women and children are also a violation of Sudan's obligation under

116 *International Commission of Inquiry on Darfur,* Report..., supra, footnote 55, para. 144.

117 *Eve La Haye,* War Crimes in Internal Armed Conflicts, Cambridge 2008, p. 67. Cp. *Michael Bothe,* "War Crimes in Non-International Armed Conflicts", in: Israel Yearbook on Human Rights, volume 25, The Hague / Boston / London 1994, pp. 241 et seqq. (on p. 248).

118 See *Hatem Elliesie,* Die Darfur-Krise im Sudan und das Völkerrecht..., supra, footnote 35, on p. 209.

119 Cp. *Noha Ibrahim,* "The Right to Fair Trial in the Light of the Interim National Constitution of Sudan: Theory and Practice", in: Recht in Afrika (Law in Africa · Droit en Afrique), volume 11, issue 1, Cologne 2008, pp. 83 et seqq.; *idem,* "The Sudanese Bill of Rights", in: The International Journal of Human Rights, volume 12, no. 4, London / et al. 2008, pp. 613 et seqq.

Article 6 CRC to ensure the protection of children. Although the objective of GoS's and their allies may be to forcibly displace the population rather than starve the population *per se*, the effect is the same. Victims arrive in other villages or areas where there are limited or no means of subsistence and no access to food. Persons are thus forced to depend on ***food aid and humanitarian assistance*** for survival where and when it is available; thus, under Customary International Law and Article 14 Protocol II as well as Article 17 ICCPR and Article 14 ACHPR, ***forcibly displace*** constitutes a breach of law. Inasmuch as the GoS attacks are aimed at forcefully displacing the civilians, such attacks also force these persons to abandon their traditional form of livelihood. These attacks, therefore, also violate the right of these persons to make their living as they have chosen to do. And even if these civilians are able to return to their villages, which is *de facto* rarely the case, the crops are usually destroyed or ruined and the livestock is gone.[120] Forcing ***abandonment of livelihood of cultivating land***, disregards Article 6 ICESCR. The forcible displacement of a civilian population also violates the rights of freedom of movement and residence ensured in Article 12 ICCPR and Article 12 (1) ACHPR. Moreover, a cause to flee is also the ***rape of women***[121], which is in itself prohibited not just under Common Article 3 Geneva Convention, clarified by Article 4 (2) (e) Protocol II but also according to Article 1 CAT and Article 5 I ICCPR. Furthermore, the effect of those attacks on civilians is the ***dispersal of families***, a violation of the positive incumbent to the GoS under Article 23 (1) ICCPR, Article 10 (1) ICESCR and Article 18 ACHPR in general, and as to the parent-child relationship under Article 24 (1) ICCPR, Article 7 (1) and Article 9 CRC.

D. Concluding Remarks on the Case Study Darfur

Without doubt, the GoS fails to meet its obligations under both Human Rights Law and Humanitarian Law. Instead of defending the civilian population in Darfur, government troops have been part of the violence or kept a blind eye to the atrocities committed by the paramilitary groups. Thus, Sudan's government has clearly defied its primary responsibility to protect its own population. Ad-

[120] Cp. *Muḥammad ʿAbdullāh ad-Dawma,* ḥimāyāt al-muwāṭinīn fī Dārfūr…, supra, footnote 34, on p. 45; *International Commission of Inquiry on Darfur,* Report…, supra, footnote 55, p. 66 et seq. (para. 233-236).

[121] Cp. *ʿĀʾiša Ṣabīra,* "al-ʿunf ḍidd an-nisāʾ fī Dārfūr", in: *Muḥsin ʿAwaḍ / ʿAlāʾ Šalabī* (Eds.), min ʾağl salām Dārfūr (buḥūṯ wa-munāqašāt nadwa ḥawla mawāqif ʾakṯar fāʿilīya li-munaẓẓamāt ḥuqūq al-ʾinsān fī Dārfūr – al-Qāhira, 11-12 May 2007), Al-Munaẓẓama al-ʿArabīya li-Ḥuqūq al-ʾInsān: Cairo 2008, pp. 109 et seqq.; *UNHCR,* Report to the United Nations High Commissioner for Human Rights and Follow-Up to the World Conference on Human Rights: Situation of Human Rights in the Darfur Region of the Sudan, UN-Doc. E//CN.4/2005/3, 7 May 2004, p. 17 et seq., para. 65-69.

mitting that the crisis is much more complex than some may wish to think or are given to believe, one has to concede that the tragedy of the Darfur crisis is that the world community continues to watch its prolonged violence. Although the human toll in Sudan is horrific – whatever numbers are used – and the elements of crime committed in the western most parts of Sudan are unambiguously covered by norms of (International) Human Rights Law and Humanitarian Law, the case of Darfur prompted some of the most puzzling contradictions in the ways in which international relations work. International state actors involved in the southern peace negotiations did not want to risk its continuation, even though the humanitarian catastrophe became more alarming. In the course of time, the geopolitical interests of the UN-Security Council's veto-power members seemed to be the pivotal aspect of adjudication. Avoidance of using the word "genocide" to describe (and determine) the events in Sudan indicate an international political reluctance to acknowledge the atrocities. The chasm that exists between the protection of citizens, an entitlement based on the legal instruments and rule, and what is taking place in reality is in large part related to strategic choices of states that favour regime protection over citizen protection. One has to admit that the solution lies in politics, rather than in law. Thus, the deplorable state of affairs surely represents a reversal for human rights advocates and scholars of international law. The risk is that we will soon consider the incident in Darfur as a low intensity conflict, handing over the responsibility to the humanitarian agencies, as was the case in many other places in Africa, once again vowing "never again", when it was within our means to ensure that it never happened on this scale in the first place.

To conclude, as already named by Barack Hussein Obama on 24 July 2008 in Berlin:[122]

The genocide in Darfur
shames
the conscience of us all!

[122] On his only public speech of his world tour at the *Siegessäule am Großen Stern* in the *Tiergarten* park as Democratic Party candidate ahead of November's US presidential election.

General Remarks on Human Rights and Islam in the Middle East

Ann Elizabeth Mayer, Philadelphia

A. Introduction

In contrast to the discussion of the theoretical debates about the relationship of Islam and Human Rights that is presented in the introductory chapter by Abdullahi Ahmed An-Na'im[1] and Assem Hefny,[2] here an attempt will be made to clarify the political background against which these debates are being carried on in the Middle East. In the background lie systems that are in large measure dominated by despotic and corrupt ruling cliques that are profoundly hostile to Human Rights, and their interests in self-preservation lead them to crush advocacy of progressive reforms and to forge alliances with institutions and groups opposed to democratization. It is the character of these regimes that has produced the grievous Human Rights deficiencies that prevail in the Middle East. Even when Islam is invoked – as it often is – as the rationale for acts and policies violative of Human Rights, upon critical assessment, it seems that in practice Islam plays a distinctly subordinate role to political agendas. Here the term "*Islam*" will be used to refer to the religion in general. However, when the subject is the widely varying national versions of Islam, they will be designated as "*Islams*." It is important to make such a distinction in the context of discussing *Islam* and Muslim countries' human rights policies.[3] Governments often speak in public as if the Islamic religion dictated their positions on Human Rights, but the fact that the *Islams* in countries like Egypt, Iran, and Saudi Arabia are so distinctive and correlate closely with the local balance of power shows that in practice "*Islam*" is a malleable concept that can be used to construct *"Islams"* that reflect government policies and priorities.

This discussion will center on the highly politicized official *Islams* sponsored by various Middle Eastern governments and the *munaẓẓamat al-mu'tamar al-islāmī* (Organization of the Islamic Conference – hereinafter OIC), an international organization to which Muslim countries belong that is discussed in the chapter "The Organisation of Islamic Conference in the Context of the Human Rights

---

1 *Abdullahi Ahmed An-Na'im,* "Islam and Human Rights: Introductory Remarks and Reflections", in: *Hatem Elliesie* (Hrsg./Editor), Beiträge zum Islamischen Recht VII, Islam und Menschenrechte (Islam and Human Rights / الإسلام وحقوق الإنسان), Frankfurt a.M. 2010, pp. 41-47.

2 *Assem Hefny,* „Hermeneutik, Koraninterpretation und Menschenrechte", in: *Hatem Elliesie* (Hrsg./Editor), ibidem, pp. 73-97.

3 Cp. *Hatem Elliesie*, "Editor's Foreword", in: Ibidem, on p. 27.

Islam und Menschenrechte (Islam and Human Rights / الإسلام وحقوق الإنسان)
Hatem Elliesie (Hrsg./Editor), © Peter Lang Verlag: Frankfurt a.M. 2010, S. 219-237

Council: Human Rights as Instruments of Government Politics" by Theodor Rathgeber.[4] Events in 2008 suggested that the trend on the part of the OIC and various Middle Eastern states to press the idea that the international human rights system had to make special accommodations for Islam, a trend that had been in motion since the 1990s, was picking up momentum and taking new directions.

B. Human Rights and Islam in the Middle Eastern Context

I. Positioning Islam against Human Rights

For many years various Middle Eastern governments have endeavoured to convince the international community that their commitment to Islam means that they deserve to be exempted from compliance with aspects of International Human Rights Law. Some of them have actively supported the OIC in its efforts to win acceptance for the idea that a separate Islamic system of Human Rights that is defined by the OIC should apply in Muslim countries, one that drastically reduces rights protections. In an ominous development, the OIC and some member states[5] have recently been winning acceptance in UN Human Rights forums for the idea that concerns related to Islam must be given paramount consideration.[6] The positions that some Middle Eastern governments and the OIC have taken in UN forums have amounted to major challenges to central premises of our modern human rights system. In insisting that protecting Islam must be accorded priority at the expense of Human Rights, they have rejected the idea that Human Rights are of such overriding importance that they trump other concerns, and in insisting on Islamic particularism, they have sought to undermine the universality of Human Rights.

These governmental pretensions to speak for Islam will strike those familiar with Islamic jurisprudence as outré. Of course, International Law gives states a central role in formulating its principles, which they establish via conventions and treaties and by consistent state conduct where it is understood to reflect requirements of International Law, which is treated as international custom. In contrast, no authoritative Islamic jurisprudential or theological principle gives the apparatus of the modern nation-state, an entity of European derivation, the

4 *Theodor Rathgeber*, "Die Organisation Islamischer Konferenz im UN-Menschenrechtsrat: Menschenrechte als Instrument staatlicher Politik", in: *Hatem Elliesie* (Hrsg./Editor), Beiträge zum Islamischen Recht VII, Islam und Menschenrechte (Islam and Human Rights / الإسلام وحقوق الإنسان), Frankfurt a.M. 2010, pp. 457-473.

5 Cp. *Theodor Rathgeber*, ibidem, Annex I (I. Mitgliedstaaten der OIC), on p. 472.

6 On more detail see section B. III. ("Efforts to Reorient Human Rights to Protect Religion") of this article, on pp. 227 et seqq.

prerogative of defining Islamic doctrine, including doctrine relevant for Human Rights. It is therefore presumptuous of states to assume the role of authorities on Islam and Human Rights. Nonetheless, various Middle Eastern governments speak as if entitled to impose their ideas on this subject, presuming that their views must be regarded as definitive.

The official *Islams* sponsored by Middle Eastern governments should be differentiated from the rich and complicated legacy of Islamic jurisprudence developed by independent scholars. In theory Islam is a universal religion, but the official *Islams* in the Middle East vary from country to country.[7] Middle Eastern states consistently speak as if they were merely deferring to settled Islamic requirements, as one can see in the Hanna Beate Schöpp-Schilling chapter on how states invoke Islam to justify denying women the equality that is mandated under the Women's Convention (CEDAW).[8] They aim to create an impression that Islam obliges them to uphold rules at odds with International Human Rights Law despite the fact that they otherwise disregard Islamic law when it suits them. Leaving aside Saudi Arabia, for the most part, Middle Eastern countries have discarded Islamic law in favour of adopting continental European laws, borrowing substantive law codes and emulating the judicial systems and other legal institutions of Western European countries like France, retaining only a small selection of Islamic rules to cover topics like family law and inheritance. Even Saudi Arabia is supplanting Islamic Law by continental European law as it adjusts to globalization. Furthermore, the various national *Islams* evolve over time, being subject to reformulation when and if governments decide to change related policies. All of this points to the primacy of politics.

True, elements taken from the vast legacy of Islamic rules do appear in laws and policies that conflict with International Human Rights Law. In certain areas one can identify the influence of Islamic rules that correlate with distinctive Human Rights violations, rules that are still accepted as authoritative by many Muslims. For example, one can trace the ideas that Muslim women are barred from marrying non-Muslims, that women are entitled to only one half the inheritance shares of males, that non-Muslims must be relegated to an inferior status, and that fornication and apostasy from Islam should be capital offenses to the lingering influence of medieval Islamic Law. In cases where states tailor laws and policies

7 Likewise *Hatem Elliesie*, "Editor's Foreword", in: *Hatem Elliesie* (Hrsg./Editor), Beiträge zum Islamischen Recht VII, Islam und Menschenrechte (Islam and Human Rights / الإسلام وحقوق الإنسان), Frankfurt a.M. 2010, on p. 27.

8 *Hanna Beate Schöpp-Schilling*, "Der „Frauenrechtsausschuss" der Vereinten Nationen in der Interaktion mit islamisch geprägten Staaten", in: *Hatem Elliesie* (Hrsg./Editor), Beiträge zum Islamischen Recht VII, Islam und Menschenrechte (Islam and Human Rights / الإسلام وحقوق الإنسان), Frankfurt a.M. 2010, on pp. 417-455.

to fit Islamic doctrines that retain considerable authority and where Human Rights violations result, the influence of Islamic Law can be linked to deviations from International Human Rights Law. However, even in such instances, it must be recognized that ultimately local politics will determine which medieval Islamic rules are endorsed or suppressed. It is no coincidence that since the establishment of Iran's reactionary theocracy after the 1979 revolution, medieval Islamic rules have been deployed in ways that cause Human Rights violations – although such rules were not in force under the far more secular monarchical regime that preceded it.[9]

II. Deploying Islam to Resist Democratization

It is important to take into account how the highly oppressive climate that prevails in most Middle Eastern countries leads to reinforcing Islamic rules at odds with Human Rights. This climate stifles the presentation and dissemination of emancipatory and progressive readings of the Islamic sources and reinforces the more reactionary interpretations of Islam. Among other things, the policies of crushing dissent and harsh censorship of reformist ideas mean that many of the most brilliant Islamic thinkers – often ones with the greatest potential to influence their fellow Muslims to recognize the potential for reconciling Islam and International Human Rights Law – are forced into exile in the West or are compelled to operate virtually under siege in dangerous and hostile environments if they elect to try to work in the Middle East.

A perfect example of the correlation between oppressive local politics and upholding reactionary views of Islamic requirements would be the official Saudi position that "Islam" bans women from driving cars.[10] The regime is an absolute monarchy that legitimizes its oppressive rule by vaunting its commitment to upholding Islam and that relies heavily on the support of an arch-conservative religious establishment that regards the subjugation and segregation of women as lying at the core of Islamic morality. The regime aggressively represses challenges to its ban on women driving, which is actually not tied to any generally

---

9 On how political changes in Iran have affected the use of Islam to justify Human Rights violations, see *Ann Elizabeth Mayer*, "Shifting Grounds for Challenging the Authority of International Human Rights Law: Religion as a Malleable and Politicized Pretext for Governmental Noncompliance with Human Rights", in: *Andras Sajo* (Editor), Human Rights with Modesty: The Problem of Universalism, Leiden 2004, pp. 349-374.

10 The Saudi custom banning women from driving reflected the distinctive version of Islamic morality sponsored by the regime – an apt example of how local "*Islams*" are tied to particular national contexts. The ban was endorsed by an Islamic edict issued by a jurist after demonstration in Riyadh on 6 November 1990. Protesting the ban, women who had qualified for driving licenses outside the kingdom briefly drove cars around the capital before being arrested and subjected to harsh sanctions.

accepted Islamic rule but instead reflects the harshly patriarchal Saudi system, under which medieval Islamic rules have been expanded to try to maintain a form of gender apartheid in the face of changes that threaten to destabilize the *status quo*.[11]

The Saudi case presents a particularly dramatic example of Islam being given a reactionary cast that reflects local politics, but elsewhere in Middle East one finds other undemocratic systems that provide hostile environments for the growth of progressive Islamic currents. Throughout the region, these systems block Middle Easterners from realizing their aspirations for development both at the national and at the personal levels. It merits mention that blocking development is by itself a Human Rights violation, violating a right established in the 1986 Declaration on the Right to Development. Since development is regarded in a positive light, no Middle Eastern governments have proposed that Islamic Law requires them to restrict or deny the right to development even as they pursue policies that destine their countries to be laggards in this category.

Recently published studies have highlighted the deeply-rooted problems that generate the Human Rights deficits afflicting Middle Eastern societies. These studies lay the blame for these deficits on political problems rather than attributing them to the influence of Islam. One of the biggest problems is the egregious corruption, which is hard to combat in the absence of democratization. As Transparency International, the prestigious anti-corruption non-governmental organisation (NGO), has observed:

> The primary challenges facing civil society organizations in the fight against corruption in the Middle East and North Africa are non-democratic government structures, coupled with little manoeuvring space for civil society amidst stagnant, heavily state-managed economies.[12]

Assessments of the poor governance records of Middle Eastern countries can be found in the Worldwide Governance Indicators released by the World Bank in June 2008. One sees 212 countries ranked in terms of voice and accountability, political stability and absence of violence, government effectiveness, regulatory quality, rule of law, and control of corruption. As a group Middle Eastern countries fare poorly in these rankings.[13]

---

11 See *Human Rights Watch,* Perpetual Minors. Human Rights Abuses Stemming from Male Guardianship and Sex Segregation in Saudi Arabia, http://www.hrw.org/reports/2008/saudiarabia0408/ (accessed on 13 September 2008).

12 *Transparency International,* Middle East and North Africa (MENA), http://www.tranparency.org/regional_pages/africa_middle_east/about/mena (accessed on 19 September 2008).

13 See *World Bank;* Worldwide Governance Indicators: 1996-2007, Released - June 2008, http://web.worldbank.org/WBSITE/EXTERNAL/WBI/EXTWBIGOVANTCOR/0,,conte

The Arab Human Development Reports (AHDR) published in 2002-2005 have attributed the poor development performance of Arab countries to systemic problems.[14] The reports, compiled by Arab intellectuals, offer insights into the nature of the contemporary Arab dystopias, pinpointing factors that have held back the region's development.[15] They have been widely recognized as constituting an important milestone in analyzing what ails Arab countries. Although the authors do not dwell on the relevant provisions of International Human Rights Law, their analyses amount to damning indictment of the Human Rights deficits in the region and the way they have impeded development.[16]

The authors rely on an expanded version of the Human Development Index designed by the economist Amartya Kumar Sen, famous for insisting that, in order to grasp a country's state of development, it is insufficient to measure economic indicators alone. He urged that statistics be gathered measuring human development in terms of life expectancy, literacy, schooling and per capita real Gross Domestic Product (GDP) to give a more complete picture of poverty, growth and inequality. The AHDR authors expand Amartya Kumar Sen's concerns, adding data on life-long knowledge acquisition – especially regarding information technology, women's access to power, and human freedom.

In the 2002 report the authors blame the lack of democracy and freedom on the structure of modern Arab states, which have been controlled by regimes opposed to democratization. They note that, as a group, Arab countries score lower than any other regional group on the index of freedoms – political and civil rights, independent media, and accountability of rulers to the ruled. They observe that many relatively poor non-Arab countries rank above Arab countries in various indices of human development, particularly with regard to women.

The 2003 report maintains that disabling constraints hamper the acquisition, diffusion and production of knowledge in Arab societies. This has consequences

---

ntMDK:20771165~menuPK:1866365~pagePK:64168445~piPK:64168309~theSitePK:1740530,00.html (accessed on 19 September 2008).

14 See the UNDP's Arab Human Development Reports (AHDR) published in 2002- 2005. Information on these reports and details for obtaining them are listed at http://hdr.undp.org/xmlsearch/reportSearch?y=*&c=r%3AArab+States&t=*&k=&ordery=year (accessed on 19 September 2008).

15 These reports do not cover Iran, but Iran suffers from many of the same failings, as the reports by Transparency International, the Governance Indicators, and various Human Rights NGOs show.

16 Among the rights denied people in the region are Human Rights stipulated in the International Covenant on Civil and Political Rights and the International Covenant on Economic, Social, and Cultural Rights, rights guaranteed women in the Women's Convention and to children in the Convention on the Rights of the Child, the protections of the ILO conventions, and the right to development.

for Human Rights: the report asserts that knowledge could help the region to expand the scope of human freedoms, enhance the capacity to guarantee those freedoms through good governance, and achieve the goals of justice and human dignity. The latter goals are, of course, central to Human Rights. The report asserts that defective structures created by human beings – social, economic and above all political structures – constitute obstacles to the pursuit of knowledge.

The 2004 report focuses on the denials of fundamental freedoms in the Arab region, discussing legal restrictions on freedom, "the vicious circle of repression and corruption", and societal structures that stifle individual freedom, trying to go beyond these to offer strategic visions of freedom and good governance.

In general, the authors do not treat Islam as a relevant factor in the lack of development and freedoms, but issues related to Islamic Law do surface in the 2005 report on women in the Arab world. It points to the need for scholars to challenge conservative readings of Islamic requirements that are used to thwart women's progress. However, even where Arab women's rights are concerned, the authors stress the problems created by systematic features other than Islam. A summary describes the report as follows:

> It situates the problematic nature of the equality of their rights, capabilities and opportunities in the context of history, culture, religion, society and the political economy. [...] Compared to their sisters elsewhere in the world, they enjoy the least political participation. Conservative authorities, discriminatory laws, chauvinist male peers and tradition-minded kinsfolk watchfully regulate their aspirations, activities and conduct. Employers limit their access to income and independence. In the majority of cases, poverty shackles the development and use of women's potential. High rates of illiteracy and the world's lowest rates of female labour participation are compounded to 'create serious challenges'. [M]any remain victims of legalised discrimination, social subordination and enshrined male dominance. Unacceptably, physical and mental violence against women often destroys their personal health and security and even their right to life. [T]he Report stresses the need to eliminate the seeds of discrimination against women in Arab tradition and to promote ijtihad (interpretative scholarship) [*iğtihād*] in religious matters to overcome cultural obstacles. It outlines changes in patterns of upbringing, education and media presentation that could revise social norms, erase harmful stereotypes and vitally transform relations between the sexes in a culture of equal treatment. It proposes a battery of legal reforms to guarantee women's political, civil and economic rights. They range from the full alignment of national legislation with the Convention on the Elimination of All Forms of Discrimination against Women (CEDAW) and with international labour treaties through time-bound quotas for women in political assemblies to the adoption of updated personal status codes. The Re-

> port also advocates measures to protect the civil and personal rights of all women in Arab countries including expatriate women. More broadly, it calls for the opening of the economic sphere to women to address income poverty and for investments in women's education, health and social safety nets to reverse the spread of human poverty.[17]

A comparison will show that the OIC approach to Human Rights has nothing in common with these critical perspectives on the acute Human Rights deficits in the Middle East. Showing no concern for the egregious Human Rights violations afflicting people in the Middle East, the OIC has emphasized the need to devise Human Rights standards that are designed to ensure respect for Islamic Law. The OIC projects are not designed to cure Human Rights deficiencies but to use Islam as a tool to solidify the *status quo* and to deflect criticisms. Upon closer examination "human rights" turns out to be a misleading rubric for OIC projects, because they deploy Islam as a justification for circumscribing and even eliminating the Human Rights afforded under International Law. Of course, this pattern of deploying Islam against Human Rights coincides with the domestic policies of various Middle Eastern states and with the policies of Saudi Arabia in particular. This is significant, because the OIC is closely tied to Saudi Arabia, which has been one of the strongest proponents of the idea that Islam must be upheld at the expense of Human Rights.

Despite the vast gulf separating the Saudi and Iranian versions of Islam, Saudi Arabia has been able to make common cause with Iran's theocracy in international forums when promoting what are supposedly Islamic versions of Human Rights. Given that the official Saudi Arabian and Iranian philosophies that Islam – or, more accurately, the Islam favoured by their respective rulers – overrides Human Rights, it is not surprising that they cooperated in promoting the OIC's 1990 Cairo Declaration on Human Rights in Islam[18], which invoked Islam in setting forth a diluted and reduced set of Human Rights provisions.[19] It is noteworthy that serious Human Rights advocates in the Middle East have criticized these Islamic versions of Human Rights, relying instead on the far more robust and extensive guarantees of Human Rights that are set forth in International Law.

---

[17] This summary by *Amat Al Alim Alsoswa* is presented in her foreword to the "The Arab Human Development Report 2005. Towards the Rise of Women in the Arab World", http://www.arab-hdr.org/contents/2005/intro-e.pdf (accessed on 19 September 2008).

[18] Hereinafter referred to as *Cairo Declaration.*

[19] See *Ann Elizabeth Mayer*, "Universal versus Islamic Human Rights: A Clash of Cultures or a Clash with a Construct?", in: Michigan Journal of International Law, volume 15, issue 2 , Ann Arbor 1994, pp. 327-350, 371-404.

III. Efforts to Reorient Human Rights to Protect Religion

Apparently not dissuaded by negative assessments of the deficiencies of the *Cairo Declaration* that had been made by human rights activists, the OIC announced in March 2008 at a Mecca summit that it was contemplating producing yet another new Islamic human rights document, an Islamic Charter of Human Rights that would conform to the values and principles of Islamic Law.[20] On that occasion the OIC chose to put the West on trial, expressing its concern for protecting Islam and asserting:

> The rising phenomena of Islamophobia and other forms of religious intolerance, defamation, and demonization of religious references and symbols, should be fully and firmly addressed.[21]

The OIC's interest in establishing the principle that Islam needed protection was not new; for years the OIC had been presenting various resolutions to the UN Commission on Human Rights, which in 2006 was reconstituted as the Human Rights Council, that were designed to combat what the OIC claimed was defamation of religions. While the text of the resolutions referred to religions, it was clear that that the real purpose was to win UN support for the notion that criticism of Islam constituted a Human Rights violation that should be prohibited.

In context, the OIC's concern seemed to be twofold. On the one hand, the OIC hoped to identify its Human Rights stance with a popular cause, which it could do by aligning itself with many ordinary Muslims who had been outraged by what were seen as grave insults to Islam on the part of various European provocateurs. Starting with the outrage over Salman Rushdie's Satanic Verses in 1988, violent controversies and protests had been engendered by what were seen as Western assaults on Islamic sanctities. In the wake of terrorist incidents like the 2001 attack on the World Trade Center, Muslims' anger was aggravated by Western stereotyping of Muslims as terrorists and by inflammatory anti-Islamic cartoons published in Denmark and films made in the Netherlands. Posing as the champion of the honour of Islam in the fight against *Islamophobia* offered the OIC a rare opportunity to espouse a principle that both gave it grounds for demanding restrictions on freedom and that also had widespread popular resonance. In addition, it seems that the OIC member states wanted to shield from criticism their own practices of using Islam as a way of justifying Human Rights violations by pressing the idea that to criticize such practices was to defame Islam. On occasion, OIC statements revealed its aim to make the UN condemn

---

20 See *International Humanist and Ethical Union*, "Organization of the Islamic Conference announces an 'Islamic Charter of Human Rights'," 11 March 2008, http://www.iheu.org/node/2997 (accessed on 19 September 2008).

21 Ibidem.

any associations of Islam with Human Rights violations. One can see an example in a 2005 OIC resolution, which was adopted by the Commission on Human Rights. The text affirmed that the commission:

> [...]
> 4. *Expresses deep concern* that Islam is frequently and wrongly associated with human rights violations and terrorism [...].
> 8. *Stresses* the need to effectively combat defamation of all religions, Islam and Muslims in particular especially in human rights forums.
>
> [...][22]

Of course, vague language of this sort potentially threatened anyone, whether Muslim or non-Muslim, who condemned Human Rights violations in Middle Eastern countries that were in some way linked to Islamic rules. For example, Iran and Saudi Arabia cling to medieval doctrines according to which Islam mandates brutal methods of execution like stoning for sexual transgressions, persecuting heretics and apostates, severe discrimination against minority religions, and stripping women of rights and treating them like children. Although condemning such governmental breaches of International Human Rights Law would normally be viewed as perfectly legitimate, according to the approach taken by the OIC, such condemnations could be classified as defamatory on the theory that they associated Human Rights violations with Islam. In the Middle East governmental policies have led to Islam becoming identified with Human Rights violations, but the OIC refuses to acknowledge its members' responsibility for this, instead trying to convince the world that connecting Islam with Human Rights violations evinces *Islamophobia*.

In 2007 the OIC succeeded in getting the UN General Assembly to pass a resolution condemning the "defamation of religions", with Islam being the only religion mentioned by name in the text. Even more ambitious initiatives were in store. In March 2008 the OIC decided to try to use the influence of the large block of OIC members in the Human Rights Council to get this UN entity to endorse a resolution denouncing the defamation of religions and specifically asserting that the need to protect Islam entailed placing curbs on freedom of expression, claiming that the right of freedom of expression was being abused. Acting on behalf of the OIC, Pakistan presented this resolution, a resolution that was passed with the support of Muslim countries in the council but with ten dissents and fourteen abstentions.[23]

---

[22] *Commission on Human Rights,* UN-Doc. E/CN.4/2005/L.10/Add.6, "Combating defamation of religions. Human Rights Resolution 2005/3", *44th meeting 12 April 2005,* chapter. VI, http://ap.ohchr.org/documents/E/CHR/resolutions/E-CN_4-RES-2005-3.doc (accessed on 19 September 2008).

[23] "ISESCO welcomes UN Human Rights Council's resolution condemning defamation of Islam", *Emirates News Agency,* 28 March 2008, available on Lexis/Nexis.

As a result of this OIC initiative, the mandate of the United Nations Special Rapporteur on the Promotion and Protection of the Right to Freedom of Opinion and Expression was dramatically changed to encompass investigating so-called "abuses" of the right of freedom of expression, obviously reflecting the OIC view that in the past protections for freedom of expression had been too expansive. Upon observing this significant alteration in the mandate of the United Nations Special Rapporteur on the Promotion and Protection of the Right to Freedom of Opinion and Expression, the media freedom organization *Reporters Sans Frontières* (RSF) strongly objected, noting that this change

> "turns someone who is supposed to defend freedom of opinion into a prosecutor whose job is to go after those who abuse this freedom."

RSF further complained about the growing influence of the OIC within the Human Rights Council, warning that

> "[a]ll of the council's decisions are nowadays determined by the interests of the Muslim countries or powerful states such as China or Russia that know how to surround themselves with allies".[24]

Amnesty International also called the measure deeply flawed, asserting that it went contrary to the main purpose of the mandate, which is to protect and promote the right to freedom of expression. According to Amnesty International, in adopting the OIC position, the Human Rights Council was departing from its mandate by deciding to police the exercise of rights rather than promote and protect them.[25]

United Nations Special Rapporteur on the Promotion and Protection of the Right to Freedom of Opinion and Expression, Kenyan lawyer Ambeyi Ligabo, warned the Human Rights Council that he was concerned about attempts to stretch the reach of defamation laws beyond protecting individuals' reputations, expanding these to include the protection of "abstract values or institutions" such as religions. He pointed out that International Human Rights documents placed limitations on freedom of expression with the aim of protecting individuals – not religions – from defamation. Ambeyi Ligabo also strongly rejected the OIC view that the use of freedom of expression has undermined people's ability to enjoy other rights, such as the freedom of religion.[26]

---

24 "RSF condemns UN Human Rights Council's approach on freedom of expression", *BBC Monitoring World Media,* 1 April 2008, available on Lexis/Nexis.

25 "Human Rights Council: Council Continues to Struggle to Establish Itself as an Effective Human Rights Body", *States News Service,* 4 April 2008, available on Lexis/Nexis.

26 *Ambeyi Ligabo,* Report of the Special Rapporteur on the Promotion and Protection of the right to freedom of opinion and expression, Human Rights Council, Seventh session, Agenda item 3, A/HRC/7/14, 7 March 2008, http://www2.ohchr.org/english/bodies/hrcouncil/docs/7session/A-HRC-7-14.pdf (accessed on 19 September 2008).

On 26 March 2009, the UN Human Rights Council adopted by a vote of 23 members in favor and 11 against, with 13 abstentions, a resolution calling for combating defamation of religions. The resolution, proposed by Pakistan on behalf of the OIC, reiterated themes in previous OIC sponsored proposals on this topic, promoting the view that defamation of religion was itself a human rights violation. It called among other things for preventing and eliminating negative stereotyping of religions and beliefs, although every indication was that shielding Islam from aspersions was the central concern. Islam was again portrayed as being frequently and wrongly defamed by being associated with Human Rights violations and terrorism.[27] The resolution was criticized by many Western countries and also condemned by independent human rights advocates. For example, the human rights NGO Women Living Under Muslim Laws (WLUML) noted the dangers that the resolution posed, commenting:

> Civil society groups have expressed that the "combating defamation of religion" Resolution may be used in certain countries to silence and intimidate human rights defenders, religious minorities and dissenters, and other independent voices. In effect this resolution has the potential to dramatically restrict the freedoms of expression, speech, religion and belief.[28]

With these initiatives, one had a clear indication that the OIC was going to try to use its members' influence in the UN Human Rights Council to advance its own agenda, which is not an agenda of promoting respect for Human Rights but one that entails invoking the need to protect Islam as a pretext to justify measures designed to curb freedoms – in the most recent instance, the freedom of expression. These efforts are part of a process in which undemocratic Middle Eastern regimes assume the prerogative of defining what respect for Islam requires and then, on the assumption that their positions reflect divine mandate, call for International Law to be adjusted to accommodate Islam.

One needs to bear in mind that when Middle Eastern countries speak about the need to protect "Islam", it is only their official *Islams* that are meant. Similarly, when they complain of *Islamophobia*, it is only negative characterizations of their official *Islams* that concern them. The same regimes feel free to defame

---

27 *Human Rights Council,* 10th session, Draft report of the Human Rights Council, Resolution 10/22, "Combating defamation of religions", A/HRC/10/L, 31 March 2009, http://www2.ohchr.org/english/bodies/hrcouncil/docs/10session/Unedited_versionL.11Revised.doc (accessed on 25 May 2009).

28 *Women Living Under Muslim Laws,* "Women Living Under Muslim Laws Demands the Resolution on Combating Defamation of Religions be revoked", 8 March 2009, http://www.wluml.org/english/newsfulltxt.shtml?cmd%5B157%5D=x-157-564223 (acess ed on 25 May 2009).

and persecute versions of Islam that they do not endorse. A dramatic example of this practice could be seen in Saudi Arabia, where high ranking clerics have regularly vilified Šīʿa-Islam with the regime's acquiescence and where Shiʿis have suffered harsh persecution, being treated as heretics and infidels. For example, a 2008 study of the public excoriations and brutal mistreatment of the Saudi Arabian Ismāʿīlī community reminded observers of the wide gulf separating Saudi Arabian domestic policies, which included demonizing disfavoured religious traditions, from official Saudi Arabian claims in the UN to be committed to halt defamation of religions and to promote religious tolerance. Not only did Ismāʿīlī in Saudi Arabia have to cope with severe repression and abuse – including imprisonment and torture – but they had to endure being labeled by powerful clerics as corrupt infidels, debauched atheists, and members of a deviant sect.[29]

Having won support for its positions in the UN, the OIC wanted still more – an international legal document backing its position that clampdowns on freedom of expression were needed. An entity called the OIC-Observatory issued a report in March 2008 concerning what was claimed to be a crisis of *Islamophobia* in the West.[30] The OIC complained of vilification, defamation, and the denigration of the sacred symbols of Islam. It called for "a binding legal instrument to fight the menace of *Islamophobia* in the context of freedom of religion and elimination of religious intolerance." It also complained that Islamophobes remained free to carry on their assaults because of the absence of legal measures that were needed to stop people from "misusing or abusing the right to freedom of expression".[31]

The OIC insistence that the UN needed to focus on modifying Human Rights in the interests of ensuring respect for Islam had ominous implications. The OIC project entailed disregarding the urgent need to address the serious Human Rights violations suffered by people in the Middle East, instead treating the interests of Islam as if these should be the paramount concern and as if excessive freedoms in the West were the real problem that most urgently required attention.

OIC invocations of the need to protect Islam from defamation turn out to be simply one facet of efforts by Middle Eastern regimes that want to avoid the

---

29 See *Human Rights Watch*, "The Ismailis of Najran: Second-Class Saudi Citizens", http://hrw.org/reports/2008/saudiarabia0908/ (accessed on 23 September 2008).

30 *Organisation of Islamic Conference*, "1st OIC Observatory Report on Islamophobia – May 2007-March 2008, www.theunity.org/en/index.php?option=com_docman&task=doc_download&gid=8&Itemid=14 – (accessed on 19 September 2008*)*.

31 See "Report Outlines Approaches to Combat Islamophobia", *The Malaysian News Agency*, 12 March 2008, available on Lexis/Nexis.

embarrassment of having their dismal Human Rights records exposed to public criticism, which leads them to seek ways to discredit Human Rights activists who shine spotlights on their terrible records. The nature of the enterprise that the OIC was engaged in can be illuminated by reviewing some recent cases that show how determined Middle Eastern OIC members have been to crush and to vilify those of their citizens who fight against great odds on behalf of the cause of Human Rights.

C. Selected Case Studies

I. Saudi Arabia

The determination of Saudi Arabian officials to deter anyone from calling attention to Saudi Arabian Human Rights violations was exemplified by a criminal case involving the victim of a gang rape who became known as "the Qatif girl." In November 2007, the appeals court in Qatif sentenced the rape victim, then nineteen, to six months in imprisonment and 200 lashes. She had originally been sentenced in November 2006 to ninety lashes by the Qatif General Court to punish her for what was termed "illegal mingling," because she had been sitting by a shopping mall in the car of a male friend who was not her relative when the rapists noticed her and undertook their assault. The "Islam" supported by the regime decrees that women may never be alone with men outside their own families. According to the judges' point of view, the rape itself was deemed a relatively minor offense and the girl's flouting of conservative Saudi mores was the more heinous crime. The ruling by the appeals court was made after the girl's lawyer, the noted Human Rights activist ʿAbd al-Raḥmān al-Lāḥim, had asked it to review the verdict of the lower court and to reverse the judgment – only to have the appeals court condemn his client to a much harsher punishment. News reports recorded that the court informed the rape victim that her sentence had been made tougher because of "her attempt to aggravate and influence the judiciary through the media."[32] That is, the judges were willing to state openly that the number of lashes had been more than doubled as punishment for the defendant and her lawyer contesting the harshness of her original sentence and contacting the media. Clearly, they felt that a gang rape victim who had been given a heavy sentence should not be allowed to challenge her punishment and that the conduct of the Saudi Arabian judiciary was not to be exposed to any embarrassing scrutiny from the media. In increasing the already severe punish-

---

[32] *Human Rights Watch,* "Saudi Arabia: Rape Victim Punished for Speaking Out Court Doubles Sentence for Victim, Bans Her Lawyer From the Case", 17 November 2007, http://hrw.org/english/docs/2007/11/16/saudia17363.htm (accessed on 19 September 20 08).

ment for this reason, the judges manifested their utter disregard for modern standards of criminal justice and provided additional evidence supporting the frequently made charges that the Saudi Arabian system allows judges to mete out penalties in completely arbitrary fashion.

The court also punished ʿAbd al-Raḥmān al-Lāḥim, the girl's lawyer, banning him from defending her, confiscating his law license, and sending him to a disciplinary hearing.[33] According to a statement issued by the prosecutor, the lawyer was accused of "misrepresenting legal subjects through the media to confuse the judicial establishment's image and thus harm the country."[34] That is, they treated ʿAbd al-Raḥmān al-Lāḥim's recourse to the media in an attempt to rescue his client from severe and undeserved punishment and to expose the injustice that was being done to her as if this amounted to a kind of defamation of the Saudi Arabian judicial system. This expressed the official policy of suppressing any discussion of the deficiencies in Saudi Arabian justice. In punishing a defense attorney for carrying out his professional responsibilities, officials in the Saudi Arabian system revealed a mindset fundamentally at odds with the rule of law.[35]

In mid-December, after enduring intense international criticism and before the lashings were carried out, King ʿAbdallāh b. ʿAbd al-ʿAzīz as-Saʿūd decided to end the controversy by issuing a pardon to the "Qatif girl" – but deliberately refrained from making even the slightest criticism of the miscarriage of justice involved. The then Saudi Arabian Justice Minister, ʿAbdallāh b. Muḥammad aš-Šaiḫ, made a point of announcing that the king fully supported the sentence but had decided to pardon her because it was in the "interests of the people."[36]

II. Iran

Iran's conservative religious establishment has shown a similar intolerance of lawyers whose activities bring to light the patterns of Human Rights violations that pervade its system. One of its most courageous Human Rights attorneys,

---

33 Ibidem.

34 See "Abdullah pardons 'Qatif girl'", *Saudi-US Relations Information Service,* 18 December 2007, http://www.saudi-us-relations.org/articles/2007/ioi/071218-qatif-girl.html (accessed on 19 September 2008).

35 See the comments by the Middle East Director at Human Rights Watch: "Saudi Arabia: Rape Victim Punished for Speaking Out Court Doubles Sentence for Victim, Bans Her Lawyer From the Case", 17 November 2007, http://hrw.org/english/docs/2007/11/16/saudia17363_txt.htm (accessed on 19 September 2008).

36 *Katherine Zoepf,* Saudi King Pardons Rape Victim Sentenced to Be Lashed, Saudi Paper Reports, New York Times, 18 December 2007, http://www.nytimes.com/2007/12/18/world/middleeast/18saudi.html?em&ex=1198126800&en=17a903231aef1a5e&ei=5087%0A (accessed on 13 September 2008).

Mehrāngiz Kār, has been forced into exile after enduring severe harassment and imprisonment. Iran's ruling theocrats have angrily observed how Nobel Laureate Shirin Ebadi (Šīrīn ʿEbādī), a renowned Human Rights attorney, has continued to use her professional skills to defend her clients and to turn the spotlight on the regime's bad Human Rights record. She has outspokenly denounced the official Islamic rationales that are used for denying Human Rights, maintaining that, correctly understood, Islamic values support Human Rights.

In July 2008 Shirin Ebadi's Defenders of Human Rights Center linked Iran's stalled development to its disregard for Human Rights, warning the Iranian leadership about what it called growing public despair over Human Rights violations and economic pressures as inflation and unemployment were soaring. It denounced the trials and punishment meted out to students, teachers, unionists, Human Rights activists, and women who were agitating for reform and criticized the regime's intolerance of peaceful protests and calls for change. It complained about the application of the death penalty to minors. The center called for the government "to take reasonable action, not just meaningless propaganda, to cure the chronic disease of human rights violations and to improve the livelihood of the people."[37]

Although her international stature has meant that the regime has hesitated to take direct steps to silence her, Shirin Ebadi has been subjected to threats and harassment – presumably engineered by agents of the regime – designed to intimidate her or to persuade her to join the legions of critics of Iran's government who have fled to safety in foreign exiles. In what appeared to be a new effort to discredit her, in August 2008 IRNA, Iran's official news agency, falsely reported that Shirin Ebadi's daughter had converted from Islam to Bahāʾīsm.[38] Bahāʾīsm is a minority faith that has been both vilified and harshly persecuted by Iran's theocracy as it pursues its Islamization program. As members of a religion that spun off from Islam, Bahāʾīs have long been denounced by Iran's clerics as apostates. In practice, under the Islamic Republic large numbers of Bahāʾīs have been executed as apostates – although the regime seeks to cloak this practice and to shield itself from criticism by pretending that the punishments were meted out for offenses like spying or treason.

Since there is strong popular animus towards the Bahāʾī faith in Iran, the regime was apparently hoping to exploit anti-Bahāʾī prejudices to discredit Shirin Ebadi.

---

[37] "Ebadi rights group warns of 'public despair' in Iran", *Agence France Presse*, 20 July 2008, http://afp.google.com/article/ALeqM5gSnlqTcMsicKQDZRPf2DiutqnlAA (acessed 19 September 2008).

[38] "Iran's Ebadi denies state media report on daughter", *Agence France Presse,* 7 August 2008, http://afp.google.com/article/ALeqM5hW1Z9zuKcNBQe0RIZpSysquDUX4w (accessed 19 September 2008).

The implication of the false story about the conversion would be that, due to her failure to uphold Islamic values in her home, her daughter had betrayed her Islamic heritage. The lies about her daughter may have had more sinister motives, as well. The clerical regime has promoted a climate of religious zealotry and intolerance. The fact that disseminating the false allegation of conversion to Bahā'īsm could prompt religious zealots to assassinate Shirin Ebadi and her daughter likely also figured among the calculations behind the defamatory allegation. Shirin Ebadi responded by lodging a complaint against IRNA, accusing it "spreading lies, insults and defamation."[39] As the "Ebadi case" illustrated, the Iranian regime did not hesitate to resort to defamation to try to harm critics of its own Human Rights performance, in this case a defamation that was linked to the regime's policy of demonizing and persecuting a beleaguered religious minority.

III. Egypt

In 2008 a related case came up in Egypt in which the government targeted Saʿd ed-Dīn Ibrāhīm, one of the most prominent critics of its dismal Human Rights record. Saʿd ed-Dīn Ibrāhīm is the founder of the *markaz Ibn Ḫaldūn li-l-dirāsāt al-inmā'īa* (Ibn Khaldun Center for Development Studies), an independent research institute promoting democratization, government accountability, minority rights, and political and social development in Egypt and the wider Middle East. He is also the founder of *al-munaẓẓama al-ʿarabīa li-ḥuqūq al-insān* (Arab Organization of Human Rights), an advisor to the Project on Middle East Democracy, and a political dissident long persecuted by the regime. He had been sentenced in 2001 to seven years on a variety of charges including the claim that his discussions of Human Rights problems amounted to harming Egypt's image, before being freed on appeal after spending ten months behind bars in bad conditions that had seriously harmed his health. By 2007, the regime's campaign to silence its critics and arrest pro-democracy activists led to a major crackdown on dissent. Fearing that he was again at risk of arrest and complaining that Egypt's climate was prejudicial to political opposition and Human Rights, Saʿd ed-Dīn Ibrāhīm left Egypt in 2007 and was living in exile when in August 2008 a court sentenced him *in absentia* to two years imprisonment for tarnishing Egypt's reputation after he published an article on repression in Egypt in The Washington Post.[40] As in the 2001 case, the ultimate reason for the sentence was Saʿd ed-Dīn Ibrāhīm's activities bringing to light Egypt's anti-democratic policies and

---

39 "Iran's Ebadi lodges complaint over Bahai claim, *Agence France Presse*, 18 August, 2008, http://afp.google.com/article/ALeqM5gJfzqCWdwMvYxW6ClesgTlNMHBLA (accessed 19 September 2008).

40 "Egyptian-American activist jailed for 'defaming Egypt'", *Agence France Presse*, 2 August 2008, http://afp.google.com/article/ALeqM5iyZxEgOFVdXaa3a0SBQNoJSwwV3g (accessed 19 September 2008).

Islam und Menschenrechte (Islam and Human Rights / الإسلام وحقوق الإنسان)
Hatem Elliesie (Hrsg./Editor), © Peter Lang Verlag: Frankfurt a.M. 2010

Human Rights violations, the discussion of which the regime wanted to suppress. However, as in the "Qatif girl case" in Saudi Arabia and the "Ebadi case" in Iran, Islamic Law was superficially implicated in his case. According to Egyptian law, Saʿd ed-Dīn Ibrāhīm's offense was at least in theory one of infringing Islamic morality.

Inspired by the Quranic command that believers should command the good and forbid the evil, the *ḥisba* statute under which the 2008 suit against Saʿd ed-Dīn Ibrāhīm was brought gave Egyptians the right to file private lawsuits in cases where they claimed that Islamic morality had been violated. Judgments rendered under this statute did not merely enforce Islamic morality but also served to implement a policy of repressing dissent. *Ḥisba* lawsuits have become tools of Egypt's Islamic conservatives, apparently acting with official connivance, and have been used to target intellectuals who challenge the *status quo*.[41] A famous earlier case had involved Cairo University Arabic Professor Naṣr Ḥāmid Abū Zaīd, who in 1993 had been ruled an apostate based on his innovative religious scholarship, which his critics claimed had heretical elements.[42] Having been declared an apostate, like so many other Islamic thinkers who offer fresh approaches to the Islamic sources – only to anger those who condemn all dissent, Naṣr Ḥāmid Abū Zaīd was forced to flee to exile, in his case to the Netherlands. Like Saʿd ed-Dīn Ibrāhīm, Naṣr Ḥāmid Abū Zaīd was being punished not really for offending Islam but for raising questions that threatened the establishment and its repressive policies.

D. Summary and Conclusion

One can see that elements of Islamic Law do figure in these cases, but the theme of governmental repression, including policies of stifling all dissent and any criticisms of Human Rights violations, definitely predominates. As usually happens, when Human Rights violations occur in the Middle East, the anti-democratic character of the regimes involved shapes the rights violations, with Islamic law playing a distinctly subordinate role. In the treatment of the "Qatif

41 "Daanish Faruqi, Egypt's Repressive 'Hisba' Lawsuits", *Middle East Times*, 28 August 2008, http://www.metimes.com/Opinion/2008/08/28/egypts_repressive_hisba_lawsuits/4699/ (accessed on 19 September 2008).

42 See also *Jörn Thielmann*, "Naṣr Ḥāmid Abū Zaīd und die wiedererfundene *ḥisba*", Würzburg 2003; *Kilian Bälz*, "Eheauflösung aufgrund von Apostasie durch Popularklage: der Fall Abû Zayd", in: Praxis des Internationalen Privat- und Verfahrensrechts (IPRax), volume 16, Bielefeld 1996, pp. 353-356; *idem*, "Die Popularklage zur Verteidigung der Rechte Gottes: Hisba im heutigen Ägypten", in: Verfassung und Recht in Übersee (Law and Politics in Africa, Asia and Latin America – VRÜ), volume 31, Baden-Baden 1998, pp. 60-69.

girl" and her attorney, in the efforts to defame and discredit Shirin Ebadi, and in the judgment against Sa'd ed-Dīn Ibrāhīm, Islam was more a tool of those controlling the system than it was the driving force behind the efforts to punish those bringing Human Rights violations to light. These examples provide good illustrations of why it is a mistake to overweight Islam as a factor shaping the Human Rights violations pervading the Middle East. Rather than viewing it as a region where a fundamental conflict between Islam and Human Rights is being waged, people who scrutinize actual developments in the Middle East recognize the political interests that underlie the use of Islam to thwart calls for respecting Human Rights.

One should focus on the contention between despotic rulers determined to crush challenges to the *status quo* and supporters of democratization and Human Rights. Throughout the Middle East, people are agitating for the rollback of despotism and the enhancement of Human Rights – some working from secular perspectives and others arguing on the basis that true Islam supports their demands for Human Rights. It will be important to bear this in mind at a time when the OIC backed by its Middle Eastern members is striving to divert attention away from the actual Human Rights struggles being waged in the Middle East and to persuade the world that the rights of the Islamic religion, not the Human Rights of the people of the region, are what matters.

Governmental Human Rights Structures and National Human Rights Institutions in the Middle East and North Africa

Anna Würth / Claudia Engelmann, Berlin

A. What are National Human Rights Institutions?

Human rights regulate state behavior *vis-à-vis* individuals and communities of individuals. Accordingly, institutional perspectives on human rights promotion and protection tend to concentrate on various state institutions, such as law enforcement, legislatives, and the judiciary on the one hand, and on civil society including the media on the other hand. National Human Rights Institutions (NHRIs) represent an interesting "in-between" – established and funded by the state, and yet independent of it, strongly related to civil society and yet different to it. The *raison d'être* for NHRIs is the conviction that systematic national implementation of human rights requires human rights education, policy advise and, above all, systematic national monitoring.[1]

For that purpose, many states have set up National Human Rights Institutions in recent years.[2] Their make-up is based on the *Paris Principles*, adopted by the United Nations' General Assembly in 1993.[3] The *Paris Principles* formulate constitutive and optional functions for NHRIs but in principle are very open, accommodating the differences in country backgrounds.[4] Whether NHRIs fulfill

---

* We wish to thank Heiner Bielefeldt and Frauke Seidensticker for their critical comments on earlier drafts of this article.

1 This is also reflected in the development of International Human Rights Law: two recent Optional Protocols (to the Convention against Torture and other Cruel, Inhuman or Degrading Treatment or Punishment and to the Convention on the Rights of Persons with Disabilities) mandate the establishment of national monitoring mechanisms.

2 The annual report of the High Commissioner for Human Rights lists 75 National Human Rights Institutions, see *Office of the High Commissioner on Human Rights*, Annual Report of the UNHCHR and Reports of the Office of the High Commissioner and the Secretary-General. UN-Doc. A/HRC/7/70, Geneva, 18 January 2008.

3 See *General Assembly*, National Institutions for the Promotion and Protection of Human Rights, Annex 1: Principles relating to the Status of National Institutions. Competence and Responsibilities, 1993, UN-Doc. A/RES/48/134, http://www.unhchr.ch/Huridocda/Huridoca.nsf/(Symbol)/A.RES.48.134.En?Opendocument (accessed on 23 April 2008), quoted as *Paris Principles.*

4 For non Mid-East regional experiences with National Human Rights Institutions: *Human Rights Watch*, Protectors or Pretenders? Government Human Rights Commissions in Africa, 2001, http://www.hrw.org/reports/2001/africa/ (accessed on 17 March 2008); *Brian Burdekin*, National Human Rights Institutions in the Asia Pacific Region, Leyden 2007; *Sonia Cardenas*, Adaptive States: The Proliferation of National Human Rights Institu-

Islam und Menschenrechte (Islam and Human Rights / الإسلام وحقوق الإنسان)
Hatem Elliesie (Hrsg./Editor), © Peter Lang Verlag: Frankfurt a.M. 2010, S. 239-256

the *Paris Principles* is peer reviewed by the international community of NHRIs, with the support of the Office of the High Commissioner for Human Rights.

The *Paris Principles* require that NHRIs should

- work for the harmonization of national laws with international human rights standards,
- encourage ratification of international human rights treaties,
- assist in human rights education,
- conduct research into human rights issues,
- submit reports or recommendations to any public administrative body on matters concerning the promotion and protection of human rights, and
- cooperate with other actors involved in human rights work at the national, regional and international level.

In addition to these responsibilities, the *Paris Principles* lay out possible additional functions of NHRIs with respect to complaints from individuals or representative organizations. Exercising these functions should be based on the following principles:

- information on available remedies,
- mediation between the parties, leading to an amicable settlement,
- transmitting the complaint to the competent authorities,
- recommending review of respective legislation or policies.

As for the constitutive elements of National Human Rights Institutions, i.e. their establishment and sufficient core funding by the state and yet their independence of it, the *Paris Principles* suggest a number of mechanisms:

- the exclusion of voting rights for government representatives in governing bodies of the institution,
- the provision of adequate core funding,
- a legal basis for the respective National Human Rights Institution, and
- a pluralist representation of social and political forces involved in the promotion and protection of human rights.

Connected to but different from the issue of independence, the *Paris Principles* also give guidance on how NHRIs should make sure that their membership and

---

tions, Carr Center for Human Rights Policy Working Paper, Cambridge 2001, http://www.hks.harvard.edu/cchrp/Web%20Working%20Papers/Cardenas.pdf (accessed on 21 April 2008); *Linda Reif*, Building Democratic Institutions: The Role of National Human Rights Institutions in Good Governance and Human Rights Protection, in: Harvard Human Rights Journal 13, Cambridge 2000, pp. 1-69; *Valentin Aichele*, Die nationale Menschenrechtsinstitution. Eine Einführung, Berlin 2006; *Gauthier de Beco*, National Human Rights Institutions in Europe, CRIDHO Working Paper 01, Louvain 2007, http://cridho.cpdr.ucl.ac.be/documents/Working.Papers/CRIDHO.WP.2007-1.pdf (accessed on 20 April 2008); for ombudspersons in Latin America see *Anja C. Gebel*, Ombudsinstitutionen in Lateinamerika. Die Kunst des Überzeugens und politische Machtinteressen, Frankfurt a.M. 2008.

governing bodies entertain consistent relationships with civil society and reflect social pluralism. In that sense, civil society activism is a precondition for a meaningful National Human Rights Institution – and conversely – a National Human Rights Institution is not a substitute for civil society.

The NHRIs in conformity with the *Paris Principles* form the International Coordination Committee (ICC).[5] While the ICC has numerous competencies,[6] the most important is the accreditation of new National Human Rights Institutions and the regular re-accreditation and review of existing ones. Re-accreditation (in a five year interval) and review (as need arises) have been introduced considering that country conditions may change and thus may affect, e.g. the independence or core funding, of the concerned National Human Rights Institution.[7] The ICC may also review a NHRI in shorter time periods and thus put a time tag on solving problematic issues, related e.g. to the legal basis, core funding, or annual reporting.[8] Until March 2008, accreditation was being done in four layers:

(A): Compliance with *Paris Principles*;
(A)R: Accreditation with reserve[9];
(B): Partial compliance or insufficient information submitted;
(C): Not compliant with *Paris Principles*.

The process of accreditation, re-accreditation and status review is a powerful (if cumbersome) peer review. The process helps the community of NHRIs to remain sensitive of the challenges of NHRI work in different political settings. It also sends signals to governments that window-dressing – i.e. just setting up a governmental unit and call it "National Human Rights Institution" – will not lead to recognition or applause by the international human rights community. For example, the UN bodies responsible for monitoring treaty compliance (the

---

5 Up to March 2008, the ICC was a 16 member committee, elected by the four regional groups of accredited NHRIs; see http://www.nhri.net/default.asp?PID=85&DID=0 (accessed on 19 June 2008) for information on the former and current set-up.

6 For details see *Frauke Seidensticker / Amrei Müller*, The Role of National Human Rights Institutions in the United Nations Treaty Body Process, Berlin 2007, pp. 34-35, http://www.institut-fuer-menschenrechte.de/uploads/tx_commerce/handbook_the_role_of_national_human_rights_institutions_in_the_un_treaty_body_process.pdf (accessed on 24 April 2008).

7 See *Office of the High Commissioner on Human Rights*..., supra, footnote 2; *International Coordinating Committee of National Institutions for the Promotion and Protection of Human Rights*, Report and Recommendations of the Sub-Committee on Accreditation, Geneva 2007, Annex 2, para. 6.2, http://www.nhri.net/2007/Report_Sub-Committee_Oct2007_E.pdf (accessed on 23 April 2008).

8 See the numerous NHRIs to be reviewed in a one year interval, http://www.ohchr.org/Documents/Countries/ChartStatusNHRIsDec2007.pdf (accessed on 14 April 2008).

9 The "accreditation with reserve" (A)R status has been abolished in March 2008.

so-called treaty bodies), may make critical remarks: Thus the Committee against Torture recommended Qatar to bring its National Human Rights Committee (B Status) in line with the *Paris Principles*, particularly with respect to its independence.[10] In addition, during accreditation procedures the respective sub-Committee may consider NGO reports and thus incorporate a local civil society perspective on how a NHRI functions and performs in its respective context.

B. Governmental Human Rights Structures and National Human Rights Institutions in the Middle East

Many if not most states in the Middle East and North Africa (MENA) established governmental human rights structures in the 1970s or earlier, most usually a department or unit in the Ministries of Foreign Affairs. Traditionally, these were responsible for the cooperation with the international human rights community, e.g. they submitted the respective state report to the UN treaty bodies and responded to letters by international human rights groups on specific human rights violations. This institutional set-up reinforced the tendency to perceive human rights as a foreign policy concern,[11] as if human rights violations were of no concern for a government's domestic legitimacy.

With increasing transnational and domestic human rights activism, MENA governments established human rights structures in ministries or state institutions with a mandate for domestic policy. In Egypt, e.g., the attorney-general established one such unit in 1999, to look into petitions demanding to know about the whereabouts and well-being of political prisoners. Today, most, if not all states in the Middle East, have a multitude of units in the state apparatus which have

---

10 *Committee Against Torture*, Conclusions and recommendations Qatar, 2006, para. 17, http://www.bayefsky.com/pdf/qatar_t4_cat_36_2006.pdf (accessed on 24 April 2008). Another example: The Committee on the Rights of the Child recommends Jordan in 2006 " [...] to ensure that National Centre for Human Rights is provided with adequate human, financial and technical resources and that it has facilities to monitor and evaluate progress in the implementation of the Convention at the national and local levels as well as to receive, investigate and address complaints from children. The Committee also recommends that the State party expand the monitoring mandate of NCHR to include all agencies of the Government, including the police and the military. [...]"; *Committee on the Rights of the Child*, Concluding Observations Jordan, CRC/C/JOR/CO/3, 2006, para. 20 at http://www.bayefsky.com/pdf/jordan_t4_crc_43.pdf. See in addition the most recent work of Human Rights Watch on NHRIs: *Human Rights Watch*, Mexico's National Human Rights Commission, A Critical Assessment, New York 2008.

11 This appears no MENA peculiarity, see e.g. *Gauthier de Beco*, National Human Rights Institutions..., supra, footnote 4, on p. 4 on the French National Advisory Commission for Human Rights; *Sonia Cardenas*, Adaptive States..., supra, footnote 4, on p. 47.

"human rights" in their title.[12] These governmental human rights structures range from departments in the respective Ministry of Justice, checking laws for consistency with international conventions, to units or commissioners in the legislative, president's or king's office, at the attorney-general etc., where citizens and residents may lodge complaints or petitions. Some states, e.g. Yemen and Iraq, have fully-fledged ministries for human rights. In some states, notably those in North Africa, the establishment of governmental human rights structures went parallel to the founding of NHRIs – in most of the Middle East, however, governmental human rights structures preceded the establishment of NHRIs (see below).

The following table shows the number and percentage of accredited NHRIs (A, A(R), and B status) in different regions. Despite the proliferation of governmental human rights structures during the past decades, member states of the Arab League and the Organization of the Islamic Conference have relatively few accredited NHRIs.

Figure 1
Accredited National Human Rights Institutions
among Member States of Different Intergovernmental Regional Organizations (2008)

Organization	number	in % of member states
African Union	21	40
Arab League	6	27
Association of Southeast Asian Nations	4	40
European Union	17	63
Organization of the Islamic Conference	19	33
Organization of American States	15	43

[12] These governmental structures are listed, inter alia, in the pledges states made to the Human Rights Council in 2006. Tunisia for example prides itself to have the following governmental human rights structure:

> *Comite supérieur des Droits de l'homme et des libertés fondamentales, le Coordinateur Général des droits de l'Homme, les Unités des droits de l'Homme au sein des ministéres de ja Justice et des droits de l'homme, de l'Intérieur et du développement local et des Affaires Entrangères, le Médiateur Administratif, le Citoyen Superviseur, la Commission Nationale pour l'Education aux droits de l'homme, l'Observatoire National des droits de l'enfant, la nouvelle fonction du juge d'exécution des peines.*

Egypt has the National Council for Childhood and Motherhood, a Permanent Human Rights Committee of the People's Assembly, specialized human rights departments in various ministries and the Office of the Public Prosecutor, and the Ombudsman Office in the National Council for Women. All documents at http://www.un.org/ga/60/elect/hrc/; accessed on 18 March 2008).

To carry this line of inquiry a little further, the following figure plots the dates of foundation for the different MENA NHRIs.

Figure 2
MENA NHRIs by date of foundation and accreditation status (2008)[13]

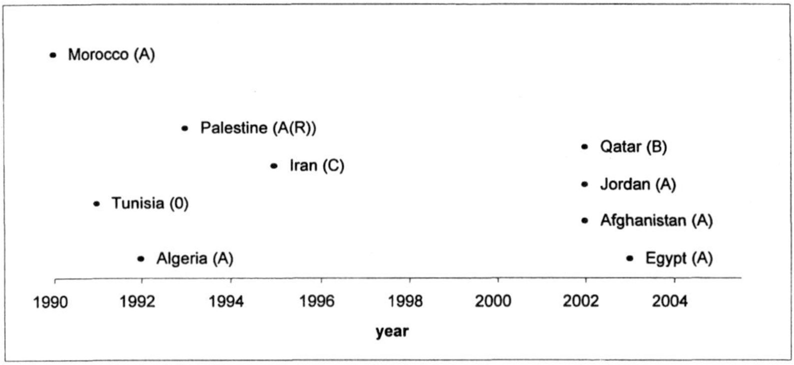

(A): Compliance with *Paris Principles*,
(A)R: Accreditation with reserve
(B): Partial compliance or insufficient information submitted
(C): Not compliant with *Paris Principles*
(0): Never applied for accreditation or accreditation pending

As illustrated in **figure 2**, Maghrib states and Palestine were the first to set up National Human Rights Institutions during the early 1990s. Iran followed suit in the later 1990s, all other countries post 2000. Despite the low percentage of states in the region with NHRIs seen in **figure 1**, the two waves of setting up NHRIs in the early 1990s and the 2000s appear to be an example of regional contagion and state adaptation to international and national pressure, so prominent in other aspects of Middle Eastern political systems.[14]

What does the establishment of a National Human Rights Institution mean for human rights practices? What is the correlation between the establishment of such an institution and the development of local human rights situations? To assess this question we used the *Cingranelli-Richards* (CIRI) *Human Rights In-*

[13] For accreditation status see: *Office of the High Commissioner on Human Rights…*, supra, footnote 2. We have not included the Bahraini NHRI established in summer 2008, due to lack of detailed information, see press release by the Office of the High Commissioner for Human Rights at http://www.ohchr.org/EN/NewsEvents/Pages/Markofprogress.aspx (accessed on 20 August 2008), nor the Iraqi one established in July 2009.

[14] See *Oliver Schlumberger*, Autoritarismus in der arabischen Welt: Ursachen, Trends und internationale Demokratieförderung, Baden-Baden 2008, on p. 157.

dex,[15] well aware of the difficulties to measure the human rights situation in a country,[16] and to assess the performance of a National Human Rights Institution.[17]

For **figures 3** and **4**, we used the *Physical Integrity Rights Index* (PHYSINT), constructed from data on measuring the occurrence of torture, extrajudicial killings, political imprisonment and disappearances by state organs, and the *Empowerment Rights Index* (EMPINX), aggregating the data for respect for the freedoms of movement and speech, for workers' rights, political participation and the freedom of religion. We looked at Algeria, Jordan, Egypt and Morocco, the four countries with (A) accredited NHRIs in the region.

Figure 3
Respect for Physical Integrity Rights in selected MENA Countries with (A) accredited NHRIs, 1981-2006

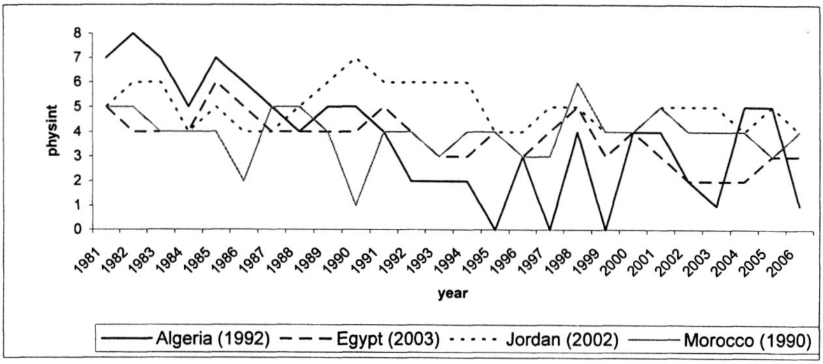

0 = no government respect for physical integrity rights
8 = full government respect for physical integrity rights
Date of foundation of NHRI in parentheses

[15] The CIRI Index codes the qualitative data from the US State and Amnesty International annual reports on human rights practices. For details, see http://ciri.binghamton.edu/ (accessed on 25 March 2008).

[16] For a brief synopsis see *Anna Würth*, Monitoring and Measuring Human Rights – a brief survey, in: Friedens-Warte (Journal of International Peace and Organization), volume 81, issue 1+2, Berlin 2007.

[17] See *International Council on Human Rights Policy*, Assessing the Effectiveness of National Human Rights Institutions, Versoix 2005, http://www.ichrp.org/files/reports/18/125_report.pdf (accessed on 1 April 2008).

Figure 4
Respect for Empowerment Rights in selected MENA Countries with (A) accredited NHRIs, 1981-2006

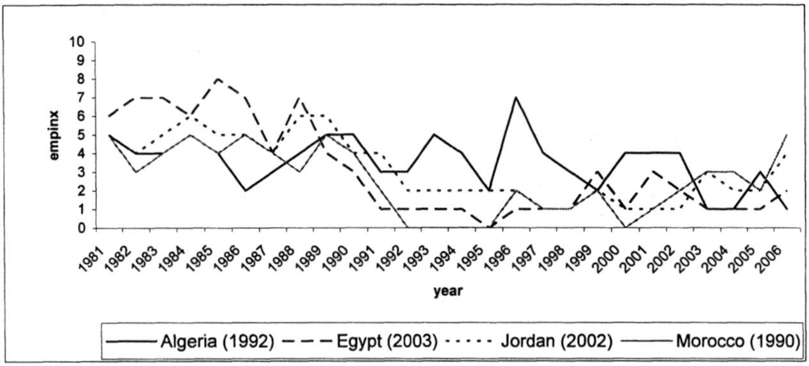

0 = no government respect for empowerment rights
10 = full government respect for empowerment rights
Date of foundation of NHRI in parentheses

Figures 3 and **4** show highly erratic developments before and after the establishment of the respective National Human Rights Institution. While the trend in respect for physical integrity rights remained erratic in Algeria, the early 1990s marked an alarming downward trend in Egypt, Morocco and Jordan. Likewise, the data show further decline in respect for physical integrity rights post 9/11, although occurring later in Jordan than in the other three countries.[18] With respect to empowerment rights (**figure 4**), developments in Algeria are again highly erratic. In the three other countries, there has been a steady decline in respect for empowerment rights, with a slight upward trend in 2005/2006.

To conclude: NHRIs in those four countries were established at a period when respect for physical integrity and empowerment rights was low or at best fairly moderate. The figures also demonstrate that there has not been any empirical relationship between the establishment of the respective National Human Rights Institution and an improvement in governments' human rights practices. However, running the same analysis with non-Middle Eastern countries with Na-

[18] For an overview of practices established worldwide in the name of counter-terrorism, see the monitoring by *Human Rights Watch* at http://www.hrw.org/english/docs/2005/04/27/china10549.htm (accessed on 13 April 2008) and the reports by the Special Rapporteur on the Promotion and Protection of Human Rights while Countering Terrorism.

tional Human Rights Institutions (we used India, Indonesia, and Malaysia) brought the same result.

While this hypothesis warrants further empirical research, we tentatively argue that NHRIs rarely, if ever, can be shown to have a direct impact on the change of governmental human rights practices, and, to take this one step further, it is overly ambitious or – rather - wrong to expect them to have one.[19] To fairly assess the contribution of NHRIs, one has to put NHRI performance in its political context and take into account how human rights situations change. As a number of authors have pointed out, such changes occur on different levels, are – if visible at all – slow, not linear, and often contradictory.[20] In what follows, we will discuss the institutional set up of MENA NHRIs against the backdrop of the *Paris Principles*. By doing this, we also attempt to flesh out a research agenda to assess the specific contributions made by NHRIs.

C. Between a rock and a hard place: Living up to the *Paris Principles* in the Middle East and North Africa

I. Basis in Law

According to the *Paris Principles*, National Human Rights Institutions shall have a foundation in a constitutional or legislative text (see above). In the MENA, NHRIs were initially founded on the basis of executive instruments, i.e. royal or presidential decrees, so prominent in MENA law-making.[21] In the

---

19 For this expectation, see *Amy Hawthorne*, Egypt's New National Council for Human Rights: Watchdog or Window Dressing?, Arab Reform Bulletin volume 1, issue 2, July 2003, Washington D.C. 2003, http://www.carnegieendowment.org/arb/?fa=downloadArticlePDF&article=21591 (accessed on 9 August 2009), *Moataz El Fegiery*, Arab World: The Effectiveness of Human Rights Commissions, in: Arab Reform Bulletin volume 6, issue 5, Washington 2008, http://www.carnegieendowment.org/arb/?fa=downloadArticlePDF&article=20521 (accessed on 9 August 2009).

20 Thomas Risse et al. use a spiral model of human rights change to explain how, when and why national governments move towards improvement of human rights conditions. The model describes five phases of states' behaviour in respect to human rights (repression, denial, tactical concession, prescriptive status, rule-consistent behaviour). See *Thomas Risse / Kathryn Sikkink*, "The Socialization of International Human Rights Norms into Domestic Practices: Introduction", in: idem (Editor), The Power of Human Rights. International Norms and Domestic Change, Cambridge 2001, pp. 1-38; *Susan Waltz / Lindsay Benstead*, "When the Time is Ripe: The Struggle to Create an Institutional Culture of Human Rights in Morocco", in: *Anthony Chase / Amr Hamzawy* (Editors), Human Rights in the Arab World. Independent Voices, Philadelphia 2006, pp. 174-195.

21 However, executive instruments establishing NHRIs are not a MENA specificity; in fact the tendency is so wide-spread that the ICC's Subcommittee on Accreditation flagged it as a major issue affecting accreditation decisions, see *International Coordinating Committee*, Report and Recommendations…, supra, footnote 7, para. 3.8 and Annex 2, para. 6.8.

meantime, however, MENA governments have reversed this trend; some have accorded NHRIs a basis in constitutions (Afghanistan, Palestine) or, more frequently, in legislation passed by parliaments.[22]

II. Funding by the State

As laid out above, the *Paris Principles* mandate that the state provides adequate funding for the operation of the NHRI, which many states do not. Qatar's National Committee, e.g. has no stable funds, Jordan's lacks financial autonomy, and the Moroccan Council had a budget cut. Again, this is no MENA specificity: NHRIs in Denmark and Greece lack sufficient core funding to name but two examples from Europe.[23]

With respect to budget size and how funds are spent, we have not been able to ascertain amounts: Annual reports cover NHRI activities and/or the human rights situation in the country, but not financial statements. In fact, this is quite comparable to NGOs in the region (and elsewhere), not all of which make their annual financial statements publicly accessible.

The requirement that states provide adequate core funding does not imply that NHRIs should not be allowed to accept funding from other sources,[24] and many NHRIs all over the world do to run specific projects. In MENA, the NHRIs of Palestine and Afghanistan are financed by donors.[25]

As with respect to local human rights NGOs, donor funding for NHRIs enables institutions to exist where otherwise they would not, given current political and economic circumstances. For NHRIs, foreign funding reduces dependency on fickle state allocation mechanisms and authoritarian inroads into the independence and autonomy of an NHRI, and thus may increase the possibilities to address particular violations.[26] But complete donor funding may also entail a spe-

22 See e.g. for Jordan *Official Gazette*, Law No 51 of 2006, http://www.nchr.org.jo/pages.php?menu_id=31 (accessed on 23 April 2008).

23 *International Coordinating Committee*, Report and Recommendations..., supra, footnote 7.

24 *International Coordination Committe,* Guidelines for Accreditation and Re-Accreditation of National Human Rights Institutions, 2008, Annex 1, para. 2.6, http://nhri.net/2008/Guidelines_for_accreditation_application_April_2008_En.pdf (accessed on 1 July 2008).

25 The lack of adequate funding is one of the reasons why the Palestinian NHRI is accredited with an A(R) status, and the NHRI of Afghanistan is being scheduled for an annual review.

26 See for this argument *Sonia Cardenas / Andrew Flibbert,* "National Human Rights Institutions in the Middle East", in: The Middle East Journal, volume 59, issue 3, Washington D.C. 2005, pp. 411-437. They argue that in the MENA dependency on domestic funding limits NHRIs' possibilities to address the most pressing and severe human rights violations committed by the governments that fund them. Accordingly, the Palestinian Com-

cific set of problems:[27] among them the unpredictability of funds and support for one-off projects with little capacity and strategy development. Current modes of donor funding also still tend to shift accountability and agenda setting to donors. Furthermore, if all funds for NHRI work come from abroad, it is hard to domesticate human rights politically: foreign funding may provide the ammunition for the knock-out argument often raised by MENA governments (and Islamist oppositions) in former decades, i.e. that human rights are a "Western" issue.

III. Complaint Handling

Most of the NHRIs in the Middle East and North Africa have been mandated to investigate violations of human rights and/or accept citizens' and residents' petitions or complaints.

Albeit different in scale in each country, deaths in custody, torture, criminalization of civil society, repression of political opposition and the press as well as impunity are the most frequent violations of civil and political rights (see above, **figures 3** and **4**). MENA judiciaries have only partially been able to address these violations, due to lack of independence in some countries, lack of capacity in others, or a combination of both. In a number of countries (e.g. Egypt, Palestine, Syria, Tunisia etc.), the state has also created and used parts of the judiciary to silence opposition in general and human rights defenders in particular.[28] In such a political context, an independent institution to receive and address citizens' complaints is undoubtedly important and may contribute, albeit in an indirect fashion, to increased state accountability.

MENA NHRIs have different powers with respect to individual complaints and differ in what they do with them. All MENA NHRIs may receive human rights-related petitions or complaints by citizens and residents, assess them for their human rights relevance and transfer them to the responsible government authori-

---

mission funded by donors is seen as the only one in the region able to address the most pressing human rights concerns. Overall it appears that this argument may warrant a more solid empirical inquiry on cause and effect, but also a legal discussion whether a NHRI funded long-term by the international community should really be considered a National Human Rights Institution.

27 See *Nicola Pratt*, "Human Rights NGOs and the 'Foreign Funding Debate' in Egypt", in: *Anthony Chase / Amr Hamzawy* (Editors), Human Rights in the Arab World..., supra, footnote 20, pp. 114-126, and http://ahrfund.org/english/about/aboutus.php (accessed on 13 April 2008).

28 *Susan Waltz*, Human Rights and Reform. Changing the Face of North African Politics. Berkeley 1995; *Eberhard Kienle*, A Grand Delusion. Democracy and Economic Reform in Egypt, London 2001; Tamir Moustafa, "Got Rights? Public Interest Litigation and the Egyptian Human Rights Movement", in: *Anthony Chase / Amr Hamzawy* (Editors), Human Rights in the Arab World..., supra, footnote 20, pp. 153-173.

ties involved in the alleged violation.[29] In addition, Morocco's Council may investigate human rights violations of its own accord.[30] This power is also foreseen for the Iraqi High Commissioner on Human Rights,[31] founded in July 2009.

Detailed statistics on how complaints are dealt with are hard to come by. The Palestinian Commission is the only MENA NHRI with its case-handling data base available at the international NHRI site.[32] Other NHRIs, e.g. in Egypt and Qatar, publish the respective numbers and a break-down of legal areas touched by the petitions received.

Some NHRIs not only address the individual complaints received but also use them for the promotion of human rights: The Egyptian Human Rights Council bases its annual report on the human rights situation on complaints about violations brought to its attention, and so do the Palestinian Commission and the Jordanian Centre.[33] Other NHRIs, e.g. the Qatari Committee, provide a breakdown of the complaints raised and how they dealt with them, but do not relate this to the human rights situation in the country.[34]

---

29 Governmental human rights structures usually hold the same powers.

30 See Royal Decree no 1.00.350 Reorganizing the Advisory Council, 10 April 2000, http://www.ccdh.org.ma/spip.php?article222 (accessed on 29 April 2008). The difference between "accepting petitions" and "suo motu investigations" is not always clear-cut. The Qatari NHRI, e.g., has the mandate "[...] النظر في التجاوزات على حقوق الانسان وحرياته إن وجدت (*an-naẓar fil-taǧāwazāt ʿalā huqūq al-insān wa-ḥuriyātihi in wuǧidat*) [...]", "to consider cases of trespassing human rights and freedoms", s. http://www.nhrc-qa.org/ar/files/downloads/NHRC_Decree.pdf, which is rendered in English as "investigation of human rights violations", see decree 25/2006 at http://www.nhrc-qa.org/ar/files/downloads/NHRC_Decree.pdf. In its reports, the Committee mentions to have received almost 600 (2005) and more than 1,200 complaints in 2006, mostly relating to the rights of migrant workers. See: *National Human Rights Committee*, The State of Qatar, Annual Reports, accessible under "Annual Reports" at http://www.nhrc-qa.org/en/news.php?item.509 (all accessed on 13 April 2008).

31 2006 Draft law on the Establishment of the Iraqi High Commissioner for Human Rights, electronic document in the possession of authors.

32 See http://www.nhri.net/nich.asp (accessed on 29 June 2008).

33 See *Egyptian National Council for Human Rights*, Third Annual Report, Human Rights Situation in Egypt 2006-2007, Cairo 2007, http://www.nchr.org.eg/en/annual_report06.html; *National Centre for Human Rights*, Status Report Human Rights 2006, Amman, 2007, http://www.nchr.org.jo/uploads/HRstatus2006-Engl.pdf; *Palestinian Independent Commission for Citizen's Rights*, The Status of Palestinian Citizens' Rights During 2006, 12th Annual Report, at http://www.ichr.ps/pdfs/ear12.pdf (all accessed on 9 August 2009).

34 See *National Human Rights Committee, The State of Qatar*, Annual Reports 2005 & 2006, supra, footnote 30. The Yemeni Ministry of Human Rights produced a similar report: Yemeni Ministry of Human Rights, Annual Human Rights Report 2004, http://www.merip.org/mer/mer235/stacher.html (accessed on 13 April 2008, website suspended).

To build on petitions and complaints received to report on the domestic human rights situation and give respective recommendations appears to be a decisive and powerful contribution of MENA NHRIs to "nationalizing"[35] human rights. A NHRI report based on citizens' complaints constitutes an acknowledgment by a government financed body that violations occur and need to be addressed systematically within the government. In the long run, this may shift human rights discourse, with respect to actors and content. Traditionally, human rights violations in MENA tend to be debated between international human rights actors and domestic civil society on the one hand and respective governments on the other hand. With NHRIs reporting on violations, the debate tends to become domestic, involving the NHRI as a government funded but independent institution, domestic civil society and different state or government agencies. With the shift in actors debating human rights performance comes a shift in the overall tone of the debate, moving from a flat-out denial ("violation did not happen") to the realm of debating different policies addressing human rights issues. It is with respect to these shifts in discourse that NHRIs have a unique potential and contribution to make. Shifts in discourse are obviously hard to be discerned, but in our view offer a promising line of future research.

EXCURSUS: Ombudspersons, or: Appropriating Islamic Tradition for Human Rights

As said above, given the current lack of the ability of MENA judiciaries to offer redress for human rights related wrongs, independent institutions – such as NHRIs and/or ombudspersons - to address complaints and petitions may be of a particular relevance. As of this writing, only the Palestinian Commission conceives of itself as a NHRI with functions of an ombudsperson, but it still lacks the enabling legislation to apply mechanisms of alternative dispute resolution in dealing with complaints. Egypt and Morocco have established ombudspersons but not in the area of human rights. Both institutions relate their mandate to the *dīwān al-maẓālim*, a prominent institution in Islamic legal history. The Egyptian Ombudsman Office for Gender Equality was established in 2001 (i.a. by EU funding). It is attached to the National Council for Women which in turn is under the authority of the Egyptian president and headed by his wife. A recent report explains:

> "While ombudsman institutions elsewhere have traditionally been granted the power to independently investigate complaints, the Egyp-

[35] This term was aptly coined by *Joshua A. Stacher*, Rhetorical Acrobatics and Reputations: Egypt's National Council for Human Rights, in: MERIP 235, Washington D.C. 2005, http://www.merip. org/er/mer235/stacher.html (accessed on 23 April 2008).

> tian Ombudsman is built on a "model of cooperation" between the various government bodies and agencies. [...] The office's affiliation with the N[ational] C[ouncil] for W[omen], chaired by H.E. First Lady Suzanne Mubarak, has facilitated the political backing and clout that further streamlines its negotiating power *vis-à-vis* other state bodies."[36]

The mandate of the Moroccan ombudsman (*wālī al-maẓālim*) is administrative in nature. It aims

> "to develop communication between citizens as individuals or groups and the administration or any public authority, and to stimulate the latter to respect the rule of law."[37]

The Swedish International Development Agency has been supporting efforts to coordinate an initiative to institutionalize ombudspersons regionally.[38] To date, it is not apparent how this initiative will connect and add to NHRI mandates to receive complaints and whether access to redress for human rights violations will be enhanced.[39]

IV. Relationship with Civil Society

A pluralist representation of social forces (e.g. civil society, opposition, minorities etc.) is a prerequisite for a National Human Rights Institution. The *Paris*

---

36 *The Egyptian Ombudsman Office for Gender Equality*, Helping Women Obtain Fair Treatment, no date (ca. 2005), on p. 4 at: http://www.wluml.org/english/news/egypt-ncw.pdf (accessed on 22 April 2008).

37 Royal Decree no 1-01-298 Establishing *dīwān al-maẓālim*, 9 December 2001. For the Islamic history of *qaḍā' al-maẓālim* as administrative justice, see *Muḥammad al-Kitābī*, Qaḍā' al-maẓālim fīl-islām baina al-māḍī wal-ḥāḍir, in: Dīwān al-maẓālim, Mağalla mutaḫaṣṣisa nisf sanawiya, 4&5, Casablanca 2006, pp. 7-10. On the development of ombudspersons in Europe, see *Linda Reif*, Building Democratic Institutions..., supra, footnote 4, pp. 7-9. Reif points out that ombudspersons in Europe were historically appointed by the legislative to check on conduct of the executive – a very different model compared to *qaḍā' al- maẓālim* or the contemporary MENA ombudspersons who are appointments of the executive to check on other parts of the executive and/or the judiciary.

38 See http://www.arabombudsman.net/en and minutes of a February 2008 meeting http://www.arabombudsman.net/ar/meetings (accessed on 13 April 2008), detailing future plans.

39 Compare, e.g., the German experience, as analyzed by the Commissioner for Human Rights at the Council of Europe: "In Germany [...] the complainant seeking a responsible body for remedying shortcomings may be daunted by the labyrinthine possibilities offered." Report by the Commissioner for Human Rights Mr Thomas Hammarberg on his Visit to Germany, CommDH(2007)14, para. 48, https://wcd.coe.int/ViewDoc.jsp?Ref=CommDH(2007)14&Language=lanEnglish&Ver=original&Site=COE&BackColorInternet=DBDCF2&BackColorIntranet=FDC864&BackColorLogged=FDC864 (accessed on 9 August 2009).

Principles suggest that this can be ensured with, or through, the presence of representatives of NGOs, trends in philosophical or religious thoughts, universities and qualified experts, the parliament and governmental departments.[40] In MENA NHRIs the latter are dominating, and as a rule, all institutions have more men than women as staff and on their boards. Islamist opposition, strong in all MENA states in or out of parliaments, appears not to be represented in any of the institutions – but this should be tested on a country-per-country basis which is beyond the reach of this article.

Morocco's Human Rights Advisory Council includes representatives from government and civil society. Though the appointment process is open to a variety of stakeholders, the king ultimately approves all candidates. Institutions in other countries show similar patterns. Members of the Jordanian National Center are appointed by Royal Decree at the recommendation of the Prime Minister.[41] The Egyptian Council is appointed by the upper house of parliament (*mağlis aš-šūrā:* Shura Council), and fairly pluralist in membership, apart from being prominent, with a former UN Secretary General heading it. The Human Rights Council includes some (non-Islamist) oppositional figures, journalists, a prominent woman's rights activist, and two human rights activists. Membership of the latter has always been controversial among civil society actors who deemed the Council a means to coopt and weaken civil society.[42] After the first three-years-term in 2006, the Shura Council made no changes to the composition of the 27 members. But two civil society members refused to serve another term, arguing that the government did not heed any of the Council's previous recommendations and that the Council adapted government discourse on essential human rights issues, e.g. with respect to anti-terrorism legislation.[43] Tunisia's Higher Committee for Human Rights and Fundamental Freedoms (as of 2008 not an accredited NHRI, see above, **figure 2**) is composed of representatives of eight

---

40 Paris Principles, para. 4; *International Coordinating Committee,* Report and Recommendations…, supra, footnote 7, Annex 1, para. 3.

41 *Official Gazette*, Law No 51 of 2006, Art. 13(a), supra, footnote 22. The degree of transparency and involvement of other stakeholders in the selection process is unclear and has been flagged by the ICC Sub-Committee on Accreditation: *International Coordinating Committee,* Report and Recommendations…, supra, footnote 7, para. 3.7.

42 See e.g. *Abdel Mawla Isma'eel*, The National Council for Human Rights. Democratic reform delusions spreading, Cairo 2004, http://www.hrinfo.net/en/discussion/2004/nchr.shtml (accessed on 10 April 2008); *Joshua A. Stacher*, Rhetorical Acrobatics and Reputations…, supra, footnote 35.

43 *Gihan Shahine*, The one you know, in: al-Ahram Weekly, Cairo, 14. February 2007, http://weekly.ahram.org.eg/2007/831/eg6.htm (accessed on 9 August 2009); *Bahey Eldin Hassan*, Ten Steps Backwards! Why did I Disapprove of the National Council for Human Rights' Annual Report?, Cairo 2006, http://www.cihrs.org/opinion_details_en.aspx?op_id=13 (accessed on 23 April 2008, link broken).

ministries (with no right to vote) and another 14-18 Committee members. All members are appointed by presidential decree.[44] In January 2008, the Tunisian President announced changes in the structure of the Higher Committee, including a revision of its composition and strengthened communication between civil society and the state,[45] maybe in view of the Universal Peer Review at the Human Rights Council in April 2008.[46]

Many observers have argued that the establishment of governmental human rights structures and NHRIs in MENA was a result of (inter)national pressure and intended to coopt and weaken civil society.[47] This argument stems, inter alia, from the observation that governmental human rights structures and NHRIs were established when civil society struggled against repressive and restrictive legislation regulating their status. Egypt's civil society, e.g., has been fighting an uphill battle for two decades to liberalize legislation regulating civil society organizations; many were forced to register as companies abroad in order to have some legal status at home; others were denied registration on technicalities.[48] For slightly different purposes, a similarly restrictive law is being debated in Jordan.[49] Iran has jailed most of its civil society activists when at the same time pledging to the Human Rights Council in 2006 "to mainstream human rights."[50]

---

44 *Republique Tunisienne*, Law no. 54-1991, para. 2, http://democratie.francophonie.org/IMG/pdf/7_TEXTES_CONST.TUNISIE_217a221_.pdf (accessed on 23 April 2008).

45 *Info Tunisie*, Le Comité supérieur des droits de l'Homme et des libertés fondamentales devient une institution autonome aux attributions renforcées, Tunis, 24 January 2008, http://www.infotunisie.com/2008/01/240108-10.html (accessed on 23 April 2008, link broken).

46 This pledge (in addition to numerous other pledges) to reform the Higher Council to conform to the Paris Principles was repeated by the Tunisian government at the Universal Peer Review, plus an indignant remark about the non-accreditation of the Council so far: http://lib.ohchr.org/HRBodies/UPR/Documents/Session1/TN/A_HRC_8_21_Tunisia_E.pdf (accessed on 29 June 2008).

47 See *Abdel Mawla Isma'eel*, The National Council for Human Rights..., supra, footnote 42; *Sonia Cardenas / Andrew Flibbert*, National Human Rights..., supra, footnote 26; *Amy Hawthorne*, Egypt's New National Council for Human Rights..., supra, footnote 19.

48 *Human Rights Watch*, Egypt: Margins of Repression: State Limits on Nongovernmental Organization Activism, 2005, http://hrw.org/reports/2005/egypt0705/egypt0705.pdf; *US Department of State*, Egypt Country Report on Human Rights Practices, Washington D.C. 2006, http://www.state.gov/g/drl/rls/hrrpt/2005/61687.htm (both accessed on 31 March 2008).

49 *Human Rights Watch*, Shutting Out the Critics, Restrictive Laws Used to Repress Civil Society in Jordan, 2008, http://hrw.org/reports/2007/jordan1207/jordan1207web.pdf (accessed on 6 July 2008).

50 *Permanent Mission of the Islamic Republic of Iran to the United Nations*, The Islamic Republic of Iran's Pledges and Commitments on Human Rights, 08 May 2006, http://www.un.org/ga/60/elect/hrc/iran.pdf (accessed on 23 April 2008).

In countries with no accredited NHRIs, the situation is equally bleak: In Tunisia, civil society can barely breathe, and activists are regularly slandered, physically assaulted, and under threat of spurious charges.[51] In Yemen, there are comparatively few outright restrictions in the 2001 NGO law, but many more in the by-law decreed in May 2004.[52]

It will take an in-depth study to assess the effect the establishment of NHRIs has on domestic civil society. From the little research available so far it appears that government motives may not have predetermined results. In Egypt, the establishment of the Council for Human Rights has led towards an increased coordination among those civil society actors who refused to cooperate with the Council.[53] On the other hand, in Algeria, activities of a rather weak and divided civil society have been further fragmented by the establishment of the National Human Rights Institution.[54] The same ambivalence can be observed with respect to governmental human rights structures: In Tunisia, institutional reforms in the 1990s, including the founding of the Higher Committee on Human Rights and Fundamental Freedoms, weakened the emerging human rights movement and led to a stabilization of a thoroughly repressive state apparatus.[55] In Yemen, human rights activists remain critical of the status and performance of the Ministry of Human Rights, but are willing to serve on its (largely defunct) advisory board.

As adequate funding discussed above, pluralist representation – including oppositional forces, minority representation, and civil society groups – are a major and continuous challenge for NHRIs worldwide.[56] With civil society activists being either criminalized and/or continuously coopted, NHRIs in MENA must

---

51 *Christopher Alexander*, Authoritarianism and Civil Society in Tunisia, in: MERIP 205, Washington D.C. 1997; *Susan E. Waltz*, Human Rights and Reform: Changing the Face of North African Politics, Berkeley 1995; *No Author*, No Rules, No Limits, Sexual assaults and fabrication of cases against journalists and activists, Tunisia, Egypt, and Bahrain, at http://www.hrinfo.net/en/reports/re2006/#3 (accessed 22 April 2008); *Sihem Bensedrine / Omar Mestiri*, Despoten vor Europas Haustür: Warum der Sicherheitswahn den Extremismus schürt (Übers. Ursel Schäfer), München 2005.

52 See *Human Rights Training and Information Centre*, The Situation of Human Rights NGOs, Sanaa 2006, pp. 42 et seqq.

53 *Sonia Cardenas / Andrew Flibbert*, National Human Rights…, supra, footnote 26.

54 *Sieglinde Graenzer*, "Changing Discourse: Transnational Advocacy Networks in Tunisia and Morocco", in: *Thomas Risse* et al. (Editors), The Power of Human Rights…, supra, footnote 20, p. 110.

55 Ibidem.

56 In fact, during its October 2007 session, the Subcommittee on Accreditation noted pluralist representation as an issue in almost all NHRIs, see *International Coordinating Committee*, Report and Recommendations…, supra, footnote 7.

find "consistent relations with civil society" a particularly difficult principle to live up to.

To sum up, the maybe intended cooptation of human rights activists and appropriation of the human rights discourse by MENA governments has had the side-effect that MENA governments are increasingly entangled in human rights discourse.[57] While this may seem modest, it is a far cry from the flat-out denials of either facts ("did not happen") or the relevance or appropriateness of human rights ("Western issue") so prominent in earlier decades. Apart from this discursive entanglement (to use a term coined by Risse[58]), the establishment of NHRIs may also serve to domesticate and nationalize human rights: it shifts human rights as a bone of contention between international human rights NGOs and the government concerned to domestic struggles over policies, legislation and redress where the main players are governmental agencies, the NHRI, and domestic civil society. Therefore, and to do justice to what NHRIs are and are there to do, it is unreasonable to expect NHRIs to be a "court above all courts" or a "voice" louder than all other voices able to bring to a halt the abuses of human rights so deeply entrenched in current political and governance systems in MENA.

57 See *Thomas Risse / Kathryn Sikkink*, "The Socialization …," supra, footnote 20.
58 Ibidem.

Zwischen Einschränkung und neuen Entwicklungen: Das Grundrecht auf heterosexuelle Selbstbestimmung in den Verfassungssystemen arabischer Staaten

Naseef Naeem, Berlin / Göttingen

A. Einführung

Das Thema Sexualität mit all seinen Aspekten gehört neben dem Herrschaftssystem und der Religion zum sog. „Tabudreieck“ des gesellschaftlichen, politischen und rechtlichen Diskurses in arabischen Staaten.[1] Trotzdem ist nicht zu übersehen, dass es in den letzten Jahren verschiedene Versuche – zumeist literarischer Natur – gegeben hat, die darauf abzielten, einen Rahmen für ein mögliches kulturelles Umdenken in diesen Bereichen auf Ebene der Politik und der Gesellschaft herbeizuführen oder zumindest die Diskussionen in diese Richtung voranzutreiben.[2] Die rechtswissenschaftliche Befassung mit der

---

1 Vgl. *Bu Ali Yasin*, Das Tabudreieck: Studie zu Religion, Sexualität und Klassenkampf *(al-Ṯālūṯ al-muḥarram: Dirāsa fī l-dīn wa-l-ğins wa-l-ṣirāʿ al-ṭabaqī)*, 7. Auflage, *Dār al-kunūz al-adabiyya*, Beirut 1999, S. 16. Begriffe wie z.B. „arabische Staaten oder Länder“, „der arabische Raum“ oder „die arabische Welt“ werden als Synonyme für die arabischsprachigen Staaten von Marokko bis Oman verwendet. Diese Länder sind völkerrechtlich in der Arabischen Liga organisiert. Siehe dazu *Herbert Baumann*, „Einführende Bemerkungen“, in: *Herbert Baumann / et al.* (Hrsg.), Die Verfassungen der Mitgliedsländer der Liga der Arabischen Staaten, Berlin 1995, S. 9; *Elizabeth Hart Rikabi-Succari*, Regional System and Political Development in the Arab Word, Louvain 1971, S. 2 ff. In diesem Aufsatz werden allerdings nur Beispiele aus Verfassungen von achtzehn Mitgliederstaaten der Arabischen Liga genannt. Andere Verfassungen von Mitgliedstaaten, die – wie die Komoren – sehr klein sind oder in denen – wie Somalia – die Staatlichkeit derzeit nur begrenzt vorhanden ist, werden hier nicht berücksichtigt, nicht zuletzt weil die analysierten Verfassungssysteme auch für sie repräsentativ sind. Zudem wurde sich hier terminologisch bewusst für Begriffe wie „Verfassungsrecht oder -system der arabischen Staaten/in den arabischen Ländern“ oder „arabische Verfassungen,“ nicht aber für „arabisches oder gemeinarabisches Verfassungsrecht“ entschieden, um zu zeigen, dass an dieser Stelle von verschiedenen Staatssystemen die Rede ist, die allgemein gesprochen durchaus mehr Gemeinsamkeiten als Unterschiede kennzeichnen. Auf der anderen Seite hat sich bis dato der Begriff „gemeinarabisches Verfassungsrecht“ noch nicht richtig entwickelt und etabliert.

2 Im Bereich der Sexualität ist unter vielen Beispielen der inzwischen ins Deutsche übersetzte arabischsprachige Roman der syrischen Exil-Autorin Salwā al-Nuʿaimī zu erwähnen: *Salwa Al Neimi*, Hamburg 2008. Zur Analyse des die Sexualität behandelten libanesischen Romans in der Periode nach dem Zweiten Weltkrieg s. *Maher Jarrar*, „Sexuality, Fantasy and Violence in Libanon's Postwar Novel“, in: *Samir Khalaf* (Hrsg.), Sexuality in the Arab World, London 2006, S. 278-298. Zum Konfliktpotenzial bezüglich

Islam und Menschenrechte (Islam and Human Rights / الإسلام وحقوق الإنسان)
Hatem Elliesie (Hrsg./Editor), © Peter Lang Verlag: Frankfurt a.M. 2010, S. 257-280

Thematik scheint allerdings marginaler Bedeutung zuzukommen. Dies betrifft insbesondere Aspekte des Sexualitätskonzepts, im weitesten Sinne des Wortes, d.h. hetero- und homosexuelle Beziehungen sowie Geschlechtsumwandlungen. Des weiteren kann man behaupten, dass eine ernsthafte rechtliche Auseinandersetzung mit der Sexualität in ihrer auf das Individuum bezogenen Dimension in den arabischen Staaten bislang noch nicht stattgefunden hat. Die Diskussion über eine neue rechtliche Orientierung im Rahmen der Sexualität wird als Tabu einer traditionell-religiösen Kollektivgesellschaft stets zum Schweigen verbannt.[3]

Als ein Teilaspekt dieser Problematik werden im vorliegenden Aufsatz die verfassungsrechtlichen Fragestellungen des Rechts von Männern und Frauen auf freie heterosexuelle Partnerschaft untersucht. Untersuchungsgegenstand ist also die staatliche Behandlung einer sexuellen Beziehung zwischen einem unverheirateten volljährigen Mann und einer ebenso unverheirateten Frau abgesehen von Inzest, Prostitution und der Erregung „öffentlichen Ärgernisses" (nachfolgend mit *Partnerschaft* bezeichnet). Mit umfasst werden dabei die Begründungsmuster im Verfassungssystem der arabischen Staaten.[4] Es geht um die

---

der Sexualität in der arabischen Gesellschaft s. außerdem *Samir Khalaf*, „Living with Dissonant Sexual Codes", in: Ibidem, S. 7 f. (7-34).

3 Die fehlende Ernsthaftigkeit bezieht sich hier insbesondere auf die fehlende Arbeit arabischer Gesetzgeber zur Schaffung eines dem Individuum dienenden Normensystems zur Regelung der oben genannten Bereiche der Sexualität. Zudem findet im allgemeinen islamischen Diskurs keine Diskussion zum Wandel vom Kollektiv hin zum Individuum im Hinblick auf sexuelle Selbstbestimmung statt. Dazu s. *Hans-Peter Raddatz,* Allahs Frauen: Djihad zwischen Scharia und Demokratie, München 2005, S. 219. Die Tendenz, Sexualität nicht zu individualisieren, zeigt sich am deutlichsten an Diskussionen über Transsexualität, die Gegenstand einiger Gerichtsfälle in verschiedenen arabischen Ländern war. Die Kernaussage der Urteile lautete: Der Mensch darf selbst nicht über sein Geschlecht entscheiden, eine Geschlechtsumwandlung muss medizinisch gerechtfertigt sein. Dazu s. *Dupret, Baudouin,* „Sexual Morality at the Egyptian Bar: Female Circumcision, Sex Change Operations, and Motives for Suing", in: Islamic Law and Society, vol. 9, 1/2002, S. 50 ff., 56 ff. (42-69).

4 Mit der Beschränkung der Untersuchung auf unverheiratete Personen soll die Analyse unabhängig von Diskussionen über den in arabischen Strafgesetzbüchern festgehaltenen Tatbestand des Ehebruches (*al-zina*) durch verheiratete Personen gestaltet werden. Der Grund für diese Entscheidung liegt u.a. in der Gewichtung des Aufsatzes, der den verfassungsrechtlichen Status unverheirateter Heterosexueller im Verfassungssystem der arabischen Staaten als eine Standardsituation zweier Personen ohne vertragliche Bindung in Form einer Ehe und die daraus entstehende Philosophie der Sünde mit ihren gesellschaftlichen und juristischen Folgen – untersuchen will. Dazu s. *ʿIzzat Muṣtafa al-Dusūqī,* Regelungen des strafrechtlichen Tatbestandes *al-zina* im positiven und islamischen Recht *(Aḥkām ǧarīmat al-zina fī l-qānūn al-waḍʿī wa-l-šarīʿa al-islāmiyya),* 2. Auflage, al-Maktab al-fannī li-l-iṣdārāt al-qānūniyya, 1999, S. 1 ff. Zur Erklärung dieser

Beantwortung der Frage, ob aufgrund des Verfassungsrechts arabischer Staaten das Recht von Männern und Frauen auf eine ungehinderte heterosexuelle Selbstbestimmung begründet werden kann und unter welchen Voraussetzungen die arabischen Staaten Partnerschaften dieser Art zulassen oder einschränken. Dabei ist darauf hinzuweisen, dass hier die sexuelle Beziehung in einer *Partnerschaft* – und nicht nur der *status quo* der sexuellen Rechte der Frau – in Betracht gezogen wird. Auf den Sonderstatus der sexuellen Rechte der Frau wird in der folgenden Untersuchung nur dann eingegangen, wenn dies für den spezifischen Kontext unerlässlich ist.[5] Außerdem soll der Versuch unternommen werden, die staatlichen Begründungen für Einschränkungen heterosexueller Freiheiten zu beleuchten und sich mit ihnen anhand von Verfassungsvorschriften sowie neuer theologischer Interpretationsansätze kritisch auseinanderzusetzen. Zum Zweck dieser Analyse werden einige Merkmale des Grundrechts auf sexuelle Selbstbestimmung nach den Vorgaben des deutschen Grundgesetzes (GG) einbezogen.

B. Das Grundrecht auf sexuelle Selbstbestimmung

Das Grundrecht auf sexuelle Selbstbestimmung ist aus dem in Art. 2 Abs. 1 GG verankerten Recht auf freie Entfaltung der Persönlichkeit in Verbindung mit der Unantastbarkeit der Menschenwürde und ihrer Achtungs- sowie Schutzpflicht seitens der Staatsgewalten, gemäß Art. 1 Abs. 1 GG, abzuleiten.[6] Der Bereich der Sexualität ist demnach Teil, der zur engeren persönlichen Lebenssphäre, die zum intimsten Bereich des Persönlichkeitsrechts gehört, zuzuschreiben.[7] In diese darf nur bei Vorliegen besonderer „öffentlicher Belange" eingegriffen werden.[8] Abgesehen von bspw. Inzest sowie, graduell, Prostitution und/oder bei Erregung „öffentlichen Ärgernisses", hat daher der Staat nach Maßgabe des Grundgesetzes in einer *Partnerschaft* nicht *per se* Eingriffsbefugnisse. Jeder einer *Partnerschaft* darf die Form der Sexualpraktik(en) frei gestalten[9] bzw. die *Partnerschaft* jenseits staatlicher Eingriffsmöglichkeiten weiterführen oder beenden. Diese Rechtsansicht hat im Verfassungssystem Deutschlands an Selbstverständlichkeit gewonnen, so dass der Status dieses Grundrechts als Teil der

Verknüpfungen im Islam s. *Jad Jiko,* „Die Idealisierung des sexuellen Triebes im Islam", in: Psyche, Jahrgang 61, Heft 11, Stuttgart 2007, S. 1136 ff. (1132-1154).

5 Zu einer in gewisser Hinsicht fokussierten Betrachtung aller Aspekte von sexuellen Rechten der Frau im islamischen Kontext s. z.B. *Farideh Akashe-Böhme,* Sexualität und Körperpraxis im Islam, 1. Auflage, Frankfurt a.M. 2006.

6 Vgl. BVerfGE 49, 286 (298); *idem,* 115, 1 (14).

7 Vgl. BVerfGE 47, 46 (73 f.).

8 Vgl. BVerfGE, 1 BvL 10/05 vom 27. Mai 2008, Abs.-Nr. 37, www.bverfg.de.

9 Vgl. *Philip Kunig,* in: Münch-Kunig, Kommentar zum GG, I. Band, 5. neubearbeitete Auflage, München 2000, S. 146.

nicht einschränkbaren Persönlichkeitsrechte außer Frage steht.[10] Es gehört zu den fundamentalen Säulen der Privatsphäre, die es seitens des Staates zu schützen gilt.[11] Im deutschen Grundgesetz wird also das Grundrecht auf heterosexuelle Selbstbestimmung zum einen vom Schutz der freien Entfaltung der Persönlichkeit und zum anderen von der Menschenwürde abgeleitet.

Im Hinblick auf Verfassungsbestimmungen in arabischen Staaten ist an erster Stelle zu untersuchen, ob und in welcher Form ein solcher doppelter Schutz explizit oder implizit vorhanden ist und ob aus dem jeweiligen Normensystem zumindest theoretisch eine uneingeschränkte heterosexuelle Partnerschaft begründet werden kann.

I. Das Grundrecht auf freie Persönlichkeitsentfaltung

Geht man von einer wörtlichen Übersetzung des Begriffes „freie Entfaltung der Persönlichkeit" in die arabische Sprache aus, dann sollte in den Vorschriften der arabischen Verfassungen nach einer Garantie des Grundrechts auf *al-tanmiyya al-ḥurra li-l-šaḫṣiyya* gesucht werden.[12] Der Terminus *al-tanmiyya* soll in diesem Zusammenhang die Bedeutung „vertikale und horizontale Ausdehnung" der Persönlichkeit haben. Um diese Bedeutung genauer zu erfassen, ist die Übersetzung um den Wortlaut *wa-l-taʿbīr al-ḥurr ʿan-hā* zu ergänzen, so dass das Grundrecht auf freie Entfaltung der Persönlichkeit *al-tanmiyya al-ḥurra li-l-šaḫṣiyya wa-l-taʿbīr al-ḥurr ʿan-hā* („freie Ausdehnung der Persönlichkeit und freier Ausdruck ihrer selbst") lauten könnte. Damit trifft die Formel im verfassungsrechtlichen Sinne genauer die Bedeutung des Wortes „Entfaltung" im deutschen Verfassungskontext:[13] *Expressis verbis* ist demgemäß das Recht enthalten, dass der Mensch seine Persönlichkeit entwickeln und gleichzeitig die mit dieser Persönlichkeit zusammenhängenden menschlichen Eigenschaften, seelischer und körperlicher Natur, zum Ausdruck bringen darf.

Eine solche juristische Formulierung als Ausdruck des Grundrechts auf freie Entfaltung der Persönlichkeit lässt sich allerdings in arabischen Verfassungsbestimmungen nicht ermitteln. Trotzdem kann nicht behauptet werden, dass die arabischen Verfassungsgeber den Bürgern dieses Grundrecht völlig aberkennen. Es ist zwar eine Tatsache, dass der oben genannte Ausdruck in den Grundrechtskatalogen der arabischen Verfassungssysteme nicht auftaucht,[14] die Mehr-

---

[10] Vgl. *Hans-Peter Raddatz,* Allahs Frauen..., a.a.O. (Fn. 3), S. 213.

[11] Vgl. *Hans D. Jarass,* in: Jarass-Pieroth, Kommentar zum GG, 8. Auflage, München 2006, S. 68; BVerfGE, 96, 56 (61).

[12] Der Begriff „freie Entfaltung der Persönlichkeit" kann auch anders übersetzt werden, z. B. *al-taṭwīr al-ḥurra li-l-šaḫṣiyya.*

[13] Vgl. Philip Kunig, a.a.O. (Fn. 9), S. 127 f.

[14] In den meisten arabischen Verfassungen sind Grundrechte und -pflichten in Katalogen zu finden: So im 2. Kapitel der jordanischen Verfassung; 3. Teil der Verfassung der Ver-

heit der arabischen Verfassungen spricht sich jedoch deutlich für eine Garantie und Gewährleistung der persönlichen Freiheit aus.[15] In anderen Verfassungen, in denen die persönliche Freiheit nicht explizit betont wird, deuten verschiedene Bestimmungen darauf hin, dass die Verfassungsgeber dennoch anstreben, eine solche Freiheit implizit zu garantieren. So spricht Art. 26 des saudischen Grundgesetzes von Gewährleistung der Menschenrechte im Allgemeinen.[16] An die Menschenrechte, wie sie von der internationalen Gemeinschaft anerkannt sind und zu denen die freie Entfaltung der Persönlichkeit dazugehört,[17] hält sich auch die Präambel der marokkanischen Verfassung. Der tunesische Verfassungsgeber weist in Art. 7 der tunesischen Verfassung (tun.Verf.) darauf hin, dass die Bürger alle Rechte genießen. Dann spricht sich Art. 8 Satz 4 tun.Verf. für eine Verpflichtung der politischen Parteien zur Respektierung der Menschenrechte aus. In der Präambel der tun.Verf. wird überdies betont, sich an die unter Völkern verbreiteten humanen Werte als Grundlage des Volkswillens zu halten. Dies kann in Verbindung mit Art. 7 tun.Verf. im Sinne einer verfassungsrechtlichen impliziten Gewährleistung der persönlichen Freiheit verstanden werden.

---

einigten Arabischen Emirate; 3. Teil der Verfassung des Königreichs Bahrain; 5. Teil des saudischen Grundgesetzes; 4. Kapitel des 1. Teiles der syrischen Verfassung; 3. Teil des omanischen Grundgesetzes; 3. Teil der Verfassung von Qatar; 3. Teil der kuwaitischen Verfassung; 2. Kapitel des 1. Teiles der libanesischen Verfassung; 3. Teil der ägyptischen Verfassung; 2. Teil der jemenitischen Verfassung. Nur in den Verfassungen von Algerien (4. Kapitel des 1. Teiles), Sudan (2. Teil), Irak (2. Teil) und Libyen (das Große Grüne Dokument für die Menschenrechte in der Volksperiode und das Gesetz Nr. 5/1991 zur Implementierung der Prinzipien des Grünen Dokumentes zur Stärkung der Freiheit) kann man eine Liste von Grundrechten und -freiheiten unabhängig von den Pflichten finden. In den Verfassungen von Tunesien, Marokko und Mauretanien hingegen sind keine gesonderten Grundrechtskataloge zu finden. Dennoch sind Letztere in den 1. Teil der drei Verfassungen über allgemeine Grundsätze und Grundprinzipien des Staatssystems integriert.

15 Vgl. Art. 7 der jordanischen Verfassung; Art. 26 Satz 1 der Verfassung der Vereinigten Arabischen Emirate; Art. 19 Abs. a der Verfassung des Königreichs Bahrain; Art. 39 der algerischen Verfassung; Art. 29, 37 der sudanesischen Übergangsverfassung; Art. 25 Abs. 1 der syrischen Verfassung; Art. 17 Abs. 1 der irakischen Verfassung; Art. 18 Satz 1 des omanischen Grundgesetzes; Art. 36 Satz 1, 37 der Verfassung von Qatar; Art. 30 der kuwaitischen Verfassung; Art. 8 der libanesischen Verfassung; das Prinzip Nr. 2, 7 des Großen Grünen Dokuments für die Menschenrechte in der Volksperiode und § 16 des libyschen Gesetzes Nr. 5/1991 zur Implementierung der Prinzipien des Grünen Dokumentes; Art. 41, 45, 57 der ägyptischen Verfassung; Art. 13 Satz 3 der mauretanischen Verfassung; Art. 48 Abs. a der jemenitischen Verfassung.

16 Auf den Vorbehalt in diesen Verfassungsbestimmungen zugunsten der Einschränkung der Menschenrechte aufgrund der islamischen *šarīʿa* wird später hingewiesen.

17 Vgl. Art. 3, 22, 29 Abs. 1 der Allgemeinen Erklärung der Menschenrechte.

Ergo ist festzuhalten, dass Verfassungsgeber in den arabischen Staaten generell darauf abzielen, zumindest grundsätzlich den Geist des Grundrechts auf freie Entfaltung der Persönlichkeit zu schützen. Dies ist insbesondere deshalb betrachtenswert, weil die Hinweise auf die Gewährleistung der Menschenrechte im Allgemeinen und dem grundrechtlich zu gewährleisteten Schutz der persönlichen Freiheit in allen Verfassungen in Kapiteln mit dem Titel „Rechte und Pflichten", „Freiheiten, Rechte und Pflichten", „Rechte und Freiheiten" oder „Allgemeine Grundsätze und Grundprinzipien" vorgesehen sind. Somit ist dieses Grundrecht entweder als Teil der Grundrechte oder als Teil der fundamentalen Grundsätze des staatlichen Systems, die Staatsgewalten binden, auch im arabischen Raum zu schützen.

II. Schutz der Menschenwürde

Der Begriff „Menschenwürde" ist wörtlich ins Arabische als *al-karāma al-insāniyya* oder *karāmat al-insān* zu übersetzen. Die arabische Übersetzung des Begriffes „Menschenwürde" deutet – neben Eigenwert, Eigenständigkeit, Subjektivität, Gattungswesen des Menschen und Wesen des Menschenseins – [18] insbesondere auf eine humanistische Verehrung hin. Im Lichte des Art. 1 Abs. 1 GG bedarf es demgemäß analog in arabischen Verfassungen der Ermittlung von

- Verehrung des Menschen;
- Erklärung zur Unverletzlichkeit menschlicher Würde;
- Verpflichtung der Staatsgewalten zu Achtung und Schutz der o.g. Würde.

Dabei ist vorwegzunehmen, dass in einigen arabischen Verfassungen (Jordanien, Saudi-Arabien, Libanon und Marokko) ein ausdrücklicher Hinweis auf die Menschenwürde fehlt. In Verfassungen anderer arabischer Länder wird der Schutz der Menschenwürde im Rahmen des Verbots der Folter und einer gegen die Menschenwürde verstoßenden Behandlung betont. Ein solches Verbot ist überwiegend in den Verfassungsbestimmungen verankert, in denen es um die Haftbedingungen, die Behandlung der Menschen seitens der Polizei und anderer Sicherheitsorgane geht.[19]

---

[18] Vgl. *Hans D. Jarass,* a.a.O. (Fn. 11), S. 40; BVerfGE, 87, 209 (228).

[19] Vgl. Art. 26 Satz 3 der Verfassung der Vereinigten Arabischen Emirate; Art. 19 Abs. d der Verfassung des Königreichs Bahrain; Art. 149 Abs. 1 Satz b der sudanesischen Übergangsverfassung; Art. 28 Abs. 3 der syrischen Verfassung; Art. 37 Abs. 1 Satz a & c der irakischen Verfassung; Art. 20 Satz 1 der omanischen Verfassung; Art. 36 Satz 2 der Verfassung von Qatar; Art. 31 Satz 2 der kuwaitischen Verfassung; das Prinzip Nr. 2 des Großen Grünen Dokuments für die Menschenrechte in der Volksperiode und § 17 Satz 2 des libyschen Gesetzes Nr. 5/1991 zur Implementierung der Prinzipien des Grünen Dokumentes; Art. 42 Satz 1 der ägyptischen Verfassung; Art. 13 Satz 3 der mauretanischen Verfassung; Art. 48 Abs. a & b Satz 2 der jemenitischen Verfassung.

Zusätzlich sieht die sudanesische Übergangsverfassung (INC) die Gewährleistung der Menschenwürde als staatliche Verpflichtung, im Zusammenhang mit einem Sonderschutz der Rechte von Frauen, Behinderten und älterer Leute sowie bei der Verteilung der öffentlichen Einnahmen auf staatlicher Ebene, vor.[20] In Anlehnung an das Prinzip Nr. 2 des Großen Grünen Libyschen Dokuments für die Menschenrechte in der Volksperiode statuiert außerdem Art. 31 Satz 2 der omanischen Verfassung die Menschenwürde als eine Schranke der Pressefreiheit und den Grund des Verbotes von Haushaltsdienstleistungen. Darüber hinaus werden die Menschenwürde und ihre Schutzpflicht in der Präambel der tun.Verf., Art. 34 der algerischen Verfassung, Art. 1 Abs. 2, 28 INC, Art. 25 Abs. 1 der syrischen Verfassung, Präambel und Art. 29 der kuwaitischen Verfassung, Nr. 4 Satz 2 des Verfassungserklärungsdokuments Ägyptens und der Präambel der mauretanischen Verfassung mehr oder minder als Abstraktum behandelt.

Insoweit kann man behaupten, dass die meisten arabischen Verfassungsgeber die Schutzpflicht der Menschenwürde in den Verfassungstexten zum Ausdruck gebracht haben. Das Fehlen einer expliziten Verankerung der Menschenwürde in den vier oben genannten Verfassungen kann nicht im Sinne einer Ignoranz interpretiert werden:

> Art. 26 des saudischen Grundgesetzes, Punkt b der Präambel der libanesischen Verfassung („Gewährleistung der allgemeinen Erklärung der Menschenrechte") und der Präambel der marokkanischen Verfassung („Gewährleistung des allgemeinen internationalen [menschenrechtlicher] Standard") enthalten menschrechtliche Schutzpflichten im Allgemeinen.

Die Menschenwürde gilt schlechthin als Kern der Menschenrechte in ihrem internationalen Kontext.[21] Jordanien war übrigens derjenige arabische Staat, der als erster die vom Gipfel der Arabischen Liga am 23. Mai 2004 verabschiedete und am 15. März 2008 in Kraft getretene sog. arabische Erklärung der Menschenrechte unterzeichnete.[22] Deshalb ist der jordanische Staat – wie alle anderen arabischen Staaten – ebenfalls an die Schutzpflicht der Menschenwürde gebunden, welche im ersten Satz der Präambel dieser Erklärung als Glaubensgegenstand der arabischen Nation ausdrücklich vorgesehen ist.

---

20 Vgl. Art. 32 Abs. 3, 45, 185 Abs. 1 der sudanesischen Übergangsverfassung.

21 Vgl. Präambel; Art. 1, 5, 22. 23 Abs. 3 der Allgemeinen Erklärung der Menschenrechte.

22 Ursprünglich wurde die arabische Erklärung der Menschenrechte in der Entscheidung des Rates der Arabischen Liga Nr. 5427 vom 15. September 1997 gefasst. Sie ist im März 2008 gem. Art. 49 Abs. 2 in Kraft getreten, nachdem sieben arabische Länder (Jordanien, Bahrain, Algerien, Palästina, Vereinigte Arabische Emirate, Libyen und Syrien) die Erklärung beglaubigt haben.

III. Ableitungsmöglichkeit des Rechts auf freie heterosexuelle Partnerschaft

Stellt man auf die normative Wirkung der o.g. arabischen Verfassungstexte ab, so kann man feststellen, dass die Verfassungsgeber der arabischen Staaten – nicht anders als der deutsche Grundgesetzgeber – die Menschenwürde und die freie Entfaltung der Persönlichkeit im allgemeinen Kontext schützen wollen. Analog zur Entscheidung des deutschen BVerfG scheint es daher in diesem Zusammenhang grundsätzlich möglich, eine Anerkennung des Grundrechts auf Selbstbestimmung der Sexualität im Verfassungssystem der arabischen Staaten abzuleiten. Ein arabischer Staat[23] darf demnach auf eine *Partnerschaft* keinen Einfluss nehmen. Eine Entscheidung des „Ob“ und „Wie“ einer *Partnerschaft* unterliegt dem geschützten Bereich der Privatsphäre und ist seitens der Staatsgewalten unantastbar. Geboten ist Rückhalt und die Gewährung des persönlichen Freiraums. Man könnte sogar weitergehen und behaupten, dass der arabische Staat nach den Bestimmungen einiger arabischer Verfassungen die Pflicht hat, die Privatsphäre einer solchen *Partnerschaft* zu schützen,[24] welche – dem Vergleich der Bestimmungen des deutschen Grundgesetzes und den arabischen Verfassungen folgend – zum Kern des Menschseins gehören sollte.

C. Staatliche Einschränkungen des Rechts auf heterosexuelle Selbstbestimmung und ihre Legitimation

Wenn die obige theoretische Ableitung des Rechts auf Selbstbestimmung der heterosexuellen *Partnerschaft* einfach in der Verfassungswirklichkeit implementiert wäre, dann gäbe es keinen Anlass für diese Analyse. In den arabischen Staaten fundieren die die *Partnerschaft* betreffenden Grundrechte auf anderen dogmatischen Säulen und Bezugsrahmen, als es im deutschen Verfassungskontext der Fall ist. Die juristischen Konzeptionen sind in diesem Zusammenhang grundsätzlich unterschiedlicher Natur. Allerdings wäre es im Gesamtkontext möglich, trotz einiger Vorbehalte,[25] zu behaupten, dass die staat-

[23] Mit dem Begriff „arabischer Staat“ wird die gesamte Konzeption der legislativen, exekutiven und judikativen Gewalt bezeichnet.

[24] Der Begriff „Privatsphäre“ ist mit *al-ḥayāt al-ḫāṣṣa* oder allgemeiner als *al-ḫuṣūṣiyya* ins Arabische zu übersetzen. Eine Betonung der Schutzpflicht dieser Privatsphäre ist insbesondere in folgenden Bestimmungen zu finden: Art. 39 der algerischen Verfassung; Art. 37 der sudanesischen Übergangsverfassung; Art. 37 der Verfassung von Qatar; §16 des libyschen Gesetzes Nr. 5/1991 zur Implementierung der Prinzipien des Grünen Dokumentes; Art. 45 Satz 1, 57 der ägyptischen Verfassung; Art. 13 Satz 3 der mauretanischen Verfassung.

[25] Die Vorbehalte betreffen in diesem Zusammenhang meistens das Ausmaß des staatlichen Eingriffes und die Begründung aus strafrechtlicher oder polizeirechtlicher Sicht. Aus verfassungsrechtlicher Sicht macht dies keinen Unterschied, da es generell zu einem staatlichen Eingriff kommt.

liche Behandlung dieses Grundrechts von Marokko bis Oman formell und materiell aus verfassungsrechtlicher Sicht Ähnlichkeiten aufweisen. Die Ähnlichkeit ist u.a. darin zu sehen, dass im gesamten arabischen Raum das Recht auf „Ob“ und „Wie“ der *Partnerschaft* lediglich im juristischen Rahmen der Ehe anerkannt wird.[26] Obgleich mit graduellen Unterschieden, lassen sich zudem im *inter-* und *intra*-verfassungsrechtlichen- und einfachgesetzlichen Kontext arabischer Staaten starke Einschränkung dieses Rechts außerhalb der Ehe nachweisen. Diese für heterosexuelle *Partnerschaften* wichtigen Einschränkungssachverhalte werden im Folgenden neben dem verfassungsrechtlichen Ehekonzept verfassungsrechtlich untersucht, ohne sich in andere Rechtsbereiche zu vertiefen.[27]

I. Schutz von Ehe und Moral als verfassungsrechtlicher Gegenspieler

Gegenüber der Garantie der freien Entfaltung der Persönlichkeit, die ja auch den vorherigen Ausführungen folgend – in manchen arabischen Verfassungen durch eine indirekte Bestimmung[28] geschützt ist, steht der Schutz von Ehe, Familie und Moral sowie der religiösen und/oder gesellschaftlichen Werte im Rahmen des familiären Konzeptes[29] als Grundsatz im Mittelpunkt des Verfassungssystems der arabischen Staaten. In den meisten arabischen Verfassungen stellt die Familie Basis und Kern der Gesellschaft dar. Sie ist auf Grundlage der moralischen, religiösen und gemeinarabischen (oder auch, je nach Land, nationalen) Werte zu bilden.[30] Eine solche Verknüpfung von Familie, Moral,

---

26 Vgl. *Christa Salamandra,* „Hierarchy and Distinction in Damascus“, in: *Samir Khalaf* (Hrsg.), Sexuality in the Arab World, a.a.O. (Fn. 2), S. 154 ff. (152-162)

27 Da hier über eine mögliche Einschränkung eines Grundrechts im Rahmen des Verfassungsrechts die Rede ist, sei darauf hingewiesen, dass in den arabischen Verfassungen, in denen von einem einheitlichen Konzept von Grundrechten und Pflichten der Personen ausgegangen wird (vgl. Fn. 14), alle Grundrechte und Pflichten einer zum Kern der Verfassung originär gehörenden Schranke unterliegen. Zur allgemeinen Problematik der Grundrechte in den arabischen Verfassungen s. *Hans-Georg Ebert,* „Arabische Verfassungen und das Problem der ‘islamischen Menschenrechte’“, in: Verfassung und Recht in Übersee, 30. Jahrgang, Heft 4, Baden-Baden 1997, S. 520-532.

28 Die Indirektheit bezieht sich hier darauf, dass das Recht auf freie Entfaltung der Persönlichkeit nicht wortwörtlich in den arabischen Verfassungen übernommen ist.

29 Vgl. *Carol J. Riphenburg,* „Changing Gender Relations and the Development process in Oman“, in: *Yvonne Yazbeck Haddad / et al.* (Hrsg.), Islam, Gender & Social Change, New York 1998, S. 153 f. (144-168).

30 Vgl. Art. 15 der Verfassung der Vereinigten Arabischen Emirate; Art. 5 Abs. a Satz 1 der Verfassung des Königreiches Bahrain; Art. 58, 63 der algerischen Verfassung; Art. 9, 10 des saudischen Grundgesetzes; Art. 15 Abs. 1 der sudanesischen Übergangsverfassung; Art. 44 der syrischen Verfassung; Art. 29 Abs. 1 Satz 1 der irakischen Verfassung; Art. 12 Nr. 3 des omanischen Grundgesetzes; Art. 21 der Verfassung von Qatar; Art. 9 der kuwaitischen Verfassung; die Prinzipien Nr. 20, 21 des Großen Grünen Dokuments für

Religion und Tradition lässt die Ehe zwischen Mann und Frau als die einzige sittlich-verfassungsrechtlich anerkannte Grundlage von familiären Verhältnissen erscheinen.[31] Diese Auffassung leitet sich von der allgemeinen religiösen und traditionellen Überzeugung im islamisch-arabischen Gesellschaftskontext ab, welcher die Bildung einer Familie ohne Ehe – jedenfalls bis dato – nicht akzeptiert.[32]

Diese Haltung gilt selbstverständlich auch für die vier Verfassungen (Jordanien, Tunesien, Marokko und Libanon), in denen keine explizite Verknüpfung dieser Zusammenhänge zu finden ist. Die Gründe für eine solche Auffassung liegen zum einen an der Sonderstellung des Islam als die Staatsreligion (wie bspw. in Art. 2 der jordanischen Verfassung, Präambel und Art. 1 der tunesischen Verfassung sowie Präambel und Art. 6, 19 der marokkanischen Verfassung)[33] zum anderen aber auch an der Betonung des arabischen Charakters (wie bspw. in der libanesischen Verfassung in Punkt b der Präambel und der Pflicht des Staates

die Menschenrechte in der Volksperiode und § 25 des libyschen Gesetzes Nr. 5/1991 zur Implementierung der Prinzipien des Grünen Dokumentes; Art. 9 Satz 1 der ägyptischen Verfassung; Präambel der mauretanischen Verfassung; Art. 26 der jemenitischen Verfassung.

31 Vgl. *Yvonne Yazbeck Haddad,* „Islam and Gender: Dilemmas in the Changing Arab World“, in: *Yvonne Yazbeck Haddad / et al.* (Hrsg.), Islam, Gender & Social Change, a.a.O. (Fn. 29), S. 15 ff. (1-29). In den Verfassungen von Sudan – Art. 15 Abs. 1 – und Syrien – Art. 44 Abs. 2 – sowie gem. dem Prinzip Nr. 21 des Großen Grünen Dokuments für die Menschenrechte in der Volksperiode und §25 des libyschen Gesetzes Nr. 5/1991 zur Implementierung der Prinzipien des Grünen Dokumentes ist die Ehe als Basis der Familie ausdrücklich verankert.

32 Zur Erklärung der Verbindung von Ehe, Sexualität und den familiären Pflichten aus muslimischer – eher islamistischer – Perspektive s. *Ismail Adam Patel,* Islam: The Choice of Thinking Women, London 1997, S. 36 ff. Andere muslimische Autoren sprechen sich dafür aus, dass Eltern in der Erziehung Sexualität als Recht jedes Menschen ansprechen sollten, welches man ausschließlich durch Heirat erhält. Dazu s. *V. A. Mohamad Ashrof,* Islam and Gender Justice: Questions at the Interface, Delhi 2005, S. 200.

33 Die Sonderstellung des Islam als Staatsreligion und seine Erwähnung an prominenterer Stelle in der Verfassung im Gegensatz zur Verankerung der Grundrechte an zweiter Stelle ist – abgesehen vom Libanon als multikonfessionellem Staat und der Betonung der Menschenwürde in Art. 1 Abs. 2 der sudanesischen Übergangsverfassung – in fast allen arabischen Verfassungen zu finden. Dazu s. Art. 7 der Verfassung der Vereinigten Arabischen Emirate; Art. 1 Abs. a, 2 der Verfassung des Königreiches Bahrain; Präambel, Art. 2 der algerischen Verfassung; Art. 1 des saudischen Grundgesetzes; Art. 3 der syrischen Verfassung; Art. 2 Abs. 1 Satz a der irakischen Verfassung; Art. 1, 2 der omanischen Verfassung; Art. 1 der Verfassung von Qatar; Art. 2 der kuwaitischen Verfassung; Nr. 2 der Erklärung der Entstehung der Volksmacht in Libyen vom 02.03.1977; Art. 2 der ägyptischen Verfassung; Art. 1 Satz 1 der mauretanischen Verfassung; Art. 1, 2, 3 der jemenitischen Verfassung.

zur Durchführung der Gottesgebote und Respektierung der religiösen Interessen im Allgemeinen in Art. 9 der libanesischen Verfassung).[34]

Mit der direkten und indirekten verfassungsrechtlichen Festlegung der Ehe als die einzige Basis zur Bildung einer Familie – in Einklang mit islamischen und arabisch-traditionellen Gesellschaftsverhältnissen –[35] streben die arabischen Verfassungsgeber danach, sexuelle Beziehungen zwischen Frauen und Männern ausschließlich in der sozialverträglichen Form der Ehe,[36] von den formellen Unterschieden und Besonderheiten des Eheschließungsverfahrens und seiner Voraussetzungen einmal abgesehen,[37] zu regeln. Ein derartiger vertraglicher Zwang als der einzige Weg zur Bildung einer staatlich anerkannten bzw. im verfassungsrechtlichen Sinne zumindest geduldeten *Partnerschaft* stellt ohne Zweifel eine theoretische und praktische Schranke des Rechts auf eine freie

---

34 Libanon könnte auf den ersten Blick ein Gegenbeispiel sein: Der Islam ist in der libanesischen Verfassung nicht erwähnt und der Libanon stellt einen Staat mit zahlreichen Religionen und Konfessionen dar, weshalb die Verknüpfung zwischen Familien und Ehe nicht zutreffen würde. Diese Annahme ist zum Teil wahr, denn die libanesische – insbesondere die christliche – Gesellschaft duldet mehr als andere arabische Gesellschaften außereheliche familiäre Verhältnisse, die verfassungsrechtliche Schranke im Sinne von Erfüllung der Gottesgebote in Art. 9 der libanesischen Verfassung bleibt jedoch bestehen, nicht zuletzt weil auch bei den meisten libanesischen Christen die Ehe die einzige anerkannte Grundlage der Familie darstellt. Zur Haltung der libanesischen Gesellschaft gegen die Lebensgemeinschaft ohne Heirat als Grundlage der Familie s. „Die Lebensgemeinschaft ohne Heirat“, in: *Balagh,* http://www.balagh.com/woman/heih/r00w6-lfh.htm (zuletzt aufgerufen am 30. August 2009). Zur Haltung libanesischer junger Studenten zum Thema Sexualität im Allgemeinen s. *Roseanne Saad Khalaf,* „Breaking the Silence: What AUB Students Really Think about Sex“, in: *Samir Khalaf* (Hrsg.), Sexuality in the Arab World, a.a.O. (Fn. 2), S. 175-198.

35 Vgl. *ʿIzzat Muṣtafa al-Dusūqī,* Regelungen..., a.a.O. (Fn. 4), S. 263 ff.; *J. Mark Halstead,* „Muslims and Sex Education“, in: Journal of Moral Education, Band 26, Heft 3, Carfax1997, S. 320 f. (317-330).

36 Die Ehe als die unverzichtbare Voraussetzung zum Geschlechtsverkehr stellt die Basis für permanente sexuelle Nöte in der islamisch-arabischen Gesellschaft dar und ist damit der Ursprung für praktische Probleme der sog. islamischen Sexualethik. Dazu und zur Bedeutung der Ehe für die Sexualität im Islam s. *Hans-Peter Raddatz,* Allahs Frauen..., a.a.O. (Fn. 3), S. 78, 91 ff.; *Yvonne Yazbeck Haddad,* Islam and Gender..., a.a.O. (Fn. 31), S. 15 ff. Einige Autoren sprechen von der Idealisierung des Sexualtriebes im Islam und versuchen sich damit aus psychischer Perspektive auseinanderzusetzen. Dazu s. *Jad Jiko,* Die Idealisierung des sexuellen Triebes im Islam, a.a.O. (Fn. 4), S. 1145 ff.

37 Zu einigen Besonderheiten des Ehevertrages in der islamischen Jurisprudenz, die auch für das positive Recht gelten können s. *Ziba Mir-Hosseini,* „Neue Überlegungen zum Geschlechterverhältnis im Islam: Perspektiven der Gerechtigkeit und Gleichheit für Frauen“, in: *Mechthild Pumpf / et al.* (Hrsg.), Facetten islamischer Welten, Bielefeld, 2003, S. 57 ff. (53-81).

heterosexuelle *Partnerschaft* dar, welches sich von einer Verknüpfung von Menschenwürde und freier Entfaltung der Persönlichkeit im Verfassungssystem der arabischen Staaten ableiten könnte. Eine Interpretation beider Zusammenhänge im Sinne einer möglichen unbeschränkten Anerkennung heterosexueller Freiheiten im Verfassungsrecht der arabischen Staaten könnte dabei zu weit gehen. Denn die erklärten Verfassungsgrundsätze Moral, Religion, Tradition und Sitten richten sich im Substrat der arabischen Gesellschaften gegen die sexuellen Selbstbestimmungsrechte der Einzelnen und im Hinblick auf die Heterosexualität gegen die Bildung einer nicht-ehelichen Beziehung.[38]

An dieser Zielbestimmung von Verfassungsprinzipien, d.h. gegen die Anerkennung einer nicht-ehelichen sexuellen Beziehung, ist festzuhalten, weil in einigen arabischen Verfassungen diesbezüglich explizite Vorbehalte mit der Gewährleistung der persönlichen Freiheit verankert sind. Damit wird eine Einschränkungsmöglichkeit des persönlichen Rahmens und der garantierten persönlichen Freiheitsrechte eröffnet. Einige arabische Verfassungsgeber haben sich deshalb einen Spielraum bei der Regelung des Rechts auf persönliche Freiheit eingeräumt. Diesbezüglich wurden Einschränkungsmöglichkeiten über den Gesetzesvorbehalt,[39] den die Grundsätze des Islam betreffenden Vorbehalt,[40] den Vorbehalt zugunsten der Rechte Anderer in Verknüpfung mit den allgemeinen Sitten und Werten der Gesellschaft[41] zugelassen. In anderen Verfassungen hingegen, in denen kein direkter Zusammenhang zwischen dem Schutz der persönlichen Freiheit und ihrer Einschränkungsmöglichkeit besteht, trägt in einzelnen Vorschriften oder in anderen Zusammenhängen die Bestimmung von Religion, Tradition und/oder Moral zur allgemeinen Grundlage der gesellschaftlichen und öffentlichen Ordnung dazu bei,[42] dass sich diese arabischen Staaten – anders als der deutsche Staat – zumeist aus dem Bereich der sexuellen Freiheit nicht

---

38 Zu einer klaren islamischen Haltung gegen die außereheliche Partnerschaften s. *Ismail Adam Patel,* Islam…, a.a.O. (Fn. 32), S. 95 ff.

39 Vgl. Art. 19 Abs. 1 der Verfassung von Bahrain; Art. 7 der tunesischen Verfassung; Art. 29, 37 der sudanesischen Verfassung; Art. 27 der syrischen Verfassung; Art. 18 Satz 1 des omanischen Grundgesetzes; Art. 37 der Verfassung von Qatar; Art. 48 Abs. a der jemenitischen Verfassung.

40 Vgl. Art. 26 des saudischen Grundgesetzes.

41 Vgl. Art. 15, 17 Abs. 1, 46 der irakischen Verfassung; Prinzipien Nr. 2 & 7 des Großen Grünen Dokuments für die Menschenrechte in der Volksperiode und § 16 des libyschen Gesetzes Nr. 5/1991 zur Implementierung der Prinzipien des Grünen Dokumentes.

42 Vgl. Art. 14 der jordanischen Verfassung; Art. 32, 44 der Verfassung der Vereinigten Arabischen Emirate; Präambel, Art. 42 Satz 2, 63 der algerischen Verfassung; Art. 10, 35, 40 Satz 1 & 3, 44 Satz 2, 49 der kuwaitischen Verfassung; Art. 9, 10 der libanesischen Verfassung; Art. 12, 56 Satz 3 der ägyptischen Verfassung; Präambel, Art. 6, 19 der marokkanischen Verfassung; Präambel, Art. 9 der mauretanischen Verfassung.

zurückziehen. Letztere wird nicht in den Bereich der Privatsphäre verwiesen, sondern seitens des Staates als ein „öffentlicher Akt" behandelt.[43]

Im Allgemeinen lässt sich also schlussfolgernd sagen, dass alle arabischen Staaten Einfluss in die *Partnerschaft* nehmen und diese als Teil der öffentlichen Ordnung betrachten. Im Rahmen dieser Einflußnahme kommt der bereits angeführte Hinweis auf graduelle Unterschiede zwischen arabischen Staaten zum Tragen. Allerdings handelt es sich dabei lediglich um nicht mehr als formelle Differenzierungen hinsichtlich der Einschränkung der heterosexuellen Freiheit. Sie wird je nach Rechtssystem explizit oder implizit einer strafrechtlichen Verfolgung ausgesetzt. Demgegenüber kann berechtigterweise behauptet werden, dass aus materieller verfassungsrechtlicher Sicht kein oder nur ein geringer Unterschied zu erkennen ist. Generell dulden arabische Staaten das Recht auf sexuelle Selbstbestimmung außerhalb der Ehe nicht.

II. Strafrechtliche Verfolgung von nicht-ehelichen heterosexuellen Partnerschaften

Bei Verwendung des Begriffes strafrechtlicher Verfolgung sind zwei Fälle zu unterscheiden:

- Einleitung des Strafverfahrens;
- Strafbarkeit nach einem Text oder richterlicher Praxis.

Dabei unterscheiden die Strafgesetzbücher der arabischen Staaten in ihrer konzeptionellen Ausgestaltung nicht-ehelicher Partnerschaften als strafrechtlich relevanter Tatbestand.[44] Manche Länder stellen diese Handlung entweder gesetzlich oder justiziable unter Strafe[45] andere nicht.[46] Es ist allerdings möglich, volljährige unverheiratete Männer und Frauen, die *in flagranti* oder einer entsprechend verdächtigen Situation in einer Wohnung angetroffen werden,

43 Vgl. *Carol J. Riphenburg,* Changing Gender Relations…, a.a.O. (Fn. 29), S. 154 f.

44 Die formellen Unterschiede im Rahmen der expliziten und impliziten Verfolgung von außerehelichen Partnerschaften betreffen nur den Fall, in dem beide Partner unverheiratet sind. Im Fall, dass eine der beiden Partien verheiratet ist, gilt in allen arabischen Strafgesetzbüchern der Straftatbestand des Ehebruches (*al-zina*). Zu *al-zina* als Tatbestand s. z.B. §§473 ff. des syrischen Strafgesetzbuches und §§273-277 des ägyptischen Strafgesetzbuches; *ʿIzzat Muṣtafa al-Dusūqī,* Regelungen…, a.a.O. (Fn. 4), 38 ff.; *Aḥmad Muḥammad Badawī,* Straftaten gegen die Ehre *(ğarāʾim al-ʿirḍ),* Saʿid Samak: Kairo 1999, S. 159 ff.

45 Als Beispiel ist die Haltung von saudischen Gerichten zu nennen. Zudem hat das libysche Gesetz Nr. 70 vom 2. Oktober 1973 ausdrücklich alle außerehelichen Partnerschaften unter Strafe gestellt.

46 Zu diesen Ländern gehören beispielsweise Syrien und Ägypten. Allerdings verlangen einige ägyptischen Strafrechtler, alle außerehelichen Partnerschaften unter Strafe zu stellen. Dazu s. *ʿIzzat Muṣtafa al-Dusūqī,* Regelungen…, a.a.O. (Fn. 4), S. 300 f.

unter dem Vorwurf der Prostitution oder der Anstiftung zu unmoralischen Taten zu verfolgen. Dies geschieht in der Regel durch die Polizei und der Staatsanwaltschaft, selbst wenn diese genau wissen,[47] dass derartige Tatbestände gar nicht vorliegen und das Paar nicht schuldig gesprochen wird. Im verfassungsrechtlichen Sinne – anders als im strafrechtlichen – genügt eine solche Verfolgungsmöglichkeit, um einen staatlichen Angriff auf das Recht auf freie heterosexuelle Selbstbestimmung und damit eine Einschränkung der Wirkung des Schutzes von Menschenwürde und freier Entfaltung der Persönlichkeit im Rahmen der sexuellen Rechte feststellen zu können.

Eine solche staatliche Handlung Haltung kann – verfassungsrechtlich gesehen – nur als ein Eingriff in den Kernbereich der Persönlichkeitsrechte gewertet werden, wenn die Handlung der arabischen Staaten in diesem Zusammenhang parallel zu Auffassungen des deutschen Bundesverfassungsgerichts – wie oben erwähnt (Fn. 8) – betrachten würde. Dem ist nicht entgegenzusetzen, dass man in manchen Staaten beide Beschuldigte von der Justiz frei sprechen würden. Das Problem in diesem Zusammenhang liegt vielmehr an der Grundstruktur der traditionell-religiösen Gesellschaft mit ihren patriarchalen Familienstrukturen.[48] Die Verfolgungsmöglichkeit einer *Partnerschaft* führt dazu, dass eine von der Gesellschaft als große Sünde geächtete,[49] aber vom Staat nicht explizit ver-

---

47 Normalerweise beginnt die strafrechtliche Verfolgung einer außerehelichen Partnerschaft zwischen unverheirateten Männern und Frauen durch Nachbarn, die Kenntnis davon erhalten, dass in dieser oder jener Wohnung eine unverheiratete Person wohnt. Sie alarmieren die Polizei, sobald sie merken, dass eine Person anderen Geschlechts in der Wohnung zugegen ist. Die Polizei kommt, nimmt beide aufgrund Gefahrenverzuges fest und leitet die Akte an die Staatsanwaltschaft weiter, zumeist mit dem Vorwurf der Prostitution oder des Verstoßes gegen die allgemeinen Sitten. Dazu s. *Ḥaiyān Nawāf,* „Ein syrischer Jurist ruft zur Kodifizierung der Lebenspartnerschaft von unverheirateten Männern und Frauen auf", in: al-Arabiya, 21. Januar 2008, http://www.alarabiya.net/articles/2008/01/21/44522.html (zuletzt aufgerufen am 30. August 2009). Die Staatsanwaltschaft klagt dann beide vor dem Untersuchungsrichter oder dem Gericht erster Instanz an. Sobald die Akte den Untersuchungsrichter oder das Gericht erreicht hat, werden die Angeklagten normalerweise freigelassen. Dennoch haben sie von der Verhaftung durch die Polizei bis zur Freilassung in der Regel ein paar Tage in der Untersuchungshaft verbracht.

48 Vgl. *Martina Sabra,* „Die Schwäche des Rechtsstaats ist die Stärke der Islamisten: Geschlechterdemokratie und politischer Islam in der arabischen Welt", in: Internationale Politik und Gesellschaft, Bonn 3/2006, S. 109 (106-118); *Dahlia Eissa,* Constructing the Notion of Male Superiority over Women in Islam, Internetpublikation von Women Living Under Muslim Laws, London 1999, S. 15 f., 19; *Farideh Akashe-Böhme,* Sexualität und Körperpraxis im Islam, a.a.O. (Fn. 5), S. 109 ff., 115 ff.

49 Vgl. *Iyman Salwa Mohammed,* „Wechselwirkung von Zuneigung, Sexualität und Liebe: Eine islamische Perspektive", in: *Klaus Nagorni* (Hrsg.), Religion und Eros, Karlsruhe, 2007, S. 50 (49-61).

botener Akt in die Öffentlichkeit gelangt, obgleich eine solche Beziehung nach einer anderen Interpretation der intimen Privatsphäre angehören sollte.

Dies hätte seitens des Staates geschützt werden, zumindest aber hätte der Staat von einem Eingriff absehen müssen. Es scheint gar so, als wäre der Staat bewusst daran interessiert, den Akt öffentlich zu machen, um *Partnerschaften* den traditionell-gesellschaftlichen Druck auszusetzen.[50] Somit kommt die zuvor erklärte verfassungsrechtliche Wirkung, also die Kombination mit den Faktoren Ehe und Familie, gleichermaßen zum Tragen. Der Staat verhält sich in diesem Zusammenhang nicht neutral und kommt weder seiner verfassungsrechtlichen Schutzpflicht, noch strafrechten Grundsätzen nach. Er entscheidet sich implizit und *per se* für die Bestrafung der *Partnerschaft*, indem er die Regelung des Sachverhaltes der internen Dynamik der Gesellschaft und Familie überlässt. Dabei ist die Wahrscheinlichkeit sehr hoch, dass entweder die Frau oder beide Parteien der *Partnerschaft* aus Ehrenmotiven umgebracht werden, oder sie zumindest Gewalt ausgesetzt werden.[51]

III. Aufhebung oder Strafminderung im Falle von sog. Ehrenmorden

Der Ehrenmord, oder im Arabischen mit dem rechtswissenschaftlichen Terminus *al-qatl bi dāfiʿ al-šaraf* bezeichneten Ausdruck, ist als ein Mord zu definieren, der von einem männlichen Täter an einer oder beiden Parteien eines sog. illegalen Sexualkontaktes verübt wird.[52] Die weibliche Partei des sexuellen Verhältnisses muss Ehefrau, Schwester, Mutter, Großmutter, Urgroßmutter, Tochter, Enkelin oder Urenkelin des Täters sein. Die Täter können also im Fall von unverheirateten Frauen ihre Brüder, Väter, Großväter oder Urgroßväter sein, die nach traditioneller und/oder religiöser Wahrnehmung ihre Ehre durch den sexuell konnotierten Akt der Frau verletzt sehen.[53] Sie verüben dabei ihrem Verständnis nach einen Akt der Verteidigung, weil die Frauen im Hinblick auf die Sexualität die (religiöse und/oder traditionelle) Ehre ihrer Eltern, Familie und

---

[50] Vgl. *Anja Wehler-Schöck*, Ehrenmorde in Jordanien: Ursache und mögliche Gegenstrategien, Frankfurt a.M. / et al. 2007, S. 49 ff.

[51] Vgl. *Farideh Akashe-Böhme,* Sexualität und Körperpraxis im Islam, a.a.O. (Fn. 5), S. 57 f.; „Ehrenstraftaten in Jemen: Die Gewalt gegen Frauen aufgrund der Ehrenfragen: rechtssoziologische Analyse“, in: Muntadā al-šaqā'iq al-ʿarabī, Sanaa 2005, S. 21 ff. http://saf-yemen.org/saf_books.asp?myid=30&safbok=79 (zuletzt aufgerufen am 30. August 2009)

[52] Vgl. *Anja Wehler-Schöck*, Ehrenmorde..., a.a.O. (Fn. 50), S. 17.

[53] Die Bezeichnung des Ehrenmörders bezieht sich im Sinne dieses strafrechtlichen Tatbestandes nur auf einen männlichen Täter. Eine eventuelle weibliche Täterin fällt meistens nicht unter diesen Sachverhalt, so dass in diesem Zusammenhang durchaus von einer Diskriminierung der Frau zu sprechen ist. Dazu s. *Laurie A. Brand,* „Women and the State in Jordan: Inclusion or Exclusion?“, in: *Yvonne Yazbeck Haddad / et al.* (Hrsg.), Islam, Gender & Social Change, a.a.O. (Fn. 29), S. 108 (100-123); *ʿIzzat Muṣṭafa al-Dusūqī,* Regelungen..., a.a.O. (Fn. 4), S. 239 ff.

Gesellschaft tragen.[54] Strafrechtlich wird generell zwischen zwei Fällen unterschieden, deren Regelung und Beurteilung unter arabischen Gesetzgebern und Gerichten einige, wenngleich unerhebliche Unterschiede verfahrensrechtlicher Art aufweisen:

- Ertappens während des Geschlechtsaktes
- Verdachtsfall ohne sexuelle Handlung

Während im ersten Fall der Täter strafausschließende Rechtfertigung der Ehrverletzung profitieren kann, besteht im zweiten Fall allenfalls die Möglichkeit einer Milderung des Strafmaßes.[55]

Dies ändert allerdings nichts an der Tatsache, dass staatlicherseits ein Mord im Namen der Ehre gerechtfertigt erscheint und damit nicht mehr der staatlichen Strafsanktion unterliegt. Allein schon die Verwendung des Begriffes „Ehre" im Strafgesetzbuch in Verbindung mit einem Tötungsdelikt deutet auf eine konkludente staatliche Akzeptanz individueller Gewaltanwendung hin. Deshalb kann eine Quadratur von Sexualität, Religion, Ehre, Gesellschaft, und Strafrecht festgestellt werden.[56]

Im selben Zusammenhang ist zu bemerken, dass vier arabische Verfassungsgeber ausdrücklich auf den Schutz der sog. Ehre in ihren jeweiligen traditionellen Konzeptionen hinweisen:

- Die **algerische Verfassung** spricht sich in Art. 39, 63 für ein absolutes Verbot jeder Ehrverletzung und für das Recht auf Ehre aus;
- Art. 37 der **Verfassung von Qatar** verbietet alle Eingriffe, die die Ehre oder den Ruf einer Person berühren.
- Das Dokument zur Erklärung der **ägyptischen Verfassung** sieht die Ehre des Menschen und der Menschheit neben dem tiefen Glauben als Element vor, auf das das ägyptische Volk stolz ist.
- In Art. 9, 13 Satz 3 der **mauretanischen Verfassung** ist die Ehre als ein Prinzip der Republik und ihre Gewährleistung als Staatspflicht verankert.

---

54 Vgl. *Hans-Peter Raddatz,* Allahs Frauen…, a.a.O. (Fn. 3), S. 77, 88 f, 96 ff.; *Dahlia Eissa,* a.a.O. (Fn. 48), S. 16 f.; *Marei Pelzer,* „Frauenrechte sind Menschenrechte - auch für Flüchtlingsfrauen? Asyl aufgrund gesellschaftlicher Verfolgung", in: Femina Politica, Jahrgang 17, Heft 1 Leverkusen 2008, S. 97 f. (93-104); *Farideh Akashe-Böhme,* Sexualität und Körperpraxis im Islam, a.a.O. (Fn. 5), S. 46 f.

55 Zum Unterschied zwischen beiden Fällen im Rahmen des jordanischen Strafgesetzbuches s. *Anja Wehler-Schöck,* Ehrenmorde…, a.a.O. (Fn. 50), S. 67 ff.

56 Vgl. *Hans-Peter Raddatz,* Allahs Frauen…, a.a.O. (Fn. 3), S. 103, 213.

Zusammenfassend lässt sich diesbezüglich feststellen, dass Verfassungsordnungen arabischer Staaten die Sexualität[57] dem Archetyp Ehre, Moral, Tradition und Religion unterstellen. Die Bedeutung dieser Faktoren für die Bestimmung des sexuellen Verhaltens ist so groß, dass die arabischen Staaten nichteheliche *Partnerschaften* nicht nur nicht dulden oder unter Strafe stellen, sondern vielmehr, als *ultima ratio,* die Todesstrafe verhängen. Diese Annahme macht in Verfassungssystemen arabischer Staaten die Ableitung eines Rechtes auf Bildung von *Partnerschaften* im Kontext des Schutzes der persönlichen Freiheit und der Menschenwürde unmöglich. Ferner ist zu bezweifeln, ob überhaupt etwas von der Menschenwürde im Gepräge des GG übrig bleibt.[58] Staatsrechtliche Abwehr- und Schutzrechte des Individuums zugunsten der traditionell-religiösen Werte der Gesellschaft werden außer Kraft setzt.[59]

D. Neue Entwicklungen im religiösen Diskurs durch Muḥammad Šaḥrūr

Betrachtet man die Art und Weise, wie die arabischen Staaten das Recht auf Bildung von sexuellen Beziehungen in *Partnerschaften* zulassen, dann erscheint es unmöglich den religiösen Diskurs auszublenden.[60] Die staatlichen Ordnungen stützen sich nämlich grundsätzlich darauf, dass der Islam nicht-eheliche sexuelle Verhältnisse verbietet und bestraft.[61] Die daraus resultierend Pönalisierung durch Staatsgewalten in arabischen Ländern entfaltet sich in zweierlei Hinsicht:

- **Aktiv** – durch positives Tun – erfolgt eine unmittelbare oder mittelbare Bestrafung;

---

57 Vgl. *Farideh Akashe-Böhme,* Sexualität und Körperpraxis im Islam, a.a.O. (Fn. 5), S. 61 ff.

58 Diese Haltung kann aus islamwissenschaftlicher Perspektive relativiert werden. Demnach kann die Menschenwürde im islamischen Kontext anders als im westlichen nur in einer Verbindung mit einer Gehorsampflicht gegenüber Gott verstanden werden. Dazu s. *Ute Gerhard,* „Einleitung: Menschenrechte sind Frauenrechte: Überlegungen zu Gleichheit und Geschlechtergerechtigkeit im Islam“, in: *Mechthild Rumpf,* Facetten islamischer Welten, Bielefeldt 2003, S.88 (85-102). Gehorsamkeit Gottes bedeutet im Rahmen der Sexualität die Zwangsbindung an einer Ehe.

59 Dass arabische Staaten durch die Garantie einer Straffreiheit oder -minderung zugunsten des sog. Ehrenmörders faktisch ihn zum Wächter der islamischen Werte erklären, ist beispielsweise am Scheitern des Versuches zur Verschärfung der Strafen für die Ehrenmorde im jordanischen Parlament im Jahr 2000 zu beobachten. Dazu s. *Martina Sabra,* Sexualität und Körperpraxis im Islam, a.a.O. (Fn. 5), S. 112; *Anja Wehler-Schöck,* Ehrenmorde..., a.a.O. (Fn. 50), S. 78 ff.

60 Zu einem Rechtfertigungsversuch der ablehnenden islamischen Haltung gegenüber der sexuellen Freiheit s. *Ismail Adam Patel,* Islam..., a.a.O. (Fn. 32), S. 84 ff.

61 Vgl. *Farideh Akashe-Böhme,* Sexualität und Körperpraxis im Islam, a.a.O. (Fn. 5), S. 53 ff.

- **Passiv** – durch Unterlassen – kommt der Staat seiner Schutzpflicht gegenüber seiner Bürger nicht nach.

Letztlich kann man behaupten, dass sich die arabischen Staaten dadurch nicht nur zu Wächtern der religiösen Grundsätze erklären, sondern vielmehr zur höheren Interpretationsinstanz des religiösen Willens im Rahmen der Sexualität gerieren.

Dieser Impetus manifestiert sich / lässt sich auch nachzeichnen, wenn man bedenkt, dass sich der Begriff *al-zina* bei nahezu allen islamischen Gelehrten und Rechtsschulen auf Sexualkontakte ohne Ehevertrag bezieht. Er wird jedoch in den meisten arabischen Strafgesetzbüchern als Bezeichnung für eine nichteheliche *Partnerschaft* angewandt, bei der mindestens ein Partner verheiratet ist.[62]

Betrachtet man darüber hinaus jedoch die Rechtswirklichkeit, wird bei der Strafverfolgung sog. *al-zina* Delikte deutlich, dass die jeweiligen staatlichen Institutionen bei der Ahndung keinen Unterschied zwischen einer ehelichen Bindung und keiner ehelichen Bindung einer der Partner macht. Der *al-zina* Tatbestand wird also ausgedehnt. Im Fall zweier Unverheirateter findet sich *expresis verbis* zuweilen nicht der Begriff *al-zina*, sondern der eines illegalen Sexualkontakts (*ṣila ǧinsiyya ġair mašrūʿa*). Diese Wendung wird insbesondere im Rahmen der Rechtfertigung von sog. Ehrenmorden verwendet.[63] Insgesamt lässt sich in diesem Kontext feststellen, dass die arabischen Staaten bemüht sind, der überwiegenden Auffassung von Gelehrten und der Rechtsschulen zu entsprechen, welche ihrerseits vorgeben die Haltung der Mehrheit der arabischen Gesellschaft zu reflektieren.

Dass sich der Staat bezüglich des Verbotes von nicht-ehelichen heterosexuellen Beziehungen auf die Auslegung der Gelehrtenmehrheit beruft, kann anhand der Reaktionen auf die Thesen des syrischen Islamforschers Muḥammad Šaḥrūr verdeutlicht werden.[64] Koranverse zugrundelegend teilt Šaḥrūr die Ehe in zwei getrennten Achsen sexueller und menschlicher bzw. sozialer Art. Seiner Auf-

---

[62] Vgl. *Isa Adeniyi,* Zina (Unlawful Sexual Intercourse) in the Modern World, Lagos 2000, S. 81 ff.; *ʿIzzat Muṣtafa al-Dusūqī,* Regelungen…, a.a.O. (Fn. 4), S. 29 ff. Allerdings strebte der libysche Gesetzgeber im Gesetz Nr. 70 vom 02. Oktober 1973 an, die Definition von *al-zina* als einem strafrechtlichen Tatbestand dem islamischen Recht anzupassen, indem in §1 alle unehelichen sexuellen Beziehungen als *al-zina* bezeichnet wurden.

[63] Vgl. §548 Abs. 1 des syrischen Strafgesetzbuches.

[64] Zur allgemeinen Information über Muḥammad Šaḥrūr und seine Methodik s. *Loay Mudhoon,* „Muhammad Schahrûr: Für ein zeitgenössisches Koran- und Islamverständnis“, in: *Katajun Amirpur / et al.* (Hrsg.), Der Islam am Wendepunkt, Freiburg / et al. 2006, S. 136-145.

fassung nach stellt die Sexualität in einer ehelichen Beziehung nicht mehr als 2% des alltäglichen Lebens gegenüber den 98% der anderen Aspekte und Aktivitäten dar, die u.a. ein für die Ewigkeit bestimmtes gemeinsames Leben, Bildung einer Familie mit Kindern, Neffen und Verwandtschaftsbeziehungen, gegenseitigen Respekts und Loyalität sowie Treue enthalten. Dieser vielschichtigen menschlichen und sozialen Seite der Heirat steht die „kleinere" Seite der Sexualität gegenüber, die ausschließlich die Erfüllung eines körperlichen Bedürfnisses des Menschen bezweckt. Jedoch kann die Erfüllung des sexuellen Bedürfnisses nach Šaḥrūr nicht nur auf einem Ehevertrag basieren, weil der Koran in Sure 23 (*al-Mu'minūn*):Verse 5-7,[65] Sure 33 (*al-Aḥzāb*):Vers 50[66] und Sure 24 (*al-Nūr*):Vers 31[67] explizit von der Heirat *und* dem sog. Besitz der rechten Hand (*milk al-yamīn*) spricht, die die Interpretationsgrundlage für den Sexualkontakt zwischen Mann und Frau bilden. Die Abschaffung der Sklaverei in der Moderne bedeutet nach Šaḥrūr, dass der Begriff „Besitz der rechten Hand" nicht mehr im Sinne eines sexuellen Verhältnisses zwischen Herrn und einer Sklavin interpretiert werden kann, sondern stattdessen die Legitimität von sexuellen Beziehungen außerhalb eines normalen Ehevertrages im Islam begründet.[68]

Dementsprechend spricht Šaḥrūr einerseits über andere Heiratsarten – wie *al-misyār* und *al-mutʿa* – als legale Formen der Regelung des Sexualkontaktes zwischen Männern und Frauen nach der islamischen Lehre.[69] Auf der anderen

---

65 *Sure 23* (المؤمنون)*:Verse 5-7:*

إلا عَلَى أَزْوَاجِهِمْ أوْ مَا مَلَكَتْ أَيْمَانُهُمْ فَإِنَّهُمْ غَيْرُ مَلُومِينَ . (المؤمنون/5)
فَمَنِ ابْتَغَى وَرَاء ذَلِكَ فَأُوْلَئِكَ هُمُ الْعَادُونَ. (المؤمنون/6)
وَالَّذِينَ هُمْ لأَمَانَاتِهِمْ وَعَهْدِهِمْ رَاعُونَ. (المؤمنون/7)

66 *Sure 33* (الأحزاب)*:Vers 50:*

يَا أَيُّهَا النَّبِيُّ إِنَّا أَحْلَلْنَا لَكَ أَزْوَاجَكَ اللاتِي آتَيْتَ أُجُورَهُنَّ وَمَا مَلَكَتْ يَمِينُكَ مِمَّا أَفَاء اللَّهُ عَلَيْكَ وَبَنَاتِ عَمِّكَ وَبَنَاتِ عَمَّاتِكَ وَبَنَاتِ خَالِكَ وَبَنَاتِ خَالَاتِكَ اللاتِي هَاجَرْنَ مَعَكَ وَامْرَأَةً مُّؤْمِنَةً إِن وَهَبَتْ نَفْسَهَا لِلنَّبِيِّ إِنْ أَرَادَ النَّبِيُّ أَن يَسْتَنكِحَهَا خَالِصَةً لَّكَ مِن دُونِ الْمُؤْمِنِينَ قَدْ عَلِمْنَا مَا فَرَضْنَا عَلَيْهِمْ فِي أَزْوَاجِهِمْ وَمَا مَلَكَتْ أَيْمَانُهُمْ لِكَيْلا يَكُونَ عَلَيْكَ حَرَجٌ وَكَانَ اللَّهُ غَفُورًا رَّحِيمًا.

67 *Sure 24* (النور)*:Vers 31:*

وَقُل لِّلْمُؤْمِنَاتِ يَغْضُضْنَ مِنْ أَبْصَارِهِنَّ وَيَحْفَظْنَ فُرُوجَهُنَّ وَلا يُبْدِينَ زِينَتَهُنَّ إِلا مَا ظَهَرَ مِنْهَا وَلْيَضْرِبْنَ بِخُمُرِهِنَّ عَلَى جُيُوبِهِنَّ وَلا يُبْدِينَ زِينَتَهُنَّ إِلا لِبُعُولَتِهِنَّ أَوْ آبَائِهِنَّ أَوْ آبَاء بُعُولَتِهِنَّ أَوْ أَبْنَائِهِنَّ أَوْ أَبْنَاء بُعُولَتِهِنَّ أَوْ إِخْوَانِهِنَّ أَوْ بَنِي إِخْوَانِهِنَّ أَوْ بَنِي أَخَوَاتِهِنَّ أَوْ نِسَائِهِنَّ أَوْ مَا مَلَكَتْ أَيْمَانُهُنَّ أَوِ التَّابِعِينَ غَيْرِ أُوْلِي الإِرْبَةِ مِنَ الرِّجَالِ أَوِ الطِّفْلِ الَّذِينَ لَمْ يَظْهَرُوا عَلَى عَوْرَاتِ النِّسَاء وَلَا يَضْرِبْنَ بِأَرْجُلِهِنَّ لِيُعْلَمَ مَا يُخْفِينَ مِن زِينَتِهِنَّ وَتُوبُوا إِلَى اللَّهِ جَمِيعًا أَيُّهَا الْمُؤْمِنُونَ لَعَلَّكُمْ تُفْلِحُونَ.

68 Vgl. *Muḥammad Šaḥrūr*, Für neue Grundsätze in der islamischen Jurisprudenz (*Naḥwa uṣūl ğadīda li-l-fiqh al-islāmī: fiqh al-mar'a*), 1. Auflage, al-Ahālī: Damaskus 2000, S. 307 ff.

69 Der Unterschied zwischen diesen beiden Heiratsarten, die nach Muḥammad Šaḥrūr als Besitz der rechten Hand zu bezeichnen sind, liegt darin, dass in der *al-mutʿa*-Heirat der

Seite betont er unmissverständlich, dass abgesehen von diesen Heiratsvertragsarten nichts im Islam einer *Partnerschaft* entgegensteht, soweit beide freiwillig eine derartige Beziehung wollen und sie keinen Sexualkontakt zu einer dritten Person unterhalten. Aus dieser Überzeugung heraus betrachtet er die Lebenspartnerschaft (*al-musākana*) von unverheirateten Männern und Frauen als legitim im Islam, wenn beide Partner der Beziehung freiwillig diese Form statt der offiziellen Heirat wählen. Diese Form sei eine Art Heirat ohne einen Vermittler oder Scheich, welche korangemäß sei und in der Zeit des Propheten zugelassen war.[70]

Dieser Auffassung von Šaḥrūr ist von fast allen islamischen Gelehrten kategorisch abgelehnt worden, nicht zuletzt weil der Heirat im Islam ein Vertrag zugrunde liegen muss, dessen Richtigkeit bestimmte Voraussetzungen – wie zwei Zeugen und die Festlegung des Brautgeldes (*al-mahr*) – benötige. Zudem überschreitet derjenige, der sexuelle Lust ohne Heirat anstrebt für manche Gelehrten die Gott gesetzten Grenzen (*hudūd Allāh*).[71] Erkennbar ist, dass Šaḥrūr mit seiner Auffassung einerseits eine Minderheitsmeinung im islamischen Kontext vertritt; andererseits repräsentiert er jedoch eine Entwicklung, die es keineswegs zu ignorieren gilt.

E. Mögliche Wirkung der Ansätze von Muḥammad Šaḥrūr

Die Vorbehalte seitens anderer islamischer Gelehrter gegenüber der Auffassung von Šaḥrūr mögen vielleicht im religiösen Diskurs gerechtfertigt sein. Aus verfassungsrechtlicher Sicht ist die von ihm vertretene Meinung hinsichtlich der Legitimation von sexuellen Beziehungen zwischen unverheirateten Männern und Frauen als Meilenstein zu werten: Arabische Staaten müssen ihre Haltung in diesem Zusammenhang überdenken.[72] Nun haben die arabischen Staaten zumindest theoretisch zu begründen, warum sie die Anerkennung des Rechts auf Selbstbestimmung heterosexueller Kontakte auf die Ehe beschränken. Sie

---

Mann allein für den Lebensunterhalt zuständig ist, während es in der *al-misyār*-Heirat die Frau ist. Dazu s. *Muḥammad Šaḥrūr*, „Definition der im Koran erwähnten Terminologien nach moderner Lesart", http://www.shahrour.info/index7.htm [Offizielle Webseite von Šaḥrūr] (zuletzt aufgerufen am 30. August 2009).

70 Vgl. „Syrischer Intellektueller wettet darum, dass seine Ideen die arabische Welt eines Tages beherrschen werden", in: al-Arabiya, 27. Januar 2008, http://www.alarabiya.net/-articles/2008/01/27/44810.htm (zuletzt aufgerufen am 30. August 2009)

71 Dazu s. die Auffassung von Scheich Ṣalāḥ Kuftārū im Artikel von al-Arabiya, s. Fn. 70.

72 Das Überdenken der staatlichen Haltung bezüglich der außerehelichen heterosexuellen Beziehungen betrifft alle oben erklärten rechtlichen Schranken, d.h. direkte oder indirekte Bestrafung und Nichtbestrafung oder die Verringerung des Strafmaßes im Fall der sog. Ehrenmorde.

können nicht einfach weiterhin behaupten, dass der Islam als Verfassungsprinzip – von der Form seiner Verankerung in der Verfassung einmal abgesehen –[73] nur die Ehe für solche *Partnerschaften* vorsehe. Durch die Auffassung von Šaḥrūr und seiner Auslegungsart ist eine solche Behauptung hinfällig. Richtigerweise sollte ein arabischer Staat seine Haltung im Prinzip nun dadurch rechtfertigen, dass er hier einer bestimmten einheitlichen Auslegung der Religion folgt.

Mit anderen Worten kann sich der Staat nicht mehr nur auf den Islam als eine Staatsreligion berufen, die *per se* solche Handlung verbietet. Der Staat untersteht *ipso jure* der Verfassung und muss sich daher auch den Auslegungsmechanismen des Islambegriffs stellen. Vor dem Hintergrund, dass Grundrechte einen Teil des Verfassungssystems in den arabischen Staaten darstellen, sollte die Auslegung auch andere Verfassungsgrundsätze miteinbeziehen, jedenfalls wenn es darum geht, die Rechte der Einzelnen zu definieren. Dabei sollten beide Auslegungsmöglichkeiten von Šaḥrūr und anderen Gelehrten hinsichtlich der Garantie der persönlichen Freiheiten, der Menschenwürde sowie die Verknüpfung von Familie, Ehe und Sexualität in ihren Funktionen als Verfassungsprinzipien in einen Kontext gebracht werden. Den Ausführungen folgend, lässt sich eine „Pattsituation" feststellen: Einerseits knüpft Šaḥrūrs Interpretation zur heterosexuellen Wahlfreiheit an die Konzeption von persönlicher Freiheit und Menschenwürde an; andererseits korreliert Šaḥrūrs Begründungsmuster mit dem Primat der Ehe im Verfassungskontext im Sinne eines Verbots der Wahlfreiheit heterosexueller Selbstbestimmung.

Diese „Pattsituation", die die erst durch die neue Entwicklung in der Auslegung des Islam durch Šaḥrūr entstehen konnte, führt in der Theorie dazu, dass die Entscheidung des Staates für die Einschränkung der Wahlfreiheit heterosexueller Selbstbestimmung einer Begründung bedarf, weshalb sich der Staat nicht für die andere, religiös begründete Alternativkonzeptionen entscheidet. Diese Begründung sollte, aufgrund divergierender Verfassungsauslegungsmuster am Verhältnismäßigkeitsprinzip gemessen werden. Der große Verdienst

---

[73] Zu den verschiedenen Formen der Verankerung des Islam als einem Verfassungsprinzip gehören z.B.: Der Staat ist islamisch, Religion des Staates ist Islam, die islamische Scharia ist die Quelle oder eine Quelle der Gesetzgebung. Dazu s. oben (Fn. 33). Zur Auswirkung des Islam als Verfassungsprinzip auf das Verfassungsrecht in den islamischen Staaten im Allgemeinen und in einigen islamischen Staaten s. *Naseef Naeem*, „Einfluss der Religionsklausel auf die Verfassungsgebung in islamisch geprägten Ländern", in: *Birgit Krawietz / et al.* (Hrsg.), Islam und Rechtsstaat zwischen Scharia und Säkularisierung, Sankt Augustin / et al. 2008, S. 77-86; *Ramin Moschtaghi*, „Die Islamische Republik als Verfassungsprinzip – Ein Vergleich der Verfassungen von Afghanistan und Iran", in: Verfassung und Recht in Übersee, 41. Jahrgang, Heft 2, Baden-Baden 2008, S. 185-220.

Šaḥrūrs ist darin zu sehen, dass sich arabische Staaten in Bezug auf die Einschränkung des Rechts auf heterosexuelle Selbstbestimmung nun in Erklärungsnot befinden. Andererseits bestünde natürlich die Möglichkeit, dass der Staat in diesem Zusammenhang weiterhin auf die arabischen Gesellschaftstraditionen und ihre Stellung in der Verfassung zurückgreifen, um seine Haltung auch ohne religiöse Konnotation zu rechtfertigen. Dieser Rechtfertigungsversuch kann allerdings nicht einfach so hingenommen werden:

- **Erstens** ist es eine menschliche, nicht eine göttliche Begründung.
- **Zweitens** entstehen zunehmend gesellschaftliche Realitäten, die berechtigterweise die Frage erlauben, ob, wie und wann die staatliche Haltung dagegen steuern sollte.

Zu den gesellschaftlichen Realitäten gehört beispielsweise die Lebenspartnerschaft (*al-musākana*), die zunehmend, z.B. in der syrischen Gesellschaft und in der medialen Auseinandersetzung, auf gesellschaftliche Anerkennung stößt.[74] Zudem hat dieses neue gesellschaftliche Phänomen auch eine außerparlamentarische juristische Debatte ausgelöst: Ein syrischer Anwalt hat sich in einer Tageszeitung dafür ausgesprochen, Lebensgemeinschaften per Vertrag staatlich beglaubigen zu lassen, zumal das syrische Strafgesetzbuch eine Partnerschaft zwischen unverheirateten Männern und Frauen nicht verbiete. Dieser Vertrag solle dazu dienen, die juristischen Rechte und Pflichten beider Partner zu definieren und mögliche künftige Konsequenzen einer solchen Beziehung, wie etwa der Geburt eines Kindes, zu regeln.[75] Es ist zu hoffe, dass der syrische Staat in absehbarer Zeit hierzu eine deutliche (juristische) Stellung bezieht. Sollte sich der Staat gegen diese Form von *Partnerschaften* positionieren, würde er in Anbetracht von Šaḥrūrs Auffassung und des durch das Phänomen „Lebenspartnerschaft" ausgelösten realen gesellschaftlichen Wandels seine Begründung außerhalb des religiösen oder traditionellen Diskurses suchen müssen. Diese Begründung dürfte demnach nicht von absoluten gesellschaftlichen oder religiösen Normen abgeleitet werden und unterstände damit der juristischen Methodik und dessen Diskurses, der Akzeptanz und Ablehnung einer Rechtsmeinung.

F. Ausblick

Der Hinweis auf die juristische Methodik als Maßstab zur Lösung einer rechtlichen Auseinandersetzung erscheint zunächst wohl eher befremdlich. Aller-

[74] Vgl. „Syrische junge Leute wählen die Lebenspartnerschaft statt der traditionellen Heirat", in: al-Arabiya, 07.Juli 2006, http://www.alarabiya.net/articles/2006/06/07/24458.html (zuletzt aufgerufen am 30. August 2009).

[75] Vgl. *Ḥaiyān Nawāf,* Ein syrischer Jurist…, a.a.O. (Fn. 47).

dings ist ein derartiger Hinweis im Rahmen dieser für die arabischen Gesellschaften und die arabisch-islamische Mentalität höchst sensible Thematik von nicht unerheblicher Relevanz für die Herausbildung neuer Debatten, die die Normativität von heterosexuellen Beziehungen erfasst. Eine solche Debatte sollte unter der Prämisse stehen, staatliche Normsetzung adäquat zu diskutieren sowie staatliche Maßnahmen an Rechtstexten zu messen und mit fundierten Auslegungskriterien zu begründen.

Das Hauptproblem in der rechtlichen Auseinandersetzung liegt dabei bisher weniger an defizitären Begründungsversuchen seitens der arabischen Staaten, sondern viel eher an ihrem beharrlichen Schweigen zur Thematik. Trotz der geäußerten Hoffnung auf eine baldige Stellungnahme durch den syrischen Staat wäre es daher nicht unwahrscheinlich, wenn man auf absehbare Zeit keine Resonanz erhält. Das „offizielle" Schweigen in den arabischen Staaten indiziert das Selbstverständnis grundrechtliche Eingriffe unreflektiert praktizieren zu können. Durch diese Haltung entzieht sich der arabische Staat konkludent seiner Schutzpflicht, speziell gegenüber der Ausübung von individuellen heterosexuellen Rechten außerhalb der herrschenden gesellschaftlichen Vorstellung. Auf diese Weise umgeht man Diskussionen, die die eigene Legitimation in Frage stellen.

Die herrschenden Eliten treten als große Patriarchen einer patriarchalischen arabischen Gesellschaft auf. Es nicht im Interesse dieser Eliten, eine individualisierende Heterosexualität gegen die patriarchalischen Strukturen der Gesellschaft durchzusetzen, weil dies auf lange Sicht zur Entmachtung oder zumindest Machtlimitierung führen kann.

Die Erlangung des Rechts auf freie heterosexuelle Selbstbestimmung und die Erzwingung seines Schutzes durch die Staatsgewalten ist im arabischen Raum als erste Stufe auf dem Weg zur völligen Herrschaft des Rechts über den Staat zu betrachten. Denn diejenigen, die selbst über ihre Körper bestimmen dürfen, werden sich nicht auf Dauer damit abfinden, dass ihr Geist in einem staatlichen System gefangen gehalten wird, welches über das menschliche Wesen allein und grenzenlos herrscht.[76] Ob eine solche Vorstellung jemals Wirklichkeit wird, bleibt abzuwarten. Den Grundstein für diesen Prozess hat Šaḥrūr jedoch gelegt. Die religiöse legitimierte Macht des arabischen Staates über das körperliche Verhalten der Menschen hat Šaḥrūr, zumindest in Fragen heterosexuellen Beziehungen, entzogen.

---

[76] Vgl. *Farideh Akashe-Böhme*, Sexualität und Körperpraxis im Islam, a.a.O. (Fn. 5), S. 79 ff.; *Elizabeth Shlala Leo*, „Islamic Female Sexuality and Gender in Modern Feminist Interpretation", in: Islam and Christian-Muslim Relations, vol. 16, London / et al. 2/2005, S. 133 ff. (129-140).

Die arabischen Staaten präsentieren sich im Konsens mit der gesellschaftlichen Mentalität als entscheidende Gegner einer paradigmatischen Trennung von Menschen und Gottesgebot, welches seinerseits eine Subjektwerdung des Menschen durch eine Entfaltung der sexuellen Identität nicht zulässt.[77]

[77] Vgl. *Jiko, Jad,* Die Idealisierung des sexuellen Triebes im Islam, a.a.O. (Fn. 4), S. 1152.

The Human Rights Dilemma in Egypt: Political Will or Islam?

Bahey eldin Hassan, Cairo

A. Introduction

Egypt has lived under an authoritarian political regime for several decades, whose roots date back to the revolution of 23 July 1952, when a group of army officers (who came to be called the *Free Officers*), the so-called *ḥarakat aḍ-ḍubbāṭ al-ʾaḥrār,* overthrew the quasi-liberal monarchy that had ruled Egypt since the 1919 revolution. Using popular nationalist slogans demanding full independence, the evacuation of the British occupying forces from the Suez Canal and the reclamation of Palestine after the establishment of the State Israel in May 1948, the *Free Officers* proceeded to erect an autocracy based on individual rule.[1] The revolution cast aside the liberal constitution of 1923, rejected the proposed 1954 liberal constitution written by a panel formed by the *Free Officers* themselves[2] and went on to eventually draft another constitution in 1956 to legitimize the new regime. The new regime banned political parties, restricted professional syndicates, and brought labour unions under complete control after executing two labour leaders in the first year of the revolution. It moreover brought the media under its complete control, ultimately nationalizing the press in 1961. It placed tight restrictions on non-governmental organisations (NGOs) until in 1964 a law was issued that officially brought NGOs under government control. During this time, the regime placed severe pressure on the judiciary and judges, who draw on a liberal legacy grounded in Egyptian legal thought. The regime introduced arbitrary changes to the judicial system and established a parallel legal system of exceptional military and quasi-military courts to prosecute its political opponents. The pressure came to a head in 1954 and 1968, in two incidents known as "the massacre of the judiciary" (*maḏbaḥat al-qaḍāʾ*), when many judges who had rejected political interference in the judiciary were dismissed. Academic freedom was also a victim of the July regime, which fired university professors it considered to be its intellectual opponents and imposed police censorship over university curricula.

Groups of the right political spectrum such as the Muslim Brothers (*al-ʾiḫwān al-muslimūn*) and the left spectrum, particularly communists, were targeted for a

---

1 Cp. *Linda D. Lau,* "Historical Setting", in: *Richard F. Nyrob* (Editor), Egypt: a Country Study, Washington D.C. 1983, on pp. 25 et seqq.

2 For a full copy of the proposed 1954 constitution and a complete analysis thereof, see *Ṣalāh ʿĪsā,* dustūr fī ṣundūq al-qumāma, Cairo Institute for Human Rights Studies: Cairo 2001, pp. 149-187.

Islam und Menschenrechte (Islam and Human Rights / (الإسلام وحقوق الإنسان)
Hatem Elliesie (Hrsg./Editor), © Peter Lang Verlag: Frankfurt a.M. 2010, S. 281-298

special share of repression. They faced campaigns of mass arrest and were jailed for years, without trial, in both military and non-military prisons. During their confinement they were subjected to the worst kinds of torture, which was not prevalent before July 1952, and many of the detainees died as a result. The vast majority of them were not brought before a court. Of those who were prosecuted, some were sentenced to death in trials that did not meet the minimum standards of fairness.

The massive military defeat of Egypt by the Israeli army in June 1967 had a tremendous impact on the cohesion of the regime, which had based its political legitimacy on its confrontation with the *West* and Israel; the army, the foundation of its authority and its tool of repression, was defeated. Protests were seen in the street for the first time since 1954, having hitherto been confined to allegorical literary works.

From 1968 to 1975, the student movement became the engine of protest and democratic aspirations, and it helped shake the pillars of the autocracy, especially that demonstrations in 1968, 1972, and 1975 were met with widespread popular support. With the death of Ǧamāl ʿAbd el-Nāṣir, the pivotal figure in the July regime, the leader of the revolution, and the President of the Republic in September of 1970, the July regime started weaken and was further enfeebled by the eruption of a power struggle within the ruling elite. Although the Sādāt regime led the country to victory in the October 1973 war, which restored Egyptians' esteem after the terrible defeat of 1967, it soon became clear that the withdrawal of Israeli occupation troops – that is, the removal of the effects of the aggression, in Nasserist political terminology – did not necessarily treat the political trauma of the defeat. This led the new ruler, Anwar el-Sādāt, to institute a limited degree of political pluralism. He allowed the establishment of three parties, one of them the *ḥizb miṣr al-ʿarabī al-ištirākī*, while *ḥizb at-taǧammuʿ al-waṭanī at-taqaddumī al-waḥdawī* and *ḥizb al-ʾaḥrār al-ištirākīyīn,* the two other parties (one on the right and one on the left political spectrum), were to play the role of handmaid. A fourth party, *ḥizb al-ʿamal al-ištirākī,* was later approved and the courts licensed a fifth party, the *Wafd* party, which had existed before the 1952 Revolution.

Each opposition party began to issue its own newspaper and certain professional syndicates were imbued with a new vigour, most importantly the Lawyers' Syndicate (*niqābat al-muḥāmīn*), which was transformed into another pulpit for the opposition.[3] Egyptian Human Rights organizations were established and a new, less autocratic constitution replaced the July constitution. Torture of political

---

[3] Cp. *Richard Hrair Dekmejian,* "Government and Politics", in: *Richard F. Nyrob* (Editor), Egypt: a Country Study, Washington D.C. 1983, on p. 205.

opponents declined, both quantitatively and qualitatively; after having evolved into a routine, systematic practice in Ǧamāl ʿAbd el-Nāṣir's age, torture in this era was reduced to ill-treatment.

The objective was to restore the legitimacy of the political regime after 1967, but the few cracks that were opened were enough to let in political winds that had been gathering for two decades. The force of these repressed political tendencies drew extra momentum from the huge vacuum resulting from the collapse of the July regime's political legitimacy, which was destroyed by the Israeli army in just a few days.

The logic of armed violence soon found its way in as well, at the hands of Islamist groups. 1978 Nobel Peace Prize Laureate Anwar el-Sādāt paid the price with his assassination on 6 October 1981, while celebrating the anniversary of Egypt's victory over Israel. The bullets that killed him literally carried several messages, the most significant being that the 1973 victory did not erase the political effects of the 1967 defeat. The regime that was defeated in 1967 could not regain its political legitimacy through victory in another war or by haphazardly seeking to mend its tattered legitimacy. Rather, what was needed was the establishment of an entirely new system of political legitimacy. This is what Egypt's former President Anwar el-Sādāt did not realize and it is what President Ḥusnī Mubārak has fiercely resisted since assuming power after Sādāt's assassination.

The resistance to democratization did not begin by President Ḥusnī Mubārak, but rather about four years before Sādāt's assassination, when he gradually began to retreat from the political liberalization he had initiated by launching an assault – using legislative, security, administrative, and media means – on the very forces he had helped unleash. The food riots of 1977 were followed by exceptional legislation, arrest campaigns targeting political activists, the confiscation of the leftist *al-Ahālī*, the most active of the partisan newspapers, and the dismissal of oppositional members of parliament (MPs) from parliament. Direct support was also given to political Islamist forces as a means of countering the left political spectrum, and this included support for physical attacks on leftist activists inside universities. President Anwar el-Sādāt then amended the constitution. On one hand, he granted a great concession to Islamists by making the principles of Islamic law *the* main source of legislation (*mabādiʾ aš-šarīʿa al-ʾislāmīa al-maṣdar ar-raʾīsī*) as opposed to simply one source among others / *a* source (*"maṣdar raʾīsī"*), while on the other hand he removed the two-term limit on the presidency. This seemed to be a mutually beneficial deal: Anwar el-Sādāt endowed the Islamist project with strategic political legitimacy in exchange for remaining president for life.[4] But the Islamists abrogated the agreement a year later and assassinated him, and the Islamist strategic project continued on its path of strength.

President Ḥusnī Mubārak did not inaugurate his tenure with repression. In fact, he began his rule with measures to allow the venting of political pressures that had built up in the final years of Anwar el-Sādāt's rule. He released hundreds of opposition figures who were arrested by Anwar el-Sādāt a few months before his assassination and widened the margin of action given to opposition parties and their newspapers by relieving certain political pressures. It was during this period, in 1985, that the *al-munaẓẓma al-miṣrīa al-ḥuqūq al-'insān* (Egyptian Organization for Human Rights – EOHR) was established,[5] after three other organizations (*al-ǧam'īya al-miṣrīya li-ḥuqūq al-'insān, ǧam'īyat 'anṣār ḥuqūq al-'insān* [in Cairo] and *ǧam'īyat 'anṣār ḥuqūq al-'insān* [in Alexandria]) were founded during Anwar el-Sādāt's rule had died or foundered. Other associations followed in the wake of the EOHR.

Professional syndicates grew increasingly active although the influence of the Muslim Brothers (*al-'iḫwān al-muslimūn*) in them also grew, until the group had assumed control of most syndicates by the late 1980s. At the same time, the terrorist violence that had begun with Anwar el-Sādāt's assassination expanded into a wider social confrontation, particularly after all limits on the security establishment's engagement with terrorism were lifted, which brought in the use of assassination and fatal torture.

The second moment of political openness in the Mubārak era was seen in 2004-2005, and it came in response to intense international pressure to engage in political reform. The right to demonstrate freely was allowed on several occasions, independent political newspapers were established, and activist political groups without legal licenses were formed, *Kifāya* group being the most prominent one. A constitutional amendment was passed replacing the presidential referendum with a system of multi-candidate elections. Nevertheless, the change was largely symbolic given the many restrictions it contained; in effect the ruling party chooses presidential candidates, a system similar to that which has existed in Tunisia for a long time.

---

4 Cp. in this particular context *Richard Hrair Dekmejian*, "Government and Politics", in: *Richard F. Nyrob* (Editor), Egypt..., supra, footnote 3, on p. 206; *Clark B. Lombardi*, State Law as Islamic Law in modern Egypt: The Incorporation of Sharī'a into Egyptian Constitutional Law, Leiden / Bosten 2006, pp. 123-135.

5 See *Tamir Moustafa*, The Struggle for Constitutional Power: Law, Politics, and economic Development in Egypt, Cambridge / New York 2007, on p. 114.

With the exception of these two periods, Ḥusnī Mubārak's rule has been characterized by widespread repression carried out using diverse tools, including the constitution, the law, the security apparatus, the media, the official religious establishment, military tribunals, and exceptional and non-exceptional courts. A state of emergency has been in effect throughout Ḥusnī Mubārak's rule (28 years), and the use of torture, against both political opponents and in non-political cases, has expanded, as has the use of brutal violence to repress social and political protest. The role of the internal security apparatus has ballooned, and it is now the primary prop in the management of the country's daily affairs, in contrast to the Ǧamāl ʿAbd el-Nāṣir era, when military intelligence was the main tool of repression.

B. Sources and Causes of the poor Human Rights Record

The exceptional rise of the security apparatus in the administration of rule is one of the most significant outcomes of the July revolution. Egypt's transformation from a monarchy to a republic after the revolution was accompanied by another, more important, transformation: the elimination of the relative independence of the legislative and judicial branches under the hegemony of the executive and the concomitant transformation into a system of one-man rule. Under the republican system of the July regime, the president did and continues to enjoy more monarchical authority than the king did under the monarchy "overthrown" by the July revolution. In light of this, it is no wonder that the current president seeks to pass on rule to his son. It may be incompatible with a republican system, but it is quite consistent with the monarchical nature of the republican system in Egypt.

The July revolution did not only overturn the liberal constitution of 1923; subsequent constitutions entrenched the hegemony of the executive over the legislative and judicial branches of government. The president enjoys absolute authority and is unaccountable to any party. This central fact has not changed, despite the number of constitutions in effect since the July revolution and the many amendments introduced to them.

I. Structural Flaw in the Edifice of Governance

This structural flaw in the edifice of governance since July 1952 is not only the ***primary source*** of assaults on Human Rights but also the source of unaccountability for Human Rights violators, a direct result of the marginalization of the legislature and the judiciary.

II. The Emergency Law

The ***second source*** of Human Rights violations in Egypt is the Emergency Law *(qānūn aṭ-ṭawāriʾ)*, in effect virtually uninterrupted since the July revolution, including the last 28 years.[6] The Emergency Law gives the security apparatus exceptional prerogatives to arrest, detain, search, and restrict public liberties, particularly the freedom of expression and freedom of assembly. The law allows for referrals to exceptional courts (emergency courts – *maḥākim aṭ-ṭawāri'*), and the military ruler (i.e., the President of the Republic or his designate) can refer civilians to military courts (*al-maḥākim al-ʿaskarīa*), which are exceptional courts that do not meet the minimum standards for fairness. The judges in such trials are in fact officers who have no independence but are rather subordinate to the top-down authority structure of the military establishment.

The ongoing state of emergency in Egypt has led UN experts to believe that Emergency Law is in fact Egypt's *de facto* constitution.[7] Under the state of emergency, this apparatus [the police] has come to possess responsibilities and functions that extend far beyond the assignment of security and rule of law as it is traditionally defined.[8] Its roles and functions in every area of social life (political, economic, trade union, etc.) have redoubled its power and deeply entrenched it in society. This development has given the police apparatus authority and prerogatives unprecedented in Egypt's modern history.[9]

III. Relationship between the Constitution and Legislation

A ***third source*** for Human Rights violations is the perverted relationship between the constitution and legislation. Legal theory views the constitution as the "father of laws" (*"'abū al-qawānīn"*) – that is, laws that draw on the constitution and do not deviate from it. But the opposite is true in Egypt, particularly in the area of public liberties and Human Rights, where the power of the law stands above the principles of the constitution.

6 From the beginning of the 20th Century until the July 1952 Revolution, the emergency law was in effect for 16 years, including for 14 years during the First and Second World Wars; since the revolution, the emergency law has been in effect for 52 of the intervening 57 years.

7 *Waǧhan li-waǧh: radd al-munaẓẓama al-Miṣrīya li-ḥuqūq al-'insān ʿalà taqrīr al-ḥukūma lil-'umam al-muttaḥida*, Arab Civilization Center for Media and Publication, Cairo 1993.

8 Correspondence between the National Council for Human Rights (*al-maǧlis al-qawmī li-ḥuqūq al-'insān*) and the the Ministry of Justice (*wizārat al-ʿadl*), the Office of the State Prosecutor (*maktab an-nā'ib al-ʿāmm*), the Ministry of Interior (*wizārat ad-dāḫilīa*) indicates that the Interior Ministry enjoys a veto over the Ministry of Justice and State Prosecutor's ability to supply information about their investigations into torture, disappearances and detainees. *See* the National Council for Human Rights' 2004 annual report, on p. 212 and p. 239.

9 *Muḥammad as-Sayyid Saʿīd,* "ḥuqūq al-'insān wa muškilat al-ḥadāṯa wal-taḥdīṯ fī Miṣr: naẓra ʿāmma li-masār ḥuqūq al-'insān", in: Center for Human Rights and Legal Information Studies (Editor), ḥuqūq al-'insān wa ta'aḫḫur Miṣr, Cairo 1993, on p. 134.

The 1971 constitution drafted in the beginning of President Anwar el-Sādāt's term was the best of the July regime's constitutions, particularly in its third section dealing with civil rights and public liberties. Yet, many of the articles in this section which uphold fine principles and the exercise of rights are undermined by related laws which erode or restrict the rights guaranteed by the constitution. Hence, the majority of laws related to liberties violate to varying degrees the spirit of the constitution and Human Rights standards, and even when they are amended, these articles tend to become more rather than less restrictive.

IV. Independence of the Judiciary

The ***fourth source*** of Human Rights violations is the executive authority's systematic assault on the independence of the judiciary, which began in the first weeks of the July revolution. These encroachments include the establishment of parallel, exceptional courts (*al-maḥākim al-istiṯnā'īya*), control over the Office of the Public Prosecutor (*maktab an-nā'ib al-ʿāmm*), daily government interference in the affairs of the judiciary (including politicization), a lack of respect for court rulings, particularly those that contradict the executive's wishes, and a refusal to implement court rulings or attempts to circumvent them by semi-legal means or security methods.[10] This state of affairs has weakened legal accountability for Human Rights violations and, in turn, indirectly encouraged violations by removing legal deterrents.

V. Parliament's oversight Role

A ***fifth source*** of Human Rights violations is the pruning of parliament's oversight role. The parliament cannot hold the head of the executive authority (the president) to account, but is rather a tool for granting him additional, absolute prerogatives that contain no checks to evaluate the exercise of these prerogatives. The parliament cannot engage in any serious oversight of the president's functionaries (ministers or the prime minister), but the president can dissolve parliament, and the executive has the tools (whether legal or illegal, administrative or security-related) that enable it to dominate the election of MPs, ensuring that opposition MPs never have more than an ineffectual third of all parliamentary seats. In terms of legislation, the parliament is simply the executor of the executive's will, passing legislation for the public eye that has already been cooked up in the government "kitchen".

10 See *Nāgad al-Burʿaī,* al-ʿadāla al-muḥtaqara: ʿadam tanfīḏ al-ḥukūma li-ʾaḥkām al-qaḍāʾ: al-dawāfiʿ wa-l-natāʾiğ, in: Cairo Institute for Human Rights Studies (Editor), al-quḍāh wal-ʾiṣlāḥ al-siyāsī, Cairo 2006, pp. 219-247.

VI. Weakness of Civil Society

The ***sixth source*** of Human Rights violations is the weakness of civil society. In the first months after the July revolution, Egyptian society was stripped of all its "weapons": political parties were banned, and trade unions, NGOs, and freedom of expression, especially the press, were restricted, the press ultimately nationalized in 1961. Positive developments in the Sādāt era were limited, and civil society regularly came under constitutional, legislative, and security assault, which does not permit to develop healthily and liberate civil society's energies.

VII. Adoption of a Security Credo

The ***seventh source*** of Human Rights violations is the July revolution's adoption of a security credo based on suspicion and doubt, and not merely of the political other, but the religious other (Christian, Jewish, Bahā'ī, non-Sunni Muslim), the ethnic other (Nubian), or even citizens in border zones who may be Sunni Arab Muslims, such as the residents of the Sinai peninsula. The adoption of such a security credo inevitably leads to the erosion of citizenship rights to varying degrees and by various methods.

VIII. Hegemony of religious Discourse

The **eighth source** of Human Rights violations is the hegemony of a religious discourse that consecrates interpretations of Islam that are inconsistent with Human Rights, including prescriptions of absolute obedience to the ruler. This discourse is adopted by the official state religious establishment, al-Azhar and Dār al-'Iftā', and the government supports it in the face of alternative discourses or academic interpretations open to Human Rights principles. Indeed, the state considers some of these interpretations to be inimical to Islam. This discourse also receives the support of Salafīsts and political Islamist groups.

IX. Political Will

Finally, if the political will of the ruling regime is the overriding factor in the first seven sources of Human Rights violations, it is a full partner in the eighth. In addition, the lack of political will for reform is reflected in the institution established by the state to strengthen Human Rights, the National Council of Human Rights. With the exception of the council's first annual report, none of the council's later reports adequately monitor the deteriorating Human Rights situation in Egypt. Indeed, the council's main mission has gradually come to be responding to international reports that criticize the Human Rights record in Egypt and attempting to provide cover for the government with foreign diplomats and international organizations and agencies.[11]

---

[11] A 2005 study of the National Council for Human Rights proceedings found that in 2004, the council held ten meetings with state officials, most of whom had no influence over po-

C. The Main Patterns of Civil and Political Human Rights Violations

Systematic Human Rights violations in Egypt help secure the continuity of the July regime – that is, they serve to further entrench individual rule, the hegemony of the executive authority, and the lack of independence for the legislative and judicial authorities, and they keep civil society weak and unable to change these political formula or positively affect them. At the same time, the regime uses legislative tools and constitutional amendments to renew the legal legitimacy of these central parameters in the midst of changing circumstances, restricting the space of action for opponents who wish to alter or develop these parameters and keeping political critique in and out of the parliament below the threshold that encourages broader public participation. When legislative tools and the media fail, the repression of opponents is left to the security establishment; opponents' freedom is curtailed behind prison walls and they are disciplined by various means, including unrestricted torture. The regular or exceptional courts may also be used to punish opponents, either by controlling the judicial process at the source – if it is a military court – or by trumping up charges or intervening to appoint "trusted" judges. "The authorities intend to respect Human Rights on one condition: that it does not threaten the stability of the authorities. This does not necessarily mean political stability, but rather the stability of power in the hands of a particular group of citizens who have linked their interests, in one way or another, to the existing system of rule embodied by the National Democratic Party (*al-ḥizb al-waṭanī ad-dīmuqrāṭī*). Thus, they allow citizens to exercise these rights when they represent no real threat to this group's survival in power; it is this group that renews the Emergency Law to guarantee the stability of their power."[12]

This does not mean that victims of Human Rights abuses are limited to actual or potential political enemies, for many regular citizens have been victimized as well. For example, criminal suspects, detainees, and wanted figures, and sometimes even their families, have been tortured with the objective of extracting confessions or sometimes without any clear justification at all,[13] but simply as a

---

litical decision-making; at the same time, the council board had 111 meetings with delegations from international agencies and foreign embassies. This illustrates where the council's efforts are largely focused. See generally *Bahey eldin Hassan,* wa māḏā law lam yakun mawǧūdan? ḥiṣād al-maǧlis al-qawmī li-ḥuqūq al-'insān fī ṯalāṯ sanawāt, http://www.cihrs.org/Arabic/NewsSystem/Articles/578 (accessed on 17 May 2009).

12 *Muṣṭafā Kāmil as-Sayyid,* "wāqiʿ ḥuqūq al-'insān fī Miṣr bayn mas'ūlīyat al-dawla wa dawr al-muǧtamaʿ", in: Center for Human Rights and Legal Information and Studies (Editor), ḥuqūq al-'insān wa ta'aḫḫur Miṣr, Cairo 1993, on p. 115.

13 There are dozens of reports that confirm this conclusion, the most recent report was published by the Egyptian Organization for Human Rights (EOHR) entitled "When will the crime of Torture come to an End in Egypt?", 11 March 2009.

consequence of the unchecked power of an unaccountable security apparatus that enjoys a growing political role and whose members are increasingly counted among the governing elite.

Since December 2005, the Egyptian state has launched a broad counter-offensive on public liberties using all the tools as diverse as constitutional and legislative amendments, administrative interference, security repression, and the character assassination of advocates of political reform and Human Rights in the state-owned media.[14]

The offensive comes in response to the unprecedented political ferment seen in 2004 and 2005 and growing American and European pressure on Egypt and other Arab governments to engage in political and cultural reform as part of the global war on terror declared after the 9/11 attacks.[15]

The counter-offensive was launched just as international pressure for reform was beginning to recede, after the US project in Iraq was set back, the Muslim Brothers (*'iḫwān al-muslimūn*) in Egypt won 20 percent of the seats in parliament in December 2005, and Ḥamās in Palestine won a parliamentary majority in January 2006 and formed a new government.[16]

Targets of the counter-offensive widened to include regional and international organizations. Having decided that offence is the best defence, the Egyptian government has moved its defensive lines to Brussels and Geneva, where it is engaged in systematic efforts to weaken regional and international mechanisms that support the role of civil society in protecting Human Rights on both the national and international levels. Its efforts are aided by Egypt's position as the co-president of the Mediterranean Union and the head of the African group in the

---

14 See generally *Bahey eldin Hassan,* "ḥarb 'ahlīya siyāsīya", in: Cairo Institute for Human Rights Studies (Editor), waṭan bilā muwāṭinīn: al-ta'dīlāt al-dustūrīya fi-l-mīzān, Cairo 2007.

15 Ibidem.

16 See also *Cairo Institute for Human Rights Studies,* "From Exporting Terrorism to Exporting Repression", Human Rights in the Arab Region, Annual Report 2008, Cairo 2009, pp. 57-65 et seqq., http://www.cihrs.org/Images/ArticleFiles/Original/382.pdf (accessed on 17 May 2009). Cp. in this context, for an evaluation and future prospects of the latest developments in Palestine, particularly with regard to the Ḥamās and Fataḥ (also referring to the 'iḫwān al-muslimūn in Egypt), *Hatem Elliesie / Naseef Naeem,* Gemeinsames Dach: Der Staatenbund – eine denkbare Lösung für den Nahen Osten, Frankfurter Allgemeine Zeitung (FAZ), 12 February, Frankfurt a.M. 2009, on p. 10; *idem,* Im Namen des Staatsrechts: Staatenbund als denkbares Lösungskonzept für den Nahost-Konflikt, in: *Hatem Elliesie / Alexander Gramsch* (Editorship / Schriftleitung), GAIR-Mitteilungen 2009/1, Berlin 2009, on pp. 34-35, http://www.gair.uni-erlangen.de/GAIR-Mitteilungen%2001-2009.pdf (accessed on 3 September 2009).

UN Human Rights Council, as well as its influential leadership within the Arab League and the Organization of the Islamic Conference.[17] As such, it is playing a major role in creating an international alliance of "global authoritarianism," which dominates the decision-making process in the Human Rights Council and has had grave repercussions that do not bode well for the future of the council.[18]

D. Indicators for Egypt's deteriorating Human Rights Situation

There is a consensus in reports from local and international human rights organizations that the Human Rights situation in Egypt is deteriorating, a sentiment echoed in the most recent report on Human Rights from the US State Department.[19]

The most prominent indicators of the worsening situation are as follows:

I. The Constitution and Human Rights

Historically speaking, the most recent constitutional amendments (March 2007) were the worst constitutional setback in Egypt's modern history, or at least since the July revolution overturned the constitution of the liberal era. On the pretext of combating terrorism, the latest amendments suspended several of the best provisions on liberties and human rights in the 1971 constitution.[20]

Using these amendments, the government is seeking to pass more legislation that restricts Human Rights, including an Anti-Terrorism Bill, a bill to regulate media broadcasting, and changes to the NGO law that will strengthen the state's hegemony over institutions of civil society, particularly advocacy non governamental organizations (NGOs).[21]

II. State of Emergency and the Right to a Fair Trial

The government's promise to lift the Emergency Law, in place since 1981, has evaporated, although there is no longer any justification for its application. At

---

17 Cp. *Theodor Rathgeber,* "Die Organisation Islamischer Konferenz im UN-Menschenrechtsrat: Menschenrechte als Instrument staatlicher Politik", in: *Hatem Elliesie* (Hrsg./Editor), Beiträge zum Islamischen Recht VII, Islam und Menschenrechte (Islam and Human Rights / الإسلام وحقوق الإنسان), Frankfurt a.M. 2010, pp. 457-473.

18 For more information, see generally *Cairo Institute for Human Rights Studies,* "From Exporting Terrorism to Exporting Repression"..., supra, footnote 16, Chapter 2, on pp. 96 et seqq.

19 *US Department of State, Bureau of Democracy, Human Rights and Labor,* 2008 Human Rights Report: Egypt, 25 February, Washington D.C. 2009, http://www.state.gov/g/drl/rls/hrrpt/2008/nea/119114.htm (accessed on 17 May 2009).

20 *Bahey eldin Hassan,* ḥarb ʾahlīya siyāsīya, supra, footnote 14, on p. 13.

21 *Cairo Institute for Human Rights Studies,* "From Exporting Terrorism to Exporting Repression"..., supra, footnote 16.

this point, the policy of extending the state of emergency is a routine matter undertaken automatically when the law expires. In May 2008, the parliament agreed to the government's request to extend the state of emergency for another two years, on the grounds that it had not yet finished writing the Anti-Terrorism Bill (*qānūn mukāfaḥat al-ʾirhāb*). The state of emergency has gone beyond the letter of the Emergency Law; indeed, it has had a negative impact on the spirit of the Egyptian legislature, which has tended to disregard several rights and freedoms guaranteed by the Egyptian constitution and international human rights conventions by granting such broad authority to the security apparatus.[22] There are still 4,000-5,000 political detainees held under the Emergency Law without charge, among them 250 members of the Muslim Brothers.[23]

In point of fact, the Anti-Terrorism Bill will preserve most of the exceptional prerogatives enjoyed by the president and the security apparatus under Emergency Law. The government is always quick to comment that it will only use these prerogatives to combat terrorism – the same thing was stated about Emergency Law – but a review of the many cases in which the government has applied the Emergency Law show otherwise. Emergency Law was used against participants in the April 2008 strike and civilians have been referred to military courts, most recently 40 leaders of the Muslim Brothers; also using the Emergency Law, the president ordered a retrial of 26 farmers from the village of *Sarāndū* who had exercised their right to peaceful protest, after they were already acquitted by a High State Security (emergency) Court (*maḥākim amn ad-dawla al-ʿulyā*). It is worth noting that the Emergency Law was broadly used from 2005 to 2008 against bloggers and activists with social protest movements, some of whom were referred to State Security Courts, emergency division (*maḥākim amn ad-dawla, ṭawāriʾ)*, although they were not charged with terrorism-related offences.

Moreover, it is worth pointing out that Egypt already has an Anti-Terrorism Law, Law 97/1992, which has also been used against non-terrorist suspects. The EOHR found that in 2007, 194 citizens were questioned by the State Security Prosecutor (*an-nāʾib al-ʿāmm al-maḥkamat ʾamn ad-dawla*) in connection with 30 separate cases, 16 of which were referred to the State Security Prosecutor from summary prosecutors.[24]

---

22 *Egyptian Organization of Human Rights*, The Human Rights Situation in Egypt, 2007 Annual Report, Cairo 2008, p. 8 et seq.

23 *US Department of State, Bureau of Democracy, Human Rights and Labor,* 2008 Human Rights Report: Egypt, supra, footnote 19.

24 *Egyptian Organization of Human Rights*, The Human Rights Situation in Egypt..., supra, footnote 22.

III. Systematic torture

UN reports on torture in Egypt describe the practice of torture as routine and systematic, which is also confirmed by reports from international and Egyptian Human Rights organizations. Torture targets in particular political opponents and those suspected of involvement in terrorism, but an increasing number of non-political citizens are being tortured for various reasons. The common element in all these cases is the lack of any serious accountability for torturers, especially if the torturer is a state security officer involved in a political case or some issue of religious freedom. Reports from local and international Human Rights groups agree that the worst forms of torture are used in Egypt, including hanging in complex positions to induce temporary or permanent paralysis of certain parts of the body, electroshocks, sexual harassments, and threats of rape.

Between 2000 and 2007, the EOHR documented 266 instances of torture, 40 of them in 2007, up ten cases from 2006. Torture has been extended to the families of suspects as well.[25] Of course, statistics do not cover all cases of torture in Egypt, but only those that have been reported and documented. Even so, from 1993 to 2008,[26] the EOHR documented 167 deaths due to torture, an average of about ten deaths a year. A report from the *markaz an-Nadīm li-tā'hīl ḍaḥāyā al-'unf* (Nadim Center for the Rehabilitation of Victims of Violence) documented 32 deaths due to torture from June 2007 to March 2008. CIHRs' Annual Report found that torture and harsh treatment had been meted out to those suspected of carrying the AIDS virus, in an effort to force them to sign statements affirming that they had engaged in homosexual behavior. The authorities have been forced to bring some police officers who have tortured citizens to court, particularly in cases of crimes that were widely reported in the press, thanks to some bloggers who were able to obtain documentary evidence of the crimes.[27]

It is also worth noting that Egypt has cooperated with the CIA in its secret prisons program. By the admission of the Egyptian prime minister, Egypt received some 70 detainees brought in on CIA planes for interrogation and the extraction of confessions under torture.

IV. Freedom of expression and the media

With the exception of permission granted for the issuance of new private newspapers, freedom of opinion and expression and press freedoms did not

---

[25] Ibidem.

[26] *Egyptian Organization for Human Rights,* When will the Crime of Torture come to an End in Egypt?, 11 March 2009.

[27] *US Department of State, Bureau of Democracy, Human Rights and Labor,* 2008 Human Rights Report: Egypt, supra, footnote 19.

substantially expand in 2007 or 2008, but were circumscribed even further.[28] According to a report from the EOHR, the Office of the Public Prosecutor sent the Journalists' Syndicate (*niqābat aṣ-ṣaḥafīyīn*) some 1,000 notices for journalists to appear before questioning authorities, while from 2000 to 2007, there were 27 cases.[29]

The CIHRS report noted that in August 2008, there were 47 cases before Egyptian courts involving journalists, with 40 journalists as defendants in the cases. The most prominent case was the two-month sentence handed down to Ibrāhīm ʿĪsā, the editor-in-chief of the independent newspaper ad-Dustūr, who was convicted of publishing false information about the president's health and thereby upsetting the public order and harming the public interest. (ʿĪsā was given a presidential pardon after his conviction and sentencing.) Well-known sociologist Dr. Saʿd ed-Dīn Ibrāhīm was also sentenced to two years in prison in absentia, with a bail of LE 10,000 set to contest the sentence, after he was convicted on charges of impugning Egypt's reputation and harming the national interest.[30] In addition, the Public Prosecutor issued gag orders in several cases, and seven journalists were questioned for violating the orders.

In 2007 and 2008, bloggers became a major target of political repression, and some were detained under the Emergency Law and tortured. *Reporters Sans Frontieres* (RSF) put Egypt on its list of the 12 worst "enemies of the internet" in the world.[31]

Satellite broadcasting was a field for a whole slew of irregular violations. Three satellite channels were shut down – al-Ḥiwār, al-Ḥikma, and al-Baraka – and the security apparatus raided the offices of the Cairo company, which handles support services for satellite broadcasting, and confiscated some of the company's equipment. In January 2008, authorities arrested Huwīdā Ṭāha, a director and editor with al-Jazeera, along with her crew, while filming a documentary about migratory laborers, farmers, other marginalized workers, even though she had obtained the necessary permits from the competent authorities. *Al-maḥkama al-ʾidāriyya* (Administrative Court) in Cairo also

28 According to the Committee to Protect Journalists, Egypt is considered to be one of the top 10 countries in which the level of freedom of expression has decreased tremendously thus raising serious concerns.

29 *Egyptian Organization of Human Rights*, The Human Rights Situation in Egypt..., supra, footnote 22.

30 For more details see *Tamir Moustafa,* The Struggle for Constitutional Power…, supra, footnote 5, pp. 202-205.

31 *Reporters Sans Frontieres, Bureau "Internet et Libertés",* Les Ennemis d'Internet, 12 March, Paris 2009, http://www.rsf.org/IMG/pdf/Les_ennemis_Internet_2009_2_-3.pdf (ac-cessed on 17 May 2009).

overturned the minister of culture's decree granting poet Ḥilmī Sālīm the state award for literary excellence, following a petition filed by a member of the Supreme Council for Islamic Affairs[32] who said that the poet had defamed the divinity in one of his poems, published in the journal *ʾIbdāʿ* in the winter of 2007; the journal was withdrawn from the market as soon as it was issued.[33]

V. Civil society and Human Rights NGOs

Advocates of political reform and Human Rights are subjected to various forms of attack and in recent years have topped the list of political targets. The assaults include the tapping of phone and electronic communications, police surveillance, bans on certain meetings and seminars, bans related to the participation in international conferences, libel and character assassination in the government-controlled visual and written media, trials (on charges of harming Egypt's reputation or providing information that damages Egypt's international standing), arrest under the provisions of Emergency Law, and violent physical assault.[34] In addition, particularly active associations may be dissolved by administrative decree, as was the case with the Human Rights Association for Legal Aid (*ǧamʿīat al-musāʿada al-qānūnīa li-ḥuqūq al-ʾinsān*) and the Center for Trade Union and Worker Services (*dār al-ḫadamāt an-niqābīa wa-al-ʿummālīa*). Although the judiciary has ruled in favor of the former organization, the government continues to refuse to implement the ruling issued in October 2008.

At the same time, the Ministry of Social Solidarity (*wizārat al-taḍāmun al-igtimāʿī*) delayed compliance with a ruling handed down by the Administrative Court on 30 March 2008, that required the ministry to confer legal status on the Center for Trade Union and Worker Services, which won the French Republic's Human Rights Award. The organization was only given a registration number on 30 June 2008, after the French intervened with the Egyptian authorities. The ministry had issued an order in August 2007 closing the group based on objections from the security apparatus, which was in itself an official admission of the security establishment's interference in civil society; such interference is not even covered under existing law.[35]

---

32 A governmental institution entitled: المجلس الأعلى للشئون الإسلامية.

33 *Cairo Institute for Human Rights Studies,* "From Exporting Terrorism to Exporting Repression"..., supra, footnote 16.

34 For more details, see: *Amnesty International*, Challenging Repression: Human Rights Defenders in the Middle East and North Africa, London 2009, http://www.amnesty.org/en/library/asset/MDE01/001/2009/en/3fe5c240-d77d-4e15-8957-5928387d1093/mde010012009eng.pdf (accessed on 11 May 2009).

35 *Cairo Institute for Human Rights Studies,* "From Exporting Terrorism to Exporting Repression"..., supra, footnote 16, pp. 93-105.

VI. Freedom of belief and minority rights

Pressures on religious freedoms are not limited to those belonging to faiths and religions that are not officially recognized, for they at times extend even to members of the Islamic faith, which is the official state religion. In May 2007 state security police arrested five "Quranists"[36] on the grounds that they denied the *sunna*. They were detained on charges of deriding religion until the High State Security Prosecutor ordered their release in late September pending a trial. Reports from rights groups in November 2007 documented more than 200 cases in which citizens went to court to contest the policy of the Interior Ministry's Civil Status Office (*maṣlaḥat al-ʾaḥwāl al-madanīya bi-wizārat al-dāḫilīya*), which considers them Muslims on official records although they belong to other religions. On 9 February 2008, the High Administrative Court (*maḥkama al-ʾidāriyya al-ʿulyā*) ruled in favor of 12 citizens who re-converted to Christianity after converting to Islam; the court ordered the competent authorities to note their Christian affiliation on their identity cards. Nevertheless, the court also ruled that their previous conversion to Islam and return to Christianity should also be noted on their identity cards, which may provide the grounds for discrimination against the converts. In addition, Egyptian Bahāʾīs still face difficulties even after the Administrative Court ruled in January 2008 that they have the right to obtain birth certificates and identity cards without any mention of their religious affiliation. The ruling has still not been implemented.[37]

VII. Religion and Human Rights

Increasingly, religion has been used in the assault on Human Rights, particularly against freedom of expression and literary and artistic expression, in addition to freedom of religion itself.

The abolition of political parties in Egypt after the July 1952 Revolution and the subsequent concerted effort to uproot politics from the public sphere and limit it to the problem of managing the confrontation with the *West* and Israel had the consequence of increasing Egyptians' identification with their religious identity. The resounding defeat in June 1967 played a decisive role in deepening this tendency, which later began to assume political expression. These developments helped strengthen the role of *al-Azhar*, the official religious establishment, particularly after the July regime began to seek its "blessing" to shore up its tattered legitimacy. Thus, the religious establishment began to play a larger political role[38] and its "oversight" of freedom of thought and literary expression was

---

36 "Quranists" are sunni muslim believers.

37 *Cairo Institute for Human Rights Studies*, "From Exporting Terrorism to Exporting Repression"..., supra, footnote 16, on pp. 93 et seqq.

38 See *Bahey eldin Hassan*, ḫalf al-ḥiǧāb: dawla dīnīya ʿalà ǧuṯṯat al-ʾiḫwān al-muslimīn, http://www.cihrs.org/Arabic/NewsSystem/Articles/1128 (accessed on 17 May 2009).

strengthened. This role is no longer limited to offering opinions on proposed legislation and the books, television series, and films that are referred to it; the religious establishment now enjoys the right of judicial seizure in inspections carried out in bookstores and exhibits. The centrality of religious identity and the growing role of the religious establishment has put increased pressure on religious freedom.

All of these elements combined – the political decay, the rise of the religious identity and official religious institutions as well as the defeat of 1967 – have in effect created the appropriate atmosphere for the rise of the tide of the political Islam whether as a terrorist or non-terrorist (the Muslim Brotherhood) tide. The constitutional amendment of May 1980, that made *the* principles of Islamic law *al-maṣdar ar-ra'īsī,* the primary source of legislation in Egypt,[39] has only added to the pressure, giving advocates of religious discrimination the strategic pretext needed to rewrite academic curricula and media programming, which has gradually entrenched a contemptuous view of other faiths and religions and their adherents among Egyptian citizens.[40] This, in addition to the lack of equal rights to establish houses of worship, has exacerbated religious discrimination in Egypt and transformed it into a social practice at the grassroots level – a practice which is not entirely free of violence and may bode grave danger.[41]

The picture is undoubtedly bleak, but some rays of light exist in the form of a gradually growing resistance of people that are ready to pay the price. Indeed, the expansion of political repression can be explained by an expansion of resistance that brought new groups and elements to the struggle and created new methods of resistance.

In the 1970s and 1980s, opposition parties and the Lawyers' Syndicate were the two most prominent platforms for resisting authoritarianism. As their role declined in the 1990s, they were replaced by Human Rights organizations, while in recent years, the latter have been eclipsed by social protest movements, the privately owned press, the electronic media (especially bloggers), and new political

39 See *Clark B. Lombardi,* State Law as Islamic Law in modern Egypt..., supra, footnote 4, pp. 11 et seqq.; *Omaia Elwan,* Gesetzgebung und Rechtsprechung, in: *Udo Steinbach / Rüdiger Robert* (Editors), Der Nahe und Mittlere Osten, Opladen 1988, on pp. 237 et seq. For further references cp. *Imen Gallala,* "Religionsfreiheit und islamisch geprägtes Erbrecht: Gesetzliche Regelungen und Rechtsprechungsauslegung im heutigen Ägypten und Tunesien", in: *Hatem Elliesie* (Editor/Hrsg.), Beiträge zum Islamischen Recht VII, Islam und Menschenrechte (Islam and Human Rights / الإسلام وحقوق الإنسان), Frankfurt a.M. 2010, on p. 505 (footnote 27).

40 *Bahey eldin Hassan,* ḫalf al-ḥiǧāb:..., supra, footnote 38.

41 See *Bahey eldin Hassan,* "ṣināʿat al-tamyīz al-dīnī", in: *Muḥammad Munīr Muǧāhid* (Editor), Miṣr lil-Miṣrīyīn, Dar al-Maḥrūsa: Cairo 2009, on p. 144.

groups, although Human Rights groups continue to play a role and there is a greater interest in minority rights.[42] There are also indications that new parties may be formed on the ashes of older opposition parties that have been contained by various methods. As for the Muslim Brothers, they have not been a major element in the resistance to authoritarianism except by dint of their role as a major competitor for power. At the same time, however, they have indirectly acted to support authoritarianism, insofar as their platform does not aim for democratic reform but rather aims for a totalitarian religious state.[43]

42 In 1992, the Egyptian Organization for Human Rights (EOHR) – of which I was the Secretary General at that time – convened a conference to discuss freedom of belief and status of minorities. As a result, it was subjected to harsh criticism. This started inside the conference hall and culminated a month later in the assassination of one of the most significant speakers of the conference, Dr. Farağ Fūdā who had presented groundbreaking research on minorities in Egypt. Two years later, the *Ibn Khaldun Center* attempted to hold a conference on minorities, but had to postpone and transfer it to Cyprus for the same reasons. Not a single day now passes in Egypt without tackling minority issues in symposia, conferences and the press. Some Human Rights NGOs have been established with agendas focusing solely on these issues. Besides, discrimination against different minorities, such as Šīʿites, Bahāʾīs and "Quranite"-Sunnis who oppose the state's Sunni doctrine – Nubians and Sinai Bedouins, have become distinct issues of public opinion. It is noteworthy that the approach to tackling and proposing solutions to minority repression has primarily been rights-based in CIHRS Annual Report: *Cairo Institute for Human Rights Studies,* "From Exporting Terrorism to Exporting Repression"..., supra, footnote 16, on pp. 24 et seq.

43 See *Bahey eldin Hassan,* barnāmağ ḥizb al-ʾiḫwān al-muslimīn fī Miṣr min manẓūr ḥuqūq al-ʾinsān, http://www.cihrs.org/Arabic/NewsSystem/Articles/1452 (accessed on 17 May 2009).

Human Rights and Islam in South East Asia: The Case of Indonesia

Tim Lindsey, Melbourne

A. Introduction

Indonesia's dramatic and far-reaching democratic transition since the fall of Soeharto's authoritarian and repressive 'New Order' in 1998 has seen the emergence of two parallel developments. The rapid adoption of international human rights norms, both through the ratification of international instruments and a wave of domestic regulation, as well through the creation of new institutions, has been accompanied by the passing of regulations at local and national levels seeking to 'Islamise' Indonesia, enforcing the observance of conservative norms inspired by Middle Eastern traditions. In many cases, these directly challenge the new human rights regime, especially in that the 'Islamising' laws often discriminate against vulnerable groups, particularly women and religious minorities. This conflict reflects longstanding disputes regarding the status of Islamic Law within Indonesia's essentially Western-derived legal system that have helped motivate communal violence and terrorism. It seems unlikely, however, that "*Syariahisation*", will succeed in altering the basic structure of the Indonesian state's legal system – and that suggests that, in the long run, the recent reforms introducing international human rights norms will likely survive.

Should "*Syariah*"[1] be enforceable law in contemporary Indonesia, and what implications does the answer to this question have for Human Rights in that country?

This question has come to matter a great deal across this sprawling archipelago of more than 17,000 islands that contains the world's largest Muslim population and ten years ago in 1998 began a transition to becoming the world's third largest democracy after India and the United States. Thousands have died over that decade in a range of violent conflicts linked to the question of whether "*Syariah* Law" should be recognised as the legitimate law of the land for Muslims (who form around 90 percent of the population), rather than 'imported' Western-derived laws – and, if so, which interpretation of *Syariah* should apply, and to what extent?

Current theological and political debate on this issue is linked to the introduction of wave of Islamising regulations (*Peraturan Daerah*, Regional Regula-

---

1 Commonly-accepted Indonesian usage is adopted in places in this chapter for the transliteration of Arabic words. The question of what is understood in Indonesia by the term 'Syariah' is considered later.

Islam und Menschenrechte (Islam and Human Rights / الإسلام وحقوق الإنسان)
Hatem Elliesie (Hrsg./Editor), © Peter Lang Verlag: Frankfurt a.M. 2010, S. 299-327

tions, or PerDa) dealing with sexuality, the rights of women and public morality at the local level and similar statutes at the national level. At its fringe, this debate is also linked to militant violence, including bombings of Western targets since 2002 (for example, the two attacks in Bali and attacks on the J W Marriott Hotel, the Ritz Carlton and the Australian Embassy in Jakarta); bombings of Indonesian targets, including government buildings and churches; and what are effectively intermittent civil wars between Muslim and Christian groups in eastern Indonesia, including, most notably, in Ambon, Maluku and Sulawesi.[2]

I. Constitutionalising Human Rights

These events have, however, happened alongside a dramatic constitutionalising of Human Rights unprecedented in Indonesian history.[3] On 10 August 2002 Indonesia's supreme sovereign body, the *Majelis Permusyawaratan Rakyat* (MPR) or People's Consultative Assembly amended the country's 1945 Constitution for the fourth time since 1999.

Before Soeharto's fall, the Constitution was a short document that had been hastily drafted as Indonesia declared its independence and prepared for revolution against the Dutch in 1945. It had never been amended. In its pristine, skeletal form it was intended as an interim measure – it was then called the "lightning constitution" – but survived to provide the framework for the successive authoritarian states created by both Soeharto and his predecessor, Soekarno, the nation's first President. The post-Soeharto amendments have now brought Indonesia a long way from the two dictatorships that had prevailed from 1959[4] to 1998. The most important of these amendments for the purposes of this paper was the second, passed in 2000, which introduced a comprehensive Bill of Rights.

The original 1945 Constitution contained few guarantees of civil and political rights. Instead it emphasised citizens' duties to the state. So, for example, Article 27 of the Constitution provided that citizens had a positive obligation "to

---

2 *Charles Coppel*, Violent Conflicts in Indonesia: Analysis, Representation, Resolution, London / et al. 2006, pp. 3-18.

3 – at least since the early 1950s.

4 In that year President Soekarno, in an act of contested Constitutional validity, unilaterally reinstated the 1945 Constitution. This, the nation's first Constituton, had been replaced - operationally at least – by, first, the Federal Constitution of 1949 and then the Provisional (parliamentary) Constitution of 1950. This 'self-coup' resulted in the formal creation of his 'Guided Democracy' (*Demokrasi Terpimpin*) dictatorship, although it had been developing since he declared effective martial law with his 'State of War & Siege' in 1957, see *Merle C. Ricklefs,* A History of Modern Indonesia since c.1300, 2nd edition, London 1993), pp. 312-323.

uphold by the law and the government without any exception", while "freedom of association and assembly and the like, shall be prescribed by law" (Article 28). The latter phrase was, of course, not a guarantee of rights at all, but the conferral on the state of the authority to deal with such rights as it saw fit. This absence of meaningful guarantees of rights was not an oversight. The chief drafter was Professor Dr Raden Soepomo, an impassioned advocate of the authoritarian, command-style, organic state, embodied in the *Integralisticstaatsidee* (integralist state idea) he espoused, a direct refutation of socialist, democratic and liberal political thinking. Soepomo therefore set out to create a Constitution that could "give the greatest accent to the government", while being itself "also accountable to the government and primarily the head of state".[5] This was based on the notion that the integralist state that he proposed – because it was 'integrated' – could never be at odds with the individuals comprising it "because the state is not a powerful body or political giant standing outside the sphere of individual freedom".[6] On this basis, there was no need for a civil (private) legal sphere independent of the state – and thus able to place checks on the state – because the state *was* all citizens and their interests were therefore identical.[7]

The failure of Soepomo's *naïve* notion of a romanticised union of state and people was obvious as soon as his Constitution came into force in 1945, because governments and citizens do not, of course, think and act as one. An obligation on citizens to "uphold the government" therefore quickly becomes the grant to the government of the right to repress them.

II. Post-Soeharto Human Rights Reforms

IN 2002, however, Indonesia's MPR found itself in a situation where the people and the government clearly had parted ways a few years earlier, in 1998, leading to the fall of Soeharto's New Order regime. The members of the MPR thus faced widespread popular demands for democratic reform and the 'rolling back' of the state. The addition to the Constitution of a new chapter on Human Rights that would protect citizens against the state was an obvious step towards achieving these objectives, by dismantling Soepomo's integralist creation. The new Articles 28A to 28J of the Constitution (which form Chapter XA) therefore delivered perhaps the most radical change to the original philosophy of the Constitution. Soepomo's paternalist and authoritarian presidential model was tempered

5 *Muhammad Ridhwan Indra,* The 1945 Constitution: A Human Creation, 1990, p. 44. Details not available. Copy on file with author.

6 *H. Muhammad Yamin,* Naskah Persiapan Undang-Undang Dasar 1945, vol. 1, Jakarta: Yayasan Prapanca, 1959, on p. 114.

7 *Adnan Buyung Nasution,* The Aspiration for Constitutional Government in Indonesia: A Socio-legal study of the Indonesian Konstituante 1956-1959, Den Haag 1992.

with clauses lifted directly from the Universal Declaration of Human Rights (UDHR). Chapter XA is a lengthy and impressive passage, granting on paper at least a full range of rights and protections extending well beyond those guaranteed in most developed states. Specific protections enshrined within the amended Constitution now include:

- Citizenship and equality before the Law (Articles 26, 27, 28D, and 28I(5));
- anti-discrimination (on any grounds) and equal opportunity (Articles 28I(2), 28D(3), 28H(2));
- the right to work with fair remuneration (Articles 27(2), 28D(2),);
- freedom of expression, assembly and organisation (articles 28, 28E(3), 28C(2), 28I(1)), although qualified by Article 28 with the caveat "according to law";
- the right to education, learning and access to information (Articles 28C(1), 28F and Chapter XIII Article 31);
- freedom of religious belief and practice (Article 28E), although qualified by Article 29 which requires the state to be based upon the belief in the "One and Only God";
- freedom from torture and other degrading or inhumane acts (Articles 28G(2), 28I(1))
- property ownership rights (Article 28H(4));
- the right to housing and adequate health services (Article 28H(1));
- the right of all citizens to state-funded social welfare services (Articles 28H(1) and 34);
- family rights and the right to procreate (Article 28B(1)) - women are equal to and have the same rights, obligations, and opportunities as men (although women face legal discrimination under other legislation such as within the Marriage and Citizenship laws);
- children's rights, including protection by state from exploitation, violence and discrimination (Articles 28B(2), Article 34);
- freedom of the press and for the expression of cultural values (Articles 28F; 28C; 32);
- the rights of indigenous people (Articles 32; 28I(2) & (3)).

Indonesia has now also ratified a large number of the international instruments that create a global framework for Human Rights, including:

- Conventions on the Elimination of All Forms of Discrimination Against Women (CEDAW), acceded to in 1984;
- Convention on the Rights of the Child (CRC), ratified in 1990;
- The Convention Against Torture and Other Cruel, Inhumane or Degrading Treatments or Punishments (CAT), acceded to in 1998;
- Convention on the Elimination of All Forms of Racial Discrimination (CERD), acceded to in July 1999;
- International Convention of Civil and Political Rights (ICCPR), acceded to in acceded to 2006;
- International Covenant on Economic, Social and Cultural Rights (ICESCR), acceded to in 2006.

It has also since established a Directorate general of Human Rights charged with developing and implementing a National Action Plan for Indonesia Human Rights (RANHAM) and has passed a large range of laws that seek to make the human rights norms embodied in these instruments and in Chapter XA of the

Constitution legally enforceable in Indonesia, in particular, by establishing institutions and mechanisms for doing so. These include:

- Presidential Decree No. 181 of 1998– regulating the National Commission for the Rights of Women (*Komnas Perempuan*)
- Law 39/1999 – Human Rights Law (regulating the National Commission for Human Rights: *KomnasHAM*)
- Law 26/2000 - Human Rights Courts (establishing these courts: *Pengadilan HAM)*
- Law 23.2002 on Child Protection
- Presidential Decree 77/2003, establishing the Commission for the Protection of Indonesian Children
- Law 27/2004 on the Truth and Reconciliation Commission
- Law 23/2004 on the Elimination of Violence in Households

The result is that since 1998 Indonesia has experienced at the same time both a strong push to 'Islamise' laws and, at the same time, a far-reaching effort to institutionalise international human rights norms in domestic law that was for it, revolutionary.

The question thus arises as to whether these parallel developments are complementary or in conflict?

Certainly, the adoption in domestic law of International Human Rights is seen as a threat to Islamic revival by the conservative proponents of legal Islamisation, although more progressive 'moderate' Muslims welcome and support such developments.

This debate must be understood against the backdrop of the somewhat idiosyncratic development of both Indonesian Islamic traditions and the Indonesian legal system; and, in particular, the complex mechanisms developed by colonial and post-colonial administrators, lawyers and scholars for reconciling Islamic and European-derived legal traditions. Both of these are traditions that were, of course, originally transplanted from outside Indonesia.

B. Web of Transplants

Borrowing, copying, adapting or refining laws from another jurisdiction in one way or another is the norm in most countries when policy requires new laws or institutions: this is 'best practice reform' or 'legal harmonisation' or, in most cases, just common sense. Modern Southeast Asian legal systems are, however, an unusually clear example of this broader pattern. Almost all legal institutions in Southeast Asia were originally drawn from common law or civil (including Socialist) law systems, whether in pure form or hybrid, and were transplanted as a consequence, direct and indirect, of 'Western' (that is, English, American and European) colonialism or post-colonial influence in the region, especially during the eighteenth, nineteenth and twentieth centuries. Over time, these regulations and institutions co-existed or overlapped with, and modified or were modified by, a large and often inchoate body of non-European legal traditions, including 'Islamic', and older non-Islamic, ones.[8] More recently, this process was revived by continuing post-colonial Western influence on law reform as a result of economic crisis 'conditionality' lending by major donors such as the World Bank and IMF. This was particularly true of Indonesia, the Southeast Asian country most severely affected by the so-called 'Asian crisis'.

I. Legal Traditions in Southeast Asia

The hugely varied and diverse range of legal traditions in Southeast Asia that are not clearly of Western origin are often identified by the classifiers of legal systems as 'non-Western', 'primitive', 'other' or, less dismissively (although no less vaguely), as 'Oriental', 'indigenous' and 'local'. All these terms speak to the fundamental alterity attributed to these systems in Anglo-European perceptions.[9] Their alien identity lies in the implicit assumption that these systems are so different, so varied and so detached from the Western Anglo-Common Law/Continental-Civil Law dichotomy that they can never sensibly be reconciled with Western systems. Yet the legal history of European colonialism in Southeast Asia can, in fact, be coherently written as an account of Dutch and British attempts to reconcile and merge European institutions with local legal traditions and institutions in what are now Indonesia and Malaysia/Singapore/Brunei, respectively.[10]

Some of these mergers were brutal and crude but others were highly sophisticated. In any case, the result of the complex, piecemeal and often uncertain processes of merger in both regions was the creation of hybrid judicial and bu-

---

8 Over the period 1998 to 2002, Indonesia's national legislative program was largely determined by IMF Letters of Intent. As a result, the argument about legal transplants and their legitimacy has been particularly political and heated in Indonesia, but that is beyond the scope of this chapter. See *Tim Lindsey / Veronica Taylor*, "Rethinking Indonesian Insolvency Reform: Contexts and Frameworks", in: *Tim Lindsey* (Editor), Indonesia: Bankruptcy, Law Reform and the Commercial Court, Sydney 2000; *William A.H. Neilson,* "Reforming Commercial Laws in Asia: Strategies and Realities for Donor Agencies", in: Ibidem.

9 On this issue, see *Annette Marfording*, "The Fallacy of the Classification of Legal Systems; Japan Examined" in: *Veronica Taylor* (Editor), Asian Laws Through Australian Eyes: Australian Perspectives on Asian Legal Systems, Sydney 1997, esp. on p. 65et seq.

10 Demonstrating this was the contribution made by Professor M B Hooker to the study of Southeast Asian legal systems. See for example, *MB Hooker*, Legal Pluralism: An Introduction to Colonial and Neo-Colonial Laws, Clarendon Press, Oxford, 1975; *MB Hooker*, Islamic Law in South East Asia, Singapore, 1984.

reaucratic institutions and hybrid doctrines. These, whatever their merits or lack thereof, have proved extraordinarily resilient and the tradition of legal eclecticism continues today across the archipelago.[11]

II. Islam and Legal Traditions in Indonesia

In formerly Dutch Indonesia, however, the reconciling and merging of Dutch legal institutions with local institutions was usually done without recognition of Islamic Law as an independent source of law, by contrast to formerly British-controlled Malaysia, Singapore and Brunei, where it was recognized, independent, albeit highly restricted, source of law. The reasons for this date from the colonial administration of the Netherlands East Indies and, in particular, what is known as 'Reception Theory.' Under the plural legal system developed by the Dutch, *Syariah* was not formally recognized as a source of law in its own right but rather was given legal effect only to the extent it was accepted by the bureaucracy or courts as having been absorbed by – or 'received' into - local traditional customary law, or *adat* (arab. *ʿāda*, pl. *ʿādāt*), as it is widely known in archipelagic Southeast Asia.[12] As Hooker[13] describes it:

> "[F]rom the 1850s it became a settled principle of Dutch colonial legal policy that each racial group should have its own law, applied only to members of that group. There were separate legal universes. For Europeans, or persons assimilated to that status, Dutch law applied. For natives it was *adat* (custom). The Syariah as such had no formal status, except to the degree or extent permitted by any of the *adat* laws. Its status was dependent on recognition by *adat,* that is, its 'reception' into *adat* law. This so-called 'reception theory' has since dominated the administration of Islamic law in Indonesia."

This approach meant that *Syariah* had force only for indigenous people if they were Muslims. It could never apply to Europeans, for example.[14] Even then, it would only apply to any Muslim member of the indigenous population to the

---

11 See, for example, *Mark Cammack / Lawrence Young / Tim Heaton*, Legislating Social Change in an Islamic Society – Indonesia's Marriage Laws, in: The American Journal of Comparative Law, 44/45, Ann Arbor 1996; *MB Hooker / Tim Lindsey* "Public Faces of *Syariah* in Contemporary Indonesia: Towards a National *Madhhab*?", in: Studia Islamika volume 10 issue 23, Jakarta 2003; *Greg Fealy / Virginia Hooker*, Voices of Islam in Southeast Asia: A Contemporary Sourcebook, Institute of Southeast Asian Studies, Singapore, 2006.

12 *MB Hooker*, Islamic Law in South East Asia, supra, footnote 11, on p. 244.

13 *MB Hooker*, "The State and Syariah in Indonesia", in: *Tim Lindsey* (Editor), Indonesia: Law and Society, Federation Press, Sydney, 1999.

14 For an engaging account of the labyrinthine and sometimes absurd complexities of this elaborate ethnically and religiously-determined legal system – especially as regards Formosan Chinese in the East Indies – see *Charles Coppel*, Violent Conflicts in Indonesia…, supra, footnote 3.

extent it could be said to form part of the traditional customary law of the ethnic group to which he or she belonged. In other words, to determine the application of *Syariah* what was required was not an enquiry into the scriptures of Islam, but into the ethnicity and folk beliefs of the *inlander*, or native, involved.

Indigenous Indonesian ethnic groups were generally regarded by Dutch scholars as being classifiable into nineteen main groups,[15] but most of these could be sub-divided many times over.[16] The result was that Islam, with its tradition of a universal Muslim identity that transcended ethnicity (the *umma*, or community of Islam), was subordinated to ethnic identity; and by this process local differences were valorized over a shared religion. The political objective of this was to counter the emergence of a unifying identity among the colonized population based around Islam or nationalism (or both) that might threaten the colonial state. In the end, the strategy failed politically: the Indonesian nationalist movement did, in fact, eventually grow out of organised Islamic chauvinism.[17] As a legal policy, however, the privileging of *adat* was remarkably effective in marginalizing Islamic Law in the East Indies.

This system of 'separate legal universes' – of different laws and legal traditions for different racial groups – had been formalized as positive law in the Netherlands East Indies in the Regeerings Reglement Staatsblad.1855 No. 2 and in Staatsbald 1929 No. 221, but it was the latter that formally confirmed that Islamic Law no longer had status as an independent source of law. Stbd. 1937 No. 116 completed the process by restricting the *Priesteraad* Islamic courts largely to dowry, marriage and divorce. The result was that regardless of whether Islamic Law was, in fact, applied more broadly by the custom of the relevant ethnic group, the Muslim judiciary's jurisdiction could not, in principle, extend outside beyond this narrow corridor.[18]

---

15 Aceh; Gayo, Alas and Batak islands; Minagkabau; South Sumatra; East Sumatra, Malaya and West Borneo; Bangka and Billiton; Borneo; Minahasa; Gorontolo; Toraja; South Sulawesi; Ternate archipelago; Ambon and the Moluccas, Irian Jaya; Timor archipelago; Bali and Lombok; Central and East Java; the Sultanates of Solo and Yogyakarta; and West Java (Sunda).

16 Some scholars even claim to have identified as many as 300 distinct groups: *MA Jaspan*, Daftar Sementara dari Sukubangsa-bangsa di Indonesia, Yogyakarta, 1958; *Hildred Geertz*, "Indonesian Cultures and Communities", in: *Ruth T McVey* (Editor), New Haven / Indonesia 1963.

17 *Harry J. Benda*, The Crescent and the Rising Sun. Indonesian Islam under the Japanese Occupation, 1942-45, The Hague / Bandung 1958; *Justus M van der Kroef*, "The Role of Islam in Indonesian Nationalism", in: Western Political Quarterly, Salt Lake City 1958.

18 *MB Hooker*, The State and Syariah in Indonesia, supra, footnote 13, on p. 98.

1. *Teori iblis*

For many Muslims, this Dutch doctrine was the devil's theory – *teori iblis* – as a renowned modern Indonesian scholar of Islamic Laws, Professor Hazairin, described Reception Theory, because it directly conflicted with the idea of Islam as *dīn wa dawla,* both religion and state, and placed non-Muslim sources of law above divine law.[19] Classic examples of the operation of reception theory given by Hazairin (and still commonly used in legal education in Indonesia) include, among others, *adat* marriage in Indramayu, whereby a women invites a man at a party to return to her home and her parents allow them to sleep together, in the morning calling a *kiyai* (*ʿulamāʾ*, or religious scholar) to marry them. Other examples include abduction 'marriages' and a variety of local traditions, for example, in Bojonegoro and Pasuruan, including where couples live together and marry only when the woman falls pregnant. For Hazairin, these practices, recognized as valid *adat* by the Dutch, were *zinā* (prohibited sex, adultery) and the law that allowed them was *hukum iblis* (devil's law),[20] because it privileged *adat* over clear *Syariah* injunctions.

In opposition to the Devil's theory, two alternative analyses have been put by advocates of a broader application of *Syariah.*

2. *Receptio in complexu*

The first, *receptio in complexu,* had it that *Syariah* had been absorbed in Indonesia, had become one with *adat* and applied in full for Muslims, at least since the coming of the Dutch. And, because *adat* and *Syariah* had merged, so-called '*adat*' practices that were contrary to *Syariah* were, in fact, deviant *adat* and should not be given legal weight. This analysis seemed – and still seems – to find little support in the routine spiritual practices of many Indonesian Muslims, although it is still argued by the more conservative proponents of Islamic revival.

3. *Receptio a contario*

The second analysis often posited as an alternative to Reception Theory is *receptio a contario*, The inversion of Reception Theory, the argument here was that *adat* and *Syariah* were, indeed, separate legal systems in Indonesia, but *adat* could only apply to the extent that *Syariah* did not apply, or, as it was usually put, to extent it was 'received into Islamic Law'.[21] In other words, *adat* could only fill gaps not filled by scriptural instruction. This view has always attracted support from Islamic reformers, and continues to do so today.

---

19 See, for example, *H M Idris Ramulyo*, Kumpulan Soal ujian Negara Cicilan Hukum Islam, Penerbit Sinar Grafika: Jakarta 2000, p.106.

20 Ibidem, p. 128.

21 Ibidem.

In any case, regardless of Muslim opposition, 'Reception Theory' was applied by the Dutch to marginalize the place of *Syariah* within an effectively secular legal system. Despite criticism, this theory still underpins Indonesian legal pluralism today, has been accepted as such by judges of Indonesia's final court of appeal, the Mahkamah Agung, or Supreme Court. It was also the underlying logic of a recent Constitutional Court decision that allowed the state to continue to restrict the right of polygamy conferred in the Qur'ān by imposing a series of legislative and judicial pre-requisites for registration of such marriages and imposing criminal penalties for non-compliance.

C. Transplantation Rejected[22]

The second aspect of Indonesian legal thinking that has been central in Indonesia's formal rejection of the transplantation of the corpus Islamic Law, or at any rate, its refusal to recognize *Syariah* as a valid, free-standing legal system in the Republic, has been the Jakarta Charter (*Piagam Jakarta*) discourse.

Indonesia is not an Islamic state and its Constitution – *Undang-Undang Dasar 1945* – does not refer to religion except in general formulae asserting freedom of religious expression. But this does not mean that Islam, or more specifically *Syariah,* has been totally distanced from the Constitution. On the contrary, Islam was an important issue – perhaps the most important issue – in the debates surrounding the drafting of the Constitution in the chaotic months preceding the declaration of independence in August 1945.

This was because the question of the relationship between Islam and the then-putative Indonesian state did not spring into being, fully formed, in the tumultuous months before the Japanese surrender that year. Rather, it was the product of decades of dispute, typified by the celebrated debate between the secularist nationalist leader (and later first President) Soekarno and the Islamic politician, Mohammed Natsir, from 1938 to the early 1940s. Their public correspondence showed the high degree of mutual incomprehension,[23] or even refusal to see the other's point of view, that was to mark the way the parties dealt with the question of Islam or secularism as the constitutional basis of the state (*dasar negara*) in 1945.

In 1945, all sides of politics agreed on a Preamble to the Draft Constitution that was an uneasy compromise between the contesting ideologies and beliefs represented among the nationalist leaders, patched together by the future first Presi-

---

22 This and the following paragraphs draw on *MB Hooker / Tim Lindsey*, Public Faces of Syariah..., supra, footnote 11.

23 Passages are reproduced in *Deliar Noer*, The Modernist Muslim Movement in Indonesia, 1900-1942, Kuala Lumpur, 1973, p. 273.

dent, Soekarno. It identified five fundamental principles (*Pancasila*) as the *dasar negara*. These are 'Belief in A Supreme God', 'Just Humanitarianism', 'Unity of Indonesia', 'Democracy guided by Consultation' and 'Social Justice'. There was, however, and remains, serious and seemingly insoluble disagreement as to the first *sila* —the implications of 'Belief in A Supreme God'.

Belief is prescribed for all Indonesians by the *Pancasila* but in 1945 the Muslim position added the words 'with obligation to carry out (implement) the *Syariah* for adherents of Islam' This, the so-called 'Jakarta Charter[24] or 'seven words',[25] did not, however, form part of the final draft of the Constitution when it was promulgated. It was dropped at Soekarno's insistence as the Constitution was being finalised. 'Belief in A Supreme God' has therefore been, and is still today, the official formulation of the first *sila,* with the Indonesian term *Tuha,n* 'capable of encompassing Christian, Islamic, Buddhist, Hinduistic and even animist notions of the supreme deity',[26] being used for 'God' in place of the identical Arabic word, *Allāh,* with its stronger Islamic connotations. So far as the state is concerned, the first *sila* also marks the outer limits of religious obligation for Indonesians, Muslim and otherwise.

Despite this official position, however, the missing words of the Jakarta Charter have never disappeared from the debate on what the state of Indonesia is supposed to represent for Islam, the religion to which the vast majority of the population adhere. The missing words are, in fact, so central that since 1945 some Muslim groups have persistently called for re-inclusion of the Jakarta Charter in the Constitution, or at any rate for the insertion of provisions to a similar effect.[27]

D. Reception Theory Revisited

After the fall of President Soeharto in 1998 and the end of his three decades of military-backed crony dictatorship, a key pillar of his regime also rapidly disin-

24 In fact, the Jakarta Charter refers to the full original draft of the Constitution with the 'seven words' included, but it is commonly used to refer simply to the 'seven words' themselves.

25 The phrase 'with the obligation to carry out the Syariah for adherants of Islam,' comprises seven words in the original Indonesian. *Michael Feener*, "Indonesian Movements for the Creation of a 'National Madhhab'", in: Islamic Law and Society, volume 9, New York 2001, p. 86.

26 *Michael van Langenburg*, "The New Order State: Language, Ideology, Hegemony", in: *Arief Budiman* (Editor), State and Civil Society in Indonesia, Melbourne 1990, p. 133.

27 It has even been argued that because the words were only removed by informal agreement they were never validly erased from the Constitution and are, in fact, therefore, in principle 'still there'. This is, however, a position that has not attracted significant political support since the 1950s.

tegrated: aggressive legislative, institutional and coercive repression of Islamic politics.

For most of his New Order, Islamic political parties other than the government-controlled *Partai Persatuan Pembangunan* (PPP) were banned, Islamic leaders censored and sometimes jailed and all organisations were obliged by the notorious '*Azas Tunggal*' (Sole Foundation) Law on Social Organisations No. 8 of 1985 to adopt *Pancasila* as their 'sole foundation' to the exclusion of, for example, the Qur'ān or '*Syariah*'. Major Islamic organisations such as *Nahdlatul Ulama* and *Muhammadiyah* – supposedly the largest Muslim organizations in the world - were required by this Law to adopt the *Pancasila* as their sole philosophical base. Refusal to do so, for example by insisting that only Islam or the Qur'ān could be the philosophical basis of a Muslim religious organisation, or, indeed, any questioning at all of the universal superiority of *Pancasila* as *Grundnorm*, was seditious. Most major Islamic organisations therefore eventually complied, acknowledging – however reluctantly or nominally— that *Pancasila* was their sole foundation on the grounds that it 'embraced' and, to use the words of the Preamble to the Constitution, was 'inspired' by Islam. Some, however, maintained defiance, even characterising *Pancasila* as un-Islamic, polytheistic and heretical. This opposition was seen by the state as political dissent and subversion and was sometimes treated as a security issue, with killings, intimidation and detentions.[28]

This array of restrictions and sometimes-violent interventions was usually effective in preventing Islamic groups from organising opposition to Soeharto's civilianized and secularizing military bureaucratic system. It was therefore not surprising that the messy and temporary coalition of groups that forced the end of the New Order in 1998 included radical Muslim politicians. Modern Indonesian history has always been characterised by tensions of differing levels of intensity between political Islam and governments of all colours, whether colonial or independent. It has thus usually been the case that major regime change has been accompanied by a temporary coalition of Islamic groups with elite secular political leaders, factions of the military and radical student groups. 1998 was no exception to this pattern.

From 1998, the calls of Islamic groups for unfettered rights of public political expression seemed at first to sit well with the liberalising and democratising rhetoric of rights and 'rolling back' the state shared by both the governments that succeeded Soeharto and the reform movement that helped topple him. It also seemed to fit with a popular human rights discourse directed at reining in

---

[28] *Michael van Langenburg*, The New Order State…, supra, footnote 26, on pp. 123, 133 et seq., note 43.

the military, which had, at times, been active in repressing (or at any rate, marghinalising) political Islam. The result was a resurgence of the Islamic identity and ideological expression that inevitably took political form. This wave of popular 'Islamisation', however, also resulted in political pressure to disaggregate the Dutch legal omelet and, in particular, to abolish Reception Theory and even to reinstate the Jakarta Charter - or, at any rate, the Charter's aim of imposing on Muslims a formal regulatory obligation enforceable by the state to observe '*Syariah*'.

E. Article 29

These issues came to a head on 29 August 2002, when the question of the status of the Jakarta Charter was put to a vote in the MPR (*Majelis Permusyawaratan Rakyat*, Indonesia's highest legislative body), as a formal proposal to amend Article 29 of the 1945 Constitution to make the practice of *Syariah* an obligation for adherents of Islam. By an overwhelming majority, however, the MPR – the first truly democratically-elected assembly in Indonesian history – vindicated Soekarno's position 57 years earlier by formally rejecting the proposal. They did this despite the initial support of the then Vice President, Hamzah Haz, his party PPP (*Partai Persatuan Pembangunan*) and several smaller Islamic parties. In the end, almost all the Muslim parties opposed the amendment.

This result demonstrated, once again, that while secular nationalist leaders and non-Muslim religious groups oppose the Jakarta Charter, there are deep divisions within Muslim society itself about the inclusion of these words in a reformed Constitution. There are various different reasons for this split within the Indonesian *umma*.

In 1945, the Charter was dropped at President Soekarno's insistence as the Constitution was being finalised in part because of fears that Christians in Eastern Indonesia would abandon the new Republic in favour of the returning Dutch colonial forces; and in part because of secular nationalist objection.[29] Fears of dividing largely Christian Eastern Indonesia from the overwhelming Muslim majority in central and western Indonesia, thus potentially provoking secession and possible collapse of the state, still played a role in the thinking of Muslim politicians in 2002, a time when East Timor had been lost to the Republic and when it seemed Aceh and Papua might follow.[30]

---

29 *Merle C. Ricklefs,* A History of Modern Indonesia..., supra, footnote 4, on p. 258 and p. 262.

30 It is also probable that international pressure on Indonesia not to support 'extremist' Islam may have played some par, in the MPR's decision, not least because the amendment's chief advocate outside the MPR was Abu Bakar Ba'asyir, widely believed to be

There were, however, other, probably more influential, reasons for rejecting the reinstatement of the Jakarta Charter. First, it is by no means clear what *Syariah* means for Indonesian Muslims. What its content should be is an issue that is no nearer settlement today than when it was hotly debated in the 1930s and 1940s by Soekarno and Natsir. Part of the reason for this relates to the meaning of the word '*Syariah*', a term that is usually used very loosely in Indonesia for a range of ideas, ranging from proposals for harsh criminal codes modeled on the Saudi system to vague notions of 'freedom' and 'democracy'.[31] In a formal sense, of course, *Syariah* refers to 'the way', the norms derived from the revalations in the Qurʾān, as understood through the *ḥadīṯ*, records of the words and deeds of Muḥammad, the Prophet of Islam. These are not legal texts in any modern sense of the term. Indeed it is often said that, despite the fact that Islam is, like Judaism, a profoundly 'legalistic' religion, only around ten per cent of the Qurʾān can be seen as 'rules' or 'laws' in the sense a lawyer would understand, the rest being largely moral theology or metaphysics.[32] On this reading, '*Syariah*' is not the same thing as *fiqh*, or Islamic jurisprudence, that is, the legal doctrines derived from 1400 years of scholarly interpretation of the basic scriptural sources by competing schools and scholars. Thus, while the content of the Qurʾān is certain for Muslims, *fiqh* is contestable. Islamic legislation or *qānūn*, positive law, is a further, highly contestable effort to reduce *fiqh* (which is already at a distance from revelation) to a set of written instruments and legal institutions, usually set firmly within the framework of a secular governmental authority. These distinctions are, however, usually lost on the bulk of the Muslim population in Indonesia for whom '*Syariah*' may often simply mean *keIslaman* or 'Islamicness' or whatever mixture of popular ideas and values – often political – have come to be associated with their religion.

Consequently, in Indonesia there are many and different interpretations of Islamic doctrine and consensus is not easily reached on legal problems. So, if *Syariah* became a constitutional obligation for Indonesian Muslims, the question would arise: what does that mean? Does it mean *fihki* (as *fiqh* is often referred to in Indonesia) and if so, which school or tradition? And whose interpretation of doctrine would prevail in the case of dispute?

---

leader of the terrorist group *Jema'ah Islamiyah*, which carried out the Bali bombings among many other attacks.

31 Pusat Pengkajian Islam dan Masyarakat' Survey Report: Jakarta ("Islam and the Culture of Good Governance"), copy on file with author.

32 *H Patrick Glenn*, Legal Traditions of the World, Oxford 2004.

The two leading popular Islamic movements in Indonesia, *Nahdlatul Ulama* and *Muhammadiyah*, are generally regarded as socially and politically moderate[33] and together they claim a membership of around 70 million, making them, as mentioned, arguably the largest Muslim organizations in the world. They have long feared the Jakarta Charter on the grounds that granting legal force to something as contested and uncertain in interpretation as '*Syariah*' would hand a political weapon to their smaller, more radical and conservative competitors, or even to each other. For these reasons, both PKB[34] (created by *Nahdlatul Ulama*) and PAN[35] (which has close links to *Muhammadiyah*) opposed the Art 29 amendment in the MPR, and this was probably fatal to the proposal.

F. Think Global, Act Local

The failure of the proposal to amend Art 29 and reintroduce a form of the Jakarta Charter – and thus effectively abolish Reception Theory, for the two ideas are sides of the same coin – seemed to prevent the formal constitutional transplantation of Islam into Indonesian law. It did it not, however, mean an end to efforts to obtain formal legal recognition of *Syariah* norms in Indonesia.

Instead, the focus of such efforts shifted from the national to the local level and involved direct challenges to the newly emerging human rights regime in post-Soeharto. This new local 'Islamisation' push was, to a significant extent, a response to major changes regarding the administration of the state that took place in the aftermath of Soeharto's fall in 1998. His successor, President BJ Habibie, formerly a member of Soeharto's inner circle and facing allegations of corruption and cronyism, was keen to win legitimacy as a reformer. He therefore presided over a period of massive reforms, unequalled in any subsequent administration. Among the most important of these was the transition of the Indonesian state from being highly-centralised and authoritarian to becoming a geographically-devolved democracy in which government was shared between the national government in Jakarta and local governments in the provinces across Indonesia's 17,000 or more islands. This process is often described as one of the most substantial re-allocation of powers inside a nation state in modern times, and was aimed at satisfying the demands of reformers for greater local autonomy and increased democratization.

As of January 2001, Law 22 of 1999 on Regional Autonomy (since replaced as Law 32 of 2004) and Law 25 of 1999 on Fiscal Balance (since replaced as Law

33 *Greg Fealy*, "Parties and Parliament: Serving Whose Interests?" in: *Grayson Lloyd / Shannon Smith* (Editors), Indonesia Today. Challenges of History, Institute of Southeast Asian Studies, Singapore 2001.

34 *Partai Kebangkitan Bangsa* (National Awakening Party).

35 *Partai Amanat Nasional* (National Mandate Party).

33 of 2004) handed government control to Indonesia's 400 regencies (*kabupaten*), transferring authority over all areas of government except foreign affairs, defence and security, justice, religion and economic policy areas to local governments. The Law on Regional Autonomy also made it clear that these local governments can issue create regional Regulations or PerDa (*Peraturan Daerah*) as their main mechanism of governance, although other, lower-level, bureaucratic instruments, such as 'circular letters' (*surat edaran*), Instructions, Decisions and the like are also common at this level, as they are throughout the Indonesian system.[36]

Of the 219 local elections that were conducted in 2005 in pursuance of the new system of regional autonomy, some 40% or so resulted in the removal of incumbents and the rise of new elites. Many of the winners in this process were male traditional leaders pushed to one side under Soeharto's New Order, who either drew authority from local tradition or looked for legitimacy to conservative and socially-regressive values linked to local identity. In many regions these groups replaced Soeharto-era bureaucrats, who, for all their many failings, often had a strongly secular nationalist bent and some commitment to a modernising agenda. The new local elites sought to differentiate themselves from their New Order predecessors and strengthen their local support by adopting agendas sponsored by conservative social groups, frequently religious in nature. One means of doing this was to support the introduction of conservative, religious and usually socially-regressive laws, and in most parts of Indonesia, that meant '*Syariah*isation' (*Syariahisasi*).

The result has since been the passing of plethora of regulations at the local level that seek to displace norms from European Civil Law with socially conservative norms from Islamic and other local traditions, often mixing the latter two together. At the time of writing, new 'PerDa Syariah' totalled around 160 and existed in at least 24 of Indonesia's 33 provinces.[37] The province of West Sumatra had the most PerDa, around 40, with South Sulawesi next, with 28, and then West Java, with 20 or so. These areas, with Aceh, are commonly regarded as the areas where Islamic traditions have had their strongest influence on local cultures in Indonesia.

Generally, the PerDa and other related local regulations seek to target perceived religious, social and moral wrongs and can be loosely divided into seven main

36 For the hierarchy of Indonesian laws and the relationship between the levels of regulation, see Law no. 10 of 2004.

37 I am grateful to Melissa Crouch for her research on PerDa as part of my ARC-funded Federation Fellowship project, which forms the basis of much of the following discussion of Regional Regulations.

categories: *zakāt*, prostitution, clothing, alcohol and drugs, social ills (*maksiat*), religious rituals and Qur'ānic literacy.

The question of what is appropriate Muslim costume, particularly for women, is an area of particular concern for the drafters of these PerDa and so more than 20 Regulations, again mostly from West Sumatra, West Java and South Sulawesi, specifically related to Muslim dress. They share similar provisions. Typically, they apply to women, students or civil servants and require head covering and, in most cases, covering of all but the hands and face. In some regions, Muslim clothing is only required to be worn on Fridays. In others it is daily wear and in some PerDa even non-Muslims are asked to comply.[38]

Other PerDa deal more directly with moral behaviour and aim to criminalise public sexuality. So, for example, the Draft PerDa of Depok 2006 on Forbidding Prostitution (which was copied from a Tangerang PerDa) bans kissing in public (Art.4). Others target targeted perceived 'social ills' commonly referred to as *maksiat*, a term that covers a wide range of areas, from gambling, begging, homelessness, immorality (*asusila*) and adultery to pornography and prostitution. One such regulation even bans children from playing Playstation.

Many PerDa also purport to establish religious police in the form of 'law enforcement teams' to enforce these regulations. For example, in Batam (South Kalimantan) a team consisting of prominent religious, *adat* and youth figures was established for this purpose.[39]

The penalty for breaches varies. Some PerDa, for example, Bulukumba 5/2003 on Muslim Clothing, simply states that a person should be disciplined 'appropriately' (Art.11). More often, the punishment is specific to the accused. For example, if the accused is a student, they may be banned from participating in class activities[40] or they may receive an oral or written warning from the school, or even be suspended or expelled.[41] If the accused is a civil servant, they are to be 'disciplined', although the details of this are not given.[42] In other cases, fines or imprisonment are applied, with the most common penalties being a maximum of 6 months jail or a fine of up to Rp 5 million (ca. 350 €uro).

---

38 See, for example, Instruction of the Walikota of Padang 451.422/Binsos-III/2005 on the Obligation to wear the Jilbab (*ǧilbāb*) and Islamic dress (for Muslims) and Suggested Attire (for Non-Muslims).

39 PerDa of Batam (South Kalimantan) 6/2002 on Social Order (Art.6).

40 PerDa of Enrekang 6/2005 on Wearing Muslim Clothing in Enrekang, Art. 11.

41 Examples include PerDa of Lima Puluh Kota 5/2003 on the Obligation to Wear Muslim Clothing Art. 11; PerDa of Agam 6/2005 on Wearing Muslim Clothing Art.5; PerDa of Pasaman 22/2003 on Muslim Clothing for Students, University Students and Workers Art.11).

42 Examples include PerDa of Sawahlunto/Sijunjung 2/2003 on Muslim Clothing, Art. 9; Perda of Solok 6/2002 on Wearing Muslim Clothing in Solok Art. 11.

The validity of these laws is, however, questionable, given that, as mentioned, 'religion' is one of the few areas of government authority that was retained by the central government and not devolved to the local level. Accordingly, to the extent that the PerDa and other local regulations can be said to be about 'religion' per se, they are probably *ultra vires* (as a common lawyer would put it) or, as Indonesians would say, lacking a 'legal basis', and thus, arguably, invalid. Interestingly, although the central government has power to strike out PerDa,[43] and has exercised that power on some occasions, it has never done so with any 'Islamic' PerDa, so far as the author is aware. Indeed, senior advisers to the president questioned by the author indicated that they had no plan to take steps against any PerDa despite acknowledging that many may be illegal and some clearly breach human rights guarantees in statutes and the constitution, on the grounds that these 'sensitive' issues are 'best dealt with informally by society (*masyarakat*)', rather than formally by the government.

G. Anti-Porno Action

Success at the local level in Indonesia encouraged proponents of legal Islamisation to revive their efforts at the national level. The *maksiat* issues of prostitution and the regulation of sexuality were raised in the national legislature, the DPR, through the introduction of the Anti-Pornography and Pornographic Acts Bill in 1999, soon after the end of New Order in May the previous year.

Largely ignored at first, the Bill became the subject of fierce debate in 2005, around the time the PerDa movement reached its peak. Its opponents argued that the Bill directly discriminated against women, religious and ethnic minorities and breached the guarantees in Chapter XA of the amended Constitution, particularly as regards religious freedom (Art 28E and 29) and freedom from discrimination (Articles 28I(2), 28D(3), 28H(2)). The Bill was, however, eventually passed as Law No.44 of 2008 despite widespread opposition and mass protests across the archipelago, especially in areas where Muslims were not the local majority and where indigenous traditions are strong, such as largely-Hindu Bali and largely-Christian Papua.

The Law as passed contains contentious provisions that purport to prohibit forms of expression that its proponents consider *pornoaksi* (pornographic actions) – mainly sexuality or women's self-expression. Public displays of affection (such as kissing and holding hands) are, for example, criminalized, as are

[43] Law No 32 of 2004 creates a complex process that among other things gives the Minister for Home Affairs 60 days to approve a new PerDa and the Minister can, in theory, require that the law be revised or cancelled. The process is, however, unclear in some respects. The DPR can also, of course, pass a statute overruling a PerDa at any time.

exposing 'sensitive' body parts such as breasts, thighs, belly and navel, as well as even hair, shoulders and legs. These were the provisions that were the focus of many of the protests, as the Law like many of the PerDa Syariah, the Law is seen by its opponents as targeting women and as another attempt to apply a very conservative and socially-regressive form of *Syariah* as positive law in Indonesia. To that extent, it can be read as, implicitly, yet another attempt to revive the ideas underpinning the Jakarta Charter/ anti-Reception Theory discourse.

Despite these successes at the local and national level in the last 5 years, support for formal legal Islamisation now seems to be declining in Indonesia. The first Islamising PerDa appeared in 1999, with the number issued across Indonesia rising to five in 2000 and peaking at just under 25 in 2003. By 2006, however, numbers of new PerDa had reportedly fallen to less than five.

I. Islam, According to Who?

Given that women in Indonesian societies have historically enjoyed far greater social freedoms than their sisters in the Middle East, it is unsurprising that both the wave of PerDa regulation and the Anti-Pornography Bill have provoked public controversy in Indonesia as to whether Islamic Law (and, in particular, its substance relating to women) is, in fact, properly to be considered 'indigenous' or 'local' (and thus not a transplant and therefore 'appropriate') or alien (and thus a transplant that, opponents argue, is not 'compatible' with 'Indonesian circumstances'). Put another way, the issue is whether Islamic Law is an alien Arab transplant being imposed on Indonesians, or whether there is a form of Islam that, despite its Middle Eastern origin, has now become somehow distinctly 'Indonesian'?

At its extremes, this is a battle between two poles. At one end are radical conservative hard-line (*garis keras*) groups who advocate an austere, orthodox understanding of Islam inspired by Middle Eastern (and, in particular, Arab al-WahhÁbÍya) practice. These include at their fringe, extremist groups who openly advocate the creation of a Caliphate, for example, Abu Bakar Ba'asyir's Majelis Mujahadin Indonesia (Indonesian Jihad Fighters' Council), and militant groups such as *Jemaah Islamiyah*.[44] These groups often see 'the West' as an enemy and as neo-colonial, depraved and corrupting. At the other pole are moderate liberal Muslims who advocate what many would consider a heterodox *madhab Indonesia*, or Indonesian national 'school' of Islam, that mixes 'orthodox' Arab interpretations of Islam with local interpretations and traditions said to be

44 *Tim Lindsey / Jeremy Kingsley*, "Talking in Code: Legal Islamisation and the MMI Shari'a Criminal Code", in: *Peri Bearman / Wolfhart Heinrichs / Bernard G Weiss* (Editors), The Law Applied: Contextualising the Islamic Shar'ia, London, 2008.

more suited to Indonesians' more open and, in many cases, less morally-strict, cultures. Many at this pole fear Middle Eastern orthodoxy as aggressive, alien and intolerant and are concerned to find readings of Islam that can accommodate Western culture and thought.

This raises a further, complex question that is intensely contested in contemporary Indonesia: who has legitimacy to decide whether to 'do' a transplant, that is, who should make the highly-subjective value judgment about whether a legal model is 'foreign' or 'local' enough to be introduced? This is highly significant for Indonesia's new, internationally-derived human rights regime, because if conservative Islamic legal traditions are indigenous and 'fitting' for Indonesia, then that suggests that they should prevail over 'foreign' human rights principles to the extent that the two are in conflict.

To pursue these interlocked problems, I now turn to the most significant experiment with Islamising PerDa and, indeed, legal Islamisation, so far conducted in Indonesia, if not, in fact, the whole of Southeast Asia: Aceh's new Qanun regime.

J. Aceh's New Qanun Regime: Islamic or Indonesian?[45]

'Qanun' is the term used by the DPRA (Dewan Perwakilan Rakyat Aceh) or Provincial Legislature in the Indonesian province of Nanggroe Aceh Darussalam for the PerDa or Regional Regulations it produces. These are unique in that Aceh is the only province in Indonesia where the decentralisation process involved devolution to the provincial government, rather than lower-level local governments. This was part of a series of major concessions granted by Jakarta in the post-Soeharto era to prevent Aceh from breaking away from the Republic in the way that East Timor did. They were confirmed by the post-tsunami Helsinki Agreement in 2005, by which conflict between GAM (*Gerakan Aceh Merdeka*, the Free Aceh Movement) and Jakarta was formally brought to an end and Aceh agreed to remain part of the Republic, and in the resulting Law on Governance in Aceh.

Aceh's history of Muslim kingdoms and its relative isolation at the northern tip of Sumatra have created an Acehnese Islamic identity seen by most Indonesians as distinguishable from other manifestations of Islam elsewhere in the country.[46] One result of this has been that in recent times '*Syariah*' has become inextricably bound up with Acehnese identity. Attempts to secularize or displace

45 This discussion of Aceh draws on *Lindsey / Hooker / Jeremy Kingsley / Clarke*, "Syari'ah Reform in Aceh: New Born or Still Born?", in: *Michael Feener / Mark Cammack* (Editors), *Islamic Law in Contemporary Indonesia,* Cambridge 2007.

46 *John R Bowen*, Islam, Law and Equality in Indonesia, Cambridge, 2003.

'*Syariah*', or rather, Achenese *fihki*, have never been successful in completely removing it from the local political agenda.

The sweeping powers of self-government granted to Aceh from 1999 onwards were a response to this and they extended to the grant of legislative capacity, the creation of a *Syariah* Court (*Mahkamah Syariat*), and the devolution of almost complete authority for the administration of the province. Other new institutions created include the MPU or Deliberative Assembly of Ulama or Religious Scholars (*Majelis Permusyawaratan Ulama*), the latest incarnation of similar bodies that existed in the past; the *Dinas Syariat* (the Governor's *Syariah* Office); and the *Wilayatul Hisbah* (religious 'police'). The DPRD, working in conjunction with the *Dinas Syariat* and, to a lesser extent, the MPU, has now introduced more than 20 Qanun that purport to cover most areas of public law and some aspects of private law, including, specifically, *syakshiyah,*[47] *muamalat*[48] and *jinayah.*[49]

Compared to most PerDa, many of which were, in fact, directly inspired by the Qanun but which are generally poorly drafted and often internally inconsistent, the Qanun are relatively sophisticated instruments that extend beyond religion to issues of general administration and governance and are capable of functioning as means of regulating a complex society. They have, however, created significant human rights problems, especially for Achenese women.

To understand these problems, some contextualization is necessary. Islam entered Indonesia in a fragmented, gradual and slow process, generally through trading routes and by royal conversion but almost never by foreign conquest, although there were certainly many wars of conquest led by local Muslim princes in Java, Sumatra and elsewhere.[50] In some places, Islam largely displaced existing traditions, while in others it penetrated only lightly, if at all. Some parts of the archipelago remain resistant, for example Bali (which became a refuge for displaced Hindu/Buddhist kingdoms from Java) or the mainly Christian islands to the east of Lombok. In a few areas, penetration was, however, significant enough to convert entire societies to Islam, although conversion in Indonesia, has never implied 'Arabisation' to the extent it has in Africa or the Middle East. The religious imperialism of Arab culture has, in the past, been

---

47 Arabic *aḥwāl aš-šaḫṣiya*: "personal affairs". As a legal category this refers in Indonesia to personal and family law for Muslims.

48 Arabic *mu'āmala* (pl. *mu'āmalāt*): this legal category includes those aspects of life dealing with human relationships and the physical world, mainly commerce and trade, that do not fall under the category of *'ibādāt* or ritual worships. It is often used in Indonesia to refer to economic law.

49 Arabic *ğinā'īya*: this legal category deals with crime and punishment.

50 *Merle C. Ricklefs,* A History of Modern Indonesia..., supra, footnote 4, pp. 8-9.

largely absent from many parts of the archipelago. In fact, in Indonesia there emerged a large range of local 'Islams'[51] saturated with influences from local traditions, many of which predate the arrival of Islam and are linked to the Indic and animist cultures that once dominated the archipelago.

It is generally accepted, however, that the deepest penetration of Islam occurred in Aceh, at the north-western tip of the archipelago. In other words, the areas closest to the Middle East remain closest to the Arabian source of the religion, while those further East developed more fragmented, diluted and unorthodox versions of Islam, often *ṣūfī* (mystical) in nature and heavily influenced by Hindu-animist mystical traditions, rather than being concerned with Arab-derived Sunni doctrinal austerity.

The island of Java, which contains the majority of Indonesians (60% of 240 million) and which is dominated by the Javanese ethnic group, is usually regarded as being, overall, one of the least orthodox Muslim societies in Indonesia. This is a highly generalized assessment, as it is also home to arch-conservative or militant groups like *Majelis Mujahadin* Indonesia, MMI, *Laskar Jihad* or *Hisbut Thahrir*, but it remains true that there is probably a higher rate of non-observant or, at any rate, non-orthodox, Muslims in Java than on other major islands with majority Muslim populations, such as Sumatra, Sunda, Sulawesi and Kalimantan. This is significant because the long-standing domination of politics, law and business by Javanese elites and those allied to them created a Java-saturated official and public culture across the New Order state.[52] In other words, under the New Order public culture in Indonesia deliberately and overtly valorised heterodox, sometimes even nominal, forms of Islam. Accordingly, the contemporary Islamic revival in Indonesia is often read by Indonesians– rightly or wrongly - as a reassertion of a more Arab-oriented, non-Javanese Islamic and regional identity, in opposition to heterodox Central Javanese cultural imperialism, associated with Soeharto and authoritarianism.

This has important implications for Islamic Law in Indonesia. The universalism of Islam is a fundamental principle of Muslim belief. In other words, in principle temporal authority can only draw such authority as it has from religious authority and it cannot be set up as an alternative source of legitimacy. In practice, of course, this principle is honoured mainly in the breach. In almost all Islamic societies since the time of the early Caliphs Muslims have accommodated dif-

---

51 For the term 'Islams', see also *Ann Elizabeth Mayer*, "General Remarks on Human Rights and Islam in the Middle East", in: *Hatem Elliesie* (Hrsg./Editor), Beiträge zum Islamischen Recht VII, Islam und Menschenrechte (Islam and Human Rights / الإسلام وحقوق الإنسان), Frankfurt a.M. 2010, pp. 219 et seq.

52 See, for example, *John Pemberton*, On the Subject of 'Java', Ithaca 1994.

ferent forms of secular authority. This has been true too in Indonesia, where *Syariah* as a functioning judicial and regulatory body has been marginalised since colonial times to highly restricted areas of family law, inheritance and charitable trusts. Its *fiqh* content has been almost entirely subsumed or distorted by secularising regulatory interventions that have replaced *fiqh* with bureaucratic process. [53] In other words, the recent Islamic political revival is – again – also essentially a legal revival, and is proclaimed as such in policy documents and legal instruments. Its proponents overtly – and, in the case of *Jemaah Islamiyah* and other militants, violently[54] – propose to re-establish a reformed Arab-style Islamic legal system throughout Indonesia, displacing secular laws and, in particular, Reception Theory.

The question now is how *Syariah* revival – and in particular, the *Qanun* of Aceh, are to be understood. Are the *Qanun* in Aceh 'native' laws, that is, are they a reassertion of Islamic legal norms that have been so deeply established within Indonesian society that they can be said to be indigenous? Or are they a transplantation of ideas from another jurisdiction, in particular, from al-Wahhābīya Arabia or from the conservative PAS (*Parti Islam Se-Malaysia*, All-Malaysia Islamic Party) governments in the Malaysian states of Kelantan or Terengganu, both of which were sources used by the drafters of the Acehnese regulations?[55] This question matters in Indonesia, because it goes to the crucial political issue of whether these laws are legitimate and should be accepted by Muslim Indonesians, or whether they are a form of subversive Arab cultural imperialism that threatens the legal identity of Indonesian Islam and thus of Indonesia itself, and thus should be subordinated to human rights laws, where they conflict.

The Acehnese, of course, assert that these *Qanun* are a revival of 17th century legal principles from the reign of Sultan Iskandar – the so-called golden age of Islam in Aceh. What little information we have regarding that period and its legal system suggests, however, that this reading is at the very least contestable and perhaps even ahistoric. Travelers' reports of the 17th century court of Sultan Iskandar, for example, tell stories of gambling and alcoholic drinking games[56] and give little sense of the application of an Islamic moral code along the lines envisaged in the *Qanun*.

---

[53] *MB Hooker*, The State and Syariah in Indonesia, supra, footnote 13.

[54] *Tim Lindsey / Jeremy Kingsley,* Talking in Code..., supra, footnote 44.

[55] *Lindsey / Hooker / Jeremy Kingsley / Clarke* "Syari'ah Reform in Aceh ...", supra, footnote 44.

[56] *Anthony Reid*, Southeast Asia in the Age of Commerce 1450-1680: The land below the Winds, Yale University press, New Haven/London, 1988, p. 40, 194.

Be that as it may, for nominal Muslim Javanese and for the Indonesian state, the Acehnese *Qanun* are not indigenous at all. Rather, the state (and certainly the judges of the Supreme Court) would say that the Reception Theory system – whereby a person can, for example, be a devout Muslim and yet follow *adat* practices that contradict accepted Islamic legal tenets (for example matrilineal inheritance) – reflects a pre-existing and authentic indigenous Indonesian form of Islam, and the so-called national *madhab* (or school of Islamic jurisprudence).[57] Implicitly, on this reading the *Qanun* are illegitimate transplants and, more significantly, their proponents – the radical conservative reformers – are 'un-Indonesian'. The *Qanun* should therefore not be exempt from the application of internationally-derived human rights rules that now apply nationally in Indonesia.

It is here that the abstract question of what is implicitly 'indigenous' and what is an alien imposition may become of critical importance for the state's attempts to respond to the challenge of resurgent Islam for Human Rights in post-Soeharto Indonesia. On this question turns the broader question of who will define the nature of Islam and the reach of conservative Islamic legal norms in Indonesia, and thus whether the radical reform movements have a claim to legitimacy among the broader Islamic community.

The answer to this question – which, in the end, will likely be political rather than legal – will have a direct and significant effect on the daily life of many Indonesians. This is demonstrated by, for example, a brief consideration of how the new *Qanun* system in Aceh deals with the rights of women, to select just one example from many.

K. Women in Aceh's Syariah Revival

The obligation of every Muslim "to wear Islamic dress" appears in Art. 13(1)) of *Qanun*11/2002. Accompanying this provision is a requirement of government, educational institutions, businesses and community organizations to "promote a culture of Islamic dress in their environments" (Art. 13(2)). The wording of these provisions has been left vague 'to allow for individual interpretation', according to their drafter, Dr. Al Yasa' Abu Bakar, the former head of Aceh's *Dinas Syariat* (government *Syariah* Office). The only guidance to what 'Islamic dress' entails is found in the Elucidation to Article 13: "Islamic dress is clothes that cover the *aurat*[58] that are not transparent, and do not show

57 See on this, *Michael Feener*, Indonesian Movements…, supra, footnote 26; *M Cammack*, Islamic Inheritance Law in Indonesia: The Influence of Hazairin's Theory of Bilateral Inheritance, in: Australian Journal of Asian Law, 4/3, 2002.

58 Ar. *awra*, the parts of a person's body that according to Islamic law should be covered when outside the family environment. The *aurat* differs between males and females.

the shape of the body." This gives only limited certainty as to what does and what does not constitute appropriate Islamic dress but for Abu Bakar the intention was simply to ensure modesty and symbolic respect for Islam:

> We do not want to force women to wear the *jilbab* [the head scarf favored in Aceh], but we do encourage people to dress modestly out of respect for Islam. We're not going to force people, but if someone wants to run naked down the street, then we can use the law to stop them. That's no different to your country, is it?[59]

On this reading, the obligation to wear Islamic dress is a reflection of the Aceh DPRD's intention to preserve a perceived 'Acehnese Islamic' culture. Indeed, for the first few years of its implementation, Article 13 had little impact on how the vast majority of Acehnese dress, which is in the common, polite Indonesian manner, albeit more conservatively than Jakarta and with a common (but certainly not uniform) use of head-coverings by women. In practice, however, attitudes on Islamic dress for women appear to have hardened very considerably as result of a perception that the catastrophic Indian Ocean tsunami that devastated Aceh on 24 December 2004 was a punishment sent by God and, in particular, that it "[...] happened because women ignored religion", or, in the reported words of one *ulama*, "The Holy Koran says that if women are good then the country is good".[60]

This reflects a changing focus by Acehnese religious authorities and, especially, the *Wilayatul Hisbah* (Aceh's religious police) on the public role of women that parallels the changes provoked elsewhere in Indonesia by the PerDa phenomenon.[61] The results of this new approach ranged from religious police raids on beauty salons and cafes looking for 'prostitutes', to pressuring women to wear the *ǧilbāb* (Indonesian: *jilbab*)and cover up visible skin other than face and hands. This has led, in one case at least, to the parading in public of women with their hair 'lopped off' as punishment for failure to wear the *jilbab*.[62] There have also been reports of prohibitions on women travelling unaccompanied on *ojek* (motorcycle taxis) driven by men, as almost all are.[63] The implications of these developments are obviously severe for women, as they restrict capacity for individual expression. Their impact goes well beyond this, however. In a poor province where most women rely on public transport, they could exclude many women from a role in public life and access to employment.

---

59 Interview with Dr. Abu Bakar, *Tim Lindsey / MB Hooker*, February 2003.

60 Times Online, "Tsunami was God's revenge for Your Wicked Ways, Women Told", Times Online *UK*, 22 December, 2005.

61 Jakarta Post, "Acehnese accuse religious police of 'arrogance' and thuggery", *Jakarta Post*, February 23, 2006.

62 Times Online, Tsunami was God's revenge..., supra, footnote 60.

63 The rationale is that the passenger on an *ojek* must necessarily embrace the driver.

The new rules regarding dress have noticeably changed how women dress and behave in Aceh's public space and have limited the freedom of expression that some chose to exercise before the *Qanun* were passed. Although many Acehnese women are not troubled by the provisions on dress, a significant group – especially younger, educated women, those who have lived outside Aceh and those involved in civil society organisations – do regard the new restrictions they impose as 'alien'. There seems little likelihood that they will be repealed, however, because the weight of Acehnese opinion so far seems still to fall in their favour (although at the time of writing new proposals for *Qanun* that would introduce more severe penalties for moral offences, including severe caning and even stoning to death for adultery were meeting strong resistance from the local government and legislature in Aceh).

The view in the Jakarta would likely be different. As women activists argue, the Acehnese PerDa on women's costume and proximity are probably in breach of other, national and superior laws that override the *Qanun*, including, again, the guarantees of freedom in religion in Art 28E of the Constitution; Art 22 of the Law on Human Rights No. 39 of 1999; and Art 18 of the International Covenant on Civil and Political Rights (ICCPR), enacted in Indonesia by Law No 12 of 2005; and the prohibitions of discriminatory treatment of women in Art 26 of the ICCPR (Law no 12 of 2005); Art 3 of the International Covenant on Economic, Social and Cultural Rights (Law No. 11 of 2005) ; and the Convention of the Elimination of All forms of Discrimination Against Women (Law No. 7 of 1984).

To date these claims have not been decided by the Indonesian courts, which, like the government, seem extremely reluctant to deal with this issue. One attempt to bring the Aceh Qanun before the Indonesian Supreme Court was reportedly rejected by the Court, but this may have been restricted to its facts and, in any case, would not bind the court in a future deliberation. [64]

L. Conclusion

The complexity of the question posed earlier is, I hope, now apparent: are the Islamising regulations in the Anti-Pornography Law, Aceh's *Qanun* and other PerDa, and the '*Syariah*' legal systems they all seek to introduce – all of which are very conservative and regressive in the Indonesian context - 'indigenous' or are they 'foreign?

64 This judgment had not been published or made publicly available at the time of writing. For the vexed question of whether the Aceh Qanun can be reviewed at all, see *Tim Lindsey /et al.,* Syari'ah Reform in Aceh…, supra, footnote 46.

Some of their substance is certainly indigenous to that extent that they draw on customary traditions (for example, in *Qanun* provisions dealing with village governance) that often predate, or may conflict with, Islam. And as for their Islamic content, surely after four or more centuries, it is inappropriate to call *Syariah* 'foreign', at least in areas like Aceh where many Islamic norms have been absorbed into local culture for much of that time? But that, of course, begs the question. What parts of Islamic legal tradition have, in fact, been so absorbed, and who is to make that judgment? And to what extent are they consistent or inconsistent with the new human rights regime? On Islamic costume, the Acehnese *Qanun*, to take one example, seem perhaps to be more alien than indigenous, at least so far as regards their severity and the vigour with which they are being enforced, if women are to be the judge. If so, then many Indonesians would feel that normatively the *Qanun* should be subordinate to the national human rights laws that would allow women to ignore the *Qanun*'s restrictions on dress and behaviour.

It is hard to avoid the conclusion that the answer to the question of whether the *Qanun* are alien depends to a great extent on what clause of which instrument is under discussion. After all, much of the *Qanun* are uncontroversial and deal with non-religious matters, such as local administration, the education system and dispute resolution. Some provisions even uphold and confirm what is acknowledged in the *Qanun* to be Acehnese *adat* derived from non-Islamic sources.[65]

The answer to the question of whether the *Qanun* should be considered 'alien' will also depend on which Indonesian is being asked the question. For most Acehnese, the legitimacy of the *Qanun* is unquestioned and that is supported by Aceh's more conservative *ulama*. For conservative Muslims outside Aceh, however, (for example, those in MMI) the *Qanun* remains anathema, in that it represents – even if only in part – a failure to fully comply with the more radical, ultra-conservative vision expressed, for example, in MMI's own extremely harsh draft Criminal Code, which would introduce gruesome *hudūd* punishments such

65 Some provisions deal, for example, with the administration of *adat* justice (*peradilan*) at the village (*desa* or *gampong*, in Aceh) level, by the *imeum munasa* or *munik* (local *ulama)* and the *keuchik* (village head). These include PerDa No, 7 of 2000 on the Administration of *Adat* Life; *Qanun* No. 4 of 2003 on Mukim Governance; *Qanun* No. 5 of 2003 on Gampong Adminstration; and MPU Decision No 2 of 2005 on Legal Protection of Rights to Land etc. The *gampong* or village is the lowest unit of government. It is equivalent of the *desa* or *dusun* outside Aceh. It is headed by a *keuchik*, or village head. The next level is the *mukim*, loosely equivalent to the *kelurahan* or *kecamatan* elsewhere in Indonesia. It is headed by a *imeum meunasah*, or local *ulama*. *Meunasah* refers to a *mushollah*, prayer room, or local mosque.

as amputation and crucifixion and, fantastically, contemplates camels and dirhams as currency.[66] For moderate mainstream Indonesian Muslims outside Aceh and outside the conservative right of Islam, however, the *Qanun*, like other Islamising regional regulations, may lack legitimacy precisely because their conservativism seems like a foreign Arab imposition on traditional Indonesian Islamic cultures.

The question now is who decides which version of Islam will apply and thus who determines to what extent human rights laws should be applied in Indonesia? The *Qanun* are thus symbols for a broader debate across Indonesia, one that involves not just the various PerDa but also the Anti-Pornography Law and continuing (but, to date, consistently defeated) proposals to amend the secularist constitution to make *Syariah* an obligation for Muslim citizens and thus also for the state, as law enforcer. Put another way, for more than a century, the Reception Theory approach of colonial policy has applied. Now that approach is fiercely contested politically and legally by groups who seek – in effect, and whether or not consistently articulated in these terms – to scrap reception theory and apply *Receptio in Complexu*, applying Islamic Law as indigenous, absorbed to such an extent that *adat* has been displaced. In Aceh, they have made their case, as elsewhere, at the local level through the local legislature, with some success. Their experiments with *Syariahisasi* continue across Indonesia, although they seem now to be perhaps waning.

Outside the political process, the more extreme proponents of the enforcement of an ultra-conservative vision of Islamic Law are likewise still making their case with guns and bombs, although the state has responding with arrests, trials and executions, to great effect. Seen in this light, both Islamic and *Western* legal traditions in contemporary Indonesia can be understood as still tied to armed struggles for power between those who see themselves as the inheritors of the legal and political traditions associated with the arrival of, on the one hand, the traders and conquerers of the modern European secular state, and, on the other, the apostles from Middle Eastern and other overseas Islamic communities credited with converting littoral city states to Islam and triggering wars of conquest.

So what then of the future? There is much anxiety among the Indonesian proponents of human rights regulation about the current success of conservative Muslim law reformers, who are seen as an influential lobby group seeking to reinvent Indonesian culture through regulatory change. Despite its willingness to turn a blind eye to legal Islamisation, the state seems as firmly wedded to the essentially secular legal and state system inherited from the Dutch in 1945 as it

66 This Code is a draft document and is not under consideration in any legislature. For details, see *Tim Lindsey / Jeremy Kingsley,* Talking in Code…, supra, footnote 44.

has ever been in its six decades of history. Indeed, since 1999, post-Soeharto governments, whatever their other differences, have generally shared a vision of Indonesia as an emerging democracy in which a public commitment to human rights plays a central rhetorical role to distinguish the current regime from its authoritarian predecessors.

It therefore seems unlikely that the post-1998 trend towards Islamisation of law, with its generally heavily conservative and discriminatory style, will ultimately defeat the new constitutionalisaton of Human Rights in Indonesia that developed alongside it. It also seems unlikely, however, that the adoption of international human rights norms will entirely displace Islamic legal traditions in the Indonesian system. The more probable development is therefore a continued, if much slower and less confrontational, Islamisation of laws accompanied by continued and gradual strengthening adoption and enforcement of international human rights norms: paradoxical, yes, but in that much also very Indonesian.

Human Rights Standards in Afghan Courtrooms: The Theory and Reality of the Right to a Fair Trial

Tilmann Röder, Kabul/Heidelberg

A. Introduction: Involuntary Court Observation

Nothing in the courtroom could disturb the two judges in their reasoning. They were sitting on simple chairs on the right hand of the door. Other than the chairs, I could see only four objects in the room – a slim court file, a ball-pen, an ink-pad and the *Qur'ān*. On our left hand side, two men were squatting on the floor, leaning with their backs against the wall. Through the large window in front of us warm sunrays and the songs of birds in the trees came drifting in from the courtyard.

The reason for my visit to the *maḥkame-ye estenāf* (provincial court) of Herāt in early April 2007 was not the observation of a criminal procedure, but only a short talk with one of the adjudicating judges about some formalities of a training course for the judiciary. The armed policeman in front of the courtroom's door had directed me and my companion, an Afghan-German lawyer, inside the room with the words, "Actually nobody should disrupt the court procedure – but you are foreigners." The judges stood up, warmly welcomed us and invited us to remain in the room until the case was decided.

The two men squatting on the floor, Bašīr and Ḥayātullāh,[1] Pashtun villagers in their late twenties, were accused of murder. Some time before the trial, four men had been killed in Bašīr's house in Šindand, a district in the insecure south of Herāt Province. The two men explained that they had been assaulted and that they had shot back into the dark in fear for their own and their families' lives. The judges, however, did not seem to believe them. One of the accused, Bašīr, turned to my companion and asked him who he was. An attorney? Bašīr asked what is that. When he understood he hauntingly prayed my companion to help him and his friend in their defence. My colleague, however, was not able to accept the case as he was not registered as an attorney in Afghanistan. Both accused turned back to the judges and complained that the court had not invited witnesses who they believed could prove that their statements were true. The younger judge replied that these witnesses would not be credible, stating that it was all too easy to instruct friends to give a testimony supporting any story presented before the court. The elder resumed and called on Bašīr and Ḥayātullāh

1 The names of the accused mentioned in this case have been changed in order to protect their security.

Islam und Menschenrechte (Islam and Human Rights / الإسلام وحقوق الإنسان)
Hatem Elliesie (Hrsg./Editor), © Peter Lang Verlag: Frankfurt a.M. 2010, S. 329-359

finally to confess that they had consciously and voluntarily killed the victims who he believed had been their enemies. When they refused again he ordered all to rise and announced that Bašīr and Ḥayātullāh were sentenced to death for quadruple murder.

The accused looked devastated. Ḥayātullāh asked my companion what they could do. The lawyer recommended appealing against the decision if they felt that it was not fair. Again, he had to explain a legal term: the notion of appeal was unknown to the two villagers. When they understood what it meant, a discouraged Bašīr commented, "What sense would it make to let other judges decide. They are the same like these."

Eventually the younger judge asked them to press their right thumbs with ink on the court file where he had registered the conviction. Both accused refused because they saw this as an admission of guilt. One last desperate dispute began at the end of which Bašīr gave up: "We all have to die one day", and pressed his thumb into the ink and onto the paper. His friend, Ḥayātullāh, insisted that a phrase was added which stated that he refused to accept the penalty. Then he thumb-signed below the words which he could not read.

Insights like this into the procedures of Afghan criminal courts are rare. The Afghan judiciary is generally reluctant to let monitors attend hearings without what the court officials see as a legitimate cause. One possible reason of the Afghan judges' reluctance to give outsiders insights into their work is their consciousness that they do not comply with the fair trial standards which they are expected to meet. Deviations from the provisions which are enshrined in the Afghan Constitution of 2004,[2] in statutory laws and in international human rights treaties were dramatically visible in the Herāt trial where a whole host of fundamental principles were violated.[3]

In this article the right to a fair trial in Afghanistan is analysed from two perspectives. The applicable legal framework which has been described by several

---

[2] Official Gazette of Afghanistan No. 818, 2004. The Official Gazette is accessible at: http://www.moj.gov.af (Dari and Pashto). English translations of Afghan laws, decrees and regulations are collected at: http://www.afghanistantranslation.com.

[3] The public were excluded from the hearing by the armed policeman. No prosecutor was present to present the indictment. Bašīr and Ḥayātullāh were neither supported in their defence by a free attorney or an employee of the state-run Legal Aid Department, nor had they been informed about their right to counsel or their right to remain silent. Even the court was not complete – an appeals panel in Afghanistan must consist of three judges. Witnesses named by the accused were not invited. The procedure was not recorded and the accused only learned about their right to appeal by chance from an outsider, the Afghan-German lawyer.

authors[4] since the fall of the Ṭālibān also serves as the focal point of orientation. The actual objective of this article is, however, to provide information about the diverging legal reality and to discuss the reasons and consequences of the Afghan courts' non-compliance with human rights standards.

The article does not examine violations of justice-related human rights standards – especially detentions – by the *riyāsat-e amniyat-e melli* (National Directorate of Security – NDS)[5] and the international military forces (IMF). These human rights violations, which are of deep concern, have been publicly discussed to some extent.[6] The gathering of information in this field is extraordinarily difficult because directs insights are almost never given to outsiders[7] and observers have to rely on the reports from former detainees.

B. Law in the Books: The Right to a Fair Trial in Theory

Art. 130 para. 1 of the Constitution of the Islamic Republic of Afghanistan (AC) provides that while deciding cases, judges must apply "the provisions of the Constitution as well as other laws". The Afghan Constitution contains the most important fair trial principles, i.e. the principle of legality (Art. 27 para. 1 AC), the principle of equality before the law (Art. 22 AC), the presumption of innocence (Art. 25 AC), the prohibition of unlawful detention (Art. 27 para. 2, 3 AC), the right to a defence including the right to an attorney or free legal aid

---

4 Notably, *Silvia Tellenbach*, "Fair Trial Guarantees in Criminal Proceedings under Islamic, Afghan Constitutional and International Law", in: ZaöRV volume 64, issue 4, Stuttgart 2004, pp. 929-941; *Fabrice Defferrard*, "L'Afghanistan et le procès pénal équitable", in: Recueil Dalloz, 182ième année, Paris 2006, pp. 1997-2001; *Alexandra H. Guhr, Ramin Moschtaghi / Mandana Knust Rassekh Afshar*, "Max Planck Manual on Fair Trial Standards", Amended 4th Edition, Heidelberg / Kabul 2009, Dari, Pashto and English languages: http://www.mpil.de/red/afghanistan (accessed on 23 July 2009); and, without a country-specific scope, *Dieter Weissbrodt / Rüdiger Wolfrum* (Eds.), "The Right to a Fair Trial", Berlin 1998.

5 The NDS is the domestic secret service of the government of Afghanistan.

6 On NDS-related detention see e.g., Amnesty International, "Afghanistan: Detainees transferred to torture: ISAF complicity?" (November 2007) http://www.amnesty.org, accessed 20 July 2009), and on IMF-related detention in Afghan facilities, see Human Rights First, "Arbitrary Justice: Trials of Bagram and Guantánamo Detainees in Afghanistan" (April 2008), http://www.humanrightsfirst.info (accessed on 20 July 2009). The journalist *Alex Gibney* produced the documentary film "Taxi to the Dark Side" (Jigsaw Productions, Inc., 2007) about the death of a terror suspect in Bagram Airbase, Afghanistan, which was broadcasted in more than 30 countries in October 2007 and directed international attention to the problem.

7 IMF usually allow staff of the International Committee of the Red Cross (ICRC) to inspect the situation of the detainees.

(Art. 31 AC), the prohibition of torture (Arts. 29, 30 AC) and the public conduct of trials (Art. 128 AC).

These rather general principles are detailed in secondary constitutional legislation. The *qānun-e eğraʾāt-e ğazāʾi-ye moʾaqqat* (Interim Criminal Code for Courts – ICCC) of 2004[8] forms the core of the criminal procedure in Afghanistan. It does not regulate the matter comprehensively, but only supersedes the pre-existing laws which are contrary to its provisions (Art. 98 para. 3 ICCC). Therefore many provisions of the *qānun-e eğraʾāt-e ğazāʾi* (Criminal Procedure Code) of 1965 (as amended in 1974)[9] and other laws passed between this period have remained in force.[10] Since 2004 several new laws have been introduced that superseded or amended provisions of the ICCC, notably the *qānun-e taškilāt va ṣalāḥiyat-e maḥākim* (Law on the Organisation and Jurisdiction of Courts – LOJC)[11], the *qānun-e pulis* (Law of the Police)[12], the *qānun-e rasidagi be taḫallofāt-e atfal* (Juvenile Code)[13], the *qānun-e maḥābis va tavqif ḫāne-hā* (Law on Prisons and Detention Centers)[14] and the *qānun-e mobāraze ʿalayhe mavvād-e moḫaddar* (Counter Narcotics Law)[15].

The application of the existing secondary constitutional legislation in the light of the Afghan Constitution produces a comprehensive concept of fairness in the Afghan criminal procedure. International instruments such as the International Covenant for Civil and Political Rights (ICCPR)[16] may be applied additionally because the state – and thus also the judiciary – shall abide by them (Art. 7 AC). There are no significant gaps in the Afghan domestic legal framework. The right

8 Official Gazette No. 820, 2003. A working group consisting of Afghan and foreign legal experts has drafted a new Criminal Procedure Law and handed it over to the Legal Drafting Department (Taqnīn) of the Ministry of Justice on 25 June 2009. This draft will, however, not be considered here because its approval by the National Assembly (*šurā-ye melli*) in the existing or another form will take months, if not longer.

9 Official Gazette No. 26, 1965.

10 E.g. the provisions on bail.

11 Official Gazette of Afghanistan No. 851, 2005.

12 Official Gazette of Afghanistan No. 862, 2005. The law extended length of time in police custody of an arrestee from 24 to 72 hours before a prosecutor must take over the case.

13 Official Gazette of Afghanistan No.846, 2005.

14 Official Gazette of Afghanistan No. 852, 2005.

15 Official Gazette of Afghanistan, No. 875, 2006. The law introduced new provisions for search, seizure and covert surveillance provisions, and increased to 30 days the arrest-to-indictment limit.

16 The ICCPR was ratified by the Islamic Republic of Afghanistan on 24 January 1983. Further relevant instruments are the Convention against Torture and Other Cruel, Inhuman or Degrading Treatment or Punishment (ratified on 4 February 1985) and the Convention on the Rights of the Child (ratified on 27 April 1994).

to have a conviction and sentence reviewed by a higher tribunal for example, which is not expressly enshrined within the Afghan Constitution, is clearly provided in Art. 63 ICCC.

These are the fair trial standards in Afghanistan in theory, law in the books. Although it may not easy to find all provisions and interpret them in a coherent manner, there lies within a flawless procedure which is almost perfectly in compliance with the relevant international human rights standards.

To take a state-oriented perspective, Islamic sources should not play any role in this field of law. Art. 130 para. 2 AC provides that Hanafi *fiqh* may be applied only if the afore-mentioned sources do not provide a legal norm which is necessary for the solution of the case, and only within the limits set by the Constitution. The courts are held to apply *šīʿī* instead of *sunnī* jurisprudence if Šiʿites are involved in the personal status case (Art.131 sent. 2 AC). As there are no apparent gaps in the legal framework safeguarding the rights of suspects, accused or convicted persons, there is no need and thus no legitimisation for courts to refer to Islamic sources.

C. Law in the Courts: The Right to a Fair Trial in Reality

A comprehensive assessment of the law in practice could not be realised due to the security situation in large parts of the country. However, information from all provinces has to some extent been included into this study. The case reports have been selected from among numerous examples because they illustrate specific problems in the implementation of human rights standards in contemporary Afghanistan. They should, however, not be taken *pars pro toto*. Even though the similarities of the problems and patterns of behavior of law enforcement officials throughout the country are striking, there are significant differences due to regional and local circumstances. Nevertheless the case reports add together into a mosaic which gives an impression of the situation of criminal justice in contemporary Afghanistan.

I. Independence of Judges

One fundamental precondition of the fair and equal treatment of any person facing criminal charges is the independence of the judiciary as an institution (Art. 116 AC) and – even more importantly – that of the single judge, which is dispersed over several provisions.[17] As to the institutional independence, the hurdles against undue influence from the executive and legislative branches of state

17 Especially Arts. 132, 133 AC, Arts. 14, 15 LOJC.

are sufficiently construed.[18] Earlier influence of conservative Islamic parties on the judiciary[19] has also been diminished since the election of the moderate scholar of law and *šarīʿa*, *ʿAbd as-Salām ʿAẓīmī,* as Chief Justice (*qāḍi l-qoḍāt*) in May 2006. In the context of criminal justice, the problems lie rather in the manifold threats to the independence of the single adjudicating judge.

The work of prosecutors (*tsārnvāl-hā*) and other law enforcement officials is not based on institutional independence. However, individual independence in the sense of freedom from undue influence is to some degree necessary also for them to fulfill their obligations. Therefore they will be mentioned in this section wherever similar problems affect their work.[20]

1. Lack of Material Resources

The provincial offices of the judiciary and the prosecutors are as badly capitalised and equipped as those of all state institutions. The justice institutions rarely possess real estate outside the provincial capitals. Major portions of their budgets are therefore spent on renting office space. In Kunduz in September 2007 the provincial budget of the prosecutors did not suffice for the payment of their office telephone bills, and the telecommunications company informed their main office that they intended to cut off all their land lines and mobile phones.[21] These financial and material shortages seriously harm the judges' and prosecutors' independence, as one report from Nūristān illustrates:

> " *The judicial power is an independent power in our state system, but we are under the influence of the District Governor and the Head of the District*

18 The reality, however, is different. There are serious doubts that the judiciary in constitutional adjudication acts independently from the government. One example is the opinion given by the Supreme Court (*stera maḥkame*) in the case of Foreign Minister Spanta. For details, see *Ramin Moschtaghi*, "Aktuelle Probleme beim Rechtsstaatsaufbau in Afghanistan: Das Gutachten des Obersten Gerichtshofes zum Misstrauensantrag des Unterhauses gegen den Außenminister", in: ZaöRV volume 68, issue 2, Stuttgart 2008, pp. 509-540.

19 *Martin Lau*, "The Independence of Judges Under Islamic Law, International Law and the New Afghan Constitution", in: ZaöRV volume 64, Stuttgart 2004, pp. 917 (on p. 926).

20 An AIHRC officer from Nangarhār reported that even coroners are threatened and bribed in order to cover up unwanted facts, such as in one case evidence of rape of a boy and, in another case, the fact that an accused is already an adult which means that juvenile law was not applicable. Oral Case Report from Jalalabad [Ǧalālabād], 18 May 2009, in: Collection of Reports and Documents from Afghanistan, Kabul Office of the Max Planck Institute for Comparative Public Law and International Law (MPIL Collection), JLB-6.

21 Oral statement of Ḥamīdullāh ʿAbed, Chief Prosecutor (*raʾis-e tsārnvāli-ye estenāf*) Kunduz Province, at the Provincial Justice Conference organised by the U.S. governmental organisation JSSP (Justice Sector Support Program), Kunduz (Pamir Hotel), 28 September 2007.

Security. There is no distinct court building, thus we are dependent on the District Governor to give us a room for a court in the District Administration's Building."[22]

This is the typical pattern of a District Governor [*valsvāl*] and a local NDS official unlawfully influencing judicial affairs. Other power brokers, especially former *muǧāhidīn* commanders, in many places join these mafia-like networks. The judges and prosecutors usually do not have much to counter such undue influence. They feel left alone by their superiors in the country's remote capital Kābul.

2. Threats and Physical Attacks

There are many reports where pressure is put on judges, and sometimes also prosecutors, in order to achieve certain decisions. Fear of violence is common in the justice institutions, especially at the district level. The following case from Taḫār Province is just one of many examples reported to the author:

> "*In Fakhar District the former jihad commander Abdul Razaq acts as NDS Commander and Head of the Police; he has received his police rank from President Karzai. This person has vast lands at his disposal. Water for land is shared in Fakhar. He arbitrarily assigned the water only for his land. The other farmers and the population complained on [date in 2007] at the district court of Fakhar. The judge, Sadeq, summoned this commander in order to inform him about the complaint (...). He [the commander] felt offended by the summons and personally attacked judge Sadeq with his guards and beat him in a way that he was injured and had to be taken to hospital. For fear of the commander nothing else was undertaken.*"[23]

From another report it becomes clear that the author who described this situation is Judge Ṣādeq himself. The other report contains much more information which produces a picture of a criminal network controlled from Kābul which extends over the whole Province of Taḫār and beyond. The informant ends his report with the sentence,

> "[...] *If this statement is published under my name, I am sure that I will be killed. Therefore I ask you to forgive me for not signing with my name.*"[24]

---

22 Written Case Report from Jalalabad, 18 May 2009, in: MPIL Collection, supra, footnote 20, JLB-7.

23 Written Case Report from Kunduz, 3 April 2007, in: MPIL Collection, KUZ-1. Names of persons and districts (but not the province) mentioned in this case have been changed in order to protect their security. In other cases, anonymous persons have been threatened by phone calls or "night letters", e.g. in the Oral Case Report from Jalalabad, 18 May 2009, in: MPIL Collection, supra, footnote 20, JLB-5.

24 Written Case Report from Kunduz, 3 April 2007, in: MPIL Collection, supra, footnote 20, KUZ-13.

Further reports describe how judges narrowly escaped from commanders who tried to kill them, in one example because the judge did not agree to release the commander's son, a murder suspect.[25] In other cases, law enforcement officials describe how the power of local strongmen leads to their *de facto* impunity. Judges from Laġmān Province – who have to rely on the District Governor for office room like their colleagues in Nūristān – wrote:

> " [...] *For example, in Alishing District of Laghman Province the PRT* [[26]] *helped with some necessary material, such as gas balloons, beans, blankets, peas etc, for poor and needy people and submitted them to the District Governor, but all the donated materials were retained by the District Governor, local commanders and the NDS. Although it was our duty to prosecute this case, we could not; if we move they can easily kill us and our life is in danger. In criminal cases and drug cases it is the District Governor with the NDS who take the decisions.*"[27]

Whenever significant values are at stake, local strongmen try to seize them. Subsequent distribution conflicts are rarely resolved within the framework provided by the legal system, but rather with pressure or even violent force. The law enforcement and justice institutions are in these cases ousted from their very function.

3. Judicial Corruption

Internal corruption has a similarly devastating effect on the administration of justice, just as the threats and attacks from outside. It hinders independent decisions and leads to biased and unequal treatment of persons involved in criminal prosecution all over the country. Judges, prosecutors and other law enforcement officials reported many cases to the author. Their salaries have recently been increased, but the monthly 10,000 Afghani paid to young district judges, for instance, is still not enough for a living even under the most modest conditions.[28] Additional sources of income are therefore necessary and corruption is one such source.

Bribery in the justice system begins with a few hundred Afghani[29] demanded by a court clerk who would otherwise not promote the case[30] and it can amount to

---

[25] Ibidem, KUZ-16.

[26] The PRT (Provincial Reconstruction Team) in Mehtarlām, Laġmān Province, is a military unit of the US Armed Forces.

[27] Written Case Report from Jalalabad, 18 May 2009, in: MPIL Collection, supra, footnote 20, JLB-3.

[28] 10,000 Afghani, equaling about 200 USD, per month is sufficient for simple food such as bread, tea and some vegetables, but not for the rent of a room for a family.

[29] 100 Afghani is equivalent to 2 USD.

[30] One report mentions 500 Afghani for a court clerk. Written Case Report from Kunduz, 3 April 2007, in: MPIL Collection, supra, footnote 20, KUZ-11.

tens of thousands of USD for the release of wealthy suspects from pre-trial detention or, if convicted, from prison.[31]

One prosecutor wrote down the case of a businessman from Kunduz who was thought to have smuggled heroin which is produced from opium in Afghanistan. The man was brought to the *maḥkame eḫteṣāṣi markazi mavvād-e moḫaddar* (Central Narcotics Tribunal) in Kābul, but released as soon as the initial suspicion was revealed errant. Back home, he was again arrested by the NDS Commander of Kunduz and forced to pay him 35,000 USD and another 7,000 USD to the *lu-ye tsārnvāl* (Head of the Attorney General's Office) at that time.

> *"The further investigations revealed that this person had nothing to do with the smuggling of drugs and that the 52 bags of heroin stemmed from Takhar Province. But despite the payments he was brought before court. The court found him not guilty. (...) After all it was detected that this person was put under pressure because he possessed capital and thus was an appropriate victim for extortion. The 42,000 USD were not handed back to him. (...) Even today the affair has not been settled."*[32]

Others report that public offices – including high ranking positions in the justice institutions – are sold for the highest bid. Besides the fact that the "buyers" use the offices to regain the bribe and make more profit, this has the negative side effect that competent professionals do not reach these positions. Especially well-educated, young professionals are frustrated by this situation. In April 2007, eleven young judges in Herāt were *de facto* banned from judicial service while the same number of positions remained open. The young judges' suspicion that some officials were waiting for payments cannot be easily refuted.[33]

One extreme and probably unusual case was reported by a police officer from Herāt Province. A notoriously violent commander who allegedly had killed hundreds of innocent persons in the time of *ğihād* had become a mayor in Kalaġa District. After shooting another innocent man, arguing he had been drug smuggler, he was arrested.

> *"Once he was in detention, the family of the dead bribed the prison officers.* [...] *[The killer] was handed over to the brother of the dead. Then they took revenge from him. They brought the person to the grave of their brother and shot him* [...]."[34]

---

31 In Laġmān Province, prosecutors were offered 50,000 USD for terminating their investigation into a corruption cases. Written Case Report from Kunduz, 3 April 2007, in: MPIL Collection, supra, footnote 20, JLB-1.

32 Written Case Report from Kunduz, 3 April 2007, in: MPIL Collection, supra, footnote 20, KUZ-9.

33 Copy of letter of young judges to the Supreme Court, MPIL Collection, Kabul.

34 Written Case Report from Herat, 17 April 2007, in: MPIL Collection, supra, footnote 20, HRT-1.

Corruption is one of the main reasons of the Afghans' lack of trust in their justice system.[35] In all annual surveys of the Afghan population's perception of their living situation and societal development organised by the Asia Foundation, respondents answered that they most frequently had encountered corruption in the judicial system. In 2008, 51% of those who had contact with courts reported corruption, compared with 49% who were asked for bribes when receiving official documents and 40% in contact with the police.[36] The *riyāsat-e tahqiq-e stera maḥkame* (Investigation Department of the Supreme Court) is trying to enforce its anticorruption strategy on the basis of a new Code of Conduct of 2007 combined with a Disciplinary Regulation of 2008, but wider effects are not yet visible.

II. Legality of Crimes and Sanctions

The principle of legality is one of the overarching principles in criminal justice. It demands that actions which are not defined by law as crimes are not the basis for investigations, prosecution, sentencing or punishment. This principle, which is recognised by Art. 27 AC[37] and Art. 15 ICCPR[38], ensures legal predictability and certainty.

The prohibition of retroactive criminal laws in the narrow sense, which is internationally understood as one of the most important consequences of the principle of legality, does not seem to constitute a problem in Afghanistan. There are, however, three other categories of cases where the principle of legality is violated.

1. Prosecution of Socially Disregarded Behaviour

Many women and girls are arrested and detained on charge of leaving home, even though this is not a criminal offence. UNAMA court observers found that

---

35 *Sudhindra Sharma / Pawan Kumar Sen*, "Institutionalisation of the Justice System", in: *The Asia Foundation* (Ed.), "State Building, Security, and Social Change in Afghanistan: Reflections on a Survey on the Afghan People", Kabul 2008, pp. 45 et seqq. (on p. 50).

36 The Asia Foundation, Afghanistan in 2008 – A Survey of the Afghan People, Kabul 2008, p. 60.

37 Art. 27 reads: "1. No act is considered a crime unless determined by a law adopted prior to the date the offence is committed. 2. No person can be punished but in accordance with the decision of an authorised court and in conformity with the law adopted before the date of offence."

38 Art. 15 no. 1 reads: "No one shall be held guilty of any criminal offence on account of any act or omission which did not constitute a criminal offence, under national or international law, at the time when it was committed. Nor shall a heavier penalty be imposed than the one that was applicable at the time when the criminal offence was committed. If, subsequent to the commission of the offence, provision is made by law for the imposition of a lighter penalty, the offender shall benefit thereby."

in several cases analysed by them the police, prosecutors and the judges failed to distinguish between a familial or social problem and an act that is defined by law as a crime. The following example from Mazār-e Šarīf is therefore not unusual:

> *"A young victim escaped violence by running away. She was arrested and charged with running away, even though this is not a crime. The presiding judge of the court rightly identified her as a victim not an accused person. The presiding judge described her situation with compassion, noting that the girl was already the victim of forced marriage and was raped during the engagement and now is suffering at the juvenile detention centre."*[39]

There is no statistical information about arrest, detention and other coercive measures taken against runaway girls and women but the number is presumably high. Unlawful action of the police in such cases may result from the lack of officers' knowledge of their own competencies, but it also seems to be supported by a considerable portion of the population. The Afghan society at large lacks the understanding that sanctioning behavior which is seen as immoral by many is not the task of law enforcement institutions.

2. Prosecution Aiming at Šarīʿa Penalties

Another element of the principle of legality is the general duty of the state to precisely define by law all criminal offences in the interest of legal certainty and to preclude the extension by analogy of the scope of criminal laws. Most international commentators hold that the definition of an offence under national law must result from a law in the strict sense of a general-abstract parliamentary law or an equivalent, unwritten norm of common law, which must be accessible to all persons subject to it.[40] This principle, however, is questioned in Afghanistan where prosecutors do in some cases base their indictments, and judges their verdicts, solely on *šarīʿa* penalties. In the past years, three trials received considerable international attention because of apostasy.[41] One of them concerned the publication of an unauthorised version of the *Qurʾān*:

---

39 Information received from Legal Systems Observation Project (LSOP), a joint initiative of the Human Rights and Rule of Law Units of the United Nations Assistance Mission in Afghanistan (UNAMA). All case reports date from 2007. The UNAMA LSOP files are preserved in the UNAMA Headquarter in Kābul. The author is grateful to the Rule of Law Unit for giving him preliminary information in 2007.

40 *Manfred Nowak*, UN Covenant on Civil and Political Rights: CCPR Commentary, Kehl am Rhein 2005, p. 360.

41 From a legal perspective the case of the Apostate ʿAbd al-Raḥmān is analysed by *Mandana Knust Rassekh Afshar*, "The Case of an Afghan Apostate – the Right to a Fair Trial Between Islamic Law and Human Rights in the Afghan Constitution", in: Max Planck UNYB, volume 10, Leiden 2006, pp. 592-605. The same case and that of the alleged blasphemist Sayyed Parviz Kāmbaḫš are discussed by *Tilmann J. Röder*, "Kollisionen

> In 2007, the renowned journalist Aḥmad Ġaws Zalmay – a former spokesman of the Attorney General – had published a translation of the *Qur'ān* in Dari language without the original Arabic verses alongside. The powerful *šurā-ye ʿolamāʾ*(ʿUlamāʾ Council) of Afghanistan soon condemned the publication as blasphemous, arguing that a translation could not considered a *Qur'ān* itself and could lead to the misunderstanding of God's word. The clerics accused Zalmay and Mušhtāq Aḥmad, a mullah who had signed a letter endorsing the translation, of setting themselves up as false prophets. In 2008 both men and four collaborators were accused of blasphemy and the prosecutor asked for the death penalty. The primary and appeals courts found the men guilty of modifying the *Qur'ān* and sentenced Zalmay and Aḥmad to imprisonment of twenty years. When reading out the sentence, Presiding Judge ʿAbdul Salām Qāżizāde said the accused were infidels and death would not have been an extreme punishment.[42]

The court based its verdict on the *šarīʿa*, referring to Art. 1 of the Afghan Penal Code of 1976[43], which reads: "This law regulates the *taʿzīr* crime and penalties. Those committing crimes of *ḥudūd*, *qiṣāṣ* and *diyāt* shall be punished in accordance with the provisions of the Hanafi understanding of Islamic law." Blasphemy belongs to the category of *ḥudūd* crimes. However, this relegating legal provision violates the later and higher ranking[44] provision of Art. 27 AC which states that "No act is considered a crime, unless determined by a law adopted prior to the date the offence is committed […]." The term which is here translated as "law", *qānūn*, exclusively refers to parliamentary law as the definition in Art. 94 (1) AC clarifies: "Law is what both Houses of the National Assembly approve and the President endorses unless this Constitution states otherwise." The criminal provisions of the *šarīʿa* could therefore only be applied if they

---

zwischen *sharīʿa*, Gesetz und Stammestradition in Afghanistan", in: *Matthias Kötter / Gunter Folke Schuppert* (Eds.), "Normative Pluralität Ordnen", Baden-Baden 2009, p. 257 et seqq (pp. 267 et seq.).

42 *Hafizullah Gardesh*, "Koran Translation Provokes Controversy", in: Institute for War and Peace Reporting (Ed.), Afghan Recovery Report No. 276 of 10 December 2007; *Rahim Faiez / Heidi Vogt*, "Afghan court upholds sentences in Quran trial", The Associated Press, February 15, 2009. The appeals court sentenced the owner of the print shop that had published the book to 15 months and three other men charged with trying to help Zalmay flee the country with just over seven months. All these sentences were already served at the time of the court decision.

43 Official Gazette of Afghanistan No. 347, 1976.

44 In the official Afghan legal order, the Constitution is the supreme law of the land which may not be violated by parliamentary law or governmental decrees.

were transferred into parliamentary law without any further violation of the provisions of the Afghan Constitution, such as the freedom of expression (Art. 34 AC).[45]

Many, if not most Afghans seem to agree with the imposing of *šarīʿa* punishments on perpetrators. Promoting this position is of essential interest to the Islamic scholars who have considerable influence on the public opinion, especially the 'Ulamā' Council. A vast majority of judges who did not receive a higher education in law but only in Islamic science are also generally ready to impose *šarīʿa* penalties.[46] The government and the parliament have not taken a clear stance on the issue.[47]

3. Incomplete Courts and Absence of Prosecutors

Art. 27 AC states in its third paragraph that "No one shall be punished without the decision of an authoritative court taken in accordance with the provisions of the law [...]". There are, however, diverse forms of violations of this principle. In some courts visited by UNAMA there were less than three judges as required and in one court in Mazār-e Šarīf two judges appeared to be the normal court presence. Even more problematic is the fact that frequently and all over the country prosecutors did not take part in the hearings as required by law. The prosecution was regularly carried out by the judge, compromising the judge's impartiality.[48] Court clerks or secretaries taking notes of the proceedings as required by the law were also rarely seen.[49]

---

45 The opposite, formalistic view arguing that Art. 1 of the *qānun-e ǧazā* (Penal Code) is a parliamentary law and thus meets the requirements of Art. 27 AC contradicts the very idea of the *nullum crimen sine lege* principle that crime and sanction themselves must be defined in the law. This contradiction is fully intentional, aiming at legitimising the application of *šarīʿa* penalties.

46 In 2006 only 11.6% of all judges had a law degree. *Livingston Armytage*, "Rebuilding Judicial Competence After the Generation of War", in: ZaöRV, volume 67, Stuttgart 2007, pp. 185 et seqq. (on p. 190).

47 The adoption by the National Assembly of a new, *šarīʿa* based family law for the Šīʿa population which would not comply with human rights standards, and the original approval by the government – subsequently withdrawn only upon international protest – even demonstrated a certain readiness to sacrifice human rights standards in violation of Art. 7 AC.

48 UNAMA LSOP staff report that only three out of ten trials observed in Kābul in July 2007 were held in the presence of a prosecutor. In Ǧalālabād in July 2007 three cases were adjourned because the prosecutor did not attend court. In Mazār-e Šarīf judges sent a letter to the prosecutor's department in July 2007 requesting regular attendance at trial hearings.

49 According to information received from UNAMA LSOP, supra, footnote 39.

One reason for the diminished presence of judges and prosecutors in criminal procedures is their small number in the country. Approximately 1850 judges and 1710 prosecutors serving 32 million citizens are certainly not enough for the administration of all cases which are brought before court.[50] Another possible reason for the prosecutors to stay away from trials seems be insufficient confidence and cooperation between the different justice institutions. The flow of information between police who usually investigate the cases, prosecutors who complete the investigation and submit indictments to the courts, and the judges who chair the hearings and finally decide the cases is a considerable problem. Prosecutors have reported feeling neutralised by judges who do not allow them to perform their role in the court procedure. Ideological differences between the judges who mainly study *šarīʿa* at a university or *madrasa*[51] and the prosecutors who in the average have a secular background[52] play a significant role in this conflict.

4. Prosecution by Tribal or Local Councils

Another conflict line is the relation between the formal judicial system of the state and the informal, traditional mechanisms of dispute resolution. The main traditional mechanisms are tribal and local councils called *ǧirga* in the Pashtun areas and *šūrā* in other regions.[53] While decades of civil war in Afghanistan weakened the state justice system, people relied more on the informal structures to resolve their disputes.[54] The *ǧirga*s and *šūrā*s have lost some of their importance since the fall of the Ṭālibān, but not in all parts of the country, especially not in the rural Pashtun areas. This is also where the punishment of alleged

50 Both figures as of 20 March 2009, according to *taškilāt-e stera maḥkame* (Organisational Charts of the Supreme Court) and the *lu-ye tsārnvāli* (Attorney General's Office) of the year 2008. About 150 young judges and 100 prosecutors annually join the service.

51 About 56% of the 160 judges who took part in a MPIL Fair Trial Trainings between March 2007 and May 2009 had studied at a Šarīʿa Faculty, 17% at a Law & Political Sciences Faculty, 13% at had visited a *madrasa*, 10% only a school and 3% had a different higher education. MPIL Collection, Kabul.

52 34% of the prosecutors attending one of the afore-mentioned trainings had studied Law & Political Sciences, 16% Šarīʿa, 36% had visited a Police Academy or other university faculties, 4% came from *madrasa*s, and 8% attended only school.

53 The Pashtun *ǧirga* is a community-based institution and process for collective decision making and is often used as a dispute settlement mechanism, including imposing agreed sanctions and using tribal forces to enforce its decisions. *Šūrā* usually refers to a group of elders or recognised leaders who make decisions on behalf of the community they represent. See, *Ali Wardak* et al., "Bridging Modernity and Tradition: The Rule of Law and the Search for Justice", UNDP Afghanistan Human Development Report 2007, Islamabad 2007, p. 91 et seq.

54 *Sudhindra Sharma / Pawan Kumar Sen*, "Institutionalisation of the Justice System", supra, footnote 35, on p. 46.

criminals by local or tribal councils seems to happen most frequently. One case of a death penalty imposed upon a female adulterer was however reported from the Spingul valley (Dare-ye Spingol) in Badaḫšān province.[55]

Some authors estimate that up to 80% of all disputes are resolved outside the court system.[56] In criminal cases the ratio seems to be lower. Of all the participants in the 2006 Asia Foundation Survey 13% had been a victim in the past 12 months and more than half of those 13% said that they had reported the incident to the police and/or another law enforcement institution. In the 2008 Asia Foundation Survey, 16% said they had been victim and all reported the incident to a formal justice institution. Even though the surveys suggest a slight trend away from the state institutions[57], these specific results indicate that that a majority of all criminal cases was referred to the formal justice system.

Sometimes the state officials themselves do not support the formal justice system. A prosecutor described criminal cases in Dur Baba District (Valsvāli-ye Dor Bābā) in the south eastern Nangarhār Province were regularly kept way from the justice institutions and referred them to a *ǧirga:*

> " [...] *the District Governor* [...] *has given all the authorities of the other institutions in the region to himself. He refers the legal and criminal cases to the jirga. When we ask him to send the cases to the relevant offices, he argues that this is a tribal matter, this a tribal area, this is custom etc and keeps the case under his control. It is worth mentioning that the Head of the District Police Department is his companion. Behind the above mentioned arguments he hides all his crimes and outrages the public goods. Who are the members of the jirga? Elders who the District Governor gathered* [...]. *So we observe that when a murder happens, the District Governor, instead of sending the case to the primary prosecutor's office or primary court, he sends it to jirga, haq Allah*[[58]] *almost forgotten* [...]. *If we take a regular*

55 Written Case Report from Kunduz, 3 April 2007, in: MPIL Collection, supra, footnote 20, KUZ-7. The case is analysed to in more detail by *Tilmann J. Röder*, "Kollisionen zwischen *sharī'a*, Gesetz und Stammestradition...", supra, footnote 41, on pp. 293 et seq.

56 *Ali Wardak* et al., "Bridging Modernity and Tradition...", supra, footnote 53, p. 9.

57 To the Afghan National Police reported 63% of respondents in 2006 and 48% in 2008; to the district/provincial authorities (governors) 10% (2006) and 29% (2008); to the tribal leader (*malik*) 21% (2006) and 24% (2008); to *šūrā*/*ǧirga*/elders 16% (2006 and 2008); to the Afghan National Army 11% (2006) and 9% (2008); to the local mullah 5% (2006) and 7% (2008): to the prosecutors 7% (2006) and 5% (2006); to local commanders/warlords 6% (2006) and 5% (2008), to local militias 6% (2006) and 3% (2008); to the *kamisiyun-e mostaqill-e hoquq-e bašar-e Afǧānestān* (Afghanistan Independent Human Rights Commission) 3% (2006) and 2% (2008), to the central government 4% (2006) and 2% (2008); to courts 4% (2006) and 2% (2008).

58 *Ḥaqq Allāh*: The right of God. The reporting prosecutor here refers to the application of *šarī*ʿ*a* penalties which are seen as *ḥaqq Allāh* by conservative Muslims. *Ḥaqq ādamī* (le-

> *step against the District Governor to stop him from these illegal activities, then that group of elders that they introduced themselves as representative of the people, stand behind him and support him. So then we can do nothing because we are civil servants who do not have guns, money, and power."*[59]

The resolution of societal conflicts by *ǧirgas* or *šūrās* is not approved by the legal order. From a human rights perspective the state institutions alone have the legitimacy to deal with crime because they alone are bound by the human rights standards. Furthermore, the state should maintain the monopoly of limiting the rights of citizens e.g. by detaining them or imposing penalties under the conditions permitted by the law.

III. Equality Before the Law

The principle of equality before the law (Art. 22 AC) prohibits any discrimination throughout all stages of the criminal prosecution. In reality, however, inequality begins with the lack of courts especially in the southern and eastern parts of the country. In the northern provinces of Kunduz, for example, there are 63 judges and 69 prosecutors in a population of 933,000 habitants. This is certainly by far not enough for a regular resolution of the many conflicts within a post war society, but at least there are currently judges and prosecutors in every district. In the vast southern province of Urūzgān a population of about 627,000 is served by only three judges and three prosecutors who all based in the provincial capital.[60] Equal access to justice is not realised as long as this structural divide between the different parts of the country and between cities and rural areas remains. Nevertheless, and surprisingly, the population's perception of the accessibility of courts has improved during the past years and in 2008, over two-thirds of the respondents (68%) in a survey answered that they felt that state courts are accessible to them. However, just less than a third (29%) do not feel that they can access state courts easily. More urban dwellers agree that state courts are accessible to them (77%) than their rural counterparts in rural areas (66%) and more men (73%) than women (63%) feel the same.[61]

Law enforcement officials in many cases discriminate between men and women, powerful and weak, rich and poor, citizens from different ethnic or religious

gal positions of humans including the modern notion of human rights) are seen as a lower category. *Clinton Bennett*, "Muslims and Modernity", New York, 2004, p. 65.

59 Written Case Report from Jalalabad, 18 May 2009, in: MPIL Collection, supra, footnote 20, JLB-2.

60 Figures as of 20 March 2009.

61 Only 64% of respondents who never went to school agree with this statement as compared to 70% who studied to sixth grade, 74% who studied to ninth grade, and 78% who studied to tenth grade or above; *The Asia Foundation*, "Afghanistan in 2008 – A Survey of the Afghan People", Kabul 2008, p. 75.

groups, Afghans and foreigners without any legal justification although the Afghan Constitution clearly states that "The citizens of Afghanistan – whether man or woman – have equal rights and duties before the law." (Art. para. 2 AC).

Women are in many recurring situations not granted the same substantial and procedural rights like men. For example, the substantial provisions of the existing family and heritance law solidify their weak social and economic position. Another example is the weight of evidence given by women in *hudūd* and *qiṣāṣ* cases when dealt with before the courts (which is in itself a violation of the principle of legality). *Šarīʿa*-educated judges tend to give a woman's testimony half of the weight given to evidence brought forth by men. Some judges apply this rule also to other cases. Nevertheless, slightly more women take their cases to state than men because they are even worse discriminated by traditional institutions in Afghanistan.[62] The state justice system does not effectively enough take its role in enforcing gender equality and redressing the shortcomings of informal mechanisms of conflict resolution with respect to women's rights and human rights more generally.

IV. Presumption of Innocence

The principle of the presumption of innocence is well established in the law in the books. Art. 25 AC states that "Innocence is the original state. An accused is considered innocent until convicted by a final decision of an authorised court."

The presumption of innocence requires independence and impartiality of judges. This is also relevant for all other law enforcement officials to the extent that they must be able to investigate a crime without any undue influence or prejudice affecting their acts and decisions.

In practice, problems begin with many police and prosecutors believing that their function is to prove the guilt of the accused and not also to search for evidence of their innocence. As a response to this problem, foreign aid agencies have introduced the Anglo-American principle of equality of arms which means that the accused in court should have the same possibilities to prove his version of the case as the prosecutor, for example, by having his own witnesses invited. This approach is, however, counterproductive in a country where most accused are illiterate, left without any legal assistance and barely understand the criminal procedure.

1. Prejudice Against Suspects and Accused

The UNAMA court observers noted in all regions of their activity that a majority of judges appeared to assume that the accused was guilty, often asking the

---

62 *Sudhindra Sharma / Pawan Kumar Sen*, "Institutionalisation of the Justice System", supra, footnote 35, on p. 55.

accused why they were lying or demanding them to confess. In a case from Herāt the judge showed bias by stating that:

> "*the facial appearance of the defendant was an indication that he was a drug addict and drug addicts usually commit any sort of crimes to obtain the means to buy their drugs.*"[63]

In Mazār-e Šarīf, a judge mentioned that he believed that the accused was an opium addict which was irrelevant as the charge was theft of a bicycle.[64] In another case from the same city, the judge told a group of accused at the very beginning of the trial that he had heard that they were famous for illegal activities. He seemed to take this as an evidence of guilt instead of hard proof of their alleged perpetrations.[65]

Women are generally at a greater risk of being judged according to their reputation, such as in the following example:

> "*A man and woman were charged with zina [adultery]. The woman claimed that she was not guilty and that she had been forcibly drugged and forced to live with the accused for three months. The man claimed to have married her believing her to be a widow with no children. At trial she was nine months pregnant which he claimed he had not noticed.*
>
> *On appeal the prosecutor argued that she was guilty because even if what she said was true, she did not escape or try to inform the police. The judge called her 'a bad woman' even before the verdict had been reached, suggesting bias against women in cases of a sensitive moral nature.*[66]

Here again legal norms are not distinguished from social norms. The accused was convicted because of assumed immoral behavior, rather than proven criminal activity.

2. Punishment Despite Doubts about the Guilt of the Accused

The principle of guilt is another fundamental element in *Western* and *Islamic* criminal law systems and in both systems guilt is strictly personal.[67] In Afghanistan, too, the court's conviction that the accused is guilty of a crime is a necessary precondition of any punishment.[68] The guilt of the accused may not be based on the judge's personal impression alone, but sufficient verifiable indications are necessary. However, in more than half of the 120 cases observed by UNAMA in 2007, the prosecutors offered no evidence at all, and in 21 cases the only evidence offered were doubtful pre-trial confessions. In none of the fifteen

---

63 According to information received from UNAMA LSOP, supra, footnote 39.
64 According to information received from UNAMA LSOP, supra, footnote 39.
65 Ibidem.
66 According to information received from UNAMA LSOP, supra, footnote 39.
67 *Silvia Tellenbach*, "Fair Trial Guarantees...", supra, footnote 4, p. 932.
68 Arts. 25, 26 AC and 14 para. 2 ICCPR.

cases observed in Herāt during March and April 2007, the nine Jalalabad cases of May 2007, the ten Kābul cases and the Kunduz four cases in July 2007 not a single witness was called, thus also depriving the accused of the opportunity of questioning any of the witnesses. Almost all of these trials ended with convictions.[69] In one case,

> "*The prosecutor could not answer the panel of judges' question why there was no evidence presented supporting the allegation that the accused was driving his motorcycle faster than the legal speed limit. Despite recognising that there was no evidence against the accused, the judges still convicted him and sentenced him for one and a half months of imprisonment.*"[70]

Evidence of guilt presented in the courtroom was in many cases improperly collected by police and prosecutors who have little knowledge of criminalistic techniques. Even worse, the testimonies and pieces of evidence are usually not sufficiently probed by the courts.[71] In singular cases individuals are even convicted against the judges' conviction that they are not guilty. One such situation was reported from Kābul:

> "*Article 310 of Penal Code prohibits the forging of an Afghan passport or knowingly using a forged passport. The accused had come from Iran with a forged passport, to visit her dead mother's grave. Going to the airport to return to her family in Iran, she was arrested at the airport but given bail.*
>
> *The judges allowed her to tell her story and were reported as being very kind to her. The report suggests the judges believed she had been a victim of a forger and did not know that her documents were forged. She was nevertheless convicted and sentenced to a fine of 5000 Afghanis.*"[72]

V. Freedom from Unlawful Detention

The presumption of innocence further requires that coercive measures taken against an accused are proportionate to the gravity of the charges brought against him. Fundamentally, detention during the investigation and trial phases should be exceptional and must be justified by compelling reasons, such as the danger of flight or obstruction of the investigation. In this respect, a change of the detention policy of all law enforcement institutions is necessary because they tend to detain suspects without any serious assessment of the justification of such a measure. Worsening this grave situation, more than 80% of all pretrial detainees are held longer than permitted by the law.[73]

---

69 According to information received from UNAMA LSOP, supra, footnote 39.

70 According to information received from UNAMA LSOP, supra, footnote 39.

71 According to information received from UNAMA LSOP, supra, footnote 39.

72 Ibidem. The amount of 5000 Afghanis equals about 100 USD.

73 JSSP Bagrām – The police may hold a suspect up to 72 hours (Art.15 and 25 Police Law). Detention may be extended by the prosecution and courts up to three months after

In Herāt,

> "*The accused was under eighteen years when arrested. His co-accused were arrested at the same time and they had been tried in the adult court within a few months of arrest, but he had been transferred to the Juvenile Correction Centre, where it seems his case was forgotten. He spent fourteen months in the Juvenile Correction Centre before his case came to trial. At trial, the prosecutor presented no evidence against the accused except a confession made to the police, but with no defence representative present to ensure the confession was genuine. The accused retracted the confession given to the police, saying the police had forced him to give the confession and it was not true.*
>
> *A defence lawyer argued the court was not allowed to consider evidence gained unlawfully and that the police confession was not reliable evidence under Art 7 ICCC. The prosecutor provided no other evidence. The judges found the accused not guilty.*"[74]

There are also cases of convicted persons who remain longer in prison than the court had imposed upon them.[75] One military prosecutor exemplified:

> "*I can give you names of prison inmates like Abdul Qahar and Hekramuddin who (...) were convicted by decision of the military tribunal to a sentence of three years and who appealed against this decision. Until now there has been no appeal decision. The appeals court demanded that the persons would be brought to the capital Kabul [which is the seat of the military appeals court], and this on their own expenses. As the persons are not able to pay the travel expenses by themselves, nobody felt responsible for bringing them to Kabul. For this reason they remained in prison although they had served their sentence.*"[76]

VI. Right to an Adequate Defence

The right to an adequate defence becomes effective immediately at the moment of arrest. It includes much more than the right to have the assistance of a private or a state-paid lawyer. The accused can defend themselves adequately only if he is informed about charges, his right to remain silent and the fact that the burden of proof was on the prosecution immediately after arrest.[77] The UNAMA court observers reported, however, that the accused often made a voluntary confession

---

the arrest (Art. 6, 39, 53 ICCC). If the time limits are not followed, the suspect or accused, respectively, shall be released (Arts. 6 para. 3 and 36 ICCC).

74 According to information received from UNAMA LSOP, supra, footnote 39.

75 Prisons are obliged to release these persons under Art. 50c *qānun-e maḥābis va tavqif ḫāne-hā* (Law of Prisons and Detention Centres).

76 Written Case Report from Herat, 17 April 2007, in: MPIL Collection, supra, footnote 20, HRT-3. The names of the prisoners have been changed in order to protect their security.

77 The information rights are provided in Arts. 5, 19, 31 ICCC.

to the court without prior information about their rights. If they were advised of the right to a defence lawyer, the courts rarely explained what this meant.[78]

A suspect awaiting trial must be granted adequate time and the means to prepare their defence.[79] During trial, the accused may only be absent under the narrow conditions defined by the law.[80] When present, he must have the opportunity to call his own witnesses and question witnesses introduced by the prosecution. This is frequently not granted and if so, it would need an experienced defence counsel who fully understands the alleged crime and the applicable law so that the charges can be refuted.[81] However, this fundamental right is mere theory due to the lack of defence counsel in Afghanistan, especially in the provinces. There are only 266 private attorneys registered with the *anǧoman-e mostaqill-e vokalā-ye madāfeʿ-e Afǧānestān* (Afghan Independent Bar Association)[82], many of which do not work in the field of criminal law, and the state-run Legal Aid Organisation (*moʾassasāt-e mosāʿadate-hā-ye hoquqi [davlati]*) has only slowly begun to operate. In 2007 the UNAMA Observers noted that defence lawyers featured in only 27 cases out of the 120 observed cases. Of those cases, 4 defence lawyers were hired privately; all others were employees of NGO legal aid organisations.[83] These figures have not considerably changed. In the 2008 survey of the Asia Foundation, two-thirds (66%) of all respondents who had taken a case to a state court reported that they pleaded their case alone or were helped by friends or relatives. Only around one in five respondents (22%) said they used the professional legal services of a lawyer. But this ratio can be seen as an improvement compared with the situation under former legal systems where no independent lawyers operated as defence attorneys at all.[84]

Defence attorneys generally seem to be of variable quality, some arguing the law effectively but others merely reading statements which consisted of their version of events without addressing the law or challenging the prosecution's arguments. Their work is hampered by limited access to case files or seeing the

---

78 According to information received from UNAMA LSOP, supra, footnote 39.

79 Art. 42 para. 2 ICCC.

80 According to information received from UNAMA LSOP, supra, footnote 39, the accused was usually present.

81 See ibid, p. 238 (241).

82 AIBA List of attorneys as of March 23, 2009.

83 Afghan NGOs, such as Qanoon Gushtonky (Qānun-e Ḫavāhān), and foreign NGOs, such as Norwegian Refugee Council, International Legal Foundation and Medica Mondiale, have established defence attorney offices.

84 *Nemat Nojumi / Dyan Mazurana / Elizabeth Stites*, "Afghanistan's Systems of Justice: Formal, Traditional, and Customary", Medford, MA: Youth and Community Program, Tufts University, 2004, p. 21.

evidence in advance.[85] More effective defence lawyers could, however, challenge the indictment. Judges do willingly accept reasonable arguments.[86]

In addition to the right to legal counsel, the accused must be assisted by an interpreter if he does not understand the language of the court. This is a relevant right in a multi-lingual country like Afghanistan. However, when there is a need of translation, an interpreter is usually not available.[87]

VII. Freedom from Torture and Other Forms of Inhuman Treatment

Another major problem in Afghanistan is the unlawful[88] use of evidence gathered by prohibited forms of examination, especially torture. In one trial held in Kābul:

> " *Three men were accused of narcotics offences after police had raided a house and found a bag of containing 1.9 kg heroin. There was no evidence against two of the accused except that they were present when the raid took place and had made a confession to the police they claimed was obtained through torture.*
>
> *The third accused said the heroin was planted as false evidence. The accused said the police informer owed his family half a million Afghanis [[89]] from land and livestock transactions in Badakhshan. The accused had come to ask for the money. The accused claimed the police informer agreed to travel back to Badakhshan with him to pay the debt. In preparation of the journey the police informer had given a bag to the accused to hold ready for the journey, saying it was clothes. The accused said he had trusted the police informer, not knowing that it contained heroin.*
>
> *At the trial all three accused showed marks of assault on their bodies, and claimed to have been tortured by the police to give false confessions. The police informer was not called as a witness and could not be questioned.*
>
> *One accused man was acquitted for lack of evidence, but the other two were convicted. There was no judicial enquiry into the allegation the tip off was false and malicious, no calls for evidence of the debt or for the police informer to give evidence, no investigation into the allegations of torture despite the marked bodies, and the confession made to the police was unlawfully admitted as evidence.* "[90]

---

[85] Both the accused and his defence have the right to see relevant documents and physical evidence prior to the trial, Art. 43 ICCC.

[86] According to information received from UNAMA LSOP, supra, footnote 39.

[87] A prosecutor reported a case from Nūristān where the accused came from the Dari-speaking province of Ǧawzǧān did not understand the local languages Pashto and Nūristāni. Oral Case Report from Jalalabad, 18 Max 2009, in: MPIL Collection, supra, footnote 20, JLB-4.

[88] Art. 7 ICCC.

[89] Equivalent of about 10,000 USD.

[90] According to information received from UNAMA LSOP, supra, footnote 39.

Besides the fact that any cruel, inhuman, and degrading treatment is strictly forbidden under Afghan law, the truthful content of testimonies given under torture or other pressure is highly doubtful. Nevertheless, widespread use of torture occurs. A study of the *kamisiyun-e mostaqill-e hoquq-e bašar-e Afġānestān* (Afghanistan's Independent Human Rights Commission – AIHRC) found evidence that most of the 398 interviewed torture victims were mistreated either by the police (65%) or by the NDS (14.8%).[91] Over 84% of the respondents stated that they were tortured because they did not confess.[92] Lack of means to prove crime is another major causal factor of torture in law enforcement institutions. At least 6.5% of the interviewed law enforcement officials believed that were allowed to torture suspects or accused to this aim. General lack of knowledge of the involved officials of the rights of suspects and accused persons is a closely related causal factor of torture in criminal prosecution.[93]

Another case was reported to the author in Badaḫšān where two accused showed the court the wounds from police torture only when the police officers had been sent out of the courtroom. The judge did not accept the alleged confessions of the accused as evidence because they had been given under torture. However,

> *"The policemen could not be convicted because they referred to their special rights and branch of the special judicial system. Here the court was powerless."*[94]

This statement of the reporting judge is not correct. It is true that he, as an ordinary judge, would not have had the permission to investigate against the police, but he could have referred the case to the competent branch of the prosecution.

The fact that torture and other cruel, inhuman, or degrading treatment does not lead to any negative consequences for the involved law enforcement officials is another reason why these cases occurs so frequently. About 99% of the officials interviewed by the AIHRC believed that torture cases are not followed up. Over 56% of interviewed victims did not complain to any institution against their torture because they did not know about their rights or believed that a complaint would not lead to any consequence.[95] Unless this situation changes they will feel free to continue with the unlawful behavior.

---

91 AIHRC Causes of Torture in Law Enforcement Institutions Report, http://www.aihrc.org.af (accessed on 20 July 2009), p. 13 et seq.

92 AIHRC Causes of Torture Report, supra, footnote 91, p. 16.

93 AIHRC Causes of Torture Report, supra, footnote 91, p. 18 et seq.

94 Written Case Report from Kunduz, 3 April 2007, in: MPIL Collection, supra, footnote 20, KUZ-5.

95 AIHRC Causes of Torture Report, supra, footnote 91, p. 20 et seq.

VIII. Trial Open to the Public

The principle that court hearings must be open to the public (Art. 128 AC) primarily aims at safeguarding the rights and interests of the accused. Furthermore, it is also a matter of public interest that justice is properly administrated. The principle comprises two components: the right to a public hearing and the right to a public judgment. There are only a few permissible exceptions, for example in juvenile cases.

Again, reality widely deviates far from the theory. The UNAMA court observers reported that in most of the courts across the country, the general public – including the media – were not encouraged to attend court hearings. In Mazār-e Šarīf, offices were used as courtrooms which were simply too small to admit members of the public. Policemen preventing the public from entering the courtroom like in the situation described in the introduction do not seem to be an exception:

> *"In some courts in Kabul, orders are given to prevent any member of the public entering the room being used as a courtroom. Sometimes armed guards are posted at the door and orders are given that only the concerned parties and officials are allowed to enter. The reason given is that there are no suitable trial facilities or courts, therefore the trials are conducted in judges' offices. These offices are too small even to accommodate the judges' panel conveniently so there is no room to provide seats for the public as well."*[96]

In another case,

> *"The trial had a high local profile and had been mentioned on local television. Relatives of the victim and accused were present at the trial. Whilst deciding a verdict, the judges ordered everyone to leave the courtroom except the UNAMA Observer. The Presiding Judge told the UNAMA Observer that by law the judicial discussion about the case and the decision on the verdict should take place in private, but the announcement of the verdict must be public. He added that he thought the public should be present as much as possible, and he would even like the judicial discussion to be public so the public can see the judges' performance as clearly as possible and see that justice was done."*[97]

Minutes of the hearings are almost never taken, reasons of decisions rarely recorded and verdicts not published.[98] Consequently, the public is not sufficiently informed about how the courts deal with crime and with the underlying societal conflicts.

---

[96] According to information received from UNAMA LSOP, supra, footnote 39.
[97] According to information received from UNAMA LSOP, supra, footnote 39.
[98] According to information received from UNAMA LSOP, supra, footnote 39.

IX. The Right to Appeal and Review

A criminal sentence can have a damaging impact on the person concerned, not only through the punishment inflicted on him, but also through its stigmatising effect. The defendant must have an opportunity to have the decision imposing such a burden reviewed. In addition, reducing the risk of erroneous criminal punishment is a matter of public interest. The right to appeal against the verdict of a first instance court and to review the decision of an appeals court is guaranteed in Afghanistan.[99] A surprisingly large number of convicted persons make use of this right. They can be successful, like in this case from Ǧalālabād:

> " *The accused appealed a conviction of using fake currency. With a defence lawyer in the appeals court, the conviction was overturned and he was acquitted. The evidence on which he was convicted by the lower court consisted of the allegation of a shopkeeper and a fake currency note provided by the shopkeeper to the police. The convicted man's defence was that the shopkeeper had been extorting money from him under threat of being falsely reported for use of false currency. Finally he refused to pay the extortion. The shopkeeper reported him to the police and handed over the fake currency. The appeals court accepted the defence arguments that it was for the prosecution to prove the shopkeeper's allegation was true, not for the accused to prove he was innocent. The prosecution had not provided any proof that the shopkeeper's allegation was true.* "[100]

Deciding is, however, difficult for the appeals court when reasons are not given by lower courts. Judges from the Supreme Court say that verdicts are rarely annulled, but sentences in many cases diminished.[101]

X. Intermediate Result: Courts of Law or Courts Without Law?

The analysis shows that all fair trial standards are violated in Afghanistan. The courts established by law do not operate on the legal basis defined by Art. 130 AC. Moreover, they are bypassed in many cases by traditional forms of conflict resolution or, even worse, unregulated exercise of power. It seems that M. Cherif Bassiouni's assessment of the human rights situation in Afghanistan of 2005 is still widely valid:

> " 26. The justice system currently suffers from severe and systematic problems related to: limited public resources; the legacy of decades of violent conflict; the absence of strong State institutions, especially in rural areas;

---

99 Art. 53 para. 4 LOJC limits the right to appeal to punishments to fine exceeding 50,000 Afghanis (1,000 USD), but such limitations are seen as acceptable under the ICCPR. *Manfred Nowak*, CCPR Commentary, supra, footnote 40, pp. 350 et seq.

100 According to information received from UNAMA LSOP, supra, footnote 39.

101 Information provided to the author by Dr. ʿAbdul Mālik Kāmawi, General Director of the Administration of the Afghan Judiciary (*Āmer-e ʿomumi-ye Edāri-ye qovve-ye qażāʾiya Afġānestān*).

> corruption; and significant problems of basic capacity and infrastructure. While the Government has sought to address these issues, the formal justice system remains inadequate and lacks public confidence and legitimacy. [...]
>
> 27. The administration of justice suffers from an array of problems including: lengthy pre-trial detentions that sometimes exceed the length of potential sentences; institutionalized corruption; violations of due process; severe lack of public defenders; capacity-building needs; and systematic inequities that negatively impact women, children, minorities and others. Problems regarding the fair and impartial administration of justice are associated with a lack of political will to enforce the law, powerful patronage relationships, systemic corruption and other factors that allow politically empowered individuals and groups to circumvent their legal responsibilities. In addition, judges and others willing to uphold the rule of law are often asked to act against factional commanders and other empowered groups without being provided with adequate security. [...]
>
> 31. [...] Decisions by customary law bodies tend to be accepted by both parties and contribute to restoring community harmony. However, from the human rights perspective, customary law raises serious concerns regarding due process protections, the uniformity of judgment and punishment, and fundamental principles of equality, especially as regards women. The independent expert urges the creation of a special governmental body to integrate the ideas and practices of customary law into the formal activities of the State, linking the legitimacy and public trust associated with customary law with a commitment to basic human rights."[102]

However, since Bassiouni wrote his report some positive developments have taken place, which allow careful hope for the gradual implementation of the fair trial standards in the Afghan court practice. Most importantly, the education of law professionals is considerably better than in 2005. Universities have modernised their law and *šarīʿa* curricula. New books and manuals about contemporary Afghan law are slowly replacing outdated Afghan and foreign, mainly Iranian literature. Only very few candidates for judicial or other legal services are not university graduates,[103] and they all attend vocational education courses of at least one year where knowledge gaps between *šarīʿa* and law graduates are closed and legal practice is explained. In the provinces, many courthouses and office buildings of the justice institutions have been repaired or are newly constructed and law sets distributed. The Afghan Bar Association was established in July 2008 and the number of registered attorneys is steadily rising. All these

---

102 *M. Cherif Bassiouni*, Report of the independent expert on the situation of human rights in Afghanistan, to the Commission on Human Rights of the Economic and Social Council of the United Nations (UN-Doc. E/CN.4/2005/122 of 11 March 2005).

103 The number of *šarīʿa* students among young judges is, however, still inappropriately high, given the fact that courts shall primarily apply parliamentary law.

steps forward are elements of the *atratiži-ye melli-ye sektur-e ʿadli* (National Justice Sector Strategy) of 2008.[104]

D. Reasons of the Non-Compliance with Fair Trial Standards

Some fundamental problems nevertheless continue to exert negative influence on the implementation of the fair trial principles in the field of criminal justice. Three reasons of the institutions' and law professionals' non-compliance with the prescribed standards can be identified.

I. Legacies from War and the Impact of the Insurgency

The common expression "rebuilding the justice system" sounds like a euphemism in a country where judicial structures never had been much developed.[105] More than a quarter of a century of war and civil strife and abrupt changes between Marxist (1979-1992), Ṭālibān (1996-2001) and democratic rule (since 2001) combined with long phases of anarchy devastated the ever-weak formal justice system. The spiral of violence led to a general increase of crime, while the capacity of the justice institutions to resolve conflicts was decreasing due to the destruction of their material resources and the emigration of a significant portion of the law professionals. First, the court structures of the communist regime (1979-1992) replaced those of the earlier monarchist and presidential regimes. They then collapsed to large extent when the communist regime was ousted by the *muǧāhidīn,* who never succeeded in setting up any functioning state structures due to internal struggles. The Ṭālibān, who took over in 1996, strengthened *šarīʿa* courts and tribal institutions, such as the *ǧirga*s and *šūrā*s. Since the end of their rule in 2001, a negligibly small number of law professionals are facing all the afore-described financial, logistical, institutional and professional difficulties in the performance of their tasks. The growing insurgency against the current state and its allies is adding to the difficulties as it hinders the justice institutions to reach out into many provinces.[106] Informal dispute resolution mechanisms and the new phenomenon of mobile Ṭālibān courts[107] fill the gaps. In relation to the professional deficiencies, the insufficient level of education of law professionals and lack of professional responsibility remain the

104 http://www.moj.gov.af (accessed on 20 July 2009).

105 *Ramin Moschtaghi*, "Organisation and Jurisdiction of the Newly Established Afghan Courts – The Compliance of the Formal System of Justice with the Bonn Agreement", in: Max Planck UNYB, volume 10, Leiden 2006, pp. 535 et seqq.

106 Many judges, prosecutors and other law enforcement officials have been killed in the past years because they are seen by the insurgents as agents of the state.

107 *Tilmann J. Röder*, „Kollisionen zwischen *sharī'a*, Gesetz und Stammestradition…", supra, footnote 41, on p. 297 et seq.

greatest concerns. While courthouses can be reconstructed and law sets distributed, it will take more than a decade to educate a new generation of law professionals who understand the legal system of their country including the fair trial standards and ably apply them in the resolution of societal conflicts. The state must win and ensure their loyalty and commitment.

The most depressing signs of widespread negligence are carelessness in accusing and sentencing persons without sufficient proof of guilt and indifference towards the fate of detainees and prisoners. One important underlying reason of these forms of professional misconduct is the lack of positive examples. Law professionals who grew up in a society which was ruled by guns, rather than by law lack a positive vision of fair justice. This vision is just visible, but slowly developing within the new generation of law and *šarīʿa* students. Only when they form a critical mass will there be a chance that unlawful patterns of behavior are overcome and human rights standards are effectively established in the Afghan justice system.

II. "Just a Theory"? Competing Normative Orders

Despite the fact that the Afghan Constitution demands judges and other law professionals to apply in the first instance the existing parliamentary laws, Islamic sources do play a significant role in legal practice. One reason for this is the fact that most judges received their higher education at *šarīʿa* faculties or *madrasa*s and their knowledge of the non-Islamic sources is limited. Another reason is that this group tends to refuse that the Constitution is the supreme law of the land, even though it strongly refers to Islamic principles. The elder judge who sentenced Bašīr and Ḥayātullāh in Herāt to death was one of the most active participants of Fair Trial Training organised by the Max Planck Institute for Comparative Public Law and International Law. After the seminar, he was most grateful, but admitted that after all, the principles enshrined in the Afghan Constitution, legislation and in the international law were in his view "just a theory": "Man-made laws come and go. Only the divine law remains."

Fortunately, the content and the objectives of the modern fair trial standards – i.e., protection of the fundamental rights which are derived from the dignity of the accused as a human being, and effective law enforcement – do widely comply with Islamic legal rules.[108] In most cases, the application of one or the other

---

[108] *Silvia Tellenbach*, "Fair Trial Guarantees...", supra, footnote 4; *Adel Omar Sherif*, "Generalities on Criminal Procedure under Islamic Sharī'a", in: *M. A. Abdel Haleem, Adel Omar Sherif, Kate Daniels* (Eds.), "Criminal Justice in Islam", London 2003, pp. 3-16; *Saeed Hasan Ibrahim / Nasir bin Ibrahim Mehemeed*, "Basic Principles of Criminal Procedure under Islamic Sharī'a", in: Ibidem, pp. 17-34; *Gamil Muhammed Hussein*, "Basic Guarantees in the Islamic Criminal Justice System", in: Ibidem, pp. 35-53; *Gamal Attia,*

would lead to very similar results. Nonetheless the inner resistance against allegedly non-Islamic sources of law remains one of the greatest problems for the implementation of the fair trial principles and the rule of law in general.

Another fundamental problem which needs to be resolved is the relation between the formal and informal mechanisms of conflict resolution. Afghanistan, like Nepal and North Yemen, belongs to the group of Asian countries which were never colonised. As a consequence the informal structures remained widely intact, differently from countries which were more or less forcibly modernised and in this course embraced *Western* legal systems. Approaches to streamline the justice system of Afghanistan began in the 1920's and enforced under the 1964 Constitution, but for various reasons such as political instability and the subsequent years of war and civil strife they broke down. The geographic terrain with its rugged mountains and the lack of road networks also played a role in delaying this process. Thus, unlike other non-colonised states which eventually came to have a unified justice system, Afghanistan continues to have a dual – or even multiple – justice system.[109] The discussion about possibly linking the formal and the informal systems has not led to any results so far.[110]

III. Strategic Mistakes in Rebuilding the Justice System

Early mistakes in the formation of the new Afghan state, such as the prioritisation of security in 2002, strengthening of illegitimate local power structures and insufficient or inadequate support to the justice institutions, undermined efforts to establish the rule of law. The difficulties described in this article are therefore the result of failures of the international community as well, which had committed to support the stabilisation of the young state. Local power structures, corruption and organised crime took a strong hold throughout Afghanistan, including the justice sector institutions. Lack of coordination of activities in the justice sector led to double and contradictory activities and waste of funding. The "Afghan ownership" of the development process remained an empty phrase where foreign experts drafted the justice sector strategies and new legislation. The ICCC is one such example. In a country where the law enforcement institutions

"The Right to a Fair Trial in Islamic Countries", in: *David Weissbrodt / Rüdiger Wolfrum* (Eds.), "The Right to a Fair Trial", supra, footnote 4, pp. 345-350.

109 *Sudhindra Sharma / Pawan Kumar Sen*, "Institutionalisation of the Justice System", supra, footnote 35, on p. 46 et seq.

110 Important contributions have been made by *Ali Wardak / et al.*, "Bridging Modernity and Tradition…", supra, footnote 53 and by the United States Institute for Peace (www.usip.org) as well as the Tribal Liaison Office (www.tlo-afghanistan.org). A mixed Afghan-international group of experts chaired by the Ministry of Justice is working on a strategy on the formal and informal justice sector.

severely lack sufficiently educated staff and material resources, the introduction of the ICCC caused legal insecurity, rather than clarity. Most judges and prosecutors did not receive copies of the new law in years and those who held it in their hands were rarely able to properly apply it.[111] The situation became even more difficult when legislation was introduced that superseded or amended provisions of the ICCC, especially the LOJC, the Law of the Police, the Juvenile Code, the Law on Prisons and Detention Centers and the Counter Narcotics Law. A similar strategic mistake was the belated decision to subvention the salaries of judges and other officials of the justice institutions, whose low salaries made them susceptible to corruption and bribery. There are, however, many positive examples, such as the establishment of attorney's offices by non-governmental organisations like the International Legal Foundation, Medica Mondiale and the Norwegian Refugee Council.

E. Final Remarks

What must be done to avoid unfair trials like that of Bašīr and Ḥayātullāh in the future?

The analysis has shown that the many singular improvements of the past years, important as they, have not yet combined into a general trend towards the protection of human rights in Afghan courtrooms. The fair trial principles can be successfully implemented only if the fundamental problems are overcome and judicial culture as a whole begins to change. Legal history demonstrates that such developments are never achieved in short periods of time. From this perspective, the few years since the fall of the Ṭālibān regime have brought remarkable steps forward. The examples of countries with similar conditions such as Nepal – another landlocked South Asian country with a non-colonial past and a recent history of insurgency (1996-2005) – show that the improvement of the courts' and justice institutions' performance is possible.[112]

While it is necessary that the older judges, prosecutors and other law professionals learn at least basics of the fair trial principles in order to avoid the worst human rights violations in the course of the criminal prosecution, the most energy must be invested into the new generation, which has begun to win back the

[111] The responsibility for this legislative failure mainly lies with the Italian Justice Project which drafted the law without considerable Afghan participation and convinced the President of the Republic to accept it. *Axel Schwarz*, "Justizreform und Islam in Afghanistan", in: ZaöRV, volume 65 Stuttgart 2005, pp. 257 et seqq. (on p. 264).

[112] *Sudhindra Sharma / Pawan Kumar Sen*, "Institutionalisation of the Justice System", supra, footnote 35, on p. 61, provide an interesting comparative analysis of the two countries.

trust of the people into the justice system. The financial and material challenges faced by the justice institutions can only be met with continuous foreign support for many more years. Donors and implementing agencies need to focus on the basic needs and coordinate better than they have so far with their Afghan partners. Last but not least, further analysis of the law in practice in Afghanistan needs to be undertaken for the renewal of the Afghan legal order.

Islam und Menschenrechte (Islam and Human Rights / الإسلام وحقوق الإنسان)
Hatem Elliesie (Hrsg./Editor), © Peter Lang Verlag: Frankfurt a.M. 2010

Shari'a and Implementation of Human Rights norms of Equality and Non Discrimination in the Family:
A Case Study of Family Law in Pakistan

Ayesha Shahid / Javaid Rehman, Hull / London

A. Introduction

This paper attempts to explore the implementation of family law in Pakistan vis-à-vis the international human rights framework and *šarīʿa* law from which it derives its legal basis. Pakistan is a signatory to various international human rights treaties and the Constitution of Pakistan includes provisions which are based on the international human rights norms of equality and non-discrimination. In this paper the inter-relationship between human rights norms and *šarīʿa*-based family law is assessed in light of four important areas of family law, i.e. marriage, custody and guardianship, polygamy and divorce.

As already demonstrated in previous articles of this volume, the *Qurʾān* and *ḥadīṯ* are the primary sources of *šarīʿa,* yet, when it comes to matters relating to family law, these sources are intermingled with customary and cultural norms. It is argued that while Islamic ideology of the roles of sexes may lie at the base of familial relations in Pakistan, the actual position of women, as manifested by social and legal attitudes towards them, is the result of overlapping customary and cultural norms. This influence of customary practices and cultural norms has halted the law reform process in legally pluralistic Muslim countries like Pakistan. Some reforms have been introduced in the area of family law by using the Islamic juristic techniques of *taḫaiyur* and *talfīq* to bring laws in conformity with basic human rights. Within the discourse, however, these reforms are considered to be half hearted, piecemeal measures because they fail to provide a complete redress to women. It is therefore argued that an inclusive approach is needed to examine *šarīʿa* law on a specific issue.

The first part of the paper looks into the jurisprudential aspects of family law by examining the primary sources of *šarīʿa*. The second part examines Pakistan's existing constitutional framework and its commitments to international human rights treaties. The third part analyses the legislative provisions in the area of family law. It examines legislation such as Child Marriage Restraint Act 1929, Dissolution of Muslim Marriages Act 1939 and Muslim Family Laws Ordinance 1961. The fourth section looks into some of the recent cases to analyse how courts have used the principles of Islamic jurisprudence in conjunction with constitutional and legislative provisions and human rights norms when deciding

Islam und Menschenrechte (Islam and Human Rights / الإسلام وحقوق الإنسان)
Hatem Elliesie (Hrsg./Editor), © Peter Lang Verlag: Frankfurt a.M. 2010, S. 361-386

cases relating to family matters. By way of conclusion, section four suggests a way forward for a fair and just implementation of family law in Pakistan.

B. Šarīʿa, Women's Rights and Family Law

Before discussing the impact of *šarīʿa* on Islamic family law it is pertinent here to look into the various meanings of the term *šarīʿa* and how it has been interpreted by contemporary Islamic scholars.

I. Šarīʿa in the contemporary Context: Views of Islamic Scholars

The traditionalist view of *šarīʿa* is that it is based on Divine revelation, is immutable and would remain unchanged for all times to come. This view has been challenged by a number of scholars. Hamid R. Kusha, John Louis Esposito, Asgharali Engineer, Riffat Hasan, Abdullahi A. An-Naʿim and Shaheen Sardar Ali argue that *šarīʿa* not only derives its authority from the Divine revelation but also consists of the Divinely inspired *sunna* of the Prophet as well echoing the opinions of early scholars who attempted to provide an interpretation of the few legal principles mentioned in the *Qurʾān*. In interpreting these legal principles the scholars used not just the *Qurʾān* text and/or *sunna* but also exercise *qiyās* and *iǧmāʿ*. The fluidity of the later sources reflects the adaptive and flexible nature of *šarīʿa*. These scholars also recognise the importance of customary practices that influence the development of *šarīʿa*.

Hamid R. Kusha argues that *šarīʿa,*

> " as an evolving legal doctrine had to confront pre-Islamic norms, beliefs and customs prevalent among Bedouin Arabs as well as when Islam spread to the other parts of the world other legal systems, customs and mores that existed in the Old world came into contact with Islam's evolving doctrine of law [as a result] this evolving doctrine neither remained a strict man-made doctrine of law [...] nor could it become one of strict theological doctrine such as that produced by medieval Christianity'.[1]

Asgharali Engineer, while emphasising the egalitarian basis of *Qurʾān*, further argues that

"šarīʿa must be seen both in its
cultural as well as *a normative and transcendental spirit.*"[2]

He is of the view that revising *šarīʿa* formulations does not mean that we are challenging the wisdom and intelligence of past jurists, rather we should remember that their works are a reflection of their own times and that they were aware of the possibilities of error of inferences.

---

1 *Hamid R. Kusha*, The Sacred Law of Islam, Aldershot / et al. 2002.

2 *Asgharali Engineer*, The Rights of Women in Islam, New York 2004, p. 17.

Abdullahi A. An-Naʿim is of the view that the term *šarīʿa* refers to

> " the general normative system of Islam as historically understood and developed by Muslim jurists, especially during the first three centuries of Islam – the eight to tenth centuries CE".[3]

He argues that

> " Islamic family law is that part of šarīʿa that applies to family relations through the political will of the state, is not šarīʿa based, and like all other laws, derives its authority from the political will of the state."[4]

Abdullahi A. An-Naʿim is opines that *šarīʿa* has never been and should never be the basis of family laws for Muslims.[5] For him, the only means of achieving equality and fairness for Muslim women within an Islamic perspective, is through human agency to understand the underlying (historically contextualized) rationale and spirit of the *Qurʾān* and *sunna* and develop equivalent social policy applicable in our modern context.[6] This, he suggests, would help Muslim countries in bringing their family law in consonance with their constitutional and international law obligations of protecting women's (human) rights.[7]

Shaheen Sardar Ali on the other hand, uses the term 'Principles of Islamic law' for *šarīʿa* as opposed to the classical concept of *šarīʿa* as immutable, unchangeable and Divine law.[8] She is of the view that this definition provides the foundation of her argument that

> " as the human interpretation of the Divine Will Shariʿa is the embodiment of a rich, dynamic, responsive living organism of norms, legal and non legal; hence transformative over time and place".[9]

Instead of using the term Islamic Law, she uses the term 'Islamic legal tradition' for the legal component of *šarīʿa* as this depicts the evolving and dynamic nature of *šarīʿa*.

---

3 *Abdullahi A. An-Na'im*, "Sharia and Islamic Family law: Transition and Transformation", in: *Abdullahi A. An-Na'im* (Ed.), Islamic Family Law in a Changing World, London 2002, on p. 1.

4 Ibidem, on p. 2.

5 Ibidem.

6 Ibidem, on p. 3.

7 Ibidem, on p. 4.

8 *Shaheen Sardar Ali*, "Systemically closed, cognitively open – A Critical Analysis of Transformative Processes in Islamic Law and Muslim State Practice", Keynote address given at the Conference 'Religion in the 21st Century' held at University of Copenhagen 19-23 September 2007, http://www.ku.dk/Satsning/Religion/copenhagenconference/index.htm (accessed on 15 February 2009), p. 6.

9 Ibidem, on p. 7.

Shaheen Sardar Ali argues that the emphasis of Muslim legal philosophy has essentially been an

> " elaboration and the analysis of Shari'a *in abstracto* rather than a science of the positive emanating from judicial tribunals. Therefore after an initially stimulating era of independent legal thought, intellectual stagnation set in, in particular at the theoretical level, creating a 'mismatch' between the rhetoric and reality of law. What has therefore been handed down as juristic legacy to succeeding generations of Muslims is not the 'living' normative and applicatory framework of Islamic law; only the fossilized theory of legal philosophy."[10]

Shaheen Sardar Ali elsewhere has argued that in Islamic legal tradition customs (*ʿurf* or *ʿada,* etc.) are also a source of law. She is of the view that

> " though a controversial source it plays an important role in the growth of the Islamic legal tradition as it speaks to the commonly held beliefs and convictions of communities."

She uses the example of some South Asian communities that have relied upon *ʿurf* to interpret Muslim laws of inheritance.[11]

As far as the notion of rights in *šarīʿa* is concerned John Louis Esposito suggests "hierarchisation of Qur'anic values" to deal with women's (human) rights in Islam.[12] He divides the Qur'ānic legislation into the ethico-religious dealing with the spiritual and moral aspects of life and socio-economic spheres dealing with the social and economic status.[13] In the former category, women are treated as equal to men in their creation as men and women, in their obligations and duties towards God as well as for all the rewards that are bestowed upon both men and women for the fulfilment of their duties. In the latter category however he finds that women are differentiated from men in their social status but such verses must be analysed in the socio-economic situation of the Arab society when the Qur'ān was revealed to the Prophet Muḥammad. Family law comes under the category of socio-economic values. In this category he finds that women are differentiated from men in their social status but such verses must be analysed in the socio-historical context of the Arab society. His analysis of law and its impact on women's lives in the Muslim societies shows that Muslim family law reflects the social mores of the time.

Following John Louis Esposito's framework of women's (human) rights in Islam, Shaheen Sardar Ali proposes to use a method of "categorisation of rights"

---

10 Ibidem.

11 Ibidem, on p. 8.

12 *Shaheen Sardar Ali*, Gender and Human Rights in Islam and International Law Equal Before Allah, Unequal Before Man?, The Hague 2000. p. 49.

13 Ibidem.

by which she divides rights into protective/ corrective, non discriminatory and discriminatory categories.[14] She argues that to achieve equality and non-discrimination, a strict implementation of the protective/corrective category is an imperative prerequisite, only then would substantive equality be possible as opposed to formal equality,[15] traditional roles of men and women and functions of an extended family.

II. Reforming Family Law: Šarīʿa as an evolving and dynamic concept

This paper draws inspiration from the theoretical perspectives of the above mentioned Islamic scholars and it is argued that the *šarīʿa as an evolving and dynamic concept* does provide room for bringing reform in the area of family law in Muslim countries. Reforms based on an analysis of Islamic legal tradition by following the categorization of rights, as suggested by John Louis Esposito Esposito and Shaheen Sardar Ali, could protect women against discrimination and unequal treatment in light of the Qur'ānic teachings of justice, equity and fairness. The above discussion also raises questions such as:

- If *šarīʿa* is dynamic and evolutionary in its nature then why are women in the present age not given the same rights?
- Why are they considered inferior to men using religious argument?
- Why is there a wide gap between the egalitarian principles of Islam and the lived realities of women in Muslim societies?
- Finally despite clear and unequivocal support for male-female equity, why are Muslim women today denied some of the basic rights, whether in the area of family law or otherwise, for example their right to education, health, employment, participation in politics and public life?

This challenging task can be achieved by following the principle of *iǧtihād* that seeks to promote freedom of thought (*ḥurrīyat al-ra'y*) and independent thinking *(iǧtihād)* when applied to Islamic legal tradition in relation to family law. The Qur'ān states "[w]e explain the signs in detail for those who reflect".[16] Islamic

---

14 *Shaheen Sardar Ali*, Systemically closed, cognitively open..., supra, footnote 8, on p. 6; *idem*, "Women's Human Rights in Islam: Towards a Theoretical Framework" in: *Eugene Cotran / Chibli Mallat* (Eds.), Yearbook of Islamic and Middle Eastern Law, volume 4, The Hague / London / Boston 1998, on p. 158.

15 *Shaheen Sardar Ali*, Women's Human Rights in Islam...", supra, footnote 14, on p. 152.

16 Cp. *Sura 10* (يونس)*: Verse 24:*

إِنَّمَا مَثَلُ الْحَيَاةِ الدُّنْيَا كَمَاءٍ أَنزَلْنَاهُ مِنَ السَّمَاءِ فَاخْتَلَطَ بِهِ نَبَاتُ الأَرْضِ مِمَّا يَأْكُلُ النَّاسُ وَالأَنْعَامُ حَتَّىٰ إِذَا
أَخَذَتِ الأَرْضُ زُخْرُفَهَا وَازَّيَّنَتْ وَظَنَّ أَهْلُهَا أَنَّهُمْ قَادِرُونَ عَلَيْهَا أَتَاهَا أَمْرُنَا لَيْلاً أَوْ نَهَارًا فَجَعَلْنَاهَا حَصِيدًا
كَأَن لَّمْ تَغْنَ بِالأَمْسِ كَذَٰلِكَ نُفَصِّلُ الآيَاتِ لِقَوْمٍ يَتَفَكَّرُونَ.

scholars argue for the use of concepts or juristic methods of change and reformation within the Islamic Law. *ʾIṣlāḥ* (reform), *ḍarūra* (necessity/duress), *maṣlaḥa* (Public Good), *taǧdīd* (renewal), *taḫaiyur* (eclecticism or process of selection) and *talfiq* (Patchwork) are a few other techniques that are being used along with *iǧtihād* by the Islamic scholars.[17] Besides these juristic techniques, *fatwās* (the learned decisions or utterances of the Muftīs) are also issued by juris-consults (*muftī*) in response to an individual question as well as the formal requests of opinions by *qāḍīs*. Since there is no hierarchical priesthood in Islam, *fatwās* are non-binding, advisory opinions. *Fatwās* have been issued from time to time throughout Muslim history on a wide range of issues and have played a vital socio-political role. With the growth of technology *fatwās* are now being circulated all over the world through the internet. Questions relating to family matters are often being posed to Muftīs or ʿĀlims (Religious scholars) on their websites and can be accessed by any one. However one has to take a very conscious and careful approach before following any of those *fatwās* as many are quite inconsistent with the overall spirit of Islam.

Shaheen Sardar Ali, while exploring these juristic techniques, argues that amongst all *taḫaiyur* or eclecticism is the most dynamic technique which has been used both by individual scholars as well as by the states to address those issues which are not directly covered by the primary sources of law.[18] Under the process of *taḫaiyur* the person chooses between the opinions of different schools of Islamic Law or chooses from the opinions of individual scholars within a single school or from amongst different schools. *Taḫaiyur* has been used to develop family law in different Muslim countries.[19] The first example of the use of *taḫaiyur* is the Maǧalla a collection of codified Ḥanafī law. In the Maǧalla, rules were derived not from the consensus of opinion of Ḥanafī scholars but from the divergent opinions of the Ḥanafī traditions. Other examples of *taḫaiyur* include the Dissolution of Muslim Marriages Act 1939, the Moroccan Code of Personal Status 1958, the Jordanian Law of Family Rights 1951, Syrian Law of Personal Rights 1953 and the Ottoman Law of Family Rights 1917 and in Pakistan the Muslim Family Law Ordinance 1961.[20] By applying the juristic concept of *taḫaiyur* cruelty has been considered as a ground for dissolution of marriage and

---

17 Cp. *Matilda Arvidsson*, Ijtihad Reformation of Islamic Law in the 21st Century: The Case of Sudan (Masters Thesis), Lund 2002.

18 *Shaheen Sardar Ali*, Systemically closed, cognitively open..., supra, footnote 8, on p. 6.

19 Cp. *James Norman / Dalrymple Anderson*, Law Reform in the Muslim World, London, 1976; *David Pearl / Werner F. Menski*, Muslim Family Law, London, 1998. See *Ihsan Yilmaz*, Muslim Laws, Politics and Society in Modern Nation States: Dynamic Legal Pluralisms in England, Turkey and Pakistan, Aldershot 2005, p. 43.

20 *Shaheen Sardar Ali*, Systemically closed, cognitively open..., supra, footnote 8, on p. 7.

stipulating conditions in the marriage contract is considered acceptable under the Ḥanbalī school of law. Shaheen Sardar Ali considers that

> " engagement with such principles of interpretation would help in advancing analytical critical thought in Muslim communities and would set some ground rules for a tolerant, non-discriminatory, democratic polity".[21]

In view of the above discussion, it is argued that if Muslims consider Islam to be a religion for all times to come, Islamic Law to be a guide for the life of millions of Muslims all over the world (belonging to diverse cultures and backgrounds) and all laws dealing with Muslims to derive their legitimacy on the basis of Islamic principles, then they have to make use of *iğtihād* and its accompanying juristic techniques so that any legislation made in the name of Islam reflects the principles of justice, fairness and equity. It is suggested that while exercising *iğtihād* to resolve an issue by interpreting Islamic legislative sources, an inclusive approach must be followed that would include taking into account the socio-political and economic conditions of the Pre-Islamic Arab society in which the Qur'ānic revelations were made to Prophet Muḥammad, analysis of all Qur'ānic verses and traditions of the Prophet on a specific subject and avoiding reliance on a single and isolated verse of the *Qur'ān* and *ḥadīṯ* of the Prophet which Shaheen Sardar Ali in her work calls a "selective use" of Qur'ānic verses.[22] Moreover we should also remember, as pointed out by Riffat Hasan,, that in Arabic language virtually every word has multiple meanings and nuances.[23] She therefore argues that Qur'ānic verses can be reinterpreted by not merely considering the literal meanings of the words but by looking deeper into the spirit and message behind the words.[24] With regard to *ḥadīṯ* literature used by early scholars, it must also be noted that it may not always be authentic and reliable and sometimes may even have been used to propagate patriarchal ideas

---

21 *Shaheen Sardar Ali*, "(Re) Claiming Our Histories: A Reflection on Women, Islam and Human Rights", in: Contemporary Muslim Communities, Paper for Human Rights Day, 10 December 2003, Islamabad, http://sachet.org.pk/home/gender_columns/webcolumn_26.asp (accessed on 25 December 2008).

22 *Shaheen Sardar Ali*, Gender..., supra, footnote 12, on p. 52.

23 *Riffat Hassan*, "An Islamic Perspective", in: *Jeanne Becher* (Editor), Women, Religion and Sexuality: Studies on the Impact of Religious Teachings on Women, Geneva 1990, pp. 93-128.

24 *Riffat Hassan*, An Islamic Perspective, supra, footnote 23, on p. 100. Cp. also *Muhammad Kalisch*, "Islam und Menschenrechte: Betrachtungen zum Verhältnis von Religion und Recht", in: *Hatem Elliesie* (Hrsg./Editor), Beiträge zum Islamischen Recht VII, Islam und Menschenrechte (Islam and Human Rights / الإسلام وحقوق الإنسان), Frankfurt a.M. 2010, pp. 49-72; *Assem Hefny*, "Hermeneutik, Koraninterpretation und Menschenrechte", in: *Hatem Elliesie* (Hrsg./Editor), ibidem, pp. 73-97.

and practices. Such interpretations of *ḥadīṯ* literature represent women as subordinate and dependent on men.

Adopting an inclusive approach would help in distinguishing between the actual teachings of the *Qur'ān* and customary practices which are adopted in the name of religion. It would help in bringing laws in conformity with international human rights standards which Pakistan and other Muslim countries have ratified and are under an obligation to follow. Furthermore, as discussed by Shaheen Sardar Ali, it would also help in creating deeper linkages and ongoing dialogue between the Islamic legal tradition and the western notion of Human Rights.[25]

C. Pakistan's Constitutional Framework and its Commitment to International Treaties

I. Pakistan's Constitutional "Spirit" and Framework

The constitution of Pakistan is a written constitution that draws inspiration from the Universal Declaration of Human Rights (UDHR).[26] It incorporates about two-thirds of the thirty rights enumerated in the UDHR. The equality provisions incorporated in the present constitution were also included in its predecessor constitutions of 1962 and 1972. The Charter of the United Nations provides for the reaffirmation of "faith in fundamental human rights" and the "equal rights of men and women". It further mentions the resolution of conflicts and disputes through the principle of justice as an objective to pursue.[27] The UDHR contains several provisions with regard to equality of rights and their effective implementation.[28]

By following the same spirit of the UDHR the chapter on fundamental rights and the principles of policy clearly state that women shall be provided with complete equality and at the same time the norm of non-discrimination is echoed in several provisions of the constitution.[29] Article 25 of the constitution specifically lays down that all citizens are equal before law and are entitled to equal protection of law and that "*[t]here shall be no discrimination on grounds of sex*

25 *Shaheen Sardar Ali*, Systemically closed, cognitively open..., supra, footnote 8, on p. 6.

26 Adopted and proclaimed by General Assembly Resolution, UN-Doc. 217 A (III), 10 December 1948.

27 Cp. Preamble and Art. 1 UN Charter.

28 Cp. Art. 1, 8 and 10 UDHR.

29 Art. 15of the 1962 Constitution and Art. 22 of the 1972 Interim Constitution deal with equality. The addition Clause 3 of the Art. 22 of the 1972 Interim Constitution states that "[n]othing in this article shall prevent the state from enacting any special provision for the protection of women". Later, in the 1973 Constitution, the equality provision appears in its Article 25 and the word "children" was added to Clause 3.

alone". It also permits the state to make special provisions for the protection of women and children. The two phrases aim at prohibiting arbitrary distinctions. It means that not all differences in treatment can be held as discriminatory and at the same time equal treatment does not mean that all persons should be treated in the same manner.[30] Article 35 states that *"[t]he State shall protect the marriage, the family, the mother and child"*. Similarly, Article 34 directs the state to take appropriate measures so as to enable women to participate fully in all spheres of national life. Despite the fact that equality norms resonate very clearly in the constitutional provisions, their implementation in terms of legislative enactments and ground realities remain limited.

Besides, the various constitutions adopted in Pakistan (including the present) over the last five decades were cast within the framework of Objectives Resolution, creating a legal hierarchy with Islam as the overarching norm. In 1985 amendments were made to the constitution and the Objectives Resolution was made part of the existing constitution in the form of Article 2-A.[31] In light of this constitutional background it is therefore pertinent to explore the extent to which a constitutional framework that derives its inspiration from international human rights instruments and is constructed in the name of Islam, upholds and implements human rights norms of equality and non-discrimination and Islamic notions of equity and justice with regard to women in the family.

II. Pakistan's Commitment to International Treaties

Until very recently Pakistan was a party to a few UN international human rights treaties, which include the UDHR, the CRC and the CEDAW. On 18 April 2008 Pakistan also ratified the ICCPR, ICESCR and the (CAT).[32]

1. The CEDAW

In this section we attempt to analyse Pakistan's position with regard to the CEDAW. It is the most important international statement on gender equality and prohibits all forms and manner of injustice and discrimination against women. It mandates the state parties to take full and effective measures legislative, execu-

---

30 *Siobhan Mullally*, Separate Spheres: Protective Legislation for Women in Pakistan, in: Asian Yearbook of International Law, issue 4, London 1994, pp. 47-67.

31 Article 2-A states that "[t]he principles and provisions set out in the 'Objectives Resolution' reproduced in the Annex are hereby made a substantive part of the constitution. [...] Whereas sovereignty over the entire universe belongs to Allah Almighty alone and the authority which He has delegated to the State of Pakistan, through its people for being exercised within the limits prescribed by Him is a sacred trust; [...]"; see web presence http://www.pakistani.org/pakistan/constitution/annex_objres.html (accessed on 20 August 2009).

32 For abbreviations, cp. pp. 9 et seqq. of this volume.

tive and judicial with proper sanctions, to ensure the protection of women. The framers of the CEDAW were also aware that culture and tradition play an important role in restricting women's enjoyment of their fundamental rights. The influence of the stereotype roles, customary and cultural practices has lead to legal, political and economic constraints on the progress of women. It therefore requires state parties to modify social and cultural patterns of conduct, to eliminate prejudice and practices that are based on the inferiority of women, to provide women with rights equal to those of men in the fields of employment and family benefits, and to recognize the difficulties faced by rural women in particular.[33] A significant feature of the CEDAW is that it defines the term discrimination in a sense that transcends the traditional public/private dichotomy by calling for the international recognition of women's human rights both inside and outside the familial sphere. The first part comprises six articles dealing specifically with the term *discrimination*. In order to eliminate discrimination against women the convention requires the state parties to adopt such measures including changes in the constitutions of the state parties and also changes in those legislative provisions which are discriminatory against women.

Shaheen Sardar Ali is of the view that as the CEDAW is based on a

> " predominanatly Western liberal discourse, Muslim countries view it as subservient to the overriding supremacy of Islamic law".[34]

She further argues that international human rights norms are perceived by Muslim countries as reflections of western values which are culturally and religiously alien to Muslim societies and hence unacceptable.[35] As a result many Muslim states have entered into reservations to various articles, in particular Article 16 which deals with the family. These reservations have been made on the basis of a diverse interpretation of *šarīʿa* as understood and applied in Muslim countries, for instance Afghanistan, Iraq Saudi Arabia and Egypt while other Muslim countries like Tunisia, Mali, Turkey, Indonesia and Senegal have not used *šarīʿa* in support of their reservations.[36]

---

[33] Cp. Art. 2, 5, 11, 13 CEDAW. See also *Hanna Beate Schöpp-Schilling*, "Der „Frauenrechtsausschuss" der Vereinten Nationen in der Interaktion mit islamisch geprägten Staaten", in: *Hatem Elliesie* (Hrsg./Editor), Beiträge zum Islamischen Recht VII, Islam und Menschenrechte (Islam and Human Rights / الإسلام وحقوق الإنسان), Frankfurt a.M. 2009, on pp. 417-455.

[34] *Shaheen Sardar Ali*, "Equal Before Allah Un Equal Before Man Gender and Human Rights", in: Islam and International law, The Hague 2000, pp. 275 et seqq.

[35] Ibidem, on p. 283.

[36] *Shaheen Sardar Ali*, A Comparative Study of CEDAW with Islamic Law and Laws of Pakistan, Peshawar 1995.

2. Pakistan's CEDAW Declaration and Reservation

Pakistan also acceded to the CEDAW on 12 April 1996, making (a) a declaration on the Convention and (b) entering a reservation on Article 29 (1):

a) Declaration: "The accession by [the] Government of the Islamic Republic of Pakistan to the [CEDAW] is subject to the provisions of the Constitution of the Islamic Republic of Pakistan."

b) Reservation: "The Government of the Islamic Republic of Pakistan declares that it does not consider itself bound by paragraph 1 of article 29 of the Convention."[37]

Pakistan unlike many other Muslim countries, for instance Bangladesh, Egypt, Iraq, Jordan and Tunisia, has not entered into any specific reservation on Article 16 of the CEDAW that relates to rights in the marriage/family. The Declaration is an overall blanket provision, carefully worded and more in the form of a compromise to enable Pakistan to accede to the Convention. It did not expressly invoke Islamic Law, as the objective was not to go against the object and purpose of the CEDAW while assuaging the concerns of those who had misapprehensions about it. However, by making it subject to the provisions of the Constitution of Pakistan, in a coveted sense it meant that the Convention should be read in light of Islamic teachings because under Article 2-A of the Constitution of Islamic Republic of Pakistan all laws have to be in conformity with Qur'ānic injunctions. Such type of a declaration has a negative impact upon the overall obligations undertaken by the state as it justifies and protects the dominant role played by customary norms adopted in the name of religion. The blanket declaration provides a cover to discriminatory laws against women framed in the name of Islam and, as such, it raises concerns with regard to its compatibility with the object and purpose of the CEDAW. This further suggests that the member states do not understand and interpret the norms of equality and non-discrimination that form part of the *jus cogens* in a uniform way. It provides the states with an easy escape from their obligation to accord women their due rights.

3. Pakistan's Country Report to the CEDAW

Pakistan, in its country report to the CEDAW, took the position that it takes its obligations and commitments very seriously, including the one that addresses

[37] The reservation to Article 29, paragraph 1 is benign in relation to women's rights. It is more political in nature and connected with Pakistan's general position on the jurisdiction of the International Court of Justice.

the position of women to empower them socially, economically and legally.[38] In response to Article 16 of the CEDAW, the Pakistani government in its country report held that various personal laws ensure the same rights of both men and women to enter into marriage. Men and women are free to enter into marriage and to marry spouses of their choice. It did, however, acknowledged the influence of customary practices and norms due to which parents exert their pressure when it comes to choosing a spouse particularly in the case of daughter's right to enter into a contract of marriage.[39] Sometimes it also happens, esp. in the more backward areas of the country, that if a girl persists in her desire to go against the wishes of her family she is ostracized, forced to seek a divorce and even killed in the name of honour.

As for the rights and responsibilities during marriage and at its dissolution, in its report the government tried to equate the right of a wife for dissolution of marriage by *ḫul'* to a husband's right to divorce. Whereas in the case of same rights and responsibilities with regard to guardianship, wardship, trusteeship and adoption of children, or similar institutions where these concepts exist in national legislation, the report says that in all cases the interests of the children is the guiding principle.

The CEDAW, in its concluding observations,[40] noted that the constitution, in Article 25 (2) and Article 27, stipulates equality before the law, irrespective of sex. However, the state party's constitution and other laws do not contain a definition of discrimination which is in accordance with Article 1 CEDAW, nor do they include provisions on equality of women with men that is in consonance with Article 2 (a) CEDAW.

The CEDAW, therefore, recommended that a definition of discrimination against women is in line with Article 1 CEDAW, which encompasses both direct and indirect discrimination, and provisions on the equality of women with men, in line with Article 2 (a) CEDAW, be included in the constitution or in other appropriate legislation.

The NGO sector in Pakistan in its Shadow Country report raised a number of issues regarding the implementation of family laws in Pakistan.[41] It expressed the concern that the vast majority remain unaware of the provisions of personal status law. Despite the commitment to create awareness of and support for

---

[38] Cp. "Pakistan's Combined Initial, Second and Periodic Report", submitted in May 2007, UN-Doc. CEDAW/C/PAK/1-3.

[39] Ibidem, on p. 12.

[40] See UN-Doc. CEDAW/C/SR.783 and 784.

[41] Cp. *Shirkat Gah-Women's Resource Centre*, Talibanisation and Poor Governance: Undermining CEDAW in Pakistan, Second Shadow Report, 15 April 2007.

women's rights,[42] little has been done to spread awareness about women's legal rights through the electronic media or by incorporation into school textbooks.[43] Information about legal amendments and changes in policy also fails to reach the implementing officer level and government forms are not easily available. For instance, many lower court judges were found to be unaware of the positive changes to facilitate women in family law matters under President's Ordinance No. LV of 2002. Simultaneously no steps have been taken to ensure that the prescribed government marriage registration forms are available.[44] Without rectifying these lacunae government actions have little chance of improving the lives of women. The Shadow Report called upon the CEDAW to inquire:

- What steps the Government of Pakistan is taking to address these vital issues.
- What steps have been taken to ensure those administering Muslim family laws are trained in the law.
- What procedures ensure the availability of government issued marriage contract forms, and that all Muslim marriages are registered accordingly.
- What conditions will enable Pakistan to withdraw its general declaration.

The Shadow Report further criticised the government for faulty planning, poor implementation and follow up of any positive initiatives taken to promote equality.

D. The Historical Evolution and Application of Šarīʿa to Family Law in Pakistan

Beginning this section with a brief historical background of legislative developments in family law in the Indian subcontinent, we then use family law in Pakistan as a case-study for *šarīʿa* law implementation through Islamic Jurisprudence and to assess its compatibility with Human Rights Law[45].

---

42 National Plan of Action (NPA), Chapter Human Rights; Strategic Objective I.5, Actions 1-4, on p. 77.

43 Ibidem, on p. 24.

44 Some forms have been deleted the bride's signature/thumbprint, a legal requirement for a valid marriage. Public ignorance combined with untrained marriage registrars commonly leads to a flouting of legal provisions to women's detriment: family-men and marriage registrars frequently delete protective clauses of the marriage contract without consulting the woman; in contrary to legal provisions, religious leaders frequently insist that a divorced woman needs an intervening marriage with a third party before she can re-marry her previous husband. Many women end up trapped in these second marriages.

45 As to the term "Human Rights Law" see *Hatem Elliesie,* "Sudan under the Constraints of (International) Human Rights Law and Humanitarian Law: The Case of Darfur", in: *Hatem*

I. Brief Historical Background

Historically speaking, the Indian subcontinent, which is now mainly constituted by India, Pakistan and Bangladesh, has been the land of diverse cultures and religions. It was home to peoples of vastly different backgrounds who mainly lived in self-contained tribal clans or communities, following their own usages and customs.[46] Islam came to the Indian subcontinent when Muḥammad b. Qāsim in 712 AD conquered Sindh. Different Muslim dynasties ruled the subcontinent such as the Tuġlaq, Mongol and, lastly, the Šāhān-e Moġul (self-designation: گورکانی Gūrkānī). But Islamic Law was firmly established in the 12th century when administration of justice through *qazi*-courts was introduced.[47] The influence of the Muslim monarchs however was limited to cities and towns and any effort on their part to introduce *šarīʿa* remained limited to the urban centres. They were quite tolerant of customary practices, in the domain of personal law, even when such practices were against the *šarīʿa* because it was against their imperial interests to challenge the people.[48] Therefore both Hindus and Muslims were governed by their own set of personal laws.

II. Legislative developments in Family Law on the Indian Subcontinent

Later, during the British period (1857-1947) customs were given a more formal status in the subcontinent.[49] When the British came into power, under the Warren Hastings Plan 1772 a hierarchy of civil and criminal courts was established according to the English legal system. Many changes were brought in the local administration of justice and Islamic Laws were replaced by the English Common Law.[50] Following British procedure and with the assistance of Indian Officers,

---

Elliesie (Hrsg./Editor), Beiträge zum Islamischen Recht VII, Islam und Menschenrechte (Islam and Human Rights / الإسلام وحقوق الإنسان), Frankfurt a.M. 2010, on p. 193.

46 *Kamran Arif*, "The Evolution of Muslim Personal Law", in: *Farida Shaheed / Sohail Akbar Waraich* (Eds.), Shaping Women's Lives, Lahore 1998, on p. 57 et seqq.

47 *Shaheen Sardar Ali*, A Comparative Study..., supra, footnote 36, on p. 140.

48 *Kamran Arif*, The Evolution of Muslim Personal law, supra, footnote 46, on p. 58.

49 The British arrived in India by forming the East India Company whose objectives were (1) to generate revenue and get economic gains and (2) to have better political control with least military involvement. For British rule in India see: *D. Washbook*, "Law, State and Agrarian Economy in Colonial India", in: Modern Asian Studies, volume 15, Cambridge 1981, p. 654; *Michael R. Anderson*, (1990). "Islamic Law and colonial encounter in British India", *Chibli Mallat / Jane Frances Connors*, Islamic Family Law, London 1990, on p. 207 et seqq.

50 Islamic law dealing with crimes and punishments, land tenancy, revenue and partly transfer of property were replace by the legislative enactments for instance the Criminal Procedure Code 1861, the Indian Evidence Act 1872, Regulation IX of 1793. For further discussion on the administration of Justice by the British in pre-partition India see *Michael R. Anderson*, supra, footnote 49; *Mahomed Ullah Ibn Sarbuland Jung*, The administration

Pandit (पन्दित) and Maūlvī (مولوی), the British rulers applied, in the early period, personal laws of the Muslims and the Hindus through courts.

But soon problems surfaced as most of the laws were written in Sanskrit and Arabic, and the Maūlvīs and Pundits were not well versed in their laws of personal status. As a result, the courts would arrive at different conclusions on similar questions of law and this led to conflict and uncertainty in law.[51] Therefore, on grounds of political expediency, the British left the personal (status) law, regarding matters of marriage and inheritance, untouched. Shaheen Sardar Ali argues that

> " although today the west bemoans the degraded status of women in our society but in fact west itself has played a negative role in the fossilization of Islamic laws which thus resulted in giving a heavy blow to women's rights in the Indian subcontinent".[52]

This uncertainty led the British, in the latter part of the 18th century, to give preference to customs over the religious laws.[53] In this way customary law was allowed to govern areas detrimental to women, for example, women were (a) denied a share in inheritance, (b) were unequal partners in marriage and (c) had little say in other matters of importance. However, this situation could not continue for long, as the conditions laid down for the application of customary law were strict and limited in nature, and due to the fact that customary law differed from place to place and tribe to tribe.[54] As a result, this process of legally enforcing the customary practices could not succeed in the Indian subcontinent.

In the early 20th century, along with their political struggle for independence, the Muslims of India started the movement to replace customary practices with religious laws. This challenge to customary laws was a political move because the Indian Muslims wanted to prove themselves as one nation governed by one law as opposed to a group of communities living under different customs and usage.

After independence from the British colonial rule in 1947, the legislation relating to Muslim family law, introduced under British rule, continued to govern the

---

of Justice in Islam, Lahore, in: *Katherine P. Ewing* (Ed.), Sharia and Ambiguity in South Asian Islam, Lahore 1988, p. 57 et seq.

51 Ibidem, on p. 60.

52 *Shaheen Sardar Ali*, Gender…, supra, footnote 12, on p. 143.

53 Several laws were enacted, the most important being Section 5 of the 1872 Punjab Law which laid down that in property cases, as well as matters relating to marriage, dower, divorce, adoption, guardianship and custody, customs applicable to the parties that are not contrary to the principles of justice, equity and good conscience, will be applied.

54 Custom had to be immemorial, reasonable and continuous, based on principles of justice, equity and good conscience.

personal status.[55] At present, the family law in Pakistan is a combination of both secular and Islamic laws. Secular laws govern the public sphere whereas Islamic laws are applied in matters relating to family, in particular with regard to women's position, rights, responsibilities and role in society.[56] Accordingly, Abdullahi A. An-Naʿim and Shaheen Sardar Ali argue that this has led to the emergence of a public/private dichotomy.

III. Case-Study: The Use Family Law in Pakistan

Along with this public/private divide the views of legal scholars in Pakistan are also divisive in the sense that there is a huge difference of opinions on the issue of adopting *šarīʿa* based laws among fundamentalists and modernists. The former emphasise on building the edifice of family law on Islamic principles, while the latter consider that women's equality can only be achieved by keeping family law out of the ambit of *šarīʿa.*

1. The CMRA and the DMMA

At the time of state formation, Pakistan inherited two statutes from pre-partitioned India, the Child Marriage Restraint Act 1929 (CMRA) and the Dissolution of Muslim Marriages Act 1939 (DMMA).

The CMRA was a norm setting legal document as the framers of the Act bearing in mind the societal norms did not invalidate the child marriage. However, under CMRA the father or the guardian may be punished for contracting their children into such marriages. Before 1939, Muslim women did not have the legal right to divorce and due to the pressure of customary practices were also denied access to the doctrine of *ḫulʿ*. Hence, the DMMA came as a relief for Muslim women who were given some protection against the wrongly interpreted and misapplied Islamic divorce laws. The DMMA laid down eight grounds for dissolution of marriage and it was for the first time that cruelty and incompatibility of temperament, hatred and adultery were considered as grounds for dissolution of marriage. A marriage dissolved under DMMA is called *fasḫ*. One important

55 In the first fourteen years of Pakistan's history, no reforms were made in family law. It inherited two statutes from pre-partitioned India, the Child Marriage Restraint Act 1929 (CMRA) and the Dissolution of Muslim Marriages Act 1939 (DMMA). The first attempt in this direction was made by the Punjab Legislative Assembly which presented a Marriage Reform Bill in 1954. Later in 1955 a Marriage and Family Law Commission was set up by the government.

56 As a former British colony, secular laws in Pakistan derive their basis from the British legal system. Matters relating to the public sector, for instance, trade and commerce, interstate relations and administrative rules, are regulated by secular laws. Islamic Law, on the other hand, covers the private sphere, i.e. family matters for which the term Muslim Personal law has been used by jurists.

aspect of the DMMA is that the dissolution of marriage does not affect women's right to dower and option of puberty and moreover the husband's consent to the dissolution is not needed.[57] These grounds have been included by adopting the juristic technique of *talfiq* as discussed before on pp. 349 et seqq.

In this context, it is interesting to note that the CEDAW, in its concluding observations on Pakistan's Country Report, has expressed concern that under the DMMA women do not enjoy equal rights with men during the dissolution of marriage.[58] It also noted with concern that under the CMRA the minimum age for marriage for boys is 18 years and for girls 16 years. The CEDAW was further concerned about the persistence of forced and early marriage. It urged that the CMRA be amended to eliminate all discriminatory provisions. The amendments must include raising the minimum legal age of marriage for girls to 18 years in order to bring it in consonance with Article 1 CRC, Article 16 (para. 2) CEDAW and its general recommendation 21 on equality in marriage and family relations. It also requested the implementation of measures to eliminate forced marriages.

2. Post DMMA Developments

After the DMMA no reforms were made in family law for a long time. The first attempt in this direction was made after the creation of Pakistan by the Punǧāb Legislative Assembly, which passed The New West Punjab Muslim Personal Law (Šarīʿat) Application Act of 1948 which was an amendment to the Šarīʿat Application Act of 1937 (ŠAA). This enlarged the scope to questions relating to succession including succession to agricultural land (where as the previous act applied only to intestate succession). Later, in 1950 amendments were made in the same ŠAA in the Province of Sindh and the wording "[...] save questions relating to agricultural land and other than charitable institutions and charitable and religious endowments [...]" were deleted from Section 2 ŠAA. Other than the amendments in the ŠAA, in 1955 a Marriage and Family Law Commission (MFLC) was set up by the government which, after a year, submitted its report.[59] The report of the MFLC was considered to be a very important document,

57 *Section 5 DMMA:*
" [n]othing contained in this Act shall affect any right which a married woman may have under Muslim Law to her dower or any part there of on the dissolution of her marriage."

58 UN-Doc. CEDAW/C/PAK/CO/3, p. 8.

59 The MFLC was headed by Justice ʿAbdul-Rāšid, including three women representatives and the Pakistani philosopher Ḫalīfa ʿAbdul-Ḥakīm. The MFLC's objective focused on a survey re laws relating to marriage, to dower, to divorce, to succession and to polygamy in order to suggest changes in these laws, in accordance with the "true teachings of Islam".

challenging contemporary Muslim thought. The report stated that Islam is a very progressive religion, not a priest dominated religion and changes in law must be brought by exercising the right to *iǧtihād*. However, the report received severe criticism from different religious groups and as a result the then government shelved the report and no action was taken on it. Later, in 1961, the Muslim Family Laws Ordinance (MFLO) was passed.

Under the MFLO registration of marriages was mandatory, polygamy was restricted, only one form of divorce was recognised and a provision was made for orphaned grandchildren to inherit from their grandparents. The MFLO, however, did not include all the recommendations of the MFLC nor were the reforms as radical as compared to reforms made in the family law in other Muslim countries.[60] The MFLO was followed by the West Pakistan Family Courts Act 1964 (WPFCA) which laid down the rules for implementation of the MFLO. The WPFCA was amended in 2002, in light of recommendations by the Pakistan Law Commission and National Commission on the Status of Women (PNCSW).

3. The MFLO and Islamic Concepts of Family Law

In the following, the aforementioned provisions of the MFLO will be examined in the light of the Islamic concept of family law in order to assess how far these provisions reflect Islamic legal principles on marriage, divorce, polygamy, custody and, moreover, to what extent the aforementioned provisions uphold the principles of equality and non-discrimination in Human Rights Law.

a. Niqāḥ

In Islamic Jurisprudence (*fiqh*), sexuality must be controlled and channelled by social institutions to prevent social breakdown. The need to regulate sexuality extends into different rights and obligations in marriage. From this, it follows that the institution of marriage is the centre piece of Muslim family law. Marriage is defined as a civil contract between the two parties and the consent of the parties is a prerequisite of the marriage contract. Specific conditions can also be stipulated in the marriage contract, although these vary amongst different schools of thought. This prerequisite of the Muslim marriage has been incorporated into the MFLO in the form of *nikāḥ*, thus emphasizing the importance of the marriage contract and abiding by its requirements. Section 5 MFLO provides that a *nikāḥ* be registered with the Union Council to be legally valid. By making the registration of a marriage contract mandatory, along with its specific

---

60 For instance, in Tunisia, Egypt and Turkey, where polygamy was outlawed and extra judicial divorce was declared invalid. For a detailed discussion see *Khawar Mumtaz / Farida Shaheed*, Women in Pakistan: Two steps forward one step back?, Lahore 1987, p. 59.

protections for women, the MFLO attempted to make marital practices more transparent and accountable to the law.

b. Polygamy (Sura 4 [النساء]: Verse 3)

Polygamy in Islam is a complicated and controversial issue. The *Qur'ān* in Sura 4 (النساء): Verse 3 states:

وَإِنْ خِفْتُمْ أَلاَّ تُقْسِطُواْ فِي الْيَتَامَى فَانكِحُواْ مَا طَابَ لَكُم مِّنَ النِّسَاء مَثْنَى وَثُلاَثَ
وَرُبَاعَ فَإِنْ خِفْتُمْ أَلاَّ تَعْدِلُواْ فَوَاحِدَةً أَوْ مَا مَلَكَتْ أَيْمَانُكُمْ ذَلِكَ أَدْنَى أَلاَّ تَعُولُواْ.

> " *If ye fear that ye shall not be able to deal justly with the orphans, Marry women of your choice, Two or three or four; but if ye fear that ye shall not be able to deal justly (with them), then only one, or (a captive) that your right hands possess, that will be more suitable, to prevent you from doing injustice.* "

Polygamy in light of Sura 4 (النساء): Verse 3 has not been completely abolished rather the practice has been restricted under the MFLO. Section 6 MFLO states that no married man can contract a second marriage without the permission of an Arbitration Council, which shall ensure that the man had good grounds for second marriage and had obtained his first wife's permission to do so. The incorporation of provisions that restrict polygamy by making it subject to prior permission of the first wife and a notice to the Arbitration Council[61] are based on the application of juristic technique of *taḫaiyur.* Inclusion of such clauses was only permissible under the classical Ḥanbalī school but not in the Ḥanafī school. In this regard, Javaid Rehman opines that

> " [t]he usage of takhayyur authorized Islamic scholars from all schools of thought to incorporate specific provisions within the marriage contracts to prohibit or at least restrict the practice of polygamy".[62]

It could be argued that whilst the Qur'ān permits men to enter into polygamous unions and could have up to four wives at the same time, it declares that a man should not enter into another marriage if he cannot treat all his wives with fairness. Sura 4 (النساء): Verse 3 also needs to be interpreted in its historical context when this permission was given after the Battle of Uḥud in which most of the Muslim men were killed and widows and orphaned children needed protection

---

61 An Arbitration Council – by definition, "a body consisting of the Chairman and a representative of each of the parties to a matter dealt with this Ordinance" –consists of a representative of the first wife or existing wife or wives, representative of the husband and a neutral chairperson.

62 *Javaid Rehman*, "The Sharia, Islamic Family Laws and International Human Rights Law: Examining The Theory and Practice of Polygamy and Talaq", in: International Journal of Law, Policy and the Family, volume 21, issue 1, Oxford 2007, pp. 108-127.

and support. Besides, there is no uniform application of Sura 4 (النساء): Verse 3 in Muslim countries such as Tunisia and Turkey, which totally prohibit polygamous unions, whereas other Muslim countries like Pakistan only restrict it and make it subject to certain conditions, which are not stringent enough to discourage the practice of polygamy.

c. Divorce

Another important area is divorce in Islam. Divorce is considered to be the most disliked act in the Qur'ān and is to be exercised as a last resort. Under Section 7 of the MFLO a divorce pronouncement becomes final and irrevocable after the expiry of ninety days. The ninety days period is, in accordance with the timeframe as set out in *ṭalāq (aḥsan),* a mode of pronouncing divorce under classical *fiqh*. The purpose of extending it to ninety days is to provide the couple an opportunity for reconciliation before the divorce becomes irrevocable. Therefore, it can be argued that the requirements of sending a written notice of divorce to a union council and a copy of it to the divorcee wife, after an arbitration council would try for reconciliation between the parties, are in accordance with principles of Islamic Jurisprudence on divorce. Moreover, the objective of introducing this procedure is to establish some restrictions to curtail the unilateral right of the husband to give extra judicial divorce.

In this regard, it is worth mentioning that amendments were made to the rules in the WPFCA as well. Currently, under Section 7 of the Family Courts Ordinance 2002 (FCO) a new provision has been added stipulating that a plaint for dissolution of marriage may contain all claims relating to dowry, maintenance, dower, personal property and belongings of wife, custody of children and visitation rights of parents to meet their children.[63] According to the amendment to Section 9 (1)(b) FCO, in a suit for restitution of conjugal rights by husband, a wife is entitled to make a claim for dissolution of marriage including *ḫulʿ*. This shall be deemed as a plaint and no separate suit shall lie for it. The time period for serving notice of the passing of the *ex parte* decree to the defendant has also been amended by the Family Court. At present, the notice has to be send conjointly with a certified copy of the decree within three days of its passing.[64]

Furthermore, pursuant to the amended FCO the courts are now directed to decide family disputes within six months from the date of institution. Judges can also exercise the powers of judicial magistrate. If a case is not disposed of

---

63 Family Courts (Amendment) Ordinance, 2002 Ordinance LV OF 2002, An Ordinance Further To Amend The Family Courts Act 1964. Cp. Gazette Of Pakistan, Extraordinary, Part-I, 1 October 2002.

64 The notice is sent by process server or by registered post, acknowledgement due, or by courier service or any other mode or manner as it may deem it.

within six months, either party shall have a right to make an application to the High Court for necessary direction as the High Court may deem fit.

In case of *ḫulʿ* under the amended FCO, the court is required to simply pass an order to that effect on return of the dower to the husband. However, this amendment has been severely criticised by the women right's activists in Pakistan. Women activists are of the view that the amendment is against those decisions of the courts in which it was held that "a wife is not bound to return her entire dower to the husband". In one of the cases the courts have reinterpreted the concept of *zar-i-ḫulʿ* and insisted that the husband too receives reciprocal benefits from the wife which thereby offset the benefits that the wife had to return.[65]

d) Custody and Guardianship

Matters relating to custody of the child in cases of dissolution of marriage are decided under Guardians and Wards Act 1890 (GWA). Under Muslim personal law, the father is considered to be the natural guardian.[66] However a positive trend has emerged in Pakistan, whereby the courts have adopted a sympathetic and lenient approach in custody cases in favour to women's (and children's) interest. In Sakīna Bībī's case, for example, the High court passed a decree in which the custody of the minor child was awarded to the mother. It is the principle of "best interest of the child" that one has been followed and not the classical Islamic legal doctrine. According to the latter, that is to say, the custody of a by when he attains the age of 7 years shall be awarded to father.[67]

E. Interpretation of Family Laws by the Superior Courts in Pakistan

For the purposes of this paper we carried out a review of cases decided by superior courts in Pakistan from 1997 to 2006. Cases on marriage, divorce, *ḫulʿ*, dower, custody and guardianship. Using various legal techniques, we are analysing the application of *fiqh* principles and their compatibility with human rights norms in the following:

I. Case: ʿAbdul-Waḥīd *versus* ʿĀṣma Ğeḥāngīr

ʿAbdul-Waḥīd versus ʿĀṣma Ğeḥāngīr[68] raised the issue of:

---

65 See *M. Saqlain Zaheer versus Zaib-un-Nisa,* as cited in *Shaheen Sardar Ali*, "Testing the Limits of Family Law Reform in Pakistan: A Critical Analysis of Muslim Family Laws Ordinance 1961", in: International Survey of Family Law, Bristol 2002, p. 334.

66 Once a boy attains the age of seven years, the custody is handed over to fathers.

67 Cp. Pakistan Criminal Law Journal (PCr.L.J.), Lahore 1987, p. 377.

68 Cp. Pakistan Legal Decisions (PLD), Lahore 1997, p. 331.

- whether a *sui iuris* woman is entitled to marry without the consent of her parents.
- whether parents have a right to be obeyed and whether this right can be judicially enforceable.

The court confirmed that, under Islamic Law, marriage is a contract and that the consent of both parties is required. Therefore, an adult Ḥanafī Muslim woman can contract herself in marriage without *wālī*'s consent, since it is the woman's consent and not that of the *wālī*. Counsel Ṣā'ima argued that any law, convention, or customary practice that conflicted with the provisions of the constitution regarding fundamental rights could not be legally sustained. She further argued that the presence of a legal guardian, or *wālī*, to mandate all matters relating to women's activities outside the home would violate basic human rights and contravene the country's constitutional guarantees provided for all citizens. The Counsel relied on the formal guarantees provided in the 1973 constitution through Articles 10, 11, 14, 20, and 25 relating to fundamental rights, to safeguards against detention in custody, to safeguards against traffic in human beings, to inviolability of the dignity of man, to freedom of religion and to safeguards against discrimination on the basis of sex alone.

However, prior their decision and despite recognising the position of a woman as *sui iuris*, the judges debated the social, religious and cultural structure of Pakistani society at length and expressed their fear and resentment of encouraging women to decide matters on their own without the consent of the guardian or *wālī*. Justice Čawḏry's *obiter dictum* considered the duty of Muslim parents to arrange the marriage of their children, in particular those of daughters, to prevent them from coming across male outsiders and sullying the 'purity' of the home. He described marriage bureaus and institutions alike "menace to society", and condemned them for encouraging women to choose their own spouse. Moreover, he referred to the *Qur'ān* verses and *aḥādīṯ* concluding that the obedience to parents as a religious duty should be legally enforced.

This specific case illustrated the judges' decision finding process: Despite recognition of Islamic principles, the views and opinions were strongly influenced by cultural norms as well as values and shows their reluctance to engage in a constitutional or human rights related discourse in family matters.[69]

---

[69] For a review of this case see *Shaheen Sardar Ali*, "Is an Adult Muslim Woman *Sui Juris*? Some Reflections on the Concept of 'Consent in Marriage' without a W*ali* (with particular reference to the *Saima Waheed* Case)", in: *Eugene Cotran / Chibli* Mallat (Eds.), Yearbook of Islamic and Middle Eastern Law, volume 3, London 1997, pp. 156-176.

II. Case: Ḥumaīrā Meḥmūd *versus* State

In Ḥumaīrā Meḥmūd *versus* State,[70] a woman married on her own choice, without seeking the consent of the parents. Thus, her father registered a case of adultery and abduction against the husband of his daughter. Although using Qur'ānic injunctions, Justice Gīlānī made clear references to constitutional provisions[71] and emphasised Pakistan's commitment to international treaties; such as Article 16 CEDAW as well as Article 5 and Article 6 of the Cairo Declaration on Human Rights in Islam 1990.[72] In his judgement he stated that

> " [a]s a member of the International Comity [sic!] of Nations we must respect the international instruments of human rights to which we are a party".

III. Case: Muḥammad Ṭāriq *versus* Šāhīn and 2 others

In Muḥammad Ṭāriq *versus* Šāhīn,[73] a suit for recovery of dower, dowry and maintenance allowance was filed by a wife after the husband took the dower ("*contra legem*") away. By referring to the Qur'ān, the judge concluded that the right of the wife to recover her dower in ordinary circumstances is an indefeasible one. The right to dower cannot be taken away or defeated. This right is extinguished only in cases where

> " [...] the wife convert to another religion or when the marriage was solemnized between two Non-Muslims and, after the marriage, the husband converts to Islam, while the wife remains Non-Muslim or, when a wife exercises the right of option of puberty for dissolution of marriage."

The fixation of dower and its payment to the wife is one of the limitations/ considerations laid down. Thus, the husband has no free hand or 'super imposing status' over the wife in marital life. Furthermore the learned judge held that while construing a statute, the court is bound to advance the cause of justice by providing relief to a party entitled to it and would not deny a right on the ground of unessential technicality.

IV. Case: Aūrangzīb *versus* Gūlnāz

In another case, *ḫulʿ* was granted by the family court, but the husband challenged the decision and filed a case for restoration of his right to repayment of dower by his wife in lieu.[74] The court held that

> " restitution of dower is not an indispensable condition for grant of ḫulʿ and non-restoration of dower and other benefits will not have any effect upon the validity

---

70 Cp. PLD, Lahore 1999, p. 495.

71 Art. 25, 35 and 4 Constitution of Pakistan.

72 PLD, Lahore 1999, para. 18, p. 512.

73 Cp. PLD, Peshawar 2006, p. 189.

74 Cp. PLD, Karachi 2006, p. 568.

> of the decree, once the family court comes to the conclusion that a wife was entitled for ḫulʿ it must pass such a decree in her favour".

In favour and in protection for the wife, the court referred to Sura 4 (النساء): Verse 20 and views expressed in the compilation Radd al-Muḫtār. The court held that

> " if the contention of the petitioner (husband) is accepted then a destitute wife who is found otherwise entitled to ḫulʿ, will stand deprived of the right simply because of her incapacity to return the benefits, which will be highly unfair and against the spirit of law and justice".

V. Case: Fazlī Subḥān *versus* Ṣābrīn

Fazlī Subḥān *versus* Ṣābrīn is another interesting case in which the learned judge interpreted the principles of *fiqh* in a progressive and liberal manner to provide protection to the wife. In this specific case, the wife came to an agreement of reunion with her husband by making an oral statement. Based upon two *fatwās* issued on the question of remarriage and the scholarly work of Mawlānā M. Ašraf ʿAlī Tahānvi, the court held that in cases of divorce through *ḫulʿ* it is not obligatory to the wife marrying a third person before entering into remarriage with her first husband. However, the remarriage would be subject to performance of another *nikāḥ*. The court, while further clarifying the issue of an intervening marriage, held that such a marriage is required only in cases where the couple has been divorced thrice and the third divorce has become lawfully effective. The objective behind such a requirement is to curtail the husband's arbitrary power of divorce. Any other kind of divorce, either in the form of *ḫulʿ* or *ṭalāq aḥsan*, does not require an intervening marriage as prerequisite to remarry the first husband.

VI. Case: Nāhīd Anwar *versus* Ǧāwīd Nāṣir

The changes made under the FCO have been implemented by the courts as well: In a recent judgement, Sindh's High Court held, in Nāhīd Anwar *versus* Ǧāwīd Nāṣir,[75] that, in light of to the added amendment in Section 10-A FCO

> " a family court, in a suit for dissolution of marriage, if reconciliation fails, shall pass decree for the dissolution of marriage forthwith and shall also restore to the husband the Haq Mahr received by the wife in consideration of marriage at the time of marriage."

According to the court, the petitioner shall be granted *ḫulʿ* or the marriage should be dissolved by the family judge, even if the woman's husband fails to attend the court proceedings.

---

[75] Cp. PLD, Karachi 2007.

VII. Case: Rūẖsana Malik *versus* ʿAbdul-ʿAzīz

Regarding custody and guardianship, yet another Pakistani a recent judgement is available: In Rūẖsana Malik *versus* ʿAbdul-ʿAzīz[76] a father sought the custody of his children on the ground that the mother has contracted a second marriage. In his finding, the judge made references to a number of *aḥādīṯ* whereupon the mother should be favoured to have custody over the child. In addition, the court held that a remarriage of a boy's mother constitutes, by itself, not a disqualification for retention of her custody. A female minor (close to) attaining the age of adolescence, may not be allowed to stay with the mother in the presence of the stepfather. However, if the father proves to be a person of "ill character", the mother grants the to guardianship of the minor. Based on of *aḥādīṯ*-literature and previous judgements, such as Fīrūz Bīgum *versus* M. Ḥusaīn's ruling, which stated that

> " the overriding and paramount consideration always is the welfare of the minor [...] and this is the sole consideration that must prevail in the final analysis and the fact that the father is the lawful guardian of his minor children does not compel the court to pass an order in his favour unless it is in their welfare to do so".

The court upheld the principle of "best interest of the child" as a paramount consideration. By adhering to this principle, the courts have, allusively, consent and approved the provisions of the CRC.

F. Conclusion

As illustrated, family law in Pakistan is influenced by various interpretations of *šarīʿa* doctrines. It is incorporated into the legislative enactments and also used by the courts in their family disputes' finding. The use of legal methodology, such as *taẖaiyur* and *talfiq,* made changes in contemporary family law possible. Hence, it is obvious that the concept of *šarīʿa* is not a static in itself but rather an *inbuilt dynamism.* By using *fiqh* methods interpreting Islamic principles, contemporary family law in Pakistan could increasingly consolidate women's (human) rights.

Pakistan's superordinate judiciary refers to principles of *fiqh* to interpret current legal issues in a progressive and liberal way. In doing so, it has not restricted itself to the narrow interpretations of a single *maḏhab*. The judiciary's interpretative approach reflects a combination of religious-, statutory-, constitutional- and human rights law.

[76] Cp. PLD, Lahore 2004, p. 801.

However, despite the progressive legislative amendments made, there are still a desiderata, thus room for further law reforms. Usually, no strict sanctions are imposed if there has been a violation of any of the aforementioned provisions. The relevant provisions in the family laws and *nikahnama* are too weak and vaguely worded to, effectively, intervene in customary marital practices that discriminate women rights. The field in family law that urges change is that of polygamy. So far, polygamy has not been abolished and the provisions restricting its exercise are unincisive. Noteworthy, the Qur'ānic directive in Sura 4 (النساء) : Verse 129

> وَلَن تَسْتَطِيعُوا أَن تَعْدِلُوا بَيْنَ النِّسَاءِ وَلَوْ حَرَصْتُمْ فَلَا تَمِيلُوا كُلَّ الْمَيْلِ فَتَذَرُ
> وهَا كَالْمُعَلَّقَةِ وَإِن تُصْلِحُوا وَتَتَّقُوا فَإِنَّ اللَّهَ كَانَ غَفُورًا رَّحِيمًا
>
> *"Ye will not be able to deal equally between [your] wives, however much ye wish [to do so]. But turn not altogether away [from one], leaving her as in suspense. If ye do good and keep from evil, lo! Allah is ever Forgiving, Merciful"*

is not used as a basis to constrain polygamy.

In addition, there are no supplemental clauses in the *nikahnama* to indicate the marital status of the bridegroom, strictly speaking,

- whether he married, never married or is classified as widower or
- whether marriage has been terminated through divorce (in any form) or
- whether there is an existing wife who is not mentioned.

Finally, there are no statutory provisions regarding post-divorce maintenance, although various Qur'ānic clauses relate to this issue, such as the respective Sura 65 (الطلاق) and Sura 4 (النساء) : Verse 20.[77] Some scholars opine that as all rights and obligations of a marriage contract discontinue once the divorce is finalized. Shaheen Sardar Ali, on the other hand, argues that refusing post divorce maintenance disregards the reality that the majority of women in Muslim countries are still not in a position to maintain themselves. This raises the question whether and in how far one should depend on (purposely) selected clauses of the Qur'ān. Instead, one should keep the main aforementioned main message in mind, clearly expressing the treatment of wives with respect, justice and fairness. On this note, Pakistan should consider the aforementioned CEDAW recommendations, as well.

---

[77] *Sura 4* (النساء) *: Verse 20:*

وَإِنْ أَرَدتُّمُ اسْتِبْدَالَ زَوْجٍ مَّكَانَ زَوْجٍ وَآتَيْتُمْ إِحْدَاهُنَّ قِنطَارًا فَلَا تَأْخُذُوا مِنْهُ شَيْئًا أَتَأْخُذُونَهُ بُهْتَانًا وَإِثْمًا مُّبِينًا.

"And if ye wish to exchange one wife for another and ye have given unto one of them a sum of money (however great), take nothing from it. Would ye take it by the way of calumny and open wrong?

Civil Society and Legislation: Development of the Human Rights Situation in Iran 2008

Irene Schneider, Göttingen

A. Introduction

On 22 July 2007 the Draft Bill for the protection of the family, which had been proposed by the judiciary and approved by the Council of Ministers, was submitted to the Iranian parliament (the *Mağles*).[1] When the text of this "Draft Bill for the protection of the family" (*lāyeḥeh-ye ḥemāyat az ḫānevādeh,* henceforth: the Draft Bill) was made public, a storm of protest broke out. This protest focused on two provisions. The first was Article 23, which allowed a husband to take a second wife only after the court had given permission, but ignoring the first wife's permission, which was necessary according to the Family Protection Act of 1975 (FPA) from the Shah's time.[2] The second was taxation of the dower (*mahrīyeh*) according to Article 25. This would have meant, that women would have to pay tax on dower, which usually is considered a means of security for women after divorce. Both articles were not drawn up by the judiciary when drafting the Bill, but were inserted in the course of the discussions by the Council of Ministers. A "Women's Movement" (*ğonbeš-e zanān*), as it was called in the press, emerged from different organisations and actors with different political and ideological backgrounds. Representatives of this "Women's Movement" went to the parliament and in the end succeeded in having these two articles deleted.[3]

In what follows, I will sketch out some legal developments in the Islamic Republic, focusing on the interaction between civil society (especially as composed of different women's organisations) and the state, in particular with regard to the Draft Bill.

The questions I will try to answer are: How can the human rights situation in connection with the Draft Bill be described, especially with regard to gender equality? What roles do the international human rights covenants, on the one hand, and the activities of civil society in the process of legislation, on the other

---

1 The Farsi text of the *lāyeḥeh-ye ḥemāyat az ḫānevādeh* can be found at http://meydaan.org/ShowArticle.aspx?arid=330 (accessed on 12 December 2008). An English translation can be found at http://www.meydaan.org/English/showarticle.aspx?ar id=375 (accessed on 19 January 2009).

2 See the Family Protection Act (*Qānūn-e ḥemāyat-e ḫānevādeh*)1975, Art.16 (1): *reżāyat-e hamsar-e avval*).

3 See, e.g., an interview with *Marżīyeh Langerūdī* at http://www.roozonline.com/archives/2008/ 09/post_8966.php (accessed on 22 January 2009).

Islam und Menschenrechte (Islam and Human Rights / الإسلام وحقوق الإنسان)
Hatem Elliesie (Hrsg./Editor), © Peter Lang Verlag: Frankfurt a.M. 2010, S. 387-414

hand, play in the public discussions of these human rights issues? The focus in this context is on Article 23 of the Draft Bill. After a description of the human rights situation in the Islamic Republic between 1979 and 2008 (B.), the rulings of the Draft Bill will be presented (C.). Furthermore, it will be asked whether there is a civil society in Iran and how it acted (D.), and what arguments were offered by the several participants of the public discourse (E.). A conclusion (F.) is given at the end.

Methodologically, I will focus on a reconstruction of the political and social process and its context (B., C., D.) and on discourse analysis, analysing the arguments put forward by the different sides (E.).

B. The Human Rights Situation in the Islamic Republic between 1979 and 2008

According to the FPA of 1975, divorce had to be decided by the court. This statute eliminated the right of the husband to extra-judicial divorce and broadened the grounds on which women could seek divorce. Custody was based on the best interests of the child, decided by Family Courts, and no longer accorded the absolute right of the father to custody of boys over two years and girls over seven years. Women were granted the possibility of custody. A married man had to obtain the permission of the court and the first wife before marrying a second wife. Nevertheless, polygamy and temporary marriage continued and women did not have equal rights for divorce, or custody and guardianship of children. Neither did the FPA ensure women's rights after divorce, to maintenance or to work outside the home. It was, however, an improved version of Islamic Law with regard to more gender equality.[4]

In her article, "Rights of Women and Children in Iran", Shirin Ebadi (Šīrīn ʿEbādī) points to the fact that after the Islamic Revolution the rights of women and children were curtailed. She argues that there is a great discrepancy between Human Rights according to the standard of the Universal Declaration of Human Rights (UDHR) and the Iranian legislation, especially with regard to the rights of women and children.[5] The FPA was suspended by Khomeini in 1979, but

---

4 *Shirin Ebadi / Henriette Sinding Aasen*, "Rights of Women and Children in Iran", in: *Uichol Kim / Henriette Sinding Aasen / Shirin Ebadi* (Eds.), Democracy, Human Rights and Islam in Modern Iran. Psychological, Social, and Cultural Perspectives, Bergen 2003, pp. 221-257 (on p. 240); see also *Parvin Paidar,* Women and the Political Process in twentieth-century Iran, Cambridge, 1997, pp. 271-276.

5 *Shirin Ebadi / Henriette Sinding Aasen*, Rights of Women..., supra, footnote 4, pp. 221-228.

parts of it remained in force.[6] After the Revolution, the state policy on marriage focused on the construction of marriage as the only legitimate site of sexual pleasure and reproduction, and its universalisation. To achieve this, the state adopted a number of strategies. The lawful age of marriage was lowered, obstacles to polygamy were removed, financial assistance was offered to newly-wed couples, and a campaign was launched to promote the virtues of marriage and Islamic matrimonial rights.[7] In 1986 a new marriage contract was introduced which spelled out the infringements of women's rights which could give them the right to initiate divorce. These included, among others, the husband's marriage to another woman without her consent.[8] In 1985 the policy changed towards greater restriction on polygamy.[9]

The main discrepancies in Iranian family law with regard to international human rights instruments and gender differences are:

- The age of marriage, which was lowered to 9 (lunar) years for girls after the Revolution, is still low after the reform of 2002: 13 for girls and 15 for boys (Art. 1041 Civil Code [CC]).[10]
- A woman marrying for the first time always needs the permission of her father or grandfather (Art. 1043 CC) but this is not true for a man. If the father/grandfather does not consent, the woman has to obtain the permission of a court.[11]
- The marriage of an Iranian woman to a non-Iranian man has to be permitted by the Iranian state (Art.1060 CC).[12] A Muslim woman cannot marry a non-Muslim man (Art. 1059 CC).
- A woman cannot contract a second marriage while she is married, but a man can be married to up to four women at the same time (Art. 16 FPA 1975).[13]
- Temporary marriage, a speciality of Shiite law, still exists (Art. 1075-1077 CC).
- The husband is the head of the family (Art. 1105 CC). He chooses the place to live (but husband and wife can stipulate something else according to Art. 1114 CC) and is

6 *Parvin Paidar,* Women and the Political Process…, supra, footnote 4, pp. 273-274. That parts were still in force can be seen from the fact that the new Draft Bill explicitly declares the FPA of 1975 as abrogated. In most works published on Family Law until 2008, the FPA was recited, see, e.g., *Ǧahāngīr Manṣūr,* Qavānīn va muqarrarāt-e marbūṭ beh ezdevāǧ va ṭalāq, 8th edition, Tehran 1386/1998.

7 *Parvin Paidar,* Women and the Political Process, supra, footnote 4, on p. 277.

8 Ibidem, on p. 284.

9 Ibidem, on p. 285.

10 *Hossein Safa'i,* "Le mariage et le divorce en droit Iranien", in: *Jürgen Basedow / Nadjma Yassari* (Eds.), Iranian Family and Succession Laws and their Application in German Courts, Tübingen 2004, pp. 69-80 (on p. 71).

11 Ibidem.

12 Ibidem.

13 Ibidem, on p. 72.

allowed to prevent his wife from working outside the home (Art. 1117 CC) in case the work is against the interests of the family.

- The wife, however, has also the right in certain situations to prevent her husband from working, but with an important restriction because the husband's work ensures the financial basis of the family (Art. 18 FPA).
- A reasonable amount of living expenses (*nafaqeh*) (Art. 1107 CC, and amendment of 1381/2003) and also the dower (*mahrīyeh*) has to be given by the husband (Art. 1078-1101 CC).
- Divorce has to be ordered by a court, and the court tries to reconcile the partners. If this is not possible, the husband obtains divorce (*ṭalāq*) (Art. 1133 CC, modified by the law of 10 November 2002). The wife has to give certain reasons for her wish for divorce (*fasḫ-e nekāḥ*), such as the husband's non-payment of living expenses (Art. 1129 CC), or that cohabiting is no longer bearable for her (hardship and distress/*ʿosr va ḥarağ*) (Art. 1130 CC).There is, furthermore, divorce by mutual consent (*ṭalāq-e ḫolʿ*) (Art. 1146-1147 CC)[14] and the woman can have a divorce, with the consent of the husband, by paying him a sum, more often the dower.
- According to Article 1169 CC, in case of divorce, a woman will be given custody (*ḥeżānat*) over her sons to the age of two years and seven years for daughters. After this, the custody devolves to the father. The parliament agreed on 28 July 2002 to a law raising the age of custody for children of both genders to seven years, effectively only raising the age of custody for the boys. This was finally accepted and came into force on 31 December 2003. If the woman remarries, then she will lose her right to custody over her children. However, if the father dies, then the custody will go to the mother, after a change in the law in 1992.[15]
- In 1997 women were given the right to partial custody, but not to guardianship *velāyat*) (Art. 1180 CC). This is the case, if, for example the husband is dead. Guardianship is the non-negotiable right of the father, or the paternal grandfather in case of the father's death.
- In inheritance law, the woman's portion is half of the man's portion (Arts. 921, 923, 931, 933 CC).[16]
- Women still do not have the chance to become judges in the Iranian judicial system, they can only act as legal consultants, and only in family matters.[17]

To summarize: The main fields of divergence from international human rights standards in family law are; polygamy, divorce, custody and women's representation in the public space.

---

[14] Ibidem, pp. 76-78.

[15] *Shirin Ebadi / Henriette Sinding Aasen*, Rights of Women…, supra, footnote 4, on p. 242.

[16] *Hossein Mehrpour,* "An overview of inheritance in the legal system of Iran", in: *Jürgen Basedow / Nadjma Yassari* (Eds.), Iranian Family…, supra, footnote 10, pp. 103-109 (on p. 107).

[17] *Martin Haars*, "Summary", in: *Jürgen Basedow / Nadma Yassari* (Eds.), ibidem, pp. 97-99 (on p. 98).

Since 1993, Iranian women have also increased their political participation considerably. Still, in 2008 there were only eight women in the parliament out of 290 members of the parliament. In 1997, however, the Council of Guardians disqualified female candidates from running for the presidency.[18]

On the international level, human rights and rights of women and children are protected by several international covenants, e.g., the Universal Declaration of Human Rights (UDHR), the International Covenant on Civil and Political Rights (ICCPR), the International Covenant on Economic, Social and Cultural Rights (ICESCR), the Convention on the Elimination of all Forms of Discrimination against Women (CEDAW) and the Convention of the Rights of the Child (CRC). These covenants, which are legally binding upon the ratifying states, represent the main international legal standards and instruments concerning Human Rights. Iran ratified the UDHR in 1948,[19] the International Covenant on Civil and Political Rights (ICCPR) of 1966, and the CRC in the time of the Islamic Republic, but not CEDAW. The goal of the CRC is to protect children and their fundamental human rights and dignity. It recognises that "childhood is entitled to special care and assistance" and that "the child, by reason of his physical and mental immaturity, needs special safeguards and care, including appropriate legal protection" (Preamble of CRC). However, the Iranian government made a general reservation upon ratification. It stated that

> " the Government of the Islamic Republic of Iran reserves the right not to apply any provision or articles of the Convention that are incompatible with Islamic Laws".[20]

Despite the ratification of CRC, thus discrepancies between the Convention and the Iranian legislation still exist.[21] CEDAW was discussed but not ratified by Iran. The Parliament agreed to accede to the Convention, but the Council of Guardians (*Šūrā-ye negahbān*) rejected its proposal of 12 August 2003 to ratify CEDAW.[22] CEDAW was then submitted to the Assessment Council and is still there (December 2008).

Furthermore, the Islamic Republic has approved Article 6 (A) of the Cairo Declaration on Human Rights in Islam. This declaration is not a legally binding con-

18 *Shirin Ebadi / Henriette Sinding Aasen*, Rights of Women…, supra, footnote 4, on p. 239.

19 See: http://www.unhchr.ch/udhr/miscinfo/carta.htm (accessed on 16 January 2009).

20 *Shirin Ebadi / Henriette Sinding Aasen*, Rights of Women…, supra, footnote 4, on p. 224 et seq.

21 *Nadjma Yassari*, "Who is a child?", in: *Susan Rutten*, (Ed.) Recht van de Islam 22, Maastricht 2005, pp. 17-30.

22 *Shirin Ebadi / Henriette Sinding Aasen*, Rights of Women…, supra, footnote 4, pp. 223-224.

tract, but it is a common declaration from the Muslim world on the concept and content of Human Rights.[23] It states that:

> " Woman is equal to man in human dignity, and has rights to enjoy as well as duties to perform."

Ebadi states:

> " Article 6 (A) may be interpreted to mean that women and men, despite equality in human dignity, enjoy different human rights: Women enjoy special rights due to their sex rather than equal rights like men."[24]

C. The Provisions of the Draft Bill

Being the object of a public discussion of high political implication, the developments around the Draft Bill have been reported meticulously.[25] The public criticism started in July 2007 and focused on Articles 23 and 25. The Draft Bill's introduction refers to the special role and status of the institution of the family in the legal and pedagogical system of Islam,

> " considering that certain parts of the laws concerning rights of the family have been found incompatible with the Sharia..[…]".

The Bill is divided into chapters: Chapter 1 concerns the family court, Chapter 2 family counselling centres, Chapter 3 marriage, Chapter 4 divorce, Chapter 5 custody and maintenance of children, Chapter 6 penal provisions. In Article 53 it is stated: "As of the date of enactment of this law, the following laws and all regulations to the contrary shall be superseded". Several laws are named, among them the FPA of 1975.

As Article 23 on polygamy is the focus of this article, the text of the article is given here:

> Marriage to a subsequent permanent wife shall depend on court authorization upon ascertainment of the man's financial capability and undertaking to uphold justice among his wives.
>
> Note: In the event of plurality of marriages and should the marriage portion mature and the wife demands it, the authorization to register the new marriage shall depend on payment of the marriage portion to the first wife.

Whereas the public protest focused on Articles 23 and 25, jurists have had more concise criticism of other articles, too. In her article, "Women: one step ahead does not make the whole way",[26] Šahīndoḫt Mawlāverdī, a jurist specialising in international law, draws attention to other points of the Draft Bill:

---

23 Ibidem, on p. 222.

24 Ibidem, on p. 224.

25 http://meydaan.org/showArticle.aspx?arid=660 (accessed on 15 January 2009).

26 *Šahīndoḫt Mawlāverdī*, "Zanān: yek gām beh pīš-e rāh-e nā-tamām", in: Šahravand-e emrūz 31, Šahrīvar 2008/September 2008, on p. 81.

- **Article 2**: Whereas the judiciary had made the presence of female judges in the family courts obligatory, the state changed this to "where possible" (*ḥattā l-maqdūr* instead of *bāyad*). Instead of "one of the members of the court must be from among women having a judicial basis (*dārandeh-ye pāyeh-ye qażā'ī*)" the text was changed to "one of the counsillors (*mostašārān*) of the court must be a woman […]". This means that a woman now cannot be an alternating judge or the head of the court, and it is in contradiction with what the judiciary wanted the counsellors to be, i.e., to be responsible just for problematic cases.
- **Article 4**, para. 8: The following affairs and claims shall be investigated by the Family Court: "Unilateral obedience and deference of the two parties (*nošūz va tamkīn-e zawǧayn*)". This is new insofar as *nošūz* (evasion) here refers to both sexes, husband and wife. Mawlāverdī justifies this by pointing to Qur'ān Verse 4 (النساء): 128[27]. It must be stated, that *nošūz* still is normally used based on Qur'ān 4 (النساء): 34[28], for women only. She clearly approves that this categorization now concerns both sexes.
- **Article 5**: the government inserted: "The Family Court shall also investigate offences the subject of Chapter 6 of this law". This was inserted instead of the judiciary's text: "Minor crimes and disputes in the family between the spouses" are to be dealt with by the Family Court. So the Family Court is now bound to deal with the problems named in Article 4 and chapter 6. This would mean that not all violence in the family will be penalized and Mawlāverdī suggests the formulation, "hitting and wounding and violence in the family" should be added to Article 4.
- **Article 11**, concerning the Family Court, the text is as follows: "The court may adjourn the hearing, no more than twice, at the request of the couple or one of the partners to provide opportunity for reconciliation and rapprochement." This text was left unaltered by the government, but Mawlāverdī suggests here that the hearing should be postponed only once to shorten the process.
- **Article 21**, note 1, provides: "Members of the Family Counselling Centres shall be chosen from among experts […]. Note 1: Counselling sessions shall be held necessarily in the presence of trustees of the two parties and preferably their relatives." Mawlāverdī suggests either removing this note, or that the counsellor should decide if it is necessary to invite the relatives, because, according to her, many differences arise from the participation of the relatives.
- Another note has been added by the state to **Article 2** (note 2): "All the family disputes and differences may be raised with Arbitration Councils (Marākez-e mošāvareh). If petitioned by the two parties, the said councils shall be established with relevant experts participating and their judgments, with the exception of divorce, shall be binding. If they decide upon a divorce judgment, the case shall be referred to court." Mawlāverdī suggests removing this because it undermines the authority of the court.

---

27 *Sura 4* (النساء), *Verse 128:*
وَإِنِ امْرَأَةٌ خَافَتْ مِن بَعْلِهَا نُشُوزًا أَوْ إِعْرَاضًا فَلاَ جُنَاْحَ عَلَيْهِمَا أَن يُصْلِحَا بَيْنَهُمَا صُلْحًا وَالصُّلْحُ خَيْرٌ وَأُحْضِرَتِ الأَنفُسُ الشُّحَّ وَإِن تُحْسِنُواْ وَتَتَّقُواْ فَإِنَّ اللّهَ كَانَ بِمَا تَعْمَلُونَ خَبِيرًا.

28 *Sura 4* (النساء), *Verse 34:*
الرِّجَالُ قَوَّامُونَ عَلَى النِّسَاء بِمَا فَضَّلَ اللّهُ بَعْضَهُمْ عَلَى بَعْضٍ وَبِمَا أَنفَقُواْ مِنْ أَمْوَالِهِمْ فَالصَّالِحَاتُ قَانِتَاتٌ حَافِظَاتٌ لِّلْغَيْبِ بِمَا حَفِظَ اللّهُ وَاللاَّتِي تَخَافُونَ نُشُوزَهُنَّ فَعِظُوهُنَّ وَاهْجُرُوهُنَّ فِي الْمَضَاجِعِ وَاضْرِبُوهُنَّ فَإِنْ أَطَعْنَكُمْ فَلاَ تَبْغُواْ عَلَيْهِنَّ سَبِيلاً إِنَّ اللّهَ كَانَ عَلِيًّا كَبِيرًا.

- **Article 22**, the note was changed by the state: "Registration of temporary marriage shall be subject to Rules of Procedure to be approved by the Minister of Justice." Mawlāverdī argues for the original text of the judiciary, according to which the registration of the temporary marriage was made clear and, in case of pregnancy, obligatory, in other cases, dependent on the will of the partners. Her aim is to give women in this kind of marriage more security and especially the children resulting from such relationships. She suggests taking the text of the judiciary and adding that, in case of registration, two documents are to be given to each party with possible stipulations.
- With regard to the Counselling Centres, the problem of a person not present in Iran has to be solved. Mawlāverdī suggests referring to a legal representative (*vakīl*).
- **Article 32**[29]: the proposed fair remuneration (*oǧrat al-meṯl*) for the wife after divorce was taken out by the state. Mawlāverdī suggests it should be restored.
- Chapter 5, from **Article 39** on, deals with "custody and maintenance" (*ḥeżānat va negahdārī-ye aṭfāl)*" of children and with special maintenance (*nafaqeh*). Mawlāverdī suggests dealing with the two topics – custody and maintenance – in an extra article and to avoid *negahdārī* being a synonym of *ḥeżānat*.
- **Article 44**: "In the event that a man takes action regarding permanent marriage, divorce, revocation and reunion, without having them registered with authorized offices, he shall be forced to register the event and be sentenced to pay a fine ranging from 20 million to 100 million Riyals and eventually be deprived of an appropriate social right." Mawlāverdī considers the fine far too lenient and would prefer a combination of fine and imprisonment.
- Mawlāverdī proposes that the original note to **Article 42**, according to which non-registration of a temporary marriage in case of pregnancy was to be punished, should be restored.
- **Article 45**: a doctor issuing a false medical certificate for the marriage (see Article 24)[30] is punished with imprisonment from 1 to 5 years, whereas the judiciary had proposed 3–5 years.
- According to **Article 46**: "Any foreign national who marries an Iranian woman without obtaining the permit mentioned under Article 1060 of the CC, shall be sentenced to from ninety-one days to one year imprisonment. In that case, the woman, if she has married of her free will, the girl's father, if the marriage has taken place with his permission, and the marriage solemniser, shall be sentenced as accomplices of the offence." Mawlāverdī suggests canceling this article because it was not in the judiciary's Draft Bill.
- According to **Article 48**: "The person charged with custody of child shall be sentenced to pay a fine from 500,000 to 5 million Riyals in the event he refuses to perform the du-

29 I think Šahīndoḫt Mawlāverdī erroneously wrote 31 instead of 32, but as I do not have the judiciary's text, I cannot justify this.

30 According to Article 24, the Ministry of Health, Remedy and Medical Education (*Vezāret-e behdāšt, darmān va āmūzeš-e pezeškī*) is required to determine and announce the diseases against which the two parties shall be immunised prior to marriage, as well as the contagious diseases dangerous to married couples and the children resulting from marriage, within one month of the passage of this law. Before registration of marriage, Marriage Offices are obliged to demand and file certificates issued by medical doctors.

ties concerning custody or prevents visitation to the child by the beneficiaries." She points to the Law with regard to custody ratified on 22 *Mehr* 1365 /13 August 1987, according to which default in custody is punished with imprisonment, and she argues that the fine is not enough of a deterrent.

- Mawlāverdī suggests that, according to Article19 of the FPA of 1975, there should be distinction between fixed rules (*aḥkām-e qaṭʿī*) and rules which can be changed (*aḥkām-e qābel-e eʿterāż*), so it could not be said that with the elimination of **Article 23 and Article 25** of this Draft Bill the work would be done.

Many points Mawlāverdī raises concern amendments by the government which were not the original Draft Bill of the judiciary. This is true for Article 2, where the presence of women in the courts had been changed from an obligation into a recommendation, and women can only be counsellors. It is true for Article 5, in which the offences the Family Court (*Dādgāh-e ḫānevādeh*) can deal with are restricted to the offences named in Article 4 and chapter 6. It is also true for Article 22, according to which the registration of temporary marriage was made obligatory in the judiciary's Draft Bill in case of pregnancy, and the fines and punishments are not hard enough in Mawlāverdī's opinion (see her suggestion with regard to Article 48). In most cases, it can be stated that the changes the government inserted were, from Mawlāverdī's point of view, negative for women or made the text less precise. Human rights standards are not mentioned by Mawlāverdī. However, the discrepancies between the regulations in the Draft Bill and, e.g., CEDAW are obvious with regard to the position of women in the judiciary (Art. 2), temporary marriage (Art. 22), and the still existing inequality with regard to polygamy and the male prerogative of divorce as well as custody. One positive remark concerns Islamic Law. The Qur'ānic concept of *nošūz*, which was often applied to women who did not behave appropriately, is used in Article 4 for both sexes.

D. Iranian Civil Society and its Reaction to the Draft Bill

Civil society as a concept has emerged in the context of western political culture. It has been defined in many different ways, but is normally understood as the third sphere, besides the state and the economy. Whereas the state is seen in relation with the political administration and administrative power, and the economy is seen in relation with money and the economic system of action, civil society is seen in connection with the public communication structure (networks) and its resource is solidarity. All three fields interact and thus display a certain kind of dynamism and development in the social and political context.[31]

31 *Jürgen Habermas*, Faktizität und Geltung. Beiträge zur Diskurstheorie des Rechts und des demokratischen Rechtsstaats, Frankfurt a.M. 1992, p. 448. Habermas states that civil so-

This third sphere, "civil society", will be analysed here in its relation to the state, not the economy. Obviously civil society does not rule, but the question arises whether it can influence the political regime through its power in a certain direction.[32] Ruling is thus understood as bound to institutional structures, whereas power functions also in other – not so organised – contexts. Several questions arise: Is there a civil society in Iran, not being a democratic state? If this question is answered in the affirmative: What power does the civil society in Iran exert?

According to Foucault, power is influenced by discourses and discourses create power. Discourse, according to Foucault, can be understood as an institutionalised way of thinking that can be manifested through language, a social boundary defining what can be said about a specific topic but also what cannot be said and is excluded from discourse.[33] Foucault speaks of the taboo of the topic, the ritual of the circumstances and the right of the speaking subject in this context.[34] Power according to him is not based on a restrictive top-down perspective. He seeks to provide the tools necessary for analysing power relations at different points in a state and society.[35] Power is thus ubiquitous and diffuse.[36] As discourses define reality, they exert power in a mutual process. The discourses thus produce power and shift power relations.[37] But can discourses shift the state authority?

I will focus on the social and political discourse on the question of the first wife's permission for polygamy and analyse on that basis, first of all, the political and social situation in Iran, and second, on the basis of the arguments used in this public discourse, how this discourse influenced the political decision making and why, i.e., on the basis of which arguments. This methodological approach seems to be fruitful in order to highlight the processes of legislation in an Islamic authoritarian state by focusing not only on the course of events but on the discursive mechanisms that shaped this course.[38]

---

ciety ("eine vitale Bürgergesellschaft") can only come into existence in a liberal political culture and its actors can only gain influence, not political power, ibidem, p. 449.

32 Ibidem, pp. 448-449; *Walter Reese-Schäfer,* Politisches Denken heute, 2nd edition, Oldenburg 2007, pp. 10-11.

33 *Michel Foucault*, The Archaeology of Knowledge, New York 1972, p. 98.

34 *Michel Foucault,* Die Ordnung des Diskurses, Frankfurt a.M. 1994, p. 11.

35 For the development of Foucault's concept of power, see *Barry Hindess*, Discourses of Power, Cambridge 1996, pp. 96-136.

36 *Michel Foucault*, The Archaeology Knowledge, supra, footnote 33, p. 98.

37 *Michel Foucault,* Der Wille zum Wissen, Sexualität und Wahrheit 1, Frankfurt a.M. 1983, p. 122.

38 For the political system, see the analysis of the constitution by *Silvia Tellenbach*, Untersuchungen zur Verfassung der Iranischen Republik Iran vom 15.November 1979, Berlin

Albrecht discusses this concept in the research for the Islamic states and concludes that civil society is a historically rooted concept as well as a phenomenon which can be described on the basis of social-political structures. The minimum conditions which have to be fulfilled by civil society organisations and actors as understood in this context are; that civil society organisations or actors have to represent individual interests in opposition to the formal state structures, that membership is voluntary, and that the civil society organisations are autonomous from state influence, that those organisations have to have a certain potential of organisation to be differentiated from purely individual relations (as structures of lobbyism, clientelism, familiar structures etc.), and single actors have to have a certain public voice.[39] According to Croissant, Lauth and Merkel, the tasks of civil society institutions or actors are; the protection of individuals against the state, mediation between the political and non-political sphere, a function of socialisation, the building of a social community and a communication function.[40]

Albrecht correctly points to the fact that civil society is an analytical concept for the explanation of social organisation and which has to be seen, instead of the alleged division between the social and the political spheres, very much in connection with or in dependence on the state. The state creates the legal and institutional frame and gives the rules thus deciding the radius of action civil society actors actually have.[41] According to Albrecht, democracy cannot exist without civil society and civil society is a constituent of the system, whereas in an authoritarian system it is an opposition force.[42]

At the same time, I will argue that persons having a prominent public position in Iranian society, like the Nobel prize winner Shirin Ebadi, can be regarded as representatives of civil society and as important actors in the public discourse, who have a voice in the public discourse, of course also internationally.[43]

1985. Separation of powers exists in Iran, but all three powers are dominated by the prominent figure of the religious leader (*rahbar*).

39 *Holger Albrecht,* "Zivilgesellschaft und der vorderer Orient: Das Prinzip Hoffnung und die Grenzen eines sozialwissenschaftlichen Konzepts", in: *Joachim Betz / Wolfgang Hein,* Zivilgesellschaft, Wiesbaden 2005, pp. 118-119.

40 *Aurel Croissant / Hans-Joachim Laut / Wolfgang Merkel,* "Zivilgesellschaft und Transformation: ein internationaler Vergleich", in: *Wolfgang Merkel* (Ed.), Systemwechsel 5, Opladen 2000, pp. 9-49 (on pp. 9-14).

41 *Holger Albrecht,* Zivilgesellschaft…, supra, footnote 37, p. 120.

42 Ibidem, p. 120 et seq.

43 *Sonja Hegasy,* Staat, Öffentlichkeit und Zivilgesellschaft in Marokko, Hamburg 1997, takes as examples the sociologist Fatima Mernissi and the philosopher Muhammad Abed al-Jabiri; ibidem, on p. 37, pp. 95-112, pp. 131-139).

In 2006 Iranian women's rights activists and different organisations, mostly women's organisations, initiated a nationwide campaign demanding an end to discrimination against women in Iranian law. The campaign, "One Million Signatures Demanding Changes to Discriminatory Laws,"[44] aims, as the name says, first of all to effect change in discriminatory laws by collecting one million signatures. It was a follow-up effort to the peaceful protest of the same aim, which took place on 12 June 2006 in Haft-eTīr Square in Tehran. The aims of this campaign are, according to their self-presentation, the promotion of collaboration and cooperation for social change, and the promotion of cooperation between a wide spectrum of social activists thus forming a kind of superstructure. The intention is to increase knowledge in the population about the legal situation of women and promote democratic actions, to carry out bottom-up reform and to create change through grassroots and civil society initiatives, to strengthen public action and empower women. The campaign strives to demonstrate that women have consistently employed a variety of means and venues to voice their objections to the laws, such as the writing of books, articles, production of films and other forms of artistic expression, and through social activism. In an effort to silence the voices of women calling for change, critics claim that these demands for legal change are expressed by a particular group of women who are out of touch with the realities of ordinary Iranian women. In response, the women campaigners argue that their organisation comprises not only elite and socially and economically advantaged women but many women from all strata of society. The state reacted with strength and suppression against the women participating in the campaign and the organisations, which are mostly illegal, i.e. not accepted officially as non-governmental organisations.[45] According to a non-govern-mental organisation's report, between March 2007 and March 2008, 63 women's rights activists were arrested, 38 women's rights activists were summoned to appear in court, and 114 female students were sentenced to exclusion from education. Two female prisoners were killed under suspicious circumstances, and 37 women were sentenced to execution and stoning. The most important feminist magazine (*Zanān*, edited by Šahlā Šerkat[46]) was forced to close in January 2008 and many women's websites and web logs are filtered.[47]

---

44 *Aḥmadī Ḫorāsānī*, Ǧonbeš-e yek millyūn emżā', Tehran 1386/2008, pp. 70 et seqq.; www.feministschool.com/campaign/ (accessed on 17 December 2008).

45 http://www.forequality.info/english/spip.php?article346; http://www.feministschool.org/english/spip.php?rubrique5 (both accessed on 16 January 2009); http://www.feministschool.org/english/spip.php?article162 from 23 October 2008 (accessed on 17 December 2008).

46 Cp. *Margot Badran*, "Gleichberechtigung auf Halbmast", in: Qantara, http://de.qantara.de/webcom/show_article.php/_c-469/_nr-833/i.html, (accessed on 22 January 2009).

47 Cp. http://www.meydaan.org/English/showarticle.aspx?arid=555 (accessed on 19 January 2009).

The campaign must be seen as opposed to the state, and organisations of civil society as defined above are independent from the state. On the level of organisation, the nationwide campaign and the revolt against the Draft Bill reveal an impressive structure of organisation. All the other functions mentioned above such as the protection of individuals against the state – in this case the women against discriminatory laws – the mediation between a political and non-political sphere, the function of socialisation and communication as well as the building of a social community are surely true for these groups. Thus, according to the definition given above, it can be stated that these groups initiating the campaign can be called civil-society organisations. An important aspect of this campaign is the composition of different women's movements with different approaches (feminist, religious, socialist).[48]

Building on this structure, the movement against the Draft Bill came into existence. In the press, they are mostly called the "Women's Movement (*Ǧonbeš-e zanān*)[49] or the coalition of women's groups against the "Draft Bill against the Family" (*E'telāf-e grūhhā-ye zanān-e ʿalayhe lāyeḥeh-ye żedd-e ḫānevādeh*).[50]

On 24 June 2007[51] the Draft Bill was dealt with by the cabinet, on 23 July 2007 it was sent to the parliament (*Maǧles*), it was published and the public criticism started. On 24 August 2007 the campaign entitled, "No to the Bill for the protection of men in the family", started officially. Shirin Ebadi, being one of the most active persons engaged in the campaign against the Draft Bill, threatened that if the bill was not withdrawn, women would take their protest to the parliament. On 7 December 2007 a *fatwā* by Āyatollāh Ṣāneʿī was published which declared polygamy without the permission of the first wife to be forbidden. On 11 December 2007 severe criticism was launched by the Parliament of the European Union against the Draft Bill. In July and August 2008 more than 2,200 persons joined the Women's Movement, carrying out activities such as public speeches and distributing information-leaflets and stickers.[52] On 23 August 2008 a media campaign started against the Women's Movement. On the afternoon of 31 August 2008 more than 100 women from different organisations went to the parliament and talked with members of parliament. Consequently, the Draft Bill

---

48 *Aḥmadī Ḫorāsānī*, Ǧonbeš-e Yek Millyūn Emżā, supra, footnote 42, on p. 70; see also http: //www.we-change.org/english/spip.php?rubrique5 (accessed on 17 December 2008), for further links.

49 http://www.roozonline.com/archives/2008/09/post_8966.php (accessed on 1 September 2008).

50 http://www.Feministschool.com (accessed on 17 December 2008); http://www.for equality.info/english/spip.php?article324 (accessed on 16 January 2008.

51 http://meydaan.org/showArticle.aspx?arid=660 (accessed on 17 December 2008).

52 http://meydaan.org/ShowArticle.aspx?arid=641 (accessed on 17 December 2008).

was withdrawn and sent back to the Legal Commission.[53] On 3 September 2008 Fāṭima Āliyā, a member of the parliament, spoke out against withdrawal of the Draft Bill. She called the women who had gone to the parliament "a small number of secular mud throwers". Others wrote a letter to the religious leader, Khamenei, to stop the legal proceedings of the Draft Bill.[54] On 5 September 2008 Ayatollah Amīnī, in the Friday prayer in Qom, demanded that the *Maǧles* reconsider Articles 23 and 25 of the Draft Bill. On 8 September 2008, Articles 23 and 25 and also paragraph 24 of Article 53 were eliminated from the Draft Bill in a session of the Judicial Legal Commission of the *Maǧles* (*Komīsyūn-e qażā'ī va ḥoqūqī-ye Maǧles*) and its chief, ʿAlī Šāhrūdī, stated that the articles would have led to the destruction of families.[55] On 9 September 2008 the whole Draft Bill, without the two articles, was approved in the parliament.[56]

E. Which Arguments were put forward? By whom and in what Contexts?

Analysis of a discourse is demanding from the perspective of methodology and sources and deserves a multilayered approach. First of all, the different parties taking part in this discourse must be identified, their arguments collected, classified and analysed. In a second step, an analysis of arguments put forward (and those that could have been advanced but were not) by the discussants as well as their contexts will be made. As public discourses are based on a broad range of actors and participants, there has to be a thematic focus as well as a selection of the "voices". The thematic focus in what follows will be on Article 23 of the Draft Bill and the issue of the necessity of the permission of the first wife for polygamy. The most important groups engaged in the discourse were (a) the civil society groups including prominent individuals, (b) the Shiite scholars, (c) the state, which in this case comprised the judiciary, members of the Ministry of Justice and members of the parliament and its different committees. The time for the analysis begins with the publication of the Draft Bill in July 2007 and the start of the broad public criticism. It ends, for this article, in December 2008. After the elimination of the two offending articles on 31 August 2008, the discussion became less intensive in the media. Sources that I have used are published articles in journals and the web, a letter to the parliament, the *fatwās,*

53 http://meydaan.org/ShowArticle.aspx?arid=652 (accessed on 17 December 2008).

54 http://meydaan.org/news.aspx?nid=2377 (accessed on 16 January 2009).

55 http://www.vol.at/news/CO:austria:politik/artikel/iranisches-parlament-kippt-gesetzentwurf-zur-polygamie/cn/news-20080909-02494174, of 9 September 2008 (accessed on 15 January 2009). See also Behrous Khosrozadeh, www.heise.de/tp/r4/artikel/28/28804/1.html (accessed on 16 January 2009).

56 http://meydaan.org/showArticle.aspx?arid=660 (accessed on 12 January 2009).

news reports on the internet and interviews conducted by me between October and December 2008.[57]

The arguments comprise legal arguments (I), meaning arguments concerning statutory law, international law and the Iranian judicial system, arguments of the Shiite *fiqh* (II), and social/psychological and cultural arguments (III).

I. The Legal Arguments

With regard to the national level, some of the civil society groups, in an open letter in November 2007, pointed to the CC and argued that no right for men to practise polygamy could be found in this text.[58] Fāṭimeh Āliyā, a member of parliament from Tehran and responsible for the parliamentary committee of women and the family (*Komīteh-ye zanān va ḫānevādeh-ye Maǧles*),[59] pointed to the positive points and achievements in the Draft Bill, such as female counsellors in the family courts (Art. 2), the right given to mothers to file a suit against their husbands for not paying maintenance for their children (Art. 7), the possibility

57 A starting point for the events in the discourse was the following website, which contains the most important events: http://meydaan.org/.showArticleaspx?arid=660, with the title *Rūzšomāreh-ye vaqāye*ʿ*-e ettefāqiyeh-ye lāyeḥeh-ye ḥemāyat-e ḫānevādeh*. Interviews were used as an additional source to articles and internet presentations. I selected some representatives of the groups taking part in the discourse (civil society, *fuqahāʾ* and state representatives) and asked them about the process of legislation with regard to the Draft Bill, about their personal opinion of the Draft Bill and their opinion with regard to the influence of international law, more specifically: CEDAW, on the national legislation. I want to express my gratitude to all of my interview partners for accepting to be interviewed, for answering my questions and discussing with me the different aspects of the process of legislation in the Islamic Republic of Iran. I have benefited greatly from these discussions.

58 The letter dates from 12 November 2007 and is to be found in: http://www.aftabnews.ir/vdccepq2b1qee.html (accessed on 19 December 2008). It was sent in the name of several women's groups: *Maǧmaʿ-e zanān-e eṣlāḥṭalab* being supporters of the former president Khatemi; *Ǧamʿīyat-e zanān-e mosalmān-e nawāndīš* (Intellectual Muslim Women's Association, also supporters of Khatemi); *Anǧoman-e rūznāmeh-negārān-e zan-e Īrān* (group of women journalists); *Komīsyūn-e zanān-e ǧabheh-ye mošārakat-e Īrān-e eslāmī* (Women Organisation of Islamic Iran Participation Front, a party headed by the supporters of the former President Khatemi) and *Ǧāmeʿeh-ye zanān-e enqelāb-e eslāmī* , founded in 1994, being originally supporters of Khomeini at the beginning of the Islamic revolution, now fighting for Reform and Democracy in an Islamic Framework. This letter deals critically with all articles of the Draft Bill. See also the report from 4 September 2007: "Bar-rasīy-e layeḥeh-ye ḥemāyat-e ḫānevādeh az manẓar-e ḥoqūqī, ǧāmeʿehšenāsī, ravānšenāsī: kam luṭfī beh zanān beh nām-e lāyeheh-ye ḥemāyat az ḫānevādeh?"; in: http://meydaan.org/wwShow.aspx?wwid=495 (accessed on 5 February 2009) in which the position of jurists, sociologists and psychologists are given.

59 http://meydaan.org/wwShow.aspx?wwid=520 (accessed on 22 December 2008).

for women to apply to the court of the city they live in, in case the husband is in another city (Art. 15), and the establishment of counselling centres for families (Art. 17-21).[60] With regard to Article 23 and the first wife's permission, she argued that there had been no legal regulation of polygamy before this Draft Bill, because Article 16 of the 1975 FPA had been suspended by Khomeini and quashed by the judgment of the Council of Guardians in 1985, which decided that punishment of a man not having the permission of his first wife was not lawful. In practice many men had married without permission or even without official registration. According to the Draft Bill this was now made illegal. The court furthermore has to invite the first wife and hear her.[61] Āliyā is convinced that the first wife's permission is implicitly meant in Article 23, but she argues that the text should be made explicit in order to reassure families and public opinion.

With regard to the judicial system, Āliyā expressed her trust in the courts and stressed the courts' competence.[62] The courts have to deal with justice on the level of finances (*ʿadālat-e mālī*) and on a subjective level (*ʿadālat-e ʿāṭefī*), which, she admits, is difficult for the judges. This subjective justice, Āliyā states, as implied in Qur'ān, Sura 4 (النساء): Verse 3[63], is difficult for men to bring about, so that it becomes evident that God himself restricted polygamy. Here Āliyā switches to an argument from Islamic *fiqh*.[64] The question of the independence of the judiciary and the courts is seen more critically by others. The judges are thought not to have an objective understanding of women's position in the legal system,[65] which, after all, is a strong criticism of the judiciary of the Islamic Republic.

---

60 For these positive arguments, see also the Interview with Ḥasan Ḥamīdiyān, Deputy Head of Justice Administration of Tehran Province and Director of the Family Judicial Complex, on 12 October 2008.

61 This, however, is just her interpretation. In Article 23 only the court's permission is mentioned, nothing is stated about the conditions under which the court has to decide upon the second marriage.

62 Others argue the same, e.g., Zaynab Rangbar in my interview with her on 15 October 2008. Being a judge herself (or rather a counsellor because women cannot be judges on their own) she argues that the court can act with justice with regard to the finances, and, on the other hand, has to act on the basis of a kind of extrinsic justice (*ʿadālat-e ẓāher*). For this the man's behaviour in the family as well as in society is examined.

63 *Sura 4* (النساء), *Verse 3:*
وَإِنْ خِفْتُمْ أَلاَّ تُقْسِطُواْ فِي الْيَتَامَى فَانكِحُواْ مَا طَابَ لَكُم مِّنَ النِّسَاء مَثْنَى وَثُلاَثَ
وَرُبَاعَ فَإِنْ خِفْتُمْ أَلاَّ تَعْدِلُواْ فَوَاحِدَةً أَوْ مَا مَلَكَتْ أَيْمَانُكُمْ ذَلِكَ أَدْنَى أَلاَّ تَعُولُواْ.

64 http://meydaan.org/wwShow.aspx?wwid=520 (accessed on 22 December 2008).

65 http://meydaan.org/wwShow.aspx?wwid=520 (accessed on 22 December 2008), and http://www.aftabnews.ir/vdccepq2b1qee.html (accessed on 19 December 2008).

Whereas these arguments concern the statutory law (CC) and the judiciary, Zaynab Rangbar,[66] judge and head of the department of public education of the judiciary (*Ra'īs-e āmūzešhā-ye mardomī-ye mo'āvanat-e āmūzešhā-ye quvveh-ye qażā'īyeh*) refers to the FPA of 1975 in which the first wife's permission is already explicit as well as the *ordre public* of the Islamic Republic of Iran. She summarizes the discussions in the judiciary stating that at the moment the protest against the Draft Bill came up it was decided by the judiciary to give in, because the Draft Bill was thought to be a Draft Bill for he protection of the family. As it was not accepted by the families, and especially by women, the two articles had to be dropped. Rangbar stated that in a situation like this, and with such heavy protest, public welfare (*maṣlaḥat*) was at stake and taken as a reason for skipping the articles.

With regard to international law, Shirin Ebadi argued in her article,[67] that Iran's legislation is not in accordance with human rights standards. Elāheh Kūlā'ī, professor at the Faculty of Law and Political Science of the University of Tehran,[68] described CEDAW as the frame of human rights discussion and argued that Muslims have a different understanding of human identity (*huvīyat-e ensān*) from western cultures. She connected the process of democratisation to the development of the status of women, seeing, however, sufficient potential in Iranian women for development (towards more democracy?). According to her opinion, the sensibility against CEDAW is based on the fear that with this convention the "Islamic identity" would be given up. Shahīndoḫt Mawlāverdī, a jurist trained in international law,[69] pointed in her article especially to the important meaning of public national welfare (*maṣlaḥat-e mellī*) for the Iranian state, not on the level of national legislation, but with regard to the international reputation of the Islamic Republic. She referred to Khomeini, who gave the government of the Islamic Republic the right to suspend the religious duty of pilgrimage in case the public welfare is in danger.[70] *Maṣlaḥat* is for her a strategy to solve the problems of the Islamic Republic of Iran.[71] Like Kūlā'ī, she is convinced that cultural differences cannot be an obstacle for admitting at least international standards of human rights. The equality of gender (*ğensīyat)* belongs to

66 Interview on 15 October 2008.

67 *Shirin Ebadi / Henriette Sinding Aasen*, Rights of Women…, supra, footnote 4.

68 *Elāheh Kūlā'ī*, Čālešhā-ye farāyand-e ta'mīn-e ḥoqūq-e zanān dar kešvarhā-ye eslāmī va češmandāz-e eğrā'ī-ye paymānnāmeh-ye Sīdā dar Īrān, UNICEF Office, Tehran, November 2007.

69 *Šahīndoḫt Mawlāverdī*, "Goftemān-e maṣlaḥatgerā va Konvensiyūn-e raf'-e kolliyeh-ye aškāl-e tab'īż 'alayhe zanān", in: Rayḥāneh 6.1383, pp. 203-217.

70 Ibidem, pp. 203-204.

71 Ibidem, p. 205.

these standards,[72] because it belongs to the nature of human beings. Islam and Human Rights have many points in common and there is no single interpretation to the Islamic texts, just as there are different possible understandings of the Human Rights.[73] Mawlāverdī sees Iran in danger of isolation on an international level because the state has not yet ratified CEDAW.[74]

Whereas Khomeini's concept of *maṣlaḥat* implied the Iranian government's right to restrict even basic religious rules in case this was deemed necessary for the welfare of the state,[75] Rangbar's statement quoted above reflects a concept of *maṣlaḥat* as an *ordre public* that can be influenced by public discourse. Civil society arguments thus changed the legislation because the public welfare and thus the social peace had to be preserved.

All three articles on CEDAW and Human Rights in Iran by Ebadi, Kūlā'ī and Mawlāverdī argue on the basis of international human rights and maintain that there are rulings in the Qur'ān and the Muslim tradition which can be seen as parallel to the western understanding of human dignity. None of them deals with the difficult verses of the Qur'ān which seem to contradict human rights standards[76] and cause hermeneutical problems.[77] The perspective and basis of the argument underlying all the articles is thus the hierarchy of laws (with international law on the top) and the role of the international community in acting as an instance of control over the national legislation.

Whereas Kūlā'ī's article is from 2007 and thus from the high point of the protest against the Draft Bill, the other articles are older. However, Kūlā'ī, who also participated actively in the Women's Movement and gave interviews, did not mention the Draft Bill in her article. The other two authors, Mawlāverdī and

---

72 Ibidem, p. 213.

73 Ibidem pp. 213-215.

74 *Ibid.*, 215

75 *Said Amir Arjomand*, "Authority in Shiism and constitutional developments in the Islamic Republic of Iran", in: *Werner Ende / Rainer Brunner* (Eds.), The Twlever Shia in Modern Times, Leiden 2001, pp. 305-336 (on p. 314).

76 Cp. *Sura 4* (النساء), *Verse 34:*

الرِّجَالُ قَوَّامُونَ عَلَى النِّسَاء بِمَا فَضَّلَ اللّهُ بَعْضَهُمْ عَلَى بَعْضٍ وَبِمَا أَنفَقُواْ مِنْ أَمْوَالِهِمْ فَالصَّالِحَاتُ قَانِتَاتٌ
حَافِظَاتٌ لِّلْغَيْبِ بِمَا حَفِظَ اللّهُ وَاللاَّتِي تَخَافُونَ نُشُوزَهُنَّ فَعِظُوهُنَّ وَاهْجُرُوهُنَّ فِي الْمَضَاجِعِ وَاضْرِبُوهُنَّ
فَإِنْ أَطَعْنَكُمْ فَلاَ تَبْغُواْ عَلَيْهِنَّ سَبِيلاً إِنَّ اللّهَ كَانَ عَلِيًّا كَبِيرًا.

For the difficult interpretation of Sura 4 (النساء), Verse 34, "Men are above women...", see, for example, *Kecia Ali*, Sexual Ethics and Islam, Oxford 2006, pp. 112-134.

77 See *Ann Elizabeth Mayer*, "Die Konvention über die Beseitigung jeder Form von Diskriminierung der Frau und der politische Charakter 'religiöser' Vorbehalte", in: *Mechthild Rumpf / Ute Gerhard / Mechthild Jansen* (Eds.), Facetten islamischer Welten, Bielefeld 2003, pp. 103-122.

Ebadi, took an active part in the Women's Movement, too, but in their published statements and interviews they did not hint at international law either. When asked in interviews, Mawlāverdī and Ebadi[78] supported the idea of Iran signing CEDAW[79], arguing that it would mean an improvement for the national legislation with regard to women's rights. Ebadi, however, conceded that the signature of an international convention did not automatically mean an improvement in the legislative activity of Iran, as seen, e.g., with regard to CRC (which Iran has signed). She confirmed that, in political contexts, she used religious, i.e. "*maẕhabī*", arguments.[80]

Asked why Iran did not sign CEDAW, Zaynab Rančbar, a representative of the judiciary, pointed to differing gender concepts in the west and Iran. According to the latter, the biological difference causes differences in the social and family life which is reflected in the legal regulations of the Islamic Law.[81] Since the rejection of CEDAW by the Council of Guardians in 2003, CEDAW is stranded in the Assessment Council and – according to the opinion of Ašraf Gerāmīzādegān, a lawyer and member of the legal committee of the Office of Women's Affairs of the Ministry of the Interior (*Komīte-ye ḥoqūqī-ye daftar-e omūr-e bānuvān-e Vezārat-e kešvar*), it will not be discussed in the near future.[82] Whereas Rančbar[83] explained the reasons for the non-ratification of CEDAW in terms of gender roles, and Sāneʿī[84] saw the main points of divergence from international human rights standards in the Iranian law of inheritance and divorce, the opinion was often expressed that ratification of CEDAW would have a positive influence on the legislation process in Iran towards more gender equality.[85]

Legal arguments are used by lawyers and persons trained in law as well as by participants of the Women's Movement, but, perhaps not surprisingly, not by scholars of *fiqh*. Legal arguments are used by jurists who are part of the civil

---

78 I did not conduct an interview with Kūlāʾī.

79 Interviews with Mawlāverdī, 29 October 2008; and with Ebadi, 1 November 2008.

80 Ebadi, interview on 1 November 2008

81 Rančbar, interview on 15 October 2008. This Islamic-justified concept of gender relations is common in Iran. See also the interviews with Alusvand on 11 November 2008. *Shaheen Sardar Ali*, Gender and Human Rights in Islam and International Law. Equal Before Allah, Unequal Before Man? The Hague, 2000, p. 61, calls this kind of right "protective" rights and makes a clear distinction between this and gender equality.

82 Gerāmīzādegān, interview on 10 November 2008.

83 Rančbar, interview on 15 October 2008.

84 Āyatollāh Sāneʿī, interview on 12 November 2008.

85 Ebadi, interview on 1 November 2008; Mawlāverdī, interview on 29 October 2008; Gerāmīzādegān, interview on 10 November 2008. All three women are jurists trained in law (not *fiqh*).

society such as Ebadi and Mawlāverdī, but also by jurists and persons who are connected to the state such as Rangbar and Āliyā.

II. The *fiqh* Arguments

An unnamed member of the judicial commission of the parliament stated that the omitted Article 23 was "absolutely Islamic" (*ʿayn-e ḫwāsteh-ye Eslām*) and that the parliament originally wanted "to solve some of the actual women's problems and the problems of society with the application of the opinion of Islam". He criticised the elimination of the article and argued that the parliament should have made the aim of the article clearer. Furthermore, Salmān Ẕāker, a member of the judicial and legal commission of the parliament (*Komīsiyūn-e qażāʾī va ḥoqūqī-ye Mağles*) stated: "Many women have no problem with the polygamous marriage of their husband, polygamy is based on (Islamic) law (*šarʿ*) and with the first wife's permission it is nothing wrong. When eliminating this Article 23 the Parliament has blocked the way for the solution of women's problems", whereas Farīdeh Ġayrat, a lawyer, answered that the actual problem for women in Iran is their difficulty to get a divorce. No woman in the world would accept a second marriage of her husband.[86]

Āyatollāh-e ʿoẓmā Ṣāneʿī,[87] who, according to the Middle Eastern newspaper *Al-Šarq al-Awsaṭ*, is the "women's Muftī"[88] and who resides in Qom, found clear words: the polygamous marriage of a man without consent of his first wife is forbidden and a sin (*ḥarām va-gonāh*) and from the viewpoint of law it is a crime (*ğorm*). It is against justice (*ḫelāf-e ʿadālat*)[89] and he expresses his hope that this injustice (*ẓolm*) will not become law.[90] He is not generally opposed to polygamy, but he wants to limit the injuries women may suffer from it, whereas Vasmaqī argues that polygamy is disapproved (*makrūh*).[91] According to the open letter of November 2007, Article 23 is to be considered a step backwards (*ʿaqabmāndeh*) in the exegesis (of the holy texts). The state is accused of con-

86 http://www.irwomen.info/spip.php?article6288 (accessed on 17 January 2008).

87 Cp. http://www.saanei.org/page.php?pg=showzanan&id=128&lang=fa: *ḥoqūq-e zanān; ezdevāğ-e muğaddad* (accessed on 17 January 2009).

88 http://www.asharqalawsat.com/details.asp?section=4&issue=10336&article=411000 of 17 March 2007, No. 10336 (accessed on 17 January 2009).

89 See also *Ṣadīqeh Vasmaqī*, Zan, fiq, Eslām, Tehran 1387/2008, 44; Fāṭima Āliyā: http://meydaan. org/wwShow.aspx?wwid=520 (accessed on 22 December 2008).

90 Husband and wife should live peacefully together and the rights the husband has towards his wife are the same the wife has towards her husband. If one has a right which is forbidden (*ḥarām*) for the other, this is against justice, see www.saanei.org/page.php?pg=show zanan&id=128&lang=fa (accessed on 22 January 2009).

91 *Ṣadīqeh Vasmaqī*, Zan, fiq, Eslām, supra, footnote 86, pp. 45-46.

sidering polygamy from a conservative point of view (*dīdgāh-e sonnatī*),[92] and of seeing polygamy (in the Draft Bill) as a fixed religious rule (*ḥokm-e dā'emī-ye dīnī*) and not a rule which can be interpreted according to the conditions of the time (*movaqqatī*), whereas in the Qur'ān the condition of justice is given (Sura 4 [النساء]: Verse 3, Sura 4 [النساء]: Verse 129).[93] It is from this point of view that it is argued in the letter, that the principle (*aṣl*) in the law is monogamy, polygamy is only allowed (*mobāḥ*).[94] It should not be seen as a fixed rule (*ḥokm-e dā'emī*) in the sense of an unchangeable interpretation of the Qur'ān.[95]

Polygamy, it is furthermore argued, might have been a habit in tribal times in the beginning of the Islam, but is not fit for the conditions of today's society.[96] Another argument focuses on the first wife's permission being a legal condition. Āyatollāh Moḥaqqeq-e Dāmād,[97] pointing to Khomeini's (d. 1989) prohibition of such a condition and Kho'ī's (d. 1992) acceptance of it, argues for accepting this condition. This is because it is a condition of the contract (*sharṭ-e ḍemn-e 'aqd-e nekāḥ*) and as such it is a *šarṭ-e 'orfī*, i.e., a customary condition usually stipulated in the marriage-contract and widely accepted in society. In consequence, he states, *'orf* – here in the understanding of a condition usually used by the people (*šarṭ-e 'orfī*) – can be changed into *fiqh-e šī'ī*. This is an important statement with regard to the process of development of Islamic Law as accepted by the Shiite clergy.[98]

Several chapters of Ṣadīqeh Vasmaqī's book *Zan, fiqh, Eslām*, which was published in December 2008 and much awaited by the Women's Movement, concern the problem of polygamy and the first wife's permission for a further marriage as a stipulation in the marriage contract.[99] Vasmaqī argues, using the clas-

---

92 Cp. http://www.aftabnews.ir/vdccepq2b1qee.html, supra, footnote 56.

93 Ibidem.

94 Ṣadīqeh Vasmaqī comes to a different evaluation and calles it *makrūh*, see *Ṣadīqeh Vasmaqī*, Zan, fiq, Eslām, supra, footnote 86, p. 44.

95 Cp. http://www.aftabnews.ir/vdccepq2b1qee.html, supra, footnote 56.

96 See Sanei www.saanei.org/page.php?pg=showzanan&id=128&lang=fa, ḥoqūq-e zanān; ezdevāǧ-e muǧaddad (accessed on 17 January) 2009; *Ṣadīqeh Vasmaqī*, Zan, fiqh, Eslām, supra, footnote 86, p. 49.

97 Interview with Moḥaqqeq-e Dāmād on 16 October 2008.

98 I was not, however, able to obtain Moḥaqqeq-e Dāmād's officially published article or fatwā on the topic. I used the information he gave me in the interview.

99 *Ṣadīqeh Vasmaqī*, Zan, fiqh, Eslām, supra, footnote 86, pp. 43-92: The chapters on polygamy and the stipulation of the first wife's permission in the contract and an empirical study on polygamous families. These eight chapters were published earlier in 2008 as a booklet under the title *Ṣadīqeh Vasmaqī*, Čandhamsarī va Eslām, Tehran 2008, and distributed free of charge by the Maǧmū'e-ye entešārāt-e anǧoman-e zanān-e pažūhešgar-e tārīḫ.

sical Islamic Law categorisation, that polygamy is disapproved (*makrūh*), because according to the Qur'ān justice might not be possible. After dealing with social and psychological arguments against polygamy as the impossibility of men to manage a polygamous family in today's Iranian society, she returns to judicial arguments and discusses the role of stipulations in contracts, arguing, with reference to Šayḫ Murtażā Anṣārī (d. 1864) that conditions are to be kept. Making illegal (*taḥrīm*) rulings that are acceptable (*mobāḥāt*) is allowed (*ğā'ez*).[100] Some jurists thought this condition in the contract is not void (*bāṭel*), but that the wife should have the right to divorce.[101] She argues, however,[102] that the condition of "not-taking another wife" has to be fulfilled,[103] because it is an inherent part of the contract (*ğozʾī az rokn-e ʿaqd*).[104] Thus, she concludes, legal measures have to be taken to anchor this condition in legislation and ignorance has to be punished.[105]

The hermeneutical discussion in Iran does not go so far as it does, for instance, in Tunisia, where polygamy was completely forbidden in the middle of the twentieth century on the basis of a new interpretation of Sura 4 (النساء):Verse 3.[106] In the text of the Draft Bill, it is stated, that certain laws have been found incompatible with the *šarīʿa* and nothing is said about different interpretations. State representatives point to the permission of polygamy. Different interpretations are used as an argument, mainly in the open letter to the parliament and by jurists and lawyers like Mawlāverdī and Vasmaqī but also by the Shiite clergy. In the letter, the state's interpretation of Islamic Law is called "backward", the Draft is seen to be against the *šarʿ*.[107] The Shiite *fuqahā'* like Moḥaqqeq-e Dāmād, Sāneʿī and Vasmaqī, being professors of *fiqh*, on the other hand, go into more detail and try to argue on the basis of new hermeneutical approaches.

---

100 *Ṣadīqeh Vasmaqī*, Zan, fiqh, Eslām, supra, footnote 86, p. 77.

101 Ibidem, on p. 81.

102 Ibidem, on p. 83.

103 Ibidem on pp. 86-87.

104 Ibidem on p. 88.

105 Ibidem, on p. 89.

106 Alusvand, interview on 11 November 2008, based her argument on the different gender roles which imply not equality but different roles in society and thus also different legal regulations for the sexes. See also Rangbar, interview on 15 October 2008, with a similar gender concept. She also did not accept the Tunisian approach, whereas more modern oriented women like Maryam Moḥaqqeq, daughter of the Āyatollāh Moḥaqqeq-e Dāmād, (interview on 1 December 2008) see in the Tunisian approach a point of orientation.

107 This is a contradiction: on the one hand, the rule is called a backward interpretation, on the other hand, it is seen to be against *sharʿ*. However, the letter requires an analysis for itself, because its arguments are not well structured but give the impression they had been collected quite by chance from different actors.

Fiqh arguments are used by all sides taking part in the discourse; the Shiite clergy, the state and civil society. It is evident that every side is anxious to show that the argument it uses is compatible with Islam.

III. Social, psychological and cultural Arguments.

Besides legal and *fiqh* arguments, arguments which concern society and the individuals as well as the whole of Iranian culture are put forward.

1. Society

The main argument is that the changing conditions of society have to be taken into consideration, that women's position in society has changed, that more women are educated and have more and more important positions in society. Ḥasan Ḥamīdiyān from the judiciary gave these changing conditions as a reason for the new family law represented by the Draft Bill.[108] This argument is often used in connection with the argument that institutions which were accepted at the Prophet's time cannot be accepted in Iranian society of the twenty-first century.[109] It is argued that fathers in polygamous marriages cannot perform their family duties correctly and thus cannot be just;[110] that the rights of the first wife have preference and the children have to be taken into consideration; that polygamy causes trouble and chaos in families; that divorce and single-parent families are the consequences;[111] and that polygamy actually concerns only 5% of men in the Iranian society, who can afford to have a second wife, and ignores the interests of 50% of Iranian society, i.e. women.[112]

---

108 Interview on 12 October 2008.

109 *Ṣadīqeh Vasmaqī*, Zan, fiqh, Eslām, supra, footnote 86, p. 22, p. 41, p. 47, p. 48, p. 56.

110 Ibidem, pp. 56-58. This is without any references.

111 Ibidem, pp. 47, pp. 56-60; see http://www.aftabnews.ir/vdccepq2b1qee.html (accessed on 19 December 2008).

112 Cp. http://www.aftabnews.ir/vdccepq2b1qee.html, supra, footnote 56. During the events it was revealed that more than 60 members of the Parliament have more than one wife, see http://meydaan.org/showArticle.aspx?arid=660 dated 24 Mordād 1387/14 August 2008 (accessed on 12 January 2009). There is no critical historical or empirical research on the traditional role of polygamy, the main social strata in which polygamy is practised or the economic or social circumstances of polygamy in Iranian history and present society. Polygamy is simply seen in many discussions as a cultural relict not fitting into the modern Iranian society, but mostly the definition of "modernity" is not given. See, however, http://sociologyofiran.com/index.php?option=com_content&task=view&id=770&Itemid=65 (accessed on 17 January 2009). According to an empirical study quoted in this report, the number of polygamous men rose between 1977 and 1987. In 67% of cases where women kill their husband it is because of another sexual relation the man had (or another wife) or at least because this was suspected by the women. Women are four times more likely to commit suicide than men.

Under the FPA of 1975 (Art. 16), polygamy was lawful, for instance, in the case of infertility or illness of the first wife. That is not always the case, however. Vasmaqī cites a sample of 23 polygamous marriages, where most men who wanted a second wife already had children (in 20 out of 23 marriages), and that they wanted a second wife after 15 years and more of marriage. Some married without informing the first wife, some even in spite of the first wife's protests. In the course of events, nine divorces occurred, two wives were sent away without being financially compensated, in three cases children were separated from their mothers, and all children were unhappy with the second marriage. One second marriage even remained undiscovered for 16 years.[113]

Generally, polygamy is said to endanger the structure of the family. The metaphor used here is "earthquake" (*zelzele*). The scenario is depicted according to which women will be divorced and Iran will face the problem, which is typical for western countries, i.e., many single-parent families with women and their children living alone, children growing up without a father. This argument, in the open letter to the parliament, is chosen with deliberation, because it supports the government's arguments against the moral decay in the West on the basis of a society based on individualism and materialism against the Islamic concept of the family as the heart of society.[114] Interestingly the "earthquake" argument was used by Maḥmūd Hāšemī Šāhrūdī when he declared the elimination of the two articles from the Draft Bill.[115]

2. Psychological Aspects

Polygamy damages society and puts women and children under pressure, because no woman can feel safe that her husband will not take a second wife, and this feeling of insecurity is also passed onto the children. Hostility, malevolence, loss of loyalty and aggression as well as violence in the family will grow. How can a woman be loyal to a polygamous husband? This is the question the women ask the women in their letter to the parliament. Men will marry young women and children will grow up with a bad example of the male sexuality.[116]

The category of "social" and "psychological" refers to an alleged disapproval of polygamy in modern Iranian society – where "modern" is nowhere defined – and plays with the government's ideological position on the Islamic family as

[113] *Ṣadīqeh Vasmaqī*, Zan, fiqh, Eslām, supra, footnote 86, pp. 91-92: these examples cannot be called an empirical study, there is no thorough analysis of the cases and no methodology referred to.

[114] Cp. http://www.aftabnews.ir/vdccepq2b1qee.html, supra, footnote 56.

[115] Cp. http://www.vol.at/news/CO:austria:politik/artikel/iranisches-parlament-kippt-gesetzentwurf-zur-polygamie/cn/news-20080909-02494174 from 9 September 2008 (accessed on 15 January 2009).

[116] Cp. http://www.aftabnews.ir/vdccepq2b1qee.html, supra, footnote 56.

opposed to the individualistic Western society, in which divorce and one-parent families are signs of the breakdown of society. And these arguments express the fear that the situation created by the Draft Bill will lead to a psychological strain for women and children.[117]

These arguments are, in the overwhelming number of cases, used by actors of the civil society and its activists. But the social context of legislation is also reflected in the judiciary, as Ḥamīdiyān and Šāhrūdī's statements show. The Islamic aspect of this argument stresses the legality and custom of polygamy in the Prophet's time, which, however, is no longer suitable for the society of today.

F. Conclusion

The elimination of Articles 23 and 25 from the Draft Bill surely can be considered as an important step in the dynamic process of negotiation between civil society and the state. A superstructure of civil society organisations emerged and succeeded in revising state legislation. Obviously the topic was important enough to bring together organisations with completely different social, political and ideological or religious backgrounds. The civil society's success caused international sensation. This was reached on the basis of non-violent means, with arguments, with discursive power. It turned out that public discourse brought forward by oppositional groups can exert a certain pressure on the government and state policy and thus lead to a revision of policy. In Islamic concepts this process was connected to the concept of *maṣlaḥat,* the public welfare.

Civil society in Iran is not only well structured – as the actions in the "One Million Signatures" and the visit to the parliament show – but also completely independent of the state. It is thus a civil society mostly composed of non-governmental organisations and many individual actors, which is in opposition to the political system. Being in an authoritarian system, the civil society actors' aim is (sometimes uttered expressly) to press for more democracy. The state hit back, accusing the civil society actors of being influenced by the west and being anti-Islam. This argument brings into discredit their request: being an Islamic Republic the state does not accept western value systems and explicitly rejects arguments based on the western discourse. As the process is still ongoing, the chances that this pressure and common activity will lead to more democracy in Iran are open. As stated above, the state gave in with regard to the elimination of the two articles, but started to harass the participants of the Campaign of "One

117 See: http://meydaan.org/wwShow.aspx?wwid=495 from 13 Šahrīvar 1386/ 4 September 2007 (accessed on 6 January 2008).

Million Signatures" as well as all participants of the discourse on the Draft Bill who were critical of the state. In this context, it is worth considering another draft Bill, which is being discussed at the time of writing in the parliament: the Draft Bill on the Penal Code. It is not possible to go into details here, but it has to be stated that this draft Bill aroused much international attention for inserting the death penalty for apostasy into the Iranian Penal Code.[118] The *ḥadd*-penalties are still given in this draft, which contradict international human rights norms. Gender inequality can be found, for instance, in the different amounts of blood-money (*diyeh*) for males and females, the blood-money for females being half the amount due for males. There is much criticism expressed by civil society, especially human rights organisations, to this draft Bill.[119] The question arises whether this criticism as in the case of the Draft Bill on Family Law will lead to substantial changes in the proposed legislation.

With regard to the Draft Bill on Family Law the question remains, why only two issues out of the many criticised provisions dominated the discourse: the permission of the first wife for the husband taking a second wife and the taxation of the dower.

The answer with regard to the first wife's permission can be seen, I think, in the history and development of this ruling in the Iranian legal system as well as in society. Despite the lack of attention in the classical *fiqh*, the ruling concerning the first wife's permission was made law in the FPA of 1975. Obviously, in the course of time, it became a custom (*ʿorf*) in Iranian society, inserted into many marriage contracts[120] and thus widely accepted as a right of women in society. The legal situation was ambivalent, because Khomeini suspended the FPA of 1975 without obviously eliminating it.[121] In spite of the decision of the Council of Guardians the first wife's permission seems to have had public prestige as

118 Often the juvenile criminals are kept in prison until they are 18 and are then hanged, see: http://www.stopchildexecutions.com/ (accessed on 17 January 2009).

119 The text of the Draft Bill on the Penal Code can be found on the internet: http://www.dadkhahi.net/law/Ghavanin/Ghavanin_Jazaee/layehe_gh_mojazat_eslami.htm, (accessed on 17 January 2008); for a critique from a feminist point of view see: http://meydaan.org/ShowArticle.aspx?arid=527 (accessed on 17 January 2008).

120 At this point a quantitative empirical study of the use of this stipulation in marriage contracts would be of use.

121 It is especially disappointing that no statistics and no empirical research exist on polygamy in Iranian society. It is simply not possible, whatever the human rights activists state, that polygamy does not play any role in Iran as there are polygamous marriages and as, as stated above, some 60 members of the parliament seem to live in polygamous marriages. But the topic of polygamy is, according to my impression, a taboo for modern sociological research in the country.

well as social acceptance. It was, after all, obviously politically not enforceable to override the need for this permission and restrict the permission of the second marriage to the court.

This is why this Article 23 can be seen as a good example of how legal rulings gain customary acceptance (*'orf*) and this can lead to an alteration of Islamic Law. Surely the social situation in Iran has to be taken into consideration. As stated above the number of educated women has increased since the Revolution and many women today have a good education. Having a good education will often lead to more critical assessment of traditional norms that are often disadvantageous for women: but the whole interaction of public discourse, education, civil society action and political pressure is still poorly understood for the lack of solid research.

The events and discussions about Articles 23 and 25 can be seen as an example of the development of law in a state that considers itself strictly Islamic, basing its legislation exclusively on Islamic principles. This framework influences the discussion: The arguments used in the political context, such as the public media and the open letter to the parliament, are first of all based on Islamic Law, which is used as an argument by all participants in this discourse. Furthermore, arguments from the Iranian legal system and social arguments play an important role, but not arguments based on international human rights standards. Even if CEDAW is dealt with in academic articles, it seems never to be used as an argument in the political context. The same persons who use Human Rights as an argument in their published books and articles do not use them as an argument in the direct confrontation with the domestic political system. There is, as Foucault would call it, a clear "taboo of the topic" concerning human rights according to the UN standard in the Iranian political discourse.

The human rights situation in Iran clearly still shows many discrepancies between the international standards and the domestic legislation. Many laws contradict gender equality and there is no official statement of the government of the Islamic Republic to change this. The discrepancy is even justified by jurists in state service, as well as scholars, as based on a distinctive, Islamic gender model (Rangbar, Alusvand). Arguments based on international human rights, which were used in Khatemi's time from 1997 to 2005[122], are not acceptable under President Aḥmadīnežād (2005-). Thus international human rights instruments cannot have any direct influence on the Iranian legislation, even if many human rights activists would still welcome Iran's signature of CEDAW. What

[122] *Said Amir Arjomand,*, "Civil society and the rule of law in the constitutional politics of Iran under Khatami", Social Research, volume 76, issue 2, New York 2000, pp. 283-301.

seems possible is the approach of civil society, which makes itself heard, redefines *maṣlaḥat* and, on the basis of an Islamic discourse, rebuilds a – social and political, but also legal – process of development in Iranian society. So that "custom" can become "law" – even against classical *fiqh* and the government's interpretation of Islamic Law.

Interaktion islamisch geprägter Länder und Organisationen mit internationalen Menschenrechtsinstitutionen

Interactions of predominantly Islamic Countries and Organisations with International Human Rights Institutions

موقف الدول والمنظمات ذات الطابع الإسلامي تجاه اوضاع حقوق الإنسان العالمية

Islam und Menschenrechte (Islam and Human Rights / الإسلام وحقوق الإنسان)
Hatem Elliesie (Hrsg./Editor), © Peter Lang Verlag: Frankfurt a.M. 2010, S. 415-473

Der „Frauenrechtsausschuss“ der Vereinten Nationen in der Interaktion mit islamisch geprägten Staaten

Hanna Beate Schöpp-Schilling, Wohltorf / New York

A. Einleitung

Es ist allgemein bekannt, dass islamisch geprägte Staaten – trotz gegenteiliger Äußerungen und obwohl männliche und weibliche Diplomaten dieser Staaten bei der Abfassung vieler der entsprechenden Dokumente eine oft positive Rolle gespielt haben[1] – weder in der Theorie noch in der Praxis ein durchgängig und eindeutig bejahendes Verhältnis zu den Menschenrechtsnormen haben, wie sie von den Mitgliedstaaten der Vereinten Nationen (VN) im Gründungsdokument der Organisation (VN-Charta), in der Allgemeinen Erklärung der Menschenrechte (AEMR) und den verschiedenen VN-Menschenrechtsverträgen[2] niedergelegt sind. Auch haben islamisch geprägte Staaten im Rahmen eigener islamisch geprägter[3] oder arabischer Organisationen und Gremien selbst eigene Menschenrechtsdokumente entwickelt.[4] Zeigen sich schon in den englischen

---

1 Mayer zitiert verschiedene Analysen über die Rolle von Vertretern islamisch geprägter Staaten bei der Formulierung der AEMR sowie der beiden Menschenrechtspakte, und Connors untersucht und belegt Positionen und Abstimmungsverhalten islamisch geprägter Staaten hinsichtlich der Erklärung zur Beseitigung der Diskriminierung der Frau (*Declaration on the Elimination of Discrimination against Women,* DEDAW, 1967) und des Übereinkommens zur Beseitigung jeder Form von Diskriminierung der Frau, *Convention on the Elimination of All Forms of Discrimination against Women,* CEDAW, 1979). S. *Ann E. Mayer*, Islam and Human Rights. Tradition and Politics, 4. Auflage, Boulder 2007, S. 13-17; *Jane Connors*, „The Women's Convention in the Muslim World“, in: *Chinkin and Others / J. P. Gardner* (Hrsg.), Human Rights as General Norms and a State's Right to Opt Out. Reservations and Objections to Human Rights Conventions, B.I.I.C.L. London 1997, S. 86-103 (87-89).

2 Die neun Verträge und die Arbeit der dazugehörigen Vertragsausschüsse sind einzusehen auf der Internetseite des Büros der Hochkommissarin für Menschenrechte (*Office of the High Commissioner for Human Rights*), www.ohchr.org. In deutscher Sprache werden sie u.a. auf der Internetseite des Deutschen Instituts für Menschenrechte aufgeführt, www.institut-fuer-menschenrechte.de.

3 Die Beschreibung der *Organisation of the Islamic Conference* (OIC) sowie die Liste ihrer derzeit 56 Mitglieder und die für die Organisation relevanten Dokumente sind auf der Internetseite http://www.oic-oci.org zu finden.

4 Charta der Organisation der Islamischen Konferenz (*Charter of the Organization of The Islamic Conference,* 1972), die Allgemeine Islamische Erklärung der Menschenrechte (*Universal Islamic Declaration of Human Rights*, 1981), die Kairoer Erklärung dieser Organisation über die Menschenrechte im Islam (*The Cairo Declaration on Human Rights in Islam,* 1990), die Arabische Charta über die Menschenrechte (*Arab Charter on Human Rights,* 1997).

Islam und Menschenrechte (Islam and Human Rights / الإسلام وحقوق الإنسان)
Hatem Elliesie (Hrsg./Editor), © Peter Lang Verlag: Frankfurt a.M. 2010, S. 417-455

Fassungen dieser Dokumente gravierende Abweichungen von den VN-Erklärungen und Verträgen, so werden diese in den arabischen Fassungen, wie Ann Elizabeth Mayer überzeugend dargelegt hat, noch verstärkt und zwar insbesondere in Fragen der Religionsfreiheit und der Gleichberechtigung von Frauen und Männern in ***allen*** Lebenssituationen, d.h. auch im Bereich der Ehe- und Familienbeziehungen.[5]

Diese fehlende Gleichberechtigung und Gleichstellung von Frauen mit Männern, die im allgemeinen mit den Geboten und Vorschriften der *Šarīʿa* begründet werden, führt immer wieder zu lebhaften Diskussionen in allen Teilen der VN, insbesondere aber im VN-Vertragsausschuss für das Übereinkommen zur Beseitigung jeder Form von Diskriminierung der Frau (*Committee on the Elimination of Discrimination against Women*; *Convention on the Elimination of All Forms of Discrimination against Women*, CEDAW, 1979, *Optional Protocol to CEDAW*, OP, 1999).[6]

Im Folgenden stelle ich zunächst kurz das Übereinkommen, das Fakultativprotokoll und die drei Durchsetzungsverfahren vor, die vom Vertragsausschuss auf der Grundlage dieser Verträge praktiziert werden. Sodann zeige ich anhand der Vertragsstaaten Ägypten, Marokko und Saudi Arabien wie sich diese Interaktion über drei Jahrzehnte hinweg entwickelt und welche Ergebnisse sie gezeigt hat. Dabei baue ich z.T. auf schon geleisteten Analysen der Verhaltens- und Argumentationsweisen islamisch geprägter Staaten hinsichtlich ihrer Umsetzung des Übereinkommens auf[7] und werte zusätzlich die Staatenberichte und die schriftlichen und mündlichen Diskussionsbeiträge der Regierungsdelegationen im Austausch mit den Sachverständigen des Ausschusses aus. Be-

---

5 *Ann E. Mayer*, Islam and Human Rights…, a.a.O. (Fn. 1), Kapitel 1 und 5, aber auch in anderen Kapiteln.

6 In der deutschen Diskussion und Literatur wird dieser Ausschuss auch „Frauenrechtsausschuss" genannt, in diesem Beitrag benutze ich jedoch den korrekten Begriff.

7 *Christine Chinkin*, „Reservations and Objections to the Convention on the Elimination of All Forms of Discrimination Against Women", in: *Chinkin and Others / J. P. Gardner* (Hrsg.), Human Rights as General Norms and a State's Right to Opt Out. Reservations and Objections to Human Rights Conventions, B.I.I.C.L. London 1997, S. 64-84; *Jane Connors*, The Women's Convention…, a.a.O. (Fn. 1); *Ann E. Mayer*, Islam and Human Rights…, a.a.O. (Fn. 1); *dies*., „Religious Reservations to the Convention on the Elimination of all Forms of Discrimination against Women: What Do They Really Mean?", in: *Courtney W. Howland* (Hrsg.), Religious Fundamentalism and the Human Rights of Women, New York 2001, S. 105-116; *dies.*, „Internationalizing the Conversation on Women's Rights: Arab Countries Face the CEDAW Committee", in: *Yvonne Yazbeck Haddad / Barbara Freyer Stowasser / et al.*, (Hrsg.), Islamic Law and the Challenges of Modernity, Walnut Creek 2004, S. 133-160.

sondere Betonung lege ich auf die jeweilige Rechtfertigung der Vorbehalte von Seiten der Vertragsstaaten, die diese gegenüber einzelnen Artikeln des Übereinkommens ausgesprochen haben. Meine Auswahl der drei Staaten gründet sich in der Tatsache, dass diese in der Umsetzung des Übereinkommens und in der Interaktion mit dem Ausschuss einerseits ähnliche, andererseits unterschiedliche Positionen und Entwicklungen aufzeigen, die, wie ich in der Bestätigung der Thesen u.a. von Ann Elizabeth Mayer und Jane Connors zu zeigen hoffe, weniger von religiösen – wie von den Staaten behauptet wird – als vor allem von politischen und ideologisch-patriarchalen Faktoren bestimmt werden. Auf andere islamisch geprägte Staaten werde ich gelegentlich verweisen, da ihre detaillierte Behandlung den Rahmen dieses Aufsatzes sprengen würde. Ebenfalls werde ich versuchen, die Frage zu beantworten, ob die Interaktion dieser Staaten mit dem Ausschuss zu Verbesserungen in der rechtlichen Situation der Frauen im jeweiligen Staat geführt hat und ob festzustellen ist, dass sich diese rechtlichen Fortschritte auch ***praktisch*** in der Anerkennung der Menschenrechte von Frauen durch alle Organe des jeweiligen Staats und durch Dritte widerspiegeln wie auch in der tatsächlichen Inanspruchnahme und Ausübung der Menschenrechte durch die weibliche Bevölkerung, wie es Artikel 1 und 2 des Übereinkommens verlangen.

B. Menschenrechte von Frauen

CEDAW gehört zu den internationalen Menschenrechtsverträgen der VN, die den Schutz bestimmter Bevölkerungsgruppen bzw. die Vermeidung bestimmter Menschenrechtsverletzungen garantieren.[8] Alle diese Verträge beruhen auf der Allgemeinen Erklärung der Menschenrechte von 1948 (AEMR), die heute als internationales Gewohnheitsrecht verstanden wird, sowie auf den auf dieser Grundlage rechtlich verbindlich formulierten Verträgen von 1966, den Internationalen Pakten für bürgerliche und politische Rechte (*International Covenant for Civil and Political Rights,* ICCPR) einerseits und für wirtschaftliche, soziale und kulturelle Rechte andererseits (*International Covenant for Economic, Social and Cultural Rights,* ICESCR). Die spezifischen Verträge leisten einen besonderen Beitrag. Sie verdeutlichen die Staatenverpflichtungen, die Menschenrechte bestimmter Gruppen bzw. ein einzelnes Menschenrecht zu achten, zu schützen und erfüllen,[9] in detaillierterer Form als dies in der Erklärung oder in den beiden Pakten geschieht.

---

8 Vgl. Fußnote 2.

9 Diese Typologie der Staatenverpflichtung, die ursprünglich von Asbjørn Eide im Hinblick auf das Menschenrecht auf Nahrung entwickelt wurde, wird heute allgemein für alle Menschenrechte akzeptiert.

Die Diskriminierung von Frauen enthält nach Auffassung vieler Wissenschaftlerinnen sowie nationaler oder internationaler Frauen(rechts)verbände gewisse qualitative und quantitative Besonderheiten im Vergleich zu anderen, nach sonstigen Kategorien oder Zuschreibungen definierten Gruppen (Rasse, Alter, Behinderung, etc.), sodass sie diesen anderen Personengruppen im Rahmen von Diskriminierungstatbeständen nicht ohne weiteres gleichzusetzen sind. Schon gar nicht sollten Frauen insgesamt undifferenziert mit diesen anderen Gruppen als besonders „gefährdete Gruppe" (*vulnerable group*) aufgeführt werden, wie es leider in vielen Dokumenten und Argumentationen immer wieder geschieht. Vielmehr ist bei dem Verständnis von geschlechtsspezifischer Frauendiskriminierung zu berücksichtigen, dass Täter und Opfer immer auch in einem intimen Verhältnis verbunden bzw. Mitglieder einer Familie sein können. Diese Tatsache verleiht dem Diskriminierungstatbestand besondere Härte. Bereits 1998 bestätigte der damalige Generalsekretär, Kofi Annan, dass es keinen Diskriminierungstatbestand ohne einen geschlechtsspezifischen Aspekt gibt.[10] Allerdings ist die Diskriminierung von Frauen verbreiteter als die von Männern und hält sich weltweit in vielfältigen Formen auf sehr hartnäckige Weise.[11] Frauen stellen zudem die Hälfte der Weltbevölkerung dar und sind immer auch Mitglieder jener als besonders gefährdet benannten anderen Gruppen. Sie erfahren ***mehrfache*** Diskriminierungen als Frauen ***und*** als Mitglieder dieser jeweiligen Gruppe, wobei sich diese mehrfachen Diskriminierungen auch wechselseitig verstärken können.[12]

CEDAW, dem eine weit gefasste, aber rechtlich nicht verbindliche Erklärung zur Beseitigung der Diskriminierung der Frau (*Declaration on the Elimination of Discrimination Against Women*, DEDAW) im Jahre 1967 vorausgegangen war, wurde am 18. Dezember 1979 von der VN-Vollversammlung verabschiedet, trat bereits am 3. September 1981 in Kraft und hat heute 185 Vertragsstaaten, d.h. es ist in fast allen VN-Mitgliedstaaten entweder direkt geltendes Recht, oder es dient als verbindliche Leitlinie für die eigene nationale Rechtssetzung. Unter den wenigen großen VN-Mitgliedstaaten, die das Übereinkommen noch nicht ratifiziert haben, sind der Iran, der Sudan und die

10 *United Nations,* Report of the Secretary General on the Question of Integrating the Human Rights of Women Throughout the United Nations System, E/CN.4/1998/49, 25 March 1998, Absatz. 9.

11 Vgl. auch Absatz 6 der Präambel von CEDAW.

12 Mark Latimer hat diese Situationen so beschrieben: „[women] often face sexism, racism and violence from the majority community, and frequently sexism and violence from within their own community (to say nothing of issues around ageism, class, disability, sexuality, etc.)"; *Mark Latimer*, „Preface", in: *Fareda Banda / Christine Chinkin*, Gender, Minorities and Indigenous People, Minority Rights Group International, London 2004, S. 2.

Vereinigten Staaten von Amerika. Von den islamisch geprägten Staaten fehlen Iran, Sudan und Katar.

C. Rechte von Frauen im Übereinkommen

Ziel und Zweck des Übereinkommens ist es, die Diskriminierung von ***Frauen*** auf der Grundlage ihres Geschlechts und ihres Familienstands zu beseitigen und auf diese Weise ihre Gleichberechtigung, Gleichbehandlung und Gleichstellung[13] mit Männern in der Ausübung und dem Genuss ihrer Menschenrechte in allen Lebensbereichen, und zwar auch in der Ehe und in den familiären Beziehungen, zu erfüllen. Mit der Ratifikation des Übereinkommens bzw. mit dem Beitritt zu demselben, verpflichten sich die Vertragsstaaten untereinander, diese Verpflichtungen für ihre jeweilige weibliche Bevölkerung nicht nur gesetzliche, sondern auch praktisch erfahrbare Realität werden zu lassen. Das Übereinkommen verpflichtet Vertragsstaaten daher auch zu gesetzlichen, institutionellen oder programmbezogenen Maßnahmen, um beide Gebote zu erfüllen, wobei die Auswahl der jeweiligen Maßnahme bei den meisten Vorschriften in ihrer eigenen Entscheidung steht.[14]

Das Übereinkommen besteht aus einer Präambel und 30 Artikeln. Davon sind 17 Artikel (1-16, 24) sog. substantielle Artikel. Die restlichen Artikel (17-23, 25-30) sind verfahrensorientierte Artikel. Sie beschreiben die Struktur und Arbeit des Ausschusses, die Berichtspflichten des Vertragsstaates sowie die Verfahren hinsichtlich der Vertragszustimmung bzw. Vertragsänderung, des Einlegens von Vorbehalten und des Gebrauchs von Schlichtungsmechanismen, die bei Streitigkeiten zwischen Vertragsstaaten über das Übereinkommen greifen können.

Die substantiellen Artikel unterscheiden sich in sog. substantielle Rahmenartikel (1-5, 24) und spezifische substantielle Artikel (6-16), die sich auf einzelne

---

13 Vgl. zu der unterschiedlichen Bedeutung der Begriffe *Doris König*, „Die Diskriminierungsverbote im Übereinkommen der Vereinten Nationen zur Beseitigung jeder Form der Diskriminierung der Frau (CEDAW)“, in: *Doris König / Joachim Lange / Ursula Rust / Hanna Beate Schöpp-Schilling* (Hrsg.), Gleiches Recht – Gleiche Realität? Welche Instrumente bieten Völkerrecht, Europarecht und nationales Recht für die Gleichstellung von Frauen, Loccumer Protokolle 71/03, Rehburg-Loccum 2004, S. 21-36 (S. 23-27).

14 Zum Übereinkommen in deutschsprachiger Literatur vgl. u.a. *Hanna Beate Schöpp*-Schilling, „Das Übereinkommen zur Beseitigung jeder Form von Diskriminierung der Frau (CEDAW) und sein Vertragsausschuss nach 25 Jahren – Bilanz und Ausblick“, in: *Andreas Zimmermann / Thomas Giegerich* (Hrsg.), Gender und Internationales Recht, Berlin 2007, S. 137-169; *Doris König*, Die Diskriminierungsverbote..., a.a.O. (Fn. 13); *dies.*, „Frauenrechte sind Menschenrechte ...und doch anders? Die UN-Frauenrechtskonvention“, in: *Beate Rudolf* (Hrsg.), Frauen und Völkerrecht, Baden-Baden 2006, S. 81-98.

Lebensbereiche von Frauen beziehen. Die Rahmenartikel enthalten folgende Elemente: Definition von Diskriminierung; Definition des Gleichheitsbegriffs; Gültigkeit des Diskriminierungsverbots und des Gleichstellungsgebots für alle Lebensbereiche von Frauen; Befürwortung von zeitlich befristeten oder unbefristeten Sondermaßnahmen; Verpflichtung zur Änderung und Beseitigung kulturell bedingter Einstellungen, Haltungen und Handlungen, mit denen die angebliche Minderwertigkeit von Frauen begründet wird; unverzügliche Achtungs-, Schutz- und Erfüllungsverpflichtungen der Staaten bezüglich des Handelns eigener Organe sowie des Handelns von Privatpersonen, Organisationen und Unternehmen.[15] Die Rahmenartikel sind nicht nur in sich selbst, sondern auch jeweils für die Umsetzung der Artikel 6-16 relevant, indem ein Vertragsstaat immer prüfen muss, ob er direkte, indirekte, strukturelle oder mehrfache Diskriminierungstatbestände mit gesetzlichen, institutionellen oder programmbezogenen Maßnahmen bekämpfen, zeitlich befristete Sondermaßnahmen einführen, Mutterschutz gewährleisten und in der Kultur bzw. Religion verwurzelte und durch diese gerechtfertigte Vorurteile über das Wesen und die Fähigkeiten von Frauen modifizieren und beseitigen muss.

Die einzelnen Lebensbereiche von Frauen, auf die sich Artikel 6-16 beziehen und in denen die Vertragsstaaten das Diskriminierungsverbot und Gleichstellungsgebot rechtlich und praktisch umsetzen müssen, umfassen:

- Frauenhandel und Ausbeutung von Frauen durch Prostitution;
- Öffentliches und politisches Leben einschließlich der Vertretung des Landes in internationalen Gremien;
- Staatsangehörigkeit;
- Bildung, Ausbildung und Fortbildung;
- Erwerbsarbeit;
- Zugang zum Gesundheitswesen;
- Zugang zum wirtschaftlichen und sozialen Leben;
- Stellung vor dem Gesetz;
- Ehe und Beziehungen in der Familie.

Das Übereinkommen bezieht sich auf ***alle*** Formen der Diskriminierung und ***alle*** Lebensbereiche von Frauen, auch wenn sie nicht ausdrücklich im Text des Übereinkommens genannt sind. Mit sogenannten Allgemeinen Empfehlungen, die dem Ausschuss nach Artikel 21 (1) erlaubt sind, interpretiert er das Übereinkommen. So hat er z.B. bereits 1989 und 1992 häusliche und andere Formen der Gewalt gegen Frauen als eine Form von Diskriminierung bestimmt, die Frauen

[15] Eine detaillierte Analyse der Rahmenartikel findet sich in *Hanna Beate Schöpp-Schilling*, Das Übereinkommen…, a.a.O. (Fn. 14).

die Inanspruchnahme und die Ausübung mehrerer ihrer Menschenrechte vereiteln.[16]

Die rechtlich nicht verbindlichen Abschlussdokumente der verschiedenen VN-Weltkonferenzen der 90er Jahre des vergangenen Jahrhunderts, insbesondere aber die „Aktionsplattform" der Vierten VN-Weltfrauenkonferenz, müssen mit ihren ausführlichen Problemanalysen und detaillierten Empfehlungen zum Handeln ebenfalls zum tieferen Verständnis der einzelnen substantiellen Artikel des Übereinkommens herangezogen werden.[17] Schon früh hat der Ausschuss nämlich festgestellt, dass die zwölf angesprochenen Bereiche in dieser Aktionsplattform mit Artikeln des Übereinkommens korrespondieren, die für die Vertragsstaaten von CEDAW die rechtlich verbindliche Grundlage für die in der Aktionsplattform geforderten staatlichen Maßnahmen bilden.

D. Durchsetzungsverfahren des Vertragsausschusses für CEDAW

Wie alle Menschenrechtsverträge der Vereinten Nationen wird auch das Übereinkommen von einem Vertragsausschuss begleitet, der von den Vertragsparteien eingesetzt wird, um die Umsetzung des Übereinkommens bei den Vertragsstaaten zu überprüfen. Diesem Ausschuss gehören dreiundzwanzig unabhängige Sachverständige an, die unterschiedliche Kulturen, Rechtssysteme und Berufe vertreten. Diese Verschiedenheit ist für das Verständnis der praktischen Anwendung des Übereinkommens in allen Lebensbereichen von Frauen von Vorteil, wenn auch in der Auseinandersetzung über die praktische Arbeit nicht immer einfach. Die Sachverständigen leisten ihre Arbeit ehrenamtlich. Sachverständige aus verschiedenen islamisch geprägten Staaten gehören dem Ausschuss seit Beginn seiner Arbeit im Jahre 1982 an.

Lange Zeit stand dem Ausschuss nur das im Übereinkommen selbst genannte Berichtsverfahren zur Verfügung, das aus der Überprüfung der Berichte der Vertragsstaaten besteht, die diese ein Jahr nach Inkrafttreten des Übereinkommens in ihrem Staat und dann alle vier Jahre vorlegen müssen. Die Ergebnisse der Prüfung dieser Staatenberichte sowie der mündlich durchgeführten Diskussion mit einer Regierungsdelegation des Vertragsstaates werden seit

---

16 Insgesamt liegen heute 25 Allgemeine Empfehlungen vor, die u.a. auf der Internetseite des Deutschen Instituts für Menschenrechte eingesehen werden können. Vgl. dazu auch *Hanna Beate Schöpp-Schilling*, „Die Allgemeinen Empfehlungen des Ausschusses für die Beseitigung der Diskriminierung der Frau: Einführung", in: *Deutsches Institut für Menschenrechte* (Hrsg.), Die ‚General Comments' zu den VN-Menschenrechtsverträgen: Deutsche Übersetzung und Kurzeinführungen, Baden-Baden 2005, S. 413-425.

17 Siehe hierzu *United Nations*, The Beijing Declaration and Platform for Action, http://www.un.org/documents/ga/conf177/aconf177-20en.htm. (zuletzt aufgerufen am 15. Juli 2009).

Mitte der 90er Jahre des vergangenen Jahrhunderts in der Form von Abschließenden Bemerkungen (*concluding observations*) formuliert, die heute kurz nach der jeweiligen Sitzung öffentlich im Internet und später in den jährlichen Berichten des Ausschusses zugänglich sind. Diese Abschließenden Bemerkungen enthalten neben positiven Stellungnahmen zur Umsetzung des Übereinkommens auch Kritikpunkte sowie Empfehlungen, in welchen Bereichen und mit welchen Maßnahmen der Vertragsstaat in den nächsten vier Jahren bis zur folgenden Berichtslegung tätig sein sollte, um dem Übereinkommen in seiner Gesetzgebung, Rechtsprechung und in der tatsächlichen Gleichstellung von Frauen und Männern zu entsprechen. Diese Empfehlungen sind rechtlich nicht verbindlich, auch hat der Ausschuss keinerlei Sanktionsmöglichkeiten, doch erwartet er, dass sie befolgt werden. Leider muss festgestellt werden, dass manche Vertragsstaaten gar nicht oder zu spät berichten, so dass dieses Durchsetzungsverfahren und damit eine konstruktive Beeinflussung hinsichtlich einer Verbesserung der Menschenrechte von Frauen im entsprechenden Land gar nicht oder nicht ausreichend greifen kann.

Forderungen nach zusätzlichen Durchsetzungsverfahren, die im Rahmen der Zweiten VN-Weltkonferenz für Menschenrechte (Wien, 1993) und der Vierten VN-Weltfrauenkonferenz (Peking, 1995) gestellt wurden, um das Frauenrechtsabkommen anderen Menschenrechtsverträgen gleichzustellen, wurden 1999 erfüllt, als die VN-Vollversammlung das Übereinkommen am 6. Oktober durch ein Zusatzprotokoll, auch Fakultativprotokoll (*Optional Protocol*, *OP*) genannt, ergänzte. Dieses Protokoll trat am 22. Dezember 2000 in Kraft und erlaubt dem Ausschuss seitdem, Beschwerden einer Frau oder einer Gruppe von Frauen über eine angebliche Menschenrechtsverletzung durch den Vertragsstaat unter bestimmten Bedingungen entgegenzunehmen und zu prüfen bzw. selbst Untersuchungen hinsichtlich schwerer oder systematischer Menschenrechtsverletzungen in einem Vertragsstaat durchzuführen, die ihm aufgrund verlässlicher Informationen bekannt werden. Im Mai 2008 hatten 90 der CEDAW Vertragsstaaten das Fakultativprotokoll akzeptiert, allerdings gehören Ägypten, Marokko und Saudi Arabien nicht dazu.

In den mehr als 25 Jahren der Arbeit des Ausschusses hat diese durch Berichte der VN-Sonderorganisationen nach Artikel 22 sowie durch Alternativberichte internationaler und nationaler Frauen- und Menschenrechtsverbände eine große Bereicherung erfahren. Sie alle liefern jene Informationen, die Regierungen in ihren Staatenberichten gerne verschweigen, indem sie auf noch bestehende gesetzliche Diskriminierungstatbestände oder auf die Diskrepanz zwischen Gesetzen und Lebenspraxis hinweisen. VN-Sonderorganisationen und zivilgesellschaftliche Verbände informieren den Ausschuss auch mündlich und sind während der Diskussion mit der jeweiligen Regierungsdelegation anwesend, obwohl sie während dieser Diskussion nicht das Wort ergreifen können. Die Anwesenheit der Verbände hilft diesen nach der Rückkehr ins eigene Land, die Regierung durch Lobbyarbeit in Richtung der Umsetzung der Empfehlungen des Ausschusses, auch unter Einschaltung der Presse, zu beeinflussen.[18] Auch in den Untersuchungs- und Beschwerdeverfahren spielen Frauen- und Menschenrechtsverbände eine unterstützende Rolle.

Es gibt viele Beispiele, die belegen, dass die Empfehlungen des Ausschusses im Rahmen des Berichtsverfahrens bzw. in jüngster Zeit auch die Empfehlungen im Rahmen der beiden anderen Durchsetzungsverfahren positive Veränderungen für Frauen im jeweiligen Land bewirkt haben. Oft geschieht dies auch im Zusammenwirken mit ohnehin im Land schon aktiven fortschrittlichen politischen und zivilgesellschaftlichen Kräften und Ansätzen. Erfolge sind zu verzeichnen auf der gesetzgeberischen und institutionellen Ebene, der Ebene von Maßnahmen zur tatsächlichen Verbesserung der Lebenssituation von Frauen sowie auf der kulturellen Ebene vieler Vertragsstaaten.[19]

I. Vorbehalte

Leider hat das Übereinkommen trotz der hohen Ratifikationsrate noch keine universelle Gültigkeit erlangt, und das Verbot der Diskriminierung von Frauen aufgrund des Geschlechts und Familienstands hat nicht den Status des *ius cogens* erreicht, der heute ohne Zweifel einem Verbot der Diskriminierung aufgrund einer rassischen Zuschreibung zukommt. Der Grund für diese Tatsache ist, dass viele Staaten Vorbehalte (*reservations*) zu bestimmten Artikeln des Übereinkommens eingelegt haben, d.h. sie erkennen die Verpflichtungen, die in diesen Artikeln enthalten sind, aus verschiedenen Gründen nicht an.[20] Zwar sind Vorbehalte nach Art. 28 (1) erlaubt, doch dürfen sie nach Artikel 28 (2) nicht gegen „Ziel und Zweck" (*object and purpose*) des Übereinkommens verstoßen.[21] Artikel 29 (2) erlaubt ebenfalls einen Vorbehalt hinsichtlich der mög-

---

[18] Vgl. dazu *Shanthi Dairiam*, „From Global to Local: The Involvement of NGOs", in: *Hanna Beate Schöpp-Schilling / Cees Flinterman* (Hrsg.), The Circle of Empowerment. Twenty-five Years of the UN Committee on the Elimination of Discrimination against Women, New York 2007, S. 313-325.

[19] Viele Beispiele sind in den Aufsätzen und persönlichen Erinnerungen von Sachverständigen aufgeführt in *Hanna Beate Schöpp-Schilling / Cees Flinterman* (Hrsg.), The Circle of Empowerment..., a.a.O. (Fn. 18).

[20] Die Vorbehalte zu CEDAW sind einzusehen im Internet unter http://www.un.org/women watch/daw/cedaw/reservations.htm und unter http://www.2.ohchr.org/english/bodies/rati fication/8.htm#declarations (zuletzt aufgerufen am 15. Juli 2009)

[21] Leider enthält das Übereinkommen nicht wie das Internationale Übereinkommen zur Beseitigung jeder Form von Rassendiskriminierung (*International Convention on the Elimination of All Forms of Racial Discrimination*, CERD, 1966) in seinem Artikel 20 (2)

lichen Verfahren (Schiedsverfahren, Internationaler Gerichtshof) bei Streitigkeiten zwischen Vertragsstaaten über die Auslegung oder Anwendung des Übereinkommens. Nur wenige Vertragsstaaten nutzen die Möglichkeit, Einspruch gegen Vorbehalte anderer Vertragsstaaten einzulegen, um zu verdeutlichen, dass diese ihrer Auffassung nach gegen Ziel und Zweck des Übereinkommens verstoßen.

Vorbehalte können u.a. das Ziel haben, einen Staat von einer Staatenverpflichtung zu befreien, wenn die eigene nationale Gesetzgebung noch nicht auf dem Stand des Übereinkommens ist. Wird dieser Stand erreicht, sollte der Vorbehalt zurückgezogen werden. Dies ist im Laufe der letzten 25 Jahre durchaus von einer Reihe von Vertragsstaaten, einschließlich islamisch geprägter Vertragsstaaten, getan worden.

Der Ausschuss hat sich ausführlich mit dem Problem der Vorbehalte befasst und in mehreren Stellungnahmen festgestellt, dass Vorbehalte gegen Artikel 2, 9 und 16 eindeutig gegen Ziel und Zweck des Übereinkommens verstoßen. Dies gilt auch seiner Meinung nach für sehr allgemein formulierte Erklärungen, die unter Bezug z.B. auf den Islam oder islamisches Recht das gesamte Übereinkommen umfassen und unklar lassen, welche Verpflichtungen eigentlich vom Vertragsstaat akzeptiert werden. Dies ist z.B. bei Saudi Arabien der Fall, wie ich weiter unten zeigen werde. Der Ausschuss fordert von allen Vertragsstaaten – zuletzt 1998 –, ihre Vorbehalte jeweils ausführlich zu begründen, deren Auswirkungen auf die menschenrechtliche Situation ihrer weiblichen Bevölkerung darzulegen und aufzuzeigen, ob die Absicht bestehe, diese zurückzunehmen und wenn ja, im Rahmen welcher Zeitpläne.[22]

Das Problem der Vorbehalte wird oft als ein Problem islamisch geprägter Vertragsstaaten gesehen. Dies ist insofern auch richtig, als bisher nur wenige der islamisch geprägten Staaten ihre Vorbehalte zurückgenommen haben, auch wenn die geänderte Gesetzeslage es ihnen erlauben würde. Islamisch geprägte Staaten selbst weisen häufig Diskussionen über Vorbehalte als gegen den Islam gerichtet zurück.

Der Ausschuss ist allerdings der Auffassung, dass es noch immer besser ist, ein Vertragsstaat des Übereinkommens mit gravierenden Vorbehalten zu sein als kein Vertragsstaat, da im letzteren Fall überhaupt kein Dialog mit dem Land möglich ist. Die Überprüfung der Umsetzung von nicht mit Vorbehalten be-

---

ein Kriterium, mit dem bestimmt werden kann, wann ein Vorbehalt gegen Ziel und Zweck verstößt.

22 *Hanna Beate Schöpp-Schilling*, „Reservations to CEDAW: An Unresolved Issue. Or, (No) New Developments?", in: *Ineta Ziemele* (Hrsg.), Reservations to Human Rights Treaties: Conflict, Harmony or Reconciliation, Leiden 2004, S. 3-39 (S. 12-27).

legten Teilen des Übereinkommens sowie das Ansprechen der Vorbehalte im Rahmen des Berichtsverfahrens eröffnen immerhin die Möglichkeit, mit den politischen (und zivilgesellschaftlichen) Kräften des Landes in ein Gespräch zu treten. Denn ungeachtet der völkerrechtlich noch immer umstrittenen Frage, ob ein Vertragsausschuss überhaupt Aussagen zu Vorbehalten machen darf, diskutiert der Vertragsausschuss für CEDAW mit dem jeweiligen Vertragsstaat dessen Vorbehalte und empfiehlt in seinen Abschließenden Bemerkungen immer die Konkretisierung derartiger Vorbehalte bzw. die Rücknahme derselben.

2. Islamisches Recht

Islamisch geprägte Staaten weisen zu Recht darauf hin, dass Frauen durch den Islam mehr Rechte zugestanden wurden als diese vorher in den arabischen Stammesgesellschaften in Anspruch nehmen oder ausüben konnten. Über heute praktiziertes islamisches Recht in islamisch geprägten Staaten kann auch nicht verallgemeinernd gesprochen werden. So sind die verschiedenen Rechtsquellen des islamischen Rechts, die Frauen betreffen, nicht immer eindeutig und werden darüber hinaus nicht nur in der sunnitischen und schiitischen Ausrichtung von Traditionalisten und Modernisten unterschiedlich interpretiert, sondern auch noch in den vier sunnitischen Schulen. Hinzu kommt, dass das heute in vielen islamisch geprägten Ländern kodifizierte Personenstandsrecht, das Situationen wie Eheschließung, Rechte der Ehegatten, Scheidung, Sorgerecht für Kinder oder auch das Erbrecht regelt, auch von anderen Faktoren bestimmt ist. Dazu gehören z.B. das im 19. und oft bis in die 2. Hälfte des 20. Jahrhunderts geltende Ehe- und Familienrecht der jeweiligen Kolonialmacht, das inzwischen in diesen Ländern selbst modernisiert wurde und dort heute dem Übereinkommen entspricht.[23] Dazu gehören auch das örtliche Gewohnheitsrecht, das oft nicht kodifiziert ist, oder aber auch traditionelle Bräuche bzw. sogar politische Einstellungen und Programme, die entweder die kodifizierten Formulierungen oder die Anwendung des Rechts beeinflussen. Saheen Sadar Ali spricht daher vom „operativen islamischen Recht“, das für Frauen in einigen islamisch geprägten Staaten – sie bezieht sich vor allem auf Pakistan und Indien – auf jeweils spezifische Weise innerhalb eines pluralistischen Rechtssystems zur Geltung komme. Dieses pluralistische System kann aus einer fortschrittlichen Verfassung, einem kodifizierten Recht mit frauendiskriminierenden Elementen, aus Bestimmungen

---

[23] Ann E. Mayer stellt dies für die Länder Algerien, Marokko und Tunesien fest; Savitri Goonesekere z.B. für Sri Lanka. *Ann E. Mayer*, „Reform of Personal Status Laws in North Africa: A Problem of Islamic or Mediterranean Laws?“, in: Middle East Journal, 49/3, Washington D.C. 1995, S. 432-446; *Savitri Goonesekere*, „Colonial Legislation and Sri Lankan Family Law: The Legacy of History“, in: *K. de Silva* (Hrsg.), Asian Panorama, New Delhi 1997.

des religiösen Rechts und aus Elementen des stammesgeprägten Gewohnheitsrechts bestehen.[24]

Islamisch geprägte Vertragsstaaten und ihr Umgang mit Vorbehalten zu CEDAW: Bei der Annahme des gesamten Übereinkommens durch die VN-Vollversammlung im Jahre 1979 enthielt sich eine Reihe islamisch geprägter Staaten der Stimme, so u.a. Marokko und Saudi Arabien. Schon vorher hatten u.a. beide in der getrennten Abstimmung über einzelne Artikel gegen Artikel 9 (2) (Weitergabe der Staatsangehörigkeit der mit einem Ausländer verheirateten Frau an ihre Kinder) gestimmt und sich der Stimme bei der ebenfalls getrennten Abstimmung über Artikel 16 (1) (c) (gleiche Rechte von Mann und Frau in der Ehe) enthalten.[25] Es ist daher nicht von ungefähr, dass außer Indonesien und der damaligen sozialistischen Demokratischen Volksrepublik Yemen,[26] den südlich der Sahara liegenden afrikanischen Staaten und den ehemaligen Staaten der Sowjetunion, alle Staaten mit muslimischer Bevölkerung bzw. mit Verfassungen und Gesetzen, die von der *Šarīʿa* inspiriert bzw. auf diese bezogen sind, Vorbehalte gegen substantielle Artikel des Übereinkommens eingelegt haben und damit sowohl seine Integrität als auch seine universelle Gültigkeit gefährden und einschränken. Einige Staaten formulieren diese Vorbehalte mit Bezug auf den Islam bzw. die *Šarīʿa* sehr allgemein und das gesamte Übereinkommen betreffend, andere beziehen sich dagegen konkret und präzise auf einzelne Artikel, z.T. mit, aber auch ohne Bezug zur *Šarīʿa*.

Im allgemeinen werden Vorbehalte zu folgenden Artikeln ausgesprochen:

- **Artikel 2** (Verpflichtung des Vertragsstaates zur Verankerung des Gleichheitsprinzips für die Geschlechter in der Verfassung; zur Änderung diskriminierender Gesetze; zur Aufhebung kulturell bedingter diskriminierender Praktiken und Gebräuche; zur Einrichtung einer funktionierenden Gerichtsbarkeit und Ermöglichung des Zugangs von Frauen zu derselben; zu Sanktionen bei Diskriminierungstatbeständen; zur Verantwortung des Staates, Frauen vor Menschenrechtsverletzungen durch private Personen, Organisationen und Unternehmen zu schützen, diese zu verhindern und zu bestrafen);
- **Artikel 9 (2)** (Recht der mit einem Ausländer verheirateten Frau zur Weitergabe der Staatsangehörigkeit an ihre Kinder);
- **Artikel 15 (4)** (Recht der Frau auf Freizügigkeit und freie Wahl des Aufenthaltsortes und Wohnsitzes);

---

24 *Saheen Sadar Ali*, Gender and Human Rights in Islam and International Law. Equal Before Allah, Unequal Before Man? The Hague / London / Boston 2000, S. 187-191.

25 *Jane Connors*, The Women's Convention..., a.a.O. (Fn. 1), S. 88 f. Das Abstimmungsverhalten ist aufgeführt in: *United Nations*, Official Records: General Assembly: Thirty-fourth Session, 107th Plenary Meeting, Agenda Item 75, 18 December 1979, S. 1995-1997.

26 Indonesien und die Demokratische Volksrepublik Yemen legten allerdings einen nach Artikel 29 (2) zulässigen Vorbehalt gegen Artikel 29 (1) ein.

- **Artikel 16 (1) (a-h), (2)** (Gleichstellung der Frau in allen Angelegenheiten der Ehe und in den Beziehungen der Ehepartner und Familienmitglieder untereinander, d.h. gleiches Recht auf Eheschließung, auf freie Wahl des Ehegatten, gleiche Rechte und Pflichten in der Ehe und bei deren Auflösung; als Eltern, im Sorge- und Vormundschaftsrecht; bei der Wahl des Familiennamens und des Berufs oder einer Beschäftigung während der Ehe; hinsichtlich des Erwerbs, der Verwaltung, der Nutzung, der Veräußerung des Eigentums; Verbot der Kindesverlobung oder -ehe, Gebot des Mindestalters für Eheschließung, der amtlichen Registrierungspflicht von Eheschließungen);
- **Artikel 29 (1)** (Regelung des Verfahrens bei Streitigkeiten unter den Vertragsstaaten über die Auslegung oder Anwendung des Vertrags, Möglichkeit eines Schiedsverfahrens einschließlich der Vorlage beim Internationalen Gerichtshof der Vereinten Nationen).

Ann Elizabeth Mayer und Jane Connors haben bereits darauf verwiesen, dass nicht alle Vorbehalte mit der *Šarīʿa* zu rechtfertigen sind.[27]

E. Islamisch geprägte Vertragsstaaten in der Interaktion mit dem Vertragsausschuss für CEDAW

Regierungsvertreter islamisch geprägter Staaten behaupten des öfteren während der Diskussion ihrer Staatenberichte im Ausschuss, dass kein Widerspruch zwischen dem Islam und dem Übereinkommen bestehe. Diese Auffassung vertreten auch Sachverständige des Ausschusses aus islamisch geprägten Ländern mit Verweis auf die Notwendigkeit, die Interpretationen der Quellen der *Šarīʿa* modernen Gegebenheiten anpassen zu müssen. Manche Regierungsvertreter gehen allerdings soweit zu behaupten, dass im Islam die wahre oder sogar noch größere Gleichberechtigung von Frauen und Männern garantiert sei als nach dem Übereinkommen. Die folgende Analyse der Interaktion Ägyptens, Marokkos und Saudi Arabiens mit dem Ausschuss wird aufzeigen, wie sich die Argumentationsmuster der Regierungsvertreter im Laufe der Zeit ändern und welche Fortschritte für Frauen im Rahmen des Übereinkommens in diesen Ländern zu verzeichnen sind.

I. Ägypten

Ägypten hatte sich aktiv an der Formulierung des Übereinkommens beteiligt, sich allerdings zusammen mit anderen islamisch geprägten Staaten 1979 bei der Abstimmung über die Artikel 9 (2) und 16 (1) (c) der Stimme enthalten, obwohl es dann dem Übereinkommen insgesamt zugestimmt hatte.[28] Ägypten hatte auch

27 *Jane Connors*, The Women's Convention..., a.a.O. (Fn. 1), S. 101, *Ann E. Mayer*, Reform of Personal Status Laws..., a.a.O. (Fn. 23).

28 *United Nations*, Official Records..., a.a.O. (Fn. 25); nach der Abstimmung ergriff u.a. die ägyptische Diplomatin das Wort, um ägyptische Vorbehalte hinsichtlich einiger Vorschriften zu erwähnen, S. 1999.

als erster arabischer islamisch geprägter Staat das Übereinkommen am 18. September 1981 ratifiziert. Von Anfang an haben Sachverständige aus Ägypten im Ausschuss mitgearbeitet, die in mindestens zwei Fällen beruflich dem ägyptischen diplomatischen Dienst angehörten.[29]

Wie Ägypten bei der Verabschiedung des Übereinkommens bereits durch sein Abstimmungsverhalten und in einer allgemein gehaltenen Erklärung angekündigt hatte, ratifizierte es das Übereinkommen mit Vorbehalten zu den Artikeln 2, 9 (2), 16 und 29 (1). Allerdings legte Ägypten keine Vorbehalte zu den entsprechenden Vorschriften hinsichtlich der Rechte in der Ehe und der Staatsangehörigkeit im ICCPR oder in der Kinderrechtskonvention (*Convention on the Rights of the Child,* CRC) ein, die es 1982 bzw. 1990 ratifizierte. Die Vorbehalte sind bis auf den Vorbehalt zu Artikel 9 (2) trotz einiger positiver rechtlicher Entwicklungen für Frauen und trotz mehrfacher Hinweise seitens der ägyptischen Regierung, dass ihre Aufhebung diskutiert und bevorstehen würde, bis heute nicht zurückgenommen worden. Die drei erstgenannten Vorbehalte verstoßen nach Auffassung des Ausschusses und einiger Vertragsstaaten gegen Ziel und Zweck des Übereinkommens.[30]

Der Vorbehalt zu Artikel 2 ist sehr allgemein formuliert und schon aus diesem Grund für den Ausschuss aufgrund seiner Beschlüsse nicht akzeptabel.[31] Die übrigen Vorbehalte sind eher argumentativ angelegt, wobei der patriarchalische Charakter der Argumentation von der Regierung nicht erkannt wird, wenn sie z.B. behauptet, dass die väterliche Staatsangehörigkeit bei unterschiedlicher Staatsangehörigkeit der Eltern die „angemessenste" (*most suitable*) für das Kind sei und diese Regelung nicht das Gleichheitsprinzip von Mann und Frau verletze, da es „üblich" (*customary*) sei, dass die Frau bei einer Heirat mit einem

---

29 Farida About El-Fetouh (1983-1986), Mervat Tallawy (1987-1998) (Vorsitzende des Ausschusses von 1991-1992), Naela Gabr (1999 ff.). Der Vorsitz im Ausschuss wechselt im allgemeinen alle zwei Jahre und rotiert zwischen Sachverständigen aus verschiedenen Regionen – Afrika, Asien, Lateinamerika, Westeuropa und andere westliche Länder, Osteuropa –, die eine Sachverständige aus ihrer Region vorschlagen, die dann im Konsens gewählt wird.

30 Die Vorbehalte und die Einsprüche dagegen sind aufgeführt in *United Nations*, Declarations, reservations, objections and notifications of withdrawal of reservations relating to the Convention on the Elimination of All Forms of Discrimination against Women, CEDAW/SP/1992/2, S. 11 f., 29-32. Einsprüche legten ein: Deutschland (1985, Vorbehalte zu Artikel 2, 9 (2), 16), Mexiko (1985, Vorbehalte zu Artikel 9, 16), die Niederlande (1990, Vorbehalte zu Artikel 2, 9, 16), und Schweden (1986, Vorbehalte zu Artikel 2, 9 (2), 16).

31 *„The Arab Republic of Egypt is willing to comply with the content of this article, provided such compliance does not run counter to the Islamic Shariah."*; *United Nations*, Declarations..., a.a.O. (Fn. 30), S. 12.

Ausländer ihre Zustimmung gebe, dass die Kinder die Staatsangehörigkeit des Vaters erhalten würden.[32] Auch der Vorbehalt zu Artikel 16 wird ausführlich mit den Vorschriften der *Šarīᶜa* begründet, die nicht in Frage gestellt werden dürften, da die wichtigste Grundlage der ehelichen Beziehungen die „Entsprechung" der Rechte und Pflichten der Ehegatten sei, um ein Gleichgewicht zu schaffen. So rechtfertige die Tatsache, dass die *Šarīᶜa* dem Mann die Pflicht auferlege, der Frau ein Brautgeld zu zahlen, sie und ihre gemeinsamen Kinder unabhängig von ihrem eigenen Vermögen und Besitz zu unterhalten und ihr bei einer Scheidung wiederum eine Zahlung zu leisten, die Einschränkung des Rechts auf Scheidung für die Frau, das nur durch die Entscheidung eines Richters wahrzunehmen sei, während der Mann keine derartige Einschränkung habe.[33] Mit diesen Erläuterungen wird der Gleichheitsbegriff hinsichtlich der Rechte von Mann und Frau des Übereinkommens durch einen Gleich***wertigkeits***begriff ersetzt, wie er im 19. Jahrhundert auch in den Erläuterungen führender Philosophen Europas und auch heute noch in den Lehren der Katholischen Kirche vertreten wird.

Als der Vertragsausschuss für CEDAW den zunächst nur zweiseitigen ersten ägyptischen Bericht und die dann auf 10 Seiten erweiterte, aber aussagekräftigere zweite Fassung im Jahre 1984 mit der ägyptischen Regierungsdelegation diskutierte, wurde er zum ersten Mal mit der Tatsache von Vorbehalten auf der Grundlage der *Šarīᶜa* konfrontiert, da die erste Fassung des Berichts die Vorbehalte zu den Artikeln 9 (2), 16, 29 (1) und deren Begründungen wiederholte,[34] und die Leiterin der ägyptischen Delegation auch mündlich auf dieselben verwies. Ansonsten stellte sie eine vollständige Übereinstimmung der ägyptischen Verfassung (Artikel 11 und 40) und der übrigen Gesetzgebung mit dem Übereinkommen fest, wobei sie nicht ausdrücklich erläuterte, dass Artikel 40 sich nur auf die Rechte und Pflichten der Staatsbürger und –bürgerinnen (*citizens*) im ***öffentlichen*** Bereich bezieht.[35] Diese Auffassung findet sich auch

---

32 „ *...since it is customary for a woman to agree, upon marrying an alien, that her children shall be of the father's nationality.*"; *United Nations*, Declarations..., a.a.O (Fn. 30), S. 11.

33 „*... women are accorded rights equivalent to those of their spouses so as to ensure a just balance between them.* [...] *one of the most important bases of these relations is an equivalency of rights and duties so as to ensure complementarity which guarantees true equality between the spouses, not a quasi-equality that renders the marriage a burden on the wife.*"; *United Nations*, Declarations..., a.a.O. (Fn. 30), S. 11 f.

34 *United Nations*, Government of the Arab Republic of Egypt, Initial Report under the CEDAW Convention, CEDAW/C/5/Add.10 (3 February 1983), S. 3. Die zweite Fassung trägt die Signatur CEDAW/C/5/Add.10/Amend.1 (20 February 1984).

35 Artikel 11 verpflichtet den ägyptischen Staat, die "Harmonie" zu garantieren, "*between women's family duties, their activity in society, and their equality with men in the politi-*

in den in späteren Jahren verfassten zweiten, dritten und kombinierten vierten/fünften Berichten Ägyptens, obwohl die Regierungsvertreter in der mündlichen Diskussion eine unterschiedliche Behandlung von Frauen und Männern in einigen Rechtsstatuten zugaben und diese als diskriminierend charakterisierten. Darüber hinaus ist die Behauptung nur aufrecht zu halten, indem das religiös fundierte Personenstandsrecht für die unterschiedlichen religiösen Bevölkerungsgruppen ausgeklammert und für die muslimische Bevölkerung mit Hinweis auf die *Šarīʿa* mit Vorbehalten belegt wird.

Die Diskussion im Ausschuss im Jahr 1984 spiegelte zum einen die Unkenntnis einiger Sachverständiger aus nichtmuslimischen Kulturkreisen bezüglich der Inhalte der *Šarīʿa* und ihrer konkreten Auswirkungen auf die Rechtslage und praktische Lebenssituation ägyptischer Frauen wider, zum anderen aber auch die Kritik der Sachverständigen gegenüber der ägyptischen Argumentation.[36] So ergriffen in diesem ersten mündlichen Austausch mit Ägypten neunzehn Sachverständige das Wort, um die positiven und fragwürdigen Punkte aufzuzeigen. Als positiv erkannten sie in der schriftlichen und mündlichen Darstellung u.a. die Anstrengungen der Regierung im Bildungsbereich, die Setzung einer minimalen Quotierung für Frauen im politischen Bereich, die angeführte Gleichstellung der ägyptischen Frauen in der Rechtsfähigkeit und hinsichtlich des Eigentums sowie die Einrichtung frauenpolitischer Institutionen durch die Regierung. Da damals kein Alternativbericht vorlag, war es für die Sachverständigen schwer, die Fragwürdigkeit mancher Behauptungen zu erkennen, die sich in späteren Darstellungen konkretisierte, wie ich aufzeigen werde. Fünf Sachverständige nahmen allerdings auch zu den Vorbehalten Stellung, während fünf weitere Fragen zum islamischen Recht stellten, sich die Vorlage der entsprechenden Textstellen wünschten, um diese besser verstehen und in ihren Auswirkungen auf die Lebenswirklichkeit von Frauen deutlicher einschätzen zu können.

---

cal, social, cultural and economic fields of life, without prejudice to the prescriptions of Ismalic [sic!] *religious law (Shari'a).*" Artikel 40 "*stipulates the complete equality of all citizens in all rights and duties, without distinction of sex, origin, language, religion or belief.*" *United Nations,* Government of the Arab Republic of Egypt..., a.a.O. (Fn. 34), S. 2, Absatz 1.

36 Laut einer heutigen Regel des Ausschusses darf sich die sachverständige Person, die aus dem Land kommt, das vom Ausschuss überprüft wird, nicht an der Diskussion beteiligen. Es gibt keine Äußerungen der damaligen ägyptischen Sachverständigen, 1990 beteiligte sich allerdings Mervat Tallawy an der Diskussion.

Die jugoslawische Sachverständige[37] begrüßte die Tatsache, dass Ägypten sich zur Ratifizierung, wenn auch mit Vorbehalten, entschlossen habe und sah dieses Verfahren als ein Modell auch für andere Länder an, die ebenfalls Schwierigkeiten mit der Anerkennung bestimmter Artikel des Übereinkommens hätten. Die portugiesische Sachverständige stellte die Logik des ägyptischen Staatsangehörigkeitsrechts in Frage, das einer Ehefrau die doppelte Staatsangehörigkeit erlauben würde, nicht aber ihren Kindern. Die Sachverständige aus Ruanda verwies auf Staatenverpflichtungen aus Artikel 5 des Übereinkommens und fragte, wie diese mit den Anforderungen des religiösen Rechts zu vereinbaren wären, da dieses u.a. dem ägyptischen Mann die Polygamie ermöglichen würde. Der schwedische Sachverständige hinterfragte – entsprechend des schwedischen Verständnisses von der Doppelrolle von Frau ***und*** Mann – die im Bericht angeführte alleinige Unterstützung von Frauen, ihre familiären Pflichten mit ihrer Berufstätigkeit zu vereinbaren. Er vermisste Informationen einer entsprechenden Unterstützung von Männern insbesondere hinsichtlich der Arbeitsteilung im Haushalt und der Verantwortlichkeit für die Empfängnisverhütung. Auch wandte er sich kritisch gegen die Substitution des Gleichheitsbegriffes hinsichtlich der Rechte und Pflichten durch Begriffe wie „Harmonie" bzw. „Entsprechung". Letztere wären kein Synonym für Gleichberechtigung und Gleichstellung, sondern würden für das Gegenteil stehen. Sie würden in von Männern dominierten Gesellschaften eingesetzt, um Anstrengungen zu vermeiden, die Gleichheit der Geschlechter zu erreichen.

Wie auch die kanadische Sachverständige kritisierte er die Vorbehalte deutlich. Er verlangte Klärung, ob die Vorbehalte gegen Artikel 2 als Kernartikel und Artikel 16, der einen fundamentalen Aspekt der Lebenswirklichkeit von Männern und Frauen betreffen würde, mit Ziel und Zweck des Übereinkommens vereinbar wären. Die kanadische Sachverständige ging noch einen Schritt weiter, indem sie deutlich die Unvereinbarkeit dieser Vorbehalte mit dem Ziel und Zweck des Übereinkommens feststellte und der Hoffnung Ausdruck verlieh, dass sie eines Tages zurückgezogen würden.

> *In ihrer Entgegnung führte die Leiterin der ägyptischen Delegation das auf der Šarīʿa basierende Personenstandsrecht in Einzelheiten aus und erklärte, dass Artikel 16, außer in der Frage der Ehe und Familienbeziehungen während der Ehe und bei Scheidung (Artikel 16 (1) (c)), mit der Šarīʿa vereinbar wäre. Im übrigen würden Ehen auf der Grundlage eines Vertrags geschlossen, in dem auch*

[37] Da die Äußerungen der Sachverständigen auch jeweils den Bewusstseins- und Diskussionsstand zu Gleichberechtigungsfragen in ihren Herkunftsländern widerspiegeln und inzwischen eine historische Dimension besitzen, identifiziere ich sie in der Analyse Ägyptens; in den Ausführungen zu Marokko und Saudi Arabien werde ich dies aus Platzgründen nicht mehr tun.

das Recht auf Scheidung für die Frau verankert werden könnte. Unabhängig davon sähe auch das Personenstandsrecht in mehreren Fällen eine Scheidung vor, die von der Frau gewünscht würde (im Falle einer zweiten Eheschließung des Ehemannes, der Verheimlichung einer schon bestehenden Ehe und der Vernachlässigung der finanziellen Unterstützungspflicht des Mannes). Im übrigen unterläge die Polygamie bestimmten Einschränkungen in Ägypten. Auch unterstrich sie mehrfach in der schon bekannten Argumentation, dass Frauen nach islamischem Recht schon viel früher Rechte hätten genießen können als Frauen in anderen Ländern bzw. als sie selbst heute in anderen Teilen der Welt genießen würden.

Die Ausschussmitglieder waren von den Ausführungen nicht vollständig überzeugt. Aus heutiger Sicht besonders relevant ist die abschließend gestellte Frage der kanadischen Sachverständigen, warum Ägypten denn einen Vorbehalt zu dem ***gesamten*** *Artikel 16 formuliert hätte, wenn es selber nur die Notwendigkeit für einen Vorbehalt zu Artikel 16 (1) (c) sähe.*[38]

Der ägyptische Staatenbericht leitete eine allgemeine Diskussion im Ausschuss über Vorbehalte im allgemeinen ein sowie hinsichtlich der Fragen, welche Vorbehalte erlaubt seien, wer dies bestimme und wie eigentlich islamisches Recht auf die Umsetzung des Übereinkommens wirke. Diese Diskussion ist bis heute weder im Vertragsausschuss für CEDAW noch in anderen VN-Gremien abgeschlossen. Eine vom Ausschuss geforderte Studie zu islamischem Recht wurde von islamisch geprägten VN-Mitgliedstaaten als Angriff verstanden und nie durchgeführt.[39]

1990 diskutierte der Ausschuss den zweiten Bericht Ägyptens.[40] *Dieser war ausführlicher als die beiden ersten Berichte, verwies wiederum auf die relevanten Verfassungsartikel 11 und 40, um die rechtliche Gleichheit von Frauen mit Männern zu belegen, enthielt jedoch keinerlei neue Informationen hinsichtlich der Vorbehalte. Allerdings wurde auf Neuerungen im Personenstandsrecht (1985) verwiesen, nachdem das Höchste Verfassungsgericht (*Supreme Constitutional Court*) das entsprechende Gesetz von 1979 für verfassungswidrig erklärt hatte.*[41]

---

38 *United Nations*, „Summary Record of the Committee on the Elimination of Discrimination against Women of its Third Session, 35th Meeting and 39th Meeting", in: *United Nations*, The Work of CEDAW. Reports of the Committee on the Elimination of Discrimination against Women, (CEDAW), 1982-1985, Bd. 1, New York 1989, S. 353-363, 405-411.

39 Vgl. dazu *Christine Chinkin*, Human Rights as General Norms..., a.a.O. (Fn. 1), S. 77-78 und *Jane Connors*, The Women's Convention..., a.a.O. (Fn. 1), S. 96 f.

40 *United Nations*, Government of the Arab Republic of Egypt, Second periodic report under the CEDAW Convention, CEDAW/C/13/Add.2 (14 May 1987) und CEDAW/C/13/Add.2/Amend.1 (4 December 1989).

41 Das neue Gesetz enthielt folgende Regelungen: Zahlung des Unterhalts der Ehefrau vom Datum des Ehevertrags an, auch wenn die Ehefrau wohlhabend oder krank ist; sofortige Scheidung, wenn der Ehemann der Unterhaltspflicht ohne Erklärung nicht nachkommt oder seinen Geldmangel nicht darlegt; Möglichkeit der Ehefrau, bei unheilbarer oder erst

Im übrigen verwies der Delegationsleiter in seiner mündlichen Einführung auf die ägyptische Verfassung, die im wirtschaftlichen und politischen Bereich eine rechtliche Gleichheit der Geschlechter garantieren würde. Allerdings wäre die faktische Gleichheit an den Stand der Kultur, den Gebräuchen, dem Kulturerbe und der Entwicklung [sic] gebunden. Zwar würde die Welt globaler, doch würde gleichzeitig die jeweilige Gruppenidentität und das Recht, diese zu bewahren, verstärkt. Übergangslos stellte er dann die Verbindung zu den in Ägypten praktizierten Religionen her, womit er diese indirekt als Quelle der jeweiligen Gruppenidentität positionierte und das jeweilige Personenstandsrecht, das sich aus diesen Quellen speist, rechtfertigte. Er betonte den Status eines Entwicklungslandes für Ägypten sowie die „zahlreichen wirtschaftlichen und sozialen Probleme", die verhinderten, dass Frauen ihre Rechte voll ausüben könnten, und verwies auf eine weltweit vorhandene Tendenz zum Konservatismus sowie auf die Existenz konservativer Gruppen in islamischen Ländern, aber auch in Ländern mit anderen Religionen (Christentum, Judentum).

Der Ausschuss, dessen Zusammensetzung sich in Teilen geändert hatte, hatte vor der Sitzung Fragen eingereicht, die Mitglieder der Regierungsdelegation mündlich beantworten sollten. Hinsichtlich der Frage, ob Ägypten überlegen würde, seine Vorbehalte zurückzuziehen, wurde der Ausschuss vom Delegationsleiter zunächst belehrt, dass es das Recht eines Staates wäre, Vorbehalte einzulegen. Dies ist zwar grundsätzlich richtig, doch dürfen diese eben nicht gegen Ziel und Zweck des Übereinkommens verstoßen, worauf er nicht einging. Er betonte auch die Auffassung der Regierung, dass es besser sei, einen Vertrag mit Vorbehalten zu ratifizieren als dies gar nicht zu tun, also eine Wiederholung der Argumentation der jugoslawischen Sachverständigen aus dem Jahr 1984. Im übrigen gäbe es eine Diskussion unter Intellektuellen und Regierungsbeamten, einige der Vorbehalte zu prüfen, z.B. den Vorbehalt zu Artikel 9 [sic!]. *Er wiederholte die Auffassung, dass die Vorbehalte zu Artikel 2 die Umsetzung dieses Artikels nicht beeinträchtigen würden, da die Verfassung die Gleichheit aller Personen ohne Ansehen des Geschlechts und der Religion garantieren würde. Er zitierte eine Reihe von Vorschriften aus verschiedenen Rechtsgebieten, die auf Frauen ohne Diskriminierung zuträfen, gab dann allerdings zu, dass Zeugenaussagen von Frauen weniger Gewicht im Vergleich zu Zeugenaussagen von Männern hätten und dass diese Tatsache Frauen diskriminieren würde.*

langfristig heilbarer Krankheit des Ehemannes um Scheidung nachzufragen; Verschärfung der Restriktionen für Polygamie, d.h. Pflicht des Ehemannes, schon bestehende Ehe(n) mit Namen und Adressen der Ehefrau(en) im Heiratsvertrag zu nennen sowie Möglichkeit der Ehefrau, um Scheidung nachzufragen, wenn sie durch eine weitere Ehe materiellen oder moralischen Schaden erleidet, der ein weiteres Zusammenleben verunmöglicht, auch wenn sie eine zusätzliche Ehe nicht bei Antritt der Ehe ausgeschlossen hat; Pflicht des Mannes, seinen Kindern aus seiner geschiedenen Ehe und ihrem weiblichen Vormund eine getrennte angemessene Behausung zu gewähren oder selbst aus der ehelichen Behausung auszuziehen, bis er die Vormundschaft übernimmt. *United Nations,* Government of the Arab Republic of Egypt, Second periodic report..., a.a.O. (Fn. 40), S. 33.

Verschiedene Sachverständige des Ausschusses ließen sich nicht beirren, die Hoffnung auf baldige Zurücknahme der Vorbehalte zu Artikel 9 [sic!] anzusprechen. Die ägyptische Sachverständige wies sogar darauf hin, dass Ägypten sich mit den Vorbehalten schaden würde. Der Vorbehalt zu Artikel 2 wäre unnötig, da ägyptisches Recht Diskriminierungen verbieten würde. Viele Absätze des Artikels 16 müssten nicht mit Vorbehalten belegt werden, da sie nicht im Konflikt mit islamischem Recht stünden. Andere Sachverständige wiesen auf Fehlinterpretationen des Korans hinsichtlich der Rechte von Frauen durch Männer hin und auf die Pflicht des Staates, den Koran richtig anzuwenden. Beides bejahte der Leiter der Delegation. Im übrigen wünschte sich die Sachverständige aus Mali, dass Ägypten ein Beispiel geben sollte, damit muslimische Frauen auf ihre Religion stolz sein könnten. Die Rollenstereotypen, die dem Artikel 11 der Verfassung zugrunde liegen, wurden diesmal von der griechischen Sachverständigen angesprochen.[42]

Den dritten sowie den kombinierten vierten und fünften Bericht Ägyptens diskutierte der Ausschuss im Frühjahr 2001. Zum dritten Bericht hatte das *Cairo Institute for Human Rights* bereits im September 1996 einen kritischen Kommentar gegeben, in dem es die Erlaubnis des ägyptischen Gesundheitsministeriums kritisierte, die weibliche Genitalverstümmelung in öffentlichen Krankenhäusern zu erlauben unter dem Vorwand, die Durchführung dieser Praktiken durch Friseure verhindern zu wollen.[43] Darüber hinaus befasste sich der Kommentar mit den Vorbehalten, die nicht nur die Diskriminierung von Frauen durch das Gesetz, sondern auch durch vorherrschende soziale und kulturelle Muster rechtfertigten. Der Kommentar verwies auf die gesetzlich verankerte Diskriminierung von Frauen im Strafrecht (unterschiedliche Bestrafung von Männern und Frauen bei Ehebruch, Strafmilderung bei sog. „Ehrenmorden") hin. Auch im Zivilrecht gäbe es noch diskriminierende Regelungen. So könnte z.B. die Ehefrau ohne Erlaubnis ihres Ehemannes keinen Pass beantragen oder reisen. Die öffentliche Verwaltung könnte Frauen im Interesse bestimmter Bedingungen diskriminieren. Obwohl kein Gesetz verbieten würde, dass Juristinnen zu Richterinnen ernannt würden, wäre dies bisher nicht geschehen. Diese Regelungen würden nicht auf der *Šarīʿa* beruhen und wären außerdem in anderen arabischen Ländern auch im Sinne der Gleichberechtigung

[42] *United Nations*, Summary Record of the Committee on the Elimination of Discrimination against Women of its Ninth Session, 164th Meeting, CEDAW/C/SR.164 (12 February 1990), S. 7-15; *United Nations*, Summary Record of the Committee on the Elimination of Discrimination against Women of its Ninth Session, 165th Meeting, CEDAW/C/SR.165 (12 February 1990), S. 2-4.

[43] *Cairo Institute for Human Rights Studies*, „Discrimination Beyond Reservations: A Critical Reading of Egypt's Report", in: SAWASIAH, 12, Kairo 1996, S. 6-9.

geregelt. Im übrigen gäbe es andere Gesetze (z.B. Zinspraxis bei Banken), die gegen die *Šarīʿa* verstießen, ohne dass darüber diskutiert würde. Die *Šarīʿa* würde darüber hinaus in viele Schulen zerfallen und würde in unterschiedlichen islamisch geprägten Ländern unterschiedlich interpretiert und angewendet. Der Kommentar schloss mit einem Vergleich der rechtlichen Situation von Frauen in Tunesien und der Türkei und mit dem Aufruf, dass die Frauen- und Menschenrechtsbewegungen Studien durchführen müssten, um die Grundlage für eine Aufhebung der Vorbehalte zu schaffen.

Der dritte sowie der kombinierte vierte und fünfte Bericht umfassten jeweils fast 60 bzw. 100 Seiten, gaben aber hinsichtlich einer möglichen Aufhebung der Vorbehalte keine neuen Informationen und unterschieden sich auch kaum in Aufbau und Darstellung der Fakten. Von Bedeutung für meine Analyse ist jedoch eine neue allgemeine und für beide Berichte wortgleiche Begründung der Vorbehalte in der jeweiligen Einleitung. Unter Hinweis auf das Abschlussdokument der Wiener Menschenrechtskonferenz (1993) der Vereinten Nationen verdeutlichte Ägypten erneut seine Auffassung, den Normen von CEDAW sowie anderen VN-Menschenrechtsverträgen zu entsprechen und mithilfe der Vorbehalte sowohl seinen vertraglich eingegangenen Verpflichtungen als auch der Bewahrung seiner „nationalen Besonderheiten" und „historischen und kulturellen Bräuche, Eigenschaften und Glaubensrichtungen" Genüge zu tun. Das komplizierte Satzgebilde verdeckt, zumindest in der englischen Version, die Widersprüchlichkeiten und Unrichtigkeit der Aussage nur mühsam.[44]

Neben dem Kommentar des Kairoer Menschenrechtsinstituts lagen dem Ausschuss zwei weitere kritische Alternativberichte vor, die von einer Koalition ägyptischer Frauenverbände bzw. von der Weltorganisation gegen die Folter

---

44 "*Egypt consistently demonstrates every respect for the full and effective implementation of international human rights treaties and conventions in all international and domestic forums. It also respects the diverse nature of societies and the heritage, cultural characteristics and prevailing values stemming from their historical development. These should not, however, conflict with the values that the international community protects by means of these instruments, as was stressed in the report of the 1993 Vienna World Conference on Human Rights. This unshakeable policy represents Egypt's national view and strategy with regard to human rights and freedoms at the domestic, regional and international levels.* ***This view has been expressed in the Egyptian reservations to some provisions of the instruments in question, which have the purpose of ensuring their implementation while at the same time preserving the national peculiarities of Egyptian society along with those of its historical and cultural customs, characteristics and creeds that do not conflict with or infringe upon the instruments but are decidedly within the scope of the protection they provide to rights and freedoms*** [Meine Hervorhebung].", *United Nations*, Government of the Arab Republic of Egypt, Combined fourth and fifth periodic reports under the CEDAW Convention, CEDAW/C/EGY/4-5 (30 March 2000), S. 3.

erstellt worden waren. In diesen Berichten wurde ebenfalls auf noch vorhandene rechtliche und materielle Diskriminierungstatbestände verwiesen.[45]

Der Ausschuss hatte zu diesem Zeitpunkt seine Arbeitsweise dahingehend geändert, dass er dem Vertragsstaat bereits einige Monate vor der mündlichen Diskussion seines Berichtes schriftliche Fragen übermittelte, die dieser vor der mündlichen Aussprache schriftlich beantworten musste.[46] Obwohl die beiden Berichte nicht auf irgendwelche Bemühungen verwiesen hatten, die Vorbehalte aufzuheben oder zumindest zu präzisieren, wie es ja in den mündlichen Verlautbarungen der Regierungsvertreter in den früheren Jahren angeklungen war, fragte der Ausschuss schriftlich konkret nach derartigen Bemühungen.

Die schriftliche Antwort, die dann auch in der mündlichen Einführung von Seiten der Regierungsdelegation weiter ausgeführt wurde, zeigte einen entscheidenden Fortschritt, wobei es nicht im Rahmen dieses Aufsatzes liegen kann, die Faktoren zu analysieren, die diese Fortschritte bewirkt haben könnten. Auf jeden Fall war aufgrund mehrerer nationaler Konferenzen, die wahrscheinlich im Rahmen der nationalen Vor- und Nachbereitungen der Vierten VN-Weltfrauenkonferenz in Peking stattgefunden hatten, ein Nationaler Frauenrat (*National Council for Women,* NCW) geschaffen worden, der aus Frauen und Männern aus Wissenschaft und Zivilgesellschaft bestand. Der Vorsitz wurde von der Frau des ägyptischen Präsidenten wahrgenommen, das ehemalige Ausschussmitglied Merwat Tallawy, die auch die Delegation anführte, hatte die Funktion der Generalsekretärin inne.

Sie berichtete in ihrer Einführung, dass sich eine Vielzahl von Ausschüssen des Nationalen Frauenrates mit der Verbesserung der Situation der ägyptischen Frauen befassen würde, einschließlich eines Ausschusses für rechtliche Fragen und die ägyptischen Vorbehalte. Mit finanzieller Unterstützung von UNICEF wäre eine Studie über die *Šarīʿa* durchgeführt worden, die aufzeigen würde, dass die Prinzipien der Gleichheit vor dem Gesetz und der Nichtdiskriminierung durch das Gesetz „von der *Šarīʿa* voll geachtet und geschützt" würden. Mit diesem Ergebnis könnte nun gezeigt werden, dass der sehr allgemein gehaltene Vorbehalt zu Artikel 2 des Übereinkommens nur als eine „Vorsichtsmaßnahme" (*precautionary in nature*) der ägyptischen Regierung zu verstehen wäre und in keiner Weise gesetzliche Frauendiskriminierung oder Einschränkungen des

---

45 *Egyptian Nongovernmental Organizations Coalition*, Shadow Report on CEDAW, Kairo 2000; *Carin Benninger-Budel*, Violence against Women in Egypt. A report prepared by the World Organization against Torture, Genf 2000.

46 *United Nations*, Government of the Arab Republic of Egypt, Responses to the list of issues and questions for consideration of the third and combined fourth and fifth periodic reports, CEDAW/PSWG/2001/1/CRP.2/Add.3 (23 October 2000).

Artikels 40 der Verfassung erlauben würde. In einem zweiten Schritt, der nun vom NCW in Gang gesetzt und weiter unterstützt würde, sollten die notwendigen Schritte durchgeführt und Zustimmungen erreicht werden, die eine Rücknahme des Vorbehalts ermöglichen würden. Hinsichtlich des Vorbehalts zu Artikel 16 würde das neue Gesetz No.1 (2000) jetzt nicht nur Männern, sondern auch Frauen die bereits in der *Šarīʿa* verankerte Möglichkeit der Scheidung durch „Zurückweisung" (*repudation*; *ḫulʿ*) eröffnen – allerdings verbunden mit finanziellen Verlusten. Die Einführung von Familiengerichten und vereinfachten Verfahrensregeln würde die Gerichtsverfahren für Scheidungen beschleunigen. Dies wäre ein erster Schritt in Richtung der Aufhebung des Vorbehalts zu Artikel 16. Hinsichtlich des Vorbehalts zu Artikel 9 (2) wurde offen zugegeben, dass das ägyptische Gesetz gegen die Verfassung verstoßen würde, dass aber die Klagen, die ägyptische Frauenverbände diesbezüglich eingereicht hätten, bisher nicht das Höchste Verfassungsgericht erreicht hätten.[47]

Im mündlichen Vortrag ergänzten die Mitglieder der Delegation diese Informationen. Zunächst wurde zum ersten Mal wirklich zugegeben, dass es in Ägypten sowohl *de jure* als auch *de facto* Diskriminierung von Frauen gäbe, und die entsprechenden Gesetze bzw. Praktiken wurden aufgezählt.[48] Während das Verfassungsgericht jetzt doch das Staatsangehörigkeitsrecht überprüfen würde, hätte ein Regierungsausschuss bereits vorgeschlagen, den Vorbehalt zu Artikel 2 zurückzuziehen, da weder die *Šarīʿa* noch andere gesetzliche Prinzipien ihn rechtfertigen würden. Nun komme es darauf an, mit Unterstützung der Regierung, der Zivilgesellschaft und der Al-Azhar Universität das Parlament zu überzeugen.

Alle Sachverständigen des Ausschusses begrüßten die Fortschritte, gaben aber auch kritische Anmerkungen und Empfehlungen, von denen hier nur die relevantesten für das Thema dieses Aufsatzes wiedergegeben werden können. Die italienische und türkische Sachverständige betonten, dass es an der Zeit wäre, die Vorbehalte zurückzuziehen; die tunesische befürwortete die „weise und dynamische Lesart der religiösen Texte", die zu dem neuen Scheidungsrecht

---

47 Manuskript der Einführungsrede; vgl. auch das Wortprotokoll in *United Nations*, Summary Record of the Committee on the Elimination of Discrimination against Women of its Twenty-fourth Session, 492nd Meeting (19 January 2001), CEDAW/C/SR.492, S. 2.

48 So wurde u.a. verwiesen auf die Unterrepräsentanz von Frauen im Parlament; das Fehlen von Richterinnen und Staatsanwältinnen; das diskriminierende Staatsangehörigkeitsrecht; das hohe Analphabetentum bei Frauen; viele Traditionen, die auf der angeblichen Minderwertigkeit der Frau basierten; das geschlechtsspezifisch unterschiedliche Strafmaß bei Ehebruch, das nirgends in der *Šarīʿa* zu finden wäre; die Regelung zum Reisepass des Innenministeriums, die für verfassungswidrig erklärt worden wäre; häusliche Gewalt gegen Frauen.

für Frauen geführt hätte. Andere Sachverständige zeigten allerdings auch Besorgnis, dass dies nur ein Recht für wohlhabendere Frauen wäre. Die türkische Sachverständige verwies auf die „patriarchale Mentalität, die sich des Vorwandes des islamischen Rechts bedienen würde, um Fortschritte für Frauen im Sinne des Übereinkommens zu verhindern". Die philippinische Sachverständige unterstrich die Wichtigkeit der Ergebnisse der Studie, dass der Islam „keine Barriere für die Freiheit von Frauen darstellen würde", war sich jedoch unsicher, inwieweit die Generalsekretärin des NCW denn wirklich für die ägyptische Regierung sprechen könnte. Ich selbst erbat u.a. die englische Übersetzung der Studie, die dem Ausschuss allerdings bis heute nicht zugestellt wurde.[49]

Diese Fragen und Empfehlungen fanden ihren Widerhall in den Abschließenden Bemerkungen (*concluding observations*), die der Ausschuss später verabschiedete und der ägyptischen Regierung zustellte.[50] Der sechste und siebte Staatenbericht (fällig in den Jahren 2002 und 2006) ist inzwischen mit Verspätung eingetroffen und wird vom Ausschuss 2009 behandelt werden. 2004 wurde das ägyptische Staatsangehörigkeitsrecht dahingehend geändert, dass ägyptische Frauen, die mit einem Ausländer verheiratet sind, ihren Kindern die ägyptische Staatsangehörigkeit geben können.[51] Der Vorbehalt gegen Artikel 9 (2) wurde 2007 zurückgezogen.

Die Interaktion Ägyptens mit dem Vertragsausschuss für CEDAW habe ich aus verschiedenen Gründen so umfassend dargestellt. Zum einen wollte ich aufzeigen, wie fortschrittliche Kräfte im Land sich in den letzten Jahrzehnten bemüht haben, die Begründungen der Vorbehalte von ihrem nicht immer zutreffenden religiösen Rechtskontext zu befreien, Widersprüche zwischen Verfassungsanspruch und einfachem Recht oder auch Diskrepanzen zwischen nichtdiskriminierenden Gesetzen und ihrer Umsetzung im Rahmen patriarchalen Denkens aufzuzeigen und die Rechtssituation für Frauen im Sinne des Übereinkommens zu verbessern. Zum anderen ist jener Ansatz dieser fortschrittlichen

---

49 *United Nations*, Summary Record…, a.a.O. (Fn. 47), S. 3, Absätze 9-12, S. 4, Absatz 19, S. 5 f., Absätze 23-31; *United Nations*, Summary Record of the Committee on the Elimination of Discrimination against Women of its Twenty-fourth Session, 493rd Meeting (19 January 2001), CEDAW/C/SR.493, S. 2-9.

50 *United Nations,* Report of the Committee on the Elimination of Discrimination against Women 2001, Twenty-fourth and Twenty-fifth Sessions, UN General Assembly, Official Documents, Fifty-sixth Session, Supplement No. 38, A/56/38, S. 33-37.

51 *Al-Ahram,* Weekly, Issue No. 697, 1-7 Juli 2004, http://weekly.ahram.org.eg/2004/697/eg10.htm (zuletzt aufgerufen am 31 August 2008). Allerdings wurde allen, die vor der Annahme des Gesetzes geboren sind, nur ein Jahr eingeräumt, sich mit den entsprechenden Dokumenten um die ägyptische Staatsangehörigkeit zu bewerben, und der Eintritt in die Armee, Polizei und den öffentlichen Dienst bleibt ihnen aus „nationalen Sicherheitsgründen" verwehrt.

Kräfte bedeutsam, das religiöse Recht und seine Quellen genau zu lesen und ggf. eine moderne Interpretation zu entwickeln, ein Ansatz, der von Sachverständigen aus islamisch geprägten Staaten im Ausschuss immer wieder vertreten und empfohlen wurde. Ob CEDAW einen Anteil an der positiven Gesetzesentwicklung hat, kann nur vermutet werden, doch wären die Aussagen des Ausschusses auf jeden Fall nur **ein** Faktor in einem Kaleidoskop von Einflüssen, zu denen auch die Auswirkungen der Weltfrauenkonferenzen der Vereinten Nationen sowie Entwicklungen in anderen arabischen islamisch geprägten Staaten gehören. Festzuhalten ist auf jeden Fall, dass die Empfehlungen des Ausschusses die fortschrittlichen Kräfte in Regierung und Zivilgesellschaft stärken und den Handlungsbedarf mit Hinweis auf die international eingegangenen Verpflichtungen als dringlich erscheinen lassen. Dass der Widerstand im Parlament und in einzelnen Ministerien nicht zu unterschätzen ist, zeigt sich immer wieder und erklärt die Langsamkeit der Entwicklung.

II. Marokko

Marokko trat dem Übereinkommen 1993 bei, allerdings mit denselben Vorbehalten wie auch andere islamisch geprägte Staaten seiner Region, d.h. mit allgemein gefassten Erklärungen zu den Artikeln 2 und 15 (4) und Vorbehalten zu den Artikeln 9 (2), 16, und 29 (1), die es mit Hinweisen auf islamisches Recht oder sonstiges nationales Recht begründete.[52] Die Vorbehalte und ihre Rechtfertigungsversuche durch die Regierung im ersten Staatenbericht sind nicht überraschend, obwohl Marokko entsprechende Vorschriften im ICCPR und in der CRC nicht mit Vorbehalten belegte.

Connors hat aufgezeigt, wie Marokko noch im Dritten Ausschuss des VN-Wirtschafts- und Sozialrats (*Economic and Social Council*, ECOSOC) zusammen mit anderen islamisch geprägten Staaten versucht hatte, den Entwurf des Übereinkommens dahingehend zu verändern, dass er islamischem Personenstandsrecht entsprechen würde. Der marokkanische Vertreter argumentierte damals, dass die unterschiedlichen Rollen von Frauen und Männern nicht „traditionell" wären, sondern sich „aus dem tiefen Bewusstsein der menschlichen Rasse ergeben würden." Würden Männer und Frauen gleiche Rechte genießen und ausüben, würde dies „das psychische und moralische Gleichgewicht der Kinder" beeinflussen.[53] Es ist daher nicht von ungefähr, dass Marokko, wie bereits erwähnt, sich bei der Abstimmung über das Übereinkommen der Stimme enthielt. In den Formulierungen der Erklärungen und Vor-

---

52 *United Nations*, Declarations, reservations, objections and notifications of withdrawal of reservations relating to the Convention on the Elimination of All Forms of Discrimination against Women, CEDAW/SP/1994/2, S. 20 f.

53 *Jane Connors*, The Women's Convention..., a.a.O. (Fn. 1), S. 94.

behalte selbst verweist Marokko auf das islamische Personenstandsrecht und seine Verwurzelung in der *Šarīʿa*, und zwar ähnlich wie Ägypten, auf die Bevorzugung der Frau im ehelichen Rahmen und auf die Notwendigkeit, ein Gleichgewicht zwischen dieser Bevorzugung und den Pflichten des Mannes zu erzielen und die Geschlossenheit der Familie zu sichern.

Ich habe 2004 eine kurze Analyse der umständlichen marokkanischen Rechtfertigungsversuche seiner Erklärungen und Vorbehalte in seinem ersten Staatenbericht aufgezeigt und analysiert, wie die biologischen Unterschiede von Mann und Frau uminterpretiert werden, um funktionale Rollenunterschiede im Sinne herkömmlicher Stereotypen (*what is most suited to them*) und damit unterschiedliche Rechte zu begründen. Gleichzeitig propagierte Marokko, dass die islamische Werteidentität mit den universalen Menschenrechten zu verbinden wäre. Unter Beibehaltung des marokkanischen Rechtssystems sollten allerdings rechtliche Fortschritte für Frauen erreicht werden.[54]

Der Ausschuss diskutierte Marokkos ersten Bericht, den es fast pünktlich im September 1994 einreichte, erst 1997. Mayer hat diese frühe Interaktion des Ausschusses mit der marokkanischen Regierungsdelegation mehrfach und zuletzt 2004 analysiert. Sie beschreibt, wie der Regierungsvertreter die Ergänzungsthese (*complementarity*) bezüglich der Gleichheit der Geschlechter bemühte, die Würde der Frauen beschwor und den Schutz derselben vor Unmoral. Die natürlichen Unterschiede zwischen den Geschlechtern und das islamische Recht rechtfertigten seiner Auffassung nach die Abweichungen von den Vorschriften des Übereinkommens. Zudem würden die Vorbehalte auf einem „nationalen Konsens" beruhen. Gleichzeitig verwies er, ähnlich wie 1990 der ägyptische Regierungsvertreter, auf die Gefahren des Fundamentalismus und Terrorismus und auf Marokkos begrenzte Ressourcen als Entwicklungsland.

Muslimische und nicht muslimische Mitglieder des Ausschusses kritisierten Marokko, da der Koran nicht vorgeschoben werden dürfe, um das Übereinkommen nicht umzusetzen, islamische Vorschriften nicht im Gegensatz zum Übereinkommen stünden und zudem andere islamisch geprägte Vertragsstaaten größere Fortschritte als Marokko gemacht hätten. Religiöser Fundamentalismus wäre nicht auf islamisch geprägte Länder begrenzt, sondern auch in christlichen Ländern vorhanden. Und von einem nationalen Konsens könnte kaum die Rede sein, wenn Frauen aufgrund von Analphabetismus und anderer Beschränkungen nur wenig im öffentlichen Raum der marokkanischen Gesellschaft präsent wären.[55]

---

54 *Hanna Beate Schöpp-Schilling*, Reservations to CEDAW..., a.a.O. (Fn. 22), S. 33.

55 *Ann E. Mayer*, Internationalizing the Conversation..., a.a.O. (Fn. 7), S. 146-149.

Die Diskussion des zweiten Berichts Marokkos, der von Marokko 1999 eingereicht und 2003 vom Ausschuss diskutiert wurde, soll hier nur kurz beleuchtet werden, da auch 2003 keine wesentlichen Änderungen hinsichtlich einer Verbesserung der Gesetze, die marokkanische Frauen diskriminieren und damit hinsichtlich der Vorbehalte, erreicht waren. Erstaunlich war allerdings zu hören, dass Marokko das Übereinkommen erst 2001 in der entsprechenden Publikation (*Official Gazette*) bekannt gemacht und ihm damit erst zu diesem Zeitpunkt den Status des geltenden Rechts gegeben hatte, so dass es oberhalb des einfachen marokkanischen Rechts, aber unterhalb der Verfassung angesiedelt war. Die Delegation verwies auch auf einen Gesetzesentwurf im Parlament, der das Staatsangehörigkeitsrecht für Frauen im Sinne des Übereinkommens verändern und damit die Rücknahme der Vorbehalte ermöglichen würde. Auch würde eine Kommission, der Frauen, religiöse Führer und andere Personen angehörten, das Personenstandsrecht überprüfen. Bei allen Neuerungen müsste eine Balance zwischen dem internationalen Recht und der *Šarīʿa* erreicht werden, die Gesellschaft dürfte nicht destabilisiert werden. Die Sachverständigen begrüßten die Fortschritte, forderten aber erneut die Rücknahme der Vorbehalte und eine Änderung der Verfassung, damit diese nicht länger im Konflikt mit dem Übereinkommen als nun geltendem Recht stehen würde.[56]

Für die Einschätzung der neuesten positiven, wenn auch widersprüchlichen frauenpolitischen Entwicklungen in Marokko gibt Salimes diskussionswürdige Analyse aufschlussreiche Einblicke. Sie war allerdings den Ausschussmitgliedern bei der Diskussion des kombinierten dritten und vierten Staatenberichts im Januar 2008 nicht bekannt, und die von Salime aufgeworfenen Thesen wurden daher auch nicht thematisiert. Sie untersucht die Chancen und Strategien, die sowohl liberal feministische als auch an der *Šarīʿa* orientierte marokkanische Frauengruppen im Rahmen der marokkanischen Terrorismusbekämpfung seit 2003 für ihre durchaus unterschiedlichen frauenpolitischen Forderungen wahrnehmen und nutzen konnten. Dies war laut Salime möglich, weil die von den USA initiierte und u.a. von Marokko nach dem Terrorattentat von Casablanca im Mai 2003 unterstützte *Greater Middle East Initiative* einerseits der Bekämpfung des Terrors dienen soll, andererseits aber auch den Bemühungen um neoliberales wirtschaftliches Denken und Handeln sowie Demokratisierung und Modernisierung. Damit wäre auch dem marokkanischen König ein größerer Handlungsspielraum für Reformen eröffnet worden. Deutlich wird

56 *United Nations*, Summary Record of the Committee on the Elimination of Discrimination against Women of its Twenty-ninth Session, 626th Meeting, CEDAW/C/SR.626 (15 July 2003); *United Nations*, Summary Record of the Committee on the Elimination of Discrimination against Women of its Twenty-ninth Session, 627th Meeting, CEDAW/C/SR.627 (15 July 2003).

jedenfalls durch Salimes Analyse, dass politisch-soziale Umbrüche immer auch Chancen für Frauen bieten.[57]

Der kombinierte dritte und vierte Staatenbericht enthielt viele positiv einzuschätzende Informationen zu gesetzlichen und institutionellen Entwicklungen sowie Programmen, die marokkanischen Frauen u.a. im Bereich der islamischen „Adoption" im Strafvollzug, im Strafgesetzbuch, im Wahlrecht, im Staatsangehörigkeits-, Ehe- und Familienrecht oder in der Förderung von Bildungs- und Erwerbschancen auf dem Lande zugute kommen sollten. Wichtig waren auch neue Informationen zu den Vorbehalten. So hatte der marokkanische König bereits 2005[58] verkündet, dass jedes marokkanische Kind ab sofort die Staatsangehörigkeit seiner Mutter erhalten würde. Das Justizministerium hatte zum Frauentag am 8. März 2006 die Rücknahme bzw. Revision und Neuformulierung von Erklärungen und Vorbehalten verkündet, und zwar Rücknahme hinsichtlich der Artikel 9 (2), 15 (4) und der Artikel 16 (1) (f)[59] und 16 (2) sowie Präzisierung der Vorbehalte zu den übrigen Teilen des Artikels 16 und des Artikels 2 (2).

Diese Information wurde im Bericht mehrfach wiederholt. In den schriftlichen Antworten auf die schriftlichen Fragen des Ausschusses verwies Marokko Ende 2007 auf eine baldige Mitteilung an den Generalsekretär der Vereinten Nationen über den geplanten Zeitrahmen für die Rücknahmen und Umformulierungen.[60] In der mündlichen Einführung berichtete die Delegationsleiterin, dass das Kabinett gerade in seiner jüngsten Sitzung die vom Justizministerium angekündigte Rücknahme der Vorbehalte und Erklärungen sowie die Revision der übrigen Vorbehalte gebilligt hätte. Tatsächlich aber waren aber im Januar 2008 noch keine entsprechenden Mitteilungen bei der Vertragsabteilung der Vereinten Nationen eingegangen, und auch in der im Mai von der VN herausgegebenen

---

57 *Zakia Salime*, „The War on Terrorism: Appropriation and Subversion by Moroccan Women", in: Signs, 33/1, Chicago 2007, S. 1-24.

58 Die englische Version ist in der Angabe des Datums widersprüchlich, in Absatz 28 wird vom 30. Juli 2006 [sic!] gesprochen, in Absatz 169 vom 30. Juli 2005. Es muss sich aber korrekterweise um das Jahr 2005 handeln, da das königliche Dekret den Äußerungen des Justizministeriums vorangegangen sein muss.

59 *United Nations*, Government of Morocco, Combined third and fourth periodic report of States Parties, CEDAW/C/MAR/4 (18 September 2006), S. 7, Absatz 29. Der Hinweis auf Artikel 16 (1) (f) ist falsch, da später davon die Rede ist, dass Ägypten seinen Vorbehalt gegenüber der Gleichberechtigung in der Familienplanung zurückzogen habe, die von Artikel 16 (1) (e) abgedeckt wird. Auch die Frauenministerin verwies auf Artikel 16 (1) (e) in ihrer mündlichen Präsentation.

60 *United Nations*, Government of Morocco, Responses to the list of issues and questions for consideration of the combined third and fourth periodic reports, CEDAW/C/MAR/Q/4/Add.1 (15 November 2007), S. 2.

Übersicht über Vorbehalte zu CEDAW waren bei Marokko noch keine Änderungen verzeichnet.[61] Offensichtlich waren also die affirmativ formulierten Informationen im Staatenbericht und in der Einführungsrede nur als Willensbekundungen und nicht als Tatsachen zu verstehen, da die politischen und gesetzgebenden Prozesse auch im Januar noch nicht abgeschlossen waren. Möglicherweise sollten derartige Bekundungen auf internationaler Ebene aber auch die Entwicklung selbst beschleunigen?

Festzuhalten ist jedoch, dass gesetzliche und andere Fortschritte gemacht wurden, die dem Ausschuss in der Sitzung sowohl elektronisch als auch mit einer Hochglanzbroschüre noch einmal vor Augen geführt wurden, auch wenn verschiedene Alternativberichte auf weiterhin bestehende Formen von Diskriminierung marokkanischer Frauen verwiesen.[62] U.a. müssen Frauen nicht mehr die Erlaubnis ihrer Ehemänner zum Erhalt eines Reisepasses oder zur Berufsausübung einholen; das Heiratsalter ist für Männer und Frauen auf 18 Jahre gesetzt; andere altersbezogene Ungleichheiten wie auch einige Ungleichheiten im Erbrecht sind aufgehoben; Frauen sind ihren Ehemännern nicht mehr zum Gehorsam verpflichtet, sondern tragen gemeinsam mit ihm alle Rechte und Pflichten. Polygamie ist zwar noch möglich, doch muss sie durch einen Richter genehmigt werden und kann auch zur für die Frau finanziell abgesicherten Scheidung führen. Die Frau kann aber auch weitere Ehen des Mannes im Rahmen des Ehevertrags von vornherein ausschließen. Auch die zweite Frau muss über die schon bestehende eheliche Situation des zukünftigen Ehemannes informiert werden und ihre schriftliche Einwilligung geben. Verstoßung der Ehefrau ist nicht mehr möglich, eine Auflösung der Ehe muss durch ein Gericht erfolgen. Neben den im islamischen Recht bekannten Gründen für einen Scheidungsantrag durch die Frau gibt es jetzt auch Scheidung aufgrund eines gemeinsamen Scheidungswillens und aufgrund unlösbarer gravierender Differenzen zwischen den Ehepartnern.[63]

In der Diskussion richteten sich die Fragen der Sachverständigen auf den offensichtlich noch immer offenen Zeitplan für die Rücknahme der Vorbehalte, auf die nicht näher spezifizierten Neuformulierungen von Vorbehalten und auf die Diskrepanz zwischen den neuen Gesetzen und Programmen und der tatsächlichen Lebensrealität marokkanischer Frauen, vor allem auf dem Lande. In Verkennung der völkerrechtlichen Situation betonte die Delegationsleiterin erneut, dass die Vorbehalte faktisch nicht mehr gültig wären, auch wenn es noch der

61 *United Nations,* Declarations, reservations, objections and notifications of withdrawal of reservations relating to the Convention on the Elimination of All Forms of Discrimination against Women, CEDAW/SP/2008/2, S. 22 f., 63.

62 U.a. der ausführliche Bericht der *Association Démocratique des Femmes des Maroc.*

63 *United Nations*, Government of Morocco..., a.a.O. (Fn. 59), S. 55-62.

Zustimmung verschiedener Regierungsgremien bedürfe.[64] In seinen Abschließenden Bemerkungen betonte der Ausschuss neben der Würdigung der vielen gesetzlichen und institutionellen Fortschritte erneut die Notwendigkeit, die Vereinten Nationen umgehend über die Rücknahme und Änderung von Vorbehalten und Erklärungen zu informieren. Darüber hinaus wiederholte er seine Auffassung, dass die verbleibenden Erklärungen und Vorbehalte weiterhin gegen Ziel und Zweck des Übereinkommens verstoßen würden, so dass auch hier eine Rücknahme geboten wäre, um marokkanische Frauen in den vollen Genuss aller Vorschriften des Übereinkommens kommen zu lassen.[65]

III. Saudi Arabien

Saudi Arabien ratifizierte das Übereinkommen erst im Jahr 2000 im Rahmen seiner vorsichtigen Reformprozesse. Die Ratifikation erfolgte allerdings mit spezifisch gefassten Vorbehalten gegen die Artikel 9 (2) und 29 (1) sowie mit einem allgemein gehaltenen Vorbehalt, dass das Königreich nicht verpflichtet sei, die Vorschriften des Übereinkommens zu befolgen, wenn diese den „Normen islamischen Rechts" widersprechen würden. Ähnlich allgemein gehaltene Vorbehalte hatte Saudi Arabien auch bei seinem Beitritt zum CERD und zur CRC gemacht. Wie ich bereits ausgeführt habe, werden Erklärungen und allgemein gehaltene Vorbehalte dieser Art vom Ausschuss als unvereinbar mit dem Ziel und Zweck des Übereinkommens angesehen. Einspruch in eben diesem Sinn legten auch eine Reihe westeuropäischer Staaten ein.[66]

Mit einiger Verspätung[67] reichte Saudi Arabien 2006 einen kombinierten ersten und zweiten Bericht ein. Dieser wurde im Januar 2008 im Ausschuss diskutiert, zusammen mit den schriftlichen Antworten zu den schriftlichen Fragen des Ausschusses, der „philosophisch-politischen" Einführungsrede der Delegations-

---

64 *United Nations*, Summary Record of the Committee on the Elimination of Discrimination of its Fortieth Session, 824th meeting, CEDAW/C/SR.824, S. 4, Absatz 25.

65 *United Nations*, Concluding Comments of the Committee on the Elimination of Discrimination of its Fortieth Session, CEDAW/C/MAR/CO/4 (8 April 2008), S. 3, Absätze 14 und 15. Das Dokument ist einsehbar unter http:www2.ohchr.org/english/bodies/cedaw/docs/CEDAW.C.MAR.CO.4_en.pdf. (zuletzt aufgerufen am 15. Juli 2009).

66 *United Nations,* Declarations, reservations, objections and notifications of withdrawal of reservations relating to the Convention on the Elimination of All Forms of Discrimination against Women, CEDAW/SP/2002/2; es handelt sich um die Vertragsstaaten Österreich, Dänemark, Finnland, Frankreich, Deutschland, Irland, die Niederlande, Norwegen, Portugal, Spanien, Schweden, Großbritannien.

67 Der erste Staatenbericht wäre im Oktober 2001, der zweite im Oktober 2005 fällig gewesen. Der kombinierte erste und zweite Bericht wurde im September 2006 eingereicht, *United Nations*, Government of Saudi Arabia, Combined initial and second periodic reports, CEDAW/C/SAU/2 (29 March 2007).

leitung sowie der elektronischen Präsentation der durchaus beachtlichen frauenspezifischen gesetzlichen, programmbezogenen und institutionellen Maßnahmen Saudi Arabiens in den Bereichen der politischen Beteiligung von Frauen, ihrer Erwerbsarbeit, ihrer Bildungschancen und in der Sozialpolitik. Insgesamt vier, z.T. vertrauliche Alternativberichte, einschließlich eines anonymen Berichts einer Frauengruppe aus Saudi Arabien, dokumentierten die Menschenrechtsverletzungen, die Frauen in diesem Land erfahren, insbesondere aufgrund des Systems der „männlichen Vormundschaft" sowie der fast vollständige Trennung der Geschlechter in allen Bereichen der Öffentlichkeit einschließlich der Bildung und Erwerbsarbeit. So wurden fünf Gebiete – eigenständige Rechtsfähigkeit, politische Partizipation, Bildungspolitik, Erwerbsarbeit, Familienrecht – aufgezeigt, in denen Frauen in Saudi Arabien auf der Grundlage ihres Geschlechts diskriminiert würden, die Diskriminierung von Wanderarbeitnehmerinnen und die rechtliche und faktische Situation der häuslichen Gewalt gegen Frauen wurden thematisiert.

Die Delegation war mit 45 Teilnehmenden, davon 18 Frauen, überraschend und außergewöhnlich groß. Frauen saßen auch mit dem Delegationsleiter, dem stellvertretenden Präsidenten der staatlichen Menschenrechtskommission, auf dem Podium. Wie bei Ägypten und Marokko werde ich auch bei Saudi Arabien aufzeigen, mit welchen Argumenten die Regierungsvertreter den allgemein gefassten und den konkret zu Artikel 9 (2) formulierten Vorbehalt verteidigten, welches Gleichheitskonzept sie verfolgten und wie der Ausschuss auf diese Argumente in seinen Fragen und seinen Abschließenden Bemerkungen reagierte. Da ich eine gewisse Variation in den Argumentationsmustern erkennen kann, werde ich diese detailliert aufzeigen, obwohl alle Argumente – in welcher Form auch immer – auf die eine Position hinauslaufen, dass es in Saudi Arabien keine Gesetze gäbe, die Frauen diskriminieren würden.

Im Bericht selbst erklärte Saudi Arabien zunächst, dass die Ratifikation des Übereinkommens in der Tatsache gründen würde, dass „sein allgemeiner Inhalt" mit dem Ansatz des Landes übereinstimmen würde, die Rechte von Frauen zu schützen. Die Ratifikation dokumentierte auch den Wunsch des Landes, durch die Vorschriften des Übereinkommens gebunden zu sein, und sie würde die Entschlossenheit des Königreichs unterstreichen, sich der Verantwortung um die Fürsorge für die Rechte von Frauen im Land im Rahmen der ausgesprochenen Vorbehalte zu stellen. Die nachfolgende Rechtfertigung, dass diese Vorbehalte im Einklang mit den Artikeln 19-23 des Wiener Übereinkommens über das Recht der Verträge (*Vienna Convention on the Law of Treaties,* VCLT) wären, „insbesondere, da sie mit dem Thema des Übereinkommens in Einklang stünden und nicht unvereinbar mit seinem Zweck wären", wie sich im Bericht zeigen würde, ist allerdings weder richtig noch verständlich angesichts der Feststellungen anderer Vertragsstaaten, die in ihrem Einspruch gegen diese Vorbehalte diese als inakzeptabel bezeichnet hatten. Diese falschen Behauptungen konnten auch nicht durch die anschließenden Ausführungen Saudi Arabiens korrigiert werden: als islamischer Staat, in dem es keine Trennung von Staat und Kirche gäbe wie in nichtislamischen Ländern, sei es an sein „Grundgesetz" (*Basic Law*) und damit an die islamische *Šarīʿa* gebunden; es könnte in seiner Gesetzgebung keine neuen Prinzipien entwickeln, die in Buchstaben oder Geist der *Šarīʿa* entgegenstünden. Die Vorbehalte hätten daher „erklärenden Charakter" (*explanatory reservation*), der diesem Sachverhalt Genüge tun sollte, dass nämlich Saudi Arabien das Übereinkommen in einem Rahmen anwenden würde, der den Prinzipien der islamischen *Šarīʿa* nicht widersprechen würde.[68] Mayer hat aufgezeigt, dass sich das *Basic Law* Saudi Arabiens in keiner Vorschrift direkt auf Frauenrechte bezieht, sondern vielmehr große Bedeutung auf die Familie legt.[69]

In den Ausführungen zu den Rahmenartikeln legte Saudi Arabien die islamischen Vorstellungen zum Gleichheitsbegriff bezüglich der Geschlechter dar. Dabei wurde auch eine offene Kritik an den nichtislamischen Bemühungen um Gleichheit deutlich. Die seit den Griechen geltende und im modernen Liberalismus eines John Locke aufgegriffene Unterscheidung zwischen einer öffentlichen und einer privaten Sphäre, in denen Frauen als das schwächere Geschlecht der letzteren zugeordnet wären, würde „im Prinzip" für den Islam nicht gelten. Implizit wurde damit auch die Notwendigkeit von Frauenbewegungen in der islamischen Welt negiert, die in der nichtislamischen Welt mit „antithetischen Haltungen ..., die für die Auflösung der Familie, den Schutz von Frauen vor Unterjochung und für das Vorrücken von Frauen in die öffentliche Sphäre plädierten, um dort Positionen zu erreichen, die bisher von Männern monopolisiert wären.[70]

Während Saudi Arabien einerseits die im Übereinkommen enthaltene Vorschrift unterstrich, dass Gleichbehandlung von Männern und Frauen aufgrund der biologisch bedingten Verschiedenheit nicht immer identische Behandlung bedeuten dürfte, also eine durchaus richtige Erkenntnis, die über den rein formalen Gleichheitsbegriff hinausgeht, fiel die Argumentation dann auf jenen Gleichheitsbegriff zurück, der die Geschlechter als komplementär sieht und ihnen sich

---

68 *United Nations*, Government of Saudi Arabia…, a.a.O. (Fn. 67), S. 10 f.

69 *Ann E. Mayer*, Islam and Human Rights…, a.a.O. (Fn. 1), S. 139.

70 "*With Locke, modern liberalism adopted this position* […] *This has had subsequent implications in the form of the antithetical attitudes of women's movements, calling for the dissolution of the family, protection of women from subjugation and the advancement of women toward the public domain to occupy the position previously monopolized by men.*"; *United Nations*, Government of Saudi Arabia…, a.a.O. (Fn. 67), S. 12.

wechselseitig bedingende Aufgaben, Pflichten und Rechte zuschreibt. Betont wurde ähnlich wie von Ägypten, dass in diesem Rahmen Frauen in der islamischen *Šarīʿa* sogar Privilegien zugestanden würden und sie laut *Šarīʿa* auch stärker an islamischen Werten partizipierten als Männer.[71] An anderer Stelle wurde festgestellt, dass „Gleichheit bezüglich von Rechten und Pflichten, der Menschlichkeit, der moralischen und anderen Pflichten" bestünde, aber nicht bezüglich der „Eigenarten und Funktionen, bei denen eine Gleichheit nicht im Interesse einer Frau sei".[72] Des weiteren zitierte Saudi Arabien diverse Artikel seines *Basic Law* und verwies auf weitere Gesetze im politischen Bereich, in der Erwerbsarbeit im privaten und staatlichen Sektor, in der Familienfürsorge, in der Bildung und Bekämpfung des Analphabetentums und in der Gesundheitsfürsorge, die den Staat verpflichteten, Geschlechtergleichheit in öffentlichen Rechten und Pflichten auf der Grundlage der *Šarīʿa* und damit volle Rechte für Frauen „seit 1400 Jahren" zu gewähren.

Im Verlauf des Berichts ging Saudi Arabien gar nicht oder nur kurz auf weitere Bereiche an, in denen jene rechtliche Ungleichheit herrscht, die auch aus anderen islamisch geprägten Staaten bekannt ist. So betonte der Vertragsstaat ausdrücklich, keinen Vorbehalt zur politischen Beteiligung von Frauen eingelegt zu haben, ein Beweis dafür, dass diese bevorstünde und nur eine Frage der Organisation sei. Auf Artikel 9 (2) – Weitergabe der Staatsangehörigkeit der Frau an ihre Kinder bei Ehe mit einem Ausländer – ging der Bericht gar nicht ein. Zu Artikel 15 (4) wurde festgestellt, dass Frauen im Vertragsstaat nach der islamischen *Šarīʿa* das Recht auf Freizügigkeit hinsichtlich des Reisens und der Wahl ihres Wohnsitzes hätten und auch in rechtlichen Verfahren den Männern gleichgestellt wären. Artikel 16 wurde nur sehr kurz behandelt, indem die unterschiedlichen Rechte nach dem Personenstandsrecht im Rahmen der *Šarīʿa* nicht thematisiert wurden (das unterschiedliche Erbrecht war vorher als Privileg, nicht als Diskriminierung behandelt worden).

Mit ähnlich ausweichenden und nicht immer logischen bzw. mit z.T. sogar widersprüchlichen Argumenten beantwortete Saudi Arabien die schriftlichen

---

71 "*These values include filial piety, the bond of kinship and the raising of children. Women enjoy a more favourable share of these than men: the Islamic Shariah has more to say about the virtue of caring for daughters than for sons, a mother's right over her children is three times that of a father's and a woman's right of custody of her infant child takes precedence over a man's, in principle.*"; *United Nations*, Government of Saudi Arabia..., a.a.O. (Fn. 67), S. 11 f.

72 "*God created mankind from Adam and Eve and between Adam and his wife eve, there was equality in respect of rights and duties, humanity and obligation but not in respect of characteristics and functions, where equality would not be in a woman's interest.*"; *United Nations*, Government of Saudi Arabia..., a.a.O. (Fn. 67), S. 14 f.

Fragen des Ausschusses nach dem konkreten Umfang der Auswirkungen der Vorbehalte auf die Umsetzung des Übereinkommens. So betonte es erneut, dass die islamische *Šarīʿa* sich mit den allgemeinen Prinzipien des Übereinkommens vertragen würde, obwohl es andererseits zugab, dass es eine „kleine Ungleichheit" bezüglich der „umzusetzenden Vorschriften" gäbe. Eine Beurteilung derartiger „Ungleichheiten" würde von den juristischen Autoritäten anhand einzelner Fälle im Vergleich mit den Texten der islamischen *Šarīʿa* vollzogen. Die im Bericht angeführte „erklärende Natur" des allgemein gefassten Vorbehalts wurde jetzt zur „Vorsorgemaßnahme" (*precautionary measure*) erklärt, allerdings anders als im Falle Ägyptens begründet. Es hätte sich gezeigt, dass Menschenrechtsinstrumente nach deren Inkrafttreten sehr schnell Interpretationen unterworfen würden, die nicht nur über den eigentlichen (wörtlichen) Inhalt (*literal content*) des Vertrages hinausgingen, sondern nach Auffassung einiger Sachverständiger des „subcommittees"[73] sogar zu einer Kernvorschrift würden.[74] Derartigen Interpretationen, die den rechtlichen Vorschriften des Königreichs widersprechen könnten, wollte Saudi Arabien vorsorglich vorbeugen. Die erneut gemachte Feststellung, dass es keinen Widerspruch gäbe zwischen den Hauptvorschriften des Übereinkommens und den Prinzipien der *Šarīʿa*, ist insofern erstaunlich, als damit das Personenstandsrecht für unwesentlich erklärt wurde.

Auch weitere konkrete, schriftlich gestellte Fragen des Ausschusses hinsichtlich der vorhandenen traditionellen Gebräuche, Praktiken und Stereotypen (Fragen 7, 11) oder der unterschiedlichen Behandlung von Frauen und Männern im Personenstandsrecht (Fragen 30 & 31) wurden nicht wirklich beantwortet. Durchgehend wurde betont, dass es keine Gesetze gäbe, die Frauen diskriminierten (z.B. hinsichtlich des Autofahrens, der politischen Beteiligung, in Gerichtsverfahren), doch wurde gleichzeitig in allgemein gehaltenen Formulierungen eingeräumt, dass es Probleme in der Praxis gäbe (Antworten zu den Fragen 8, 16).[75]

---

[73] Es ist unklar, ob hier die im Zusammenhang mit der Menschenrechtskommission aufgelöste *Sub-Commission on the Promotion and Protection of Human Rights* gemeint ist, oder ob es sich um einen Übersetzungsfehler handelt, so dass doch der Vertragsausschuss für CEDAW gemeint ist.

[74] Wahrscheinlich spielt Saudi Arabien hier auf die Bemühungen einiger VN-Mitgliedstaaten in der Nachfolge der Vierten VN-Weltfrauenkonferenz an, das Diskriminierungsverbot auf der Grundlage des Geschlechts um die sexuelle Orientierung zu erweitern, wie es inzwischen auch in Richtlinien der Europäischen Union (EU) und damit auch in Antidiskriminierungsgesetzen von EU Mitgliedstaaten enthalten ist. Diese Ausweitung oder „Interpretation" trifft auf heftigen Widerstand nicht nur islamisch geprägter, sondern auch katholischer Staaten und der Vereinigten Staaten von Amerika.

[75] *United Nations*, Government of Saudi Arabia, Responses to the list of issues and questions contained in document number CEDAW/C/SAU/Q/2, A.H.1428 (A.D. 2007), CEDAW/C/SAU/Q/2/Add.1 (18 December 2007).

Eine entsprechende Haltung zeigte die Delegation auch im mündlichen Austausch mit den Ausschussmitgliedern. Eingeleitet wurde dieser durch die Einführung der Delegationsleitung, in der u.a. dem Ausschuss eine erfolgreiche Arbeit nur dann zugestanden wurde, wenn er „objektiv" arbeiten und ein „angemessenes" (*proper*) Verständnis der Kulturen der Nationen und Völker besitzen würde. Ein derartiger Hinweis, den ich in meiner 20jährigen Erfahrung im Ausschuss noch nie gehört habe, bevor der „konstruktive Dialog" überhaupt begonnen hat, konnte nur als Warnung verstanden werden. Diese wurde mit dem Hinweis auf nicht näher spezifizierte „Mächte" (*powers*) verbunden, welche die Menschenrechte im Rahmen persönlicher Ziele politisch ausbeuteten und durch eine „Einseitigkeit" gefährden würden.[76] Es folgten längere Ausführungen über Rechte im Islam auf der Grundlage des Korans mit entsprechenden Zitaten und ein Hinweis auf die UNESCO, deren Vollversammlung in ihrer 14. Sitzungsperiode die kulturelle Eigenart eines jeden Volkes als Wert an sich proklamiert hätte. Daraus ergäbe sich, dass die in Saudi Arabien herrschende Gleichheit der Geschlechter im Rahmen ihrer Ergänzung (*complementarity*) akzeptiert werden müsste, wenn auch zuzugeben wäre, dass menschliche Haltungen, Verhaltensweisen sowie Bräuche und Traditionen diese nicht immer zur Verwirklichung brächten. Es ist bezeichnend, dass Saudi Arabien die UNESCO von 1966 und nicht, wie Ägypten, die Wiener Erklärung der Menschenrechte von 1993 zitiert, wird doch in der letzteren deutlich zum Ausdruck gebracht, dass bei aller Anerkennung kultureller Eigenarten, diese nicht eine Verletzung der Menschenrechte rechtfertigen dürfe.

Unbeeindruckt von diesen Ausführen verfolgten die Sachverständigen des Ausschusses in der Diskussion mit der Delegation ihre Fragen hinsichtlich der Konkretisierung dieser Bräuche und Traditionen und wiesen wiederholt auf offensichtliche Widersprüche zwischen der Gesetzeslage und der gesellschaftlichen Wirklichkeit des Landes hin. Sie stellten auch den genannten Gleichheitsbegriff in Frage und forderten die Rücknahme des allgemein gehaltenen

---

76 *„The success of your Committee's work depends on the extent of its objectivity and its proper understanding of the cultures of nations and peoples, especially since human rights are facing numerous challenges including, in particular, a selectivity inconsistent with the motives underlying the promotion of human rights which, unfortunately, have been subjected to political exploitation by some Powers seeking to achieve personal aims incompatible with the natural requirements of human beings who share a common origin (Adam and Eve) and a common home (the Earth) and are headed, for better or for worse, towards a common future and shared destiny."*; in: Statement of the Kingdom of Saudi Arabia, Delivered by H.E. Dr. Zaid bin Abdul Mushin Al Hussein, Geneva 17 January 2008, S. 1. Die Rede ist in arabischer Sprache eingestellt unter http://www2.ohchr.org/english/bodies/cedaw/docs/statement/statsaudiarabia.pdf (zuletzt aufgerufen am 1. Juni 2009).

Vorbehalts und des Vorbehalts zu Artikel 9 (2).[77] Diese Forderungen fanden auch ihren Niederschlag in den Abschließenden Bemerkungen. Neben den positiven Einschätzungen vieler frauenpolitischer Maßnahmen empfahl der Ausschuss, die im Übereinkommen enthaltenen Definitionen der Diskriminierung, des formalen und materiellen Gleichheitsbegriffs und der Staatenverantwortlichkeit hinsichtlich staatlicher und privater Akteure in den Gesetzen des Landes zu verankern, das Staatsangehörigkeitsrecht im Sinne des Übereinkommens zu reformieren, die Vorbehalte zu überprüfen, vor allem aber den allgemein gefassten Vorbehalt zurückzunehmen, da er gegen Ziel und Zweck des Übereinkommens verstoßen würde und auch nicht notwendig wäre, „da die Delegation versichert hätte, dass die Substanz des Übereinkommens der islamischen *Šarīʿa* nicht widersprechen würde."[78]

Es ist abzuwarten, welche der Empfehlungen Saudi Arabien bis zur nächsten Berichterstattung umsetzen wird. Zeitungsmeldungen seit dem Januar 2008 verweisen auf neue Dekrete hinsichtlich der Freizügigkeit von Frauen bzw. auf Anstrengungen politischer und religiöser Kräfte zur Verhinderung von häuslicher Gewalt und von einer Verheiratung minderjähriger Mädchen. Wie im Staatenbericht ausgeführt wurde, ist das Übereinkommen gültiges Recht in Saudi Arabien mit der Einschränkung durch die Vorbehalte. Vor Gericht oder anderen juristischen Strukturen oder Strukturen der Verwaltung können Frauen sich angeblich darauf beziehen, doch ist ein Erfolg fraglich, da der allgemein gehaltene Vorbehalt jedem islamischen Text den Vorrang vor dem Text des Übereinkommens gibt und derartige Rechtsdokumente, wie Mayer analysiert hat, sich von CEDAW und anderen international anerkannten menschenrechtlichen VN-Verträgen gravierend unterscheiden.

---

[77] *United Nations*, Summary Record of the Committee on the Elimination of Discrimination against Women of its Fortieth Session, 815th Meeting (17 January 2008), CEDAW/C/SR.815, und 816th Meeting (17 January 2008), CEDAW/C/SR 816, beide sind einsehbar unter http:www2.ohchr.org/English/bodies/cedaw/docs/CEDAWSR815.pfd und .../CEDAWSR816.pdf (zuletzt aufgerufen am 1. Juni 2009).

[78] *United Nations*, Committee on the Elimination of Discrimination, Fortieth Session, Concluding Comments, CEDAW/C/SAU/CO/2, S. 3, Absätze 14 und 15, S. 6, para. 29, S. 3, para. 14, S. 2 para 11. Das Dokument ist einsehbar unter http:www2.ohchr.org/english/bodies/cedaw/docs/CEDAW.C.SAU.CO.2_en.pdf (zuletzt aufgerufen am 1. Juni 2009). Auch die beiden anderen Vertragsausschüsse, zu deren Übereinkommen Saudi Arabien allgemein jeweils einen allgemein gehaltenen Vorbehalt eingelegt hatte, hatten die Prüfung der Rücknahme (CERD, 2003) (CERD/C/62/CO/8, S. 2, Abs. 9) bzw. die Prüfung der Rücknahme oder die Präzisierung empfohlen (CRC, 2006) (CRC/C/SAU/CO/2, S. 2f, Abs.7 und 8).

F. Ausblick

Meine Analyse der Interaktion des Ausschusses mit Ägypten, Marokko und Saudi Arabien kann in diesem Rahmen nicht erschöpfend sein. Es wäre reizvoll, sie noch detaillierter durchzuführen. Darüber hinaus könnte sie für jene islamisch geprägten Vertragsstaaten von CEDAW für die letzten Jahre fortgeschrieben werden, deren erste oder zweite Präsentation ihrer Staatenberichte im Ausschuss bereits von Mayer und anderen beschrieben wurde bzw. auf jene auszudehnen, die nicht dem arabischen Kulturkreis angehören. Aufschlussreich könnte in diesem Zusammenhang auch ein Vergleich der in arabischer Sprache geschriebenen Staatenberichte mit ihren englischen oder französischen Übersetzungen sein. Auffallend ist nämlich, dass in den englischen Versionen häufig der Begriff des „sozialen Geschlechts" (*gender*) verwendet wird, obwohl es dieses Wort im Arabischen nicht gibt. Auch wäre zu prüfen, ob die Tatsache, dass das arabische Wort „جنس" (*ğins*) sowohl biologisches Geschlecht als auch Rasse bedeuten kann, Auswirkungen auf die Argumentation bzw. auf die Frauenpolitik der betreffenden Staaten hat.[79]

Diese unklare Begrifflichkeit mag auch mit ein Grund dafür sein, dass die hier besprochenen Vertragsstaaten weiterhin die Unterschiede der Geschlechter nicht nur im biologischen Sinn, sondern auch bezüglich der Einstellungen und Fähigkeiten vertreten und diese nie in Frage stellen. Zwar ist es einleuchtend, dass eine aus der Offenbarung begründete Position nicht auf historisch oder kulturell determinierte Einflüsse eingehen will, doch ist in meiner Analyse auch deutlich geworden, dass selbst in einem Bereich wie dem Staatsangehörigkeitsrecht, in dem ein Bezug auf religiöses Recht gar nicht versucht wird, die Verankerung in traditionellen Rollenstereotypen nicht wahrgenommen wird.

Meine Analysen Ägyptens, Marokkos und Saudi Arabiens haben gezeigt, dass sowohl religiöse als auch politische Gründe die Vorbehalte bestimmen, und dass grundsätzlich immer ideologisch-patriarchale Haltungen und Auffassungen Fortschritte verhindern, selbst wenn nach dem Gesetz keine Diskriminierung erlaubt ist. Gleichzeitig sind zwei Ansätze deutlich geworden, die fortschrittliche Entwicklungen im Hinblick auf nichtdiskriminierende Gesetze ermöglichen. Zum einen kann das Übereinkommen, wenn es im Vertragsstaat geltendes Recht ist, als Druckmittel eingesetzt werden, um Diskrepanzen in

79 Diesen Hinweis verdanke ich Anna Würth wie auch den Hinweis auf eine entsprechende Literaturstelle: *Nathalie Bernard-Maugiron*, „La Haute Cour Constitutionelle Egyptienne, gardien de libertés publiques", in: Le prince et son juge, Sondernummer Egypte / Monde Arabe, 1999 (2), S. 28 und Fußnote 45.

anderen Gesetzen aufzuheben. Zum anderen werden – auch mit Hilfe fortschrittlicher islamischer Kräfte – die religiösen Quellen genau gelesen und ggf. anders interpretiert und zur Rechtfertigung gesetzlicher Änderungen herangezogen. Auch die Beobachtung der Entwicklungen in einem anderen islamisch geprägten Staat kann hilfreich sein.

Die Interaktion der Vertragsstaaten mit dem Vertragsausschuss für CEDAW ist ohne Zweifel auch von Bedeutung für fortschrittliche Entwicklungen. Gerade die Sachverständigen des Ausschusses, die selbst aus islamisch geprägten Ländern kommen, wirken am glaubwürdigsten auf die jeweiligen Regierungsvertreter ein. Letztlich sind es aber politische, wirtschaftliche und soziale Entwicklungen im jeweiligen Land selbst, die den Raum schaffen, dass fortschrittlich politische Kräfte und nationale Frauen- und Menschenrechtsbewegungen die Aussagen der unabhängigen Sachverständigen auf der internationalen Ebene der Vereinten Nationen für ihre Ziele einsetzen können. Die vor allem im letzten Jahrzehnt erreichten Fortschritte stimmen durchaus hoffnungsvoll, wenn auch noch viel zu tun und für die Frauen Saudi Arabiens der Weg gerade erst betreten worden ist. Die Tatsache, dass es außerordentlich schwierig ist, die politischen Prozesse zur Rücknahme der Vorbehalte überhaupt einzuleiten oder zu Ende zu bringen, wie es im Fall Ägyptens und Marokkos offen angesprochen wurde, deutet allerdings auch darauf hin, dass es politisch vielleicht sogar weiser ist, die Vorbehalte beizubehalten und gleichzeitig rechtliche und institutionelle Fortschritte zu verwirklichen, um unterschiedliche politische Gruppierungen zu befriedigen. Dies scheint z.B. in Tunesien der Fall zu sein. Die vorsichtigen Modernisierungsprozesse allgemeiner und frauenpolitischer Art in islamisch geprägten Staaten, die von vielen Faktoren beeinflusst werden, müssen immer auch mit einer negativen Gegenreaktion rechnen. Für die männlichen Verlierer bei diesen Modernisierungsprozessen ist das Festhalten an patriarchalen Mustern immer noch ein letzter Halt, der unterstützt wird durch andere Muster, in denen Frauen zu den symbolischen Trägerinnen der Ideen von Moral, Kultur und nationalen Identität werden[80] und denen gerade aus diesem Grund eine Gleichstellung in allen Lebensbereichen verweigert wird.

Der Ausschuss wird zwar mit der Diskrepanz zwischen den Normen des Übereinkommens und der gesellschaftlichen Realität in islamisch geprägten Ländern noch lange leben müssen, doch werden seine Durchführungsmechanismen auch einen Beitrag leisten, Fortschritte zu erzielen. Das Gespräch

80 *Zakia Salime*, The War on Terrorism, a.a.O. (Fn. 57), S. 20, zitiert in diesem Zusammenhang *Valentine Mogdaham*, Gender, National Identity, and Citizenship: Reflections on the Middle East and North Africa, in: Hagar: International Science Review, 1/1, 2000, S. 41-70.

zwischen diesen Vertragsstaaten und den Sachverständigen im Vertragsausschuss für CEDAW ist ein notwendiger Baustein in einem internationalen Dialog, dem sich islamisch geprägte Länder unterwerfen und einem Dialog innerhalb der Länder selbst.[81] Das Berichtsverfahren unterstützt die auf Änderungen dringende Zivilgesellschaft als auch fortschrittliche Kräfte in Justiz und Politik. Es legitimiert, stärkt und beschleunigt ihre Bemühungen und ist manchmal auch von Erfolg gekrönt.

81 Es muss beobachtet werden, ob und in welchem Umfang die im Rahmen des Menschenrechtsrats (*Human Rights Council*, HRC) durchgeführte „allgemeine periodische Überprüfung" (*Universal Periodic Review*) von Mitgliedstaaten, in die auch die Empfehlungen der Vertragsausschüsse einfließen, ebenfalls Veränderungen bewirken wird.

Die Organisation Islamischer Konferenz im UN-Menschenrechtsrat:

Menschenrechte als Instrument staatlicher Politik

Theodor Rathgeber, Kassel

A. Die Organisation Islamischer Konferenz

Die Organisation Islamischer Konferenz (*Organisation of the Islamic Conference* / OIC; arab. *munaẓẓamat al-mu'tamar al-islāmī*) ist eine zwischenstaatliche Organisation und wurde am 25. September 1969 in Rabat (Marokko) gegründet. Saudi-Arabien hatte zur Konferenz eingeladen. Ein zentraler Beweggrund war die Besetzung der West Bank und Ost-Jerusalems durch Israel im Sechstagekrieg 1967. Nun lagen dem Islam wichtige, heilige Stätten – vor allem die Al-Aqsa-Moschee – im direkten Einflussbereich Israels. Den unmittelbaren Anlass gab Israel durch seinen Angriff auf in der Al-Aqsa-Moschee verschanzte Aufständische am 21. August 1969. Dies war in der muslimischen Welt als Entweihung der drittwichtigsten heiligen Stätte interpretiert worden.[1] Nach der militärischen Niederlage kann die Einrichtung der OIC auch als Akt der Selbstvergewisserung und als Institutionenbildung unter arabisch-islamischen Vorzeichen verstanden werden.

Über den konkreten Anlass hinaus, haben zwei Entwicklungen im internationalen Kontext wesentlich zur Entstehung und Bedeutung der OIC beigetragen. In den 1960er Jahren – im Zuge der Entkolonialisierung – begannen die USA, muslimische Bewegungen zu unterstützten, um das Vordringen des damaligen Blockrivalen, der Sowjetunion bzw. des ‚Marxismus' zu verhindern oder einzudämmen. Der Islam wurde zu einem politischen Instrumentarium. Zum zweiten wertete die erste Erdölkrise, vor allem die Erdöl produzierenden Staaten im Nahen Osten, strategisch auf. Ölressourcen verbrauchende und nachfragende Länder wie die USA oder westeuropäische Staaten bemühten sich um gute Beziehungen, insbesondere zu Saudi Arabien, stärkten der dortigen Regierung den Rücken und trugen wiederum dazu bei, deren Rückgriff auf die islamische Religion als Orientierung für das Regierungshandeln politisch hoffähig zu machen.

---

1 Zu weiteren Details der Geschichte und des Aufbaus der Organisation vgl. die Selbstdarstellung auf http://www.oic-oci.org/oicnew (zuletzt aufgerufen am 17. März 2009); *Abdullah Al-Ahsan*, The Organization of the Islamic Conference. An Introduction to an Islamic Political Institution. International Institute of Islamic Thought, Kuala Lumpur 1988.

Islam und Menschenrechte (Islam and Human Rights / الإسلام وحقوق الإنسان)
Hatem Elliesie (Hrsg./Editor), © Peter Lang Verlag: Frankfurt a.M. 2010, S. 457-473

Die 25 Gründungsmitglieder der OIC sahen in der Befreiung der Moschee und Jerusalems die zentrale Aufgabe der Organisation. Die erste Konferenz der Außenminister im saudi-arabischen Ǧidda im März 1970 beschloss die Einrichtung eines ständigen Generalsekretariats, um zwischen den Mitgliedsstaaten eine ständige Verbindung zu gewährleisten und die Aktivitäten zu koordinieren. Ǧidda wurde als vorläufiger Sitz der Organisation – bis zur geplanten Befreiung Jerusalems – festgelegt. Heute umfasst die OIC 57 Staaten[2] und fünf Staaten mit Beobachterstatus.[3]

Das dritte Treffen der Außenministerkonferenz der OIC im Februar 1972 verabschiedete die Charta der Organisation. Diese nennt als wichtigste Ziele:

- Die Stärkung der islamischen Solidarität, der politischen, ökonomischen, sozialen, kulturellen und wissenschaftlichen Kooperation unter den Mitgliedsstaaten, des Kampfs der Muslime für ihre Würde, Unabhängigkeit und nationalen Rechte.
- Die Koordinierung der Aktivitäten zum Schutz der heiligen Stätten sowie die Unterstützung der Palästinenser im Kampf um ihre Rechte und ihr Bemühen, die besetzten Gebiete zu befreien.
- Die Eliminierung jeder Form von ethnischer Diskriminierung und Kolonialismus, die Förderung der Kooperation und des Verständnisses zwischen den Mitgliedstaaten und anderen Staaten.

Die Prinzipien der Zusammenarbeit bestehen laut Charta:

- in der Gleichheit aller Mitglieder;
- im Recht auf Selbstbestimmung und Nichteinmischung in die internen Angelegenheiten eines Mitgliedsstaates;
- in der Souveränität, Unabhängigkeit und territorialen Integrität eines jeden Staates;
- in der friedlichen Konfliktlösung zwischen den Mitgliedsstaaten, etwa in Form von Verhandlungen, Mediation, Versöhnung und Schiedsgerichten;
- im Verzicht auf Gewalt in den Beziehungen zwischen den Mitgliedsstaaten.

---

2 Vgl. Annex I (I. Mitgliedstaaten der OIC), S. 472.

3 Vgl. Annex I (II. Staaten mit Beobachterstatus), S. 472.

I. Hauptorgane der OIC

Um die Aufgaben zu bewältigen, verfügt die OIC über verschiedene Organe, Institutionen und Sonderauschüsse. Die Gipfeltreffen der Staatsoberhäupter (alle drei Jahre) bestimmen die Richtlinien der OIC-Politik. Ein zweites bedeutsames Gremium ist die jährliche Konferenz der Außenminister der Mitgliedsstaaten (*Islamic Conference of Foreign Ministers*). Sie legt gemeinsame Positionen zu politischen, wirtschaftlichen und anderen Fragen fest und kontrolliert die Umsetzung der Gipfelbeschlüsse. Das Generalsekretariat ist das dritte Hauptorgan der OIC, die Exekutive, die die Beschlüsse der beiden vorgenannten Gremien umzusetzen hat.

II. Unterorganisationen der OIC

Neben den Hauptorganen existieren zahlreiche Unterorganisationen; ähnlich den Ausführungsorganen der Europäischen Union (EU). So beobachtet das islamische Friedenskomitee (*Islamic Peace Committee*) die für die OIC-Länder wichtigen Konfliktzonen des Sahel, in Afghanistan und in Kaschmir. Im kulturellen Bereich kümmert sich die islamische Organisation für Erziehung, Kultur und Wissenschaft (*Islamic Educational, Scientific and Cultural Organization*) darum, die islamische Lehre in den Lehrplänen der Bildungseinrichtungen muslimischer Staaten zu verankern und die islamische Kultur vor der kulturellen Überlagerung aus dem *Westen* zu schützen. Im wirtschaftlichen Bereich von Bedeutung ist u.a. die islamische Entwicklungsbank (*Islamic Development Bank*) und der ständige Ausschuss für Wirtschaft und Handelsbeziehungen (*Standing Committee for Economic and Trade Cooperation* – COMCEC). Die Entwicklungsbank wird im Wesentlichen durch die Öl exportierenden Staaten finanziert. Insbesondere Saudi-Arabien versucht, hierüber seinen Einfluss und seinen Politikansatz in der islamischen Staatenwelt geltend zu machen. Ärmere Länder sehen in der OIC und der Entwicklungsbank eine Möglichkeit, Hilfe außerhalb von Weltbank und Internationalem Währungsfond zu erhalten. In vielen Bereichen der Entwicklungshilfe für islamisch geprägte Staaten arbeitet die OIC mit den Vereinten Nationen zusammen.

Insgesamt unterhält die OIC einen komplexen Apparat internationaler Konsultation und Kooperation. Die OIC selber weist eine große Vielfalt in ihrer Mitgliederstruktur auf. Zur OIC gehören Monarchien, Republiken, Konservative, Radikale, Verbündete *westlicher* Länder und Kritiker *westlicher* Länder.[4] Innerhalb der Mitgliedsstaaten gibt es u.a. einen Wettbewerb der Golfstaaten mit Saudi Arabien. Trotz der Vielfalt in der Mitgliederstruktur gelingt es der OIC, in den offiziellen Äußerungen ein beachtliches Maß an grundlegender Übereinstimmung und konzertiertem Handeln zum Ausdruck zu bringen.

---

[4] Vgl. Annex I (I. Mitgliedstaaten der OIC), S. 472.

In den Deklarationen der Gipfel und der Außenminister wurde regelmäßig die Okkupation Palästinas und Jerusalems verurteilt, aber auch z. B. der Krieg in Bosnien und im Kosovo behandelt. So beteiligten sich die Mitgliedsstaaten der OIC an der Entsendung internationaler Schutztruppen und der Bewaffnung der Bosnier bzw. Albaner zur Selbstverteidigung. Unbeschadet der strategischen Vernetzung islamischer Staaten und der gemeinsamen Definition der politischen Identität und Zugehörigkeit durch den islamischen Glauben versteht sich die OIC wiederum nicht als Einrichtung, um eine islamische Weltgemeinschaft (*umma*) anzustreben. Die größte Kohärenz der OIC existiert beim Thema Palästina.

III. Kairoer Erklärung der Menschenrechten im Islam

Im Jahr 1990 beschloss die 19. Außenministerkonferenz der OIC die Kairoer Erklärung zu Menschenrechten im Islam. Sie gilt als Leitlinie der OIC-Mitgliedstaaten in Sachen Menschenrechte und stellt in wesentlichen Teilen eine Kombination aus Genfer Konvention und allgemeiner Erklärung der Menschenrechte dar. Mit einem gewichtigen Unterschied: In den Artikeln 24 und 25 wird die islamische Gesetzgebung, die *šarīʿa*, als Grundlage zur Interpretation dieser Erklärung festgelegt. Dies steht in Konkurrenz zur Allgemeingültigkeit der 1948 durch die Generalversammlung der Vereinten Nationen beschlossenen Erklärung der Menschenrechte; die im Übrigen die damaligen OIC-Staaten im Rahmen der Erklärung der Wiener Menschenrechtskonferenz 1993 als gültig anerkannt haben.

B. Die OIC im Kontext des UN-Menschenrechtsrates

I. Allgemeine Anmerkungen

Die OIC tritt wirkungsmächtig im Wesentlichen im UN-Menschenrechtsrat (UNHRC; im folgenden MRR) in Genf auf. Dort agiert die OIC als Staatenblock und verhandelt mit anderen Blöcken wie den offiziellen Regionalgruppen,[5] der informellen, sogenannten *Like-Minded Group* (von gleichen Interessen geleitet) und der Blockfreienbewegung. Pakistan nimmt die Sprecherrolle ein, da Pakistan innerhalb der OIC wesentlich zur Gründung der Arbeitsgruppe Menschenrechte beigetragen hat. Bisher gehörten 17 der 47 Mitgliedsstaaten des MRR der OIC an.[6] In New York bestehen in der UN-Generalversammlung andere Mehrheitsverhältnisse, und im UN-Sicherheitsrat verfügen die OIC-

---

5 Afrika, Asien, Osteuropa, Lateinamerika und Karibik (GRULAC) sowie Westeuropa und andere Staaten (WEOG).

6 Vgl. Annex II (I. Mitglieder im Menschenrechtsrat der Sitzungsperiode 2007/2008); zum Stand der Mitglieder im Menschenrechtsrat seit Juni 2009 vgl. II., S. 473.

Länder über keine direkte Vetomacht. Insgesamt ist der MRR in Genf der für die OIC günstigere Schauplatz für das geo- und machtpolitische Kräftemessen.[7]

In den Verhandlungen in Genf um Resolutionstexte und den Einsatz des menschenrechtlichen Instrumentariums spiegelt sich häufig eine Nord-Süd-Konfrontation wider, in der die Länder des Südens bzw. die OIC etwa die Themen faire Entwicklung, Rassismus oder Migration besetzen, während die *westliche* Staatengruppe die politischen und staatsbürgerlichen Menschenrechte betont und von einem verbindlichen Recht auf Entwicklung oder von kollektiven Rechten nichts wissen will. Ebenso drängen OIC und Blockfreienbewegung darauf, das Regierungshandeln in Asien und Afrika in Sachen Menschenrechte im Lichte von Armut, bewaffneten Konflikten, Internationalem Währungsfonds, Weltbank, Welthandelsorganisation sowie Globalisierung zu bewerten.

Den internationalen Finanzagenturen haftet zurecht der Makel an, mit ihren *qua* Staatskredit erzwungen Eingriffen in nationale Haushalte und ihrer dogmatischen Privatisierungspolitik wesentlich dazu beigetragen zu haben, landwirtschaftliche Kleinststrukturen und andere Subsistenzwirtschaften in armen Ländern zu zerstören. Umgekehrt verweigern die *westlichen* Staaten, die für diesen Politikansatz der Agenturen wesentlich Verantwortung tragen, bis heute ihre Mitarbeit an einer menschenrechtlichen Auswertung dieser Strukturanpassungspolitik. Natürlich sind die Beschwerden der OIC und der Blockfreienbewegung über die Folgen der neoliberalen Politik – die soziale Exklusion vieler Entwicklungsländer aus der Globalisierung – nicht frei von instrumentellem Interesse, etwa in Form von angestrebten internationalen Entschädigungszahlen auch für verfehlte Binnenpolitik. Gleichwohl vernachlässigt die kategorische Verweigerung schutzwürdige Anliegen. Der Schutz und die Förderung von Menschenrechten im Sinne der wirtschaftlichen, technologischen und wissenschaftlichen Entwicklung wird in Genf häufig von der OIC geltend gemacht. In New York ist dieser Themenkomplex in der Regel von der Blockfreienbewegung besetzt.

Bislang sind die 17 MRR-Mitglieder der OIC überwiegend wohl koordiniert und bei vielen Abstimmungen geschlossen aufgetreten. Gleichwohl lassen vertrau-

---

7 Die umfangreichen Stellungnahmen der OIC, in der Regel durch Pakistan, vor der UN-Menschenrechtskommission können über die Website der OIC nachgelesen werden, s. http://www.oic-oci.org/oicnew (zuletzt aufgerufen am 17. März 2009). Die Mitschriften der Stellungnahmen während der regulären Sitzungen des UN-Menschenrechtsrates sind einsehbar u.a. über die Website des UN-Konferenzservice unter http://www.unog.ch/News%20and%20Media/Press%20Releases&Summaries/Human%20Rights%20Council/Meeting%20Summaries (zuletzt aufgerufen am 17. März 2009). Weitere Quellen bilden die persönlichen Aufzeichnungen des Autors.

liche Bemerkungen darauf schließen, dass nicht alle diplomatischen Missionen gleichermaßen konsultiert werden. So klafft ein deutliches Gefälle etwa zwischen Staaten aus dem arabischen Raum und Länder aus der Sub-Sahara-Region. Einmütig fallen die Stellungnahmen zum Thema Palästina aus; der zentralen Aufgabe der OIC. So gelang es der OIC, den Tagesordnungspunkt „Palästina und besetzte arabische Gebiete" auch im MRR zu verankern; der einzige Tagesordnungspunkt auf der Agenda (TOP 7), der *expressis verbis* ein Land behandelt.

Die Position der OIC zu Palästina innerhalb des MRR ist schlicht als beschönigende, einseitige politische Unterstützung zu bezeichnen, die auch die Konflikte innerhalb der palästinensischen Führung ausklammert.[8] Eine sachlich fundierte und die Machtverhältnisse widerspiegelnde Kritik aus menschenrechtlicher Perspektive an Israel wie an den palästinensischen Parteien erfolgte bislang einzig durch thematische Mandatsträger der UN-Sonderverfahren (*Special Procedures*). So gehört der gemeinsame Bericht von Philip Alston (Sonderberichterstatter zu extralegalen, massenhaften und willkürlichen Hinrichtungen), Paul Hunt (Sonderberichterstatter zu Gesundheit), Walter Kälin (Repräsentant des UN-Generalsekretärs zu intern Vertriebenen) und Miloon Kothari (Sonderberichterstatter zu angemessenem Wohnen) vom September 2006 mit zum Besten, was im Kontext des UN-Menschenrechtsystems zu diesem Komplex geschrieben wurde.[9]

II. Diffamierung von Religion und Meinungsfreiheit

Ein zweites zentrales Themenfeld für die OIC bildet der Kontext Diffamierung der Religionen, die Eliminierung aller Formen religiöser Intoleranz sowie Fremden- und Religionsfeindlichkeit vor allem in *westlichen* Staaten.[10] Zu letzterem gehört auch das Thema Gewalt gegen Muslime. Die OIC greift den kritikwürdigen, insbesondere nach den Anschlägen auf das World Trade Centre in New York am 11. September 2001 verbreiteten Generalverdacht gegen Muslime in *westlichen* Ländern auf und bewertet den Politikansatz *westlicher* Länder zur Meinungsfreiheit gegenüber dem Schutz für Angehörige des Islam

---

8 Siehe bspw. *Hatem Elliesie / Naseef Naeem*, Gemeinsames Dach: Der Staatenbund – eine denkbare Lösung für den Nahen Osten, in: Frankfurter Allgemeine Zeitung (Rubrik: "Staat und Recht"), Donnerstag, den 12. Februar 2009, S. 10, die u.a. wegen des Konflikts innerhalb der palästinensischen Führung(en) – jedenfalls vorübergehend – eine Staatenbundlösung zur Debatte stellen.

9 UN-Dok. Nr. E/CN.4/2006/7, Genf 2006.

10 Vgl. an dieser Stelle auch *Ann Elizabeth Mayer*, „General Remarks on Human Rights and Islam in the Middle East, in: *Hatem Elliesie* (Hrsg./Editor), Beiträge zum Islamischen Recht VII, Islam und Menschenrechte (Islam and Human Rights / الإسلام وحقوق الإنسان), Frankfurt a.M. 2010, S. 219 (227 f.).

als parteilich und dysfunktional. In allen *westlichen* Ländern gibt es parteipolitische und gesellschaftliche Gruppierungen, die diesen Konflikt im Kampf gegen den Terrorismus bewusst schüren. Auch einschlägige Mandatsträger der UN-Sonderverfahren wie Asma Jahangir[11] (zu Religionsfreiheit) und Doudou Diène[12] (zu rassistischer Diskriminierung) mahnten mehrfach, Meinungsfreiheit nicht zur bewussten Diskriminierung von Ethnien oder Angehörigen einer Religion zu missbrauchen.[13]

Die Diffamierungen gegenüber dem Islam etwa in westeuropäischen Ländern benennt eine real existierende Lücke im Menschenrechtsschutz.[14] Die Identifizierung dieser Lücke gerät der OIC jedoch zur ebenso fragwürdigen Vereinseitigung, indem die Religion als solche – etwa der Islam – unter Schutz gestellt werden soll. Insbesondere Asma Jahangir warnt in ihren Berichten davor, die Religion statt die individuelle Freiheit der Religions- und Glaubensausübung zu schützen. Sie appelliert an die Regierungen, sich Zurückhaltung bei Maßnahmen gegen die Diffamierung von Religion auf zu erlegen. In aller Regel gehe damit eine Politisierung des Rechts auf Religionsfreiheit einher.

---

11 *Asma Jahangir,* Report of the Special Rapporteur on freedom of religion or belief, UN-Dok. Nr. E/CN.4/2006/5, Genf 2006; *idem,* Report of the Special Rapporteur on Freedom of Religion or Belief, UN-Dok. Nr. A/HRC/4/21, Genf 2007; *idem,* Report of the Special Rapporteur on Freedom of Religion or Belief, UN-Dok. Nr. A/HRC/6/5, Genf 2007.

12 *Doudou Diène,* Report of the Special Rapporteur on Contemporary Forms of Racism, Racial Discrimination, Xenophobia and related Intolerance on the Situation of Muslim and Arab Peoples in various Parts of the World, UN-Dok. Nr. E/CN.4/2006/17, Genf 2006; *idem,* Political Platforms which promote or incite Racial Discrimination – Updated Study, UN-Dok. Nr. E/CN.4/2006/54, Genf 2006; *idem,* Report of the Special Rapporteur on Contemporary Forms of Racism, Racial Discrimination, Xenophobia and related Intolerance on the Manifestations of Defamation of Religions and in particular on the serious Implications of Islamophobia on the Enjoyment of all Rights, UN-Dok. Nr. A/HRC/6/6, Genf 2007.

13 Zur Substanz solcher Vorkommnisse vgl. *European Monitoring Centre on Racism and Xenophobia* (EUMC), Muslims in the European Union: Discrimination and Islamophobia, Wien 2006, http://eumc.europa.eu/eumc/material/pub/muslim/Manifestations_EN.pdf (zuletzt aufgerufen am 13. März 2009); *idem,* Perceptions of Discrimination and Islamophobia: Voices from Members of Mulsim Communities in the European Union, Wien 2006, http://fra.europa.eu/fra/material/pub/muslim/Perceptions_EN.pdf (zuletzt aufgerufen am 13. März 2009); jüngere Berichte der Sonderberichterstatter Asma Jahangir und Doudou Diène aus den Jahren 2006 und 2007.

14 *Heiner Bielefeldt,* Das Islambild in Deutschland: Zum öffentlichen Umgang mit der Angst vor dem Islam, Berlin 2007, Kapitel III, S. 20 ff. Zur Onlineausgabe s.: http://files.institut-fuer-menschenrechte.de/437/IUS-040_E_Islam_RZ_WEB_ES.pdf (zuletzt aufgerufen am 15. März 2009).

Ihre Mahnung ist nur allzu berechtigt. Im März 2008 erneuerte der MRR das Mandat der Sonderverfahren zur Meinungsfreiheit.[15] Die OIC brachte allerdings ihre Ergänzung durch,[16] wonach das Mandat zukünftig auch darüber berichten soll, inwieweit das Recht auf freie Meinung zur Diffamierung von Individuen oder Gruppen mit spezifischem religiösem Hintergrund missbraucht wird. Was nachvollziehbar scheint, verkehrt das bisherige Prinzip des Mandats ins Gegenteil. Mittels der Ergänzung wird der Mandatsträger aufgefordert, verstärkt auf die Einschränkung statt auf die Wahrung der Meinungsfreiheit zu achten und darüber dem Menschenrechtsrat zu berichten. So wird die Meinungsfreiheit gefährdet.

Beide, Doudou Diène und Asma Jahangir, setzten sich außerdem im September 2006 in einer Studie mit dem Verhältnis von Meinungs- und Religionsfreiheit auseinander.[17] Darin fordern sie zum einen die entschiedene Umsetzung der Beschlüsse der Durban-Konferenz aus dem Jahre 2001 gegen Rassismus, Diskriminierung, Fremdenfeindlichkeit und darauf bezogene Formen der Intoleranz, um der Diffamierung und Hasspropaganda zu begegnen. Ihre Mahnung richtet sich *de facto* vor allem an *westliche* Staaten, deren Regierungshandeln hier bislang kaum messbar gewesen ist. Der Nationale Aktionsplan der deutschen Regierung ist bis *dato* (Mitte 2008) nicht verabschiedet. Die Islamfeindlichkeit wird tendenziell heruntergespielt. Die *westlichen* Länder sind von einer menschenrechtlich konsistenten Beschäftigung mit dem Thema religiöse Diffamierung einiges entfernt.

Zum anderen warnen Asma Jahangir und Doudou Diène ebenso davor, Religionskritik unter Strafe zu stellen und religiösen Pluralismus durch Strafandrohungen (Blasphemiegesetze) oder Nachteile etwa im Familien- und Erbschaftsrecht zu unterlaufen; z.B. im islamisch orientierten Pakistan. Dies schränke die Freiheit der Person ein, oder mache es gar unmöglich, sich für eine (oder keine) Religion zu entscheiden und diese Entscheidung frei, ohne Nachteile oder Repression, zu praktizieren. Darüber ist von der OIC regelmäßig nur zu hören, dass es der Souveränität der Regierung überlassen bleiben muss, wie sie die nationale Gesetzgebung entsprechend der Geschichte und Kultur des Landes gestaltet. Außerdem schweigt die OIC konsequent zu Judenverfolgungen.

Die Entwicklung der Resolutionstexte zur Diffamierung von Religion von den Zeiten der früheren UN-Menschenrechtskommission bis in die heutigen Tage des Menschenrechtsrates legt den Schluss nahe, dass neben der Sorge um den

---

15 UN-Dok. Nr. A/HRC/7/L.24, Genf 2008.

16 UN-Dok. Nr. A/HRC/7/L.39, Genf 2008.

17 UN-Dok. Nr. A/HRC/2/3, Genf 2006.

Schutz von Muslimen gegen voreingenommene *westliche* Gesellschaften ganz eigene Ziele verfolgt werden. Die OIC stellt

a) die Schutzlosigkeit der Muslime fest,

b) präsentiert die OIC als geborenen Hort für diese Angelegenheit, und

c) fordert nachdrücklich die Entwicklung von Institutionen zum Schutz und zur Förderung der Menschenrechte für Menschen islamischen Glaubens.

In den Sitzungen des MRR im September 2007 sowie im März 2008 verwies die OIC auf ihre Erklärung von Kairo als Referenzrahmen für ein zukünftiges eigenes Instrumentarium zum Schutz der Menschenrechte von Muslimen. Seit der Konferenz der Blockfreienbewegung Anfang September 2007 in Teheran gibt es dazu öffentlich wahrnehmbare, ernst zu nehmende Absprachen. Die OIC betreibt die Umkehrung bisheriger Werteannahmen und strebt die Meinungsführerschaft im Sinne muslimischer Auslegung des Rechts auf Religionsfreiheit an: die vermeintliche, einseitig christliche Grundlegung der UN-Menschenrechte soll durch eine islamische Referenz ergänzt, wenn nicht ersetzt werden. Die Religionsfreiheit wird letztlich dadurch unterhöhlt.

C. Autoritäres Politikmuster und Universalität der Menschenrechte

Der vorgenannte Politikansatz stellt die Universalität der Menschenrechte substanziell in Frage. Obwohl die teilnehmenden Staaten an der Wiener Menschenrechtskonferenz 1993 die Universalität der Menschenrechte ausdrücklich bestätigten, hörten die Versuche nie auf, die fehlende Umsetzung dieser Menschenrechte in den Ländern mit kulturellen Besonderheiten und nationalen Rechts- und Wertesystemen zu begründen. Dieses Ansinnen verstärkte sich ab der zweiten Hälfte der 1990er Jahre um so mehr, je deutlicher die *westlichen* Staaten erkennen ließen, dass sie an der Umsetzung des Gegenstücks zur Vereinbarung der Wiener Erklärung, des Rechts auf Entwicklung, nicht wirklich interessiert waren. Nicht nur die OIC, sondern auch Länder aus der Blockfreienbewegung bemühen kulturelle Besonderheiten, um die Bewertung der Lage der Menschenrechte in ihren Ländern zu relativieren.

Ein zweiter Argumentationsstrang fokussiert auf den Vorrang der sozialen und wirtschaftlichen Entwicklung der Bevölkerung als Grundvoraussetzung für die faktische Inanspruchnahme der Menschenrechte. Eine dritte Argumentation hebt auf das Gemeinwesenkonzept u.a. in islamisch geprägten Ländern ab, das die Inanspruchnahme von Menschenrechten an die gleichzeitige Erfüllung von „Pflichten“ gegenüber der Gemeinschaft abhängig macht. Demgegenüber zeichnen sich die 1948 verkündeten Menschenrechte dadurch aus, dass sie bedingungslos zu garantieren und als vorstaatliche Rechte konzipiert sind.[18]

Auch hier greift die OIC eine Lücke im Menschenrechtssystem auf, wenn sie kollektive Rechte als unabgegoltenen Schutz einfordert. Indigene Völker etwa sind Subjekte einer solchen Norm, und die 2007 von der UN-Generalversammlung mit großer Mehrheit – einschließlich *westlicher* Staaten – verabschiedete Erklärung zu den Rechten indigener Völker öffnet dieser Rechtsfigur den Zugang zum internationalen Recht. Die Art und Weise der Geltendmachung durch die OIC und einzelne ihrer Mitglieder legt jedoch die Vermutung nahe, dass individuelle Rechte gegen kollektive Rechte ausgespielt werden, um den Staat vor – berechtigten – Ansprüchen zu schützen und die mangelnde Umsetzung bestehender Standards zu kaschieren.

Die Mischung aus realer Problemanzeige und politisch-instrumentellem Eigeninteresse fußt auf einem vorherrschenden Staatsverständnis in der OIC-Welt, das Wohl und Wehe der einzelnen Person in die Hände des gemeinschaftlich orientierten Akteurs legt, d.h. Regierung und autorisierte Geistlichkeit. Menschenrechte als „Abwehrrecht" gegen einen nicht wohlmeinenden Staat zu konzipieren, scheint meines Erachtens bei OIC-Mitgliedern eine kaum verstandene Erfahrung aus der europäischen Geschichte. Im Rahmen der Globalisierung, im Umfeld von drohendem Verlust bisheriger Sicherheiten in Politik und Kultur, kommt hinzu, dass die intendierte Neuordnung eher mit Hilfe expliziter Normen und Sanktionen gesucht wird. So stellen sich Kontrolle und Vorgaben dem einzelnen Subjekt gegenüber weiterhin als unabdingbarer Bestandteil des staatlichen Instrumentariums für ein gutes, gesegnetes Leben dar.[19] Von der Regierung unabhängige Einrichtungen wie das UN-Hochkommissariat für Menschenrechte, die UN-Sonderverfahren oder regierungskritische Zivilgesellschaften sind einem solchen normativen Politikansatz und autoritären Verständnis gesellschaftlicher Prozesse nicht geheuer.

Fatal wird ein solches Verständnis, wenn dem Staat der Schutz von Menschen anvertraut ist, denen seiner eigenen Auffassung nach selbst biologisch kein Existenzrecht zukommt; etwa Homosexuellen. Allein ihrer Existenz wegen ist diese Bevölkerungsgruppe im Iran vom Tode bedroht. Diese extreme Variante

---

[18] Eine knappe Darstellung der Regierungsführung unter islamischen Vorzeichen leistet *Muqtedar Kahn,* Demokratie und islamische Staatlichkeit, in: Aus Politik und Zeitgeschichte (APuZ) 26-27, Bonn 2007, S. 17-24; zum politischen Diskurs vgl. Bernard Lewis: Die Politische Sprache des Islams, Hamburg 2002.

[19] Zum Hintergrund vgl. *Naika Foroutan,* Kulturdialoge in der politischen Anwendung, in: APuZ 28-29, Bonn 2006, S. 17-25; *Olivier Roy,* Der Islam in Europa- eine Ausnahme?, in: Ibidem, S. 5-11; *Wolfgang Günter Lerch,* Der Islam in der Moderne, in: Ibidem, S.11-17.

der gesellschaftlichen Exklusion findet sich nicht in allen Mitgliedsländern der OIC, aber dort wird gleichgeschlechtliche Identität generell als verwerflich erachtet und mit dem Entzug grundlegender (Menschen-) Rechte bedroht. So überrascht die Vehemenz nicht, mit der vor allem Pakistan und Malaysia im Namen der OIC allein die Erörterung eines von Brasilien eingebrachten Resolutionstextes in der früheren Menschenrechtskommission verhinderten, die die Diskriminierung aufgrund sexueller Orientierung ächten sollte. Mit allen Tricks der Geschäftsordnung legten die Botschafter der beiden Länder die letzte Sitzung der 59. Periode im Jahr 2003 lahm. Bis heute hat es kein Land vermocht, erneut einen Resolutionsentwurf zu diesem Thema vorzulegen. Pakistan und Malaysia hatten schon im Vorfeld deutlich gemacht, dass dieses Thema die Grundfesten ihrer Gesellschaften erschüttert und mit allen Mitteln unterbunden würde.

Weniger vehement aber inhaltlich ähnlich restriktiv verhält sich die OIC zu *Gender*-Fragen. Die OIC spricht sich zwar, wie alle anderen auch, für eine *Gender*-Perspektive aus. OIC-Länder weigern sich aber beharrlich, die Kritik der Sonderberichterstatterin zu Frauen zur Kenntnis zu nehmen, dass gerade in muslimisch geprägten Staaten eine systematische Benachteiligung bzw. Diskriminierung von Frauen etwa beim Familien- und Erbrecht erfolgt. Zu viel ‚Frauen-Power' würde vermutlich die traditionell verstandene Familie als erklärten Hort von Schutz und Rechten in Gefahr bringen; darin dem dogmatischen Christentum durchaus ähnlich. Darüber hinaus lassen einige OIC-Staaten die Frauen-Verstümmelung[20] zu; wenn nicht *de jure* so doch *de facto*.[21]

D. Staatenorientierte Analyse und Bewertung der Menschenrechte

Als folgerichtige Ergänzung des zuvor skizzierten, autoritären, normativen Staatsverständnisses betreiben die OIC-Mitglieder im MRR ein zunehmend an den Interessen der Staaten orientiertes Verfahren zur Analyse und Bewertung der Lage der Menschenrechte. Manifester Ausdruck davon ist das neue Instrument des MRR in Form der universellen periodischen Überprüfung (*Uni-*

---

20 Vgl. hierzu *Dörthe Engels,* Die islamrechtliche Beurteilung der Mädchenbeschneidung: Eine kritische Analyse des Beschlusstextes der Gelehrtenkonferenz „Verbot des Missbrauchs des weiblichen Körpers" vom 22. bis 23. November 2006 an der Azhar-Universität in Kairo im Kontext moderner Entwicklungen in der islamischen Rechtsfindungspraxis [Magisterarbeit am Institut für Islamwissenschaft an der Freien Universität Berlin], Berlin 2008.

21 Vgl. auch *Muhammad Kalisch,* „Islam und Menschenrechte: Betrachtungen zum Verhältnis von Religion und Recht", in: *Hatem Elliesie* (Hrsg./Editor), Beiträge zum Islamischen Recht VII, Islam und Menschenrechte (Islam and Human Rights / الإسلام وحقوق الإنسان), Frankfurt a.M. 2010, S. 49 ff. (S. 51).

versal Periodic Review, UPR) aller Mitgliedsstaaten der UNO innerhalb von vier Jahren. Zum UPR-Verfahren lässt sich einiges auch an positiven Aspekten anführen. In diesem Zusammenhang von Interesse ist jedoch die Ausgestaltung des Verfahrens, in dem nicht-staatliche Akteure buchstäblich nur am Rande vorkommen, und wesentliche Verfahrensschritte wie Anhörung, Beratung und Bewertung allein den Staaten vorbehalten bleiben.[22] Saudi Arabien (damals als Sprecher der Asien-Gruppe), Pakistan (OIC), Malaysia, Algerien (damals Sprecher der Afrika-Gruppe) und Russland machten bei der abschließenden Beratung des Verfahrens im Jahr 2007 deutlich, dass die aus dem UPR-Verfahren abgeleiteten Schlussfolgerungen und Empfehlungen an den untersuchten Staat eigentlich im Konsens mit diesem zu fassen seien.

Umgekehrt sprechen sich neben China oder Kuba Ländern der OIC wie Pakistan, Ägypten, Algerien aber auch Indonesien vehement gegen die herausgehobene Evaluierung einzelner Länder und öffentliche Benennung von Menschenrechtsverletzungen aus; zumindest, solange keine gleichgewichtige Berücksichtigung der Länder des Südens und des Nordens / Westens erfolgt. Pakistan sieht in den Länderevaluierungen und -Resolutionen die hauptsächlichste Quelle für den Unfrieden im MRR. Auch hier kann über doppelte Standards etwa in Bezug auf die Menschenrechtslage im Irak oder in Afghanistan und das kollektive Schweigen des Westens dazu, einiges gesagt werden, das das Anliegen einer gleichgewichtigen Länderauswertung stützt. Gleichwohl steht den zuvor genannten Ländern weniger der Sinn nach einer gründlichen Auswertung der Menschenrechtslage in einzelnen Ländern als vielmehr das allgemeine Kaschieren mangelnder Regierungsführung.

So ist in all den Jahren der völkermordähnlichen Verbrechen in der sudanesischen Region Darfur[23] keine kritische Bewertung durch die OIC erfolgt.

---

[22] Zu einer ersten Auswertung des UPR-Verfahrens siehe *Theodor Rathgeber,* The HRC Universal Periodic Review: A Preliminary Assessment. Dialogue on Globalization (FES Briefing Paper), Genf, Juli 2008, http://library.fes.de/library/fr-voll-digbibnew.html (zuletzte aufgerufen am 17 März 2009).

[23] Hierzu ausführlich *Hatem Elliesie,* „Die Darfur-Krise im Sudan und das Völkerrecht: Eine Herausforderung für die Vereinten Nationen (UN) und den Internationalen Strafgerichtshofes (ICC)“, in: Verfassung und Recht in Übersee (VRÜ), Jahrgang 40, Heft 2, Baden-Baden 2007, S. 199-229; *idem,* „Sudan under the Constraints of (International) Human Rights Law and Humanitarian Law: The Case of Darfur“, in: *Hatem Elliesie* (Hrsg./Editor), Beiträge zum Islamischen Recht VII, Islam und Menschenrechte (Islam and Human Rights / الإسلام وحقوق الإنسان), Frankfurt a.M. 2010, S. 193-217. Ferner *Hatem Elliesie / Urs Behrendt / Niway Zergie Aynalem,* „Different Approaches to Genocide Trials under National Jursidiction on the African Continent – The Rwandan, Ethiopian and Sudanese Cases“, in: Recht in Afrika (Law in Africa · Droit en Afrique), 12. Jahrgang, Heft 1, Köln 2009, S. 21-67.

Im Gegenteil: dem guten Bericht der Expertengruppe zu Darfur vom Juni 2007[24] wurde von der OIC aufgrund einer nebensächlichen Formalie die Legitimation als offizielles UN-Dokument abgesprochen.[25] Demgegenüber mahnten in diesem Fall auch einige afrikanische Staaten vermehrt Aktivitäten des MRR an, um sowohl die Lage der Menschen zu verbessern als auch die Instabilität der Region zu überwinden.[26] Soweit alles unter staatlicher Kontrolle bleibt, spielt die OIC durchaus eine konstruktive Rolle wie in der Mediation auf den Philippinen zwischen Regierung und aufständischen Muslimen.

Zum staatenorientierten Procedere gehören die Versuche nicht nur der OIC, das vom MRR formal unabhängige Hochkommissariat für Menschenrechte (UNHCHR) und die vom MRR zu berufenden Mandatsträger der Sonderverfahren an die kurze Leine – um nicht zu sagen: das Gängelband – zu nehmen. Dem Hochkommissariat wird bei der Besetzung von Führungspositionen mangelnde geographische Ausgewogenheit, unausgewogene Länderberichte und insgesamt intransparentes Management vorgeworfen. Bei der technischen Unterstützung für einzelne Länder oder der Eröffnung lokaler Büros seitens des UNHCHR müssten nicht nur die beteiligten Staaten sondern auch die dafür zuständigen Regionalgruppen im MRR konsultiert werden. Pakistan kritisierte im Namen der OIC mehrfach den strategischen Rahmenplan des UNHCHR, da nach Pakistans Auffassung nicht die Stärkung der Mechanismen zum Schutz der Menschenrechte im Vordergrund zu stehen habe, sondern „Entwicklung" im Sinne des Rechts auf Entwicklung müsse als entwicklungspolitische Maßnahme verstanden werden. In gleicher Weise sollte das UNHCHR seine Länderteams strikt nach Gesichtspunkten der technischen Hilfeleistung organisieren. Die bis Juni 2008 amtierende Hochkommissarin Louise Arbour konnte diesem gewaltigen Druck noch einigermaßen widerstehen.

Die Sonderverfahren mussten hingegen im Juni 2007 einen Verhaltenskodex als Ergebnis der Institutionenbildung des MRR hinnehmen.[27] Dieser *Code of*

---

24 UN-Dok. Nr. A/HRC/5/6, Genf 2007.

25 Die Expertengruppe umfasste die Sonderberichterstatterin für den Sudan, die Sondergesandte des UN-Generalsekretärs zu Kindern in bewaffneten Konflikten, den Sonderberichterstatter zu extralegalen, summarischen oder willkürlichen Hinrichtungen, die Sondergesandte des UN-Generalsekretärs zu Menschenrechtsverteidigern, den Sondergesandten des UN-Generalsekretärs zu intern Vertriebenen, den Sonderberichterstatter zu Folter und die Sonderberichterstatterin zu Gewalt gegen Frauen.

26 Kamerun, Burundi, Gabun, Ghana, Sambia.

27 Realiter bedürften, wenn überhaupt jemand, die Regierungen eines Verhaltenskodexes: viele kommen Berichtspflichten nicht nach, beantworten Anfragen der Experten nur unvollständig oder gar nicht, verweigern oder verzögern Mandatsträgern die Einreise zwecks Feldaufnahme soweit, bis der Anlass entfallen ist, oder erschweren Mandatsträgern die Kontaktaufnahme mit Opfern. Es ist nicht ungewöhnlich und nicht auf OIC-

Conduct legt den Mandatsträgern eine enge Auslegung des Mandats nahe, reglementiert den Zugang der Sonderverfahren zur Presse und fordert zur Beachtung bestimmter Vorgaben bei der Kommunikation mit Regierungen sowie der Einbeziehung nicht-staatlicher Akteure und nicht-regierungsamtlicher Informationen auf. Länder und Ländergruppen wie China (*Like-Minded Group*), Kuba (Blockfreienbewegung), Ägypten (derzeit Sprecher der Afrika-Gruppe) sowie Pakistan (OIC) versuchen nach Kräften, die bisherige, als zu weitgehend empfundene Unabhängigkeit und unbequemen Bewertungen der Sonderverfahren einzuhegen und durch regierungsnahe Mechanismen der Auswahl und inhaltlichen Engführung mindestens zu ergänzen, wenn nicht auf mittlere Frist zu ersetzen. Im Juni 2008 wurde der *Code of Conduct* durch eine von den vorgenannten Staatengruppen erzwungene Entscheidung des Ratspräsidenten ergänzt, wonach Mandatsträger nicht wie bislang automatisch für eine zweite Mandatszeit (drei Jahre) berufen werden, wenn sie sich nicht gemäß des Kodex‘ verhalten.

Die Partizipation von Nichtregierungsorganisationen (NGOs) oder nationalen Menschenrechtsinstitutionen (NHRIs)[28] im Rahmen des MRR wird von der OIC nicht prinzipiell in Frage gestellt. Einzelne Mitgliedsländer wie Aserbeidschan forderten und förderten sogar die Beteiligung zivilgesellschaftlicher Akteure. Natürlich müssen sich NGOs gegebenenfalls mit Vorwürfen auseinandersetzen, die Lage der Menschenrechte in den Ländern einseitig darzustellen, zu übertreiben, staatliche Informationen nicht zu berücksichtigen, unautorisiert zu sprechen. Noch sensibler reagieren OIC-Staaten auf Kritik aus dem Kreis der NHRIs, die als dem Regierungslager zugehörig empfunden werden; was sie in der Tat häufig genug sind. Im Zuge der Institutionenbildung des MRR schlugen Pakistan im Namen der OIC sowie China vor, in den Debatten um Länderresolutionen NGOs allenfalls in einer getrennten Sitzung zu Wort kommen zu lassen. Zunehmend werden Debattenbeiträge von NGOs durch Anträge zur Geschäftsordnung seitens der betroffenen Staaten unterbrochen und Vortragende mürbe gemacht.

Länder beschränkt, dass etwa der Sonderberichterstatter zu Folter z.B. für die Hinfahrt zum Besuch eines Gefängnisses mehrere Stunden braucht, während die Rückfahrt in kürzester Zeit bewältigt wird.

28 Zu NHRIs siehe *Anna Würth / Claudia Engelmann*, „Governmental Human Rights Structures and National Human Rights Institutions in the Middle East and North Africa“, in: *Hatem Elliesie* (Hrsg./Editor), Beiträge zum Islamischen Recht VII, Islam und Menschenrechte (Islam and Human Rights / الإسلام وحقوق الإنسان), Frankfurt a.M. 2010, S. 239 ff.

E. Fazit

Die Aktivitäten der OIC in Genf sind als erfolgreich zu bewerten, da die OIC inzwischen zu allen wesentlichen Aspekten der Menschenrechte das Wort ergreift, zu Teilen den Diskurs mit bestimmt und ein zentraler Verhandlungspartner geworden ist. Mit Themen wie Armut, Recht auf Entwicklung, Recht auf Selbstbestimmung (nicht zuletzt im Kontext der Globalisierung), Fremdenfeindlichkeit und religiöser Intoleranz spielt die OIC geschickt die Klaviatur der Länder des Südens. Wobei der eigene Einflussbereich in der Regel komplett ausgeblendet bleibt. Aus Sicht vieler NGOs spielt die OIC eine verheerende Rolle in Bezug auf die Unabhängigkeit der Sonderverfahren und des Hochkommissariats sowie in der versuchten Gängelung zivilgesellschaftlicher Akteure (NGOs, NHRIs).

Es wäre meines Erachtens jedoch verkehrt, der OIC und vielen ihrer Mitgliedsstaaten ausschließlich eine instrumentell-böswillige Absicht zwecks Begrenzung von Menschenrechten zu unterstellen. Das Verständnis zu Staat und Politik sowie über handelnde Akteure in gesellschaftlichen Prozessen muss in Rechnung gestellt werden; zumal bei Überlegungen, welches OIC-Land wie zur konstruktiven Auseinandersetzung mit Menschenrechtsverletzungen gebracht werden kann. Einige Aussagen im UPR-Verfahren zu Bahrain und Marokko lassen darauf schließen, dass dort bspw. ernsthaft über mehr zivilgesellschaftliche Beiträge zur Bewertung und Umsetzung der Menschenrechte nachgedacht wird.

Zum anderen ist es gleichzeitig unabdingbar, die von der OIC und anderen Staaten geltend gemachten Schutzlücken, doppelten Standards und politischen Vorbehalte gegenüber bestimmten Menschenrechten auf Seiten *westlicher* Regierungen ebenfalls ins Visier zu nehmen und dort auf Änderung zu drängen. Dabei sind Herrschaftszweifel auch auf Seiten *westlicher* Regierungen nicht selbstverständlich. So klingt die Schlussfolgerung insgesamt nach Utopie, und die bisherige Praxis weist in der Tat eine Präferenz nicht zuletzt der *westlichen* Staaten dafür aus, im Bestehenden zu verharren und die Unabänderlichkeit der Verhältnisse zu beklagen. Auch hier ist also vermehrt zivilgesellschaftliche Einmischung notwendig, um die Erkenntnis in praktische Politik ummünzen zu können.

F. Annex I:

I. Mitgliedsstaaten der OIC (Stand Anfang 2008)

Nr	MITGLIEDSSTAAT	seit	Nr	MITGLIEDSSTAAT	seit
1.	Arabische Republik ÄGYPTEN	1969	30.	Republik MALEDIVEN	1976
2.	Islamischer Staat AFGHANISTAN	1969	31.	Republik MALI	1969
3.	Republik ALBANIEN	1992	32.	Königreich MAROKKO	1969
4.	Demokrat. Volksrepublik ALGERIEN	1969	33.	Islamische Republik MAURETANIEN	1969
5.	Republik ASERBEIDSCHAN	1992	34.	Republik MOZAMBIQUE	1994
6.	Königreich BAHRAIN	1972	35.	Republik NIGER	1969
7.	Volksrepublik BANGLADESH	1974	36.	Bundesrepublik NIGERIA	1986
8.	Republik BENIN	1983	37.	Sultanat OMAN	1976
9.	BRUNEI-DARUSSALAM	1984	38.	PALÄSTINA	1969
10.	BURKINA-FASO (früher Obervolta)	1974	39.	Islamische Republik PAKISTAN	1969
11.	Union der COMOREN	1976	40.	QATAR	1972
12.	Republik ELFENBEINKÜSTE	2001	41.	Königreich SAUDI ARABIEN	1969
13.	Republik DJIBOUTI	1978	42.	Republik SENEGAL	1969
14.	Republik GABUN	1974	43.	Republik SIERRA LEONE	1972
15.	Republik GAMBIA	1974	44.	Republik SOMALIA	1969
16.	Republik GUINEA	1969	45.	Republik SUDAN	1969
17.	Republik GUINEA-BISSAU	1974	46.	Republik SURINAME	1996
18.	Republik GUYANA	1998	47.	Arabische Republik SYRIEN	1972
19.	Republik INDONESIEN	1969	48.	Republik TADSCHIKISTAN	1992
20.	Islamische Republik IRAN	1969	49.	Republik TOGO	1997
21.	Republik IRAK	1975	50.	Republik TSCHAD	1969
22.	Haschemit. Königreich JORDANIEN	1969	51.	Republik TÜRKEI	1969
23.	Republik KAMERUN	1974	52.	Republik TUNESIEN	1969
24.	Republik KASACHSTAN	1995	53.	Republik TURKMENISTAN	1992
25.	KUWAIT	1969	54.	Republik UGANDA	1974
26.	Republik KIRGISIEN	1992	55.	Republik USBEKISTAN	1996
27.	Republik LIBANON	1969	56.	VEREINIGTE ARAB. EMIRATE	1972
28.	Sozialistische Volksrepublik LIBYEN	1969	57.	Republik YEMEN	1969
29.	Islamische Republik MALAYSIA	1969			

II. Staaten mit Beobachterstatus

Nr	BEOBACHTERSTATUS	seit	Nr	BEOBACHTERSTATUS	seit
1.	Nordzypern[29]	1979	4.	Thailand	1998
2.	Bosnien und Herzegowina	1994	5.	Russland	2005
3.	Zentralafrikanische Republik	1997			

29 Seit 1979 als Muslimische Gemeinschaft Zyperns, ab 2004 als Türkisch-Zyprischer Staat.

III. Internationale Organisationen mit Beobachterstatus

Nr	Beobachterstatus	seit	Nr	Beobachterstatus	seit
1.	Arabische Liga	1975	4.	Bewegung der blockfreien Staaten	1977
2.	Vereinte Nationen	1976	5.	Economic Cooperation Organization	1995
3.	Afrikanische Union (vormals OAU[30])	1977			

IV. Muslimische Gemeinschaften und Organisationen mit Beobachterstatus

Nr	Muslimische Gemeinschaften und Organisationen mit Beobachterstatus	seit
1.	Moro National Liberation Front (MNLF)[31]	1977

V. Islamische Institutionen mit Beobachterstatus

Nr	Islamische Institutionen mit Beobachterstatus	seit
1.	Parlamentarische Union der OIC Mitgliedsstaaten (PUOICM)	2000
2.	Jugendforum der Islamischen Konferenz für Dialog und Kooperation (ICYFDC)	2005

G. Annex II:

I. Mitglieder im Menschenrechtsrat der Sitzungsperiode 2007/2008

Nr	Staat	Nr	Staat	Nr	Staat	Nr	Staat	Nr	Staat
1.	Ägypten	5.	Burkina Faso	9.	Jordanien	13.	Nigeria	17.	Senegal
2.	Aserbaidschan	6.	Djibouti	10.	Kamerun	14.	Pakistan		
3.	Bangladesch	7.	Gabun	11.	Malaysia	15.	Qatar		
4.	Bahrain	8.	Indonesien	12.	Mauritius	16.	Saudi Arabien		

II. Stand der Mitglieder im Menschenrechtsrat seit Juni 2009

Nr	Staat	Nr	Staat	Nr	Staat	Nr	Staat
1.	Ägypten	5.	Djibouti	9.	Kamerun	13.	Pakistan
2.	Bangladesch	6.	Gabun	10.	Kirgisien	14.	Qatar
3.	Bahrain	7.	Indonesien	11.	Mauritius	15.	Saudi Arabien
4.	Burkina Faso	8.	Jordanien	12.	Nigeria	16.	Senegal

30 Die Organisation für Afrikanische Einheit (englisch: *Organisation of African Unity, OAU*; französisch: *Organisation de l'Unité Africaine*, OUA) war eine von 1963 bis 2002 bestehende Organisation fast aller afrikanischer Staaten. Sie ist die Vorgängerorganisation der Afrikanischen Union.

31 Bei der Moro National Liberation Front (MNLF) handelt es sich um eine ehemalige Rebellen- und Guerillagruppe, die zwischen 1970 und 1997 im Süden der Philippinen für einen eigenständigen muslimischen Staat kämpfte.

Menschenrechte und Islamisches Recht unter dem Blickwinkel des (Internationalen) Privatrechts

Human Rights and Islamic Law in the View of the (International) Private Law

حقوق الإنسان والشريعة الإسلامية من وجهة نظر القانون الدولي الخاص

Islam und Menschenrechte (Islam and Human Rights / الإسلام وحقوق الإنسان)
Hatem Elliesie (Hrsg./Editor), © Peter Lang Verlag: Frankfurt a.M. 2010, S. 475-521

Ordre Public, Menschenrechte und Scharia*

Peter Scholz, Berlin

A. Menschenrechtskritik an der Anwendung islamischen Rechts

I. Einführung

Die Aktualität der Auseinandersetzung mit dem Islam und im Namen des Islam ausgeführten Handlungen hat seit dem 11. September 2001 nicht nachgelassen. Fast täglich berichten die Medien über Terrorakte unter Berufung auf den Islam fast überall auf der Welt und Verletzungen von Menschenrechten in den islamischen Staaten. Innerstaatlich steht der religiös und kulturell gelebte Islam in Deutschland und Europa unter dem Generalverdacht verfassungsfeindlicher Aktivitäten und potenzieller Gewaltbereitschaft. Dabei wird die öffentliche Diskussion den Realitäten vielfach nicht gerecht. Der Islam wird zumeist klischeehaft mit Gewalt und Terror, Menschenrechtsverletzungen und Unterdrückung in einer Art und Weise in Verbindung gebracht, die ihn als Ursache allen Übels erscheinen lässt; nichtreligiöse politische, ökonomische und soziale Ursachen werden weitgehend vernachlässigt.[1] Eine differenzierende und multikausale Betrachtungsweise unter Berücksichtigung auch gelebter Toleranz im europäischen und islamischen Kulturraum sowie liberalen Gedankenguts muslimischer Intellektueller findet sich nur selten.

II. Kritik an der Anwendung islamischen Rechts

Unter rechtlichen Gesichtspunkten steht die Anwendung traditionellen islamischen oder islamisch geprägten Rechts international im Kreuzfeuer der Kritik. Mit Ausnahme der Türkei, die ihr Rechtssystem unter Mustafa Kemal, genannt Atatürk, vollständig säkularisiert hat, gilt in den islamisch geprägten Staaten des Vorderen Orients traditionelles islamisches Recht zumindest in bestimmten Bereichen fort, und zwar teils in seiner traditionell von Rechtsgelehrten überlieferten Form, teils in mehr oder weniger reformierter und kodifizierter Form.[2] Die Kritik richtet sich zunächst einmal ganz besonders gegen

---

* Der Aufsatz basiert zu einem großen Teil auf dem Manuskript meiner Antrittsvorlesung als Honorarprofessor an der Freien Universität Berlin am 31. Januar 2008.

1 Ähnlich bereits *Heiner Bielefeldt*, „Muslim Voices in the Human Rights Debate“, in: Human Rights Quarterly (HRQ), Baltimore 1995, S. 587 (595); *idem*, „Menschenrechte und Menschenrechtsverständnis im Islam“, in: Europäische Grundrechte-Zeitschrift (EuGRZ), Kehl 1990, S. 489 (494).

2 Vgl. nur *Peter Scholz*, „Scharia in Tradition und Moderne“, in: JURA, Berlin 2001, S. 525 (530 f.), und *Hans-Georg Ebert*, „Tendenzen der Rechtsentwicklung“, in: *Werner Ende / Udo Steinbach* (Hrsg.), Der Islam in der Gegenwart, 5. Auflage, Bonn 2005, S. 199 ff., jeweils m.w.N.

Islam und Menschenrechte (Islam and Human Rights / الإسلام وحقوق الإنسان)
Hatem Elliesie (Hrsg./Editor), © Peter Lang Verlag: Frankfurt a.M. 2010, S. 477-498

das in einigen Staaten noch geltende[3] oder wieder eingeführte[4] islamisch geprägte Strafrecht.[5] In ihrem Fokus stehen insbesondere die sog. koranischen Strafen, drakonische Strafen an Leib und Leben wie die Steinigung, das Abschlagen von Extremitäten und das Auspeitschen, die vor allem im Iran, in Saudi-Arabien und im Sudan auch vollstreckt werden. Heftig kritisiert werden aber auch die Praxis der Wiedervergeltung bei Tötungen und Körperverletzungen in diesen Ländern sowie die weit verbreitete Anwendung der Todesstrafe in der islamischen Welt.[6]

Kritisch diskutiert wird darüber hinaus das islamisch geprägte Familien- und Erbrecht,[7] das in seiner traditionellen Ausgestaltung die Frau zur Sicherung patriarchalischer Gesellschaftsstrukturen benachteiligt. In den meisten islamischen Staaten des Vorderen Orients ist es noch stark vom traditionellen islamischen Recht geprägt,[8] auch wenn es mehr oder weniger stark reformiert und zumeist in staatliche Gesetze gegossen worden ist. Die familienrechtlichen Reformen haben zwar in vielen islamischen Staaten die rechtliche Stellung der Frau verbessert, an der strukturellen Benachteiligung der Frau aber nur wenig zu

---

3 Das gilt insbesondere für Saudi-Arabien.

4 Ihr Strafrecht reislamisiert haben vor allem Libyen, Pakistan, Iran Sudan und Nigeria. Zu letzterem vgl. *Isa Hayatu Chiroma / Hatem Elliesie,* „Islam, Islamic Law and Human Rights in the Nigerian Context", in: *Hatem Elliesie* (Hrsg./Editor), Beiträge zum Islamischen Recht VII, Islam und Menschenrechte (Islam and Human Rights / الإسلام وحقوق الإنسان), Frankfurt a.M. 2010, S. 155 ff.

5 *Heiner Bielefeldt*, Muslim Voices…, a.a.O. (Fn. 1), S. 600; *idem*, Menschenrechte…, a.a.O. (Fn. 1), S. 494 f.

6 Zum Strafrecht in den islamisch geprägten Staaten siehe nur *Peter Scholz,* Scharia in Tradition…, a.a.O. (Fn. 2), S. 533 f.; *Hans-Georg Ebert,* Tendenzen der Rechtsentwicklung, a.a.O. (Fn. 2), S. 199 ff.; *Rudolph Peters*, „The Islamization of Criminal Law: A Comparative Analysis", in: Die Welt des Islams, München 1994, S. 246 ff.; jeweils m.w.N. Vgl. ferner *Mathias Rohe*, „Islamisches Recht und Menschenrechte – eine Problemskizze", in: *Petra Bendel / Thomas Fischer* (Hrsg.), Menschen- und Bürgerrechte: Perspektiven der Region, Arbeitspapier Nr. 7 des Zentralinstituts für Regionalforschung, Erlangen 2004, S. 439 (448 ff.).

7 *Heiner Bielefeldt*, Muslim Voices…, a.a.O. (Fn. 1), S. 596 f.; *idem*, Menschenrechte…, a.a.O. (Fn. 1), S. 495; *Imen Gallala,* „Religionsfreiheit und islamisch geprägtes Erbrecht: gesetzliche Regelungen und Rechtsprechungsauslegung im heutigen Ägypten und Tunesien", in: *Hatem Elliesie* (Hrsg./Editor), Beiträge zum Islamischen Recht VII, Islam und Menschenrechte (Islam and Human Rights / الإسلام وحقوق الإنسان), Frankfurt a.M. 2010, S. 499 ff.

8 Eine gewichtige Ausnahme stellt insoweit die Türkei dar, in der das Familien- und Erbrecht einheitlich im Zivilgesetzbuch geregelt ist, das auch in seiner neuen Fassung vom 8.12.2001, die am 1.1.2002 in Kraft getreten ist, säkulares Recht schweizerischer Prägung enthält, hierzu siehe *Christian Rumpf,* „Das neue türkische Zivilgesetzbuch", in: StAZ, Frankfurt a.M. 2002, S. 97 ff.

ändern vermocht.[9] Grundlegendere Ansätze muslimischer Intellektueller zu einer Reformierung des islamisch geprägten Rechts werden zwar zuweilen gesellschaftlich diskutiert, haben sich aber bisher gesetzgeberisch kaum durchsetzen können.[10]

III. Ausrichtung der Kritik an den internationalen Menschenrechten

Die internationale Kritik am geltenden Recht in islamisch geprägten Staaten und seiner Anwendung richtet sich insbesondere an den internationalen Menschenrechten aus, zu deren Einhaltung sich viele Staaten, unter ihnen auch Deutschland und zahlreiche islamisch geprägte Staaten, in völkerrechtlichen Übereinkommen und Verträgen auf internationaler oder regionaler Ebene mehr oder weniger verbindlich verpflichtet haben.

B. Menschenrechtsschutz durch Anwendung des *ordre public*

I. *Ordre public* als Instrument des Menschenrechtsschutzes

Der Durchsetzung der internationalen Menschenrechte dienen in völkerrechtlichen Verträgen vereinbarten Kontrollmechanismen, die von der Überwachung durch einen Ausschuss bis zur Durchsetzung durch ein Gericht reichen können. Zur Durchsetzung der Menschenrechte können aber auch die nationalen Rechte mittels ihrer jeweiligen *ordre public*-Klausel beitragen. Diese stellt die Anwendung ausländischen Rechts unter den Vorbehalt, dass sie nicht gegen den unantastbaren Kernbereich der eigenen Rechtsordnung verstößt. Die deutsche Vorbehaltsklausel des Art. 6 S. 1 EGBGB normiert einen Vorbehalt für die wesentlichen Grundsätze des deutschen Rechts.[11] Solche stellen nach Art. 6 S. 2

---

9 Zum Familien- und Erbrecht in den islamisch geprägten Staaten siehe nur *Peter Scholz*, „Islamisches Recht im Wandel“, in: Fachbereich Rechtswissenschaft der Freien Universität Berlin (Hrsg.), Sommersemester 2002. Fachbereichstag, Berlin 2003, S. 46 ff.; *Peter Scholz*, „Islam-rechtliche Eheschließung und deutscher ordre public“, in: StAZ Frankfurt a.M. 2002, S. 321 (321 f. und 326 ff.); *idem*, Scharia in Tradition…, a.a.O. (Fn. 2), S. 530 f. und S. 533; *idem*, Erbrecht der maghrebinischen Staaten und deutscher ordre public, Hamburg 2006, S. 4 ff., jeweils m.w.N.; *Hans-Georg Ebert*, Das Erbrecht arabischer Länder, Frankfurt a.M. 2004, S. 29 ff.; *idem*, Das Personalstatut arabischer Länder: Problemfelder, Methoden, Perspektiven, Frankfurt a.M. 1996, S. 31 ff. Zur Gleichberechtigung der Geschlechter siehe ferner *Mathias Rohe*, Islamisches Recht und Menschenrechte…, a.a.O. (Fn. 6), S. 439 (442 ff.) m.w.N.

10 Zu diesen Ansätzen siehe nur *Heiner Bielefeldt*, Muslim Voices…, a.a.O. (Fn. 1), S. 606 ff.; *idem*, Menschenrechte…, a.a.O. (Fn. 1), S. 495; *idem*, „‚Western' Versus ;Islamic' Human Rights Conceptions? A Critique of Cultural Essentialism in the Discussion on Human Rights“, in: Political Theory, Thousand Oaks 2000, S. 101 ff., jeweils m.w.N.

11 Der Bundesgerichtshof stellt in ständiger Rechtsprechung darauf ab, ob das Ergebnis der Anwendung des ausländischen Rechts zu den Grundgedanken der deutschen Regelung

EGBGB insbesondere die Grundrechte dar, gemeint sind die Grundrechte des Grundgesetzes und der Länderverfassungen.[12] Zu den wesentlichen Grundsätzen werden aber allgemein auch die europa- und völkerrechtlich garantierten Menschenrechte gezählt, soweit sie als allgemeine Regeln des Völkerrechts nach Art. 25 GG unmittelbar oder als Inhalt eines völkerrechtlichen Vertrags aufgrund eines Zustimmungsgesetzes nach Art. 59 Abs. 2 GG Bestandteil des deutschen Rechts geworden sind.[13]

In der Praxis hat man die Anwendungsergebnisse ausländisch geprägten Rechts bisher fast ausschließlich an den einschlägigen Grundrechten des Grundgesetzes gemessen. Die europa- und völkerrechtlichen Gewährleistungen der Menschenrechte dagegen wurden im Rahmen des *ordre public* weitgehend vernachlässigt. In letzter Zeit mehren sich jedoch die Stimmen, die die internationalen menschenrechtlichen Verpflichtungen Deutschlands im Rahmen des *ordre public* verstärkt berücksichtigen wollen.[14] Sie berufen sich auf den Grundsatz der Völkerrechtsfreundlichkeit, der verlangt, den völkerrechtlichen Bindungen Deutschlands im Rahmen des *ordre public* Rechnung zu tragen, um eine völkerrechtliche Verantwortlichkeit Deutschlands zu vermeiden.[15]

II. Einschlägige Menschenrechte für islamisch geprägtes Familien- und Erbrecht

Betrachtet man den universellen Menschenrechtsschutz, der für ein islamisch geprägtes Familien- und Erbrecht relevant und Bestandteil des deutschen Rechts geworden ist, so sind international gewährleistet die Diskriminierungsverbote

---

und der in ihnen liegenden Gerechtigkeitsvorstellungen in so starkem Widerspruch steht, dass es von uns für untragbar gehalten wird, z.B. BGHZ 50, S. 370 (376); 54, S. 123 (130); 75, S. 32 (43); 118, S. 312 (330); BGH IPRax 2001, S. 586 f.

12 *Dirk Looschelders,* Internationales Privatrecht, Art. 3-46 RGBGB, Berlin 2004, Art. 6 Rz. 22; *Andreas Heldrich* in: Palandt, Bürgerliches Gesetzbuch, 65. Auflage, München 2006, Art. 6 EGBGB Rz. 7.

13 Vgl. *Jan Kropholler*, Internationales Privatrecht, 5. Auflage, Tübingen 2004, § 36 III 1 und IV 2; *Christian von Bar / Peter Mankowski*, Internationales Privatrecht, Band I, 2. Auflage, München 2003, § 7 Rz. 269 ff.; *Bernd von Hoffmann / Karsten Thorn*, Internationales Privatrecht, 8. Auflage, München 2005, § 6 Rz. 147 ff.; *Peter Scholz,* Erbrecht der maghrebinischen Staaten…, a.a.O. (Fn. 9), S. 219; *Christoph Engel*, „Ausstrahlungen der Europäischen Menschenrechtskonvention auf das Kollisionsrecht", in: RabelsZ, Tübingen 1989, S. 3 ff.

14 *Markus Voltz,* Menschenrechte und ordre public im Internationalen Privatrecht, Frankfurt a.M. 2002, S. 385; *Peter Scholz*, „Islamisch geprägtes Erbrecht und deutscher ordre public", in: *Hans-Georg Ebert/Thoralf Hanstein* (Hrsg.), Beiträge zum Islamischen Recht VI, Frankfurt a.M. 2007, S. 9 (14 ff.).

15 *Markus Voltz,* Menschenrechte und ordre public…, a.a.O. (Fn. 14), S. 385; *Peter Scholz*, Islamisch geprägtes Erbrecht und deutscher ordre public, a.a.O. (Fn. 14), S. 14.

wegen der Abstammung einschließlich deren Ehelichkeit, des Geschlechts und der Religionszugehörigkeit sowie die Religionsfreiheit im Übrigen. Geschützt sind weiter die Freiheit der Eheschließung und die Eheschließung aufgrund beiderseitigen freien Willens, die Familie vor allem vor willkürlichen Eingriffen und hinsichtlich der Freiheit ihrer Gründung sowie das Recht auf Achtung des Privat- und Familienlebens. Ferner sind die Berücksichtigung des Kindeswohls, Schutz und Fürsorge für das Kind sowie die Aufgaben, Rechte und Pflichten der für das Kind gesetzlich verantwortlichen Personen garantiert. Die Erbrechtsgarantie ist allenfalls im Rahmen des Eigentumsschutzes international gewährleistet. Einschlägig sind insoweit folgende Erklärungen, Übereinkommen, Grundsätze und gewohnheitsrechtliche Gewährleistungen:

- Internationaler Pakt über Bürgerliche und Politische Rechte vom 19.12.1966[16]
- Internationaler Pakt über Wirtschaftliche, Soziale und Kulturelle Rechte vom 19.12.1966[17]
- Übereinkommen zur Beseitigung jeder Form von Diskriminierung der Frau vom 18.12.1979[18]
- Übereinkommen über die Rechte des Kindes vom 20.11.1989[19]
- III. Genfer Abkommen über die Behandlung der Kriegsgefangenen vom 12.8.1949[20]
- IV. Genfer Abkommen zum Schutze der Zivilpersonen in Kriegszeiten vom 12.8.1949[21]
- Allgemeine Erklärung der Menschenrechte vom 10.12.1948[22], deren menschenrechtlicher Gehalt teilweise als bindendes Völkergewohnheitsrecht eingestuft wird[23]
- Konvention zum Schutze der Menschenrechte und Grundfreiheiten (Europäische Menschenrechtskonvention) vom 4.11.1950[24]
- Völkerrechtlicher Grundsatz der Achtung wohl erworbener Privatrechte[25]
- gewohnheitsrechtliche Geltung - wenn auch streitig - des Verbots der Diskriminierung aufgrund des Geschlechts und der Religionszugehörigkeit[26], der Religionsfreiheit[27] und des Schutzes des Eigentums[28].

---

16 BGBl. 1973 II S. 1534; Art. 2 Abs. 1, 3, 17, 18 Abs. 1, 23 Abs. 1, 2, 3 und 4, 24, 26, 27.

17 BGBl. 1976 II S. 428; Art. 2 Abs. 2, 3, 7, 10 Nr. 1, Nr. 2, Nr. 3 1, 11 Abs. 1.

18 BGBl. 1985 II S. 648; Art. 2 Abs. 1, 14 Abs. 1.

19 BGBl. 1992 II S. 121; Art. 2 Abs. 1, 3 Abs. 1 und 2, 5, 8 Abs. 1,14 Abs. 1, 16, 18 Abs. 1 und 2.

20 BGBl. 1954 II S. 838; Art. 34.

21 BGBl. 1954 II S. 917 und 1956 II S. 1586; Art. 24 Abs. 1, 27 Abs. 1, 38 Nr. 3 und 93 Abs. 1.

22 United Nations-Documents A/811; Art. 2, 14 Abs. 1, 16 Nr. 1 und 2, 17 Nr. 1, 18.

23 *Horst Dreier,* Vorbem. Rz. 25 m.w.N., in: *Horst Dreier* (Hrsg.), Grundgesetz, Kommentar, Band I, 2. Auflage, Tübingen 2004.

24 BGBl. 1952 II S. 685; nach Änderungen neu bekannt gemacht BGBl. 2002 II S. 1055; Art. 8, 9 Abs. 1 und Abs. 2, 12, 14.

25 *Rudolf Streintz,* Art. 25 Rz. 69, in: *Michael Sachs,* (Hrsg.), Grundgesetz, Kommentar. 3. Auflage, München 2003.

26 *Markus Voltz,* Menschenrechte und ordre public..., a.a.O. (Fn. 14), S. 248. Dagegen *Bernhard Kempen / Christian Hillgruber,* Völkerrecht, München 2007, S. 323. Nicht ein-

Von Bedeutung kann auch die völkerrechtlich geschützt Menschenwürde sein:

- in der Präambel der UN-Charta vom 26.6.1945[29]
- in den Präambeln der Internationalen Pakte über Bürgerliche und Politische Rechte sowie über Wirtschaftliche, Soziale und Kulturelle Rechte
- in der Präambel des Übereinkommens zur Beseitigung jeder Form der Diskriminierung der Frau
- in der Präambel der Satzung der UNESCO vom 16.11.1945[30] sowie
- in der Präambel und in den Art. 1 und 22 der Allgemeinen Erklärung der Menschenrechte.

III. Verbindlichkeit der Menschenrechte für islamisch geprägte Staaten

Wenngleich der deutsche *ordre public* auf die wesentlichen Grundsätze des deutschen Rechts abstellt und es folglich für seine Anwendung allein auf die völkerrechtliche Verbindlichkeit des Menschenrechts für die Bundesrepublik Deutschland ankommt, ist auch die Gebundenheit des entsprechenden islamisch geprägten Staats von Bedeutung. Der Grundsatz der größtmöglichen Schonung des fremden Rechts gebietet es nämlich, im Rahmen des *ordre public* vorrangig auf diejenige Verbürgung des Menschenrechts abzustellen, die auch für den Staat maßgebend ist, dessen Recht vom deutschen *ordre public* verdrängt wird.[31] Folglich ist hinsichtlich der islamisch geprägten Staaten primär auf die für sie verbindlich gewordenen universellen Menschenrechtspakte und die für sie geltenden einschlägigen völkergewohnheitsrechtlichen Grundsätze zurückzugreifen.

Die Allgemeine Erklärung der Menschenrechte wurde seinerzeit von der Generalversammlung ohne Gegenstimmen verabschiedet; von den neun islamischen Staaten, die damals der UNO angehörten.[32] enthielt sich lediglich Saudi-Arabien.[33] Den Internationalen Pakten über Bürgerliche und Politische

deutig hingegen *Juliane Kokott*, „Der Schutz der Menschenrechte im Völkerrecht“, in: *Hauke Brunkhorst / Wolfgang Köhler / Matthias Lutz-Bachmann* (Hrsg.), Recht auf Menschenrechte, Frankfurt a.M. 1999, S. 176 (179).

27 *Rainer Hofmann*, in: *Dieter C. Umbach / Thomas Clemens* (Hrsg.), Grundgesetz, Mitarbeiterkommentar und Handbuch, Band I, Heidelberg 2002, Art. 25 Rz. 13; *Juliane Kokott*, Der Schutz der Menschenrechte..., a.a.O. (Fn. 26), S. 180.

28 *Rudolf Streintz*, in: *Michael Sachs* (Hrsg.), Grundgesetz, a.a.O. (Fn. 25), Art. 25 Rz. 69.

29 BGBl. 1980 II S. 1252.

30 BGBl. 1971 II S. 473, 1978 II S. 987, 1983 II S. 475, 1979 II S. 419.

31 So auch *Markus Voltz*, Menschenrechte und ordre public…, a.a.O. (Fn. 14), S. 270 f. und S. 283 f.

32 Afghanistan, Ägypten, Irak, Iran, Libanon, Pakistan, Saudi-Arabien, Syrien und die Demokratische Volksrepublik Jemen.

33 Saudi-Arabien wandte sich insbesondere gegen die in Art. 18 verankerte Religionsfreiheit, soweit sie es einem Muslim gestatte, seine Religion zu wechseln, *Donna E. Arzt*,

Rechte sowie über Wirtschaftliche, Soziale und Kulturelle Rechte, auch den Übereinkommen zur Beseitigung jeder Form der Diskriminierung der Frau und über die Rechte des Kindes sowie den genannten III. und IV. Genfer Abkommen sind jeweils über 15, teilweise sogar über 20 islamische Staaten beigetreten. Soweit einzelne islamisch geprägte Staaten dem einen oder anderen Abkommen nicht beigetreten sind, haben sie sich vor allem darauf berufen, dass die in ihm gewährleistete Religionsfreiheit bzw. die Gleichberechtigung von Mann und Frau nicht mit dem islamischen Recht vereinbar sei.[34]

IV. Bedeutung eines am Völkerrecht ausgerichteten *ordre public*

Die Ausrichtung des *ordre public* an den völkerrechtlichen Gewährleistungen stärkt den internationalen Menschenrechtsschutz, indem sie den *ordre public* zu einem Instrument der Durchsetzung der internationalen Menschenrechte macht. Sie gibt dem *ordre public* eine übernationale moralisch-ethische Dimension und befreit ihn damit aus dem Geruch, ein bloßes Vehikel nationaler Interessen zu sein. Dies gilt umso mehr, als die international verbürgten Menschenrechte keinerlei Relativierung ihres Schutzes vertragen, insbesondere nicht in Gestalt des Inlandbezugs, den das Eingreifen des *ordre public* grundsätzlich verlangt.

Nach allgemeinem Völkerrecht bedarf die Anwendung inländischen Rechts auf einen Sachverhalt mit Auslandsbezug grundsätzlich einer sachlichen Rechtfertigung.[35] Dementsprechend setzt die Anwendung der Vorbehaltsklausel regelmäßig eine hinreichende Inlandsbeziehung des Sachverhalts zum Zeitpunkt der Entscheidung voraus.[36] Im Falle der Grundrechtsbetroffenheit aufgrund aus-

---

„The Application of International Human Rights Law in Islamic States", in: HRQ, Baltimore 1990, S. 202 (216). Ausführlich zur Haltung der islamischen Staaten zur Menschenrechtserklärung siehe *Alexandra Petersohn*, Islamisches Menschenrechtsverständnis unter Berücksichtigung der Vorbehalte muslimischer Staaten zu den UN-Menschenrechtsverträgen, Bonn 1999, S. 162 ff. speziell zur Haltung Ägyptens siehe *Hatem Elliesie,* Rezension von Holger Scheel: Die Religionsfreiheit im Blickwinkel des Völkerrechts, des islamischen und ägyptischen Rechts, in: Recht in Afrika (Law in Africa · Droit en Afrique), Köln 2009, Heft 1, S. 149-154 (152).

34 So beispielsweise Saudi-Arabien und Pakistan, vgl. *Donna E. Arzt*, The Application of International Human Rights..., a.a.O. (Fn. 33), S. 217 ff.

35 *Peter Scholz,* Erbrecht der maghrebinischen Staaten..., a.a.O. (Fn. 9), S. 225; *idem*, Islamisch geprägtes Erbrecht und deutscher ordre public, a.a.O. (Fn. 14), S. 15; *Christian von Bar / Peter Mankowski,* Internationales Privatrecht, Band I, a.a.O. (Fn. 13), § 7 Rz. 263 m.w.N.

36 *Peter Scholz,* Erbrecht der maghrebinischen Staaten..., a.a.O. (Fn. 9), S. 224 f.; *Dieter Blumenwitz,* in: Staudinger, Kommentar zum Bürgerlichen Recht, 13. Auflage, Berlin 1993 ff., Art. 6 EGBGB Rz. 154; *Hans Jürgen Sonnenberger*, in: Münchener Kommentar zum BGB, Band VII, EGBGB/IPR, 4. Auflage, München 2006, Art 6 EGBGB Rz. 82 ff.; *Gerhard Kegel,* in: *Soergel*, Bürgerliches Gesetzbuch, Band X, 12. Auflage, Stuttgart et

ländischer Rechtsanwendung kommt es auf die Inlandsbeziehung allerdings lediglich im Rahmen der Prüfung an, ob und inwieweit der Schutzbereich des jeweils betroffenen Grundrechts auch Sachverhalte mit Auslandsberührung erfasst; für eine weitere Relativierung des Grundrechtsschutzes ist kein Raum.[37] Es ist anhand von Wortlaut, Sinn und Zweck des betroffenen Grundrechts das im Einzelfall gebotene Maß an Inlandsbeziehung zu bestimmen, das den Schutzbereich des Grundrechts berührt sein lässt.[38]

Demgegenüber ist bei den international verbürgten Menschenrechten weder für eine inhaltliche noch für eine räumliche Relativierung ihrer Gewährleistung Raum.[39] Diese Rechte sind bereits inhaltlich und funktionell auf eine internationale Geltung im Rahmen ihres völkerrechtlichen Umfangs angelegt. Ihren Anwendungsbereich durch nationales Recht zu beschränken, wie es für ein lediglich innerstaatliches Schutzgut grundsätzlich geboten ist, verstieße gegen

---

al. 1996, Art. 6 EGBGB Rz. 27; *Andreas Spickhoff,* Der ordre public im internationalen Privatrecht, 1989, 97 ff., jeweils m.w.N.; *Gerhard Kegel/Klaus Schurig,* Internationales Privatrecht, 9. Auflage, München 2004, § 16 II, III 2 b; *Jan Kropholler*, Internationales Privatrecht, a.a.O. (Fn. 13), § 36 II 2; *Bernd von Hoffmann/Karsten Thorn,* Internationales Privatrecht, a.a.O. (Fn. 13), § 6 Rz. 152; vgl. BGHZ 63, S. 219 (226); 120, S. 29 (34).

37 Liegt infolge einer hinreichenden Inlandsbeziehung eine Grundrechtsverletzung vor, greift nach der zutreffenden Rechtsprechung des Bundesverfassungsgerichts die Vorbehaltsklausel immer ein, da angesichts der Grundrechtsbindung des Art. 1 Abs. 3 GG für eine Differenzierung zwischen tragbaren und untragbaren Grundrechtsverletzungen kein Raum ist, vgl. BVerfGE 31, S. 58 (86).

38 *Peter Scholz,* Erbrecht der maghrebinischen Staaten..., a.a.O. (Fn. 9), S. 226; *idem*, Islamisch geprägtes Erbrecht und deutscher ordre public, a.a.O. (Fn. 14), S. 18; vgl. BVerfGE 31, S. 58 (86); *Dieter Blumenwitz,* in: Staudinger, a.a.O. (Fn. 36), Art 6 EGBGB Rz. 13, 104; *Dirk Looschelders,* a.a.O. (Fn. 12), Art. 6, Rz. 26 ff.; *Gerhard Kegel / Klaus Schurig,* Internationales Privatrecht, a.a.O. (Fn. 36), S. 471; *Jan Kropholler* Internationales Privatrecht, a.a.O. (Fn. 113), § 36 IV 1; *Dirk Looschelders,* „Die Ausstrahlung der Grund- und Menschenrechte auf das Internationale Privatrecht", in: RabelsZ 2001, S. 463 (484 ff.), jeweils m.w.N.; *Andreas Spickhoff,* „Eheschließung, Ehescheidung und ordre public", in: JZ, Tübingen 1991, S. 323 (325). A.A. aber insbesondere *Alexander Lüderitz,* Internationales Privatrecht, 2. Auflage 1992, Rz. 209.

39 Im Ergebnis ebenso *Dieter Blumenwitz,* in: Staudinger, a.a.O. (Fn. 36), Art. 6 EGBGB Rz. 68, 76 f., 161 m.w.N.; *Gerhard Kegel / Klaus Schurig,* Internationales Privatrecht, a.a.O. (Fn. 36), § 16 III 2 b; *Christian von Bar / Peter Mankowski,* Internationales Privatrecht, Band I, a.a.O. (Fn. 13), § 7 Rz. 269; a.A. *Hans Jürgen Sonnenberger*, in: Münchener Kommentar zum BGB, a.a.O. (Fn. 36), Art. 6 EGBGB Rz. 80; *Andreas Spickhoff,* Eheschließung, Ehescheidung und ordre public, a.a.O. (Fn. 38), S. 98 f. m.w.N.; vgl. *Herbert Kronke,* Die Wirkungskraft der Grundrechte bei Fällen mit Auslandsbezug, in: *Dagmar Coester-Waltjen / Herbert Kronke / Juliane Kokott,* Die Wirkungskraft der Grundrechte bei Fällen mit Auslandsbezug, Heidelberg 1998, S. 33 (52 f.), m.w.N.

den Grundsatz der Völkerrechtsfreundlichkeit, der als allgemeine Regel des Völkerrechts nach Art. 25 S. 2 GG den staatlichen Gesetzen vorgeht und unmittelbare Geltung hat.[40] Nach dem genannten Grundsatz ist der nationale *ordre public* so anzuwenden, dass die innerstaatliche Rechtsanwendung nicht von den menschenrechtlichen Verpflichtungen abweicht. Nur so kann ein völkerrechtswidriges Verhalten Deutschlands mit entsprechenden Verantwort-lichkeiten vermieden werden.[41]

Demnach kommt der deutsche *ordre public* auf der Grundlage zu innerstaatlichem Recht gewordener international verbürgter Menschenrechte bereits dann zur Anwendung, wenn deutsche Gerichte international zuständig sind und somit den Fall mit Auslandsbezug weiter zu prüfen haben. Das gilt auch, wenn die internationale Zuständigkeit durch eine Gerichtsstandsvereinbarung oder durch rügeloses Verhandeln begründet wird, wie es vor allem in vermögensrechtlichen Fällen der Fall ist. Allerdings darf nicht übersehen werden, dass bereits die internationale Zuständigkeit im Familien- und Erbrecht eine nicht unerhebliche Inlandsbeziehung erfordert. Deren schwächste Ausprägungen stellen vor allem der gewöhnliche Aufenthalt einer Person im Inland[42] und das nur von inländischen Behörden erfüllbare Bedürfnis nach Fürsorge einer Person im Inland[43] dar.

V. Grenzen eines am Völkerrecht ausgerichteten *ordre public*

Inhalt und Umfang der völkerrechtlichen Verpflichtungen zur Gewährleistung von Menschenrechten sind nach den völkerrechtlichen Auslegungsregeln zu bestimmen.[44] Oft eröffnen die menschenrechtsgewährleistenden Normen und ihre Schrankenregelungen ausdrücklich oder konkludent Auslegungsspielräume. Auch billigen die internationalen Überwachungsgremien den Vertragstaaten regelmäßig Beurteilungsspielräume (*margins of discretion*) zu, damit ihr Ver-

---

40 Vgl. *Markus Voltz,* Menschenrechte und ordre public..., a.a.O. (Fn. 14), S. 292 ff., allerdings nur zum Inlandsbezug.

41 BVerfGE 74, 358, 370; *Markus Voltz*, Menschenrechte und ordre public..., a.a.O. (Fn. 14), S. 262 ff. m.w.N.; *Peter Scholz*, Islamisch geprägtes Erbrecht und deutscher ordre public, a.a.O. (Fn. 14), S. 20 m.w.N.

42 Z. B. §§ 606 a Abs. 1 S. 1 Ziff. 3 und 4, 640 a Abs. 2 S. 1 Ziff. 2 ZPO, 35 b Abs. 1 Ziff. 2, 43 b Abs. 1 S. 1 Ziff. 2 FGG, Art. 1 MSA.

43 Z. B. § 35 b Abs. 2 FGG.

44 Zur Auslegung von Menschenrechtspakten siehe nur *Karl Doehring*, Völkerrecht, 2. Auflage, Heidelberg 2004, Rz. 980; *Bernhard Kempen / Christian Hillgruber,* Völkerrecht, a.a.O. (Fn. 26), S. 325 ff.; zur Auslegung der Europäischen Menschenrechtskonvention siehe nur *Matthias Herdegen*, Völkerrecht, 5. Auflage, München 2006, § 49 Rz. 4; *Theodor Schilling*, Internationaler Menschenrechtsschutz, Tübingen 2004, Rz. 27 ff.; *Markus Voltz*, Menschenrechte und ordre public..., a.a.O. (Fn. 14), S. 79 ff. m.w.N.

halten bei den Vertragsstaaten auf die erforderliche Akzeptanz stößt.[45] In allen diesen Fällen sind aber die Grenzen dieser Spielräume zu ermitteln und zu beachten. Insbesondere ist der Mindeststandard an menschenrechtlicher Gewährleistung einzuhalten, der der entsprechenden Verpflichtung im Wege der Auslegung zu entnehmen ist.[46]

Hinsichtlich des räumlich-personalen Schutzbereiches eines völkerrechtlichen Abkommens ist für den Menschenrechtsschutz charakteristisch, dass dieser einer jeden der Hoheitsgewalt eines Vertragstaates unterworfenen Person unabhängig von ihrer Staatsangehörigkeit zuteil wird.[47] Der Hoheitsgewalt der Bundesrepublik Deutschland unterfällt bereits jede Person, die vor einem deutschen Gericht klagt oder verklagt wird und damit der Rechtsprechung eines deutschen Gerichts unterliegt.

In ihrem Wirkungsgrad unterscheiden sich völkerrechtliche Verpflichtungen je nach der Art und Weise ihres Inhalts.[48] Sind sie auf Unterlassung staatlicher Eingriffe in Individualrechte gerichtet, unterliegen sie wesentlich geringeren Beschränkungen als solche Verpflichtungen, die auf Gewährung einer Leistung wie beispielsweise Schutz und Fürsorge gerichtet sind.[49] Die Realisierung dieser Rechte hängt nämlich von der Existenz der dafür erforderlichen staatlichen Mittel ab und hat vor der Verwirklichung solcher Werte zurückzustehen, die mit diesen Mitteln vorrangig zu bedienen sind.[50]

Trotz bestehender Auslegungsspielräume und eingeschränkten Wirkungsgrades kann sich der Menschenrechtsschutz durch eine jahrzehntelange Praxis verdichtet haben. Für diese ist insbesondere die Tätigkeit von Organen maßgebend,

---

45 Vgl. *Markus Voltz*, Menschenrechte und ordre public…, a.a.O. (Fn. 14), S. 134 ff. und S. 92 ff., jeweils m.w.N. Zum Europäischen Gerichtshof für Menschenrechte weitere Nachweise bei *Eckart Klein*, „Universeller Menschenrechtsschutz – Realität oder Utopie", in: EuGRZ 1999, S. 109 (113, dort Fn. 72).

46 Vgl. *Markus Voltz*, Menschenrechte und ordre public…, a.a.O. (Fn. 14), S. 277 f. und 280 f. Zum menschenrechtlichen Mindeststandard siehe ferner *Looschelders*, Die Ausstrahlung der Grund- und Menschenrechte…, a.a.O. (Fn. 38), S. 483 f.

47 Vgl. *Karl Doehring*, Völkerrecht, a.a.O. (Fn. 44), Rz. 982; *Markus Voltz*, Menschenrechte und ordre public…, a.a.O. (Fn. 14), S. 129 ff., und für die Europäische Menschenrechtskonvention S. 106 ff.

48 So enthält beispielsweise das Übereinkommen über die Rechte des Kindes in weiten Teilen nur wenig verbindliche Bestimmungen, die zudem oft noch inhaltlich unbestimmt ausgestaltet sind, vgl. *Markus Voltz*, Menschenrechte und ordre public…, a.a.O. (Fn. 14), S. 195 f.

49 Vgl. *Juliane Kokott,* Der Schutz der Menschenrechte..., a.a.O. (Fn. 26), S. 184 ff.; *Karl Doehring*, Völkerrecht, a.a.O. (Fn. 44), Rz. 977 f.; *Markus Voltz*, Menschenrechte und ordre public…, a.a.O. (Fn. 14), S. 121 ff., S. 101 ff.

50 Vgl. *Juliane Kokott,* Der Schutz der Menschenrechte..., a.a.O. (Fn. 26), S. 184.

denen die Menschenrechtspakte die Aufgabe übertragen haben, die Einhaltung der Pakte zu überwachen. Bei diesen Organen handelt es sich um spezielle Gremien (z. B. Ausschüsse)[51] oder bestimmte Gerichte,[52] wobei die Auslegung der Gremien grundsätzlich nicht verbindlich ist und die Entscheidungen der Gerichte regelmäßig nur *inter partes* wirken.

Eingeschränkt wird die Geltung von internationalen Menschenrechtspakten ferner durch rechtlich zulässige Vorbehalte der Mitgliedstaaten.[53] Von derartigen Erklärungen, die Geltung einzelner Vorschriften für sich auszuschließen, haben zahlreiche Staaten, unter ihnen auch die Bundesrepublik Deutschland, Gebrauch gemacht.[54] Dabei ist der Prüfung der Vorbehalte auf ihre völkerrechtliche Wirksamkeit hin besondere Aufmerksamkeit zu widmen, wie noch darzulegen sein wird.

Die zwischen den Vertragsstaaten zu überbrückenden Differenzen im Verständnis der Menschenrechte, den daraus resultierenden Auslegungen und den Vorbehalten sind immens. Während abendländisch geprägte Rechtsvorstellungen den Menschen und seine Freiheitsrechte in den Vordergrund stellen, betonen afrikanische und asiatische Rechtskonzeptionen die Gemeinschaftsbindung des Einzelnen. In diesen sind folglich die Individualrechte weniger stark ausgeprägt

---

51 Zu nennen ist beispielsweise die Praxis des Ausschusses für Menschenrechte nach Art. 28 ff. des Internationalen Paktes über Bürgerliche und Politische Rechte durch die Formulierung abstrakter General Comments und eine jahrzehntelange Praxis in Individualbeschwerdeverfahren, vgl. *Markus Voltz*, Menschenrechte und ordre public..., a.a.O. (Fn. 14), S. 115 ff.

52 Von überragender Bedeutung ist die Rechtsprechungstätigkeit des Europäischen Gerichtshofs für Menschenrechte für die Durchsetzung des Menschenrechtsschutzes der Europäischen Menschenrechtskonvention, vgl. *Markus Voltz*, Menschenrechte und ordre public..., a.a.O. (Fn. 14), S. 78 ff.; *Karl Doehring*, Völkerrecht, a.a.O. (Fn. 44), Rz. 997 ff.; *Bernhard Kempen / Christian Hillgruber*, Völkerrecht, a.a.O. (Fn. 26), S. 317 ff.; *Juliane Kokott*, Der Schutz der Menschenrechte..., a.a.O. (Fn. 26), S. 193 ff., jeweils m.w.N.

53 Zu Vorbehalten siehe nur *Karl Doehring*, Völkerrecht, a.a.O. (Fn. 44), Rz. 350 ff.; *Bernhard Kempen / Christian Hillgruber*, Völkerrecht, a.a.O. (Fn. 26), S. 66 ff.; *Monika Bauer*, Vorbehalte zu Menschenrechtsverträgen, München 1994, und *Alexandra Petersohn*, Islamisches Menschenrechtsverständnis..., a.a.O. (Fn. 33), S. 167 ff.

54 So beispielsweise die für das Familien- und Erbrecht nicht relevanten Vorbehalte zum Internationalen Pakt über Bürgerliche und politische Rechte, BGBl. 1976 II S. 1068, Ziff. 1, und zur Europäischen Menschenrechtskonvention, BGBl. 1954 II S. 14 f., vgl. *Markus Voltz*, Menschenrechte und ordre public..., a.a.O. (Fn. 14), S. 139 ff. und S. 109, und die durch Gesetzesänderungen inzwischen weitgehend bedeutungslos gewordene Erklärung der Bundesrepublik zum Übereinkommen über die Rechte des Kindes, BGBl. 1992 II S. 990, vgl. *Markus Voltz*, Menschenrechte und ordre public..., a.a.O. (Fn. 14), S. 191 ff.

bzw. stärkeren Beschränkungen unterworfen.[55] Von besonderem Interessen sind in diesem Zusammenhang die islamisch geprägten Sichtweisen und Konzeptionen von den Menschenrechten sowie der Umgang der islamischen Staaten mit den internationalen Menschenrechten.

C. Islamisches Verständnis von den internationalen Menschenrechten

I. Islamisch geprägte Sichtweisen der Menschenrechte

Ausgangspunkt für die in der islamischen Welt vertretenen Auffassungen zu den internationalen Menschenrechten ist das vom modernen europäischen Verständnis grundsätzlich abweichende Verhältnis des Staates zum Bürger im traditionellen Islam. Der Islam hat aufgrund der Doppelrolle des Propheten als Religionsstifter und politischer Führer eine religiöse und eine politische Dimension, die miteinander verwoben sind. Die Ausübung des islamischen Glaubens und seine Verbreitung über die Welt können nach islamischer Auffassung nur von einem islamischen Gemeinwesen auf der Grundlage des von Gott gesetzten religiösen Rechts, der *šarīʿa*, garantiert werden. Ist der islamische Staat das Instrument des allmächtigen Gottes zur Durchsetzung seines Willens auf Erden, geht alle irdische Macht von ihm aus und kommt der Aufrechterhaltung seiner Funktionsfähigkeit die höchste Bedeutung zu. Für individuelle Rechte des Einzelnen gegenüber dem Staat wie die Menschenrechte und für Institutionen zur Kontrolle des Staates lässt dieses Staatsverständnis grundsätzlich keinen Raum.[56]

Vor diesem Hintergrund vertreten die Gelehrten in der islamischen Welt heute die unterschiedlichsten Standpunkte zu den universalen Menschenrechten, je nachdem, wie eng sie sich an das traditionelle Verständnis von Staat und Recht im Islam gebunden fühlen und wie offen sie gegenüber Ansätzen einer

---

55 Vgl. *Bernhard Kempen / Christian Hillgruber,* Völkerrecht, a.a.O. (Fn. 26), S. 331; *Karl Doehring*, Völkerrecht, a.a.O. (Fn. 44), Rz. 980; *Bassam Tibi*, Im Schatten Allahs. Der Islam und die Menschenrechte, 1994, S. 103 ff.; *Ann Elizabeth Mayer*, Islam and Human Rights, Boulder 1991, S. 47.

56 Vgl. nur *Udo Steinbach*, Die Menschenrechte im Verständnis des Islam, VRÜ 1975, S. 47 (S. 47 ff.); *Martin Forstner,* Das Menschenrecht der Religionsfreiheit und des Religionswechsels als Problem der islamischen Staaten, Kanon 1991, S. 119 und S. 130, jeweils m.w.N., ferner *Noel J. Coulson*, The State and the Individual in Islamic Law, in: ICLQ, Oxford et al. 1957, S. 49 ff.; *Sharifoddin Pirzada*, „Concept of Islamic State and Human Rights in Islam“, in: The Iranian Journal of International Affairs, Teheran 1991/1992, S. 679 ff; *Alexandra Petersohn*, Islamisches Menschenrechtsverständnis…, a.a.O. (Fn. 33), S. 63 ff. Zur fehlenden Tradition des Individualismus im Islam siehe *Ann Elizabeth Mayer*, Islam and Human Rights, a.a.O. (Fn. 55), S. 47; kritisch dazu *Alexandra Petersohn*, Islamisches Menschenrechtsverständnis…, a.a.O. (Fn. 33), S. 157 ff.

modernen Interpretation islamischer Inhalte sind.[57] Die Mehrheit der

[57] Vgl. *Bassam Tibi*, Im Schatten Allahs, a.a.O. (Fn. 55), S. 104; *Heiner Bielefeldt*, „Die Menschenrechte zwischen Universalitätsanspruch und kultureller Bedingtheit", 22.-24. September 1992 in Hamburg, ORIENT (Deutsche Zeitschrift für Politik, Wirtschaft und Kultur des Orients), Berlin 1992, S. 367 (369) – zum Verhältnis des Islam zu den Menschenrechten siehe außer den in diesem Aufsatz zitierten Autorinnen und Autoren ferner: *Khalid M. Ishaque*, „Human Rights in Islamic Law", in: RevICJ (Review of the International Commission of Jurists), Genf 1974, S. 30 ff.; *Malik*, „Islamic Concept of Human Rights", in: *S. M. Haidar* (Hrsg.), Islamic Concept of Human Rights, Lahore 1978, S. 59 ff.; *Allamah Abu Al-A'la Mawdudi*, „Human Rights in Islam", Al-Tawhid, Qum 1987, S. 56 ff.; *Abdul Aziz Said*, „Human Rights in Islamic Perspective", in: *Adamantia Pollis / Peter Schwab* (Hrsg.), Human Rights: Cultural and Ideological Perspectives, New York 1979, S. 92 ff.; *Bassam Tibi / Miklos Muranyi*, Streitgespräch: Die Menschenrechte im Islam, in: *Gerhard Schult* (Hrsg.), Islamische Herausforderung an West und Ost, Altenberge 1981, S. 68 ff.; *Mohamed Charfi*, Islam et droits de l'homme, in: Islamochristiana, Rom 1983, S. 13 ff.; *Jan Hjärpe*, „The Contemporary Debate in the Muslim World on the Definition of ‚Human Rights'", in: *Ferdinand Klaus / Mozaffari Mehdi* (Hrsg.), Islam: State and Society, London 1988, S. 26 ff.; *Abdullahi an-Na'im*, Toward an Islamic Reformation. Civil Liberties, Human Rights and International Law, Syracuse 1990; *Christine Lienemann-Perrin*, „Anmerkungen zum Verständnis der Menschenrechte im Islam", in: CIBEDO – Beiträge zum Gespräch zwischen Christen und Muslimen, Frankfurt a.M. 1991, S. 162 ff.; *Bassam Tibi*, Im Namen Gottes?, „Der Islam, die Menschenrechte und die kulturelle Moderne", in: *Michael Lüders* (Hrsg.), Der Islam im Aufbruch, München / Zürich 1992, S. 144 ff.; *Mohamed Charfi*, „Die Menschenrechte im Bezugsfeld von Religion, Recht und Staat in den islamischen Ländern", in: *Johannes Schwartländer* (Hrsg.), Freiheit der Religion. Christentum und Islam unter dem Anspruch der Menschenrechte. Sunnitische Muslime zwischen Islamismus, Säkularismus und Modernismus, Mainz 1993, S. 93 ff.; *Tore Lindholm / Kari Vogt* (Hrsg.), Islamic Law Reform and Human Rights, Oslo / Kopenhagen 1993; *Stefan Batzli* (Hrsg.), Menschenbilder, Menschenrechte. Islam und Okzident: Kulturen im Konflikt, Zürich 1994; *Reza Afshari*, „An Essay on Islamic Cultural Relativism in the Discourse of Human Rights", in: HRQ 1994, S. 235 ff.; *Sami A. Abu-Salieh Aldeeb*, Les musulmans face aux droits, de l'homme, Bochum 1994; *Gamal ad-din Mahmud*, „Menschenrechte im Islam", in: Concilium 30, Einsiedeln-Zürich / Mainz 1994, S. 248 ff.; *Gudrun Krämer*, „Menschenrechte und islamische Gesellschaftsordnung", in: Politische Studien, Sonderheft 1, 1995, S. 56 ff.; *Abdullahi Ahmed An-Na'im*, „Islamic Law and Human Rights Today", in: Interights Bulletin, London 1996, S. 3 ff.; *Udo Steinbach*, „Menschenbild, Menschenrechte und Demokratie in Europa und der islamischen Welt – einige vergleichende Anmerkungen", in: *Rainer Brunnder / Monika Gronke / Jens P. Laut / Ulrich Rebstock* (Hrsg.), Islamstudien Ohne Ende. Festschrift für Werner Ende zum 65. Geburtstag, Würzburg 2002, S. 449 ff.; *Maimul Ahsan Khan*, Human Rights in the Muslim World. Fundamentalism, Constitutionalism and International Politics, Durham 2003; *Susan Eileen Waltz*, "Universal Human Rights: The Contribution of Muslim States", in: HRQ 2004, S. 4 ff.; *Mashood A. Baderin*, "Identifying possible mechanisms within Islamic law for the promotion and protection of human rights in Muslim states", in: Netherlands

muslimischen Gelehrten tut sich mit den universalen Menschenrechten schwer, da sich ihre Konzeption und ihre Inhalte mit dem traditionellen Recht nicht vereinbaren lassen. Viele Gelehrte halten die internationalen Menschenrechtspakte für Instrumente eines kulturellen Hegemoniestrebens des Westens und die Einforderung ihrer weltweiten Beachtung für Menschenrechtsimperialismus. Folglich stellen diese Gelehrte die internationalen Menschenrechte unter einen generellen Šarīʿavorbehalt oder konzipieren ein islamisches Menschenrechtsverständnis, indem sie Herkunft und Inhalt der Menschenrechte im Sinne des traditionellen Islam interpretieren.[58] Ihren Ausdruck haben derartige Sichtweisen beispielsweise auch in der „Allgemeinen Islamischen Menschenrechtserklärung" des „Islamrat von Europa" von 1981[59] und dem Entwurf einer „Menschenrechtserklärung im Islam" der Organisation der Islamischen Konferenz (OIC) von 1990[60] gefunden.[61] Lediglich eine Minderheit der Gelehrten sieht die uni-

Quarterly of Human Rights 2004, S. 3 ff.; *Norbert Müller*, Islam und Menschenrechte, Köln 2004.

58 Vgl. hierzu ausführlich *Heiner Bielefeldt*, „Western" Versus „Islamic" Human Rights Conceptions?, a.a.O. (Fn. 10), S. 16 ff.; *idem*, Muslim Voices..., a.a.O. (Fn. 1), S. 606 ff.; *idem*, „Der Universalitätsanspruch der Menschenrechte und die Pluralität der Kulturen", in: *Eduard J. M., Kroker* und *Bruno Dechamps* (Hrsg.), Das Menschenbild der freien Gesellschaft: Globalisierung und europäische Integration, Frankfurt a.M. 2000, S. 43 (59 ff.); *Martin Forstner*, „Menschenrechte zwischen Geltungsuniversalität und Inhaltspartikularität – ein Problem für den Islam in Europa?", in: *René Pahud de Mortanges / Erwin Tanner* (Hrsg.), Muslime und schweizerische Rechtsordnung. Les musulmans et l'ordre juridique suisse, Freiburg 2002, S. 479 (491 ff.); *Lorenz Müller*, Islam und Menschenrechte, Hamburg 1996, S. 141 ff.; *Alexandra Petersohn*, Islamisches Menschenrechtsverständnis..., a.a.O. (Fn. 33), S. 79 f. und 232 ff., jeweils m.w.N. Siehe ferner *Boubker Bennani*, L'islamisme et les droits de l'homme, Lausanne 1984.

59 Zur „Allgemeinen Islamischen Menschenrechtserklärung" von 1981 siehe *Ann Elizabeth Mayer*, Islam and Human Rights, a.a.O. (Fn. 55), S. 27 ff., 86 ff., 120 ff., 153 ff. und 173; *Heiner Bielefeldt*, Menschenrechte..., a.a.O. (Fn. 1), S. 496 f.; *Martin Forstner*, „Inhalt und Begründung der Allgemeinen Islamischen Menschenrechtserklärung", in: *Johannes Hoffmann* (Hrsg.), Begründung von Menschenrechten aus der Sicht unterschiedlicher Kulturen, Frankfurt a.M. 1991, S. 249 ff.; *M. Salim Abdullah*, „Die Allgemeine Islamische Menschenrechtserklärung", in: *Hermann Weber* (Hrsg.), Die Menschenrechte – unsere Verantwortung, Jahresakademie (KAAD) 25.-27. April 1991, Bonn 1991, S. 113 ff.; *Ali Merad*, Überlegungen zur „Allgemeinen Islamischen Menschenrechtserklärung", in: *Johannes Schwartländer* (Hrsg.), Freiheit der Religion. Christentum und Islam unter dem Anspruch der Menschenrechte. Sunnitische Muslime zwischen Islamismus, Säkularismus und Modernismus, Mainz 1993, S. 443 ff.; *Lorenz Müller*, Islam und Menschenrechte..., a.a.O. (Fn. 58), 1996, S. 120 f., und *Alexandra Petersohn*, Islamisches Menschenrechtsverständnis..., a.a.O. (Fn. 33), S. 240 ff., jeweils m.w.N.

60 Zum Entwurf einer „Menschenrechtserklärung im Islam" von 1990 siehe *Ann Elizabeth Mayer*, „Universal Versus Islamic Human Rights: A Clash of Cultures or a Clash with a Construct?", in: Mich. JIL, Ann Arbor 1994, S. 307 (327 ff.); *Lorenz Müller*, Islam und

versalen Menschenrechte auch für islamische Staaten als verbindlich an, sei es auf der Grundlage eines säkularen Rechtsverständnisses, sei es auf der Grundlage einer modernen Auslegung des Islam. Säkulare Ansätze werden heute nicht zuletzt auch aus Angst vor Repressalien in den islamischen Staaten nur selten vertreten. Ihre Vertreter fordern zumeist eine klare Trennung von Staat und Religion in der Weise, dass der Staat, seine Aufgaben und sein Verhältnis zu seinen Bürgern nicht mehr im Sinne des traditionellen islamischen Rechts, sondern im Sinne der modernen westlichen Staatslehre verstanden werden, die sich mit der Idee unveräußerlicher grundlegender Rechte menschlicher Individuen gegenüber staatlicher Gewalt vereinbaren lässt.[62] Andere liberale Gelehrte fordern eine Neuinterpretation der Quellen Koran und Sunna, die unter Rückbesinnung auf ihren Bedeutungsgehalt den Anforderungen an eine moderne Gesellschaft besser gerecht wird. Dabei wird regelmäßig der ethisch-religiöse Gehalt der Quellen betont, während ihre rechtliche Bedeutung vernachlässigt oder sogar negiert wird. Auch wird vertreten, die Quellen in allgemeingültige Passagen und solche Passagen aufzuteilen, die lediglich historischen Gehalt haben und aktuell nicht mehr von Bedeutung sind.[63] Diese Gelehrten halten die internationalen Menschenrechte für vereinbar mit dem Geist des Islam.[64]

Menschenrechte, a.a.O. (Fn. 58), S. 120, und *Alexandra Petersohn*, Islamisches Menschenrechtsverständnis..., a.a.O. (Fn. 33), S. 242 ff., jeweils m.w.N.

61 Vgl. an dieser Stelle zum OIC *Theodor Rathgeber*, „Die Organisation Islamischer Konferenz im UN-Menschenrechtsrat: Menschenrechte als Instrument staatlicher Politik", in: *Hatem Elliesie* (Hrsg./Editor), Beiträge zum Islamischen Recht VII, Islam und Menschenrechte (Islam and Human Rights / الإسلام وحقوق الإنسان), Frankfurt a.M. 2010, S. 457-473.

62 Vgl. hierzu ausführlich *Heiner Bielefeldt*, „Western" Versus „Islamic" Human Rights Conceptions?, a.a.O. (Fn. 10), S. 20 f.; *idem*, Muslim Voices..., a.a.O. (Fn. 1), S. 606 ff.; *idem*, Der Universalitätsanspruch der Menschenrechte und die Pluralität der Kulturen, a.a.O. (Fn. 58), S. 61; *Martin Forstner*, Menschenrechte zwischen Geltungsuniversalität und Inhaltspartikularität..., a.a.O. (Fn. 58), S. 499; *Lorenz Müller*, Islam und Menschenrechte, a.a.O. (Fn. 58), S. 213 ff.; *Alexandra Petersohn*, Islamisches Menschenrechtsverständnis..., a.a.O. (Fn. 33), S. 81 f., jeweils m.w.N.

63 Zum Gesamtkontext vgl. auch *Abdullahi Ahmed An-Na'im*, "Islam and Human Rights: Introductory Remarks and Reflections", in: *Hatem Elliesie* (Hrsg./Editor), Beiträge zum Islamischen Recht VII, Islam und Menschenrechte (Islam and Human Rights / الإسلام وحقوق الإنسان), Frankfurt a.M. 2010, S. 41-47; *Muhammad Kalisch*, „Islam und Menschenrechte: Betrachtungen zum Verhältnis von Religion und Recht", in: *Hatem Elliesie* (Hrsg./Editor), ibidem, S. 49-72; *Assem Hefny*, „Hermeneutik, Koraninterpretation und Menschenrechte", in: *Hatem Elliesie* (Hrsg./Editor), ibidem, S. 73-97; *Heiner Bielefeldt*, „‚Westliche' versus ‚islamische' Menschenrechtskonzeptionen", ibidem, S. 99-119.

64 Vgl. hierzu ausführlich *Heiner Bielefeldt*, „Western" Versus „Islamic" Human Rights Conceptions?, a.a.O. (Fn. 10), S. 16 ff.; *idem*, Muslim Voices..., a.a.O. (Fn. 1), S. 606 ff.;

II. Stellung der islamisch geprägten Staaten zu den internationalen Menschenrechten

Mit Ausnahme der Türkei, die sich nach dem ersten Weltkrieg konsequent säkularisierte, gründen auch heute islamisch geprägte Staaten ihre Legitimation auf den Islam und ihre Rechtsordnung auf das islamische Recht. In den Verfassungen der meisten islamisch geprägten Staaten ist der Islam als Staatsreligion oder offizielle Religion verankert[65] und wird die *šarīʿa*, werden die Grundsätze der *šarīʿa* oder wird die Rechtswissenschaft als Hauptquelle oder eine Quelle der Gesetzgebung festgeschrieben.[66]

Dieses Selbstverständnis hindert die islamisch geprägten Staaten nicht, internationalen Menschenrechtspakten beizutreten, führt aber dazu, dass sie ihre menschenrechtlichen Verpflichtungen regelmäßig šarīʿakonform auslegen.[67] Zudem machen die islamisch geprägten Staaten wesentlich öfter und umfänglicher von der Möglichkeit Gebrauch, Vorbehalte zu internationalen Menschenrechtspakten zu erklären, um die Vereinbarkeit der völkerrechtlichen Verpflichtungen mit der *šarīʿa* zu gewährleisten.[68] Das gilt vor allem hinsichtlich des Übereinkommens zur Beseitigung jeder Form von Diskriminierung der Frau, und zwar insbesondere in Bezug auf das allgemeine Verbot der Diskriminierung der Frau und die Maßnahmen zur ihrer Beseitigung, die entsprechende Regelung hinsichtlich der Rechte und Pflichten in Ehe und Familie, die Gleichheit in Erwerb, Wechsel und Beibehaltung der Staatsangehörigkeit sowie deren Über-

---

idem, Der Universalitätsanspruch der Menschenrechte…, a.a.O. (Fn. 58), S. 60 f.; *Martin Forstner*, Menschenrechte zwischen Geltungsuniversalität und Inhaltspartikularität…, a.a.O. (Fn. 58), S. 501; *Lorenz Müller*, Islam und Menschenrechte, a.a.O. (Fn. 58), S. 213 ff. und 239 ff.; *Alexandra Petersohn*, Islamisches Menschenrechtsverständnis…, a.a.O. (Fn. 33), S. 80 f. und 236 ff., jeweils m.w.N.

65 *Hans-Georg Ebert*, Die Interdependenz von Staat, Verfassung und Islam im Nahen und Mittleren Osten in der Gegenwart, Frankfurt a.M. 1991, S. 130 ff.; *idem*, „Arabische Verfassungen und das Problem der „islamischen Menschenrechte"", in: VRÜ, Baden-Baden 1997, S. 520 (524); *Martin Forstner*, Das Menschenrecht der Religionsfreiheit…, a.a.O. (Fn. 56), S. 105; 152; *Heiner Bielefeldt*, Menschenrechte…, a.a.O. (Fn. 1), 495.

66 *Martin Forstner*, Das Menschenrecht der Religionsfreiheit…, a.a.O. (Fn. 56), S. 105 und S. 152; *Hans-Georg Ebert*, Arabische Verfassungen…, a.a.O. (Fn. 65), S. 525; eine Klassifizierung der Staaten vornehmend *Alexandra Petersohn*, Islamisches Menschenrechtsverständnis…, a.a.O. (Fn. 33), S. 40 ff; *Imen Gallala*, Religionsfreiheit… a.a.O. (Fn. 7), S. 480 (Fn. 8), S. 484-485 (jeweils m.w.N.).

67 Vgl. *Bernhard Kempen / Christian Hillgruber*, Völkerrecht, a.a.O. (Fn. 26), S. 331 f.; *Donna Arzt*, The Application of International Human Rights…, a.a.O. (Fn. 33), S. 214 ff.

68 Vgl. *Alexandra Petersohn*, Islamisches Menschenrechtsverständnis…, a.a.O. (Fn. 33), S. 173 ff.; *Donna E. Arzt*, The Application of International Human Rights…, a.a.O. (Fn. 33), S. 218 ff.; *Martin Forstner*, Menschenrechte zwischen Geltungsuniversalität und Inhaltspartikularität, a.a.O. (Fn. 58), S. 490 f.

tragung auf die Kinder.[69] Allerdings haben einige Staaten, unter ihnen die Bundesrepublik Deutschland, gegen diese Vorbehalte nach einer entsprechenden Option im Wiener Übereinkommen über das Recht der Verträge vom 23.5.1969,[70] dem auch einige islamische Staaten beigetreten sind,[71] Einspruch eingelegt, weil die Vorbehalte mit Ziel und Zweck des Paktes nicht vereinbar und aus diesem Grunde unzulässig[72] sind.[73]

Ferner gibt es zahlreiche Vorbehalte islamisch geprägter Staaten hinsichtlich des Übereinkommens über die Rechte des Kindes, um die Vereinbarkeit der Verpflichtungen mit der *šarīʿa* zu gewährleisten, und zwar vor allem in Bezug auf die nachfolgend noch einer vertiefenden Betrachtung unterworfene Religionsfreiheit und die im islamischen Recht verbotene Adoption.[74] Auch gegen diese

---

69 Art. 2, 9 und 16. Ausführlich hierzu *Hanna Beate Schöpp-Schilling*, „Der ‚Frauenrechtsausschuss' der Vereinten Nationen in der Interaktion mit islamisch geprägten Staaten", in: *Hatem Elliesie* (Hrsg./Editor), Beiträge zum Islamischen Recht VII, Islam und Menschenrechte, (Islam and Human Rights / الإسلام وحقوق الإنسان), Frankfurt a.M. 2010, S. 417-455; *Alexandra Petersohn*, Islamisches Menschenrechtsverständnis…, a.a.O. (Fn. 33), S. 184 ff.; *Christine Chinkin*, „Reservations and Objections to the Convention on the Elimination of All Forms of Discrimination against Women", in: *J. P. Gardner* (Hrsg.), Human Rights as General Norms and a State's Right to Opt Out. Reservations and Objections to Human Rights Conventions, London 1997, S. 64 (67 ff.); *Jane Connors*, „The Women's Convention in the Muslim World", in: *J. P. Gardner* (Hrsg.), Human Rights as General Norms and a State's Right to Opt Out. Reservations and Objections to Human Rights Conventions, London 1997, S. 85 (89 ff.); *Belinda Clark*, „The Vienna Convention Reservations Regime and the Convention on Discrimination Against Women", in: AJIL, New York 1991, 281 ff.; *Donna E. Arzt*, The Application of International Human Rights…, a.a.O. (Fn. 33), S. 218 ff.; *Rebecca J. Cook*, „Reservations to the Convention on the Elimination of All Forms of Discrimination Against Women", in: Virg. JIL, Charlottesville 1990, S. 643 ff.

70 Art. 19 a) und c) und Art. 20 Abs. 4 b). BGBl. 1985 II S. 926.

71 *Donna E. Arzt*, The Application of International Human Rights…, a.a.O. (Fn. 33), S. 220.

72 Die Unzulässigkeit folgt schon aus Art. 28 Abs. 2 des Paktes.

73 *Alexandra Petersohn*, Islamisches Menschenrechtsverständnis…, a.a.O. (Fn. 33), S. 197 ff.; *Christine Chinkin*, Reservations and Objections to the CEDAW, a.a.O. (Fn. 69), S. 75; *Jane Connors*, The Women's Convention in the Muslim World, a.a.O. (Fn. 69), 95 f.; *Donna E. Arzt*, The Application of International Human Rights…, a.a.O. (Fn. 33), S. 220.

74 *Alexandra Petersohn*, Islamisches Menschenrechtsverständnis…, a.a.O. (Fn. 33), S. 209 ff.; *Martin Forstner*, Menschenrechte zwischen Geltungsuniversalität und Inhaltspartikularität, a.a.O. (Fn. 58), S. 491; *Jenny Kuper*, „Reservations, Declarations and Objections to the 1989 Convention on The Rights of the Child", in: *J. P. Gardner* (Hrsg.), Human Rights as General Norms and a State's Right to Opt Out. Reservations and Objections to Human Rights Conventions, London 1997, S. 104 (106 ff.).

Vorbehalte haben mehrere Staaten einschließlich der Bundesrepublik Deutschland Einspruch eingelegt.[75]

III. Islam und Menschenrechte am Beispiel der Religionsfreiheit

Im traditionellen Islam sind Gemeinwesen und Religion derart untrennbar miteinander verbunden, dass der Staat seine wahre Legitimation nur im Islam finden und eine gerechte Gesellschaft nur von einem islamischen Gemeinwesen garantiert werden kann.[76] Religionsfreiheit kann es allein im Rahmen der göttlichen Ordnung zum Wohle des Islam geben.[77] Die Freiheit, sich eine religiöse Überzeugung zu bilden, kommt dem Muslim nur insoweit zu, als er nicht vom Islam abfällt. Denn die Apostasie vom Islam ist bei Androhung der Todesstrafe und Verlust des Vermögens verboten.[78] Nichtmuslimen steht es lediglich frei, den Islam anzunehmen.[79] Die Freiheit, sich zu ihrer Religion zu bekennen und sie auszuüben, steht neben den Muslimen auch den Angehörigen der anderen Buchreligionen[80] (*ahl al-kitāb*) zu, soweit sie sich in einem – zumeist fiktiven – Schutzvertrag mit dem islamischen Staat dazu verpflichtet haben, die Souveränität des islamischen Gemeinwesens anzuerkennen und eine besondere Steuer zu

---

75 *Alexandra Petersohn*, Islamisches Menschenrechtsverständnis…, a.a.O. (Fn. 33), S. 216 ff.; *Jenny Kuper*, Reservations, Declarations and Objections to the 1989 Convention on The Rights of the Child, a.a.O. (Fn. 74), S. 107 ff.

76 Vgl. *Udo Steinbach*, Die Menschenrechte im Verständnis des Islam, a.a.O. (Fn. 55), S. 47 ff.; *Martin Forstner*, Das Menschenrecht der Religionsfreiheit…, a.a.O. (Fn. 56), S. 119 und S. 130 m.w.N.

77 Vgl. *Martin Forstner*, Das Menschenrecht der Religionsfreiheit…, a.a.O. (Fn. 56), S. 142.

78 *Adel El Baradie*, Gottes-Recht und Menschen-Recht, Baden-Baden 1983, S. 123 f.; *Rudolph Peters / Gert J. J. de Vries*, Apostasy in Islam, Die Welt des Islams, Leiden 1976/77, S. 1 ff.; *Ann Elizabeth Mayer*, Islam and Human Rights, a.a.O. (Fn. 55), S. 163; *Martin Forstner*, Das Menschenrecht der Religionsfreiheit…, a.a.O. (Fn. 56), S. 105, S. 112 ff. m.w.N.; *Alexandra Petersohn*, Islamisches Menschenrechtsverständnis…, a.a.O. (Fn. 33), S. 137 ff. m.w.N.; vgl. *Hans-Georg Ebert*, Arabische Verfassungen…, a.a.O. (Fn. 65), S. 527.

79 Vgl. *Hans-Georg Ebert*, Arabische Verfassungen…, a.a.O. (Fn. 65), S. 527.

80 Grundsätzlich sind dies Christen und Juden, denen aber von den Rechtsgelehrten auch andere Religionsangehörige gleichgestellt wurden, vgl. *Martin Forstner*, Das Menschenrecht der Religionsfreiheit…, a.a.O. (Fn. 56), S. 153; *Hans-Georg Ebert*, Arabische Verfassungen…, a.a.O. (Fn. 65), S. 527.

entrichten.[81] Die religiösen Überzeugungen und Praktiken von Atheisten und Polytheisten sind demgegenüber in keiner Weise geschützt.[82]

Dass der Islam und die *šarīʿa* in den Verfassungen der meisten islamischen Staaten verankert sind, bedeutet allerdings nach überwiegender Auffassung der muslimischen Gelehrten keine Theokratie im Sinne der Herrschaft von Religionsgelehrten, sondern ist durchaus mit einem zivilen Staatsverständnis vereinbar.[83] Zwar widerspricht die Statuierung des Islam als Staatsreligion einer umfassenden Freiheit, sich eine religiöse Überzeugung zu bilden, sich zu ihr zu bekennen und den religiösen Kultus auszuüben, nicht grundsätzlich.[84] So enthalten die meisten[85] Verfassungen im Zusammenhang mit der Abhandlung von Rechten und Pflichten des Bürgers auch die Rechte auf Glaubens- oder Religionsfreiheit und die Ausübung des religiösen Kultus, letztere zumeist beschränkt durch den *ordre public* oder die guten Sitten,[86] und statuieren Diskriminierungsverbote auch hinsichtlich der Religionszugehörigkeit.[87] Diese Rechte werden jedoch innerstaatlich regelmäßig so ausgelegt, dass sie entsprechend der verfassungsmäßigen Bedeutung von Islam und *šarīʿa* lediglich innerhalb der von der *šarīʿa* gesetzten Schranken gewährleistet werden.[88] Dogmatisch wird zumeist der aus dem Französischen stammende *ordre public* herangezogen, mit islamisch-rechtlichen Inhalten versehen und auf alle Rechts-

---

81 *Hans-Georg Ebert,* Arabische Verfassungen…, a.a.O. (Fn. 65), S. 527; vgl. *Martin Forstner,* Das Menschenrecht der Religionsfreiheit…, a.a.O. (Fn. 56), S. 153; *Ann Elizabeth Mayer*, Islam and Human Rights, a.a.O. (Fn. 55) S. 147 ff.; *Lorenz Müller*, Islam und Menschenrechte, a.a.O. (Fn. 58), S. 159 f.; *Alexandra Petersohn*, Islamisches Menschenrechtsverständnis…, a.a.O. (Fn. 33), S. 19 f. und 123 ff., jeweils m.w.N.

82 *Martin Forstner,* Das Menschenrecht der Religionsfreiheit…, a.a.O. (Fn. 56), S. 108; *Hans-Georg Ebert,* Arabische Verfassungen…, a.a.O. (Fn. 65), S. 527, und *Ann Elizabeth Mayer*, Islam and Human Rights, a.a.O. (Fn. 55), S. 148.

83 Vgl. *Gudrun Krämer,* „Islam, Menschenrechte und Demokratie", in: *A. Zunker* (Hrsg.), Weltmacht oder Chaos? Beiträge zur internationalen Politik, Festschrift zum 75. Geburtstag von Professor Dr. K. Ritter, Baden-Baden 1993, S. 340; *Hans-Georg Ebert,* Arabische Verfassungen…, a.a.O. (Fn. 65), S. 526.

84 *Hans-Georg Ebert,* Arabische Verfassungen…, a.a.O. (Fn. 65), S. 526; vgl. *Heiner Bielefeldt*, Menschenrechte…, a.a.O. (Fn. 1), 495 f. mit Verweis auf die Staatskirchen in Großbritannien und in den skandinavischen Staaten; *Mohamed Charfi*, Die Menschenrechte im Bezugsfeld von Religion, Recht und Staat in den islamischen Ländern, a.a.O. (Fn. 56), 107 ff.

85 Eine Ausnahme stellt beispielsweise Saudi-Arabien dar, vgl. *Ann Elizabeth Mayer*, Universal Versus Islamic Human Rights…, a.a.O. (Fn. 59), S. 356 ff.

86 *Martin Forstner,* Das Menschenrecht der Religionsfreiheit…, a.a.O. (Fn. 56), S. 105 und S. 151 f.

87 *Martin Forstner,* ibidem, a.a.O. (Fn. 56), S. 151 f.

88 Vgl. *Martin Forstner,* ibidem, a.a.O. (Fn. 56), S. 108 f. m.w.N. für Ägypten.

gebiete einschließlich des Verfassungsrechts erstreckt und auf diese Weise das gesamte nationale Recht unter den Vorbehalt der Vereinbarkeit mit der *šarīᶜa* gestellt.[89] Dementsprechend werden die Religionsfreiheit und das Diskriminierungsverbot wegen der Religion grundsätzlich nur unter dem Primat des Islam und der Bevorzugung seiner Angehörigen sowie in den von der *šarīᶜa* dargelegten Grenzen gewährleistet.[90]

Dieser Šarīᶜavorbehalt prägt auch die Einstellung der meisten islamischen Staaten zu den Gewährleistungen der internationalen Menschenrechte. Das lässt sich abgesehen von den internationalrechtlich gewährleisteten Diskriminierungsverboten unter anderem auch wegen der Religionszugehörigkeit,[91] mit denen die islamisch geprägten Staaten regelmäßig ebenso wie mit den nationalen Diskriminierungsverboten umgehen, besonders bei den entsprechenden Gewährleistungen der Religionsfreiheit sehen:

Bereits gegen Art. 18 der Menschenrechtserklärung der Vereinten Nationen, der nicht nur allgemein die Religionsfreiheit, sondern ausdrücklich auch die Freiheit des Religionswechsels sowie unbeschränkt auch der Religionsbekundung feststellt, wurden von Afghanistan, Irak, Pakistan, Saudi-Arabien und Syrien unter anderem mit der Begründung Bedenken erhoben, die Norm sei mit dem islamischen Recht nicht vereinbar.[92] Den Bedenkenträgern gelang es, in Art. 18 des Internationalen Paktes über bürgerliche und politische Rechte eine schwächere Fassung der Religionsfreiheit durchzusetzen, die nunmehr ausdrücklich neben der Religionsbekundungsfreiheit lediglich die Freiheit garantiert, eine Religion eigener Wahl zu haben oder anzunehmen. Wie es sich mit der Religionsaufgabe oder dem Religionswechsel verhält, überließ man der insoweit strittigen Auslegung.[93] Im Übrigen wird die Freiheit der Religionsbekundung

---

89 *Martin Forstner,* ibidem, a.a.O. (Fn. 56), S. 121 ff. m.w.N.; neuerdings *Imen Gallala,* Religionsfreiheit… a.a.O. (Fn. 7), S. 479 ff.

90 *Heiner Bielefeldt*, Menschenrechte…, a.a.O. (Fn. 1), 496 m.w.N.; vgl. *Ann Elizabeth Mayer*, Islam and Human Rights, a.a.O. (Fn. 55), S. 143 ff. und 163 ff.

91 Art. 2 Nr. 1 der Allgemeinen Erklärung der Menschenrechte, Art. 2 Abs. 1, 24 Abs. 1, 26 des Internationalen Paktes über Bürgerliche und Politische Rechte, Art. 2, Abs. 2, Art. 10 Nr. 3 S. 1 des Internationalen Paktes über Wirtschaftliche, Soziale und Kulturelle Rechte, Art. 2 Abs. 1 des Übereinkommens über die Rechte des Kindes.

92 *Martin Forstner,* Das Menschenrecht der Religionsfreiheit…, a.a.O. (Fn. 56), S. 110 und 156 f.; *idem*, Menschenrechte zwischen Geltungsuniversalität und Inhaltspartikularität, a.a.O. (Fn. 58), S. 490 m.w.N.; vgl. *Lorenz Müller*, Islam und Menschenrechte, a.a.O. (Fn. 58), S. 144 m.w.N.

93 Vgl. *Alexandra Petersohn*, Islamisches Menschenrechtsverständnis…, a.a.O. (Fn. 33), S. 175 ff.; *Brice Dickson*, „The United Nations and Freedom of Religion“, in: ICLQ (The International and Comparative Law Quarterly), Cambridge 1995, S. 327 (342); *Martin*

gesetzlichen Beschränkungen unterworfen, unter anderem zum Schutz der öffentlichen Ordnung, unter die die islamisch geprägten Staaten ihren Šarī'avorbehalt subsumieren.[94] Entsprechend verhält sich das Ergebnis der Verhandlungen hinsichtlich Art. 1 Abs. 1 der – unverbindlichen – Erklärung der Vereinten Nationen über die Beseitigung aller Formen von Intoleranz und Diskriminierung aufgrund der Religion oder der Überzeugung vom 25.11.1981. Allerdings gelang es den westlichen Staaten, in dessen Art. 8 festzuschreiben, dass die Bestimmungen der Allgemeinen Menschenrechtserklärung von 1948 nicht beschränkt oder aufgehoben werden dürfen. Da diese Erklärung keinen rechtsverbindlichen Charakter hatte, konnten die islamisch geprägten Staaten mit dieser Regelung leben.[95] Im Lichte dieser Bestimmungen dürfte auch Art. 5 Abs. 3, nach dem das Kind vor allen Formen der Diskriminierung aufgrund der Religion und der Überzeugung zu schützen ist, der Erklärung von den islamisch geprägten Staaten einerseits und den westlichen Staaten andererseits unterschiedlich verstanden werden.

Šarī'avorbehalte ausgesprochen haben islamisch geprägte Staaten auch gegen das Übereinkommen über die Rechte des Kindes, das in Art. 14 Abs. 1 ganz allgemein die Religionsfreiheit des Kindes und in Art. 14 Abs. 3 die Religionsbekundungsfreiheit schützt, allerdings wiederum eingeschränkt unter anderem durch die öffentliche Ordnung, das Einfallstor für die *šarī'a*; die Freiheit des Religionswechsels wird erneut nicht erwähnt. Die Vorbehalte beziehen sich zuweilen auf das gesamte Abkommen, wie beispielsweise die Vorbehalte Mauretaniens, Irans, Kuwaits, Qatars und auch Pakistans, das die Bestimmungen des Abkommens im Lichte der Prinzipien islamischer Rechts- und Wertvorstellungen ausgelegt wissen will. Andere Erklärungen bzw. Vorbehalte hingegen betreffen einzelne Artikel wie die Erklärungen bzw. Vorbehalte Algeriens, Marokkos, Jordaniens, Syriens und Indonesiens in Bezug auf Art. 14.[96]

Forstner, Das Menschenrecht der Religionsfreiheit..., a.a.O. (Fn. 56), S. 110; *Eibe H. Riedel*, „Der völkerrechtliche Mindeststandard der Religionsfreiheit", in: *Johannes Schwartländer* (Hrsg.), Freiheit der Religion. Christentum und Islam unter dem Anspruch der Menschenrechte, Mainz 1993, S. 421 (423).

94 Vgl. *Martin Forstner*, Das Menschenrecht der Religionsfreiheit..., a.a.O. (Fn. 56), S. 126; *Brice Dickson*, The United Nations and Freedom of Religion, a.a.O. (Fn. 93), S. 327 (342).

95 *Martin Forstner*, Das Menschenrecht der Religionsfreiheit..., a.a.O. (Fn. 56), S. 110 und S. 157 m.w.N; *Eibe H. Riedel*, Der völkerrechtliche Mindeststandard der Religionsfreiheit, a.a.O. (Fn. 93), S. 424.

96 *Alexandra Petersohn*, Islamisches Menschenrechtsverständnis..., a.a.O. (Fn. 33), S. 209 ff.; *Jenny Kuper*, Reservations, Declarations and Objections to the 1989 CRC, a.a.O. (Fn. 74), S. 106 ff., und *Jeremy McBride*, „Reservations and the Capacity to implement Hu-

C. Fazit

Trotz der nur beschränkten Bedeutung eines am Völkerrecht ausgerichteten *ordre public* sollte auch das nationale Zivilrecht seinen Beitrag zur Durchsetzung der international gewährleisteten Menschenrechte leisten. Die völkerrechtliche Aufladung des *ordre public* befreit diesen aus der Provinzialität eines bloßen Instruments zur Durchsetzung nationaler Egoismen und gibt ihm eine übernationale moralisch-ethische Dimension. Die konsequente Berücksichtigung der völkerrechtlichen Gewährleistungen der Menschenrechte im Rahmen des *ordre public* stärkt den internationalen Menschenrechtsschutz. Sie macht einerseits Ernst damit, dass die völkerrechtlichen Verpflichtungen Deutschlands zu innerstaatlichem Recht geworden sind – und schärft übrigens auch den Blick für die Beachtung der internationalen Menschenrechte bei reinen Inlandssachverhalten. Andererseits nimmt sie die islamischen Staaten beim Wort, die den einschlägigen völkerrechtlichen Abkommen beigetreten sind. Da sie sich selbst den vertraglichen Verpflichtungen – gegebenenfalls eingeschränkt durch rechtlich zulässige Vorbehalte – unterworfen haben, kann auch keine Rede davon sein, dass ihnen ein bestimmtes Verständnis der Menschenrechte aufgezwungen wird.

Das weltweit unterschiedliche Verständnis der Menschenrechte und ihrer völkerrechtlichen Gewährleistungen bleibt allerdings eine der großen Herausforderungen des internationalen Menschenrechtsschutzes. Das gilt insbesondere für religiös-rechtlich ausgerichtete Staaten, die wie die meisten islamischen Staaten ihr Rechtssystem einschließlich ihrer völkerrechtlichen Verpflichtungen unter einen „Vorbehalt" des religiösen Rechts stellen. Bei den islamisch geprägten Staaten schlägt sich dieser in einer šarīʿakonformen Auslegung der menschenrechtsgewährleistenden Vertragsbestimmungen und der Geltendmachung entsprechender völkerrechtlicher Vorbehalte nieder. Durch Herausarbeitung und Beachtung der Grenzen noch zulässiger Auslegung und noch erlaubter Vorbehalte gilt es sicherzustellen, dass sich der internationale Menschenrechtsschutz nicht in der Beliebigkeit seines Verständnisses verliert. Nur auf diese Weise kann unter Anerkennung der unterschiedlichen Rechtskulturen der universelle Anspruch der Menschenrechte gewahrt werden.[97]

---

man Rights Treaties", in: *J. P. Gardner* (Hrsg.), Human Rights as General Norms and a State's Right to Opt Out. Reservations and Objections to Human Rights Conventions, London 1997, S. 120 (150).

97 *Vgl. Heiner Bielefeldt*, „Die Menschenrechte zwischen Universalitätsanspruch und kultureller Bedingtheit", a.a.O. (Fn. 57), S. 370; *idem*, „Western" Versus „Islamic" Human Rights Conceptions?, a.a.O. (Fn. 10), S. 22 ff.

Religionsfreiheit und islamisch geprägtes Erbrecht: Gesetzliche Regelungen und Rechtsprechungsauslegung im heutigen Ägypten und Tunesien *

Imen Gallala, Hamburg

A. Einleitung

Das klassische islamische Recht, die *šarīʿa*, übt immer noch einen starken Einfluss auf die rechtssetzenden und die rechtsanwendenden Akteure aus,[1] wobei seine Bedeutung je nach Rechtsbereich variieren kann. Die meisten islamischen Länder haben ihre Rechtssysteme modernisiert und sich dabei von westlichen Gesetzbüchern inspirieren lassen. Die Fragen des Personalstatuts werden jedoch nach wie vor von dem klassischen islamischen Recht geprägt.[2] Der Gesetzgeber und der Richter befinden sich in den islamischen Ländern in einem Dilemma. Nach ihrer Unabhängigkeit von den Kolonialmächten entschieden sich die postkolonialen, islamisch-geprägten Länder für Staatsmodelle westlicher Prägung: sie erließen moderne Verfassungen mit Menschenrechtskatalogen, ratifizierten völkerrechtliche Menschenrechtskonventionen, und dennoch konnten sie sich des kulturellen Erbes des islamischen Rechts nicht völlig entziehen, da die *šarīʿa* nicht nur als Recht betrachtet wird, sondern als ein wesentliches Element der Identität islamischer Staaten.[3]

Diese Dichotomie, die darin besteht, dass *šarīʿa* und Menscherechtskonventionen in einem Nebeneinander existieren, hat oft zu Unstimmigkeiten innerhalb einzelner islamischer Rechtsordnungen geführt. Dies soll im folgenden Beitrag anhand des Beispiels der Religionsverschiedenheit als Erbhindernis bei der gesetzlichen Erbfolge im Recht Ägyptens und in Tunesien veranschaulicht werden, welches mit dem Postulat der Religionsfreiheit kollidiert.

Alle Rechtsordnungen kennen das Institut des Erbhindernisses oder der Erbunwürdigkeit. Es bestand schon im Römischen Recht, das die Erbunwürdigkeit und ihre Rechtsfolgen detailliert geregelt hatte.[4] Erbunwürdigkeit bedeutet stets,

---

* Dieser Aufsatz beruht auf einem Vortrag der Verfasserin im Rahmen der *Aktuellen Stunde* des Max-Planck-Institutes für ausländisches und internationales Privatrecht.

1 *Yadh Ben Achour*, L'Etat nouveau et la philosophie politique et juridique occidentale, Tunis 1980, S. 69.

2 In den islamischen Ländern gilt eine breite Definition der Personalstatutsfragen *al-aḥwāl aš-šaḫsiya*. Diese schließt Familien- und Erbrechtfragen mit ein; dazu *Jamal J. Nasir*, The Islamic Law of Personal Status, Den Haag/London/New York 2002, S. 34-35; sowie *Hans-Georg Ebert*, Das Personalstatut arabischer Länder, Problemfelder, Methoden, Perspektiven, Frankfurt am Main 1996, S. 11.

3 *Wael B. Hallaq*, The Origins and Evolution of Islamic Law, Cambridge 2005, S. 1-7.

4 *Pasquale Voci*, Diritto ereditario romano, Mailand 1967, S. 465 ff.

Islam und Menschenrechte (Islam and Human Rights / الإسلام وحقوق الإنسان)
Hatem Elliesie (Hrsg./Editor), © Peter Lang Verlag: Frankfurt a.M. 2010, S. 499-521

dass eine Person, obwohl sie aus Gründen der Verwandtschaft oder Ehe zur Erbfolge berufen wäre, wegen Vorliegens eines Erbhindernisses von der Erbfolge ausgeschlossen ist.[5] In den Rechtsordnungen „westlicher" Staaten gelten die Erbhindernisse meistens sowohl für die gesetzliche als auch für die gewillkürte Erbfolge. Weder die Religionsverschiedenheit gegenüber dem Erblasser noch der Religionswechsel stellen hierbei ein Erbhindernis dar.[6] Die Erbunwürdigkeit erfüllt in erster Linie die Funktion einer zivilrechtlichen Strafe wegen Verfehlungen gegenüber dem Erblasser.[7] Das vom klassischen islamischen Recht herrührende Erbhindernis der Religionsverschiedenheit gilt in fast allen islamisch geprägten Staaten. Danach wird ein eigentlicher Erbe von der Erbfolge ausgeschlossen, weil er einer anderen Religion als derjenigen des Erblassers angehört. Es liegt auf der Hand, dass das Erbhindernis der Religionsverschiedenheit die Religionsfreiheit der Erben verletzt und auf diesem Wege eine Spannung innerhalb der Rechtsordnungen islamisch geprägter Staaten verursacht.

Die Religionsfreiheit als Ausprägung der Menschenrechte ist sowohl in der ägyptischen als auch in der tunesischen Verfassungen verankert.[8] Ferner haben beide Länder völkerrechtliche Menschenrechtsinstrumente, die die Religionsfreiheit anerkennen und die Diskriminierung wegen der Religion verbieten, ratifiziert. Der Allgemeinen Erklärung der Menschenrechte vom 10. Dezember 1948 haben sowohl Ägypten als auch Tunesien zugestimmt. Außerdem haben sie den internationalen Pakt über bürgerliche und politische Rechte vom 16. Dezember 1966 und den internationalen Pakt über wirtschaftliche, soziale und

---

5 Zur Erbunwürdigkeit im deutschen Recht *Hans Brox*, Erbrecht, Köln/Berlin 2003, S. 163.

6 So bestimmt etwa § 2339 Abs. 1 BGB, dass derjenige erbunwürdig ist, der den Erblasser vorsätzlich und widerrechtlich getötet oder zu töten versucht oder in einen Zustand versetzt hat, infolge dessen der Erblasser bis zu seinem Tode unfähig war, eine Verfügung von Todes wegen zu errichten oder aufzuheben. In Spanien sieht Art. 756 *Código Civil* vom 24. Juli 1889 die Erbunwürdigkeit u. a. eines Vaters oder einer Mutter vor, welche ihre Kinder im Stich gelassen, der Prostitution anheimgegeben oder diese zur Unzucht verleitet haben. In Argentinien ist nach Art. 3294 und Art. 3295 *Código Civil* erbunwürdig die Person, die den Erblasser getötet hat oder versucht ihn zu töten, die Person, die wegen Ehebruchs mit dessen Frau verurteilt wurde, sowie die Person, die nicht Hilfe geleistet hat, als der Erblasser diese gebraucht hätte.

7 *Ricardo Omodei-Salé*, „Indegnità a succedere", in: *Rodolfo Sacco* (Hrsg.), Digesto delle Discipline Privatistiche, Sezione Civile, Turin 2006, S.7.

8 Art. 46 der ägyptischen Verfassung von 1971 besagt, dass der Staat die Glaubens- und Religionsfreiheit gewährleistet. Siehe dazu *Nathalie Bernard-Maugiron*, Le politique à l'épreuve du judiciaire: La justice constitutionnelle en Egypte, Brüssel 2003, S. 190 ff.; Art. 5 der tunesischen Verfassung von 1959 besagt, dass die tunesische Republik die Glaubensfreiheit gewährleistet.

kulturelle Rechte vom 19. Dezember 1966 ratifiziert.[9] Diese völkerrechtlichen Menschenrechtsinstrumente erkennen die Freiheit des Einzelnen, einer Religion anzugehören und diesbezüglich keinem Zwang zu unterliegen, an.[10] Ferner wurde in diesen Instrumenten die Diskriminierung aufgrund der Religion verboten.[11]

Die Untersuchung konzentriert sich auf diese beiden Länder wegen der Bedeutung ihrer Gesetzgebung für die *arabische* bzw. *islamische Welt*:

- Ägypten ist für viele islamisch geprägte Staaten zum gesetzgeberischen Vorbild geworden und
- Tunesien hat bereits im Jahre 1956 das Gesetzbuch zum Personalstatut eingeführt, das in der *islamischen Welt* den größten Abstand vom Islamischen Recht genommen hat.

B. Das Erbhindernis der Religionsverschiedenheit in der Šarīʿa und ein rechtsvergleichender Überblick

I. Erbhindernisse in der Šarīʿa

Die vier sunnitischen Rechtsschulen (*maḏhab*), die Hanafiten, Malikiten, Schafiiten und Hanbaliten, kennen in der Regel dieselben Erbhindernisse. Unterschiede zwischen den sunnitischen Schulen betreffen lediglich die Ausgestaltung und die Rechtsfolgen der Erbhindernisse. Bedeutendere Unterschiede bestehen zwischen den sunnitischen und den schiitischen Rechtsschulen. Die klassischen Erbhindernisse der sunnitischen Rechtsschulen sind:[12]

---

9 http://www.unhchr.ch/pdf/reportfr.pdf (zuletzt aufgerufen am 23.Juli 2008). Ägypten hat jedoch eine Erklärung dazu abgegeben, dass die Vereinbarkeit der in den Pakten verankerten Rechte mit der *šarīʿa* vorausgesetzt wird. Ausführlicher zu den sogenannten *šarīʿa*-Vorbehalten der islamisch geprägten Länder siehe *Peter Scholz,* „Ordre Public, Menschenrechte und Scharia“, in: *Hatem Elliesie* (Hrsg.), Beiträge zum Islamischen Recht VII, Islam und Menschenrechte (Islam and Human Rights / الإسلام وحقوق الإنسان), Frankfurt a.M. 2010, S. 477 ff. (u.a. S. 492 ff.).

10 Art. 18 des internationalen Pakts über bürgerliche und politische Rechte lautet:

(1) Jedermann hat das Recht auf Gedanken-, Gewissens- und Religionsfreiheit. Dieses Recht umfasst die Freiheit, eine Religion oder eine Weltanschauung eigener Wahl zu haben oder anzunehmen [...],

(2) Niemand darf einem Zwang ausgesetzt werden, der seine Freiheit eine Religion oder eine Weltanschauung seiner Wahl zu haben oder anzunehmen [...].

11 Bspw. Art. 2 Abs. 1 des internationalen Paktes über bürgerliche und politische Rechte und Art. 2 Abs. 2 des internationalen Paktes über wirtschaftliche, soziale und kulturelle Rechte.

12 Die erbrechtliche Stellung des Kindes aus illegitimem Geschlechtsverkehr und des Kindes eines gegenseitigen Verfluchungsschwurs werden nicht im islamischen Recht unter den Erbhindernissen geregelt, sondern der Erbfähigkeit. Dieses Kind darf lediglich

- vorsätzliche Tötung des Erblassers
- Religionsverschiedenheit zum Erblasser
- Apostasie, der Abfall vom islamischen Glauben
- Sklaverei
- unterschiedliche Staatsangehörigkeit[13].

Was die Religionsverschiedenheit betrifft, sind sich die vier sunnitischen Rechtsschulen darüber einig, dass Muslime und Nichtmuslime einander nicht beerben dürfen. Sie berufen sich dabei auf einen dementsprechenden Prophetenspruch, nämlich

لاَ يَرِثُ الْمُسْلِمُ الكَافِرَ
وَلاَ الكَافِرُ الْمُسْلِمَ

Dieses Erbhindernis wird mit dem Argument begründet, dass die Berufung zur Erbfolge aufgrund der Beistandspflicht unter Muslimen erfolgt. Da zwischen Muslimen und Nichtmuslimen diese Pflicht nicht bestehe, könne es zwischen ihnen keine erbrechtlichen Ansprüche geben.[14]

Im Gegensatz dazu ist bei den Schiiten das Erbhindernis der Religionsverschiedenheit nur im Hinblick auf den nichtmuslimischen Erben relevant: Ein schiitischer Muslim kann seinen nichtmuslimischen Ehegatten oder Verwandten beerben und ist von der Erbfolge aus Gründen der Religionsverschiedenheit nicht ausgeschlossen. Dafür berufen sich die Schiiten auf den Prophetenspruch „الإسلام يعلو ولا يُعلى عليه“, nach welchem der Islam stets die dominierende Stellung haben müsse.[15] Deswegen könnten Muslime bezüglich der Religionsverschiedenheit bevorzugt behandelt werden. So begründet die Religionsverschiedenheit im Iran gemäß Art. 881a Zivilgesetzbuch (*qānūn-e madanī*) kein gegenseitiges Erbhindernis.[16]

Die Frage, ob Nichtmuslime einander beerben dürfen, ist von den klassischen Rechtsschulen unterschiedlich beantwortet worden. Die Hanafiten ordnen alle

---

seine Mutter und seine Verwandten mütterlicherseits beerben und sie ihn; dazu bei *Ramaḍān Šaranbāṣī / Ǧābir Aš-šāfiʿī*, masāʾil al-aḥwāl aš-šaḫsiya al-ḫāṣṣa bi-ʾl-mīrāṯ wa-ʾl-waṣiya wa-ʾl-waqf, Beirut 2003, S. 271; ʿAbd-al-Muṭṭalib Ḥamdan, Aḥkām al-laqīt fiʾl-fiqh al-islāmī, Alexandria 2006, S. 20.

13 Unterschiedliche Staatsangehörigkeit *iḫtilāf ad-dāraīn* stellt für die malikitische Rechtsschule kein Erbhindernis dar.

14 *Ramaḍān Šaranbāṣī / Ǧābir Aš-šāfiʿī*, masāʾil al-aḥwāl…, a.a.O. (Fn. 12), S. 85.

15 Ibidem, S. 86.

16 *Nadjma Yassari*, „Iran“, in: *Murad Ferid / Karl Firsching / Heinrich Dörner / Rainer Hausmann* (Hrsg.), Internationales Erbrecht, Lfg. LXIII, Frankfurt am Main, Stand: 1. Januar 2006, S. 7-8.

Nichtmuslime in eine Gruppe und räumen ihnen das Recht ein, einander zu beerben. Im Gegensatz dazu vertreten die Malikiten die Meinung, dass Christen, Juden und Nichtgläubige jeweils eigene Religionsgemeinschaften bilden und deswegen einander nicht beerben dürften.[17] Für alle klassischen Rechtsgelehrten ist der Zeitpunkt des Erbfalls, also der Tod des Erblassers, entscheidend für die Feststellung, ob die Religion des Erblassers mit der des Erben übereinstimmt. Als Ausnahme gestatten die Hanbaliten dem Nichtmuslim, vor der Verteilung des Nachlasses zum Islam zu konvertieren und dann an der Erbschaft teilzuhaben.[18]

Nach herrschender Meinung der klassischen Rechtsgelehrten ist das Erbhindernis der Religionsverschiedenheit nur solange relevant, wie es sich um die gesetzliche Erbfolge handelt.[19] Der muslimische Erblasser darf Nichtmuslime im Rahmen der gewillkürten Erbfolge in der Grenze des erlaubten Drittels bedenken. Dies ist auf die unterschiedliche Ratio der gesetzlichen und der gewillkürten Erbfolge zurückzuführen. Die gesetzliche Erbfolge soll das Vermögen des Erblassers in seiner Familie halten. Im Gegensatz dazu dient das Vermächtnis primär der Realisierung des Erblasserwillens.

Neben der Religionsverschiedenheit gegenüber dem Erblasser halten alle klassischen Rechtsgelehrten die Apostasie für ein Erbhindernis. Ein Apostat, *murtadd,* ist eine Person, die vom islamischen Glauben abgefallen ist. In der *šarīʿa* ist seine Erbunwürdigkeit weit gefasst. Er darf niemanden beerben, weder Muslime, noch Nichtmuslime, noch andere Apostaten. Die Rechtsschulen unterscheiden sich allerdings bezüglich der erbrechtlichen Stellung eines vom Islam abgefallenen Erblassers. Nach den malikitischen, hanbalitischen und schafiitischen Rechtsgelehrten muss das Vermögen des Apostaten dem Fiskus des islamischen Gemeinwesens zufallen. Im Gegensatz dazu unterscheidet die hanafitische Rechtsschule zwischen dem vor der Apostasie erworbenen Vermögen und dem danach angefallenen. Hiernach stehe nur das letztgenannte Vermögen dem Fiskus zu. Die muslimischen Erben kämen dann in den Genuss des restlichen Nachlasses.[20]

II. Erbhindernisse in islamisch geprägten Staaten

Das Erbrecht islamisch geprägten Staaten ist stark vom klassischen islamischen

---

17 *Badrān Badrān*, al-mawāriṯ waʾl-waṣiya waʾ-l-hiba fiš-šarīʿa al-islāmiya wa-ʾl-qānūn, Alexandria 1985, S. 30.

18 *Hans-Georg Ebert*, Das Erbrecht arabischer Länder, Frankfurt a.M. 2004, S. 88 ff.

19 Mit Ausnahme der Hanafiten und der Schiiten, die dem nichtmuslimischen Begünstigten sein Vermächtnis versagen, wenn er Angehöriger eines nichtmuslimischen Staates ist; vgl. *Peter Scholz*, Erbrecht der maghrebinischen Staaten und deutscher Ordre Public, Hamburg 2006, S. 116-117.

20 *Hans-Georg Ebert*, Das Erbrecht arabischer Länder, a.a.O. (Fn. 18), S. 90.

Recht geprägt.[21] Dies betrifft auch die Regelungen der Erbhindernisse. Unterschiede innerhalb der einzelnen Länder sind auf die unterschiedlich dominierenden Rechtsschulen zurückzuführen.[22] Überall in den islamischen Ländern schließt die vorsätzliche Tötung des Erblassers den Täter von der Erbfolge aus.[23] In ähnlicher Weise ist die Religionsverschiedenheit gegenüber dem Erblasser als Erbhindernis in fast allen einschlägigen Gesetzen vorgesehen.[24] Algerien stellt hierbei eine Ausnahme dar. Dort wird die Religionsverschiedenheit nicht ausdrücklich als Erbhindernis geregelt. Art. 138 des algerischen Familiengesetzbuches schließt nur den Apostaten von der Erbfolge aus.[25] In Kuwait und in den Vereinigten Arabischen Emiraten wird die erbrechtliche Stellung des Apostaten sowohl als Erblasser als auch als Erbe geregelt.[26]

Die besondere Stellung der *šarīʿa* in den Rechtsordnungen der islamischen Länder erklärt das Vorhandensein der Religionsverschiedenheit unter den Erbhindernissen.

C. Stellung der Šarīʿa in den Rechtsordnungen von Ägypten und Tunesien

I. Verfassungsrechtliche Betrachtung

1. Ägypten

Nach Art. 2 der ägyptischen Verfassung von 1971 ist der Islam die Staatsreligion Ägyptens. Nach einer Verfassungsänderung im Jahre 1980 stellen die Prinzipien der *šarīʿa* nicht nur *eine* der wesentlichen Quellen (*maṣdar raʾīsī*) der

---

21 Ibidem, S. 20.

22 *Peter Scholz,* Erbrecht der maghrebinischen Staaten…, a.a.O. (Fn. 19), S. 52.

23 Algerien: Art. 135 Familiengesetzbuch Nr. 84-11 vom 9. Juni 1984; Marokko: Art. 333 *Mudauwana* in der Fassung vom Gesetz Nr. 2003-70; Syrien: Art. 264-a Gesetzesverordnung Nr.59 vom 17. September 1953; Kuwait: Art. 229 Gesetz Nr. 51 von 1984 über das Personalstatut; Sudan: Art. 350 Gesetz zum Personalstatut der Muslime Nr.42 von 1991; Jemen: Art. 304 Präsidialbeschluss über das Gesetz Nr. 20 von 1992 über das Personalstatut; Oman: Art. 238 Dekret des Sultans Nr.32/97 über die Veröffentlichung des Gesetzes zum Personalstatut.

24 Syrien: Art. 264; Marokko: Art. 332; Kuwait: Art. 293 a und b; Sudan: Art. 351; Jemen: Art. 305; Oman: Art. 239. Diese Artikel sind aus den jeweiligen Gesetzen in Fn. 23 entnommen.

25 *Peter Scholz,* Erbrecht der maghrebinischen Staaten…, a.a.O. (Fn. 19), S. 53.

26 Art. 294 des kuwaitischen Gesetzes Nr. 51 von 1984 über das Personalstatut, dazu *Hans-Georg Ebert*, Das Erbrecht arabischer Länder, a.a.O. (Fn. 18), S. 66; In den Vereinigten Arabischen Emiraten besagt Art. 318 des Gesetzes Nr. 28 von 2005 über das Personalstatut, dass die Religionsverschiedenheit ein Erbhindernis darstellt. Das Erläuternde Memorandum zu diesem Gesetz bekräftigt, dass der Apostat niemanden beerben darf. Im Gegensatz dazu dürfen seine muslimische Verwandte ihn beerben, in: al-ǧarīda ar-rasmiya [Gesetzesblatt] Nr. 439, 35/2005, S. 362-363. Dazu *Hilmar Krüger*, „Grundzüge des Privatrechts der Vereinigten Arabischen Emirate", in: *Hans-Georg Ebert / Thoralf Hanstein* (Hrsg.), Beiträge zum islamischen Recht VI, Frankfurt a.M. 2007, S. 101 (133).

Gesetzgebung, sondern *die* wesentliche Quelle (*al-maṣdar ar-ra'īsī*) dar. Die Verfassungsänderung sollte die Stellung der *šarīʿa* in der ägyptischen Rechtsordnung stärken und wurde insbesondere auf politischen Druck eingeführt.[27] Der ägyptische Oberste Verfassungsgerichtshof, *al-maḥkama ad-dustūriya al-ʿulīya,* (im Folgenden: ägypt.OVerfG) hat die Rechtsfolgen dieser Verfassungsänderung in zahlreichen Entscheidungen erläutert. Zunächst betonte er, dass die Erhebung der *šarīʿa* zu der Hauptquelle der Gesetzgebung keine Rückwirkung habe. So konnte der ägypt.OVerfG es ablehnen, Regelungen die vor Verabschiedung des neuen Art. 2 Verfassung in Kraft waren, wie Art. 226 des ägyptischen Zivilgesetzbuches über die Verzugszinsen, auf ihre Vereinbarkeit mit der *šarīʿa* zu prüfen.[28] Ferner betont der ägypt.OVerfG, dass die Prinzipien der *šarīʿa* keine unmittelbare Geltung in der ägyptischen Rechtsordnung haben. Vielmehr stellten sie eine Aufforderung an den Gesetzgeber dar, schrittweise die Rechtsvorschriften mit den Prinzipien der *šarīʿa* in Einklang zu bringen. Gestützt auf diese Argumente hat der ägypt.OVerfG es auch abgelehnt, erbrechtliche Vorschriften auf ihre behauptete Unvereinbarkeit mit der *šarīʿa* zu prüfen.[29] Außerdem stellte der ägypt.OVerfG klar, dass nur die absoluten und unveränderlichen Prinzipien der *šarīʿa* den Gesetzgeber binden. Dazu gehören die islamrechtlichen Regelungen über die Verteilung der Erbanteile und die Übertragung des Eigentums auf die Erben.[30] Die Erhebung der *šarīʿa* zu *der* Hauptquelle der Gesetzgebung führt zu ihrer Vereinnahmung durch den Staat. Dies wird u.a. dadurch belegt, dass der ägypt.OVerfG für sich in Anspruch genommen hat, die *šarīʿa* zu interpretieren und ihre Normen nach deren Bedeutung zu klassifizieren, ohne dabei Rat bei den religiösen Instanzen, wie den Rechtsgelehrten der Al-Azhar Universität, einzuholen.[31]

---

27 Der damalige ägyptische Staatspräsident Muḥammad Anwar as-Sādāt versuchte das Verhältnis seiner Regierung zu den islamischen Bewegungen, insbesondere zu der Muslimbruder(schaft) (*ǧamāʿat al-iḫwān al-muslimīn*), zu verbessern. Er suchte ihre Unterstützung gegen das linke politische Spektrum und die Nasserianer; Ausführlicher *Clark B. Lombardi*, State Law as Islamic Law in Modern Egypt: The Incorporation of Shari'a into Egyptian Constitutional Law, Leiden / Boston 2006, S. 126. Zu der Stellung der *šarīʿa* und des Islams in den Verfassungen islamisch geprägter Länder siehe u.a. auch *Peter Scholz*, Ordre Public, Menschenrechte und Šarīʿa..., a.a.O. (Fn. 9), S. 472; *Hatem Elliesie,* „Quo vadis bilad as-Sūdān? The Contemporary Framework for a National Interim Constitution", in: Recht in Afrika (Law in Africa · Droit en Afrique), 8/1, Köln 2005, S. 63ff. (77-78); *idem,* „Friedensprozess und Verfassungsentwicklung im Sudan", in: Verfassung und Recht in Übersee (VRÜ), 38/3, Baden-Baden 2005, S. 276 ff. (292-294).

28 *Nathalie Bernard-Maugiron*, Le politique à l'épreuve du judiciaire..., a.a.O. (Fn. 8), S. 343; *Omaia Elwan*, „Überblick über die Entwicklung des ägyptischen Staatsrechts seit den 70er Jahren", in: VRÜ, 23, Baden-Baden 1990, S. 297 ff.

29 *Nathalie Bernard-Maugiron,* ibidem, a.a.O. (Fn. 8), S. 347.

30 Ibidem, S. 366-367.

31 Ibidem, S. 91.

2. Tunesien

Nach Art. 1 der tunesischen Verfassung von 1959 ist der Islam die Staatsreligion Tunesiens. Außer Art. 40, nach welchem das Staatsoberhaupt Muslim sein muss, gibt es in der tunesischen Verfassung jedoch keinen weiteren Bezug auf den Islam. Im Gegensatz zur ägyptischen Verfassung bezeichnet die tunesische Verfassung die *šarīʿa* weder als *eine* Quelle, noch als *die* Hauptquelle der Gesetzgebung. Es geht aus den *travaux préparatoires* der verfassungsgebenden Versammlung hervor, dass diese zwischen dem Begriff muslimischer Staat (*dawlatun muslima*) und dem Ausdruck „die Staatsreligion ist der Islam" (*al-islām dīn ad-dawla*) zu entscheiden hatte. Der Begriff „islamischer Staat" wurde abgelehnt, weil es bedeutet hätte, dass das staatliche Recht immer in Einklang mit dem islamischen Recht hätte sein müssen.[32] Die verfassungsgebende Versammlung hat sich für die Formulierung „Der Islam ist die Staatsreligion" (*al-islām dīn ad-dawla*) entschieden. Dies bedeutet lediglich, dass das islamische Recht eine der Inspirationsquellen des tunesischen Rechts darstellt.[33]

II. Im Hinblick auf einfachgesetzliche Vorschriften

1. Ägypten

Verschiedene ägyptische einfachgesetzliche Vorschriften verleihen der *šarīʿa* die Rolle einer subsidiären Rechtsquelle. Diese Vorschriften sind von einer allgemeinen Reichweite oder beziehen sich auf ein bestimmtes Rechtsgebiet.

Nach Art. 1 Abs. 2 des ägyptischen Zivilgesetzbuches von 1949 (*al-qānūn al-madanī*; nachfolgenden ägypt.ZGB) hat der Richter bei einer fehlenden gesetzlichen Regelung auf das Gewohnheitsrecht (*al-ʿurf*), hilfsweise auf die Grundsätze des islamischen Rechts (*mabādiʾ aš-šarīʿa al-ʾislāmīa*) zurückzugreifen.[34] Für das Erbrecht sieht allerdings Art. 875 ägypt.ZGB ausdrücklich vor, dass die Bestimmung der Erben, die Festlegung ihrer Anteile an der Erbschaft und der Übergang der Nachlassgegenstände auf sie unter die entsprechenden Regelungen der islamischen *šarīʿa* und die entsprechenden nationalen Gesetze fallen. Zudem bestimmt Art. 3 Abs. 1 des Gesetzes Nr. 1/2000 über die Regelung einiger Grundsätze und Maßnahmen der Prozessführung in den Angelegenheiten des Personenstatuts, dass bei fehlender gesetzlicher Regelung der Richter bei Angelegen-

---

[32] *M. Neifar*, Constitution tunisienne et Islam, Tunis 1986, S. 279.

[33] *Mohamed Charfi*, Introduction à l'étude de Droit, Tunis 1983, S. 93 ff.; *idem*, „Influence de la religion dans les pays musulmans", in: Recueil des Cours, Den Haag 1987, S. 329 (346).

[34] *Baudouin Dupret*, „A Return to the Sharīʿa? Egyptian Judges and the Reference to Islam", in: *Nadjma Yassari* (Hrsg.), The Sharīʿa in the Constitutions of Afghanistan, Iran and Egypt- Implications for Private Law, Tübingen 2005, S. 161 (163).

heiten des Personenstatuts auf Grundlage der herrschenden Meinung in der hanafitischen Rechtsschule entscheiden muss.[35]

2. Tunesien

Wie im ägyptischen Recht enthält das Recht Marokkos und Algeriens einfachgesetzliche Vorschriften, die der *šarīʿa* die Rolle einer subsidiären Rechtsquelle einräumen.[36] Im marokkanischen und algerischen Recht finden sich Klauseln, nach denen zur Auslegung oder bei Fehlen gesetzlicher Bestimmungen auf das traditionelle islamische Recht oder auf eine bestimmte Rechtsschule zurückzugreifen ist.[37] Tunesien stellt eine Ausnahme unter den maghrebinischen sowie den islamisch geprägten Ländern dar, da solche Klauseln in seinen einfachgesetzlichen Vorschriften nicht zu finden sind.[38]

III. Aus der Perspektive der Rechtsprechung

1. Ägypten

Die Bedeutung der *šarīʿa* in der Rechtsprechung kann anhand des Instituts des *ordre public* illustriert werden. So führte der ägyptische Kassationsgerichtshof, *maḥkamat an-naqḍ,* (nachfolgend: ägypt.KassGH) aus, dass der *ordre public* Grundsätze enthalte, die aus einer politischen, sozialen und wirtschaftlichen Perspektive, dem öffentlichen Interesse, *al-maslaḥa al-ʿāmma,* dienen. Der *ordre public* solle auf einer säkularen Doktrin beruhen, die als allgemein gültige Doktrin angewendet werden müsse und zu welcher sich die ägyptische Gesellschaft in ihrer Gesamtheit bekenne. Er dürfe nicht von Vorschriften des religiösen Rechts abhängen. Trotzdem schließt der ägypt.KassGH nicht aus, dass in einigen Fällen der *ordre public* auf religiösen Grundsätzen beruhen kann. Dies sei der Fall, wenn der betroffene religiöse Grundsatz mit der recht-

---

35 Ausschnittsweise abgedruckt bei *Peter Scholz*, „Ägypten“, in: *Murad Ferid / Karl Firsching / Heinrich Dörner / Rainer Hausmann* (Hrsg.), Internationales Erbrecht, Lfg., Frankfurt a.M., Stand: 1. Januar 2003, S. 70 (72); ausführlich zu diesem Gesetz *Mathias Rohe*, „Das neue ägyptische Familienrecht: auf dem Weg zu einem zeitgemäßen islamischen Recht“, in: StAZ, Frankfurt a.M. 2001, S. 193 ff.

36 Zur Geschichte des Familienrechts in den maghrebinischen Ländern siehe *Maurice Borrmans*, Statut personnel et famille au Maghreb de 1940 à nos jours, Paris / Den Haag 1977.

37 Für Algerien ist dies in Art. 222 des algerischen Familiengesetzbuches und in Marokko in Art. 400 der *Mudauwana* geregelt. Die marokkanische Klausel verweist auf den malikitischen Ritus, aber zudem auch auf die Rechtsfortbildung *iǧtihād* zur Durchsetzung der Islam-Grundsätze der Gerechtigkeit, der Gleichheit und des gedeihlichen Zusammenlebens; dazu *Peter Scholz,* Erbrecht der maghrebinischen Staaten…, a.a.O. (Fn. 19), S. 9 ff.; *Marie-Claire Foblets / Jean-Yves Carlier*, Le code marocain de la famille, incidences au regard du droit international de la famille, Brüssel 2005, S. 120-121.

38 *Sāssī Ben Ḥalīma*, „al-fiqh al-islāmī min ḫilāl fiqh al-qaḍāʾ at-tūnisī fī māddat al-aḥwāl aš- aš-šaḫsiya“, in: Mélanges offerts au Doyen Sadok Belaid, Tunis 2004, S. 51 (89).

lichen und gesellschaftlichen Ordnung eng verbunden und im Bewusstsein der Gesellschaft verwurzelt sei, so dass die Gefühle und Ansichten verletzt würden, wenn er nicht befolgt würde.[39] In den letzten Jahren ist der Bezug auf die *šarīʿa* im Zusammenhang mit dem *ordre public* deutlicher und aussagekräftiger geworden.[40]

Nach dem ägypt.KassGH gilt diese Definition des *ordre public* sowohl für das ägyptische interreligiöse Kollisionsrecht als auch für Fälle mit Auslandsbezug. In Ägypten unterliegen die Angelegenheiten der Ehe und der Scheidung für nichtmuslimische Ägypter den Bestimmungen ihres religiösen Rechts.[41] Trotzdem setzt die Anwendung des nichtstaatlichen religiösen Rechts im Rahmen der inländischen Rechtsspaltung dessen Vereinbarkeit mit dem *ordre public* voraus.[42] So hat das Eingangsgericht von Kairo eine Leviratsehe des jüdischen Rechts[43] mit der Begründung aufgehoben, dass sie gegen das Konsensprinzip des islamischen Rechts für die Eheschließung verstöße und deswegen *ordre public*-widrig sei.[44]

In internationalprivatrechtlichen Fällen benutzen die Gerichte den *ordre public,* um der Zugehörigkeit der Betroffenen zum Islam Vorrang vor deren Staatsangehörigkeit zu verleihen und auf sie statt ihres Heimatrechts – wie dies nach den ägyptischen Kollisionsnormen geboten wäre – islamisches Recht anzuwenden. So wurde die Scheidung der Ehe eines zum Islam konvertierten Italiener mit einer italienischen Frau durch Verstoßung als rechtens gewertet: Der Berufungsgerichtshof, *maḥkamat al-ʾistiʾnāf*, von Kairo entschied, dass ein

---

39 *Ägypt.KassGH,* Entscheidung Nr. 16 und 26 vom 17. Januar 1979, gerichtliches Jahr 48, bei *Maurits S. Berger* (ins Englische übersetzt), Sharia and Public Policy in Egyptian Family Law, Groningen 2006, S. 128-130.

40 *Ägypt.KassGH,* Entscheidung Nr. 85 vom 2. Februar 1997, gerichtliches Jahr 63, in welcher der ägypt.KassGH betont, dass das islamische Recht für Muslime ein unantastbares Recht und deswegen Teil des Ordre Public ist; dazu *Maurits S. Berger,* ibidem, a.a.O. (Fn. 39), S. 35.

41 Art. 3 Abs. 2 des Gesetzes Nr. 1/2000 über die Regelung einiger Grundsätze und Maßnahmen der Prozessführung in den Angelegenheiten des Personenstatuts; *Maurits S. Berger,* ibidem, a.a.O. (Fn. 39), S. 28 ff.

42 *Bruno Menhofer*, Religiöses Recht und internationales Privatrecht – dargestellt am Beispiel Ägypten, Heidelberg 1995, S. 85 ff.

43 Nach Art. 32 der Gesetzessammlung des Ben Schomuʾim wird die Witwe eines Verstorbenen kraft Gesetzes die Frau seines Bruders, wenn sie ohne Nachkommen geblieben ist. Von dieser Ehe kann sie nur durch eine Geldsumme befreit werden; dazu bei *Bruno Menhofer,* Religiöses Recht..., a.a.O. (Fn. 42), S. 90.

44 Eingangsgericht Kairo Entscheidung vom 25. Juni 1956 zitiert von *Bruno Menhofer*, ibidem, a.a.O. (Fn. 42), S. 90.

Muslim in einem islamischen Land stets die Möglichkeit zum Ausspruch der Verstoßung, *ṭalāq,* haben müsse.[45]

2. Tunesien

Auch in der tunesischen Rechtsprechung ist die Tendenz zu beobachten in Angelegenheiten des Personalstatuts auf das islamische Recht bzw. den Islam sowohl in Inlandsfällen als auch in internationalprivatrechtlichen Fällen Bezug zu nehmen. Für Inlandsfälle bedient sich die Rechtsprechung des islamischen Rechts, um einige von diesem Recht inspirierte Vorschriften des tunesischen Rechts auszulegen.[46] Dieser Bezug auf die *šarīʿa* ist allerdings dort nicht nachvollziehbar, wo er *contra legem* erfolgt, wie dies am Beispiel der Adoption deutlich wird. Im Gegensatz zum islamischen Recht erlaubt und regelt das nationale tunesische Recht die Adoption.[47] Nichtsdestotrotz bezieht sich die Rechtsprechung ausdrücklich auf die *šarīʿa*, um die Möglichkeit der Adoption einzuschränken. So hält die Rechtsprechung die Religionsverschiedenheit zwischen Adoptiveltern und Adoptivkind für ein Adoptionshindernis, obwohl das Gesetz lediglich den Schutz der Interessen des Kindes fordert.[48]

Die tunesische Rechtsprechung erachtet – im Gegensatz zu der ägyptischen – in Fällen mit Auslandsbezug das islamische Recht[49] nicht als Teil des *ordre public*. Es sieht allerdings den Islam und die islamischen Werte als wesentliche Bestandteile der nationalen Identität, wie dies in der Verfassung vorgesehen ist.[50] In diesem Zusammenhang haben tunesische Gerichte die Anerkennung ausländischer Gerichtsentscheidungen, bei denen das Sorgerecht der nichtmuslimischen Mutter erteilt wurde, verweigert und ihre Entscheidung auf den

45 Berufunsgerichtshof Kairo, Entscheidung vom 12. Juni 1952 zitiert von *Bruno Menhofer*, ibidem, a.a.O. (Fn. 42), S. 89.

46 Vgl. nachfolgend unter Gliederungspunkt D.II./1./a.: Die Religionsverschiedenheit als Erbhindernis in Ägypten und Tunesien / Tunesien / Die *šarīʿa*konforme Rechtsprechung / Die Ḥūriya-Rechtsprechung, Seite 513 f.

47 *Loi N°. 58-27 du 4.3.1958 relative à la tutelle publique, à la tutelle officieuse et à l'adoption,* in: Journal Officiel de la République Tunisienne (JORT) Nr. 19/ 1958 du 7.3.1958, dazu *Kalthoum Méziou*, „Approche critique du code du statut personnel", in: Mélanges offerts au Doyen Abdelfattah Amor, Tunis 2005, S. 815 (819 ff.); *Sassi Ben Halima* [Sāssī Ben Ḥalīma], „Religion et statut personnel en Tunisie", in: Revue Tunisienne de Droit 2000, S. 107 (S. 123 ff.).

48 *Sāssī Ben Ḥalīma*, al-fiqh al-islāmī min ḫilāl fiqh al-qaḍā'..., a.a.O. (Fn. 38), S. 71-72.

49 Ganz im Gegenteil wird z.B. in Tunesien die Verstoßung nicht anerkannt, obwohl sie islamrechtlich erlaubt ist. Grund hierfür war die Verstoßung gegen den tunesischen *ordre public*, dazu siehe *Souhaima Ben Achour*, „L'ordre juridique tunisien face à la répudiation islamique", in: Polygamie et répudiation dans les relations internationales, Tunis 2006, S. 43 (54 ff.).

50 *Cour de Cassation*, Entscheidung vom 15. Mai 1979, in : Revue de Jurisprudence et de Législation 1980, S. 79 ff.

ordre public gegründet.[51] Danach steht es nicht im Interesse des Kindes, in einem nichtmuslimischen Land aufzuwachsen und von seiner gewohnten muslimischen Umwelt und muslimischen Werten abgetrennt zu sein, da damit die Gefahr einhergehe, dass das Kind sich vom Islam abwende und zum Apostat werde.[52]

D. Die Religionsverschiedenheit als Erbhindernis in Ägypten und Tunesien

I. Ägypten

Die Erbhindernisse bei der gesetzlichen Erbfolge sind in Ägypten im Gesetz Nr. 77 von 1943 über die Erbschaft (im Folgenden: ÄEG) geregelt.[53] Dabei lehnt sich der ägyptische Gesetzgeber weitgehend an die hanafitische Rechtsschule an.[54] Folgende Erbhindernisse sind im ÄEG vorgesehen: die vorsätzliche Tötung des Erblassers (Art. 5 ÄEG), die Religionsverschiedenheit zwischen Erben und Erblasser (Art. 6 Satz 1 und 2 ÄEG) und die unterschiedliche Staatsangehörigkeit (Art. 6 Satz 3 und 4 ÄEG). Die folgenden Erläuterungen befassen sich mit der Religionsverschiedenheit als Erbhindernis und mit der Apostasie.

1. Religionsverschiedenheit

Muslime und Nichtmuslime dürfen einander nicht beerben. Art. 6 ÄEG S.1 benutzt das Wort *tawāruṯ* welches in der arabischen Sprache auf ein Reziprozitätsverhältnis hinweist: Die Religionsverschiedenheit begründet im ägyptischen Recht ein gegenseitiges Erbhindernis.[55] Demzufolge darf z.B. weder die nichtmuslimische Ehefrau ihren muslimischen Mann beerben noch er sie. Zur Bestimmung der Religionszugehörigkeit für den Zweck der Erbwürdigkeit ist der Zeitpunkt des Erbfalles entscheidend.[56] Die ägyptische Rechtsprechung entspricht diesen Prinzipien, wie anhand der nachfolgenden Beispiele belegt wird:

- „Das Kind gehört der jeweils besseren Religion seiner Eltern [dem Islam] an und es braucht daher zum Zeitpunkt seiner Volljährigkeit seine Zugehörigkeit zum Islam nicht zu bestätigen. Deswegen beerbt

---

51 Art. 11 Code de droit international privé, in: JORT vom 1. Dezember 1998, S. 2332 ff.: Hiernach ist die Beachtung des *ordre public* eine Voraussetzung zur Anerkennung ausländischer gerichtlicher Entscheidungen.

52 *Cour de Cassation*, Entscheidung vom 15. Oktober 1985, Bull. Civ. 1985 T. II, S. 61 ff.; dazu *Monia Ben Jémia*, „Ordre public, constitution et Exequatur", in: Mélanges en l'honneur de Habib Ayadi, Tunis 2000, S. 271 ff.

53 Qānān raqm 77 li-sana 1943 bi-ša'n al-mawārīt, in: al-waqā'iʿ al-miṣrīya vom 12. August 1943, Nr. 92, S. 33.

54 Vgl. oben: B. Das Erbhindernis der Religionsverschiedenheit in der *šarīʿa* und ein rechtsvergleichender Überblick (I. Erbhindernisse in der Šarīʿa), Seite 501 ff.

55 *Ramaḍān Šaranbāṣī / Ǧābir Aš-šāfiʿī*, masā'il…, a.a.O. (Fn. 12), S. 85.

56 *ʿAmr-ʿIsā' al-Fiqī*, al-mīrāṯ, Alexandria 2002, S. 50.

derjenige, dessen Mutter, als er noch jung war, zum Islam übergetreten ist, seinen christlichen Bruder nicht […]".[57]

- „Der Christ darf seinen Sohn, der zum Islam konvertiert ist, nicht beerben".[58]
- „Da die verstorbene Tochter acht Jahre alt war, als ihr Vater sich zum Islam bekannt hat, folgt sie ihrem Vater in seiner neuen Religion und ist ebenfalls Muslim."[59]

Nichtmuslime dürfen einander beerben, auch wenn sie verschiedenen Glaubensrichtungen angehören.[60] Laut dem Erläuternden Memorandum zum ÄEG werden sie diesbezüglich als Angehörige derselben Religion betrachtet.[61]

2. Apostasie

Dem Status des Apostaten ist in Ägypten in den letzten Jahren größere Aufmerksamkeit gewidmet worden.[62] Dies ist insbesondere der Affäre der Zwangsscheidung von Naṣr Ḥāmid Abū Zaīd wegen Apostasie zuzuschreiben.[63] Das ÄEG enthält keine ausdrücklichen Regelungen bezüglich der erbrechtlichen Stellung des Apostaten. Diesbezügliche Ausführungen finden sich jedoch im Erläuternden Memorandum zum ÄEG. Nach diesen Erläuterungen erben die muslimischen Verwandten des Apostaten (ob Mann oder Frau) nur das vor der Apostasie erworbene Vermögen. Das danach erworbene Vermögen fällt dem Fiskus an. Diese Regelung unterscheidet sich jedoch von der Position der hanafitischen Rechtsschule, die den muslimischen Verwandten einer Frau, die

---

57 *Al-ʿulīyā šarʿiya*, Entscheidung vom 8. November 1948, zitiert von *Anwar al-ʿAmrūsī*, uṣūl al-murāfaʿt aš-šarʿiya fī masāʾil al-aḥwāl aš-šaḫsiya, Alexandria 2005, S. 430-431.

58 *Al-ʿulīyā šarʿiya*, Entscheidung vom 6. November 1942, zitiert von *Anwar al-ʿAmrūsī*, ibidem, a.a.O. (Fn. 57), S. 434.

59 *Maḥkamat an-naqḍ*, taʿn raqm 44, aḥwāl šaḫsiya vom 29. Januar 1975, zitiert von *ʿAbd al-Munʿim Dasūqī*, qaḍāʾ an- naqḍ fī ʾl-mawādd al-madaniya, muǧallad 1, 1992, S. 143 ff.

60 Art. 6 Satz 2 ÄEG.

61 Das Erläuternde Memorandum zum ÄEG, abgedruckt u. a. bei *ʿAmr-ʿIsāʾ al-Fiqī*, al-mīrāṯ, a.a.O. (Fn. 56), S. 222 ff.

62 Zur rechtlichen Stellung des Apostaten in den Rechten islamischer Länder siehe *Abdullah Saeed / Hassan Saeed*, Freedom of Religion, Apostasy and Islam, Aldershot 2004, S. 123 ff. Zu einer rein (klassisch) islamrechtlichen Erörterung der Apostasie bzw. Apostaten siehe *Assem Hefny*, „Hermeneutik, Koraninterpretation und Menschenrechte", in: *Hatem Elliesie* (Hrsg.), Beiträge zum Islamischen Recht, Islam und Menschenrechte (Islam and Human Rights / الإسلام وحقوق الإنسان), Frankfurt a.M. 2010, S. 73-97.

63 *Kilian Bälz*, „Eheauflösung aufgrund von Apostasie durch Popularklage: der Fall Abu Zayd", in: IPRax, Bielefeld 1996, S. 353 ff.; *Ramaḍān Šaranbāṣī / Ǧābir Aš-šāfiʿī*, masāʾil…, a.a.O. (Fn. 12), S. 88. Vgl. auch *Ann Elizabeth Mayer*, "General Remarks on Human Rights and Islam in the Middle East", in: *Hatem Elliesie* (Hrsg.), Beiträge zum Islamischen Recht VII, Islam und Menschenrechte (Islam and Human Rights / الإسلام وحقوق الإنسان), Frankfurt a.M. 2010, S. 219 ff. (236).

vom Islam abgefallen ist, gestatten, ihr gesamtes Vermögen zu erben. Nach Ramaḍān Šarabāṣī hat die hanafitische Meinung Vorrang vor dem Erläuternden Memorandum.[64]

Die hanafitische Rechtsschule und das Erläuternde Memorandum zum ÄEG stimmen insoweit überein, dass der Apostat niemanden beerben kann, weder Muslime, noch Nichtmuslime, noch weitere Apostaten. Dies ist auf den Gedanken zurückzuführen, dass der Apostat zum Tode verurteilt ist, früher oder später umgebracht wird und „ein verstorbener Mensch niemanden beerben kann".[65] Bezüglich der Apostasie im Zusammenhang mit dem Erbrecht hat der ägypt.KassGH beispielsweise folgende Ausführungen gemacht:

> „ Der Apostat darf keine Ehe eingehen. Die Ehe zwischen einer Muslima und einem Nichtmuslim ist religionswidrig und daher nichtig. Deswegen ist die von einer Apostatin geschlossene Ehe nichtig und begründet keine Abstammung, die erbrechtliche Ansprüche nach sich zieht".[66]

Kehrt der Apostat zum Islam zurück, darf er von den Erben das, was sich von seinem Anteil noch im deren Besitz befindet, herausverlangen. Seine Rechtslage gleicht demjenigen des lebend wieder erschienenen Verschollenen.[67]

II. Tunesien

Art. 88 des tunesischen Gesetzbuches zum Personalstatut[68] vom 13.8.1956 (im Folgenden: TPersG) befasst sich wie folgt mit den Erbhindernissen:[69]

> „ Die vorsätzliche Tötung des Erblassers gehört zu den Erbhindernissen. Der Mörder erbt nicht, unabhängig davon, ob er Täter, Teilnehmer oder falscher Zeuge ist, dessen Zeugnis zu einem Todesurteil und dessen Vollstreckung geführt hat".[70]

In der arabischen Fassung dieser Bestimmung heißt es: *„al-qatl al-ʿamd min mawaniʿ al-ʾirṯ"*. Dabei ist das Wort *„min"* für die Entstehung eines Auslegungsstreits dieser Bestimmung verantwortlich. Es bedeutet „zu den" oder „von" bzw. „unter" und seine Verwendung wird von einigen so interpretiert,

---

64 *Ramaḍān Šaranbāṣī / Ǧābir Aš-šāfiʿī*, ibidem, a.a.O. (Fn. 12), S. 91.

65 *Ramaḍān Šaranbāṣī / Ǧābir Aš-šāfiʿī*, ibidem, a.a.O. (Fn. 12), S. 90; *ʿAmr-ʿIsāʾ al-Fiqī*, al-mīrāṯ, a.a.O. (Fn. 56), S. 45.

66 Aṭ-ṭaʿn raqm 162 vom 16. Mai 1995, aḥwāl šaḫsiya, zitiert von *ʿAmr-ʿIsāʾ al-Fiqī*, ibidem, a.a.O. (Fn. 56), S. 336.

67 *Ramaḍān Šaranbāṣī / Ǧābir Aš-šāfiʿī*, masāʾil…, a.a.O. (Fn. 12), S. 94.

68 Maǧallat al-aḥwāl aš-šaḫsiya, manšūrāt al-maṭbaʿa ar-rasmiya li-l-ǧumḥūriya at-tūnisiya, Tunis 1998, S. 4 ff.

69 Zum tunesischen Erbrecht siehe *Kalthoum Méziou*, „Approche iconoclaste du droit des successions, in: Mélanges offerts au Professeur Sassi Ben Halima", Tunis 2005, S. 907 ff.

70 Deutsche Übersetzung bei *Peter Scholz*, „Tunesien", in: *Heinrich Dörner / Rainer Hausmann*: Internationales Erbrecht, Lfg. XL VII, Stand: 1. Januar 2002, S. 12 (40).

dass es nach Art. 88 TPersG neben der vorsätzlichen Tötung noch andere Erbhindernisse gibt. Es geht allerdings aus Art. 88 TPersG nicht klar hervor, aus welcher Rechtsquelle diese weiteren Erbhindernisse hervorgehen sollen.[71]

Rechtsprechung und Lehre sind bezüglich der Auslegung dieser Bestimmung gespalten. Während die herrschende Lehre Art. 88 TPerG eng auslegt und die Erbhindernisse auf die vorsätzliche Tötung beschränkt, hat die Rechtsprechung in Art. 88 TPersG lange Zeit einen stillschweigenden Verweis auf die *šarīʿa* hineingelesen und daraus geschlossen, dass weitere, auf islamische Grundlage beruhende Erbhindernisse im tunesischen Recht Geltung haben. Es ist allerdings zu beobachten, dass sich die Gerichte zum Teil in den letzten Jahren deutlich von dieser *šarīʿa*konformen Rechtsprechung entfernt haben.

1. Die šarīʿakonforme Rechtsprechung

Der wichtigste Fall hier ist die am 31. Januar 1966 ergangene Entscheidung im Fall Ḥūriya. Dort hat der tunesische Kassationsgerichtshof, *Cour de Cassation,* (im Folgenden: CC) die Religionsverschiedenheit zum Erbhindernis erklärt.[72] Diese Rechtsprechung war während der ersten dreißig Jahre seit dem Erlass des TPersG herrschend.[73] Sie soll im Folgenden als die Ḥūriya-Rechtsprechung bezeichnet werden.

a. Die Ḥūriya-Rechtsprechung

Ḥūriya war eine Tunesierin, die 1945 einen Franzosen geheiratet hatte. In einem Rechtsstreit über die Erbfolge ihrer Mutter brachte ihr Bruder das Argument vor, dass Ḥūriya – da sie einen Nichtmuslim geheiratet habe – vom islamischen Glauben abgefallen sei, und als Apostatin ihre muslimische Mutter nicht beerben könne.[74] Wie oben erwähnt ist das Abfallen vom Glauben bzw. die Religionsverschiedenheit nicht ausdrücklich in Art. 88 TPersG als Erbhindernis erwähnt. Trotzdem führt die CC aus, dass die Religionsverschiedenheit und die Apostasie Erbhindernisse seien, wie dies so im islamischen Recht gelte.[75] Sie rechtfertigt den Rückgriff auf das islamische Recht damit, dass das TPersG von ihm inspiriert sei. In späteren Entscheidungen stellt die CC auf Art. 1 der

---

[71] Über weitere Lücken, Mehrdeutigkeiten und Widersprüche innerhalb des TPerG siehe *Stephanie Waletzki*, Ehe und Ehescheidung in Tunesien, zur Stellung der Frau in Recht und Gesellschaft, Berlin 2001, S. 137 ff.

[72] *Cour de Casstion*, arrêt n°3384 du 31.1.1966, in: Revue Tunisienne de Droit 1968, S. 114.

[73] *Sassi Ben Halima* [Sāssī Ben Ḥalīma], „Religion et statut personnel en Tunisie", in: Revue Tunisienne de Droit 2000, S. 134 (S. 135 ff.).

[74] *Emilie De Lagrange*, Le législateur tunisien et ses interprètes, in: Revue Tunisienne de Droit 1968, S. 11; *Yadh Ben Achour*, Introduction générale au Droit, Tunis 2005, S. 156.

[75] Deswegen hat Krüger festgestellt, dass die Brautgabe die einzige vermögensrechtliche Sicherung für die christlichen oder jüdischen Ehefrauen darstellt: *Hilmar Krüger*, „Ehe und Brautgabe", in: FamRZ, Bielefeld 1977, S. 114 (S. 117 ff.)

tunesischen Verfassung ab, wonach der Islam die Staatsreligion ist, um die Einbeziehung der islamrechtlichen Erbhindernisse in das tunesische Recht zu rechtfertigen.[76]

Im Fall Ḥūriya betonte die CC, dass laut der *šarīʿa* die Eheschließung zwischen einer Muslima und einem Nichtmuslim nichtig und eine „unverzeihliche Sünde" sei. Dies führe aber nicht automatisch zum Abfall vom islamischen Glauben. Dieser müsse unabhängig von der Eheschließung mit einem Nichtmuslim bewiesen werden. Die CC begründet ihre Meinung über die Nichtigkeit einer solchen Ehe mit dem islamischen Recht, ohne die Bestimmungen über die Ehehindernisse im TPersG zu erwähnen.[77] Im konkreten Fall Ḥūriya hat der CC es

---

[76] Siehe dazu *Ali Mezghani*, „Note sous Tribunal de Première Instance de Tunis n° 7602 du 18 mai 2000", in: Revue Tunisienne de Droit 2000, S. 251 (S. 258 ff.).

[77] Nach der *šarīʿa* ist die Ehe zwischen einer muslimischen Frau und einem Nichtmuslim nichtig. Sowohl die Schiiten als auch die Sunniten berufen sich auf zwei Verse des Korans [Übersetzung nach *Rudi Paret,* Der Koran: Kommentar und Konkordanz, 2. Aufl., Stuttgart 1980], um die Nichtigkeit einer solchen Eheschließung zu begründen. Laut dieser Auffassung(en) müssen diese Eheleute getrennt werden, gleichwohl ob die Ehe vollzogen wurde oder nicht:

• Sure 2 (البقرة), Vers 221:

وَلاَ تَنكِحُواْ الْمُشْرِكَاتِ حَتَّى يُؤْمِنَّ وَلأَمَةٌ مُّؤْمِنَةٌ خَيْرٌ مِّن مُّشْرِكَةٍ وَلَوْ أَعْجَبَتْكُمْ الْمُشْرِكِينَ حَتَّى يُؤْمِنُواْ وَلَعَبْدٌ مُّؤْمِنٌ خَيْرٌ
مِّن مُّشْرِكٍ وَلَوْ أَعْجَبَكُمْ أُوْلَئِكَ يَدْعُونَ إِلَى النَّارِ وَاللّهُ يَدْعُوَ إِلَى الْجَنَّةِ وَالْمَغْفِرَةِ بِإِذْنِهِ وَيُبَيِّنُ آيَاتِهِ لِلنَّاسِ لَعَلَّهُمْ يَتَذَكَّرُونَ

[...]

„Und heiratet nicht heidnische Frauen, solange sie nicht gläubig werden! Eine gläubige Sklavin ist besser als eine heidnische Frau, auch wenn diese euch gefallen sollte. Und gebt nicht gläubige Frauen an heidnische Männer in die Ehe, solange diese nicht gläubig werden! Ein gläubiger Sklave ist besser als ein heidnischer Mann, auch wenn dieser euch gefallen sollte [...]";

• Sure 60 (الممتحنة), Vers 10:

يَا أَيُّهَا الَّذِينَ آمَنُوا إِذَا جَاءكُمُ الْمُؤْمِنَاتُ مُهَاجِرَاتٍ فَامْتَحِنُوهُنَّ اللَّهُ أَعْلَمُ بِإِيمَانِهِنَّ فَإِنْ عَلِمْتُمُوهُنَّ مُؤْمِنَاتٍ فَلَا تَرْجِعُوهُنَّ
إِلَى الْكُفَّارِ لا هُنَّ حِلٌّ لَّهُمْ ولا هُمْ يَحِلُّونَ لَهُنَّ [...]

„Ihr Gläubigen! Wenn gläubige Frauen als Auswanderer zu euch kommen, dann prüft sie (ob sie auch wirklich gläubig sind)! –Gott weiß allerdings besser über ihren Glauben Bescheid (als ihr). – Wenn ihr (auf Grund der Prüfung) festgestellt habt, dass sie (wirklich) gläubig sind, dann schickt sie nicht zu den Ungläubigen zurück! Die gläubigen Frauen (Sie) sind diesen (ihnen, d.h. den ungläubigen Männer) nicht (zur Ehe) erlaubt und umgekehrt [...]".

In den meisten islamisch geprägten Ländern ist diese Konstellation der Religionsverschiedenheit unter den zeitweiligen Ehehindernissen erwähnt; ausführlich dazu *Dawoud S. El Alami*, The Marriage Contract in Islamic Law in the Shariʿia and Personal States

abgelehnt, die Apostasie von Ḥūriya zu ermitteln. Dies sei eine Tatsachenfrage, die von den unteren Instanzen entschieden werden solle. Deswegen hat die CC die Entscheidung bestätigt, die Ḥūriya für erbberechtigt gehalten hatte.

In weiteren Entscheidungen haben die Richter es für notwendig erachtet, die Lücken im TPersG durch Normen aus dem islamischen Recht zu füllen, mit dem Argument, dass dieses die Hauptquelle dieses Gesetzes darstelle.[78] Zur Rechtfertigung dieses Ansatzes haben die Gerichte betont, dass trotz seiner Modernität das TPersG keinesfalls gegen die Prinzipien und die Ziele des Islams verstoßen dürfe.[79]

b. Bewertung der Ḥūriya-Rechtsprechung

Die Tendenz in der Rechtsprechung die Religionsverschiedenheit als Erbhindernis zu erachten, entspricht einem traditionellen islamischen Familienmodell, wo der Nichtgläubige nicht als gleichberechtigt behandelt wird.[80] Die Richter des CC, die sich als Verteidiger der traditionellen Werte sehen, haben durch ihre Rechtsprechung dieses Familienmodell aufrechterhalten wollen.[81]

In der Lehre wurde diese Rechtsprechung von Anfang an scharf kritisiert, insbesondere mit dem Argument, dass der unmittelbare Rückgriff der Gerichte auf die *šarīʿa* rechtswidrig sei. Dabei greift die Lehre insbesondere auf positivrechtliche Argumente und die Ausgestaltung des tunesischen Rechtssystems zurück. Dass der tunesische Gesetzgeber bei der Abfassung des TPersG sich vom dem islamischen Recht inspirieren habe lassen, gestatte den Gerichten nicht, sich bei fehlender gesetzlicher Regelung auf die unmittelbare Anwendung der *šarīʿa* zu berufen. Hierbei zieht die tunesische Lehre zu Recht eine Parallele zum Römischen Recht. Zahlreiche europäische Zivilgesetzbücher haben Institutionen dieses Rechts übernommen. Trotzdem erlaubt dies den (kontinental) europäischen Richtern nicht, jedes Mal wenn sie in ihren Rechten eine Lücke feststellen, direkt auf das Römische Recht zurückzugreifen.[82] Zudem

---

Laws of Egypt and Morocco, London / Dordrecht / Boston, 1992, S. 43 ff.; *Jamal J. Nasir*, The Islamic Law of Personal Status…, a.a.O., S. 69-70; a.A. *Mohamed Charfi*, Influence de la religion dans les pays musulmans…, a.a.O. (Fn. 33), S. 411 ff.

78 *Tribunal de Première Instance* (hiernach:TPI) Sfax (Safāqis) n° 37853, vom 11. Oktober 1996, zitiert von *K. Sghaier*, L'héritage de la non-musulmane devant les tribunaux tunisiens, mémoire de DEA en sciences juridiques fondamentales, Faculté des Sciences juridiques, politiques et sociales, Tunis 2001-2002, S. 83.

79 *TPI Sfax*, a.a.O., (Fn. 78), S. 82.

80 Über die Stellung des Nichtmuslims im Koran siehe *Sadok Belaid*, Islam et Droit, une nouvelle lecture des versets prescreptifs du Coran, Tunis 2000, S. 143 und S. 167.

81 *Sana Ben Achour*, „Figures de l'altérité: A propos de l'héritage du conjoint «non-musulman»", in: Mélanges offerts au Professeur Sassi Ben Halima, Tunis 2005, S. 823 (834 ff.)

82 *Ali Mezghani*, „Note sous TPI Tunis n° 7602… ", a.a.O. (Fn. 76), S. 257- 258.

wird angemerkt, dass der tunesische Gesetzgeber sich in wesentlichen Punkten deutlich von der *šarīᶜa* distanziert habe.[83]

Darüber hinaus bedient sich die Lehre der Auslegungsprinzipien des tunesischen Rechts, um die Ḥūriya-Rechtsprechung zu kritisieren. Nach Art. 532 des Gesetzbuches für Obligations- und Vertragsrecht, *mağallat al-iltizāmāt wa-'l ᶜuqūd,* (nachfolgend: COC), sind gesetzliche Bestimmungen nach ihrem Wortlaut und der Absicht des Gesetzgebers auszulegen. Zwar sah der Vorentwurf zum TPersG die Religionsverschiedenheit als Erbhindernis neben der vorsätzlichen Tötung vor, dennoch hat der Gesetzgeber dann lediglich die vorsätzliche Tötung in Art. 88 TPersG als Erbhindernis festgelegt. Das Weglassen der Religionsverschiedenheit zeige eindeutig den Willen des Gesetzgebers, ausschließlich die vorsätzliche Tötung des Erblassers als Erbhindernis verankern zu wollen. Ferner zählt Art. 535 COC die formellen Rechtsquellen auf, auf welche zurückgegriffen werden soll, wenn eine Lücke in den Gesetzen besteht. Diese sind abschließend die Anwendung des Analogieprinzips, *mabda' al-qīyās*, und der allgemeinen Rechtsvorschriften, *al-qawāᶜid al-qānūniya al-ᶜāmma.*[84] Die *šarīᶜa* sei somit keine Rechtsquelle des tunesischen Rechts.

Auch müssten die Bestimmungen über die Erbhindernisse eng ausgelegt werden, da sie Ausnahmen zu den grundsätzlichen erbrechtlichen Ansprüchen der Verwandten und Ehegatten darstellten (Art. 240 COC). Außerdem wird argumentiert, dass die unmittelbare Anwendung des islamischen Rechts zur Lückenfüllung im TPersG die Rechtssicherheit gefährde. In manchen Fällen würden die Richter die herrschende Meinung der malikitischen Rechtsschule anwenden, in anderen die der hanafitischen Rechtsschule. Dies schaffe Unsicherheit bezüglich des anzuwendenden Rechts.[85]

Schließlich, so die Lehre, rechtfertige Art. 1 der Verfassung, wonach der Islam die Staatsreligion bilde, nicht die unmittelbare Anwendung islamisch-rechtlicher Institute. Es bestehe ein Unterschied zwischen dem Islam als Religion und dem Islamischen Recht. Das Islamische Recht hat seine Wurzeln zwar in der Religion, es wurde jedoch mittels Exegese und Analogien aus den religiösen Texten wie dem Koran und der Sunna, gewonnen und ist damit ein theoretisches Konstrukt. Es ist daneben gleichermaßen eine Ansammlung von Institutionen, lokalen Bräuchen und gerichtlichen Präzedenzen und mithin geprägt von der islamischen Gesellschaft, in der diese entstanden sind.[86] Im Ergebnis teilt das islamische Recht daher nicht den göttlichen und deswegen un-

---

[83] Die Abschaffung der Privatscheidung, Verstoßung, und der Polygamie belegen deutlich die Autonomie des TPersG gegenüber der *šarīᶜa.*

[84] *Monia Kari*, Note à propos d'un texte ambigu: L'article 535 du C.O.C., in: Revue Tunisienne de Droit, Tunis 1992, S. 203 (S. 205 ff.).

[85] *Sāssī Ben Ḥalīma*, al-fiqh al-islāmī min ḫilāl fiqh al-qaḍā'…", a.a.O. (Fn. 38), S. 92.

[86] *Yadh Ben Achour*, Introduction générale au Droit…, a.a.O. (Fn. 74), S. 164.

abdingbaren Charakter des Korans und der Sunna und kann nicht für alle Zeiten Geltung und Verbindlichkeit beanspruchen.

2. Neue Ansätze zum Ausschluss der Religionsverschiedenheit von den Erbhindernissen

Die beharrliche Kritik der Lehre an der *šarīʿa*konformen Rechtsprechung hat in den letzten Jahren in der Rechtsprechung zu einer säkularen Neuorientierung geführt. Eine neue Generation junger Richter vor allem in den unteren Instanzen hat neue Argumente für den Ausschluss der Religionsverschiedenheit aus den Erbhindernissen entwickelt. Diese neuen Ansätze haben Konsequenzen, die über die Frage der Erbhindernisse hinausgehen. Sie offenbaren ein Selbstverständnis der tunesischen Rechtsordnung, das insbesondere auf seine säkularen Fundamente und eine Normenpyramide baut, in der die *šarīʿa* keine Rechtsquelle ist. Diese neuen Ansätze haben sich insbesondere in zwei Entscheidungen heraus gebildet, die im Weiteren erörtert werden sollen. Eine weitere Entscheidung vom 29. Juni 1999 hat auch in der Diskussion um das Verhältnis zwischen der *šarīʿa* und der tunesischen Rechtsordnung neue Einsichten gebracht. Sie befasste sich mit der Rechtmäßigkeit der Eheschließung zwischen einer tunesischen muslimischen Frau und einem Nichtmuslimen. Diese Frage hat eindeutige Folgen auf die Erbwürdigkeit des Ehemannes.

a. Ausschluss der Religionsverschiedenheit von den Ehehindernissen

Nach der *šarīʿa* ist die Ehe zwischen einer Muslimin und einem Nichtmuslimen rechtswidrig. Im tunesischen Recht ist die Rechtmäßigkeit einer solchen Ehe umstritten. Art. 5 TPersG bestimmt, dass bei den Eheschließenden keine „gesetzlichen" Ehehindernisse vorliegen dürfen. Der dabei verwendete Begriff *mawāniʿ šarʿiya* hat Auslegungsschwierigkeiten bereitet. Das Adjektiv *šarʿiya* ist doppeldeutig. Mit dem Begriff können die in der *šarīʿa* vorgesehenen Hindernisse gemeint sein. Das Wort *šarʿiya* kann aber auch gesetzlich bedeuten. Das hat dazu geführt, dass ein Teil der Lehre darin einen Verweis auf die Ehehindernisse nach dem islamischen Recht hineingelesen und daraus geschlossen hat, dass die Ehe zwischen einer tunesischen Muslimen und einem Nichtmuslim nichtig sei.[87] Gestützt wird diese Leseart auch durch einen Runderlass des Justizministeriums an die Standesbeamten, der ihnen verbietet, Ehen zwischen einer muslimischen Tunesierin und einem Nichtmuslimen zu schließen.[88] Dieses

[87] *M. Kerrou*, „Le mariage de la musulmane avec un non musulman et la ratification par l'Etat tunisien de la Convention de New York du 10-12-1962", in: Revue de la Jurisprudence et de la législation, Tunis 1972, S. 11 ff.

[88] Circulaire du 15.11.1973 portant interdiction de célébrer le mariage d'une Tunisienne musulmane avec un non- musulman, in: Revue de la jurisprudence et de la législation, Tunis 1973, S. 83 ff. Dazu *Stephanie Waletzki*, Ehe und Ehescheidung in Tunesien..., a.a.O. (Fn. 71), S. 174.

Verbot der Religionsverschiedenheit ist durch eine Verwaltungsverordnung des Außenministers vom 24. Februar 1998 bekräftigt worden.[89]

In seinem Urteil vom 29. Juni 1999 hat das Gericht erster Instanz von Tunis, *al-mahkama al-ʾibtidāʾiya*, klärende Ausführungen bezüglich der Religionsverschiedenheit als Ehehindernis gemacht. In diesem Fall handelte es sich um einen Belgier, der die Scheidung von seiner muslimischen tunesischen Ehefrau beantragt hatte. Die Ehefrau setzte sich dagegen mit der Begründung zur Wehr, dass eine Scheidung nicht möglich sei, da die Ehe wegen Religionsverschiedenheit zwischen den Eheleuten erst gar nicht zu Stande gekommen sei. Die Ehe wurde allerdings in Kenntnis der Religionsverschiedenheit geschlossen und hatte jahrelang gedauert. Hier versuchte die Ehefrau eine Unklarheit im tunesischen Recht über die Ehehindernisse auszunutzen, um die Scheidung und insbesondere die vermögensrechtliche Abwicklung der Ehe zu verhindern.[90] Das Tribunal folgte dem Argument der Ehefrau nicht und hielt fest, dass Ehehindernisse im Sinne von Art. 5 TPersG nur in den einschlägigen Gesetzen geregelt seien. Nach Art. 14 TPersG sei die Ehe zwischen einer Muslima und einem Nichtmuslim nicht rechtswidrig, die Religionsverschiedenheit zwischen den Eheschließenden sei nicht als Ehehindernis erwähnt.[91] Außerdem berief sich das Tribunal auf das Übereinkommen der Vereinten Nationen über die Erklärung des Ehewillens, des Heiratsalters und die Registrierung von Eheschließungen vom 10. Dezember 1962.[92] Die Präambel dieses völkerrechtlichen Vertrags verweist auf Art 16 der Allgemeinen Erklärungen der Menschenrechte, der die Ehefreiheit gewährleistet. Tunesien hat dieses Übereinkommen ohne Vorbehalte ratifiziert.[93] Das Gericht wies darauf hin, dass völkerrechtliche Verträge sich an der Spitze der Normenhierarchie befänden und vor den einfachgesetzlichen Bestimmungen Vorrang hätten. In diesem Urteil legte das Gericht

---

[89] Arrêté du ministre des affaires étrangères du 24 février 1998, relatif aux prestations administratives rendues par les services relevant du ministère des affaires étrangères et aux conditions de leur octroi, veröffentlicht in: JORT Nr. 19 vom 6. März 1998. Siehe zur Anwendung dieser Verordnung durch die tunesischen Konsulate *Hilmar Krüger*, Zur Eheschließung von Tunesierinnen mit Nichtmuslimen, in: StAZ, Frankfurt a.M. 1998, S. 251 ff.

[90] *Mālek Ġazwānī*, „min fiqh al-qaḍāʾ ḥawla al-ḥuqūq al-asāsiya", in: Revue Tunisienne de Droit, Tunis 2002, S. 1 (S. 11 ff.).

[91] TPI Tunis n° 26-855 du 29.6.1999, in: Revue Tunisienne de Droit 2000, S. 405 ff.

[92] *Michel Durupty*, „La Convention de New York du 10 décembre 1962 sur le consentement au mariage, l'âge minimum du mariage et l'enregistrement du mariage", in: Revue Tunisienne de Droit, Tunis 1968, S. 45 ff.

[93] Décret du 4.5.1968 portant publication de la Convention de New York du 10 décembre 1962 sur le consentement au mariage, l'âge minimum du mariage et l'enregistrement du mariage, in: JORT du 10.5.1968, S. 476 ff.

Art. 5 TPersG ohne jeglichen Rückgriff auf das islamische Recht aus und betonte damit die Autonomie des TPerG gegenüber der *šarīʿa*.[94]

b. Ausschluss der Religionsverschiedenheit von den Erbhindernissen

Die Entscheidung des Tribunals erster Instanz von Tunis, *al-mahkama al-ʾibtidāʾiya*, Nr. 7602 vom 18. Mai 2000 und die Entscheidung des Berufungsgerichtshofes von Tunis, *maḥkamat al-ʾistiʾnāf*, Nr. 82861 vom 14. Juni 2002 haben verfassungsrechtliche Argumente in die Diskussion um die Reichweite der Erbhindernisse im tunesischen Recht eingebracht. In beiden Entscheidungen haben es die Richter abgelehnt, Art. 88 TPersG isoliert von den weiteren Rechtsvorschriften der tunesischen Rechtsordnung, insbesondere der Verfassung, auszulegen. Damit wollten sie die Harmonie der gesamten Rechtsordnung aufrechterhalten. Die Beachtung der Normenhierarchie stellt das wichtigste Mittel dar, um dieses Ziel zu erreichen.[95]

Die in den beiden Entscheidungen vorgebrachten Begründungen stimmen beinahe überein. Das Tribunal erster Instanz führte aus, dass die Einbeziehung der Religionsverschiedenheit in Art. 88 TPersG den allgemeinen Rechtsgrundsatz der Nicht-Diskriminierung wegen Religionsangehörigkeit verletze. Zunächst qualifizierte das Tribunal die Nicht-Diskriminierung als allgemeinen Rechtsgrundsatz.[96] Dann erläuterte es, dass die Betrachtung der Religionsverschiedenheit als Erbhindernis gegen dieses Prinzip verstöße. Das Tribunal fügte hinzu, dass das Verbot der Diskriminierung aus religiösen Gründen eine Folge der Religionsfreiheit sei, wie diese in Art. 5 der tunesischen Verfassung verankert ist. Ferner bezog sich das Tribunal auf die von Tunesien unterzeichneten internationalen Erklärungen und ratifizierten völkerrechtlichen Verträgen, in welchen die Religionsfreiheit verbürgt ist, wie die Allgemeine Erklärung der Menschenrechte, der internationale Pakt über bürgerliche und politische Rechte und der internationale Pakt über wirtschaftliche, soziale und kulturelle Rechte. Das Gericht wies darauf hin, dass diese ratifizierten völkerrechtlichen Instrumente sich in der tunesischen Normenhierarchie zwischen der Verfassung und den Gesetzen befänden und einen höheren Rang als die letztgenannten genossen.[97]

Das Tribunal erster Instanz war der Meinung, dass die Betrachtung der Religionsverschiedenheit als Erbhindernis die erbrechtlichen Ansprüche von der religiösen Überzeugung des Erbberechtigten abhängig mache. Diese Anknüpfung könne auf den Erben Druck ausüben, so dass er sich zur Änderung seiner Religion gezwungen fühle, um seine erbrechtlichen Interessen nicht zu

---

94 *Souhayma Ben Achour*, Note sous affaire n°26-855, Tribunal de première instance de Tunis, 29.6.1999, in: Revue Tunisienne de Droit, Tunis 2000, S. 404 (S. 416 ff.).

95 Ausführlich zur Normenhierarchie *Hans Kelsen*, Reine Rechtslehre, Wien 1976.

96 *TPI de Tunis*, jugement n°7602 du 18.5.2000..., a.a.O. (Fn. 76), S. 247.

97 Art. 32 der tunesischen Verfassung von 1959.

gefährden. Ferner würde dies die Streitparteien dazu zwingen, sich über ihre religiösen Gefühle und Zugehörigkeit zu äußern, was der Achtung dieser Gefühle entgegenstünde.[98]

Der Berufungsgerichtshof von Tunis hat sich in seiner Entscheidung auf ein weiteres verfassungsrechtliches Prinzip berufen. Eine Einbeziehung der Religionsverschiedenheit unter die Erbhindernisse würde das Gleichheitsprinzip (Art. 6 der Verfassung) verletzen, da er die Tunesier in zwei Kategorien trennen würde: diejenigen, die erbberechtigt sind, weil sie der Religion des Erblassers angehören, und jene die von der Erbfolge ausgeschlossen sind, weil sie eine der Grundfreiheiten, nämlich die Religionsfreiheit, ausüben würden.[99]

Durch eine verfassungsorientierte Auslegung des TPersG und den Ausschluss der Religionsverschiedenheit von den Erbhindernissen wollten die Richter zum einen die verfassungsrechtlich gewährleisteten Menschenrechte schützen[100] und zum anderen die Instrumentalisierung der Religion bei vermögensrechtlichen Streitigkeiten verhindern. Das erste Ziel entspricht einem steigenden Bewusstsein in der Zivilgesellschaft über die Notwendigkeit, den Menschenrechten in den verschiedenen Rechtsgebieten mehr Geltung zu verschaffen. Zum zweiten soll einer Tendenz bei den Streitparteien und deren Anwälten entgegengewirkt werden, die Glaubenszugehörigkeit zu instrumentalisieren, um vermögensrechtliche Interessen durchzusetzen. So widersprüchlich es erscheinen mag, die neuen säkularen Ansätze sollen der Instrumentalisierung der Religion entgegenwirken.

Bisher hat sich die CC nicht ausdrücklich zu dieser Auslegungstendenz der Rechtsprechung der unteren Instanzen geäußert. Das Zögern der CC, die säkulare Auslegung des TPersG zu bestätigen, hat insbesondere sozio-politische Gründe, die auch in anderen islamischen Ländern die Justiz prägen.[101] Es wird befürchtet,

---

98 *TPI de Tunis…*, a.a.O. (Fn. 76), S. 249 ff.

99 *Cour d'appel de Tunis*, arrêt n° 82861 du 14.6.2002, in: Revue de jurisprudence et de législation, Tunis 2002, S. 75 ff.

100 Dies stellt eine relative neue Tendenz in der Rechtsprechung tunesischer Gerichte in der letzten Dekade dar, sich auf die Grundrechte zu berufen, um Rechtsstreitigkeiten zu lösen. Dies erfolgte meistens *ex officio*, ohne dazu von den Parteien angespornt zu sein; dazu *Mālek Ġazwānī*, min fiqh al-qaḍā'…, a.a.O. (Fn. 90), S. 1 ff.

101 *Chibli Mallat*, Comparative Law and the Islamic (Middle Eastern) Legal Culture, in: *Mathias Reimann / Reinhard Zimmermann* (Hrsg.), The Oxford Handbook of Comparative Law, New York 2006, S. 610 (621). Er vergleicht die Bedeutung der Gesetze in den Begründungen der gerichtlichen Entscheidungen in den islamisch geprägten Ländern mit denen der westlichen Staaten wie folgt: „[…] as a rule of thumb, the elusive answer might best be sought in those countries where the rule of law functions reasonably well-for example in the UK, Sweden, or New Zealand. There the people lawyering *feel* that the adjudication of cases is based almost entirely on legal and judicial independence and fairness, with the remaining uncontrolled factors being politics, luck quality of legal repre-

dass eine offensichtlich säkulare Auslegung der Gesetze zum Personalstatut den islamisch-konservativen Kräften in der Gesellschaft und der Politik Grund zur Kritik an der Regierung gibt.

E. Fazit

Wie in allen anderen islamisch geprägten Ländern besteht auch in der ägyptischen und tunesischen Rechtsordnung ein Spannungsverhältnis zwischen den von der *šarīʿa* übernommenen Rechtsinstituten einerseits und den in den Verfassungen sowie in den ratifizierten völkerrechtlichen Menschenrechtsinstrumenten verankerten Menschenrechten andererseits.[102] Das in der *šarīʿa* vorgesehene Erbhindernis der Religionsverschiedenheit steht nicht im Einklang mit der Religionsfreiheit, die sowohl in den Verfassungen der untersuchten Länder als auch in den ratifizierten völkerrechtlichen Verträgen anerkannt ist. Diese Unstimmigkeit zeigt jedoch in den beiden Ländern unterschiedliche Ausprägungen auf. Grund dafür ist die in diesen Ländern unterschiedliche Stellung der *šarīʿa*. Im Gegensatz zu Ägypten stellt die *šarīʿa* in Tunesien keine formelle Rechtsquelle dar. Im ägyptischen Recht gilt die Religionsverschiedenheit gegenüber dem Erblasser ausdrücklich als Erbhindernis. In Tunesien dagegen besteht keine Rechtsvorschrift, die der Religionsverschiedenheit ausdrücklich eine solche Rechtsfolge zukommen ließe. Das hat allerdings die Rechtsprechung in Tunesien nicht daran gehindert, auf die *šarīʿa* zurückzugreifen und andersgläubigen Erben das Bestehen ihrer erbrechtlichen Ansprüche abzusprechen. Diese Diskrepanz zwischen Gesetz und Rechtsprechung ist auf die Bedeutung der Religion als Identitätsfaktor in der tunesischen Gesellschaft und bei den Richtern zurückzuführen. Die neuen rechtsstaatlichen Argumente haben jedoch einen Weg aufgezeigt, wie die richterlichen und gesellschaftlichen Mentalitäten und Werte im Sinne der Grundrechte geändert werden können. Die erörterten neuen Ansätze zur Beachtung der Religionsfreiheit bei der Auslegung der Bestimmungen Erbhindernisse belegen diese Dynamik.

---

sentation, and 'X' factor, sometimes referred to as the length of the judge's foot. In the Muslim world, by and large, the picture is exactly the opposite, with law *stricto sensu* comprising perhaps no more than 20 per cent of the factors underlying a judicial decision. The remaining factors are a combination of will-power, corruption, and executive intervention".

102 Speziell zum Spannungsverhältnis in Ägypten vgl. die Ausführungen von *Hatem Elliesie,* Rezension von Holger Scheel: Die Religionsfreiheit im Blickwinkel des Völkerrechts, des islamischen und ägyptischen Rechts, in: Recht in Afrika (Law in Africa · Droit en Afrique), Köln 2009, S. 149-154.

Beitragende Autorinnen und Autoren

Abdullahi Ahmed An-Na'im, *Charles Howard Candler Professor of Law*, führt den akademischen Grad LL.B. der Universität Khartum sowie einen LL.B. und ein Diplom in Kriminologie der *Cambridge University* und einen *PhD* in Rechtswissenschaft der *Edinburgh University*. Zu seinen vorherigen Anstellungen zählen u.a. Extraordinarius an der Universität Khartum, Gastprofessur für Rechtswissenschaft an der *University of California, Los Angeles, Ariel F. Sallows Professor of Human Rights* an der *University of Saskatchewan, Olof Palme* Gastprofessur an der Universität von Uppsala. Bevor er der Fakultät der *Emory Law School* im Jahre 1995 beitrat, fungierte er als geschäftsführender Direktor von Human Rights Watch / Africa. Er publizierte zahlreiche Bücher und mehr als fünfzig Artikel und Buchkapitel zu Menschenrechten, Konstitutionalismus, Islamischem Recht und Politik. Seine jüngste Buchpublikation lautet „Islam and the Secular State: Negotiating the Future of Shari'a", Harvard University Press, Cambridge / et al. 2008.

Mashood Baderin, LL.B. (Hons.), BL, LL.M., PhD, ist Professor für Rechtswissenschaft an der *School of Oriental and African Studies* (SOAS), *University of London.* Er lehrte zuvor an der *Brunel University London, University of the West of England Bristol, University of Southampton,* und *University of Nottingham.* Er ist *Barrister* und *Solicitor* am obersten Gerichtshof (Supreme Court) von Nigeria. Prof. Baderin forscht in den Bereichen des Islamischen Rechts, der Menschenrechte und Völkerrechts mit spezifischem Interesse für die Wechselwirkung zwischen Völkerrecht, Menschenrechten und Islamischen Recht in muslimisch geprägten Staaten. Er ist der Verfasser des Buches „International Human Rights and Islamic Law", Oxford University Press, Oxford 2003 und Gründungsmitherausgeber des *Muslim World Journal of Human Rights* (http://www.bepress.com/mwjhr/).

Heiner Bielefeldt, Prof. habil., Dr. phil., ist Direktor des Deutschen Instituts für Menschenrechte in Berlin. Von 1983 bis 1990 arbeitete er als wissenschaftliche Hilfskraft, später als wissenschaftlicher Angestellter, am *Interdisziplinären Forschungsprojekt Menschenrechte* an der philosophischen Fakultät der Universität Tübingen. Anschließend war er wissenschaftlicher Mitarbeiter an den Lehrstühlen für Öffentliches Recht und Rechtsphilosophie an den juristischen Fakultäten Mannheim (1990-1992) und Heidelberg (1992-1995) mit einem Forschungs- und Lehraufenthalt (1993/1994) an der *University of Toronto*. Heiner Bielefeldt verfasste und gab zahlreiche Bücher rechtsphilosophische, menschenrechtliche sowie die politische Moral und Religionsphilosophie betreffenden Themen heraus. Eines seiner (Haupt) forschungsbereiche ist die Stellung von muslimischen Minderheiten, die in europäischen, säkular freiheitlichen Demokratien leben.

Isa Hayatu Chiroma, Professor für Rechtswissenschaft, promovierte an der *University of Jos* in Nigeria. Er war Unterdekan and Leiter des *Šarīʿa*-Fachbereichs und ist momentan Dekan an der Universität von Maiduguri in Nigeria. Er initiierte die Schaffung einer *Law Clinic* um Zugang zur Justiz durch zur Verfügungsstellung von Rechtsdiensten für Unterprivilegierte und Benachteiligte zu ermöglichen. Zusätzlich zu seiner Lehrtätigkeit und wissenschaftlichen Aktivität fungierte er von 1997 bis 1999 als Rechtsberater für Umweltrecht und Politik und

Islam und Menschenrechte (Islam and Human Rights / الإسلام وحقوق الإنسان)
Hatem Elliesie (Hrsg./Editor), © Peter Lang Verlag: Frankfurt a.M. 2010, S. 523-528

war von 2001 bis 2004 für das Bundesministerium für Umwelt tätig. Er ist ein Mitglied des *Presidential Advisory Committee on Prerogative of Mercy* und des Rates für die juristische Bildung (*Council of Legal Education*) in Nigeria. Seine Lehr- und Forschungsinteressen liegen im Bereich der Menschenrechte, dem Islamischen Recht sowie Recht und Entwicklung.

Bahey eldin Hassan ist Direktor des *Cairo Institutes for Human Rights Studies*, Mitglied des Vorstandes der *EuroMed Human Rights Foundation* (EMHRF) sowie Dozent und Autor mehrerer Artikel und wissenschaftlicher Veröffentlichungen, welche Menschenrechte und Demokratietransformation im arabischen Raum betreffen. Er ist ferner Herausgeber etlicher Bücher in Arabisch und steuerte zu anderen bei, wie zum Beispiel „A Question of Human Rights Ethics: Defending the Islamists“, in: *Anthony Chase / Amr Hamzawy* (Hrsg.), Human Rights in the Arab World: Independent Voices; sowie „Regional Protection of Human Rights in the Arab States In Statu Nascendi“, in: *Janusz Symonides* (Hrsg.), Human Rights: International Protection, Monitoring, Enforcement, UNESCO 2003.

Hatem Elliesie ist Mitglied des Vorstandes der Gesellschaft für Arabisches und Islamisches Recht sowie des Vorstandes der Gesellschaft für afrikanisches Recht und Gründungsmitglied der *Lawyers' Group* in der Hong Kong Sektion von Amnesty International. Er war Mitglied des *Sudan Peace Projects* (bis 2005) und unterstützte das Projekt *„Reconstruction of the Judiciary and the Public Administration Sector in Afghanistan“* (bis 2004) am Max-Planck-Institut für ausländisches öffentliches Recht und Völkerrecht in Heidelberg. Hatem Elliesie, der Rechtswissenschaften sowie Islamwissenschaft, Semitistik und Äthiopistik an den Universitäten in Mannheim, Oxford, Heidelberg, Kairo, Hannover und Berlin studierte, war *Research Fellow* an der Universität in Malta und ist gegenwärtig Doktorand an der Freien Universität Berlin. Er war Mitglied der Berufungskommissionen für die Professuren Islamisches Recht und Islam in Europa an der Freien Universität Berlin.

Claudia Engelmann ist Praktikantin am Deutschen Institut für Menschenrechte und Masterstudentin im Studiengang *International Human Rights Law* der Universität Oxford. Im Jahr 2007 graduierte sie in Literaturwissenschaft, Rechts- und Politikwissenschaft an der Universität Konstanz. In den Jahren 2006 und 2007 war sie in menschenrechtliche Bildungsarbeit, Forschung und Lobbyaktivitäten bei der Deutschen Gesellschaft für die Vereinten Nationen e.V. (Berlin) und der *„Conference of NGOs in Consultative Relationship with the UN“* (Genf) involviert.

Imen Gallala, Dr. iur., LL.M. (Heidelberg), ist wissenschaftliche Mitarbeiterin im Referat für das Recht islamischer Länder am Max-Planck-Institut für ausländisches und internationales Privatrecht in Hamburg. Sie hat an der juristischen Fakultät der Universität Heidelberg den Grad LL.M. erlangt und dort promoviert. Frau Imen Gallala hat an der Rechtsfakultät Tunis II studiert, wo sie eine *Maitrîse en Sciences Juridiques* und ein *Diplôme des Etudes Approfondies en Droit Public et Financier* erwarb. In derselben Fakultät hat sie als wissenschaftliche Mitarbeiterin Völkerrecht unterrichtet. Ihre Schwerpunkte sind nationales und internationales Familien- und Erbrecht in den islamischen Ländern.

Assem Hefny wurde 1972 in Ägypten geboren. Er studierte Germanistik und Islamwissenschaft an der Al-Azhar Universität in Kairo. Er erhielt seinen B.A. mit Auszeichnung und führte sein Ausbildung im Bereich der dieser Fachbereiche überschneidenden, wissenschaftlichen Schnittmenge fort. Seine Masterarbeit verfasster er zu spezifisch-kulturellen arabischen Bezeichnungen in Karl May Erzählungen. Er arbeitete als wissenschaftlicher Assistent am

Fachbereich der Germanistik und Islamwissenschaft an der Al-Azhar Universität. Assem Hefny ist zurzeit Doktorand am Orientalischen Institut an der Universität Leipzig und ist in Forschungsprojekte zum *Islamic Banking* in Deutschland sowie in der Edition und Übersetzung des ägyptischen Familienrechts beschäftigt. Als Vorstandsmitglied der „Vereinigung arabischer Studenten und Wissenschaftler“ (VASA) in Leipzig ist er zudem verantwortlich für den Kulturaustausch und den interkonfessionellen Dialog. Zurzeit arbeitet er als Lehrbeauftragter für das Fach Islamwissenschaft und Arabistik am Centrum für Nah- und Mittelost-Studien (CNMS) an der Universität Marburg.

Muhammad Kalisch ist Professor für „Religion des Islam“ und Direktor am Centrum für Religiöse Studien an der Universität Münster. Er studierte in Hamburg und erhielt seinen Doktorgrad in Darmstadt für eine Dissertation zur „Vernunft und Flexibilität in der islamischen Rechtsmethodik“. Seine Habilitation erlangte er durch die Arbeit „Fiqh und Uṣūl al-Fiqh in der Zaidīya – Die historische Entwicklung der Zaidīya als Rechtsschule“ (2002). Seine speziellen Forschungsgebiete sind Geschichte und Methode des Islamischen Rechts, die Theologie der *muʿtazila* und der *zaidīya*, islamischen Philosophie, theoretisches *ʿirfān* (islamische Gnosis) sowie *philosophia perennis.*

Javaid Rehman ist Professor für Rechtswissenschaft an der juristischen Fakultät der Brunel Universität in London. Sein besonderes Forschungsinteresse umfasst das Islamische Recht, Minderheitenrechte und internationaler Terrorismus. Er hatte zahlreiche gastwissenschaftliche Positionen u.a. in Pakistan, Bangladesch, der Türkei, Frankreich, Japan und den USA inne. Ferner wurde ihm die Ehre zuteil in das Hochschulbildungskomitee Pakistans eingeladen zu werden, um eine umfassenden Bewertung zur Lehre der Rechtsausbildung zu erstellen. Er veröffentlichte und gab zahlreiche Bücher heraus und steuerte in großem Umfang in akademischen Fachzeitschriften bei. Er ist Mitglied des Herausgebergremiums der Zeitschrift *„Religion and Human Rights“*, dem *„Asian Journal of International Law“* sowie dem *„Central European Journal of International and Security Studies“*. Darüber hinaus ist er Mitglied des Komitees Internationales Recht und Islamisches Recht der Internationalen Rechtsvereinigung (ILA) und Herausgeber des *„Journal of Islamic State Practices in International Law“*.

Ann Elizabeth Mayer ist *Associate Professor* für Rechtswissenschaften und Unternehmensethik an der *Wharton School* der *University of Pennsylvania.* Sie erwarb ihren *PhD* in Geschichte des Nahen Ostens an der *University of Michigan* und erhielt ein Abschluss in islamischem und vergleichenden Recht an der *School of Oriental and African Studies* (SOAS) der *University of London* sowie einen *JD* von der *University of Pennsylvania.* Ihr Forschungsgebiet umfasst Islamisches Recht in zeitgenössischen nahöstlichen und nordafrikanischen Ländern sowie Konstitutionalismus, Rechtsstaatlichkeit und internationale Menschenrechtsvorschriften. Sie hat zahlreiche Artikel in wissenschaftlichen Zeitschriften und Sammelbänden verfasst. Die vierte Auflage ihres Buches *Islam and Human Rights: Tradition and Politics* erschien 2007.

Naseef Naeem legte nach dem Studium der Rechtswissenschaft von 1992 bis 1996 an der Universität Aleppo 1998 das Diplom für Öffentliches Recht und 1999 das Diplom der Finanz- und Verwaltungswissenschaften an der Universität Damaskus ab. Von 1999 bis 2002 war er als selbständiger Anwalt in Syrien tätig, 2001-2002 auch als wissenschaftlicher Assistent an der Universität Damaskus. 2007 wurde er mit der Arbeit „Die neue bundesstaatliche Ordnung des Irak“ an der juristischen Fakultät der Universität Hannover promoviert. Die Dissertation erschien 2008 in der Reihe „Leipziger Beiträge zur Orientforschung“ des Peter Lang Verlags. Der Autor habilitiert sich momentan an der Universität Göttingen. Gemeinsam mit Prof. hon.

Dr. iur. Dr. phil. Peter Scholz hielt er an der Freien Universität Berlin in den vergangenen beiden Semestern Seminare über die Staatsorganisation islamisch geprägter Staaten sowie zur Grundrechtsordnung in den Verfassungen islamisch geprägter Staaten.

Chris Maina Peter, Professor für Rechtswissenschaft an der Universität von Dar es Salam, promovierte zum Dr. iur. an der Universität Konstanz und verfügt über einen LL.M.- sowie einen LL.B.-Abschluss von der Universität in Dar es Salam in Tansania. Er war Gastwissenschaftler und Gastprofessor an verschiedenen Universitäten und akademischen Instituten wie bspw. an der Universität Hamburg, dem *Raoul Wallenberg Institute of Human Rights and Humanitarian Law,* Max-Planck Institut für ausländisches öffentliches Recht und Völkerrecht in Heidelberg und dem Institut für Völkerrecht und Internationale Beziehungen in Graz. Seine Lehrtätigkeit umfasst Völkerrecht, Menschenrechte, Flüchtlingsrecht und Kriegsvölkerrecht, zu welchen er auch als externer Prüfer in verschiedenen Universitäten in Kenia, Uganda und Südafrika Prüfungen abnahm. Des Weiteren ist er Mitglied des *Advisory Boards* des *Yearbook of the International Humanitarian Law* und Mitglied im *United Nations Committee on Elimination of Racial Discrimination* (CERD).

Theodor Rathgeber, Politikwissenschaftler (Dr. rer. pol.), ist Dozent an der Universität Kassel am Fachbereich für Gesellschaftswissenschaften (Fachbereich 05). Seit 1990 ist er als Consultant und seit 2001 als freiberuflicher Consultant für Menschenrechte, Völkerrecht und Entwicklungspolitik mit Fokus sowohl auf Indigene- und Minderheitenrechte als auch auf Menschenrechtsverantwortungen von transnationalen Unternehmen („Transnational Companies"). Der Autor war offizieller Beobachter für die Menschenrechtskommission der Vereinten Nationen und, anschließend, seit 2006, für den Menschenrechtsrat der Vereinten Nationen im Auftrag des Deutschen Nichtregierungsorganisationsnetzwerkes „Forum Menschenrechte". Eine Liste seiner Publikationen zu den angeführten Themen ist auf Anfrage erhältlich.

Tilmann Röder leitet die Nahost- und Zentralasienprojekte des Max-Planck-Instituts für ausländisches öffentliches Recht und Völkerrecht in Heidelberg. Er hat sich wissenschaftlich mit Afghanistan, Libyen, Israel/Palästina, Iran, Aserbaidschan, Sudan, Somalia und Kaschmir befasst und in den meisten dieser Länder aufgehalten. Ein Schwerpunkt seiner Arbeit sind Rechts- und Justizreformen mit besonderem Blick auf die Relevanz von Verfassungs- und Völkerrecht. Er ist *Managing Editor* der Reihe von *Max Planck Manuals*, die in den Institutsprojekten als Unterrichtsgrundlage eingesetzt werden. Gemeinsam mit Dr. Rainer Grote hat er in Heidelberg eine laufende Serie von Vorträgen zu Recht im Entwicklungskontext initiiert. Daneben schreibt er zu rechtshistorischen Themen und hat die internationale *Association of Young Legal Historians* (AYLH) mitgegündet. Dr. Röder absolvierte das Studium der Rechtswissenschaften an der Humboldt-Universität zu Berlin, promovierte an der Johann Wolfgang Goethe-Universität in Frankfurt am Main und erlangte das Zweite Staatsexamen in Berlin.

Mathias Rohe, M.A., Dr. iur., Prof. habil., hat den Lehrstuhl für Bürgerliches Recht, Internationales Privatrecht und Rechtsvergleichung an der Rechts- und Wirtschaftswissenschaftlichen Fakultät der Universität Erlangen-Nürnberg inne. Darüber hinaus ist er Gründungsdirektor des Zentrums für Islam und Recht in Europa an dieser Fakultät, an welcher er auch als Dekan fungierte. Er ist Gründungsmitglied der Gesellschaft für Arabisches und Islamisches Recht in welcher er Erster Vorstandsvorsitzender ist. Mathias Rohe ist Autor von zahlreichen Publikationen, welche sich sowohl mit dem Rechtsstatus von Muslimen in Deutschland und Europa beschäftigen als auch Aspekte des Islamischen Rechts und Zivilrechtsangelegenheiten beleuchten. Zusätzlich zu seinen akademischen Engagements in Europa und Übersee arbeitete Mathias Rohe von 2000 bis 2006 als Richter am Oberlandesgericht Nürnberg. 2009 erschien sein Buch „Das Islamische Recht: Geschichte und Gegenwart".

Irene Schneider, Dr. phil., ist Professorin für Arabistik und Islamisches Recht an der Universität Göttingen. Bevor sie sich eingehend mit einer Studie zur frühen islamischen Rechtsgeschichte in ihrer Habilitationsarbeit beschäftigte, befasste sie sich in ihrer Doktorarbeit mit der *adab al-qāḍī*-Literatur. Ihr akademischer Werdegang beinhaltete eine Anstellung als wissenschaftliche Assistentin an der Universität zu Köln, *Research Associate* an der National Science Foundation/USA im Projekt *Constitutional Law and the Politics of Modernization in the Islamic Middle East* an der *State University of New York* sowie weitere Tätigkeiten für in Deutschland ansässige Forschungsprojekte. Ihre Forschungsbereiche sind Islamisches Recht und Rechtsgeschichte sowie die Rekonstruktion der frühislamischen Geschichte und *ḥadīṯ* als Quelle islamischer Geschichte; darüber hinaus auch Geschlechterforschung in arabischen Ländern, in Iran und Afghanistan sowie die (verfassungsrechtliche) Interdependenz von Staat und Gesellschaft; und auch Islam in Deutschland.

Ayesha Shahid ist Dozentin an der juristischen Fakultät der *University of Hull*. Ihr Lehr- und Forschungsinteresse richtet sich auf die Bereiche des Islamischen Rechts, Öffentlichen Rechts, der Frauen- und Geschlechterforschung und Recht, sowie der Menschenrechte. Neben ihren zahlreichen Publikationen in renommierten Fachzeitschriften bearbeitet Dr. Ayesha Shahid derzeit eine Monographie mit dem Titel *„Silent Voices, Untold Stories, Women Domestic Workers and their Struggle for Empowerment"*. Dabei handelt es sich um eine rechtssoziologische Studie, die sich mit der Stärkung und dem Zugang zur Justiz von weiblichen Hausangestellten in Pakistan beschäftigt. Die Studie hinterfragt die Wirksamkeit des Rechts als Mittel der Stärkung dieser spezifischen sozialen Gruppe in ihrem Kampf gegen die ausbeuterische Behandlung am Arbeitsplatz. Die Autorin erhielt im Jahre 2002 den angesehenen *Warwick Postgraduate Fellowship Award* und auch ein postgraduierten Diplom für die Lehre ‚Human Rights Law' von der *Columbia University* in den USA.

Hanna Beate Schöpp-Schilling, Dr. phil., ist Mitglied des Kuratoriums des Deutschen Instituts für Menschenrechte (Stellvertretende Vorsitzende von 2001-2004) sowie Mitglied des Nationalen Instituts für Menschenrechte in der Region von Sverdlovsk in Rußland und Kuratoriumsmitglied der deutschen Stiftung „filia. die Frauenstiftung". Sie ist seit 1989 Mitglied im *United Nations Committee on the Elimination of Discrimination Against Women* (CEDAW) der Vereinten Nationen, in welchem sie unterschiedliche Positionen, einschließlich Sachverständige und Vize-Vorsitzende, inne hatte, neben verschiedenen Dozenturen und Gastprofessuren in Deutschland, den Vereinigten Staaten von Amerika, Japan und Bosnien-Herzegowina, u.a. als Generaldirektorin für Frauenangelegenheiten im Bundesministerium für Familie, Frauen und Jugend. Ihre Publikationen betreffen Frauenstudien, Arbeitsmarktstudien und Menschenrechte. Frau Schöpp-Schilling erhielt kürzlich für ihr Engagement im CEDAW den Margherita-von-Brentano-Preis der Freien Universität Berlin 2008.

Peter Scholz, Prof. hon. Dr. jur. Dr. phil., studierte Jura, Islamwissenschaft und Kunstgeschichte an der Universität Hamburg. Im Jahre 1995 schloss er seine Doktorarbeit in der Islamwissenschaft ab und erhielt 2006 einen Doktor der Rechtswissenschaft an der Freien Universität Berlin. Seit 1995 arbeitet er als Richter in Berlin, wo er 2007 zum Richter am Kammergericht berufen wurde und seit 2009 Vizepräsident des Amtsgerichts Tiergarten ist. Nachdem er einige Jahre Lehrveranstaltungen mit Bezügen zum Islamischen Recht durchgeführt hatte, ernannte ihn die Freie Universität Berlin zum Honorarprofessor für Islamisches Recht und Internationales Privatrecht. Er publiziert viel zu diesen Themen und ist Mitglied von verschiedenen wissenschaftlichen Vereinigungen. Herr Scholz ist Mitglied des Kuratoriums der Gesellschaft für Arabisches und Islamisches Recht.

Anna Würth, Dr. phil, studierte Ethnologie und Islamwissenschaft in Berlin und ist wissenschaftliche Mitarbeiterin am Deutschen Institut für Menschenrechte. Von 1994 bis 1998 war sie in der Entwicklungszusammenarbeit tätig und war von 2000 bis 2002 *Finberg Fellow* bei *Human Rights Watch.* Sie lehrte an der *University of Richmond* in Virginia, USA, ebenso wie an der Freien Universität Berlin. Zu ihren jüngsten Publikationen zählt u.a. der in Mitherausgeberschaft veröffentlichte Band *Yemen into the Twenty-first Century: Continuity and Change*, Ithaca Press, Reading 2007, als auch „Investigating and Prosecuting Police Abuse in Egypt“, in: Baudouin Dupret / et al. (Hrsg.) *Narratives of Truth in Islamic Law*, I.B. Tauris/CEDEJ, London 2008.

ZUSAMMENFASSUNGEN

BEITRÄGE ZUR ISLAMRECHTLICHEN METHODIK SOWIE ZUR RECHTSPHILOSOPHIE

Islam und Menschenrechte: Einführende Anmerkungen und Reflexionen

Abdullahi Ahmed An-Na'im, Atlanta

In diesem einführenden Beitrag plädiert der Autor für eine kontextabhängige und kreative Analyse des wechselseitigen Verhältnisses zwischen Islam und Menschenrechten, um die theoretische Legitimität und praktische Wirksamkeit von Menschenrechten in allen Gesellschaften, jeweils in der Beziehung zu ihrer eigenen Religion, zu verbessern.

Der angeregte Ansatz in Bezug auf den Islam basiert auf der unvermeidlichen Rolle der menschlichen Interpretation von religiösen Texten, welche zwangsläufig im spezifischen sozioökonomischen und politischen Kontext von Gläubigen auftreten und sollte daher nicht nur auf die theologischen Ideale beschränkt werden. Der Islam ist relevant für die Validität und Wirksamkeit von Menschenrechten unter Muslimen, nämlich in dem Sinne, wie diese ihre Religion heutzutage verstehen und praktizieren und nicht so, wie es vermutlich Muslime vor vielen Jahrhunderten verstanden haben könnten.

Sein Fokus auf den Islam ist nach eigenen Angaben nicht nur darin zu sehen, dass er muslimischer Advokat für Menschenrechte ist, sondern auch in der Notwendigkeit vergleichbarer Analysen und der Möglichkeit adäquater Ansätze Menschenrechte in Einklang zu bringen, welche in allen anderen religiösen Traditionen gelten.

Islam und Menschenrechte: Betrachtungen zum Verhältnis von Religion und Recht

Muhammad Kalisch, Münster

Die Frage, ob der Islam und die Menschenrechte miteinander vereinbar seien, ist in den letzten Jahren zunehmend Diskussionsgegenstand auch in der westlichen Welt geworden. Hintergrund des Interesses an ihr ist die Angst vor einem Konflikt der Zivilisationen und vor allem wohl auch die Angst vor muslimischen Minderheiten in westlichen Gesellschaften sowie deren zukünftiger Rolle dort. Unter den Muslimen selbst wird sie ohnehin diskutiert.

In diesem Beitrag soll nicht nur der Frage nachgegangen werden, ob Islam und Menschenrechte miteinander vereinbar sind – dies ist eine Frage, zu der schon viel geschrieben worden ist –, sondern vielmehr ganz radikal die Frage gestellt werden, ob die Fragestellung überhaupt sinnvoll ist.

Islam und Menschenrechte (Islam and Human Rights / الإسلام وحقوق الإنسان)
Hatem Elliesie (Hrsg./Editor), © Peter Lang Verlag: Frankfurt a.M. 2010, S. 529-537

Hermeneutik, Koraninterpretation und Menschenrechte

Assem Hefny, Kairo / Leipzig / Marburg

Die Hermeneutik als die Kunst des Verstehens bzw. der Auslegung ist dem *ta'wīl* vom Ziel und Verfahren her ähnlich. *Ta'wīl* beschäftigt sich sowohl mit der sprachlichen Dimension des koranischen Textes als auch damit, was im Text hinsichtlich des historischen Kontexts verborgen ist. Im Laufe der islamischen Geschichte erfuhr der Begriff *ta'wīl* eine negative Konnotation, da er als Textverfälschung verstanden wurde, was ihn zu Gunsten von *tafsīr* – die Suche nach der direkten Wortbedeutung – in den Hintergrund gedrängt hat.

Die Wiederbelebung des historischen Aspektes *(asbāb an-nuzūl)* und die Durchführung des *iǧtihād* gelten daher für eine zeitgerechte Koraninterpretation und somit für die Entwicklung der islamischen Jurisprudenz als eine unabdingbare Notwendigkeit. Ferner sollen sich die islamischen Vorschriften bezüglich der weltlichen Angelegenheiten basiert auf den „Zielen der *šarīʿa*" begründen lassen, wobei das Wohl und das Interesse des Menschen das Hauptziel der *šarīʿa* darstellen. Auf dieser Basis erhöhen sich die Stellung und Würde des Menschen auf die höchste Stufe, was seine Denkens- und Glaubensfreiheit voraussetzt.

„Westliche" *versus* „islamische" Menschenrechtskonzeptionen?

Heiner Bielefeldt, Berlin

Politische Konflikte um das Verständnis und die Umsetzung der Menschenrechte spitzen sich im Rahmen der UNO seit einigen Jahren vor allem zwischen der westlichen Gruppe und der Organisation der Islamischen Konferenz zu. Eine Teilkomponente dieser Konflikte besteht in der beidseitigen Tendenz, die Idee der Menschenrechte kulturalistisch zu vereinnahmen, d.h. sie entweder aus den religiösen oder philosophischen Quellen der abendländischen Tradition oder eben aus den Quellen des Islams schlicht „abzuleiten". Gegen diese doppelte Vereinnahmung gilt es, zunächst die Modernität der Menschenrechte – als einklagbarer universaler Freiheits- und Gleichheitsrechte – klarzustellen. Des Weiteren geht es darum, die Entwicklung der Menschenrechte als eine unabgeschlossene Lerngeschichte zu begreifen, deren sachlicher Ursprung in Erfahrungen strukturellen Unrechts liegt. Als eine moderne Antwort auf strukturelle Unrechtserfahrungen stehen Menschenrechte von vornherein auch für eine Würdigung aus unterschiedlichen kulturellen bzw. religiösen Perspektiven offen, wie sich in freiem Anschluss an die von John Rawls entwickelte Figur des „overlapping consensus" zeigen lässt.

MENSCHENRECHTSSITUATIONEN IN AUSGEWÄHLTEN ISLAMISCH GEPRÄGTEN REGIONEN UND LÄNDERN

Islam und Menschenrechte in Verfassungen afrikanischer Staaten: Agenda für *Good Governance*

Mashood Baderin, London

Einige afrikanische Staaten räumen „dem" Islam als eine Religion und „dem" Islamischen Recht als Rechtsordnung, in der einen oder anderen Form, eine Rolle in ihren modernen Verfassungen ein. Dies wirft die Frage auf, inwieweit die Doktrinen von Konstitutionalismus und

Rechtsstaatlichkeit verfassungsrechtlich mit beiden, „dem“ Islam als einer Religion und „dem“ Islamischen Recht als Rechtsordnung, koexistieren können. Daraus resultiert nach Abdullahi Ahmed An-Na'im ein unumgänglicher Diskurs über „das Verhältnis zwischen Islam, als eine alte und überaus facettenreiche religiöse Tradition, einerseits und Konstitutionalismus [und Rechtsstaatlichkeit], als eine moderne säkulare Doktrin des [Konzepts] *Governance* und Rechten, andererseits.“ Wie kann dieses Verhältnis verstanden werden? Kann man die verfassungsrechtliche Rolle von Islam und Islamischem Recht in Afrika eher als eine Herausforderung zum perzipierten säkularen Wesen des Konzepts von Konstitutionalismus und Rechtsstaatlichkeit begreifen oder ist es *per se* als eine Abweichung zum Konzept zu verstehen?

Der Artikel befasst sich mit diesem Diskurs und untersucht in dieser Hinsicht kritisch die Dynamik von Konstitutionalismus und Rechtsstaatlichkeit in afrikanischen Staaten. Der Beitrag analysiert die theoretischen und praktischen Schwierigkeiten und Perspektiven von einschlägigen Regelungen zur Förderung und Realisierung der Rechtsstaatlichkeit in Afrika.

Islam, Islamisches Recht und Menschenrechte im nigerianischen Kontext

Isa Hayatu Chiroma / Hatem Elliesie, Maiduguri / Berlin

Als Nigeria 1999 zu einer demokratischen Herrschaftsform zurückfand, nutzten Muslime in einigen nördlichen Staaten Nigerias, die sich seit langem für die Wiedereinführung und vollständige Umsetzung des Islamischen Rechts einsetzten, die Gelegenheit und führten das Islamische Recht wieder ein. Die Wiedereinführung des Islamischen Rechts wurde mit gemischten Gefühlen von den unterschiedlichen Bereichen aufgrund vieler umstrittener Angelegenheiten aufgenommen. Dazu zählten und zählen die folgenden fraglichen Problemkreise:

- Ob die Einführung von strafrechtlichen Aspekten des Islamischen Rechts mit der Verfassung von 1999 konform ist oder nicht?
- Ob das Islamische Recht Menschenrechte und die Freiheit innerhalb ihres Wirkungskreises in einer rechtsstaatlichen Demokratie gewährleistet, oder nicht?

Dieser Artikel versucht einige dieser umstrittenen Kernpunkte zu beantworten.

Die Mufti Gesetzgebung in Sansibar und die Grundrechte und Freiheiten der Muslime auf der Insel

Chris Maina Peter, Daressalam

Im Jahre 2001 erließ das Abgeordnetenhaus Sansibars ein Gesetz um das Amt des Muftis von Sansibar zu schaffen. Dies erwies sich als eine äußerst kontroverse Gesetzgebung. Das Gesetz mindert das Amt des Mufti, welchem im Wesentlichen spiritueller Charakter zukommt, in eine Verwaltungsabteilung der *Revolutionary Government of Zanzibar*. Es wird daher nun auch durch den Steuerzahler finanziert. Der Mufti wird vom Präsidenten Sansibars ernannt und einige der Funktionäre seiner Kanzlei werden von dem für religiöse Angelegenheiten zuständigen Minister berufen. Dies wirft eine Anzahl von Fragen auf wie beispielsweise:

- Ist es angemessen, dass ein Amt einer bestimmten Religionsgemeinschaft mit einer Budgetzuordnung finanziert wird, zu welcher alle Sansibaris unabhängig ihrer religiösen Zugehörigkeit beisteuern?
- Wie hat man die Möglichkeit zu bewerten, dass eine gewählte, nicht-muslimische Präsidentschaft den spirituellen islamischen Führer ernennt?

Dies sind nur einige Fragen, mit denen sich diese Arbeit befasst.

Der Sudan in den Grenzen der (internationalen) Menschenrechtsordnung und des humanitären Völkerrechts: Der Fall Darfur

Hatem Elliesie, Berlin

Sudans westlichste Region, Darfur, erlangte in den letzten Jahren traurige Berühmtheit und wurde im Verlauf der Zeit als „die schlimmste humanitäre Krise der Welt" bekannt. Zu Lasten der Zivilbevölkerung spielen sich in Darfur besorgniserregende Vorgänge menschenrechtlicher und kriegsvölkerrechtlicher Verstöße sowohl seitens der sudanesischen Streitkräfte und ihnen verbundener Milizen einerseits als auch seitens der Rebellentruppen andererseits ab. In Erwiderung auf die bewaffneten Auseinandersetzungen und speziell aufgrund der Anschläge auf Zivilisten verurteilte der Sicherheitsrat der Vereinten Nationen „alle Akte der Gewalt und Verstöße gegen Menschenrechte und Kriegsvölkerrecht aller Parteien der Krise". Die internationale Resonanz auf vergangene und gegenwärtige Verbrechen waren bisher zu gering, waren zu spät. Angesichts der halbherzigen diplomatischen Bemühungen und des politischen Widerwillens werden in diesem Artikel *de facto* in prägnanter Form die Entwicklungen, die zu dem humanitären Desaster geführt haben, und die *de jure* Richtlinien und Verpflichtungen, welchen die Beteiligten im Wesentlichen verpflichtend nachkommen müssen, dargestellt.

Anmerkungen zu Menschenrechten und Islam im Nahen Osten

Ann Elizabeth Mayer, Philadelphia

Auch wenn man die Bedeutung der theoretischen Debatten über Islam und Menschenrechte würdigen sollte, so ist dennoch eine sorgfältige Bewertung, inwieweit Islam im gegenwärtigen Ringen um Menschenrechte im Nahen Osten eine Rolle spielt, erforderlich. Derartige Bewertungen lassen erkennen, dass die Tendenz Menschenrechten gegenüber resistent zu sein, viel eher auf Politik als auf Religion zurückzuführen ist. In den vergangenen Jahren haben Studien umfangreiche Schwierigkeiten offenbart, die von Korruption, undemokratischer Regierungsführung sowie Beschneidungen von Rechten und Freiheiten herrühren. In Anbetracht ihrer Menschenrechte betreffenden Unzulänglichkeiten ist es nicht überraschend, dass zahlreiche nahöstliche Staaten und die Organisation der Islamischen Konferenz (OIC), welche Interessen von Ländern wie Saudi Arabien nachkommt, bemüht sind die Welt zu überzeugen, dass sie nicht durch die Internationalen Menschenrechtsvorschriften geleitet werden, sondern von alternativen islamischen Prinzipien. Der offizielle Anspruch, dass diese „verwässerten" Menschenrechte „dem" Islam unterstehen, bedarf, angesichts der politischen Agenden der Regierungen, die diese protegieren, einer kritischen Überprüfung.

Staatliche Menschenrechtsstrukturen und Nationale Menschenrechtsinstitutionen im Nahen Osten und Nordafrika

Anna Würth / Claudia Engelmann, Berlin

In den vergangenen Jahrzehnten sind auch im Nahen Osten und Nordafrika sowie in anderen islamisch geprägten Ländern staatliche Menschenrechtsstrukturen und nationale Menschenrechtsinstitutionen gegründet worden. Wie sehen derartige Strukturen und Nationale Menschenrechtsinstitutionen in Ländern aus, deren politische Systeme vornehmlich durch Autoritarismus geprägt sind? In denen zivilgesellschaftlicher Aktivismus entweder eingeschränkt oder kriminalisiert wird und in denen Amtsträger regelmäßig Menschenrechtsverletzungen begehen?

In diesem Beitrag wird argumentiert, dass die Aneignung des Menschenrechtsdiskurses durch nahöstliche Regierungen Auswirkungen hatte, die in verschiedene, oft auch widersprüchliche Richtungen weisen. Im ersten Teil werden die Funktionen von nationalen Menschenrechtsinstitutionen erläutert und, im zweiten Teil, wird ein Überblick über die bestehenden staatlichen Menschenrechtsinstitutionen und nationalen Menschenrechtsinstitutionen im Nahen Osten und Nordafrika gegeben. Der dritte Teil untersucht schließlich nationale Menschenrechtsinstitutionen im Hinblick auf die international vereinbarten Prinzipien, auf denen diese Institutionen beruhen, und bietet Anregungen für die weitere Forschung.

Zwischen Einschränkung und neuen Entwicklungen: Das Grundrecht auf heterosexuelle Selbstbestimmung in den Verfassungssystemen arabischer Staaten

Naseef Naeem, Berlin / Göttingen

Das Grundrecht auf heterosexuelle Selbstbestimmung könnte man über die den Schutz der Menschenwürde und der persönlichen Freiheit betreffenden verfassungsrechtlichen Bestimmungen in arabischen Staaten als Teil des allgemeinen Grundrechts auf Selbstbestimmung der Sexualität ableiten. Allerdings schränken die arabischen Staaten dieses Recht außerhalb der Ehe ein, indem sie die sexuellen Beziehungen zwischen volljährigen Nichtverheirateten unter Verweisen auf (verfassungsrechtliche) Verknüpfungen von Ehe, Familien, Moral, Sitten, Ehre, Tradition und insbesondere der Religion unter Strafe stellen.

Der Autor setzt sich in diesem Kontext mit *Muḥammad Šaḥrūrs* Thesen auseinander, wonach die religiöse Rechtfertigung des Verbotes von außerehelichen heterosexuellen Partnerschaften einen Rückschlag erlitten hat. Nach *Muḥammad Šaḥrūr* sind diese Partnerschaften, unter bestimmten Voraussetzungen, islamkonform. Insofern können sich die arabischen Staaten aus verfassungsrechtlicher Sicht nicht mehr auf eine einheitliche islamische Doktrin im Sinne eines absoluten Verbotes berufen. Rechtsdogmatisch untersteht diese starre Position arabischer Staaten demgemäß vielmehr einer Verhältnismäßigkeitsprüfung.

Das Menschenrechtsdilemma in Ägypten: Politischer Wille oder Islam?

Bahey eldin Hassan, Kairo

Diese Abhandlung setzt sich kritisch mit der Menschenrechtssituation in Ägypten auseinander und versucht auf verschiedene Fragestellungen einzugehen. Dazu zählen:

- Was sind die Hauptmuster von Menschenrechtsverletzungen in Ägypten?
- Bessert sich der Stand der Dinge oder verschlechtert er sich? Wieso? Welche Zukunftsaussicht(en) gibt es?
- Weshalb besteht ein derart schlechtes Menschenrechtsprotokoll? Muss man es auf einen Mangel an politischem Willen zurückführen? Oder ist es vielmehr ein religöses/kulturelles Problem? Oder gar eine Vermischung?
- Was ist der Einfluss des wachsenden politischen Islams in Ägypten auf die Menschenrechtssituation?

Menschenrechte und Islam in Südostasien: Das Fallbeispiel Indonesien

Tim Lindsey, Melbourne

Aus Indonesiens dramatischem und weitreichendem demokratischen Wandel bildeten sich seit dem Niedergang von Soehartos autoritärer und repressiver „Neuen Ordnung" im Jahre 1998 zwei parallele Entwicklungen heraus. Die rasche Verabschiedung – sowohl durch Ratifikation internationaler Vertragsurkunden als auch durch eine Welle innerstaatlicher Rechtsvorschriften, aber auch durch Schaffung neuer Institutionen – wurde durch den Erlass von Rechtsvorschriften auf lokaler und nationaler Ebene begleitet, die eine „Islamisierung" Indonesiens anvisierte, um dem Brauch konservativer, durch nahöstliche Traditionen inspirierte Normen, Geltung zu verschaffen. Dies stellte in vielen Fällen das neue Menschenrechtsregime insbesondere dadurch unmittelbar vor Herausforderungen, dass die „islamisierten" Regelungen zuweilen die in diesem Milieu verwundbaren Gruppen, wie Frauen und religiöse Minderheiten, diskriminierte. Dieser Konflikt spiegelt den langjährigen Disput bezüglich der Stellung des islamischen Rechts innerhalb Indonesiens im Wesentlichen aus dem *Westen* abgeleiteten Rechtssystems wider, welches dazu verhalf die kommunale Gewalt und Terrorismus anzuregen. Es scheint allerdings unwahrscheinlich, dass „Syariahisation" sich in einer Änderung der Grundstruktur des indonesischen Staatsrechtssystems durchsetzen wird. Dies deutet darauf hin, dass auf lange Sicht die gegenwärtigen Reformen, welche internationale Menschenrechtsnormen einleiten, voraussichtlich bestehen werden.

Menschenrechtsstandards in afghanischen Gerichtssälen: Theorie und Wirklichkeit des Rechts auf ein faires Verfahren

Tilmann Röder, Heidelberg / Kabul

Das Recht auf ein faires Strafverfahren ist nicht nur in den Menschenrechtsverträgen garantiert, die von der Islamischen Republik Afghanistan oder ihren Vorgängern ratifiziert wurden, sondern auch in der afghanischen Verfassung und im einfachen Gesetzesrecht. Die Gerichtspraxis weicht jedoch weit von diesen Standards ab. Die Mehrheit der Strafverfolgten wird länger inhaftiert als es rechtlich zulässig wäre, viele werden von der Polizei oder dem Geheimdienst gefoltert und wer angeklagt wird, findet selten einen Rechtsbeistand. Die meisten

Verfahren finden ohne Staatsanwalt statt und viele enden mit Verurteilungen, die auf zweifelhafter Beweisführung beruhen. Die Gründe dieses bedauerlichen Zustandes sind vielfaltig; unzureichende Rechtskenntnisse der Juristen und Mangel an materiellen Ressourcen sind dabei nur zwei von vielen Hindernissen.

Der Aufsatz analysiert die Gründe für diesen unzureichenden Strafprozess und erörtert mögliche Lösungsansätze. Er stützt sich in erster Linie auf Interviews mit Richtern und Staatsanwälten aus allen Landesteilen, unveröffentlichte Ergebnisse eines Gerichtsbeobachtungsprogramms der Vereinten Nationen (UNAMA) und auf eigene Beobachtungen des Autors in afghanischen Gerichten.

Scharia und Implementierung von Menschenrechtsnormen der Gleichberechtigung und Nichtdiskriminierung in der Familie: Am Fallbeispiel des Familienrechts in Pakistan

Ayesha Shahid / Javaid Rehman, Hull / London

Šarīʿa ist das zugrundeliegende Prinzip des größten Teils der Gesetzgebung in Pakistan, insbesondere im Familienrecht. Das Familienrecht betreffend leitet sich dessen Rechtsgrundlage allerdings nicht nur vom *Šarīʿ*atsrecht ab, sondern wird eben auch von gewohnheitsrechtlichen und kulturellen Normen beeinflusst, wodurch sich das Familienrecht als Frauen diskriminierend herausstellt. Pakistan ist indes Unterzeichner vieler internationaler Verträge und die pakistanische Verfassung enthält sowohl in ihren Bestimmungen internationale Menschenrechtsstandards der Gleichberechtigung und Nichtdiskriminierung als auch in den Prinzipien der Politik.

Dieser Artikel untersucht das gegenseitige Verhältnis von Menschenrechtsnormen und *šarīʿ*atsrechtlich basierendem Familienrecht in vier wesentlichen Bereichen, nämlich Eheschließung, Sorgerecht sowie Vormundschaft, Polygamie und Ehescheidung. Dabei wird erörtert, dass – um einen vollständigen Rekurs für Frauen in familiären Angelegenheiten zu gewährleisten – ein umfassender (neuer) Ansatz erforderlich ist, um die *šarīʿ*atsrechtlichen Prinzipien von Gerechtigkeit und Gleichberechtigung mit internationalen Menschenrechtsnormen der Gerechtigkeit und Gleichberechtigung in Einklang zu bringen.

Zivilgesellschaft und Gesetzgebung: Entwicklungen in Bezug auf die Menschenrechtslage in Iran im Jahr 2008

Irene Schneider, Göttingen

Dieser Artikel behandelt die neuesten Entwicklungen zur Situation der Menschenrechte in Iran. Im Vordergrund stehen dabei die Beziehung zwischen der iranischen Zivilgesellschaft (insbesondere den Frauenorganisationen) und dem Staat, die anhand der Diskussion um den Gesetzesentwurf zum neuen Familienrecht untersucht werden. Die zentralen Fragen, welche die Autorin aufwirft, sind:

- Wie stellt sich die Menschenrechtslage in der Islamischen Republik Iran im Herbst 2008 mit Bezug auf das neue Familienrecht dar?
- Wie müssen in diesem Zusammenhang die Regelungen des Familienrechtsentwurfes beurteilt werden?
- Welche Rolle spielen a) die internationalen Abkommen, wie z.B. das Übereinkommen zur Beseitigung jeder Form von Diskriminierung der Frau (CEDAW), das allerdings

bisher in Iran nicht unterzeichnet worden ist? b) die Aktivitäten der Zivilgesellschaft im Bezug auf den Prozess der Gesetzgebung?

Methodisch werden neben einer Rekonstruktion des Ablaufes des politischen und sozialen Prozesses auf der Grundlage der Diskurstheorie diejenigen Argumente untersucht, die von den verschiedenen Seiten vorgebracht wurden.

INTERAKTION ISLAMISCH GEPRÄGTER LÄNDER UND ORGANISATIONEN MIT INTERNATIONALEN MENSCHENRECHTSINSTITUTIONEN

Der Frauenrechtsausschuss der Vereinten Nationen in der Interaktion mit islamisch geprägten Staaten

Hanna Beate Schöpp-Schilling, Wohltorf / New York

Das Übereinkommen zur Beseitigung jeder Form von Diskriminierung der Frau (CEDAW) ist der wichtigste internationale Menschenrechtsvertrag auf internationaler Ebene. Der dazugehörige Vertragsausschuss (CEDAW Committee) mit 23 unabhängigen Experten aus allen Weltregionen überprüft anhand von drei Durchsetzungsverfahren (Berichts-, Beschwerde- und Untersuchungsverfahren) die Umsetzung des Übereinkommens im einzelnen Vertragsstaat. Von den 185 Vertragsstaaten haben vor allem islamisch geprägte Staaten eine Reihe von Artikeln, welche die Staatenverpflichtungen allgemein und in spezifischen Lebensbereichen von Frauen (Staatsangehörigkeit, Freizügigkeit der Bewegung, Gleichberechtigung und Gleichstellung in Ehe und familiären Beziehungen) betreffen, mit Vorbehalten belegt.

Aufbauend auf früheren Analysen wird in diesem Aufsatz untersucht, wie ausgewählte islamisch geprägte Vertragsstaaten (z.B. Ägypten, Marokko, Saudi Arabien) ihre Vorbehalte vor dem Ausschuss rechtfertigen, welche Stellungnahmen der Ausschuss abgibt und ob in der Folge Veränderungen zur Verbesserung der Menschenrechte von Frauen in diesen Staaten geschehen.

Die Organisation Islamischer Konferenz im UN-Menschenrechtsrat: Menschenrechte als Instrument staatlicher Politik

Theodor Rathgeber, Kassel

Dieser Artikel setzt sich mit drei Handlungsebenen auseinander. Zum einen tritt die Organisation Islamischer Konferenz (OIC) wirkmächtig im Wesentlichen in Genf auf, Schauplatz für ein geo- und machtpolitisches Kräftemessen entlang des Nord-Süd-Konflikts. Zum zweiten steht die OIC in Genf für das Anliegen, die Menschenrechte von 1948 durch eine islamisch geprägte Perspektive zu ergänzen. Zum dritten strebt die OIC die Meinungsführerschaft in Sachen Religion an, da der Schutz für Muslime nach Meinung der OIC gerade in westlichen Ländern unterentwickelt ist, und Religion an sich Schutz benötigt.

In allen drei Argumentationsebenen spricht die OIC vergessene oder vernachlässigte Anliegen innerhalb des UN-Menschenrechtsregimes an. Die Art der Geltendmachung legt jedoch die

Vermutung nahe, dass individuelle Rechte gegen kollektive Rechte ausgespielt werden, um den Staat vor Ansprüchen zu „schützen“.

Dieser Beitrag plädiert dafür, diese Anliegen auf der Basis der universellen Menschenrechte in der Tat stärker zu berücksichtigen.

MENSCHENRECHTE UND ISLAMISCHES RECHT UNTER DEM BLICKWINKEL DES (INTERNATIONALEN) PRIVATRECHTS

Ordre Public, Menschenrechte und Scharia

Peter Scholz, Berlin

Islamisch geprägten Staaten werden oft Verstöße gegen internationale Menschenrechte vorgehalten. Zu deren Schutz in zivilrechtlichen Fällen kann der nationale *Ordre Public* herangezogen werden, wenn in das nationale Recht transformierte international gewährleistete Menschenrechte verletzt werden.

Der Nutzen einer solchen Verfahrensweise ist allerdings begrenzt durch verschiedenartige Vorstellungen und Konzepte der Menschenrechte, unterschiedliche Auslegungen der Menschenrechtspakte und einen extensiven Gebrauch von Vorbehalten gegenüber menschenrechtlichen Verpflichtungen. Dieses Problem wird am Beispiel des islamischen Konzepts der Religionsfreiheit und der Praxis der islamischen Staaten in Bezug auf die einschlägigen internationalen Verpflichtungen erläutert.

Religionsfreiheit und islamisch geprägtes Erbrecht: Gesetzliche Regelungen und Rechtsprechungsauslegung im heutigen Ägypten und Tunesien

Imen Gallala, Hamburg

Die islamischen Länder befinden sich seit der Erlangung ihrer Unabhängigkeit von den Kolonialmächten in einem Dilemma. Einerseits möchten sie die *Šarīʿa* befolgen, andererseits möchten sie in ihren Verfassungen Menschenrechtskataloge aufnehmen und völkerrechtliche Menschenrechtsverträge ratifizieren. Diese Menschenrechte stehen aber nicht selten in Widerspruch zu den islamrechtlichen Normen.

Dieser Beitrag untersucht diese Problematik anhand des Beispiels der Religionsfreiheit im Verhältnis zum islamisch geprägten Erbrecht in Ägypten und Tunesien. Die Religionsfreiheit ist zwar sowohl in der ägyptischen als auch in der tunesischen Verfassung verankert, trotzdem betrachten die ägyptischen Gesetze und die in Tunesien vorherrschende Rechtsprechung die Religionsverschiedenheit zwischen Erblasser und Erbe als Erbhindernis. Einen Ausweg bietet möglicherweise die jüngste Rechtsprechung in Tunesien, die neue Ansätze zur Auslegung des Erbrechts im Einklang mit der Religionsfreiheit aufzeigt.

CONTRIBUTING AUTHORS

Abdullahi Ahmed An-Na'im, Charles Howard Candler Professor of Law, holds an LLB from Khartoum University, as well as an LLB and Diploma in Criminology from Cambridge University and a PhD in Law from Edinburgh University. His previous positions include Associate Professor at the University of Khartoum, Visiting Professor of Law at the University of California, Los Angeles, Ariel F. Sallows Professor of Human Rights at the University of Saskatchewan, and Olof Palme Visiting Professor at Uppsala University. Before joining the Faculty of Emory Law School in 1995, he served as Executive Director of Human Rights Watch/Africa. He has published several books and more than fifty articles and book chapters on human rights, constitutionalism, Islamic law and politics. His most recent book is "Islam and the Secular State: Negotiating the Future of Shari'a", Harvard University Press, Cambridge / et al. 2008.

Mashood Baderin, LL.B. (Hons.), BL, LL.M., PhD, is Professor of Law at the School of Oriental and African Studies (SOAS), University of London. He previously taught Law at Brunel University London, University of the West of England, Bristol, University of Southampton, and University of Nottingham. He is a Barrister and Solicitor of the Supreme Court of Nigeria. Prof. Baderin conducts research in the areas of Islamic Law, Human Rights and International Public Law; with particular interest in the interaction between International Public Law, Human Rights Law and Islamic Law in Muslim States. He is the author of "International Human Rights and Islamic Law", Oxford University Press, Oxford 2003 and a founding Co-Editor of the "Muslim World Journal of Human Rights" (http://www.bepress.com/mwjhr/).

Heiner Bielefeldt, Prof. habil., Dr. phil., is the Director of the German Institute for Human Rights in Berlin. From 1983 until 1990, he held the position of Research Assistant, and then of Research Fellow, at the "Interdisciplinary Research Project Human Rights" (*"Interdisziplinäre Forschungsprojekt Menschenrechte"*) in the Faculty of Philosophy at the University of Tübingen. After, he held the position of staff member at the Chairs for Public Law and Philosophy of Law at the Law Faculties in Mannheim (1990-1992) and Heidelberg (1992-1995), while being, at the same time, on sabbatical in 1993/1994 to do research and to teach at the University of Toronto. Heiner Bielefeldt authored and edited a number of books on issue-related matters of Legal Philosophy and Human Rights, as well as that of Political Ethics and Philosophy of Religion. One of his main fields of research is the situation of Muslim minorities living in European secular liberal democracies.

Isa Hayatu Chiroma is a Professor of Law and holds a Ph.D. in Law from University of Jos, Nigeria. He was Sub-Dean as well as Head of the Department of *Šarīʿa* and currently holds the position of Dean of Law at the University of Maiduguri. He pioneered the establishment of a Law Clinic to facilitate access to justice by providing legal services to the underprivileged and disadvantaged. In addition to his teaching and scholarly activities, he served as a legal consultant on Environmental Law and Policy (1997-1999), and to the Federal Ministry of Environment (2001-2004). He is a Member of the Presidential Advisory Committee on Prerogative of Mercy, and Council of Legal Education in Nigeria. His teaching and research interests are in the area of Human Rights, Islamic Law as well as Law and Development.

Islam und Menschenrechte (Islam and Human Rights / الإسلام وحقوق الإنسان)
Hatem Elliesie (Hrsg.), © Peter Lang Verlag: Frankfurt a.M. 2010, S. 539-543

Bahey eldin Hassan is the director of the Cairo Institute for Human Rights Studies, member of the Board of the EuroMed Human Rights Foundation (EMHRF) and lecturer and author of several articles and papers on Human Rights and Democratic Transformation in the Arab Region. He is also the editor of several books in Arabic, and contributed to others, such as 'A Question of Human Rights Ethics: Defending the Islamists', in: *Anthony Chase / Amr Hamzawy* (Eds.), "Human Rights in the Arab World: Independent Voices"; and 'Regional Protection of Human Rights in the Arab States In Statu Nascendi', in: *Janusz Symonides* (Ed.), "Human Rights: International Protection, Monitoring, Enforcement", UNESCO 2003.

Hatem Elliesie is a member of the Board of the Arabic and Islamic Law Association as well as a member of the Executive Committee of the African Law Association and founding member of the Lawyers' Group of Amnesty International, Hong Kong Section. He was a staff-member of the 'Sudan Peace Project' until 2005 and supported the Project "Reconstruction of the Judiciary and the Public Administration Sector in Afghanistan" until 2004 at the Max Planck Institute for Comparative Law and International Law in Heidelberg, Germany. Hatem Elliesie, who studied Law as well as Islamic-, Semitistic- and Ethiopian Studies at the Universities of Mannheim, Heidelberg, Hannover, Oxford, Cairo and Berlin, has been a Research Fellow at the University of Malta and is currently a doctoral candidate at the Free University of Berlin. He has been a member of the Appointments Committees for the Professorships for 'Islamic Law' as well as 'Islam in Europe' at the Free University Berlin.

Claudia Engelmann is an intern at the German Institute for Human Rights and a student of the MSt in International Human Rights Law at Oxford University. In 2007, she graduated from the University of Konstanz focusing on Literature, Law and Political Science. In 2006 and 2007, she has been involved in research, education and lobby activities at the United Nations Association of Germany (*Deutsche Gesellschaft für die Vereinten Nationen* – DGVN) in Berlin and in the "Conference of NGOs in Consultative Relationship with the UN" (Geneva).

Imen Gallala, Dr. iur., LL.M. (Heidelberg), is a Senior Research Fellow at the Department of the Law of Islamic Countries at the Max Planck Institute for Foreign Private Law and Private International Law in Hamburg. She holds an LL.M. and a Ph.D. from the University of Heidelberg. She studied Law at the Department of Law Tunis II from where she holds a *Maîtrise en Sciences Juridiques* and a *Diplôme des Etudes Approfondies en Droit Pulic et Financier*. She also taught there as a Teaching Assistant for Public International Law. Her main field of research is National and International Family and Succession Laws of Islamic Countries.

Assem Hefny was born in Egypt in 1972. He studied German and Islamic Studies at Al-Azhar University in Cairo. He received his B.A. "with honours" and continued his education fusing these fields, writing his master's thesis on 'specific cultural Arabic terms in Karl May's stories'. He has been working as a Teaching Assistant in the German and Islamic Studies Departments at Al-Azhar University. Mr. Assem Hefny is currently a doctoral candidate at the Institute of Oriental Studies at the University of Leipzig and is engaged in research projects on Islamic Banking in Germany as well as the edition and translation of the Egyptian Family Law. As Board Member of the "Association of Arab Students and Academics" (*VASA*) in Leipzig, he is also responsible for cultural exchange and interfaith dialogue. He is currently a lecturer for Arabic and Islamic studies in the Center for Near and Middle Eastern Studies (CNMS) at the University of Marburg.

Muhammad Kalisch is a Professor for Religion of Islam and Director of the Centre for Religious Studies at the University of Münster, Germany. He studied Law in Hamburg and received his doctoral degree in Darmstadt with the dissertation on *"Vernunft und Flexibilität in der islamischen Rechtsmethodik"* (Reason and Flexibility in the Methodology of Islamic Law). His postdoctoral thesis (*Habilitation*) was obtained in the field of Islamic Studies with a thesis on *"Fiqh und Uṣūl al-Fiqh in der Zaidīya – Die historische Entwicklung der Zaidīya als Rechtsschule"* (Fiqh and Uṣūl al-Fiqh in the Zaidīya – The historical Development of the Zaidīya as a School of Islamic Law) in 2002. His special areas of research are the history and methodology of Islamic Law, the theology of the *muʿtazila* and the Zaidīya, Islamic Philosophy, theoretical *ʿirfān* (Islamic Gnosis), and *perennial philosophy*.

Javaid Rehman is a Professor of Law at Brunel Law School, Brunel University in London. His special research interests include Islamic Law, minority rights and international terrorism. He has held several visiting positions, e.g. in Pakistan, Bangladesh, Turkey, France, Japan, USA. In addition, he had the honour of being invited by the Higher Education Commission in Pakistan to formulate a comprehensive review of the Teaching of Legal Education. He edited and published several books, contributed extensively to scholarly journals and is a member of the editorial board of the journals "Religion and Human Rights", "Asian Journal of International Law", and "Central European Journal of International and Security Studies". Moreover, he is a member of the International Law Association's Committee on International Law and Islamic Law and the Editor of the "Journal of Islamic State Practices in International Law".

Ann Elizabeth Mayer is an Associate Professor of Legal Studies and Business Ethics at the Wharton School of the University of Pennsylvania. She earned a PhD in Middle Eastern History from the University of Michigan and obtained a Certificate in Islamic and Comparative Law from the School of Oriental and African Studies (SOAS), University of London, and a JD from the University of Pennsylvania. Her research areas include Islamic Law in contemporary Middle Eastern and North African countries; problems of constitutionalism and the rule of law; and international human rights Law. She has published extensively in scholarly journals and edited collections, and the fourth edition of her book "Islam and Human Rights" appeared in 2007.

Naseef Naeem obtained a diploma in public law in 1998 after studying law at the University of Aleppo between 1992 – 1996, as well as a diploma in financial and administrative sciences in 1999 at the University of Damascus. From 1999 until 2002, he worked as an advocate in Syria and from 2001 to 2002 as a Graduate Research Assistant at the Law Faculty of the University of Damascus. In 2007, he earned his Doctorate (*Dr. jur.*) at the Law Faculty of the University of Hannover with the thesis *"Die neue bundesstaatliche Ordnung des Irak"* which has been published by the Peter Lang Publishing Group. The author is currently working on his postdoctoral thesis (*Habilitation*) at the University of Göttingen. Together with Prof. hon. Dr. iur. Dr. phil. Peter Scholz, he conducted seminars on state organisation of Islamic countries and on Basic Right's system within constitutions of Islamic countries at the Free University of Berlin in the previous two semesters.

Chris Maina Peter is a Professor of Law at the University of Dar es Salaam He holds a Dr. iur. from Konstanz University in Germany, as well as an LL.M. and LL.B. from the University of Dar es Salam in Tanzania, and has been a Visiting Professor at various Universities and academic Institutions such as the University of Hamburg in Germany, the Raoul Wallenberg Institute of Human Rights and Humanitarian Law in Sweden, the Max Planck Institute for Comparative Public Law and International Law in Germany and the Institute of International Law and International Relations at the University of Graz in Austria. He teaches Public International Law, Human Rights, Refugee Law and Humanitarian Law and acted as external examiner to various Universities in Kenya, Uganda and South Africa. Furthermore, he is a member of the Advisory Board of the *Yearbook of the International Humanitarian Law* and a Member of the United Nations Committee on Elimination of Racial Discrimination (CERD).

Theodor Rathgeber, Political Scientist (*Dr. rer. pol.*), is a lecturer at the University of Kassel in Germany at the Department on Social Sciences (*Fachbereich 05*). From 1990 on, he has been a Consultant, and since 2001 consultant on a freelance basis, on Human Rights, International Law and Development Policies, focusing on Indigenous and Minority Rights as well as on transnational companies' Human Rights responsibilities. The author was an official observer to the UN Commission on Human Rights since 2003 and, since 2006, to that of the UN Human Rights Council (2006) on behalf of the German NGO network "*Forum Menschenrechte*". A list of his publications on the mentioned topics is available upon request.

Tilmann Röder is Head of the Middle East and Central Asia Projects of the Max Planck Institute for Comparative Public Law and International Law in Heidelberg, Germany. Recently, he has been researching on, and working in Afghanistan, Libya, Israel/Palestine, Iran, Azerbaijan, Sudan, Somalia and Kashmir. Dr. Röder has published in the area of legal and judicial reform (with a focus on constitutional and international law). He is the managing editor of the series of Max Planck Manuals used as training materials for Max Planck projects. Together with Dr. Rainer Grote he initiated an ongoing series of lectures on Law & Development held in Heidelberg. In addition, he has been published in the field of legal history and has co-founded the international Association of Young Legal Historians (AYLH). Dr. Röder holds a law degree from Humboldt University (Berlin) and a doctor degree from Johann Wolfgang Goethe University (Frankfurt). He also practiced as *Rechtsreferendar* in Berlin.

Mathias Rohe, M.A., Dr. iur. Prof. habil., holds the Chair of Civil Law, Private International Law and Comparative Law at the Faculty of Law and Economics at the University of Erlangen-Nuremberg. He is also the Faculty's founding Director of the Centre for Islam and the Law in Europe (*"Zentrum für Islam und Recht in Europa"*), where he acted as Dean. He is a founding member of the Arabic and Islamic Law Association of which he is currently the Chairman of the Board. Mathias Rohe is an author of numerous publications dealing with the legal status of Muslims in Germany and Europe as well as focusing on aspects of Islamic Law and on Civil Law issues. In addition to his academic endeavour in Europe and overseas, he has also worked as a Judge of the Court of Appeal of Nuremberg from 2000 until 2006. His latest book *"Das Islamische Recht: Geschichte und Gegenwart"* was published in 2009 (Beck Verlag: München).

Irene Schneider, Dr. phil., is Professor for Arabic Studies and Islamic Law at the University of Göttingen. Before focusing on a study on the early Islamic History of Law in her postdoctoral thesis (*Habilitation*), she dealt with the *adab al-qāḍī*-literature in her doctoral thesis. Her previous positions include Assistant Professor at the University of Cologne, Research Associate of the National Science Foundation/USA's project: "Constitutional Law and the Politics of Modernization in the Islamic Middle East" at the State University of New York, and has held additional functions in respective research projects based in Germany. Her fields of research are Islamic law, its history, the reconstruction of early Islamic history and *ḥadīṯ* as a source of Islamic history, as well as Gender Studies in Arab countries, in Iran and Afghanistan and the (constitutional) interdependence of state and society; and, lastly, that of Islam in Germany.

Ayesha Shahid is a lecturer at the Law School of the University of Hull. Her teaching and research interests focus on areas of Islamic Law, Public Law, Gender and Law, and International Human Rights Law. Besides numerous publications in journals, Dr. Ayesha Shahid is currently working on a monograph entitled "Silent Voices, Untold Stories, Women Domestic Workers and their Struggle for Empowerment", a socio-legal study about law, empowerment and access to justice for women domestic workers in Pakistan. The study questions the efficacy of law as a tool for empowering this specific social group in their struggle against exploitative treatment in the workplace. In 2002, the author received the prestigious Warwick Postgraduate Fellowship Award and also a Postgraduate Diploma in teaching 'Human Rights Law' from Columbia University, USA.

Hanna Beate Schöpp-Schilling, Dr. phil., is a member of the Board of Trustees of the German Institute for Human Rights (Vice-Chairperson from 2001-2004) as well as member of the National Institute for Human Rights in the region of Sverdlovsk, Russia and of the Board of Trustees of the German women's foundation, "filia. die frauenstiftung". Since 1989, she has been a member of the UN Committee on the Elimination of Discrimination Against Women (CEDAW), where she held numerous positions, including Rapporteur and Vice-Chair. Besides different lectureships and guest professorships in Germany, U.S.A., Japan and Bosnia-Herzegovina, she acted, among other appointments, as Director General for Women's Affairs at the German Federal Ministry of Family, Women and Youth. Her publications are in the areas of Women's Studies, Labor Market Studies and Human Rights. Just recently, Dr. Schöpp-Schilling received the *Margherita-von-Brentano-Preis 2008* of the Free University Berlin for her commitment in the CEDAW.

Peter Scholz, Prof. hon. Dr. jur. Dr. phil., studied law, Islamic Studies and history of art at the University of Hamburg. In 1995 he finished his doctoral-thesis in Islamic Studies and in 2006 he received a Doctor of Laws at the Free University of Berlin. Since 1995 he is working as a judge in Berlin, where he was appointed *Richter am Kammergericht* in 2007 and, just recently, since 2009, assigned as *Vizepräsident des Amtsgerichts Tiergarten.* After conducting courses covering Islamic Law for some years, the Free University of Berlin appointed him to a Honorary Professor of Islamic Law and Private International Law. He publishes widely on these issues and is a member of different academic associations as well as one of the curators of the Association for Arabic and Islamic Law.

Anna Würth, Dr. phil., studied Anthropology and Middle Eastern Studies in Berlin, is a Researcher at the German Institute for Human Rights. From 1994 to 1998 she worked in development cooperation and, from 2000 to 2002, acted as Finberg Fellow at Human Rights Watch. She taught at the University of Richmond (Virginia, USA) and at the Free University in Berlin. Among her recent publications is the co-edited volume "Yemen into the Twenty-first Century: Continuity and Change", Ithaca Press, Reading 2007, as well as 'Investigating and Prosecuting Police Abuse in Egypt', in: Baudouin Dupret / et al (Eds.) "Narratives of Truth in Islamic Law", Tauris/CEDEJ, London, I.B. 2008.

SUMMARIES

CONTRIBUTIONS TO ISLAMIC LEGAL AND THEOLOGICAL APPROACHES AND PHILOSOPHY OF LAWS

Islam and Human Rights: Introductory Remarks and Reflections

Abdullahi Ahmed An-Na'im, Atlanta

In this article, the author is calling for a contextual and creative analysis of the relationship between religion and Human Rights in order to enhance the theoretical legitimacy and practical efficacy of Human Rights in all societies, each in relation to its own religion.

The proposed approach in relation to Islam is premised on the unavoidable role of human interpretation of religious texts, which will necessarily occur in the specific socio-economic and political context of believers, and should not be limited to purely theological ideals. Islam is relevant to the validity and efficacy of Human Rights among Muslims in terms of how they understand and practice their religion today, as distinguished from how it may have been understood and practiced by Muslims many centuries ago.

According to the author, the focus on Islam here is not purely because he is a Muslim advocate of Human Rights, but because of the need for similar analysis and the possibility of appropriate approaches to reconcile how Human Rights relates to all other religious traditions.

Islam and Human Rights: Considerations on the Relationship of Religion and Law

Muhammad Kalisch, Münster

The question, whether Islam and Human Rights can conform to each other has become a subject of discussion, even in the *Western World*. The basis of this interest is the fear of a clash of the civilizations and especially the anxiety towards Muslim minorities in *Western* societies and their future role. This is also a widely discussed within the Muslim minority community itself.

This article ought not to simply look into the question of whether Islam and Human Rights are conformable to each other – itself a much-discussed issue – but, rather, if posing this controversial question in and of itself makes any sense.

Islam und Menschenrechte (Islam and Human Rights / الإسلام وحقوق الإنسان)
Hatem Elliesie (Hrsg./Editor), © Peter Lang Verlag: Frankfurt a.M. 2010, S. 545-553

Hermeneutics, Quran interpretation and Human rights

Assem Hefny, Cairo / Leipzig / Marburg

Hermeneutics as the art of text understanding resembles the *ta'wīl* in method and goal. *Ta'wīl* aims for the understanding of texts by applying all linguistic instruments with regard to its historical context. Therefore, both methods may found a basis for a contemporary Quran interpretation. *Ta'wīl* was originally highly esteemed as it was used by rational *Mu'tazilites* in approaching the Quran. In course of political history, *ta'wīl* later acquired a negative connotation and was replaced by the method of *tafsīr* which focused on lexical interpretation.

A re-establishment of *ta'wīl* combined with the opening of *iǧtihād*-gate would allow for a renewal of the Quran interpretation based on the *asbāb an-nuzūl* and goals of *šarī'a* as foundation of regulations with the human well-being as a main concern. Thus, the human values and rights will gain more significance and the human being will take the responsibility of his earthy existence by implementing the Trust which requires his freedom of thinking and belief.

'Western' *versus* 'Islamic' Concepts of Human Rights?

Heiner Bielefeldt, Berlin

Political conflicts about the understanding and implementation of Human Rights has gradually grown more acute in the context of the United Nations, primarily between the 'Western Group' and the OIC (Organisation of Islamic Conference). A partial element of the conflicts consists of the bilateral tendency to allow oneself to take the concept of Human Rights culturally, respectively: That is, either to simply "derive" them from the religious or philosophic sources of the occidental tradition, or from sources of the Islam. Contrary to this twofold appropriation, it is initially essential to clarify the modernity of Human Rights as an enforceable universal right for freedom and equality. Because the origin of Human Rights' development comes from the experience of structural injustice, its apprehension as a learning process remains open. At the onset, as a modern answer to structural unjust experiences, Human Rights struggle for the appreciation and receptions to different cultural and religious perspectives, as the doctrine "overlapping consensus", coined by John Rawl, shows.

HUMAN RIGHTS SITUATIONS IN PREDOMINANTELY ISLAMIC REGIONS AND COUNTRIES

Islam and Human Rights in the Constitutions of African States: Agenda for Good Governance

Mashood Baderin, London

Some African states provide a role for Islam as a religion and for Islamic law as a legal system, in one form or another, in their modern constitutions. This raises the question of how the doctrines of constitutionalism and rule of law can constitutionally co-exist with both Islam as a religion and Islamic law as a legal system. Out of this question results the necessary discourse about "the relationship between Islam, as an ancient and extremely diverse religious tradition, on the one hand, and constitutionalism [and rule of law] as a modern secular doctrine of governance and rights, on the other", as stated by Abdullahi Ahmed An-Na'im. How can this relationship be perceived? Is one able to consider the constitutional role for Islam and Islamic law in Africa as a challenge to the perceived secular nature of the concepts of constitutionalism and rule of law, rather than an aberration to the concepts *per se*?

This article will engage with this discourse and, in that regard, critically analyse the dynamics of constitutionalism and rule of law in African states. The contribution will analyse the theoretical and practical problems and prospects of relevant provisions for the promotion and realisation of the rule of law in Africa.

Islam, Islamic Law and Human Rights in the Nigerian Context

Isa Hayatu Chiroma / Hatem Elliesie, Maiduguri / Berlin

When Nigeria returned to democratic rule in 1999, Muslims in some of its Northern States who had long been agitated about the reintroduction and full implementation of Islamic Law took advantage of the situation and reintroduced Islamic Law in all its ramifications. The reintroduction of Islamic Law was received with mixed feelings from different quarters because of many questionable issues. Among them were, and are, the following:

- Whether the implementation of the criminal aspect of Islamic Law is in conformity with the 1999 Constitution, or not?
- Whether Islamic Law guarantees Human Rights and freedom within the sphere of its operation in a Constitutional Democracy, or not?

This paper attempts to answer some of these contending issues.

Mufti Act of Zanzibar and the Fundamental Rights and Freedoms of Moslems on the Isles

Chris Maina Peter, Dar es Salaam

In 2001, the Zanzibar House of Representatives enacted an Act to establish the office of the Mufti of Zanzibar. This turned out to be very controversial legislation. The Act reduces the office of the Mufti, which inheres an essentially spiritual character, into an administrative Department of the Revolutionary Government of Zanzibar, and thus funded by the taxpayer. The Mufti is appointed by the President of Zanzibar and some of the functionaries of his office are appointed by the Minister responsible for religious affairs. This raises a number of questions; such as:

- Is it adequate for an office of a certain religious community to be funded by an allocation to which all Zanzibaris are contributing to, irrespective of their respective beliefs?
- How should one evaluate the possibility of an elected non-Muslim presidency appointing an Islamic spiritual leader?

These are just some of the questions addressed in this work.

Sudan under the Constraints of (International) Human Rights Law and Humanitarian Law: The Case of Darfur

Hatem Elliesie, Berlin

Sudan's westernmost region, Darfur, gained notoriety in recent years and has been known as "the world's worst humanitarian crisis" in the course of time: At the expense of its civilian population, a disturbing pattern of disregard for Human Rights and Humanitarian Law is taking place by both the armed forces of the Sudan and its proxy militia on one hand, and rebel forces on the other. In response to the armed conflicts and especially due to attacks on civilians, the UN-Security Council condemned "all acts of violence and violations of Human Rights and Humanitarian Law by all parties to the crisis". However, the international response to the past and current crimes committed has been too little, too late. In the face of the ineffectual diplomatic efforts and political unwillingness, this article concisely elucidates, *de facto,* developments leading to the humanitarian disaster and, *de jure,* exemplifies benchmarks and obligations the parties hereto are essentially bound to comply with.

Remarks on Human Rights and Islam in the Middle East

Ann Elizabeth Mayer, Philadelphia

While the importance of theoretical debates about Islam and Human Rights should be recognized, the careful assessments of how Islam figures into the actual Human Rights struggle in the Middle East is also needed. Such assessments reveal that the patterns of resisting Human Rights owe more to politics than to religion. In the last years, studies have revealed extensive problems created by corruption, undemocratic governance, and curbs on rights and freedoms. Given their Human Rights deficiencies, it is not surprising that various Middle Eastern states and the OIC (Organisation of Islamic Conference), which is responsive to the interests of countries like Saudi Arabia, should be trying to convince the world that they are led not by International Human Rights Law, but by alternative Islamic principles. The official claims that these diluted Human Rights are mandated by Islam deserve to be critically scrutinized in light of the political agendas of the governments sponsoring them.

Governmental Human Rights Structures and National Human Rights Institutions in the Middle East

Anna Würth / Claudia Engelmann, Berlin

All over the Middle East, North Africa (MENA) and the "Islamic" beyond, governmental Human Rights structures, and – to a lesser degree – National Human Rights Institutions (NHRIs) have been established during the past decades. This article assesses the make-up and contribution of MENA governmental Human Rights structures and NHRIs. What is the make-up of such institutions in semi- or fully authoritarian political systems, where government 'over-regulates' or criminalizes Human Rights civil society activism, and where government agents' regularly violating Human Rights?

This article argues that the governmentalization of Human Rights has had effects pointing in different, at times contradictory, directions. Part one explains the particular functions of NHRIs. Part two gives an overview of existing governmental Human Rights structures and NHRIs in MENA, and discusses them in the context of each country's Human Rights situations. Part three examines NHRIs in the Middle East with respect to the international principles informing NHRIs, and suggests further avenues for research into the specific contributions of NHRIs.

Between Limitation and new Developments: The Basic Right of heterosexual Self-Determination in the constitutional Systems of Arabic States

Naseef Naeem, Berlin / Göttingen

The basic right of heterosexual self-determination as an aspect of the general right of sexual self-determination could be deduced from the provisions of the constitutions of the Arabic States regarding the protection of human dignity as well as of personal liberty. However, the Arabic States limit this right out of wedlock through the penalization of sexual relations between unmarried adults, justifying their position according to a constitutional nexus between marriage, family, moral, customs, honor, tradition and especially religion.

The author deals with the theses of *Muḥammad Šaḥrūr* in this context, in whose opinion the religious justification of the prohibition of heterosexual partnerships outside of wedlock has suffered a setback. *Muḥammad Šaḥrūr* argues that such partnerships in certain circumstances, conform with the rules of Islam. As a result, the Arabic States can no longer, from a constitutional perspective, base these restrictions upon a unified Islamic doctrine in the sense of an absolute prohibition. Accordingly, the rigid position of Arabic States must dogmatically be subject to the principle of proportionality.

The Human Rights Dilemma in Egypt: Political Will or Islam?

Bahey eldin Hassan, Cairo

This paper reviews the Human Rights situation in Egypt and tries to respond to several questions; of which are:

- What are the main patterns of Human Rights' violations in Egypt?
- Is the state of affairs improving or deteriorating? Why? What prospect(s) is/are there for the future?
- Why this poor Human Rights record? Is it to be traced back to a lack of political will, or is it, rather, a religious/cultural problem? Or even, a fusion of two?
- What is the impact of the growing pressure of Islam in the nation's politics and the Human Rights Situation?
- Why does the Human Rights protection not receive the support it deserves and requires?

Human Rights and Islam in South East Asia: The Case of Indonesia

Tim Lindsey, Melbourne

Indonesia's dramatic and far-reaching democratic transition since the fall of Soeharto's authoritarian and repressive 'New Order' in 1998 has seen the emergence of two parallel developments. The rapid adoption of International Human Rights norms, both through the ratification of international instruments and a wave of domestic regulation, as well as through the creation of new institutions, has been accompanied by the passing of regulations at local and national levels seeking to 'Islamise' Indonesia, enforcing the observance of conservative norms inspired by Middle Eastern traditions. These, in many cases, directly challenged the new Human Rights regime, especially in that the Islamising laws often discriminate against vulnerable groups in this milieu, such as women and religious minorities. This conflict reflects longstanding disputes regarding the status of Islamic law within Indonesia's essentially *Western*-derived legal system that has helped motivate communal violence and terrorism. It seems unlikely, however, that 'Syariahisation', will succeed in altering the basic structure of the Indonesian state's legal system – and that suggests that, in the long run, the recent reforms introducing international Human Rights norms will likely survive.

Human Rights Standards in Afghan Courtrooms: The Theory and Reality of the Right to a Fair Trial

Tilmann Röder, Heidelberg / Kabul

The right to a fair penal trial is enshrined not only in human rights instruments ratified by the Islamic Republic of Afghanistan or its predecessors, but also in the Afghan constitution and sub-constitutional legislation. Court practice, however, deviates far from these standards. The majority of suspects are detained beyond the time limits defined by law, many are tortured by the secret service police and once they are accused, they are rarely provided with the assistance of a defence counsel. Most court hearings take place in the absence of a prosecutor and many end with a conviction based on doubtful evidence. The reasons for this deplorable situation are manifold; insufficient legal knowledge among professionals and lack of material resources being only two of the main obstacles.

The article aims to analyse reasons for the deficient penal court procedures and to elaborate possible solutions. Beyond this, the context of a country fighting a war against militant insurgents demands a closer look at the particular situation of terror suspects detained by Afghan and foreign forces. The article is based mainly on interviews with judges and prosecutors from all parts of the country, unpublished results of a court monitoring program organized by the United Nations (UNAMA), and the author's own observations in Afghan courtrooms.

Sharia and Implementation of Human Rights norms of Equality and Non Discrimination in the Family: A Case Study of Family Law in Pakistan

Ayesha Shahid / Javaid Rehman, Hull / London

Šarīʿa is the underlying principle of most legislation in Pakistan. However, when it comes to family law, it derives its legal basis not only from *šarīʿa* (law) but also from customary and cultural norms. In contrast to this, Pakistan at the same time is a signatory to many international treaties and the Constitution of Pakistan incorporates international Human Rights standards of equality and non-discrimination in its provisions as well as in the principles of policy.

This article seeks to explore the interrelationship between the Human Rights norms and *šarīʿa*-based family law in four important areas of family law, i.e. marriage, custody and guardianship, polygamy and divorce. It is argued that to provide a complete redress to women in family matters, an inclusive (new) approach is needed to bring the *šarīʿa* principles of justice and equity in conformity with international Human Rights norms of equality and non-discrimination.

Civil Society and Legislation: Developments of the Human Rights Situation in Iran in 2008

Irene Schneider, Göttingen

This article will sketch the latest legal developments with respect to Human Rights in the Islamic Republic of Iran on the basis of interactions between what can be called a "civil society" (especially composed of different women's organizations) and the state, drawing on the Draft Bill for the Protection of the Family. The central questions the author raises:

- What is the Human Rights situation in the Islamic Republic of Iran in autumn 2008 with regard to the Family Law?
- How are the rulings of the Draft Bill to be seen in this context?
- What is the role of a) international Human Rights covenants, such as CEDAW, which so far has not been ratified by Iran and b) the activities of civil society in the process of legislation.

The article delivers a reconstruction of the political and social process, thereby focusing on discourse analyses pertaining to some arguments brought forward by the different sides.

Interactions of Predominantly Islamic Countries and Organisations with International Human Rights Institutions

The UN Committee on the Elimination of Discrimination and its Interaction with Muslim States

Hanna Beate Schöpp-Schilling, Wohltorf / New York

The Convention on the Elimination of All Forms of Discrimination Against Women (CEDAW) is the most important international Human Rights treaty for women. Its Monitoring Committee of 23 independent experts from all regions of the world observes its implementation through three procedures (reporting, communication and inquiry procedures). Of the 185 States Parties, many Muslim States entered reservations to articles which contain general state obligations or obligations in specific areas (nationality, freedom of movement, equality in marriage and family relations).

This essay builds on previous analyses of this issue and examines with what arguments selected Muslim States Parties (in particular, those of Egypt, Morocco and Saudi Arabia) justify their reservations, how the CEDAW Committee reacts and whether, following this interaction, any improvements take place in these states with respect to women's rights.

The Organisation of Islamic Conference in the Context of the Human Rights Council: Human Rights as Instruments of Government Politics

Theodor Rathgeber, Kassel

The text deals with three levels of activities. Firstly, the OIC (Organisation of Islamic Conference) plays an important role, particularly in Geneva. Secondly, the OIC in Geneva is promoting an Islamic-orientated approach in order to adapt the Human Rights Declaration of 1948. Thirdly, the OIC strives for leadership on religious issues, because, according to OIC, the protection for Muslims is underdeveloped, particularly in *Western* countries.

All three levels of argumentation are taken by OIC in stressing forgotten or neglected concerns within the UN Human Rights System. However, the mode of stressing raises concerns as well; as it is presumed that a conflict between individual and collective rights is instrumental in protecting the government against demands of Human Rights victims.

The article proposes to address these neglected concerns on the basis of universal Human Rights.

Human Rights and Islamic Law in Light of the (International) Private Law

Ordre Public, Human Rights and Sharia

Peter Scholz, Berlin

Islamic states are very often criticized for a lack of compliance with International Human Rights. In civil law cases their enforcement can be supported by appliance of the national *Ordre Public*, when in national law transformed international Human Rights are violated. But the advantage of this practice is restricted, especially by different ideas and conceptions of Human Rights, different interpretations of the International Human Rights' treaties and an extensive use of reservations to Human Rights' obligations. This problem is demonstrated especially by the Islamic concept of freedom of religion and the practice of the Islamic states concerning relevant international obligations.

Freedom of Religion and Islamic Law-based Succession Law: Statutes and Judicial Interpretations in contemporary Egypt and Tunisia

Imen Gallala, Hamburg

Since their independence from the colonial powers, Islamic countries have been confronted by a dilemma: On one hand, they inted to respect the *šarīʿa*, while on the other, they mean to provide for Human Rights in their constitutions and ratify the relevant international conventions. Both aims might, and often do, lead to discrepancy.

This essay examines this conflict in the matter of freedom of religion in relation to *šarīʿa*-based Succession Laws in Egypt and Tunisia. Both the Egyptian and the Tunisian Constitutions guarantee this freedom. Nevertheless, Egyptian statutes and the dominant Case Law in Tunisia consider the difference of religion between the deceased and the heirs as an impediment to inheritance. Recent judicial decisions in Tunisia may represent a possible solution: They are developing new approaches in interpreting inheritance rules in accordance with freedom of religion.

التابعة للأمم المتحدة. في هذه اللجنة تولت مناصب عدة من بينها منصب خبيرة ونائبة الرئيس. كما عملت مدرسة وأستاذة زائرة في المانيا والولايات المتحدة الامريكية واليابان وبوسنا- هرسجوفنا. بالإضافة إلى مناصبها العديدة تولت كذلك منصب مدير عام لقسم شؤون المرأة في وزارة شؤون الأسرة والمرأة والشباب في المانيا. لها اصدارات عديدة تتعلق بدراسات المرأة وسوق العمل وحقوق الإنسان. ولجهود الباحثة أثناء عملها في لجنة القضاء على جميع اشكال التمييز عن المرأة التابعة للأمم المتحدة حصلت في عام ٢٠٠٩ على جائزة Margherita-von-Brentano من جامعة برلين الحرة لعام ٢٠٠٨.

هاينربيليفلد

أستاذ دكتور، مديرالمعهد الالماني لحقوق الإنسان في برلين. من عام ١٩٨٣ إلى عام ١٩٩٠ عمل مساعد باحث وتدريس ثم باحث في مشروع البحث العلمي الخاص بحقوق الإنسان في كلية الفلسفة في جامعة توبينجن. بعد ذلك عمل باحثا في قسم القانون العام وفلسفة القانون في كلية الحقوق في جامعة مانهايم (١٩٩٠ إلى ١٩٩٢) وفي هايدلبرج (١٩٩٢ إلى ١٩٩٥) وباحثا ومدرسا في جامعة تورونتو (١٩٩٣/١٩٩٤). هاينربيليفلد كاتب وناشر للعديد من الكتب المتعلقة بفلسفة القانون وحقوق الإنسان واخلاقيات السياسية وفلسفة الدين. أهم مجالات بحثه تتركز في أوضاع الاقليات المسلمة في المجتمعات الاوروبية والعلمانية ذات الطابع الديمقراطي.

كلاوديا انجلمان

متدربة في المعهد الالماني لحقوق الإنسان وطالبة ماجستير في فرع دراسات حقوق الإنسان العالمية في جامعة اوكسفورد. في سنة ٢٠٠٧ أتمت دراستها في الآداب والقانون والسياسة في جامعة كونستانس. خلال سنة ٢٠٠٦ و ٢٠٠٧ عملت في مجال تعليم حقوق الإنسان وبحث انشطة الضغط (اللوبي) في الجمعية الالمانية للأمم المتحدة (برلين) ومؤتمر المنظمات غير الحكومية الإستشارية المرتبطة بالأمم المتحدة في جنيف.

ماتياس روهي

أستاذ في القانون المدني والقانون الدولي الخاص والقانون المقارن في كلية القانون والعلوم الإقتصادية في جامعة إرلانجن - نورنبرج. فضلاً عن ذلك يُعد المدير المؤسس لمركز الدراسات الإسلامية والقانونية في أوروبا التابع لهذه الكلية. تقلد أيضاً منصب العمادة في الكلية. وهو كذلك عضواً مؤسس ورئيس جمعية دراسات الشريعة الإسلامية وقوانين البلاد العربية. ماتياس روهي مؤلف للعديد من الإصدارات التي تلقي الضوء على المسلمين في المانيا وأوروبا والشريعة الإسلامية والموضوعات المتعلقة بالقانون المدني. إلى جانب عمله الأكاديمي في أوروبا وما وراء البحار عمل ماتياس روهي قاضياً ايضاً في محكمة المقاطعة العليا في نورنبرج خلال سنوات ٢٠٠٠ الى ٢٠٠٦. في عام ٢٠٠٩ نشر الباحث كتابه حول الشريعة الإسلامية تحت عنوان: "Das Islamische Recht: Geschichte und Gegenwart".

محمد كاليش

أستاذ في الديانة الإسلامية ومدير لمركز الدراسات الدينية في جامعة مونستر. درس في هامبورج ونال درجة الدكتوراه في دارمشتات وذلك عن بحثه الموسوم بـ: (العقل و المرونة في منهج الفقه الإسلامي). في عام ٢٠٠٢ نال درجة الأستاذية عن إطروحة (الفقه وأصول الفقه عند الزيدية والتطور التأريخي للمدرسة الفقهية الزيدية). مجال ابحاثه العلمية يتركز في التأريخ ومناهج الفقه الإسلامي والفكر الديني عند المعتزلة والزيدية والفلسفة الإسلامية والمعرفة الإلهية (الغنوصية) وفلسفة الوجود.

مشهود بدرين

أستاذ قانون في قسم الدراسات الشرقية والإفريقية التابع لجامعة لندن (SOAS) عمل محاضراً في جامعة برونيل (لندن)، وفي جامعة غرب إنجلترا بريستول وفي جامعة ساوثهامب وفي جامعة نوتنغهام. وكذلك محامي ومستشار قانوني في المحكمة العليا في نيجيريا. الأستاذ بدرين باحث في الشريعة الإسلامية وحقوق الإنسان والقانون الدولي ويتركز اهتمامه في التأثير المتبادل بين هذه المجالات المذكورة في الدول ذات الطابع الإسلامي. من مؤلفاته "حقوق الإنسان العالمية والشريعة الإسلامية" (OUP / Oxford University Press، أوكسفورد ٢٠٠٣) فضلاً عن ذلك يعد من أحد الناشرين المؤسسين لمجلة العالم الإسلامي لحقوق الإنسان \ http://www.bepress.com/mwjhr.

ناصيف نعيم

درس القانون في جامعة حلب خلال الفترة من سنة ١٩٩٢ إلى ١٩٩٦. حاصل على دبلوم في القانون العام سنة ١٩٩٨ ودبلوم العلوم الادارية والمالية سنة ١٩٩٩ من جامعة دمشق. خلال سنوات ١٩٩٩ الى ٢٠٠٢ عمل محامياً في سوريا. فضلاً عن ذلك عمل في الفترة من ٢٠٠١ إلى ٢٠٠٢ معيداً في كلية الحقوق في جامعة دمشق. في سنة ٢٠٠٨ نال شهادة الدكتوراه من كلية الحقوق في جامعة هانوفر عن بحثه الموسوم بـ: النظام الاتحادي الجديد في العراق. البحث نُشر من قبل دار نشر بيتر لانج في فرانكفورت. حالياً يقوم الكاتب بإعداد دراسة في معهد الدراسات العربية والإسلامية في جامعة جوتنجن من أجل الحصول على درجة أستاذ. إضافة إلى ذلك سيقوم بالاشتراك مع الأستاذ بيتر شولتس بتنظيم محاضرات في جامعة برلين الحرة خلال الفصل الشتوي ٢٠٠٨/٢٠٠٩ تحت عنوان: قواعد تنظيم الدولة في دساتير الدول ذات الطبيعة الإسلامية.

هانا بياتا شوب - شيليج

د. هانا بياتا شوب - شيلينج عضوة في الهيئة المشرفة للمعهد الالماني لحقوق الإنسان (نائبة الرئيس من سنة ٢٠٠١ إلى ٢٠٠٤)، وكذلك عضوة في معهد حقوق الإنسان القومي في مقاطعة سفرد لوفسك الروسية، وعضوة في الهيئة المشرفة لمؤسسة الوقف الالمانية النسائية فيليا منذ سنة ١٩٨٩، عضوة كذلك في لجنة القضاء على جميع اشكال التميز عن المرأة

عاصم حفني

ولد في مصرسنة ١٩٧٢وأتم دراسة اللغة الالمانية والدراسات الإسلامية في جامعة الأزهر عام ١٩٩٥ بتقدير "ممتاز" مع مرتبة الشرف. حصل على الماجستير بتقدير"ممتاز" من الجامعة نفسها حيث عمل معيداً ثم مدرس مساعد بقسم اللغة الالمانية والدراسات الإسلامية في الفترة من عام ١٩٩٦ حتى عام ٢٠٠٤ تخللتها زيارات علمية عدة لالمانيا. يعد الآن رسالة دكتوراه في معهد الدراسات الشرقية بجامعة لايبزج بألمانيا حول"إشكالية ترجمة الخطاب الإسلامي السياسي"، له عدة مقالات في مجالات تفسير القرآن وحقوق الإنسان والبعد الحضاري في الترجمة بين اللغة العربية والألمانية ومحاضرات دورية في إطار الحوار الديني والحضاري بوصفة مسؤول العلاقات الثقافية في مجلس إدارة"اتحاد الطلاب والدارسين العرب". مشارك في كثير من المشاريع البحثية مثل المعاملات الإسلامية في البنوك الألمانية وانتهى من دراسة وترجمة قانون الأحوال الشخصية المصري إلى الألمانية، ويعمل حالياً محاضراً للدراسات الإسلامية والعربية في مركز الدراسات الشرق أوسطية بجامعة ماربوج.

عائشة شاهد

محاضرة في كلية الحقوق بجامعة هول، يتركز عملها في التدريس والبحث العلمي في مجالات الشريعة الإسلامية، القانون العام، حقوق المرأة والجنسانية، فضلاً عن حقوق الإنسان بشكل عام. الدكتورة شاهد قامت بنشر العديد من الأبحاث المتصلة بهذه المواضيع في المجلات المختصة البارزة، وفي الوقت الحاضر تقوم بإعداد دراسة في مضمار علم الاجتماع القانوني حول مساندة حق الإدعاء لخادمات البيوت في باكستان. الدراسة تهدف إلى البحث في فاعلية حق الادعاء كوسيلة لدعم هذه الفئة الاجتماعية في كفاحها ضد المعاملة السيئة والاستغلال في اماكن العمل. في عام ٢٠٠٢ حصلت الكاتبة على جائزة جمعية وارويك المرموقة للدراسات العليا وأيضاً على دبلوم الدراسات العليا من جامعة كولومبيا لتدريس قانون حقوق الإنسان.

عبد الله أحمد النعيم

يشغل وظيفة "Charles Howard Candler Professor of Law". حائز على بكالوريوس القانون من جامعة الخرطوم، ودبلوم في علم الإجرام من جامعة كامبريج، ودكتوراه في القانون من جامعة إدنبرة. تقلد وظائف عدة من بينها أستاذ في جامعة الخرطوم وأستاذ زائر في قسم القانون بجامعة كاليفورنيا في لوس أنجلوس وكذلك في جامعة ساسكتشوان وجامعة اوبسالا. قبل أن ينضم إلى كلية إموري للقانون في سنة ١٩٩٥، عمل مديراً للشؤون الإفريقية في منظمة هيومن رايتس وتش (مراقبة حقوق الإنسان). قام بنشر العديد من الكتب، وأكثر من ٥٠ مقالاً عن حقوق الإنسان والمسائل الدستورية والشريعة الإسلامية والسياسة. في عام ٢٠٠٨ نشر الباحث كتابه " Islam and the Secular State Negotiating the Future of Shari'a".

عيسى حياتو خيروما

أستاذ في القانون وحاصل على شهادة الدكتوراه من جامعة جوس في نيجيريا. عمل معاوناً للعميد ورئيساً لقسم الشريعة، حالياً يشغل منصب عميد في جامعة مايدوكوري في نيجيريا. وهو صاحب فكرة إنشاء دائرة قانونية تُمكن طبقات المجتمع المستضعفة من الإستفادة من خدمات القضاء. فضلاً عن عمله في السلك التدريسي والعلمي من عام ١٩٩٧ إلى عام ١٩٩٩ عمل مستشاراً في قانون البيئة والسياسة من عام ٢٠٠١ إلى عام ٢٠٠٤ في وزارة البيئة. عضو في اللجنة الرئاسية الاستشارية من اجل Prerogative of Mercy وعضو في الهيئة الاستشارية للمنهج الدراسي للقانون في نيجيريا. مجال بحثه العلمي واهتماماته العلمية يتركز في حقوق الإنسان والشريعة الإسلامية والقانون والتنمية.

كريس ماينا بيتر

أستاذ قانون في جامعة دار السلام. حاصل على الدكتوراه في القانون من جامعة كونستانس الالمانية وحاصل على الماجستير والبكالوريوس من جامعة دار السلام في تنزانيا. كان أستاذاً وباحثاً زائراً في العديد من الجامعات والمراكز العلمية من بينها هامبورج ومعهد راؤول ولنبرج لحقوق الإنسان ومعهد ماكس بلانك للقانون الدولي العام والقانون المقارن في هايدلبرج ومعهد القانون الدولي العام والعلاقات الدولية في كراتس (النمسا). محاضر في القانون الدولي العام وحقوق الإنسان وحق اللجوء والحرب في القانون الدولي العام وهو عضو خارجي في اللجان الإمتحانية لجامعات مختلفة في كينيا واوغندا وجنوب إفريقيا، فضلاً عن كونه عضواً في اللجنة الاستشارية للتقرير السنوي للقانون الانساني الدولي وعضواً في لجنة القضاء على جميع إشكال التمييز العنصري في الأمم المتحدة.

بيتر شولتس

درس القانون والدراسات الإسلامية وتأريخ الفن في جامعة هامبورج. في سنة ١٩٩٥ إنتهى من كتابة إطروحة دكتوراه في الدراسات الإسلامية ونال في سنة ٢٠٠٦ درجة الدكتوراه في القانون من جامعة برلين الحرة، منذ ١٩٩٥ يعمل قاضياً في برلين، في ٢٠٠٧ تولى مهمة القضاء في محكمة الإستئناف (Kammergericht) وفي عام ٢٠٠٩ أصبح نائب رئيس لمحكمة تيرجارتن (Amtsgericht Tiergarten) في برلين. بعد قيامة بتدريس الشريعة الإسلامية لعدة سنوات تم منحة لقب أستاذ من جامعة برلين الحرة وذلك في إختصاص الشريعة الإسلامية والقانون الدولي الخاص. يعمل حالياً على نشر الكثير من الكتابات المتعلقة بمواضيع اختصاصه. وهو عضو في العديد من الجمعيات العلمية وفي الهيئة المشرفة على جمعية دراسات الشريعة الإسلامية وقوانين البلاد العربية.

تيلمان رودر

مسؤول قسم الشرق الأوسط ووسط آسيا في معهد ماكس بلانك للقانون العام المقارن والقانون الدولي العام في هايدلبرج. نطاق أبحاثه يشمل إلى الآن افغانستان وليبيا واسرائيل/فلسطين وايران واذربيجان والسودان والصومال وإقليم كشمير وقد زار الكاتب معظم هذه الأماكن. يعد الكاتب خبيراً في مسائل تطوير القانون والقضاء وبشكل خاص فيما يتعلق بالقانون الدستوري والدولي. وهو يشرف ايضاً على إصدار سلسلة المؤلفات المتعلقة بهذه الموضوعات في معهد ماكس بلانك. إذ تستخدم كمنهج دراسي في المشاريع التي يتم تنظيمها من قبل المعهد المذكور. ساهم كذلك وبالاشتراك مع رايتز كروتي في إصدار سلسلة من المقالات الخاصة بمسألة تطوير القانون. فضلاً عن مساهماته العديدة في نطاق تاريخ القانون. ومن الجدير بالذكر أنه عضو مؤسس لرابطة فقهاء تاريخ القانون AYLH. الكاتب درس القانون في جامعة هومبولد في برلين وحاصل على درجة الدكتوراة من جامعة فرانكفورت.

ثيودور راتجبر

د. ثيودور راتجبر خريج قسم العلوم السياسية ويعمل معيداً في قسم علم الإجتماع في جامعة كاسل الالمانية. منذ سنة ١٩٩٠ يعمل مستشار ومنذ عام ٢٠٠١ مستشاراً حراً للحقوق الإنسان والقانون الدولي وسياسة التنمية وخاصة فيما يتعلق بحقوق سكان البلاد الأصليين وحقوق الأقليات ومسؤولية "Transnational Companies / الشركات المتعددة الجنسيات" تجاه حقوق الإنسان. الكاتب كذلك مراقب رسمي في مجلس حقوق الإنسان التابع للأمم المتحدة ومنذ سنة ٢٠٠٦ مراقب ايضاً في لجنة حقوق الإنسان التابعة للأمم المتحدة وذلك بتكليف من الشبكة الالمانية للمنظمات غير الحكومية. وبالإمكان طلب كتاباته المنشورة.

جواد رحمن

أستاذ قانون في كلية الحقوق بجامعة برونل في لندن. مجال دراساته العلمية يتركز في الشريعة الإسلامية وحقوق الأقليات و الإرهاب الدولي. تقلد العديد من الوظائف بصفته باحثاً علمياً زائراً حيث زار العديد من البلاد من ضمنها باكستان وبنقلاديش وتركيا وفرنسا واليابان والولايات المتحدة. بالإضافة إلى ذلك كان عضواً في لجنة التعليم العالي في باكستان بغية إعطاء تقييم شامل لدراسة القانون. قام بإصدار ونشر العديد من الكتب وكان له دوره في التأثير على المجلات الاكاديمية المختصة. الكاتب كذلك عضو في هيئة التحرير لمجلة "الدين وحقوق الإنسان" و "المجلة الاسيوية للقانون الدولي" و "المجلة الاوروبية المركزية للدراسات الدولية والامنية" وهو عضو ايضاً في لجنة القانون الدولي والشريعة الإسلامية العائدة للرابطة الدولية للقانون (ILA) وناشر لمجلة "تطبيقات الحكم الإسلامي في القانون الدولي".

حاتم الليثي

عضو في الهيئة الإدارية لجمعية دراسات الشريعة الإسلامية وقوانين البلاد العربية، وعضو في الهيئة الإدارية لجمعية الدراسات الافريقية، فضلاً عن كونه عضواً مؤسساً لجمعية المحامين في منظمة العفو الدولية، فرع هونك كونك. عمل في مشروع السودان للسلام حتى عام ٢٠٠٥، وساند مشروع إعادة بناء القضاء والإدارة العامة الافغانية، وذلك برعاية معهد ماكس بلانك للقانون الدولي العام والقانون المقارن في هايدلبرج وكان عضواً في اللجان الإستشارية لتعيين الاساتذة في اختصاص الشريعة الإسلامية والدراسات الإسلامية في اوربا في جامعة برلين الحرة. درس القانون والدراسات الإسلامية والشرقية والسامية والاثيوبية في جامعات مانهايم وأوكسفورد وهايدلبرج والقاهرة وهانوفر وبرلين ومالطا. يعمل حالياً مساعد بحث وتدريس في جامعة برلين الحرة ويحضر للحصول على درجة الدكتوراه في الجامعة ذاتها.

المؤلفون المشاركون

أن إليزابث ماير

أستاذة في القانون وإخلاقية الأعمال التجارية في Wharton School في جامعة بنسيلفانيا. حصلت على درجة الدكتوراه (PhD) في تأريخ الشرق الأوسط من جامعة مشيجن. درست الشريعة الإسلامية والقانون المقارن في قسم الدراسات الشرقية والإفريقية (SOAS) التابع لجامعة لندن. حصلت كذلك على درجة الدكتوراه (JD) في القانون من بنسيلفانيا. يشمل مجال بحثها العلمي الشريعة الإسلامية في الشرق الأوسط وشمال إفريقيا، بالإضافة إلى القانون الدستوري وحقوق الإنسان. قامت بنشر العديد من المقالات في الكثير من الدوريات والمجالات العلمية. صدر لها سنة ٢٠٠٧ الطبعة الرابعة من كتابها الإسلام وحقوق الإنسان.

أنا فيرت

د. أنا فيرت درست الانثروبولوجيا ودراسات الشرق الأوسط في برلين. تعمل باحثة في المعهد الالماني لحقوق الإنسان. خلال السنوات من ١٩٩٤ إلى ١٩٩٨ عملت في مجال التعاون الإنمائي، وفي الفترة من سنة ٢٠٠٠ إلى ٢٠٠٢ مع منظمة هيومن رايتس ووتش (مراقبة حقوق الإنسان). عملت كذلك في التدريس في جامعة ريتشموند (فيرجينيا، الولايات المتحدة) و في جامعة برلين الحرة. من إصداراتها الحديثة مساهمتها في إصدار"اليمن نحو القرن الواحد و العشرين: الإستمرارية والتحول" (Ithaca Press, Reading 2007) و"التحقيق في سوء المعاملة من قبل الشرطة ومحاكمتها في مصر" من إصدارات باودوين (عن دار تاوريس) و " حكايات عن الحقيقة في الشريعة"، لندن ٢٠٠٨.

ايرني شنايدر

أستاذة في قسم الدراسات العربية والشريعة الإسلامية في جامعة جوتينجن. قبل حصولها على درجة الأستاذية في تأريخ الشريعة الإسلامية تناولت في إطروحة الدكتوراه أدب القاضي. خلال مسارها العلمي عملت باحثة في جامعة كولونيا وكذلك باحثة في المؤسسة الوطنية الامريكية وذلك في مشروع (القانون الدستوري وسياسة التجديد في الشرق الأوسط) في (State) جامعة نيويورك، عملت في الكثير من مشاريع الأبحاث العلمية في المانيا. يتركز مجال بحثها العلمي في الشريعة الإسلامية، وتاريخ القانون والتاريخ الإسلامي القديم، والحديث كمصدر للتأريخ الإسلامي، والدراسات الجنسانية (Gender Studies) في الدول العربية وايران وافغانستان، والآثار المتبادلة للحقوق الدستورية بين الدولة والمجتمع، والإسلام في المانيا.

إيمان قلالة

د. إيمان قلالة تعمل باحثة في قسم قوانين البلاد الإسلامية في معهد ماكس بلانك للقانون الدولي الخاص والمقارن في هامبورج. حصلت على درجة الماجستير (.LL.M) والدكتوراه من كلية الحقوق في جامعة هايدلبرج. درست القانون في كلية الحقوق تونس II حيث حصلت على الماجستير (maîtrise en sciences juridiques) في القانون وعلى دبلوم في القانون العام والقانون المالي. كما درست في الكلية نفسها كمعيدة في مادة القانون الدولي العام. مجال بحثها العلمي يتركز بصورة خاصة في نطاق قوانين الأسرة والميراث الدولية والوطنية للبلاد الإسلامية.

بهي الدين حسن

مدير مركز القاهرة لدراسات حقوق الإنسان وعضو في الهيئة الإدارية للمؤسسة الاورو- متوسطية لحقوق الإنسان. بالإضافة إلى أنه مدرس وكاتب للعديد من المقالات والإصدارات العلمية التي تتعلق بحقوق الإنسان والديمقراطية في العالم العربي، وناشر للعديد من الكتب العربية والانجليزية من بينها، "A Question of Human Rights Ethics Defending the Islamists", in: *Anthony Chase / Amr Hamzawy* (Editors), Human Rights in the Arab World: Independent Voices; Regional Protection of Human Rights in the Arab States In Statu Nascendi", in: *Janusz Symonides* (Editor), Human Rights: International Protection, Monitoring, Enforcement, UNESCO 2003.

الحرية الدينية وقانون الإرث المستمد من الشريعة الإسلامية في القانون والقضاء المصري والتونسي

إيمان قلالة (هامبورج)

تجد البلدان الإسلامية نفسها منذ حصولها على استقلالها من السلطة الإستعمارية في موقف صعب، إذ أرادت من جهة الالتزام بالشريعة ومن جهة أخرى تكريس حقوق الإنسان في دساتيرها والمصادقة على المعاهدات الدولية التي تعرضت لهذا الشأن. وغالباً ما تكون هذه الحقوق متعارضة مع الشريعة. هنا يتم بحث هذه المشكلة بتناول مثال الحرية الدينية وقانون الميراث المستمد من الشريعة في كل من تونس ومصر. لقد كرّس الدستور المصري والتونسي هذه الحرية ولكن القوانين المصرية وأحكام القضاء السائدة في تونس تُعد إختلاف الدين بين المتوفي والورثة سبباً مانعاً للإرث. ويمكن أن تشكل القرارات الحديثة في القضاء التونسي حلاً لهذه المشكلة وذلك بتفسيرها قوانين الميراث بما يوافق حرية الدين.

» موقف الدول والمنظمات الإسلامية تجاه اوضاع حقوق الإنسان العالمية «

لجنة حقوق المرأة في الامم المتحدة وتأثيرها في الدول الإسلامية

هانا بياتا شوب ـ شيليج (نيويورك / فولتورف – المانيا)

تعد إتفاقية القضاء على أشكال التمييز كافة ضد المرأة أهم معاهدة دولية في مجال حقوق الإنسان. وتعمل لجنة حقوق المرأة المنبثقة من هذه الإتفاقية والتي تضم ٢٣ خبيراً مستقلاً من مختلف انحاء العالم من أجل تحقيق وضمان تنفيذ الإتفاقية في الدول الأعضاء وذلك بواسطة آليات تنفيذ ثلاثة (كتابة التقارير وإيصال الشكاوى وإجراء التحقيقات). في هذه الإتفاقية التي تضم ١٨٥ عضواً أعلن بعض الأعضاء وخاصة من الدول الإسلامية تحفظاتهم على بنود عديدة من الإتفاقية وعلى وجه الخصوص ما يتعلق بالتزامات الدولة في بعض المجالات الحياتية للمرأة مثل الجنسية وحرية التنقل والسفر والمساواة وعدم التمييز في الزواج والعلاقات العائلية. هذه المقالة تبحث بناءاً على بحوث سابقة ايضاً كيف أن بعض الدول مثل مصر والمغرب والكويت والسعودية وتونس تحاول تبرير تحفظاتها أمام اللجنة المذكورة، ويُبين البحث كذلك ماهية المواقف التي تتخذها اللجنة أزاء هذه التبريرات، وهل من الممكن إحداث تغييرات في صالح حقوق المرأة في هذه الدول.

منظمة المؤتمر الإسلامي ولجنة حقوق الإنسان
في الأمم المتحدة
حقوق الإنسان كأداة في السياسة

ثيودور راتجبر (كاسل)

هذه المقالة تتناول قضايا ثلاث: أولاً الحضور اللافت للنظر لمنظمة المؤتمر الاسلامي في جنيف حيث مسرح تمثيل القوى السياسية بين طرفي الأزمة الشمال والجنوب. ثانياً موقف منظمة المؤتمر الإسلامي بطلب إصلاح أو إكمال الإعلان العالمي لحقوق الإنسان سنة ١٩٣٨ من خلال وجهات النظر الإسلامية. ثالثاً محاولة منظمة المؤتمر الإسلامي إثارة المسائل المتعلقة بالدين وهي ترى أن الحماية التي يتمتع بها المسلمين في الغرب ضعيفة جداً وأن من الضروري القيام بحماية الدين.

إن منظمة المؤتمر الاسلامي تركز على هذه القضايا وتطالب بعدم اهمالها. لكن تنفيذ هذه المطالب يعني في أغلب الأحوال ترجيح كفة الحقوق العامة على كفة الحقوق الفردية. هنا يكون من الضروري تقييم الأمر على ضوء مباديء حقوق الإنسان العالمية.

» حقوق الإنسان والشريعة الإسلامية من وجهة نظر القانون الدولي الخاص «

النظام العام وحقوق الإنسان والشريعة

بيتر شولتس (برلين)

كثيرا ما تُرتكب إنتهاكات حقوق الإنسان في الدول الاسلامية. و يُمكن هنا أن يلعب النظام العام دوراً في الحماية إذا ما عجزت القوانين الوضعية من تقديم هذه الحماية. ولكن ما يجعل المشكلة أكثر تعقيداً هو الإختلاف في فهم حقوق الإنسان وتفسيرها. هذه المقالة تحاول معالجة هذه المشكلة من خلال استعراض الفهم الإسلامي لمسألة حرية الدين والالتزامات الدولية للدول الإسلامية في التطبيق العملي.

الحلول الممكنة مع إمعان النظر في الحالة الخاصة فيما يتعلق بالمتهمين بالإرهاب الموقوفين من قبل قوات الأمن الأفغانية والأجنبية. المقالة تستند اساساً إلى مقابلات مع القضاة والمدعين العامين في مختلف انحاء افغانستان، ونتائج برنامج الامم المتحدة لمراقبة المحاكم (UNAMA) والتي تنشر هنا لأول مرة، فضلاً عن مشاهدات الكاتب الشخصية للمحاكم الافغانية.

الشريعة وتبني أحكام حقوق الإنسان في المساواة وعدم التفرقة في مضمار قانون العائلة النموذج الباكستاني

عائشة شاهد / جواد رحمن (هول / لندن)

تعد الشريعة مبدأ أساسياً في أكثر التشريعات الباكستانية وخاصة في قانون العائلة. لكن قانون العائلة لا يستمد أساسه القانوني من أحكام الشريعة فقط، بل يقع تحت تأثير القواعد العرفية وثقافة المجتمع أيضاً. لهذا السبب فإن قانون العائلة يخل بالمساواة بين المرأة والرجل، في الوقت الذي وقعت فيه باكستان الكثير من المعاهدات والمواثيق الدولية فضلاً عن تبني الدستور الباكستاني لمبادئ حقوق الإنسان الدولية المتعارف عليها بخصوص المساواة وعدم التمييز أو التفرقة في المعاملة، علاوة على تأكيد ذلك في المبادئ الأساسية للسياسة الباكستانية.

هذا المقال يبحث في العلاقة المتبادلة بين حقوق الإنسان وأحكام الشريعة في أربعة مجالات تنضوي تحت قانون العائلة، هي: انعقاد الزواج، الحضانة والولاية وتعدد الزوجات والطلاق. من خلال ذلك يتم بيان كيفية إمكانية ضمان حقوق المرأة كاملة في تلك المسائل، الأمر الذي يتطلب فهماً جديداً شاملاً لمبادئ الشريعة المتعلقة بالعدالة والمساواة بصورة تتلائم مع ما هو متعارف عليه في مواثيق حقوق الإنسان الدولية.

المجتمع المدني وعملية التشريع عرض للتطورات المتعلقة بأوضاع حقوق الإنسان في إيران لسنة ٢٠٠٨

إيريني شنايدر (جوتينجين)

تتناول هذه المقالة آخر التطورات لأوضاع حقوق الإنسان في إيران ودور المجتمع المدني في ذلك، وخاصة المنظمات النسوية في ضوء المناقشة الدائرة حول مشروع قانون العائلة الجديد. الباحثة تركز هنا على ثلاث نقاط رئيسة:

- أوضاع حقوق الإنسان المتصلة بقانون العائلة الجديد في الجمهورية الإسلامية الإيرانية، تحديداً في خريف عام ٢٠٠٨.
- كيفية تقييم أحكام قانون العائلة بهذا الخصوص؟
- ما هو الدور الذي تلعبه المعاهدات الدولية مثل معاهدة القضاء على كافة أشكال التمييز ضد المرأة (CEDAW) والتي لم توقع عليها إيران، وما هو دور المجتمع المدني في عملية التشريع هذه؟

بعد تقديم عرض للتطورات السياسية والاجتماعية يبحث هذا المقال في الآراء والحجج المتعارضة التي يتم تبنيها من جهات مختلفة.

مُعضلة حقوق الإنسان في مصر:
خيار سياسي او الإسلام؟

بهي الدين حسن (القاهرة)

هذا البحث نظرة نقدية من زوايا مختلفة لأوضاع حقوق الإنسان في مصر. أبرز نقاط البحث تتمثل بالآتي:

- ما هي أهم اشكال انتهاكات حقوق الإنسان في مصر؟
- هل إن الوضع يتجه نحو الأحسن او الأسوء؟ ولماذا؟ وما هي آفاق المستقبل؟
- ما هو السبب في وجود سجل سيء لحقوق الإنسان؟ هل يعود هذا إلى اسباب سياسية؟ أو تكمن المشكلة في الاسباب الدينية والخلفية الحضارية؟ أو أن المعضلة تكمن في مزيج من هذه الاسباب مجتمعة؟
- ما هي اسباب ضعف حماية حقوق الإنسان؟ وما هي سُبل المعالجة؟

حقوق الإنسان والإسلام في جنوب شرق آسيا:
إندونيسيا مثالاً على ذلك

تيم ليندسي (ملبورن)

نتيجة للتغيير الديمقراطي الجذري الذي حدث في إندونيسيا جراء زوال الحكم الشمولي للرئيس سوهارتو في عام ١٩٩٨ شهدت إندونيسيا تطوراً في اتجاهين متوازيين. إذ أنه في الوقت نفسه الذي سارت فيه عملية تصديق المعاهدات والاتفاقات الدولية بصورة فائقة السرعة قامت السلطات بسن مجموعة من التشريعات على الصعيدين الوطني والمحلي بهدف دفع عملية الأسلمة في إندونيسيا إلى الأمام، وذلك من خلال الأخذ بروح القواعد المحافظة ذات الأصول التقليدية الشرق أوسطية وإضفاء صفة الإلزام عليها. هذا الأمر شكل تحدياً لمسائل حقوق الإنسان، خاصة فيما يتعلق بالتمييز ضد حقوق المرأة والأقليات الدينية. ويمكن النظر إلى هذا الصراع على أنه مرآة عاكسة للصراع الدائر حول مدى أهمية الشريعة في النظام القانوني الإندونيسي المماثل أساساً للأنظمة القانونية الغربية. فضلاً عن ذلك كان من شأن هذا الجدل إثارة العنف المحلي والإرهاب. على أنه يبدو من غير المحتمل حدوث تغيير في البناء الأساسي للنظام القانوني الإندونيسي، مما يعني بأن الإصلاحات التي تمت وتتم متبنية حقوق الإنسان كما هي في المواثيق الدولية ستبقى إلى أجل بعيد قائمة.

معايير حقوق الإنسان في المحاكم الافغانية "حق المحاكمة العادلة بين النظرية والتطبيق"

تيلمان رودر (هايدلبرج)

حق المحاكمة العادلة حق منصوص عليه في معاهدات حقوق الإنسان التي صادقت عليها جمهورية افغانستان الإسلامية، فضلاً عن التأكيد على هذا الحق ايضاً في الدستور الافغاني والقوانين الافغانية. لكن واقع المحاكم الافغانية يشير إلى الاخلال الجسيم بهذا الحق، إذ يبقى المتهمون قيد التوقيف لفترة تتجاوز المدة المسموح بها قانوناً علاوة على ذلك ممارسة التعذيب من قبل رجال المخابرات والشرطة على الكثير من السجناء الذين نادراً مايجدوا من يدافع عنهم، فضلاً عن سير الإجراءات دون وجود الإدعاء العام، ناهيك عن أصدار الكثير من الأحكام التي يشوبها الخلل لعدم توفر الأدلة الكافية.

هذا الوضع المؤسف يعود إلى أسباب عدة منها على سبيل المثال لا الحصر: عدم توفر الخبرة القانونية للمحامين ونقص الموارد المادية. في هذه المقالة يتم تحليل عيوب الإجراءات الجنائية فضلاً عن تقديم

الرسمية التي تتمثل بإعتبار حقوق الإنسان "المائعة" تخضع لمبادئ الشريعة الإسلامية تتطلب نظرة نقدية خاصة تأخذ بعين الإعتبار الأجندة السياسية لأنظمة الحكم السائدة.

التركيبة الحكومية لحقوق الإنسان والمؤسسات الوطنية لحقوق الإنسان في الشرق الأوسط وشمال افريقيا

أنا فيرت / كلاوديا انجلمان (برلين)

خلال العقود الماضية أنشأت في الشرق الأوسط وشمال افريقيا ودول إسلامية أخرى العديد من الأجهزة الحكومية والوطنية ـ الأهلية المختصة بحقوق الإنسان. كيف تبدو تركيبة هذه المؤسسات في دول معروفة بأنها ذات أنظمة حكم شمولية؟ دول تفرض قيوداً على انشطة المجتمع المدني أو تقضي بتجريمها وتُرتكب هناك خروقات حقوق الإنسان بإستمرار. هذا البحث يتناول بالإدلة التأثيرات المختلفة والإتجاهات المتعارضة الناتجة عن قضية صراع حقوق الإنسان مع انظمة الحكم في الشرق الأوسط. الجزء الأول يوضح عمل المؤسسات الوطنية ـ الأهلية لحقوق الإنسان. الجزء الثاني يقدم صورة عامة عن المؤسسات الحكومية لحقوق الإنسان والمؤسسات الوطنية ـ الأهلية لحقوق الإنسان في الشرق الأوسط وشمال افريقيا. الجزء الثالث يبحث في المؤسسات الوطنية ـ الأهلية لحقوق الإنسان على ضوء المبادئ الدولية المتفق عليها والتي على أساسها انشأت هذه المؤسسات ويُقدم هذا الجزء مقترحات للبحوث الجديدة في هذا المجال.

بين التقييد والتطورات الجديدة: الحق الأساسي في التقرير الذاتي للعلاقة الجنسية بين الرجل والمرأة في الأنظمة الدستورية للدول العربية

ناصيف نعيم (برلين / جوتينجين)

ان الحق الأساسي في التقرير الذاتي للعلاقة الجنسية بين المرأة والرجل كجزء من الحق الأعم في التقرير الذاتي في مضمار الجنس بشكل عام يُمكن اشتقاقه من المواد المتعلقة بحماية كرامة الإنسان وحريته الشخصية في دساتير الدول العربية. لكن ومن الملاحظ بأن الدول العربية تُقيد هذا الحق خارج مؤسسة الزواج من خلال فرض العقوبات على العلاقات الجنسية بين العازبين من النساء والرجال البالغين، معللة موقفها هذا من خلال ربط دستوري بين مؤسسة الزواج وتكوين العائلة والأخلاق والأعراف والشرف والتقاليد وبشكل خاص الدين. في هذا المضمار يناقش الكاتب فرضيات محمد شحرور التي يستشف منها بأن التعليل الديني لمنع العلاقات الجنسية بين النساء والرجال خارج مؤسسة الزواج قد أصابه التصدع. فمحمد شحرور يرى بأن مثل هذه العلاقات، وبمراعاة بعض الشروط، متوافقة مع تعاليم الإسلام. يتبين من ذلك بأن الدول العربية من وجهة نظر القانون الدستوري لم تعد قادرة على بناء موقفها على أساس قاعدة مجمع عليها في الدين الإسلامي تتمثل في المنع المطلق لمثل هذه العلاقات. من زاوية النظرية القانونية يؤدي ذلك إلى الجزم بأن موقف الدول العربية المتزمت من هذا الموضوع وفي ضوء طرق التفسير في القانون الدستوري يجب أن يخضع للمحاكمة على ضوء ما يُسمى مبدأ تناسبية فعل المنع وعدمه.

قانون المفتي في زنجبار والحريات والحقوق الإنسانية للمسلمين في الجزيرة

كريس ماينا بيتر (دار السلام)

في سنة ٢٠٠١ أقر برلمان زنجبار قانوناً تم بموجبه إيجاد وظيفة المفتي. هذا القانون مثير للجدل لأن الإفتاء في جوهره أمر متعلق بالجانب الروحاني ولكن الحكومة الثورية في زنجبار انشأت على أساسه دائرة مدنية على حساب دافعي الضرائب. المفتي يتم تعيينه من قبل رئيس زنجبار وكذلك بعض موظفي ديوان الرئاسة يتم تعيينهم من قبل وزير الشؤون الدينية الأمر الذي يثير أسئلة عديدة من بينها:

- بعد كل هذا هل يُمكن الإدعاء بأن زنجبار دولة علمانية يتم فيها الفصل التام بين الدولة والدين؟
- هل من اللائق أن يتم تأسيس وظيفة لطائفة دينية معينة ويدفع كل مواطني زنجبار نفقات هذه الوظيفة وبغض النظر عن انتمائهم الديني؟
- هل يجوز لرئيس منتخب غير مسلم أن يقوم بتعيين الزعيم الروحي الأعلى للمسلمين؟

هذه الاسئلة غيض من فيض المسائل التي يتم تناولها في هذا البحث.

رؤية في الدولة السودانية من منظور حقوق الإنسان والقانون الدولي الإنساني: قضية دارفور

حاتم الليثي (برلين)

بادئ ذي بدء يمكن الجزم بأن دافور، إقليم السودان الغربي، قد ذاع صيته المحزن سوداوي الجوهر بشكل واسع في السنوات الأخيرة، إلى حد أن وضعه المأساوي أصبح يوصف بمرور الوقت بأنه الكارثة الإنسانية الأكثر فظاعة في العالم. إذ أن السكان المدنيين في دارفور عانوا ويعانون الكثير من المآسي الناتجة عن ألافعال المثيرة للقلق التي تُرتكب من أطراف النزاع كافة (الحكومة والجماعات المسلحة الموالية لها وجماعات المتمردين) والتي تنتهك حقوق الإنسان وقواعد القانون الإنساني وقوانين وأعراف الحرب. ورداً على العمليات المسلحة وخصوصاً الهجمات على المدنيين قام مجلس الأمن الدولي بالتنديد بكل أشكال العنف والخروقات ضد حقوق الإنسان والقانون الدولي الإنساني وقوانين الحرب وأعرافها والمرتكبة من أطراف الأزمة. مع ذلك يأتي الرد الدولي على الخروقات السابقة والحالية في دارفور حتى الآن متأخراً وقليل الفاعلية. بالنظر إلى المساعي الدبلوماسية غير الجدية وعدم توفر الإرادة السياسية لحل الأزمة. في هذه المقالة سيتم وبشكل موجز ودقيق معالجة التطورات على أرض الواقع والتي أدت إلى حدوث الكارثة الإنسانية في دارفورمن ناحية، ومن ناحية اخرى توضيح القواعد والالتزامات القانونية التي يجب مراعاتها بشكل جوهري من قبل جميع أطراف النزاع.

ملاحظات على حقوق الإنسان والإسلام في الشرق الأوسط

آن إليزابث ماير (بنسيلفانيا)

على الرغم من عدم إنكار أهمية النقاش النظري حول موضوع الإسلام وحقوق الإنسان، فإن ضرورة تحديد مدى أبعاد دور الإسلام في الصراع من أجل حقوق الإنسان في الشرق الأوسط لا يقل أهمية عن ذلك. من خلال تقييم هذا الدور يُمكن الاستنتاج بأن عوائق حقوق الإنسان تعود لأسباب سياسية أكثر من كونها دينية. في السنوات الماضية تم توضيح كثير من هذه الأسباب: كالفساد والحكم الشمولي وعدم إحترام الحقوق والحريات. وفي هذا السياق ليس من الغريب أن كثير من الدول في الشرق الأوسط ومعها منظمة المؤتمر الإسلامي بإعتبارها تمثل مصالح دول مثل السعودية تبذل كل ما تستطيع من جهود بهدف إقناع العالم بأنها لا تخضع لمواثيق حقوق الإنسان العالمية بل لمبادئ الشريعة الإسلامية. إن هذه الرؤية

هل العرب ضد التصور الإسلامي لحقوق الإنسان؟

هاينر بيليفلد (برلين)

الصراع السياسي حول مفهوم حقوق الإنسان وتطبيقاتها ازداد حدة في السنوات الأخيرة لدى منظمة الامم المتحدة وخاصة بين الجماعات الغربية ومنظمة المؤتمر الإسلامي. جزء من هذه المشكلة يكمن في الإتجاه المشترك للطرفين المتصارعين بربط حقوق الإنسان مع الحضارة. وهذا يعني تحديد هذه الحقوق وتعريفها إما على أساس المصادر الدينية او الفلسفية في اوروبا أو على أساس المصادر الإسلامية. وهذا ما يناقض المفهوم العصري لحقوق الإنسان بإعتبارها حقاً عالمياً واضحاً قائماً على مبدأ الحرية والمساواة في الحقوق للجميع. فضلاً عن ذلك يجب إدراك حقيقة أن حقوق الإنسان إنما هي في طور النمو والتطور وأنها نشأت كرد فعل على الظلم وأدواته. بإعتبار أن حقوق الإنسان تشكل جواباً عصرياً على الظلم المتفشي في واقعنا وهذا لا يناقض كونها تنسجم مع الحضارات العالمية المختلفة خاصة ما يتعلق بوجهات النظر الدينية وهذا ما يعرفه جون رولز بفكرة الإجماع المتشابك.

» اوضاع حقوق الإنسان في عدد من الدول والمناطق ذات الطابع الإسلامي «

الإسلام وحقوق الإنسان في الدول الإفريقية
اجندة من اجل *Good Governance*

مشهود بدرين (لندن)

دساتير بعض الدول الإفريقية تعتبر الإسلام دين الدولة الرسمي والشريعة الإسلامية بمثابة نظام قانوني بشكل أو بآخر. هنا يثار السؤال: حول كيفية إنسجام هذا الأمر مع المذاهب الدستورية ودولة القانون. عبد الله أحمد النعيم يلقي الضوء على التناقض بين الإسلام كدين عريق ذو تقاليد عريقة من جانب، ومبدأ الدستورية ودولة القانون كمذهب حديث يقدم مشروعاً متكاملاً عن نظام الحكم والحقوق من جانب آخر. كيف يُمكن فهم هذه العلاقة؟ هل يُمكن فهم دور الإسلام والشريعة الإسلامية في الدستور على أنه يشكل تحدياً للطبيعة العلمانية للنظام الدستوري ودولة القانون، أو أنه في حد ذاته يُشكل إنحرافاً عن هذا النظام؟

الإسلام والشريعة الإسلامية وحقوق الإنسان في نيجيريا

حياتو خيروما / حاتم الليثي (مايدوكوري– نيجيريا / برلين)

حينما اتجهت نيجيريا سنة ١٩٩٩ نحو السير في النظام الديمقراطي إنتهز المسلمون الفرصة في بعض المدن الواقعة في شمال نيجيريا فقاموا بتطبيق الشريعة الإسلامية. وكان صدى هذا التطبيق مزيجاً من إنفعالات متعارضة لأن هذا الأمر يُشكل خلافاً كبيراً ويُثير اسئلة حول المشاكل الآتية:

- هل أن العقوبات الموجودة في الشريعة الإسلامية تنسجم مع دستور ١٩٩٩؟
- هل يكفل تطبيق الشريعة الإسلامية الحماية لحقوق الإنسان والحرية في دولة القانون ذات النظام الديمقراطي أم لا؟

هذا البحث محاولة للإجابة على هذه المسائل الخلافية.

خلاصة الموضوعات

» مساهمات في منهج بحث القانون والشريعة وفلسفة القانون «

الإسلام وحقوق الإنسان: تأملات وملاحظات تمهيدية

عبدالله أحمد النعيم (أتلانتا)

في هذه المساهمة يدعو المؤلف إلى عمل دراسة تحليلية بناءة للعلاقة المتبادلة بين الإسلام وحقوق الإنسان بهدف تدعيم هذه الرابطة في النظرية والتطبيق. هنا يؤكد المؤلف على أهمية الدور الذي يلعبه التفسير البشري للنصوص الربانية، وهنا يظهر تأثير الخلفيات الإجتماعية والإقتصادية والسياسية في هذا الدور. الإسلام يشكل أهمية كبيرة في بناء شرعية حقوق الإنسان وتحسين فعاليتها لدى المسلمين وهذا يعني فهم الدين وتطبيقه على أساس عصري حديث لا على أساس ما فهمه السلف قبل العديد من القرون المنصرمة. يقول المؤلف أن نظرته هذه مدافعاً عن حقوق الإنسان لا تقتصر على الإسلام وحده ولكنها تشمل جميع الأديان ولهذا يدعو إلى نهج هذا السبيل في التعامل مع الأديان الأخرى كذلك.

الإسلام وحقوق الإنسان: تأملات حول العلاقة بين الدين والقانون

محمد كاليش (مونستر)

هل تتوافق حقوق الإنسان والإسلام معاً؟ هذا السؤال كان مدار نقاش في العالم الغربي خلال السنوات العشر الاخيرة. يعود السبب في الاهتمام بهذا الموضوع إلى الخوف من صراع الحضارات والخوف من الأقليات المسلمة في المجتمعات الغربية، وأي دور ستلعبه في المستقبل وكذلك كانت هذه الموضوعات تناقش في المجتمعات الاسلامية. في هذا البحث سوف يتم التطرق إلى هذا السؤال الذي نوقش وكُتب عنه الكثير وتحليله ودراسة مدى الفائدة من طرحه أصلاً.

حقوق الإنسان انطلاقاً من النظرية التأويلية في تفسير القرآن

عاصم حفني (ليبزج / ماربورج / القاهرة)

تتشابه الهرمينوطيقية بوصفها فناً لفهم النص مع التأويل منهجاً وهدفاً؛ فالتأويل يرمي إلى فهم النص بإستخدام كل الوسائل اللغوية كالحذف والتقديم والتأخير والمجاز وربطها بالسياق التاريخي؛ ولذا فكلاهما أساس لفهم وتفسير عصريين للقرآن الكريم. وللتأويل تاريخ ناصع باعتباره أداة الإتجاه العقلي المعتزلي في تعاطيه مع النص القرآني ولكنه ولأسباب سياسية أكثر منها فكرية اكتسب ظلالاً سلبية وارتبط بالتحريف مما أعلى من قيمة التفسير الذي يهتم فقط بشرح معاني الكلمات. وتمثل إعادة إحياء التأويل مع فتح باب الإجتهاد طريقاً لفهم موضوعي لقدسية النص ومدى قدرة الإنسان على تجديد التفسير بما يتفق مع روح العصر، تفسيراً يقوم على نظرية "أسباب النزول" التي تتشابه مع "نظرية النقد التاريخي" ويفرق بين آيات العبادات وآيات المعاملات ويعتمد على مقاصد الشريعة في تعليل الأحكام الدنيوية واضعاً مصلحة الإنسان في بؤرة الاهتمام انطلاقاً من "وما أرسلناك إلا رحمة للعالمين". على هذا الأساس تعلو قيمة الإنسان وحقوقه ويتخذ دوراً مركزياً في الكون بوصفه حاملاً للأمانة مما يستلزم حريته الفكرية والعقائدية.

والسلوك والخبرة العملية للبشر من جهة أخرى. مثل هذا المنهج لا يجد فقط المبررات، ولكنه في الواقع مطلوباً أيضاً إذ دعا القرآن في آيات عدة إلى التدبر والتمعن بشكل مستقل. وبالفعل، فإن هذه الآيات القرآنية:

"إِنَّا أَنْزَلْنَاهُ قُرْآنًا عَرَبِيًّا لَعَلَّكُمْ تَعْقِلُونَ"
(يوسف: ٢)

"إِنَّا جَعَلْنَاهُ قُرْآنًا عَرَبِيًّا لَعَلَّكُمْ تَعْقِلُونَ"
(الزخرف: ٣)

تشير إلى أن التأمل والفهم الإنساني هو الغرض الكلي من إنزال القرآن. إن التنوع الثري للآراء بين الفقهاء المسلمين في كل مبدأ شرعي تقريباً أو قضية من السياسة العامة إنما ينصّ بوضوح على وجود علاقة ديناميكية بين القرآن والسنة من ناحية، وبين الفهم والتخيل والخبرة البشرية من ناحية أخرى.

نظراً لأن السياق التاريخي للجماعة والخبرات الشخصية للمؤمنين تؤثر جوهرياً على الإدراك والسلوك البشري، فإن التغيرات العنيفة في ظروف الحياة الفردية والجماعية يجب أن تؤدي إلى إعادة النظر في معنى الرسالة الإلهية ودلالاتها. للسبب ذاته، يجب على المرء أن يقدّر الأثر الاختلافي لهذه العوامل على إدراك وتوجيه كل المجتمعات المسلمة اليوم. إن التأكيد على أهمية السياق التاريخي المعين الذي تُفهم المبادئ الإسلامية وتمارس من خلاله يعني الدعوة إلى فهم واضح لطبيعة هذه العوامل، والنظر بعين الاعتبار لعواقبها بالنسبة لكل مجتمع. بعبارة أخرى، ينبغي على المرء أن يتناول الموضوع فيما يخص كل مجتمع إسلامي في سياقه الخاص، بدلاً من معاملة جميع هذه المجتمعات بالطريقة نفسها.

إن وضع هذا السياق هو على درجة من الأهمية نظراً لدور الدولة كإطار لوضع وتطبيق السياسة العامة للمجتمعات الإسلامية اليوم. ومهما كان الدور الذي قد تضطلع به الشريعة في حياة المسلمين المعاصرين، فإن هذا الدور سيقع بالضرورة على عاتق دولهم الوطنية، وليس من خلال الفعل الذاتي للمجتمع العالمي على هذا النحو. باعتبارها مؤسسة سياسية أساسية، فإن على أي دولة أن توازن بين مختلف المطالب والمصالح المتعارضة. رغم أن بعض هذه المطالب والمصالح قد تعبّر عن العواطف الدينية للجماهير، لكن بالنظر إلى التنوع الديني والسياسي للشعوب الإسلامية اليوم، وتداخل اهتماماتهما الإقليمية والعالمية الاقتصادية والأمنية، فإنه من غير الواقعي إطلاقاً أن نتوقع من أي دولة أن تضطلع بهذه الأمور من باب العواطف الدينية فقط، حتى ولو كانت هذه عواطف الغالبية العظمى من سكانها.

لهذا أناشد الى توسيع الحوار الديني من أجل دعم الشرعية القانونية والأهمية العملية لحقوق الإنسان في جميع المجتمعات مهما اختلفت الاديان السائدة فيها. على هذا النحو استعرضت الدين الإسلامي باعتباري محامياً مسلماً ينحاز لحقوق الإنسان، على أمل أن يسلك الآخرون هذا الطريق أيضاً في إنجاز أبحاث مماثلة عن معتقداتهم وتقاليدهم. إن إمكانية وضرورته هذا الأمر لايقتصر على الإسلام وحده ولكنه ينطبق كذلك على كل التقاليد الدينية.

دوراً إيجابياً في حياة المسلمين اليوم. ففي ظل التغيرات العنيفة في الأوضاع الاجتماعية والاقتصادية والسياسية للمجتمعات الإسلامية في أنحاء العالم، فإن فهم الشريعة الذي تطور منذ ما يربو على الألف عام مرتبط بمواجهة بعض الصعوبات العملية اليوم. مع ذلك، فلا يمكن حدوث إصلاح جاد لأي جانب من الجوانب الإشكالية للشريعة طالما أن صيغ حقوق الإنسان المسبقة ينظر إليها على أنها إلهية. نتيجة لهذا الطريق المسدود "من صنع الإنسان"، فالمسلمون في كل مكان لا يزالون يقرّون بمفهوم للشريعة لا يرغب أيّ منهم أو لا يقدر أن يتعايش معه. فعلى سبيل المثال، يُنظر إلى الإدانة الدينية للربا على أنها تحريم دفع أي فوائد على القروض بالكلية. وبالمثل، فإن الاعتراضات الدينية على "الغرر" يُستند إليها في إبطال عقود التأمين، حيث تتوقف الضرورات على إمكانية حدوث أمر ما في المستقبل أم لا. إلا أنه على المستوى العملي، نجد أن المسلمين وحكوماتهم يقومون على نحو روتيني بتقاضي ودفع فائدة على القروض، ويعقدون ويفرضون عقود التأمين لأن من المستحيل أن يكون لديهم أنظمة اقتصادية قابلة للتطبيق المعاصر دون تلك الممارسات. هذا التناقض بين النظرية والتطبيق يمكن احتواءه من خلال تقدير أن كل التعريفات الخاصة بمفاهيم مثل "الربا" و "الغرر"هي بالضرورة نتاج الفهم البشري في سياق تاريخي معين، وليست حكماً إلهياً.

نتيجة للإخفاق في التمييز بين كلا المعنيين لحقوق الإنسان المشار إليهما أعلاه، يدّعي المسلمون أن الصيغ التاريخية للشريعة قد أمّنت دائماً حقوق الإنسان نظرياً، على الرغم من أن مثل هذا الموقف ربما لم يتجسد عملياً. في تصوري، من خلال تأمين درجة متقدمة نسبياً من الحماية لحقوق المرأة وغير المسلمين، فإن الصيغ التاريخية للشريعة قد وفرت حماية أفضل لحقوق الإنسان أكثر من أي أنظمة معيارية أخرى في الماضي. فعلى سبيل المثال، منذ البداية الأولى، فُهم أن الشريعة تتطلب شخصية قانونية مستقلة للمرأة، وحماية أبسط الحقوق لها في الميراث والعلاقات الأسرية، وذلك بمستوى يفوق ما كان متاحاً تحت أكبر الأنظمة المعيارية الأخرى حتى القرن التاسع عشر. وبالمثل، فإن الشريعة تضمن حقوقاً معينة لأهل الكتاب أكثر مما كان متوفراً تحت الأنظمة المعيارية للأغلبية الأخرى في الماضي. مع ذلك، فنظراً لأن حقوق المرأة وغير المسلمين بموجب الشريعة ليست مساوية للرجل وللمسلمين على التوالي، فإن مستوى حماية الحقوق بموجب الشريعة ليس كافياً عندما يُحكم عليها بالمعايير التي حددها الإعلان العالمي لحقوق الإنسان، والتي تدعو للحقوق المتساوية لجميع البشر، دون تفرقة على أساس الجنس أو الدين أو العقيدة.[5]

الإجابة الممكنة على هذا النقد للشريعة هو الدفع أنه ينبغي للمسلمين (والمؤمنين الآخرين) النضال للعيش وفقاً لأوامر دينهم، وليس وفقاً لعدد من معايير حقوق الإنسان، البشرية الوضع والقابلة للخطأ. مع ذلك، فنظراً لأن الوصايا الإلهية دائماً ما تُفهم وتطبق على يد البشر، فإن التناقض بين الإدراك الأرثوذكسي "لأوامر الدين" والنظرات الجديدة أو غير الأرثوذكسية للموضوع، هو في واقع الأمر بين "فهمين بشريين" لما يتطلبه الدين من أتباعه. وفقاً لذلك، فإن إعادة تفسير المصادر الإسلامية التي توضح الاتفاق مع مبادئ حقوق الإنسان يجب أن يُنظر إليها بألفاظها الخاصة، وليس استبعادها باعتبارها غير إسلامية لأنها غير متسقة مع التفهمات البشرية التي أسست سابقاً للشريعة. ما أريد التأكيد عليه هنا هو إمكانية إنشاء شرعية دينية لمثل هذا التفسير من خلال ما يمكن أن يُدعى منهجاً أنثروبولوجياً للإسلام.

كما أوضحتُ في موضع آخر،[6] فإن هذا المنهج مبني على وجود علاقة عضوية وديناميكية بين النصوص المقدسة لأي دين من الأديان، القرآن والسنة في حالة الإسلام، من جهة، وبين الاستيعاب والتخيل والحكم

---

[5] للمزيد من النقاش حول التناقضات بين التكوين التاريخي للشريعة والمقاييس الدولية الحديثة، انظر عبد الله أحمد النعيم، من أجل تطوير الإسلام: الحقوق المدنية، حقوق الإنسان والقانون الدولي، سيراكوس، ١٩٩٠، ص ٤-٧.

[6] عبد الله أحمد النعيم، نحو تفسير إسلامي لحقوق الإنسان، عبد الله أحمد النعيم (المحرر)، حقوق الإنسان والقيَم الدينية: علاقة معقدة، أمستردام (وآخرون)، ١٩٩٥، الفصل ١٦.

كما لاحظنا سابقاً، فإنني لستُ أفترض وجود اتساق بين الدين وحقوق الإنسان، أو اعتباره من المسلمات في أي جزء من العالم. بل على العكس من ذلك، ففي وسع المرء بسهولة أن يكتشف بعض النزاعات الأساسية، إن لم تكن فروقات صارخة بين التعاليم الدينية ومعايير حقوق الإنسان. من ثم، فإن السؤال الأساسي عند الباحث حول العالمية هو ما إذا كانت الأصول الغربية العلمانية لحقوق الإنسان، كما حددها الإعلان العالمي لحقوق الإنسان، تعني بالضرورة أن هذه الحقوق ليست عالمية حقاً أو لا ينبغي لها أن تكون كذلك.

الإجابة التي أقدمها على هذا السؤال مبنية على الفرضيات المترابطة الآتية:

١- ان الأساس الأخلاقي أو الفلسفي والتبرير السياسي لمفهوم حقوق الإنسان كما هو منصوص عليه في الإعلان العالمي لحقوق الإنسان مبطن في مختلف التقاليد الدينية والثقافية. إلا أنه نظراً لأن العقائد التقليدية للديانات الكبرى في العالم، بما فيها المسيحية، ليست متسقة مع هذا التصور المحدد لحقوق الإنسان، فإن التوفيق المطلوب قد يستدعي إعادة تفسير بعض التعاليم الموجودة في هذه الديانات.

٢- يُعد التوفيق أمراً ضرورياً نظراً للقيمة الأساسية لحماية حقوق الإنسان على المستوى الدولي في التحقق من سوء استغلال الدولة لسلطاتها. وبالنظر لأن النموذج الأوروبي للدولة قد عُمّم على يد الاستعمار، لذا فإن هناك حاجة ماسة إلى وجود حماية فعّالة ضد سلطة الدولة المفرطة أو المسيئة.

٣- سيكون هناك بالضرورة بُعد عقائدي لإعادة تفسير التعاليم الدينية، ولكن ينبغي فهم العملية نفسها في السياق السياسي والاجتماعي والاقتصادي الخاص بأتباع الديانة. ويعتبر السياق التاريخي المادي الذي يعيش فيه أتباع الديانة مكملاً لكل التفهمات الإنسانية للدين، والتي يفسرها المنهج العقائدي للدين. هذا السياق هو أيضاً الإطار الذي يمكن من خلاله إعادة تفسير التعاليم الدينية وقبولها عملياً.

سعى المسلمون، شأنهم شأن أتباع الديانات الأخرى، إلى ممارسة إيمانهم من حيث الامتثال الفردي والجماعي بنظامه المعياري، والمعروف بـ"الشريعة"، والتي يُفترض بها أن تنظم حياتهم اليومية باعتبارهم مسلمين. ولئن كان المسلمون يميلون إلى أن يعزوا السلطة الإلهية إلى صيغ تاريخية للشريعة على يد فقهاء القرنين الثامن والتاسع، إلا أنه من الواضح أن المضمون الدقيق لهذا النظام المعياري دائماً - ما كان وسيكون- هو نتاج الفهم البشري في سياق تاريخي معين.[2] كما أوضح برنارد فايس (Bernard Weiss) في السنة نفسها التي عقدت فيها الجمعية الألمانية لدراسات الشريعة الإسلامية وقوانين البلاد العربية اجتماعها السنوي الأول، والذي تناول أيضاً بشكل جزئي مسألة نسخة اليوبيل هذه[3] قائلاً: "على الرغم من أن الشريعة من مصدر إلهي، إلا أن البناء الفعلي للشريعة نشاط بشري، ونتائجه تمثل شريعة الله كما يفهمها البشر. ونظراً لأن الشريعة لم تنزل من السماء جاهزة، فإن الفهم البشري للشريعة – الفقه البشري – هو الذي يجب أن يكون معيارياً للمجتمع".[4]

على الرغم من أن الشريعة قد يسهل فهمها، إلا أن الخلط الشائع بين الشريعة الموحى بها من ناحية، والجهود البشرية لاكتشاف ما تعنيه من ناحية أخرى، يحتاج إلى التوضيح إذا ما أراد الإسلام أن يلعب

---

[2] للمزيد عن الأصول والتطور التاريخي للشريعة، انظر عبد الله أحمد النعيم، من أجل تطوير الإسلام: الحقوق المدنية، حقوق الإنسان والقانون الدولي، سيراكوس، ١٩٩٠، الفصل ٢.

[3] انظر حاتم الليثي (المحرر)، كلمة مسؤول التحرير، الإسلام وحقوق الإنسان. فرانكفورت، ٢٠١٠، ص ١-٣.

[4] برنارد فايس، روح القانون الإسلامي، أثينا، ١٩٩٨، ص ١١٦.

مستخدم هنا، فيشيرُ إلى التصور المحدد للحرية والعدالة الاجتماعية المنصوص عليها في الإعلان العالمي لحقوق الإنسان لسنة ١٩٤٨، والذي تم تفصيله في المعاهدات اللاحقة، وتفعيله عبر مجموعة متباينة من الآليات التطبيقية.

إن السمة الأساسية لحقوق الإنسان كما نصّ عليها الإعلان العالمي لحقوق الإنسان، هي أن هذه الحقوق مكفولة لكل البشر بحكم بشريتهم دون تفرقة على أساس العرق أو الجنس أو الدين أو اللغة أو الأصل القومي. مما لا شك فيه أن سوابق التعبير عن هذا المفهوم لحقوق الإنسان قد ظهرت من الخبرات الغربية (الأوربية والأمريكية) منذ أواخر القرن الثامن عشر. ومعلوم أن هذه الخبرات إنما استندت إلى ثقافة التنوير وليس العقائد المسيحية أو اليهودية، على الرغم من أن هذه الأخيرة تسعى للتوافق مع الأولى بمرور الوقت. على وجه التحديد، فإن مفهوم حقوق الإنسان كما هو منصوص عليه في الإعلان العالمي لحقوق الإنسان هو في الأساس "تعميم عالمي" لفكرة الحقوق الدستورية الأساسية كما تطورت في الدول الغربية، رغم أن منظومة الحقوق الفعلية التي ينادي بها الإعلان تتجاوز ما يمكن أن نجده في ظل أي نظام دستوري لأي دولة، غربية كانت أم غير غربية.

من الأهمية ملاحظة أنه رغم أن الإعلان العالمي لحقوق الإنسان بصيغته الحالية غير مُلزم بموجب القانون الدولي، إلا أنه يُعد الوثيقة الأساس لتفعيل الجهود لتحديد حقوق الإنسان ووضع الآليات والاستراتيجيات اللازمة لتطبيقها تطبيقاً فعلياً. وفي ضوء واقع السيادة الوطنية والعلاقات الدولية، نجد ضرورة خلق توازن بين الحاجة إلى الإشراف الدولي واحترام سلطة القضاء الوطني. لذا وفي إطار تعميم بعض أفكار الحقوق الأساسية، فإن أنظمة حقوق الإنسان الدولية تسعى لجعل هذه الحقوق إلزامية بموجب القانون الدولي، في حين أنها تترك مسؤولية التطبيق على عاتق الدولة. إن تخفيف هذه المفارقة الخاصة بالرقابة الذاتية للدول على ممارساتها الخاصة لحقوق الإنسان يتطلب فهماً واضحاً للعوامل والعمليات الوطنية والدولية، يشمل الدين ودور المؤسسات الدينية التي تؤثر على السلوك الفعلي للدول بهذا الخصوص.

ونظراً لعدم وجود آلية دولية معتمدة لـ"فرض" معايير حقوق الإنسان ضد إرادة الحكومات الوطنية،[1] يبرز سؤال مهم: كيف يمكننا تشجيع الحكومات على المصادقة على معاهدات حقوق الإنسان، وتحفيزها على الالتزام بحماية هذه الحقوق داخل أراضيها. ان أحد الطرق الفعّالة لتحقيق هذا الهدف يتمثل في تكوين جبهة محلية تناصر المصادقة على حقوق الإنسان وتطبيقها في السياق الوطني. وحتى لو أرادت النخبة الحاكمة أن تحترم بعض حقوق الإنسان، فليس من المتوقع أن تفعل ذلك ضد رغبة جماهيرها. لإقامة مثل هذه الجبهة المحلية وتفعيلها في الدفاع عن حقوق الإنسان، يجب أن تنظر الجماهير إلى هذه الحقوق باعتبارها متسقة مع معتقداتها الدينية. أي أن الحكومات قد توافق على معايير حقوق الإنسان الدولية باعتبارها ملزمة قانوناً وتحترم ممارستها، دون شرعنة قوية في السياسة الوطنية. إن الإدراك الشعبي لحقوق الإنسان باعتبارها متسقة مع المعتقدات الدينية للجماهير هو أمر أساسي لشرعنة هذه الحقوق في كل دولة. بل إن الفهم الواضح لأهمية الدين السياسية والاجتماعية في الدول التي يُقال عنها علمانية، مثل الولايات المتحدة وفرنسا، يعد أمراً أساسياً لأية جهود ترمي إلى التأثير على سياسات حقوق الإنسان وممارساتها في الدولة.

[1] رغم أنه يمكن الإشارة إلى "التدخلات الإنسانية" وأفعال مجلس الأمن التابع للأمم المتحدة باعتبارها أدلة على الإجراءات الإلزامية لحماية حقوق الإنسان ضد إرادة الحكومات الوطنية، إلا أن تلك الآليات يمكن تطبيقها فقط في الحالات الأكثر أهمية، وتعتمد أيضاً على الحسابات السياسية للقوى العظمى. بذلك لا يمكن اعتبارها جزء من نظام معتمد للإرغام الدولي على تطبيق معايير حقوق الإنسان.

الإسلام وحقوق الإنسان: تأملات وملاحظات تمهيدية *

عبد الله أحمد النعيم (أتلانتا)

يُعَد تطبيق المعايير الدولية لحقوق الإنسان أمراً ضرورياً في أي مجتمع، وهذا ما يستدعي إشراك الدين (بمعناه الواسع) إشراكاً واعياً وحكيماً لما له من تأثير كبير على سلوك الأفراد وأنظمة اعتقادهم، طبعاً بغض النظر عن التوصيف الرسمي للعلاقة بين الدين والمجتمع في الدولة. بالرغم من أن سلوك المؤمنين لا يكون دائماً نابعاً من التزامهم التام بإيمانهم، وتبقى للاعتبارات الدينية أهميتها البالغة لدى أغلب الناس لدرجة لا يجوز معها لدارسي حقوق الإنسان وأنصاره أن يواصلوا إهمالها واعتبارها أموراً ليست ذات قيمة غير مرتبطة بالموضوع أو تمثل إشكالية.

أود أن أؤكد على أن أنصار حقوق الإنسان بحاجة إلى إشراك الدين إشراكاً جدّياً، إلا أنني لستُ أفترض أن هناك توافقاً فورياً أو تعارضاً بين حقوق الإنسان وأي دين من الأديان. بل على العكس من ذلك، فطرحي مبنيّ على مفارقة واقع التوتر بينهما من ناحية، وعلى أهمية التوفيق بينهما من ناحية أخرى. هذه المفارقة غالباً ما تتمثل في الحدود القصوى التي تفرضها شمولية حقوق الإنسان ونسبية الدين. إن افتراض مثل هذا الانقسام هو في تصوّري أمر مضلل، نظراً لارتباط كل منهما بالآخر. فالمؤمنون لا يمكنهم الاعتراف بعالمية حقوق الإنسان وقبولها ما لم تكن متسقة مع معتقداتهم الدينية، كما أن تكامل الإيمان الديني وأهميته في حياة معتنقيه إنما يعتمد على الحماية الفاعلة لحقوق الإنسان. لذا فإن من الأجدى أن ننظر إلى هذه العلاقة من باب التفاعل والتأثير المتبادل، بدلاً من تصورها على أنها إحدى نقاط العداء الدائمة.

ما أذهبُ إليه هو أن هناك ضرورة لتوسيع مناحي هذا الجدل لتشمل دور العوامل المحلية والعالمية الاجتماعية منها والاقتصادية والسياسية، بدلاً من الانشغال بالتحليلات العقائدية المنصبّة على العلاقة بين الدين وحقوق الإنسان. من شأن هذا المنهج في تصوّري أن يقودنا إلى التوسط بين الحدود القصوى للعالمية وبين النسبية، وذلك من خلال التأكيد على السمات المشتركة للخبرات الإنسانية أكثر من مجرد الاختلافات حول المصطلحات العقائدية المطلقة. بإمكان هذا التوسط أن يصبح فاعلاً إذا ما انصبّ التركيز على مدى الإدراك والممارسة الفعليَّين للمسلمين وأتباع الديانات الأخرى في سياقهما الخاص. أي أنني أدعو إلى فهم العوامل الدينية في إطارها أو سياقها السليم، بدلاً من تجاهلها بالكلية أو التهويل من أثر النماذج العقائدية.

لعرض هذه الملاحظة التمهيدية لنسخة اليوبيل للجمعية الألمانية لدراسات الشريعة الإسلامية وقوانين البلاد العربية في ذكراها السنوية العاشرة، أجد من الضروري أن نفرق بين كلا المعنيين اللذين يُستخدم فيهما مصطلح "حقوق الإنسان". ففي أحد المعنيين، يشير مصطلح "حقوق الإنسان" إلى النضال التاريخي من أجل الحرية والعدالة الاجتماعية بوجه عام. غير أن هذا المعنى العام للمصطلح، على شيوعه وذيوعه، غير مجدٍ لأي تحليل للتوافق بين حقوق الإنسان والتقاليد الدينية أو السياسية أو الفكرية، إذ إن كلاً من هذه النماذج لها فهمها الخاص لحقوق الإنسان. أما مصطلح "حقوق الإنسان"، كما هو

* هذه المقالة هي نسخة منقحة ومعدلة من ورقة قُدمت في الاجتماع السنوي الرابع والتسعين للجمعية الأمريكية للقانون الدولي والذي عقد في واشنطن في الفترة ٥ إلى ٨ أبريل ٢٠٠٠.

شخصياً، أسعدني أن أجد نتاجنا العلمي في مكتبات هارفارد، لندن وطوكيو. ومن الجدير بالذكر هنا أن الجمعية قامت بتنظيم عدد من الندوات والحفلات التكريمية، كالحفلة التي أقيمت في هايدلبرج لتكريم الأستاذ المتقاعد أمية علوان في سنة ١٩٩٩، كما نظمت ندوة بخصوص القانون العربي-الإسلامي في سنة ٢٠٠٢، وندوة اخرى في سنة ٢٠٠٥ عن القانون الإيراني-الإسلامي في جامعة مانهايم بالتعاون مع رابطة الطلاب الأوروبيين وبعض الشبان النشطين من أعضاء جمعيتنا ،ونخص هنا بالذكر الدور البارز الذي لعبه حاتم الليثي باعتباره صاحب الفكرة والمعد والمنظم. أخيراً وليس آخراً نذكر هنا الندوة التي تناولت موضوع النظام العقابي في الإسلام على ضوء القانون المقارن، والتي أقيمت أثناء المؤتمر العالمي الأول للدراسات الشرق أوسطية في ماينز في العام ٢٠٠٢.

ان جمعيتنا ليست رابطة لتمثيل المصالح ولا هي جماعة ضغط، إنما جمعية علمية تهدف إلى العمل في مجال البحث العلمي الرصين الذي يأخذ الواقع العملي بعين الاعتبار. وحسب نصوص النظام الأساسي لجمعيتنا فإننا نرمي إلى المساهمة في تحقيق التفاهم المتبادل بين الثقافة القانونية الأوروبية والثقافة الإسلامية، خاصة في التطبيق العملي المتعلق بالوضع القانوني في الدول العربية، الامر الذي لا يمكن تحقيقه إلا عن طريق تقديم التحليلات الموضوعية المستندة إلى المعرفة الدقيقة بتفاصيل الأمور والمشاكل واجبة الحل.

ثلاث خصائص تميز جمعيتنا: أولاً: قيامها منذ تأسيسها بتقديم الدعم اللازم للباحثين والعاملين في المجال القانوني، ثانياً: مد الجسور بين العاملين في مجال الدراسات المتعلقة بالشريعة الإسلامية والإسلام عموما. وأخيراً وليس آخراً، إن جمعيتنا هي جمعية شابة تضم بين أعضائها الكثيرمن الطلاب والباحثين الشباب الذين ينتظرهم مستقبل زاهر.

حرّرت هذه السطور في مدينة جراز أثناء وجود كاتبها في جامعة ليوبولد فرانزنس لغرض إلقاء محاضرة هناك. وأخيراً لابد من الإشارة هنا إلى أمنيتنا في أن يمتد عمل الجمعية إلى الدول الأخرى في العالم بحيث يتاح لنا بناء شبكة واسعة تمكننا من توسيع نطاق عمل الجمعية.

جمعية دراسات الشريعة الإسلامية وقوانين البلاد العربية في العشر سنين الماضية

ماتياس روهي (إرلانجن)

هل من الممكن تأسيس جمعية مكونة من سبعة أشخاص، الحد الأدنى اللازم توفره قانوناً لتأسيس الجمعيات؟ وهو السؤال الذي طرح سنة ١٩٩٧ عندما عقد عدد من الباحثين والمهتمين بقوانين البلاد العربية والشريعة الإسلامية العزم على تأسيس جمعية في هذا الاختصاص.

وكان أن اجتمع ثمانية وعشرون شخصاً بتاريخ ١٩٩٧/١٠/٢٤ وقاموا بتأسيس جمعية دراسات الشريعة الإسلامية وقوانين البلاد العربية مؤكدين بذلك أن الوقت قد حان والزمن قد نضج لعمل كهذا. اليوم يبلغ عدد أعضاء الجمعية أكثر من مئة وسبعين عضواً، مما يشير إلى الاهتمام المتزايد باختصاص الجمعية. إن العمل في مجال الشريعة الإسلامية وقوانين البلاد العربية يعترضه كثير من الصعوبات والعقبات التي يمكن إزالتها عن طريق التعاون والتعاضد في ظل جمعية مختصة. هنا لابد من الإشادة بدور الرواد الأوائل في جمعيتنا وفي مقدمتهم أ.د. أرنست كلينجمولر، الذي كان لي شرف خلافته في الرئاسة حين اضطر في سنة ٢٠٠١ إلى التنحي لأسباب صحية. تلك الأسباب لم تمنعه من مساندة عمل الجمعية إذ ترأس مجلسها الإستشاري. ولقد استمرت مساندته تلك إلى ما بعد وفاته حيث كان للجمعية شرف الإستفادة من دعمه عن طريق المؤسّسة الخيرية "كلينجمولر". ولمزيد من المعلومات يرجى الاطلاع على صفحة الانترنت الآتية: www.gair.uni-erlangen.de/Klingmueller-Stiftung.html يرأس المجلس الاستشاري في الوقت الحالي أ.د. هيلمر كروجر المشهود له بالكفاءة العالية.

جمعية دراسات الشريعة الإسلامية وقوانين البلاد العربية تنبض بالحياة والحيوية بفضل أعضائها المتطوعين. لاتوجد للجمعية أرصدة مالية، رصيدها هو هذا العمل التطوعي، كما هو متعارف عليه لدى الجمعيات العلمية في ألمانيا. الإمكانات المادية المحدودة لم تعيقنا عن تنظيم مؤتمرات سنوية ناجحة في مناطق مختلفة من ألمانيا. غالباً ما كانت تلك المؤتمرات تستمر لمدة يومين، كل مؤتمر كان يتناول موضوعاً قانونياً مختلفاً عن دولة أو دول متعددة. في السنوات الماضية تناول البحث الوضع القانوني في العديد من الدول كأفغانستان، مصر، العراق، إيران، لبنان، نيجيريا، باكستان، السودان، سوريا، تركيا والإمارات العربية المتحدة، إضافة إلى موضوعات مختلفة في نطاق الشريعة الإسلامية، وتأريخها، وتأثير الإسلام على القوانين المعاصرة (خاصة في الدول العربية)، موضوع الإفتاء قديماً وحديثاً، أحكام القصاص في الإسلام، حقوق الإنسان في الإسلام، القانون الدولي الخاص في الدول الإسلامية، البنوك الإسلامية، النظام المالي الإسلامي، التحكيم، حماية الملكية الفكرية وحقوق الاختراع، القوانين التجارية والاقتصادية للدول الإسلامية في الشرق الأدنى والأوسط. علاوة على ذلك تم تناول موضوع الشريعة الإسلامية وآفاق مستقبلها في ألمانيا وأوروبا من وجهة نظر علمية وتطبيقية.

في السنة الماضية قامت جمعيتنا بالتعاون مع المعهد الألماني لحقوق الإنسان في برلين بتنظيم مؤتمرها السنوي العاشر. في هذه السنة ستقوم الجمعية بالتعاون مع الرابطة الحقوقية الألمانية-التركية والرابطة الحقوقية الألمانية-الإيرانية بتنظيم حفل تكريمها للأستاذ د. هيلمر كروجر إحياءاً لذكرى ميلاده السبعين.

يرجع الفضل في إخراج المحاضرات وإعدادها التي تُلقى في مؤتمراتنا واجتماعاتنا على هيئة كتب مجلدات إلى أ.د. هانز-جورج إبرت، مما اتاح الفرصة للكثير من الجمهور الاطلاع على هذه المؤلفات.

Islam und Menschenrechte (Islam and Human Rights / الإسلام وحقوق الإنسان)
Hatem Elliesie (Hrsg./Editor), © Peter Lang Verlag: Frankfurt a.M. 2010, S. 575-576 / ص ٤-٥

المشاركين كافة الذين ابدوا استعدادهم وتعاونهم للكتابة والمشاركة في حلقة البحث والنقاش هذه وخصصوا قسماً ثميناً من وقتهم وجهودهم في خدمة هذا العمل.

شكراً جزيلاً! Many thanks! Vielen Dank!

حاتم الليثي

برلين في صيف ٢٠٠٩
برلين في ١٤٣٠ هـجري

تمهيدية"، ومحمد كاليش "الإسلام وحقوق الإنسان: تأملات حول العلاقة بين الدين والقانون"، وعاصم حنفي "حقوق الإنسان انطلاقاً من النظرية التأويلية في تفسير القرآن" وهاينز بيليفلد "هل الغرب ضد التصور الإسلامي لحقوق الإنسان".

وفي الجزء الثاني ركزت المساهمات على فهم الاهمية العملية والنظرية للوظيفة التي تؤديها حقوق الإنسان في عالمنا الذي يتجه أكثر فأكثر باتجاه العولمة والتقارب بين المجتمعات المعاصرة المختلفة، وعليه فانه من الضروري وضع النقاط على الحروف فيما يتعلق بالواقع الراهن لبلدان العالم الإسلامي. وهنا يتحتم علينا البحث والتحليل لثلاث مناطق رئيسية: عن افريقيا (مشهود بدرين)، وعن الشرق الاوسط وشمال افريقيا (أن إليزابث ماير)، وعن آسيا (تيم ليندسي)، فضلاً عن بحوث خاصة بدول معينة، وعن نيجيريا (عيسى حياتو جيروما)، وعن زنجبار (كريس ماينا بيتز)، وعن السودان (حاتم الليثي)، وعن مصر (بهاء الدين حسن)، وحول "التركيبة الحكومية لحقوق الإنسان والمؤسسات الوطنية لحقوق الإنسان في الشرق الاوسط وشمال افريقيا" (انا فيرت وكلاوديا انجلمان)، وحول "بين التقييد والتطورات الجديدة: الحق الأساسي في التقرير الذاتي للعلاقة الجنسية بين الرجل والمرأة في الأنظمة الدستورية للدول العربية" (ناصيف نعيم)، وعن افغانستان (تيلمان رودر)، وعن باكستان (جواد رحمن وعائشة شاهد)، وعن ايران (ايرني شنايدر)، والتي تبحث في مساهمتها الواقع الخاص بحقوق المرأة في ايران.

وفي الجزء الثالث تلقي الضوء هانا بياتا شوب - شيليج على حقوق المرأة ولكن على صعيد عالمي وذلك فيما يتعلق بلجنة حقوق المرأة التابعة للامم المتحدة وتأثيرها في العالم الإسلامي، وتبحث مساهمة تيودور راتجبر موضوع "منظمة المؤتمر الإسلامي ولجنة حقوق الإنسان في الأمم المتحدة وحقوق الإنسان كأداة في السياسة" وبذلك يتناول هذا الجزء موضوع حقوق الإنسان على صعيد المنظمات الدولية .

وتوخينا في الجزء الأخير (الجزء الرابع) ان نختم كتابنا بالمساهمات القيّمة لكل من بيتر شولتز عن "النظام العام وحقوق الإنسان والشريعة"، وايمان جلالة "الحرية الدينية وقانون الارث المستمد من الشريعة الإسلامية:الاحكام القانونية والتفسير القضائي المعاصر في مصر وتونس"، وباور بامرني"حقوق الأقليات الدينية في مسائل الاحوال الشخصية في شمال العراق". وهو الجزء الذي يبحث مسألة حقوق الإنسان والإسلام على ضوء القانون الدولي الخاص.

تجدر الإشارة هنا إلى ان كل الآراء الواردة في المساهمات المذكورة اعلاه تعبر فقط عن رأي اصحابها، وهذه الاراء لا تطابق بالضرورة آراء مسؤول التحرير او آراء جمعية قوانين البلاد العربية والشريعة الإسلامية. ان المصطلحات والتعابير العربية واللغات الاخرى تمت كتابتها بالحروف اللاتينية حسب القواعد العلمية المعمول بها في المانيا (المعمول بها في Deutsche Morgenländische Gesellschaft)، وكذلك الحال بالنسبة لكتابة الهوامش والمصادر، وفيما يخص الاسماء فقد كُتبت كما وردت في المساهمات او مثل ما هو متعارف عليها إذا كانت الأسماء سائدة ومشهورة. وينطبق الشئ نفسه على الأسماء الانجليزية والألمانية التي ترجمت الى العربية.

وفي الختام يُسرني ان أُعبر عن خالص شكري وتقديري لكل من ساهم في إصدار هذا الكتاب وبالاخص ناشر هذه السلسلة "Leipziger Beiträge zur Orientforschung" الاستاذ الدكتور هانز جورج ابرت إذ قام بتبني اصدار الجزء السابع من هذه السلسلة تحت عنوان "حقوق الإنسان والإسلام"، جدير بالشكر والامتنان هنا أيضاً الدعم و المساندة التي قدمها عدد من الأصدقاء فمن دونهم ما كان في الإمكان إصدار هذا الكتاب بهذا الشكل. هنا اخص بالذكر النصائح الفنية القيّمة، والتصحيح والنقد اللغوي، والإرشادات البنّاءة التي قدمها سينا نيكولايف وجوي جبهاردت وباور بامرني وتسيوس فلان هوفر، واشكر كذلك السيد بينامين كلوس من دار نشر بيتر لانج لجهوده وتعاونه. كما اعبر عن عميق الشكر والامتنان للكاتبين

كلمة مسؤول التحرير

تُمثل حقوق الإنسان مجالاً خصباً للبحث العلمي فيما يتعلق بمحتواها المادي او اطارها الشكلي القانوني، وذلك لاختلاف وجهات النظر القانونية والفلسفية التي تتناول شرعية حقوق الإنسان وعالميتها وأهميتها في القوانين الوطنية وخاصة في نطاق الحماية الدستورية للحقوق المدنية، بالاضافة الى كيفية اطارها التنظيمي في الانظمة الدستورية المختلفة، رغم ان مصطلح حقوق الإنسان يوحي للوهلة الأولى بانه تعبير قانوني مادي واضح، لكن التمعن العميق فيه يبرهن خلاف هذا الامر، فعملية ربط الإسلام بهذا السياق لا يؤدي الى تسهيل المعضلة بل الى تعقيدها لا سيما وانه لا يوجد في الواقع إسلاماً موحداً وإنما مناهج اسلامية متعددة تختلف فيما بينها حسب الزمان والمكان؛ لهذا فإن من الخطأ إطلاق احكام غير دقيقة بصدد تناقض الإسلام مع حقوق الإنسان وتصنيف حقوق الإنسان تبعاً لذلك إلى "حقوق الإنسان الإسلامية" و "حقوق الإنسان الغربية"، فحقوق الإنسان تعد من حيث المبدأ مرآة عاكسة للقيم الحضارية التي قد تتشابه او تختلف، وبالرغم من التأثير الديني الكبير لا يمكن اعتبار خروقات حقوق الإنسان نتيجة طبيعية او حتمية للثقافة الاجتماعية والتقاليد الاجتماعية الدينية .

ان بلورة حقوق الإنسان ليس فقط في العالم الإسلامي مبني على أساس العوامل الثقافية السائدة والمرتبطة بالعقائد الدينية والأهداف الإيديولوجية، الأمر الذي يجب أخذه بعين الاعتبار دائماً في النظرة النقدية، كما ان تنوع الآراء واختلافها يعمل على توسيع الآفاق الفكرية وهذا لا يعني ان كل الأمور نسبية وإنما الإشارة إلى الاختلاف في تفسير النصوص القانونية على خلفية التنوع الحضاري والديني؛ لهذا يجب بحث مسألة حقوق الإنسان والإسلام ومناقشتها مع المفكرين المسلمين مباشرة وليس خلف ظهورهم.

يعد موضوع حقوق الإنسان والإسلام منذ سنوات عدة من الموضوعات التي حظيت باهتمام كبير، وان اختيار هذا الموضوع من قبل جمعية القوانين العربية والشريعة الإسلامية لمؤتمرها السنوي العاشر ليس الا دليلا على هذا الاهتمام المتزايد والمستمر، فبعد مضي عشر سنوات على مؤتمرها الاول في بون، اختارت هذه الجمعية وللمرة الثانية ان تكون مسألة حقوق الإنسان والإسلام الموضوع الرئيسي والوحيد لمؤتمرها المنعقد في الذكرى السنوية العاشرة لتأسيسها المصادف يوم ١٩ و٢٠ أكتوبر ٢٠٠٠ في برلين والذي أقيم بالتعاون مع المعهد الألماني لحقوق الإنسان.

بناء على ما ورد في هذه المقدمة تم اختيار موضوعات هذا الكتاب لتكون خدمة متواضعة في سبيل فتح آفاق جديدة للبحث العلمي، وقد توخينا من ذلك فتح باب المناقشة على صعيد عالمي يمكن من خلاله التعرف على الارآء المختلفة. يضم هذا الكتاب جزءاً من البحوث موضوع المناقشة في المؤتمر وجزءاً آخر من بحوث إضافية مما يعني ان هذا الكتاب لا يمكن عده إصداراً عادياً وإنما عدداً تذكارياً.

يقع هذا الكتاب في مقدمة واربعة اجزاء، ومما يُسعدني ان تكون المقالة الموسومة بـعنوان "جمعية دراسات الشريعة الإسلامية وقوانين البلاد العربية في العشر سنوات الماضية" لكاتبها ماتياس روهي العضو المؤسس ورئيس الجمعية، المقالة الافتتاحية لهذا الكتاب، والذي يلقي الضوء من خلالها على نشاطات الجمعية في الفترة الماضية. يتضمن الجزء الاول من الكتاب المساهمات المتعلقة بالفقه واصوله والعقائد الإسلامية والفلسفة للكتّاب: عبدالله احمد النعيم " الإسلام وحقوق الإنسان: تأملات وملاحظات

Islam und Menschenrechte (Islam and Human Rights / الإسلام وحقوق الإنسان)
Hatem Elliesie (Hrsg./Editor), © Peter Lang Verlag: Frankfurt a.M. 2010, S. 577-579 / ص ١-٣

LEIPZIGER BEITRÄGE ZUR ORIENTFORSCHUNG

Herausgegeben von Hans-Georg Ebert
Begründet von Günter Barthel

Band 1 Lutz Knörnschild: Zur Geschichte der Nilwassernutzung in der ägyptischen Landwirtschaft von den Anfängen bis zur Gegenwart. 1993.

Band 2 Henner Fürtig / Rolf Müller-Syring (Hrsg.): Ursachen gewaltförmiger Konflikte in der Golfregion. Internationale und zwischenstaatliche Faktoren. 1993.

Band 3 Ingelore Goldmann (Hrsg.): Beiträge zur Fachdidaktik Arabisch. Didaktische und methodische Probleme des modernen Arabischunterrrichts. 1993.

Band 4 Roland Kühnel: Die sprachliche Situation an Hochschulen des Maghreb und die offizielle Sprachpolitik – Eine soziolinguistische Untersuchung. 1995.

Band 5 Henk Knaupe / Ulrich G. Wurzel: Aufbruch in der Wüste. Die Neuen Städte in Ägypten. 1995.

Band 6 Wolfgang Reuschel: Aspekt und Tempus in der Sprache des Korans. 1996.

Band 7 Hans-Georg Ebert: Das Personalstatut arabischer Länder. Problemfelder, Methoden, Perspektiven. Ein Beitrag zum Diskurs über Theorie und Praxis des Islamischen Rechts. 1996.

Band 8 Uwe Pfullmann: Politische Strategien Ibn Sa^{c}ūds beim Aufbau des dritten saudischen Staates. Eine historische Studie unter besonderer Berücksichtigung deutschen Archivmaterials. 1996.

Band 9 Hans-Georg Ebert (Hrsg.): Beiträge zum Islamischen Recht. 2000.

Band 10 Anja Wünsch: Innenansichten ökonomischer Restrukturierung. Wirkungen und Wirksamkeit der Strukturanpassung in Jordanien, 1989-1999. 2001.

Band 11 Thoralf Hanstein: Islamisches Recht und Nationales Recht. Teil 1 und 2. Eine Untersuchung zum Einfluß des Islamischen Rechts auf die Entwicklung des modernen Familienrechts am Beispiel Indonesiens. 2002.

Band 12 Hans-Georg Ebert / Thoralf Hanstein (Hrsg.): Beiträge zum Islamischen Recht II. 2003.

Band 13 Hans-Georg Ebert / Thoralf Hanstein (Hrsg.): Beiträge zum Islamischen Recht III. 2003.

Band 14 Hans-Georg Ebert: Das Erbrecht arabischer Länder. 2004.

Band 15 Silvia Tellenbach / Thoralf Hanstein (Hrsg.): Beiträge zum Islamischen Recht IV. 2004.

Band 16 Almut Hinz: Die Sanktionen gegen Libyen. Sanktionen im modernen Völkerrecht und in der Staatenpraxis sowie ihre Anwendung am Beispiel Libyen. 2005.

Band 17 Hüseyin Demir: Die osmanischen Medresen. Das Bildungswesen und seine historischen Wurzeln im Osmanischen Reich von 1331–1600. 2005.

Band 18 Sebastian Maisel: Das Gewohnheitsrecht der Beduinen. Der Stellenwert von Urf in den Rechtsvorstellungen tribaler Gruppen im Norden der Arabischen Halbinsel. 2006.

Band 19 Irene Schneider / Thoralf Hanstein (Hrsg.): Beiträge zum Islamischen Recht V. 2006.

Band 20 Anja Wehler-Schöck: Ehrenmorde in Jordanien. Ursachen und mögliche Gegenstrategien. 2007.

Band 21 Hans-Georg Ebert / Thoralf Hanstein (Hrsg.): Beiträge zum Islamischen Recht VI.

Band 22 Naseef Naeem: Die neue bundesstaatliche Ordnung des Irak. Eine rechtsvergleichende Untersuchung. 2008.

Band 23 Hans-Georg Ebert: Die Qadrî-Pâshâ-Kodifikation. Islamisches Personalstatut der hanafitischen Rechtsschule. 2010.

Band 24 Hans-Georg Ebert / Assem Hefny: *Der Islam und die Grundlagen der Herrschaft*. Übersetzung und Kommentar des Werkes von Alî Abd ar-Râziq. 2010.

Band 25 Nedim Zahirović: Murteza Pascha von Ofen zwischen Panegyrik und Historie. Eine literarisch-historische Analyse eines osmanischen Wesirspiegels von Nergisi (El-vaṣfü l-kāmil fī-aḥvāli l-vezīri l-'ādil). 2010.

Band 26 Hatem Elliesie (Hrsg./ed.): Beiträge zum Islamischen Recht VII. Islam und Menschenrechte / Islam and Human Rights / الإسلام وحقوق الإنسان. 2010.

www.peterlang.de

Hans-Georg Ebert / Assem Hefny

Der Islam und die Grundlagen der Herrschaft

Übersetzung und Kommentar des Werkes von Alî Abd ar-Râziq

Frankfurt am Main, Berlin, Bern, Bruxelles, New York, Oxford, Wien, 2010.
115 S.
Leipziger Beiträge zur Orientforschung. Herausgegeben von Hans-Georg Ebert. Bd. 24
ISBN 978-3-631-59613-5 · geb. € 22,80*

Alî Abd ar-Râziqs Werk *Der Islam und die Grundlagen der Herrschaft* gehört zu den Schriften muslimischer Autoren des frühen 20. Jahrhunderts, die den Diskurs um das Verhältnis von Staat und Politik im Islam wesentlich mitgeprägt haben. Der Verfasser, selbst Azhar-Gelehrter und Richter am Islamischen Gericht von al-Mansûra (Ägypten), begründet aus der islamischen Tradition heraus die politische Verankerung des Kalifats und der Kalifen. Das Kalifat verliert damit seinen religiösen Schein und wird zur einfachen Herrschaftsform. Diese Theorie wirkte zunächst schockierend auf viele Muslime und auf die Mehrheit der islamischen Rechts- und Religionsgelehrten. Alî Abd ar-Râziq verlor alle Ämter, sein Buch wurde auf den Index gesetzt. Auch in den aktuellen Auseinandersetzungen innerhalb und außerhalb der islamischen Welt um Demokratie und Menschenrechte vermittelt das Werk bis heute interessante Ansatzpunkte.

Aus dem Inhalt: Das Kalifat als Herrschaftsform · Alî Abd ar-Râziq: Leben und Werk · Text und Kommentar *Der Islam und die Grundlagen der Herrschaft* · Das Verhältnis von Islam und Politik · Gottesstaat und menschliche Herrschaft

Frankfurt am Main · Berlin · Bern · Bruxelles · New York · Oxford · Wien
Auslieferung: Verlag Peter Lang AG
Moosstr. 1, CH-2542 Pieterlen
Telefax 0041(0)32/3761727

*inklusive der in Deutschland gültigen Mehrwertsteuer
Preisänderungen vorbehalten

Homepage http://www.peterlang.de